INFLATION THEORY AND ANTI–INFLATION POLICY

OTHER INTERNATIONAL ECONOMIC ASSOCIATION PUBLICATIONS

MONOPOLY AND COMPETITION AND THEIR REGULATION
THE BUSINESS CYCLE IN THE POST-WAR WORLD
THE THEORY OF WAGE DETERMINATION
THE ECONOMICS OF INTERNATIONAL MIGRATION
STABILITY AND PROGRESS IN THE WORLD ECONOMY
THE ECONOMIC CONSEQUENCES OF THE SIZE OF NATIONS
ECONOMIC DEVELOPMENT FOR LATIN AMERICA
THE THEORY OF CAPITAL
INFLATION
THE ECONOMICS OF TAKE-OFF INTO SUSTAINED GROWTH
INTERNATIONAL TRADE THEORY IN A DEVELOPING WORLD
ECONOMIC DEVELOPMENT WITH SPECIAL REFERENCE TO EAST ASIA
ECONOMIC DEVELOPMENT FOR AFRICA SOUTH OF THE SAHARA
THE THEORY OF INTEREST RATES
THE ECONOMICS OF EDUCATION
PROBLEMS IN ECONOMIC DEVELOPMENT
THE ECONOMIC PROBLEMS OF HOUSING
PRICE FORMATION IN VARIOUS ECONOMIES
THE DISTRIBUTION OF NATIONAL INCOME
ECONOMIC DEVELOPMENT FOR EASTERN EUROPE
RISK AND UNCERTAINTY
ECONOMIC PROBLEMS OF AGRICULTURE IN INDUSTRIAL SOCIETIES
INTERNATIONAL ECONOMIC RELATIONS
BACKWARD AREAS IN ADVANCED COUNTRIES
PUBLIC ECONOMICS
ECONOMIC DEVELOPMENT IN SOUTH ASIA
NORTH AMERICAN AND WESTERN EUROPEAN ECONOMIC POLICIES
PLANNING AND MARKET RELATIONS
THE GAP BETWEEN RICH AND POOR NATIONS
LATIN AMERICA IN THE INTERNATIONAL ECONOMY
MODELS OF ECONOMIC GROWTH
SCIENCE AND TECHNOLOGY IN ECONOMIC GROWTH
ALLOCATION UNDER UNCERTAINTY
TRANSPORT AND THE URBAN ENVIRONMENT
THE ECONOMICS OF HEALTH AND MEDICAL CARE
THE MANAGEMENT OF WATER QUALITY AND THE ENVIRONMENT
AGRICULTURE POLICY IN DEVELOPING COUNTRIES
THE ECONOMIC DEVELOPMENT OF BANGLADESH
ECONOMIC FACTORS IN POPULATION GROWTH
CLASSICS IN THE THEORY OF PUBLIC FINANCE
METHODS OF LONG-TERM PLANNING AND FORECASTING
ECONOMIC INTEGRATION
THE ECONOMICS OF PUBLIC SERVICES
THE ORGANIZATION AND RETRIEVAL OF ECONOMIC KNOWLEDGE
THE MICROECONOMIC FOUNDATIONS OF MACROECONOMICS

Inflation Theory and Anti-inflation Policy

Proceedings of a Conference held by the International Economic Association at Saltsjöbaden, Sweden

edited by
ERIK LUNDBERG

M

First published 1977 by
THE MACMILLAN PRESS LTD
London and Basingstoke
Associated companies in
Delhi Dublin Hong Kong
Johannesburg Lagos Melbourne New York Singapore Tokyo

ISBN 0 333 21618 0

Text set in 10/11 pt IBM Press Roman, printed by photolithography,
and bound in Great Britain at The Pitman Press, Bath

Contents

Acknowledgements

The conference that is recorded in this volume derived its initial impetus and choice of subject from the Jubilee of the Swedish Riksbank which was being celebrated in 1975. As part of that celebration, the International Economic Association was invited to organise a conference on the very topical subject of inflation—a subject of great concern to the banking community in all countries—and the Riksbankens Jubileumsfund bore the largest share of its expenses. We are greatly indebted to Mr Kristen Rickman, Governor of the Sviriges Riksbank, for his interest and support in all the work of the conference.

The International Economic Association conference followed immediately after another conference on a kindred subject organised by the Institute for International Economic Studies; by permission of that Institute we print in this volume two papers—those by Dr. Corden and by Dr. Claassen—which were available to both conferences and received interesting and important discussion in our own.

The planning of the I.E.A. conference was primarily the responsibility of Professor Erik Lundberg, one of the most distinguished of Swedish economists and formerly President of our Association, whose name very properly appears on the title-page.

Finally we record, as always, our debt to our two chief sponsors, UNESCO whose regular support and annual contribution has been vitally important to our work, and the Ford Foundation whose grant has again contributed significantly to making it possible to hold this and the whole series of conferences in which economists from a very wide variety of countries have attempted to wrestle with the major problems of the world.

List of Participants

Professor Odd Aukrust, Central Bureau of Statistics, Oslo, Norway
Professor Alexander Bajt, University of Ljubljana, Yugoslavia
Professor Oleg Bogomolov, Institute of Economics of the World Socialist System, Academy of Sciences of the USSR, Moscow
Professor H. William Branson, Woodrow Wilson School, Princeton University, USA.
Mr. Reuven Brenner, Hebrew University Jerusalem, Israel
Professor Martin Bronfenbrenner, Duke University, Durham, N.C., USA
Professor Emil-Maria Claassen, University of Paris, Dauphine, France
Dr. W. M. Corden, Oxford University, England
Dr. France Cotula Banca d'Italia, Rome, Italy
Professor Bela Csikós-Nagy, Hungarian Economic Association, Budapest, Hungary
Professor Wim Driehuis, Universiteit van Amsterdam, Amsterdam, Holland
Professor James S. Duesenberry, Harvard University, Cambridge, USA
Professor Revold Entov, Institute of the World Economy and International Relations, Moscow
Professor Luc Fauvel, Université de Paris, France
Professor Stanley Fischer, Massachusetts Institute of Technology, Cambridge, USA
Professor Jean Paul Fitoussi, Université Louis Pasteur, Strasbourg, France
Professor Marcus Fleming, International Monetary Fund, Washington, USA
Professor Helmut Frisch, Technical University of Vienna, Austria
Professor Hans Genberg, Institute of International Studies, Geneva, Switzerland
Professor Herbert Giersch, Institut für Weltwirtschaft, German Federal Republic
Professor Robert J. Gordon, Northwestern University, Evanston, USA
Professor Douglas Hague, Manchester Business School, England
Professor Dwight M. Jaffee, Princeton University, USA
Professor Lars Jonung, Nationaleknonmiska Institutionen, Lunds Universitet, Sweden
Mr. Michael Kaser, Oxford University, England
Professor Ephraim Kleiman, Hebrew University, Jerusalem, Israel
Professor David Laidler, University of Western Ontario, Canada
Professor David Levhari, The Hebrew University, Jerusalem, Israel
Professor Nissan Liviatan, Hebrew University, Jerusalem, Israel
Professor Erik Lundberg, Stockholm School of Economics, Sweden
Professor Fritz Machlup, New York University, USA

Professor Edmond Malinvaud, I.N.S.E.E., Paris, France
Professor Fritz Neumark, J. W., Goethe-University, Frankfurt/Main, German Federal Republic
Professor Adolf Nussbaumer, Institute of Economics, University of Vienna, Austria
Mr. P. M. Oppenheimer, Christ Church, Oxford, England
Professor Michael Parkin, University of Western Ontario, Canada
Professor Don Patinkin, Hebrew University, Jerusalem, Israel
Professor J. J. Paunio, University of Helsinki, Finland
Mr. Nicolas Plessz, OCED, Paris, France
Professor Stanislaw Polaczek, Warsaw University, Poland
Professor Sir Austin Robinson, Cambridge University, England
Professor Ingemar Stahl, Lund University, Sweden
Professor Alexander K. Swoboda, Institute of International Studies, Geneva, Switzerland
Professor Shigeto Tsuru, Hitotsubashi University, Tokyo, Japan
Professor Pieter de Wolff, University of Amsterdam, Holland

Observers

Mr. John P. Hardt, Library of Congress, Washington, USA
Professor Yoshio Miyake, Rikkyo University, Tokyo, Japan
Professor Franco Modigliani, Massachusetts Institute of Technology, Cambridge, USA
Dr. Michael Mussa, University of Rochester, Rochester, USA
Mr. Goran Wikner, Swedish Savings Banks, Stockholm, Sweden
Professor Gosta Rehn, Institute of Social Research, Stockholm, Sweden
Mr. John R. Stark, Joint Economic Committee, US Congress, Washington, USA
Mr. R. Dornbusch, Massachusetts Institute of Technology, Cambridge, USA
Mr. Lars Caimfors, Stockholm
Mr. Lars Svensson, University of Stockholm, Sweden
Professor V. Mshvenieradze, UNESCO, Paris, France

Introduction

Erik Lundberg
STOCKHOLM SCHOOL OF ECONOMICS

The I.E.A. conference on 'Inflation and Anti-Inflationary Policy' took place in Saltsjöbaden (August 28–September 3, 1975). A number of economists from many countries, plagued by inflation in varying degrees, participated. The conference was partly linked to another meeting, a Seminar on 'Flexible Exchange Rates and Stabilization Policy,'[1] which took place just before at the same venue. Some of the participants (and some of the papers) were common to both meetings.

The economic and social problems of inflation are serious in many respects and on several levels of difficulty: first, it is difficult to give precise meaning to an account of the origin or causes of inflation; second, the consequences of inflation are manifold, economic, social and political; third, there are many types of analysis and alternative models to assist an understanding of the process of inflation, both on a national and on a world level.

Inflation, simply defined as a significant rate of rise of the general price level, is undesirable as such. It is generally regarded as a kind of malfunctioning of the working of an economy as well as a failure of economic policy.

There is in all countries a kind of general learning process of how to live with a certain rate of inflation varying within relatively narrow margins over the business cycle. That was the experience of most Western countries over nearly two decades after the Korean war. But then came an unexpected acceleration of the price rise from the end of the sixties, followed by great uncertainty as to the future course after 1974.

There are various kinds of welfare costs following especially from unexpected accelerations and retardations of the rate of inflation. These are nearly always unexpected by most people, and even a stable inflation rate is not often planned for by large groups of people, who are thus not prepared to meet the repercussions of inflation.

We economists construct models to help us in understanding better, and if possible measuring, the main effects of inflation on welfare, paying special attention to changes in income and wealth distribution. We observe and theorise about leads and lags in the price-wage spiral and like to emphasise effects from changing relative prices on profits as well as on profitability expectations. Consequences for investments, resource allocation and productivity may be considered among the welfare effects from an inflationary process. There are good possibilities of model building and theorising about these effects; but there remain great difficulties of actually measuring losses compared with some hypothetical development without inflation.

There are also possibilities of benefits arising out of inflation. To the extent that social unrest has roots in unjust income distribution and unemployment, a high rate of inflation may minimise social and political frictions when solving parts of the unemployment and distribution problems. Inflation may therefore to some extent appear as an instrument (or catalyst) when reducing unemployment and stimulating investment to attain more rapid growth. On the other hand when dampening too rapid inflation is an important aim of economic policy, then the conflict with the targets of full employment and growth will imply the type of unhappy compromise of *stagflation* that the Western world has been suffering from during the 1970s.

In countries with high progressive direct taxes income, inflation has brought about a relative lowering of wages and salaries in higher income groups. Such an evening out of income differences – regarded as an aim in itself – would not have been possible in a democratic way without a high rate of inflation. On the other hand inflation has meant capital gains and other often less productive ways of earning money that may have had inequitable effects on income and wealth distribution.

An intricate problem belonging to the welfare implications of inflation is the costs of anti-inflationary policies. Depending on methods used, these costs may appear as increased unemployment over a considerable time. Restrictive policies may take the form of slower growth of productivity and have adverse effects on investments. Income policy supported by price and wage controls may have distorting effects on the allocation of production. Here again there arise difficult issues of balancing shorter-term costs against possible but uncertain longer-term gains.

Western economists have not been very successful in analysing the effects of price control measures and various forms of income policies designed to dampen wage and profit inflation. There are no adequate explanation models, and the empirical evidence is insufficient and unclear. It is not within the competence of an economist to judge the effectiveness or administrative competence of price and wage control boards on the one hand or find out the reaction of business firms and trade unions on the other. The apparent successes of price and wage control in the eastern socialist countries, to judge from the relatively low rate of open inflation, can only partly be understood by means of normal economic analysis. There are big question marks as to how much repressed inflation there is and what its effects are on production and allocation of resources.

The alternative to a successful anti-inflationary policy is to live with inflation, possibly with the risk of successive periods of acceleration of the price–wage spiral. The problems of adjusting to inflation can be nicely assumed away by means of an hypothesis of perfect foresight and adequate expectations by all groups in society. As information and correlated expectations will always be imperfect and information badly distributed, the introduction of *indexation* is one natural possibility of living with inflation. Indexation can be very partial, for example, only including interest rates and amortisations of loans in varying degrees, or be extended to cover also wage agreements and many kinds of contracts. We can theorise a lot about the results of such ways of living with inflation. There is, however, much too little of empirical evidence to test all the alternative hypotheses that seem possible, governing a wide range of different outcomes. The experiences of various countries as to very partial indexation measures – including index loans – all seem to refer to developments under very special circumstances.

All these various problems of inflation I have mentioned only in order to illustrate the wide range of issues that can only be adequately treated on the basis of good theory – tested by sufficient supply of relevant empirical evidence. It is perhaps especially in this respect that we are failing as economists. The conference in Saltsjöbaden gave very clear and useful evidence of this type of failure. Professor Hague, the 'rapporteur' of our discussion, has in the final summing-up given a number of examples of such failures.

I think the papers and discussions succeeded in giving a fairly complete survey of all possible problems that are closely related to the inflation issue of modern economies. There may be very different views on the appropriate emphasis to be given to the various problems. But it seems to me that they are all observed and mentioned in this record from the conference. From this point of view this volume should be useful.

Disappointments over our various ways of analysing inflation problems are well presented in the final summary by Professor Hague. I agree in most respects with him and could add yet more. The point is, however, that even these disappointments as here exposed may prove valuable. The volume may even be accepted as an exposé of what may be regarded as failures of economic analysis and model building designed to throw light on the phenomenon of inflation in all its ramifications.

Many kinds of theories of inflation are presented and discussed in this volume, monetarist, Keynesian, Phillips-curves approaches, microeconomic models, and others; but no agreement on a synthesis was attained. There was, however, no disturbing confrontation between 'schools' of inflation theory – as between monetarist and wage-push explanations. Instead there was much mutual understanding of the usefulness of different approaches.

There is in the field of inflation theory a kind of dilemma. There is an urge to find simple explanations, stressing one or a few factors and relations as being especially strategic. This urge seems to arise out of a need to find simple recommendations as to effective anti-inflationary policy. But I think the papers, and even more the discussions, reveal our dissatisfaction with the present state of inflation research.

Take as an example the treatment of expectations that is so important for the formation of rational hypotheses. There was noticeable dissatisfaction with the elegant theories based on simple assumptions of unified expectations of price level changes, formed *a priori* or from past experiences. We need much more knowledge of the dispersion of expectations regarding strategic groups (business men, trade unions, consumers, government). There is inadequate knowledge about formation of expectations from experience and from government declarations of policy intentions. We need to pay much more attention to variability of expectations. Consciousness of great uncertainty as to the future course of prices should also be taken into account when analysing trade union behaviour, wage formation, price fixing, and the like. The same type of dissatisfaction is felt as to the treatment of government anti-inflationary policies including the analysis of the actual reaction pattern of governments. These include such political factors as election prospects.

There are waves of fashion in economic theorising. The monetarist revival and the new micro-approach are examples. This is unavoidable and is part of the process of developing our analytical tools. The fashions of model building are well represented in this volume. But as already mentioned the wide spectrum of varying approaches at the same time demonstrates the present state of bewilderment of how to reach a real understanding of the world's very grave inflation dilemma and find solutions that are also acceptable from a political point of view. Another very important complication that the economists at this conference fully appreciated is the extent to which inflation is a world phenomenon that cannot merely be treated as a given exogenous variable for studies of national inflations. Research problems as to world inflation are well represented and discussed in this volume.

[1] Subsequently published in book form under the same title by Macmillan (U.K.) and Westview Press (U.S.A.).

Part 1

Problems of Inflation and its Analysis

1 Inflation: a Review of the Issues

Michael Parkin
UNIVERSITY OF WESTERN ONTARIO
and
Alexander Swoboda
INSTITUTE OF INTERNATIONAL STUDIES, GENEVA

INTRODUCTORY

This paper seeks to provide a basis for a constructive discussion and work on the major outstanding and unsettled questions concerning the causes, consequences and appropriate policies for dealing with inflation. At a time when the world continues to experience relatively high and variable inflation rates and the various 'schools' in the economics profession continue to hold such sharply conflicting and strongly held views, the most pressing need appears to be to attempt to reach a greater measure of professional agreement not so much on answers but on questions and on procedures for answering these questions. Our objective is to help achieve such a clarification of the questions. One ingredient in the pursuit of this objective would be a detailed and comprehensive survey of the existing body of literature on these problems. We do not provide that here, but, for a survey, refer the reader to Laidler and Parkin [29] and Gordon [16]. Rather, we try to provide an agenda for discussion by attempting to identify those aspects of the inflation problem which are settled and on which there is a widely accepted body of literature and those aspects which are in an unsettled state and require further work. Since there are so many unsettled problems a selection process is inevitable and it has been necessary to focus on those aspects of the problem which seemed to us to be the most important ones. To a large extent therefore, the content of this paper reflects our own prejudices as to what is and is not important. Further, the paper tends to be thin on what might be called hard analysis and rather heavy on less formal and more intuitive attempts to clarify the issues and state as clearly as possible the major outstanding questions and problems.

An agenda for a discussion of the main issues surrounding inflation is given by the programme for this conference. The papers to be presented (June 1975 version of programme) fall naturally into the three well-defined and often used headings: 'Causes', 'Consequences', and 'Cures' and this paper is organised around these three aspects of the inflation problem. In Section I we deal with the origins of, and transmission mechanisms which generate inflation. In Section II we analyse the effects or costs and consequences of inflation.

Section III deals with policies towards inflation. There are various ways in which these three areas interact and overlap and this will become apparent as the paper proceeds.

I. ORIGINS AND TRANSMISSION MECHANISMS OF INFLATION

(1) THE PROBLEM OF DEFINING INFLATION.

First we must deal with two semantic matters. The question which we address in this section could be posed as 'What causes inflation'. However posed in this way we have a question which is essentially unanswerable and for two reasons. First, the term 'inflation' is too ill-defined and secondly, assuming that we had a definition on which we were all willing to agree, any explanation would either be partial or would involve a chain with an infinite number of links, or be a closed loop which contained its internal dynamic momentum – a particular example of the general but helpful proposition that 'everything depends on everything else'. The first problem is easily overcome. All we have to do is to agree on a well-defined phenomenon, or set of well-defined phenomena, for which we want an explanation. A useful starting point is to recognise that 'inflation' is the first difference of the logarithm of some price index. However, the breadth of the index and the length of time over which the change is considered are both matters on which choice may be exercised Hence, there is no unique measure of the rate of inflation and the precise definition chosen must reflect the particular problem at hand. The choice of the index has, historically, been dominated by two specific problems; changes in the 'cost of living' and in the 'purchasing power of money'. Analysis of the former problem would dictate the use of a consumer price index while the latter would require a broader price index taking in not only the whole of G.N.P. (current production) but also of assets (both real and financial). Of course, these two types of indexes will not be independent of each other and it seems appropriate to keep both in focus. The time aggregate over which we measure inflation is a more troublesome matter. Simply because information is costly to amass and price indexes costly to compute, the most frequently available indexes in most advanced countries are at monthly frequencies. It is, therefore, as a matter of arithmetic, possible to compute first differences of price indexes on a month-by-month basis.

Will we want to concern ourselves with an explanation of month-by-month variations? For some purposes, some people perhaps would, but this seems likely to be too fine a time-period for most purposes and one which would involve a large amount of noise relative to signal. The same is also almost certainly true of quarterly variations. We would think therefore, that to measure changes in prices at such frequencies would pick up a large amount of randomness and would not be very interesting or important to explain. The longer the period of time over which the rate of change is calculated, the less does it become subject to the almost infinite number of small factors which from time to time are very important, but which, over time, tend to cancel each other out. The point at which one should stop depends on the precise question under consideration. Decade average rates of change are very important and interesting for long-run historical analysis (see Schwartz [40]); however, they are too long for a wide class of political–economic problems concerning inflation in modern societies, in which the typical life of parliament or of a democratically elected administration runs for only four to five years. In these cases a year is probably as long a period as it makes sense to consider. We suspect that on some occasions rates of change of prices indexes over a year will themselves be subject to many random events which, over a longer period, would tend to cancel out. However, we would regard any change in prices over a period as long as a year as of political and social as well as individual importance and therefore, would regard it as a variable which we ought to be interested in explaining.

(2) FOR WHAT PURPOSE IS AN EXPLANATION SOUGHT?

The second semantic problem concerns the nature and purpose of the explanation of the phenomenon which is being sought. Clearly, any explanation must contain an analysis of the process whereby prices are set. Regardless of the explanation provided, an additional set of variables which affect price-setting behaviour will be identified. It will then become necessary to ask how they are determined? This will take us one step further back to yet another set of variables and so on and so on. Two concrete but very different examples will serve to illustrate the problem here.

Consider first a rather conventional excess demand-expectations-monetary analysis of inflation. Prices are assumed to be set by firms, who raise their prices by the amount which they expect other firms will be raising theirs plus some adjustment depending on the state of excess demand in the market. Thus, in proximate terms, inflation depends on the expected rate of inflation and on excess demand. Expectations of inflation may be postulated as depending, via an error-learning process, on the past history of the actual rate of inflation. Hence, the rate of inflation (proximately) depends on the entire history of the economy's state of excess demand. Excess demand in turn depends on monetary and fiscal policy. However, monetary and fiscal policy do not just 'drop from the air'. They are made by governments who have their own objectives. A detailed analysis of the behaviour of governments would produce an explanation of monetary and fiscal policy which ran in terms of the constraints imposed by the electoral system and the constitution and the preferences of the voters. This however, would not be the end of the matter, it would then be necessary to explain why the economy had adopted a particular constitution and electoral procedure . . . , and so on.

The other illustrative example is that of the wage-push view of the origins of inflation. This view begins by identifying firms as price setters, but supposes that they raise their prices primarily in response to rising wages. Rising wages are seen as the outcome of a sociopolitical struggle for increased relative shares. However, it is recognised that monetary and fiscal policy have to be sufficiently elastic to permit an inflation thereby generated to proceed without producing an ever-deepening recession. Under this view it becomes necessary therefore, to explain monetary and fiscal policy (just as it does under the monetary explanation) but, additionally, it is necessary to explain the evolution of the various social and political mores which give rise to the (variable) desire to be persistently increasing relative shares.

These two concrete examples serve not only to illustrate the general point concerning the impossibility of arriving at a straightforward explanation of inflation which has an identifiable starting point and an identifiable ending point. They also show that such an explanation is not only not available, but also that it is not necessary. To see this, consider the question 'why do we want an explanation of inflation?' Of course there are many potential answers but that which appears most relevant and capable of providing a practical solution to the epistemological problem is one which regards the control of inflation as the central objective (see Gray and Parkin [17]). It becomes necessary simply to cast the alternative theories in a positive policy orientation identifying points in the chain of transmission where policy could make a difference and then asking the conditional policy question: what would happen to the rate of inflation, other things equal, if a certain well-defined policy action was taken? In other words, where may we break the loop and modify the course of inflation with well-defined acts of policy. Adopting a policy-orientated approach to explanations of inflation automatically provides us with a defined starting point, the starting point being the policy instrument itself. We can move both backwards and forwards from that, moving forwards and asking what is the effect of the policy instrument on the rate of inflation, and moving backwards to ask what are the constraints preventing us from manipulating or making for difficulties in manipulating the policy instrument. Additionally, it is worthwhile noting that the adoption of a policy-orientated approach, such as that suggested here guarantees, providing sufficient data are available, that the alternative competing hypotheses about the 'causes' of inflation may be discriminated between empirically.

(3) WHAT ARE THE OUTSTANDING QUESTIONS?

Let us now move to the substance of this section. What is settled and what are the main outstanding questions in this broad area? It seems to us that the matters which are definitively settled are a set of theorems concerning long-run equilibrium relationships between the rate of monetary expansion, the rate of inflation, the rate of growth of output, and real and nominal interest rates for a closed economy, and the behaviour of the balance of payments or the foreign exchange rate for an open economy. The theorems in question are too well known to require restatements here. They become empirically relevant if there exists a stable demand function for real balances. The existence of such a stable demand function is a further matter which seems to us to be settled. (See Laidler [24], Bank of England [1] for surveys of the relevant literature.) The long-run equilibrium theorems are empirically relevant in the sense that they would predict the rate of inflation only if the rate of monetary expansion had been held constant for a sufficiently long time for the actual and expected rates of inflation to be brought to equality. They remain relevant however when expectations are falsified as statements about the rate of inflation towards which, given a stable system, the economy is moving.

The major unsettled questions in this area are perhaps empirically more relevant and politically more important than the settled questions. These concern the details of the transmission mechanism from the creation of nominal demand through to inflation and also an analysis of what other variables are affected both en route and as permanent side-effects. Second, the process whereby monetary and fiscal policy itself is generated to give rise to a particular evolution and nominal demand is not well understood. The first of these matters is much better understood than the second.

(4) THE TRANSMISSION MECHANISM

Possibly the major reason why there is a lack of agreement on the nature of the transmission mechanism is that we do not have available a single and accepted procedure for modelling short-run adjustment processes. To see this, consider the following three alternative hypotheses, concerning the transmission from monetary and fiscal policy to the rate of inflation. One story would run as follows. First a rise in the money stock would raise real balances and lead to people holding excess real balances. This excess of real balance can be put into terms of relative price theory by noting that the implicit rate of return (non-pecuniary) on real balances is an inverse function of the stock of real balances and hence other things being equal, an increase in the stock of real balances will lower the implicit yield on money thereby creating a portfolio disequilibrium. Holders of real balances will seek to eliminate the excess by acquiring alternative assets or goods. In this process further changes in relative asset yields and prices will take place thereby feeding back onto a generalised stock adjustment process. To the extent that this stock adjustment spills over into real consumption and real capital accumulation, current output flows will be affected and in an upward direction. The rise in output will generate excess demand for goods and services. Price-setters in the face of such excess demands will initially meet them by an inventory decumulation or, by overtime working. However, as both of these activities result in an increase in marginal costs above their minimum (or, more generally optimum) levels, there will eventually be an incentive to adjust prices upwards. The upward adjustment of prices will, if a continuous one, lead to an increase in expectation of price rises which will further feed onto the actual rate of price inflation. Eventually prices will have risen by sufficient and be continuing to rise by sufficient, to eliminate the excess demand creating effects of the excess money balances.

This is a very conventional story and perhaps is a reasonable stylisation of one of the most widely held, but by no means universally held, views of the nature of the transmission mechanism. It can be formalised in very simple terms as follows (see Laidler [25], Dornbush (1975[9]), Mussa [34], Parkin [37]). The demand for money is given by

$$m^d = \alpha + \beta y - \gamma \Delta p^e + p$$

where m = $\ln$ of nominal money
y = $\ln$ of real output
p = $\ln$ of price level
Δ = first difference operator
d = demand
e = expectation

$\alpha, \beta, \gamma > 0$

The supply of money, m, is exogenous and equal to the demand for money. That equality is achieved by a market process in which expenditure increases until excess balances are eliminated. Thus,

$$y = -\frac{\alpha}{\beta} + \frac{1}{\beta}(m - p) + \frac{\gamma}{\beta}\Delta p^e \qquad (1')$$

is the proximate determinant of aggregate demand. Prices are set for finite periods by firms in accordance with

$$\Delta p = \delta(y - y^*) + \Delta p^e \qquad (2)$$

where y^* = 'natural' output

$\delta > 0.$

Inflation expectations are generated by an error learning process, the simplest example of which would be

$$\Delta p^e = \lambda \Delta p_{-1} + (1 - \lambda)\Delta p^e_{-1} \qquad (3)$$

where the subscript −1 indicates a one-period time-lag. This model will produce a rate of inflation given by

$$\Delta p^* = \Delta m^* - \beta \Delta y^* \qquad (4)$$

in long-run equilibrium provided the condition

$\gamma\lambda < 1$

is satisfied and will generate a cyclical response of Δp and $y - y^*$ to changes in the rate of monetary expansion.

An alternative 'story', vividly presented by Irving Fisher [14] is that an increase in the money supply which leads to excess real balances will instantaneously lead to a bidding up of the price level as the outcome of the process whereby people rid themselves of excess balances. This will lead to an increase in the actual rate of inflation relative to the expected rate of inflation. This discrepancy between actual and expected inflation will give producers inappropriate signals about relative prices and will lead them to increase their output. The stimulation of output which results from the mismatching of actual and expected inflation will tend to lower the inflation rate and the continuation of inflation will lead to a gradual rise in expectations of inflation. Eventually (if the economy is stable) the expected inflation rate will come to match the actual rate and there will be no tendency for producers to misread relative prices and produce at an output level different from its full long-run equilibrium volume. When this has occurred the actual rate of inflation will be equal to the rate of monetary expansion minus the real growth rate times the income elasticity of demand for money. On this view then monetary expansion leads directly to inflation and a mismatch between actual and expected inflation leads to output fluctuations.

This view can be formalised simply by reinterpreting the equations written above. Now equation (1) determines the price level as

$$p = m - \beta y + \gamma \Delta p^e - \alpha \tag{1''}$$

and equation (7) determines output as

$$y = y^* + \frac{1}{\delta}(\Delta p - \Delta p^e). \tag{2'}$$

However the dynamics are identical in both 'stories' and, from an empirical and policy point of view, the two are identical.

The third approach to the transmission system does produce (at least potentially) predictions which conflict with the above two results. It arises from an appropriate concern that the expectations generation procedure (equation 4) is both lacking in theoretical foundations and, except for very special case stochastic processes, guaranteed to provide systematic forecasting errors. This approach would replace 'error learning' with 'rational expectations'. At its most general, the 'rational expectation' hypothesis is that expectations will be formed by computing the mathematical expectation of the variable in question given all the 'relevant' information available to the agent forming the expectation. For operational purposes, what is 'relevant' information is taken to be the exogenous and predetermined variables of the particular economic model under review and the structure of that model. By the way of illustration, suppose the world is as described by equations (1) and (2) above, i.e.

$$m = \alpha + \beta y - \gamma \Delta p^e + p \tag{1}$$

and

$$\Delta p = \delta(y - y^*) + \Delta p^e \tag{2}$$

and that expectations are formed rationally on the basis of this model and on the assumption that m and y^* grow at constant rates. Then the rational expectation of Δp is given by

$$\Delta p^e = \frac{1}{1-\gamma}(m - \beta y^* - p_{-1}) \tag{5}$$

and (apart from random disturbances not explicitly introduced in the above),

$$y = y^* \tag{6}$$

and

$$\Delta p = \frac{1}{1-\gamma}(\Delta m - \beta \Delta y^*) - \frac{1}{1-\gamma}\Delta p_{-1} \tag{7}$$

which will approach the stable equilibrium rate

$$\Delta p^* = \Delta m^* - \beta \Delta y^*$$

if

$$\gamma < \tfrac{1}{2}. \tag{8}$$

Of course, this set of results depends crucially on the assumption that Δm is and is believed to be constant. If Δm follows a first-order moving average process then the above model immediately reduces to the model presented previously (see Mussa [34]).

The above examples have all been developed in the context (implicit) of a closed economy.

(5) INTERNATIONAL TRANSMISSION WITH FIXED EXCHANGE RATES

Similar considerations arise in the context of the international transmission mechanism under fixed exchange rates. Here the most common 'monetary' story, in recent (and older) times is to treat the world economy as a closed economy in which the overall rate of inflation is determined by the transmission process from money to prices following on the possible schemes outlined above. The story is most simple if one assumes that various countries produce similar goods (or at least that a substantial subset of goods produced and consumed are traded and that substitutability in both consumption and production with non-traded goods is fairly high). With commodity arbitrage the money prices (expressed in a common unit) – and rates of change in the prices of traded goods will be kept equal by the law of one price and the elimination by traders of the profit available to arbitrages arising from price differences. In the absence of 'real changes' in the structure of tastes and in relative productivity, the rate of change of the non-traded goods prices must eventually fall into line with that of traded goods prices.

An alternative explanation of the transmission mechanism under fixed rates, one that was most popular in textbooks until recently, begins by assuming, implicitly or explicitly, that countries are specialised in production but not in consumption – they both consume and produce their export goods but only the rest of the world produces the import goods they consume. Suppose the rate of monetary expansion increases in one country; this puts upward pressure on prices at home; with a fixed exchange rate this results in an increase in the price of exports relative to imports and, through substitution effects in home and foreign production and consumption, in a payments deficit for the home country. Growth of the money supply moderates at home and increases abroad as a result of the reserve flows. The process ends when price levels and inflation rates are again equalised. Thus, though in the short-run rates of inflation can differ in this second model in the long run they will converge and be determined by the world rate of monetary expansion just as they are in the first model.

These accounts of the spread and determination of world inflation remain silent, except perhaps by implication, about the determinants of the division of money income changes into price and output variations in the short run. There have been a few attempts at modelling short-run output, price and balance-of-payments dynamics for the small open economy under fixed exchange rates; see Laidler [26], Parkin [37] and Jonson [19]. The last-named also includes empirical estimates for the United Kingdom but for rather longer time-spans than those at issue here. The problems involved in the analysis are even more difficult in the open than in the closed economy case. Consider the effects of an attempt by the domestic authorities to increase the rate of monetary expansion through open-market purchases of securities. There are many added slips 'twixt' the cup and the lip. The link between a change in the domestic source component of the base, the base itself, and the money stock depends, in addition to other slippages, on the effects of the increase in the rate of domestic credit creation on the foreign source component of the base. These, in turn, depend on how sensitive capital movements (or jumps in a stock approach) are to monetary disturbances, and on how rapidly the balance of trade reacts to whatever effect has been transmitted through the supply of money, interest rates, etc., to money income. Thus, the first link of closed economy macroanalysis, that between an expansive monetary measure of the central bank and nominal income, should not be expected to hold with great strength in an open one. Furthermore, the division of money income changes into their price and output components is not easy to analysis. The outcome will depend in part on how long the rise in money income can be sustained before spilling over into a payments deficit large enough to reduce substantially the rate of monetary expansion. In addition, goods arbitrage will put a limit to the extent to which the domestic rate of inflation can differ from the foreign one (unless the exchange rate is changed). This raises a number of delicate issues on the proper handling of expectations and on disentangling inflationary impulses originating at home from those originating abroad, a topic that is receiving increasing attention in recent empirical literature (see for instance, Korteweg [23]).

It is still possible to suggest some lines along which the inflation–output division in an open economy under fixed exchange rates could be modelled in a spirit analogous to the closed economy analysis outlined above. Consider a 'small' open economy which has no influence on the world, and hence home, price of traded goods but produces and consumes some non-traded goods. An increase in the money stock leads to the usual increase in nominal spending; this falls on both home and traded goods raising, at first, output and employment in the latter sector and resulting in a current account deficit (or reduced surplus). As the increase in nominal demand is gradually perceived not to be purely temporary (random ?) prices rise in the non-traded goods sector. This, however, switches demand away from, and production towards, non-traded goods eventually leading to excess supply and a decline in prices in that sector and a return of output to its 'normal' level (and a return of the rate of monetary expansion consistent with payments equilibrium). Depending on the interplay of actual and expected prices overshooting on the downside may occur. Alternatively, prices of non-traded goods may be bid up before output changes significantly, as in the second 'story' above; producers raise output and equilibrium is restored after a process in which the actual rate of inflation falls, the expected rate rises to catch it up, and both eventually fall back to their previous level (the world rate of inflation).

In a recent paper, Branson [3] had proposed a 'Phillips-curve' explanation of why inflation rates should converge under fixed exchange rates. In a comment on that paper, Dornbusch [7] has recast the argument to an 'augmented Phillips-curve' version. Dornbusch's reformulation is reproduced below (with the ratio of traded goods to non-traded goods prices replacing that of import prices – given in world markets – to export prices)

$$\Delta p = \mu(p_W - p) + \Delta\pi^e, \mu > 0 \tag{9}$$

$$\Delta\pi^e = \lambda\Delta\pi_{-1} + (1 - \lambda)\Delta\pi^e_{-1} \tag{10}$$

$$\Delta\pi = \phi\Delta_p + (1 - \phi)\Delta p_W \tag{11}$$

where p = $1n$ non-traded goods price
p_W = $1n$ traded goods price
π = price Index

Equation (14) is the open-economy Phillips-curve. It states that home prices are rising more rapidly than the general price level is *expected* to rise when the relative price of traded to non-traded goods is above its equilibrium level (at which $\mu(p_W - p) = 0$), and vice versa. In other words, in the analysis, p_W/p, an indicator of excess demand for home goods, replaces the deviation of unemployment from its natural rate, the indicator of excess supply in conventional Phillips-curve analysis. Equation (15) is a Cagan-type adaptive expectations scheme and equation (16) defines the general price level as a weighted average of traded and non-traded goods prices. The point of reproducing this 'model' here is that it illustrates the difficulty of extending the conventional output–price division analysis to the open economy. A 'natural relative price ratio' replaces the 'natural level of unemployment'. This suggests three problems. First, the microeconomic underpinnings of macro-relationships may be even harder to derive than in the one (admittedly heterogeneous) good case of the closed economy. Second, fluctuations in relative prices, in addition to those in the general price level, need to be translated into output changes in the short run to come to grips with the policy issues at hand; in the present context, this requires setting up, at least implicitly, a two-sector model. Third, the rate of domestic credit creation should be introduced as an exogenous variable in addition to the exogenous world inflation rate, the rate of monetary expansion being endogenised, at least for some purposes.

These difficulties account partly for the fact that empirical studies of the adjustment mechanism in open economies have not followed the augmented Phillips-curve or rational expectations route. It seems more promising to postulate more conventional fairly complete – though not necessarily very large – macroeconomic models where prices and quantity variations result from various adjustments lags. Many of the questions raised above can be posed either in terms of alternative structures or in terms of alternative prior assignment of relative speeds of adjustment in various markets. This suggests that one possible way to resolve some of these issues is the formulation of differential equation systems in continuous time, using, for instance, the exact discrete approximation estimation methods developed by C. R. Wymer and applied to open-economy problems by Jonson [20] and Knight and Wymer [22].

(6) INTERNATIONAL TRANSMISSION WITH FLEXIBLE EXCHANGE RATES

If our empirical understanding of the transmission of inflation under fixed exchange rates is still in its adolescence, our theoretical and factual grasp of transmission of disturbances under flexible rates is barely in its infancy. The view that, under flexible rates, monetary disturbances are 'bottled' within countries and that one could assimilate national economies to closed economies in the study of output and price fluctuations, is not convincing except for steady states where expected and actual rates of inflation are equal, where nominal interest rates reflect these expected rates of inflation, and actual and expected rates of exchange-rate changes are equal and reflected in the difference between spot and forward rates, i.e. when output is at full employment! Some time ago, Laurensen and Metzler [29] pointed to the terms-of-trade effects of exchange-rate changes (brought about by autonomous expenditure changes) as a mechanism for translating prosperity at home into depression abroad in the face of rigid domestic price-levels – though they relied on a number of special assumptions that rob their analysis of much practical importance. Mundell [31] stressed the role of capital movements in arguing that monetary expansion at home may cause contraction abroad. Practical considerations, however, suggest that, contrary to the implications of these two studies, inflation may often get transmitted from country to country. One obvious reason is to be found in official reactions that take the exchange rate, or international interest differentials as targets of monetary policy. If authorities expand the money supply to prevent appreciation of their currency in foreign-exchange markets or in order to prevent the domestic rate of interest from rising above nominal interest rates abroad, the behaviour of the flexible-rate system will in fact simulate that of a fixed-rate one.

Recent developments in the flexible exchange-rate literature suggest a number of interesting hypotheses concerning the transmission mechanism under that exchange-rate regime.[1] One of their distinguishing characteristics is their emphasis on the role of exchange-rate variations in clearing asset markets in the short run and on the role of expectations about future exchange rates. Only two of these contributions will be mentioned here. Genberg and Kierzkowski [14] present a model of the small economy under flexible exchange rates which incorporates both traded and non-traded goods and assets. Impact and long-run effects of various disturbances are derived and the dynamics of adjustment, driven by a saving function that adjusts actual to desired wealth, are outlined. Domestic monetary expansion leads to a permanent change in real magnitudes (here mainly relative prices) because of the feedback of exchange-rate variations on wealth held in the form of foreign assets; furthermore short-run fluctuations in output and prices occur as the exchange rate overshoots its long-run equilibrium value to ensure clearing of asset markets in the short run. An increase in foreign prices will not be reflected in an instantaneous compensating fall of the price of foreign exchange for the initial impact effect is to raise both traded and non-traded goods prices – the latter less than the former – at the given exchange rate. The resulting fall in actual real wealth leads to asset accumulation, to a fall in non-traded goods prices and to appreciation of the home currency until all nominal (except the exchange rate) and real magnitudes return to their initial values. The point here is not the details of the working of the model but its broader implications, namely, that real magnitudes may be affected by nominal changes through interactions arising from the international integration of goods and asset markets even under perfectly flexible exchange rates, especially in the short run.

The lack of homogeneity of the economy in the short run under flexible exchange rates is also emphasised by Dornbusch [8] in a very interesting recent paper. Whereas Genberg and Kierzkowski assume static expectations and, by implication, continuous equality between spot and forward rates, Dornbusch stresses the role of expectations about future spot rates (reflected in the forward rate) and of interest arbitrage. He shows that, with 'rational' expectations about forward rates (in the long run exchange rates are governed by purchasing power parity) and temporary departures from purchasing power

[1]Several of the contributions were presented at an earlier conference that also took place in Saltsjöbaden.

parity in the short run, monetary policy leads, in the short run, to overshooting of the spot exchange rate. With sticky prices, monetary expansion leads to a fall in the domestic rate of interest; the home currency depreciates on forward markets reflecting rational expectations and must depreciate even more in spot markets to create the forward discount on foreign exchange required to maintain interest parity. As home prices begin to rise the home currency begins to appreciate back to its new (lower) long-run equilibrium value. Again, the relevant point here is that changes in the rate of monetary expansion lead to abrupt changes in exchange rates in the short run and are also likely to lead to short-run fluctuations in output and its allocation among traded and non-traded goods. For instance, in the preceding story, one would expect an increase in the rate of monetary expansion to lead first to an increase in output as the domestic currency first depreciates abruptly, then to a decline as it (and the price level) rises again. Dornbusch also discusses the transmission of an increase in the foreign price level to the domestic economy under the assumption that expectations are adaptive rather than 'rational'. The immediate implication is that inflation will tend to get transmitted to the domestic economy since speculators only realize with lags that the domestic currency must appreciate eventually by the full amount of the foreign price rise. They will therefore initially prevent full appreciation of the home currency on forward markets and keep its appreciation on spot markets below what it will eventually be. In the meantime, part of the inflation will have been imported from abroad. Note that this argument bears a certain resemblance to that advanced in explanation for the transmission of inflation between Canada and the United States by various authors, in particular Caves and Reuber [5]. Note also that if domestic authorities validate the transitional increase in the rate of inflation, short-run transmission may be transformed into long-run transmission.

This new strand of analysis of flexible rates points to a number of interesting issues for further thoretical and empirical research, within a framework that is more akin to that familiar from study of the closed-economy transmission process, in particular through its stress on short-run fluctuations in real variables and its emphasis on asset markets and expectations formation.

Despite the admitted unsettled state of problems in this area it would be wrong to create the impression that all the problems referred to above are in the same state of fluidity. In terms of the closed-economy transmission mechanisms it is worth re-emphasising that, from an empirical point of view, it is impossible to distinguish between the expectations augmented excess demand view, and that of Fisher. Further, if the money supply growth process is given an appropriate stochastic structure then rational expectations also produce a similar set of predictions to those of the other two models. Models based on one variant or another of the above 'stories' with an appropriate role for fiscal policy (missing in the above examples) have been estimated for a large number of economies and apparently are capable of accounting for a large amount of the variability of inflation (see Laidler and Parkin [29] for a survey).

The area where least is known concerns the behaviour of flexible exchange rate open economies. Here, both theoretical and empirical work is required, but primarily at this stage, theoretical work (on this see Genberg and Kierzkowski [15]).

Thus in the area of unravelling the details of the transmission mechanisms from monetary policy to inflation a great deal of progress has already been made in the context of both the closed economoy and fixed exchange-rate open economy, but most progress is now required for the flexible exchange-rate case.

In the above discussion virtually no mention has been made of fiscal policy. This is not because we do not believe it to have important effects on the economy. On the contrary, we recognise the existence of a large body of analysis and an enormous amount of empirical evidence indicating predictable and sizeable impact effects of such policies on the level of demand and therefore, on the rate of inflation. These policies work rather more directly than monetary policies in the sense that they immediately change disposable income and thereby set up expenditure adjustments. However, at the end of the day their effects are entirely reallocative. They can change the price level but they cannot change its rate of change in long-run equilibrium. They could of course, change its rate of change in long-run equilibrium if the overall level of public expenditure was so high that it became impossible to meet that expenditure by conventional taxes so that there was a sustained increase in the money supply. However, in that case, all the above discussion about the effects of monetary policy on inflation would be relevant even though the money supply growth rate would itself not have been exogenously controlled.

(7) THE DETERMINANTS OF MONETARY AND FISCAL POLICY

This naturally leads us to the second major unsettled problem in this area, namely an analysis of the determinants of monetary and fiscal policy. Why do governments pursue inflationary, monetary and fiscal policies? Further, why do they pursue cyclical policies? Suggested answers to these questions can usefully be grouped under three headings: (a) taxation; (b) vote-seeking; and (c) response to the behaviour of pressure groups. The taxation argument is the classical one. Since the printing of additonal money produces a revenue for the government equivalent to a tax equal to the absolute rate of increase in the money supply divided by the price level the government clearly would be tempted to use inflation as one of the many alternative sources of taxation. Since the demand for money depends inversely on the opportunity cost of holding it and since that opportunity cost is related one for one to the rate of inflation, the higher the rate of inflation generated by an inflation tax the smaller the stock of real money balances which people will wish to hold. There is thus, a revenue maximising rate of monetary expansion which, in general, will be finite. A government seeking to raise taxes in the least painful way could be presumed to use the inflation tax to raise the optimum amount of revenue from that source.

This will involve comparing the welfare loss arising from the inflation tax with the welfare loss arising from other taxes and equalising the marginal effects of all taxes on welfare loss. On the face of it, it would appear that the taxation argument for the pursuit of inflationary policies would lead to steady inflations. However, Sjaastad [41] has recently suggested that the optimum taxation regime is one in which inflation rates are unstable. This will arise if the government could, for part of the time, fool the electorate as to what the inflation rate is going to do and thereby cash in on subsequently falsified expectations.

In an international context the inflation tax argument has been put forward with respect to the holding of foreign-exchange reserves by central banks under the heading of the 'seignorage problem'.[1] Under a dollar standard, the United States could receive seignorage even at a stable price level. In addition, it could increase its seignorage by issuing money at an inflationary rate since the rest of the world would demand additional nominal balances to compensate for the rise in inflation. As the demand for real balances decreases with the rate of inflation there is a finite inflation rate that maximises seignorage. The optimum rate of inflation will be below this rate since account has to be taken of the welfare cost of inflationary finance, part of which, however, is shifted to the rest of the world. There are three options open to countries in the rest of the world to defend themselves against such a policy in the centre country. They can, first, reduce their rate of domestic credit expansion and thus bring down the overall rate of inflation but only at the cost of paying more seignorage through increase payments surpluses. Second, they can increase their rate of domestic credit expansion and thus reduce seignorage but at the cost of greater inflation in the world economy. Third, they can let their currencies appreciate. The second solution may appeal to an individual small country since it avoids the transitional unemployment costs (especially in the export sector where it might upset powerful vested interests), provides the vote-seeking advantages associated with a domestic boom generated by competitive credit expansion, and since the inflationary consequences of a small country doing so get diluted in the world economy.

We would not put too much store in the above explanation for the evolution of money and inflation in the world economy since the second world war. In the first place, the United States does pay interest on a large proportion of its monetary liabilities to non-residents and, in the second place, the behaviour of monetary authorities seems to have been motivated much more by internal considerations than by attempts at taxing foreigners in this indirect way. Nevertheless, such considerations do illuminate some of the issues involved in the struggle to change the international monetary system and points to

[1] See in particular the paper by Grubel and the note by Johnson in Mundell and Swoboda [32]. See also Mundell [33] for a formal analysis of the optimum deficit of a reserve-currency country (and hence its optimum rate of monetary expansion and inflation).

elements to be taken into account when studying the policy reactions of monetary authorities.

Of course, the optimum taxation justification for inflationary monetary policy is one aspect of the vote-seeking behaviour of governments. There is however, another which perhaps can more readily explain *variations* in the rate of inflation. This runs in terms of an analysis of government preference, which are presumed to be myopic with the time horizon equal to the time until the next election, a horizon which therefore shortens as the next election approaches and which preferences are optimised subject to the constraint that the changes in the rate of monetary expansion lead first to changes in real economic activity and only subsequently to variations in the inflation rate. This would lead to governments pursuing expansionary monetary policies on the run to an election suffering the inflationary consequences of those policies after the election and having to tighten up policy in the interelection period to make room for the next pre-election real boom. A detailed and rigorous analysis of such a process has been provided by Nordhaus [35].

It has also been suggested that policy-makers could generate inflation and a path of inflation and unemployment consistent with observed Phillips-curve loops when following and optimal control programme destined to maximise a welfare function over time. This idea is incorporated in a paper by Kierzkowski [21] in which output fluctuations are determined by the behaviour of demanders and suppliers of labour in response to changes in actual and expected prices, and in which the inflation rate is treated as a control variable and also enters (negatively, along with a fall in employment) the policy-makers' utility function to be maximised over a given number of periods. Note that, to the extent that policy-makers adopt what they perceive to be the public's utility function in their control operation, this approach is not inconsistent with the vote-maximising hypothesis.

There are two further aspects of vote-seeking behaviour which would appear to be worthy of detailed incorporation into an explanation of government monetary policy. Governments may feel that they gain political credit from achieving and maintaining extremely low rates of unemployment. If they seek to achieve such rates of unemployment by monetary policies then in order to get below and stay below the 'natural' unemployment rate it becomes necessary to pursue a montary policy which will be associated with a persistently accelerating trend rate of inflation. In proximate policy terms this would probably take the form of the government and its economic advice machine setting a target for the unemployment rate and real growth rate and shooting for that target using a mixture of fiscal, interest rate, credit and monetary policies. The outcome of such a procedure would on the average achieve the lower unemployment rate for a period but at the expense of increasing rates of inflation. Further, the rate at which the money supply expanded would increase alongside the rate of inflation.

The second aspect of vote-seeking behaviour which would tend to make for a trend increase in the rate of inflation concerns interest rate policy. It seems reasonable to suppose that governments aim to capture the votes of the new generation of young voters. The easiest way of doing that is to raise the income of young voters relative to those of older more committed voters. This can only be achieved by a redistribution of income between the two groups. To achieve such a redistribution openly and blatantly would probably backfire. However, it may be possible to achieve such a redistribution in a manner which at least for a number of years perhaps will not be resented by those who are losing and that is to ensure that rates of interest are kept low or even negative. This helps the young because they are typically net debtors whilst the old are net creditors. Low or negative rates of interest therefore, provide a return to borrowers (young people) and place a burden on lenders (older people). The only way in which low interest rates can be made to stick is by having a sufficiently expansive credit and monetary policy. The inflation process that would ensue from the holding of interest rates below their 'natural' rate is exactly that outlined by Wicksell [43]. The difference is that he told the analytical story in terms of the *banks* holding the rate of interest below the equilibrium rate, whereas the story here has the government as the dominant interest-rate setting agency.

The third source of monetary policy variations and inflationary monetary policies that has been suggested is the response of the monetary authorities and governments to various political pressure groups. The most often identified of such groups is organised labour. The story here would be that trade unions seeking to maintain or improve their relative shares, generate a particular rate of wage rise which, given the rate of productivity growth, implies a certain rate of price inflation. The analysis would go on to argue that the trade union movement is sufficiently powerful to put direct day-to-day pressures and indirect longer-term pressure through the ballot box to ensure that the government produces a monetary policy that is sufficiently expansive to validate whatever rate of inflation emerges from the rate of wage change which the unions initiated. A second and recent group who have been indentified as providing this type of inflationary impulse is the cartel.

Formalising hypotheses concerning the alternative sources of variations in monetary policy, testing those hypotheses and discriminating amongst them is very much in its infancy at this stage and clearly a great deal more work in this area is required.

II. THE CONSEQUENCES AND COSTS OF INFLATION

Almost everyone agrees that inflation is an evil, that it is costly, that it inflicts major burdens on a society. However, there is a good deal of confusion as to what these costs are precisely, how they may be measured, how large they actually are and on whom they fall.

The one relatively settled issue in this area of inflation analysis concerns a very narrow aspect of the costs of inflation, the welfare cost of fully anticipated inflation. If an economy is experiencing a rate of inflation which it has always experienced and which everyone fully expects with complete certainty to continue for ever, and if all prices are adjusted continuously at a rate equal in the rate of inflation so that relative prices are never misaligned even as a temporary matter, then the only effect of inflation is to act as a tax on real cash balances and to increase the velocity of circulation. In other words, the tax on real cash balances acts as an incentive to economise on real cash balances since it raises the private opportunity cost of holding the latter. Assuming the social opportunity cost of producing real cash balances to be zero and money to bear no interest, an obvious deadweight loss arises from the wedge that inflation drives between the private opportunity cost of holding money and its social production cost. This loss can be measured in the conventional manner using standard welfare triangles.

This standard welfare analysis developed at the University of Chicago and originating with Bailey's classic article has, for the most part, been based on a loosely specified indirect utility approach to the derivation of the demand for money function. In a recent contribution, Barro [2] makes matters more explicit by considering a stochastic transactions cost approach to the derivation of the demand for money function. He is therefore able to show (as were Feige and Parkin [10]) the effects of changes in the velocity of circulation induced by changes in the opportunity cost of holding money on the volume of transactions and therefore on the resources devoted to transactions. This more explicit approach has the virtue of making clear the source of the welfare loss referred to above; it is in its effects on transactions frequencies and on the real resources devoted to transactions that anticipated inflation impinges on the 'Chicago story'.

It should also help to make clear that there are many costs of inflation, even anticipated inflation, which are completely overlooked by this approach. If the loss of a welfare triangle – that is relatively small at anything but very high rates of inflation by existing calculations and which could anyway be eliminated by payment of interest on money balances – was all there was to the cost of inflation, we would be hard put to explain present concern about inflation and would gaily propose, as some did a few years back, that stopping inflation is definitely not worth the trouble of the transitional unemployment it is likely to cause. The nature and importance of the other costs of inflation is very much a 'soft' area in the literature. We will nevertheless venture a few suggestions as to possible lines for further enquiry below.

In the first place, it is possible for the rate of inflation to be fully anticipated in the sense that the expected and actual rate are equal but for the expectation not to be held with full certainty, the dispersion of the expectation being reflected in its variance. To the extent that economic agents are risk averters an increase in the variance should lead to a decrease in welfare. As Alvin Marty points out, whether the standard welfare triangles change systematically with the rate of inflation depends on whether the variance and covariance structure of the expected rate of inflation is heteroskedastic or not. The matter, however, is not simple. As Stanley Fischer's work on indexed bonds (Fischer [11]) indicates, the welfare loss due to variance in expected inflation depends also on its covariance with the rate of returns on alternative assets including human capital.

In his contribution to this conference, Laidler [28] emphasises three elements in the cost of inflation that are not taken into account by the conventional analysis of the welfare cost of inflationary finance. He argues first, that the social productivity of money is higher than the sum of individual consumer surpluses, if only because larger money holdings by others contribute to reducing the random element in an individual's payments and receipts patterns. Second, an increase in the expected rate of inflation and the opportunity cost of holding money induces changes in the structure of economic activity, co-ordination through markets giving way to co-ordination through institutions with resulting real resource costs. Third, inflation impairs the unit-of-account role of money making it a less efficient substitute for devoting other resources to 'the generation of information upon which plans can be based' (p. 324 below)

These types of considerations are better analysed within the Brunner and Meltzer [4] type of framework for discussing the role of money than within the neoclassical one, even if the former does not lead to easily quantifiable propositions. In our view, the issues here hinge on two key concepts, *information* and *search*, the central problems arising from the fact of costly price adjustment.

Since the cost of price change is finite it will always be optimal for firms to enter into contracts or commitments of finite duration at pre-announced or declared prices. If there is no inflation, prices will have to be adjusted from time to time in the light of underlying changes in technology and tastes which have given rise to the need for a changed relative price structure. Given a certain rate of change of the pattern of technology and tastes there will be an optimum frequency for price revision. This will involve trading off the gains from having an 'equilibrium' price against the losses of incurring the costs of adjusting the prices. However, in a period of inflation prices will have to be adjusted over and above the adjustment for changes in technology and tastes because of the change in the absolute price level. The faster the rate of inflation, either the more frequently will prices have to be adjusted, or the bigger will the steps of adjustment have to be, or some combination of the two. If prices are adjusted more frequently, purely because of inflation, then it will typically be the case that at any point in time some firms have just raised their prices to allow for inflation and others not. If firms maintain the same frequency of price adjustment, but adjust in bigger steps then it will be the case that at any point in time relative price disparities between firms will be larger than under a non-inflationary regime. In either event there will be increased returns to additional search activity. This will not show up, or at least not necessarily show up, as a change in the velocity of circulation. Transactions may still go through with the same frequency and average real money balance holdings be unaffected, but the amount of productive work time available or the amount of leisure time available after the increased search activity will be reduced. The welfare cost of this activity is not captured by the standard welfare triangle which does not distinguish the loss due to the effect of a higher opportunity cost of holding money, given the frequency and distribution of changes in relative prices from that due to an increase in their variability[1].

An additional aspect of the cost of inflation not captured either by the transactions frequency analysis or by the search analysis concerns the information content in posted prices. If the price level is stable and known to be stable then the posted prices contain a great deal of information and make it immediately possible to compute relative prices accurately. However, if the price level is itself changing at a rapid rate and furthermore at a variable and unpredictable rate it becomes less easy to make direct inferences from sequential sampling of nominal prices about the rate of inflation. If we observe a price of x today and the price of y tomorrow we may not infer that the relative price is px_{t-1}/py_t, rather we have to make an inference about what the price of x will be at t in order to compute the relative price of x and y at t, based on our observation of x_{t-1}, and y_t. Sampling must also be increased to disentangle general from relative price changes. The extra amount of effort which has to go into this activity and the amount of uncertainty to which it gives rise will lead to resource misallocations of a pervasive and difficult-to-evaluate nature, but possibly adding up to a sizeable welfare loss.[2]

It is possible that the costs associated with inflation arising from these last two sources – search costs and information costs – though not from the first (transactions frequencies) do not increase monotonically with the rate of inflation. It seems likely that these costs are not serious in very low rates of inflation. However, at intermediate rates of inflation, rates between say ten and thirty, forty and even fifty per cent per annum, these costs could be very heavy indeed; but for rates of inflation in excess of, to pick a number, 50 per cent per annum may eventually give rise to less costs of this type since there will be an incentive to institutionalise the inflation and find procedures for avoiding the costs just identified.

Considerations concerning search costs and the loss of information or content in relative prices lead to the conjecture that in the long run, far from there being a tradeoff between inflation and unemployment, there may well be a direct relationship between those two variables. As the rate of inflation

[1] It may even be that the demand for money would increase with an increase in the variability of relative prices – especially if one takes a buffer-stock view of the demand for money. This effect would tend to be offset by the effect of inflation on the opportunity cost of holding money.

[2] Genberg and Swoboda [14] note the costs of frequently changing price tags in terms of increased search and loss of information and add that '. . . zero *is* a magic number in the context of inflation; it is the only number at which the price *level* is fixed and thus minimises 'menu-changing' costs, costs that are far from trivial when the rate of inflation departs significantly from zero' (page 15).

increases, the return from search increases and the informational content in prices decreases and one would expect to see the increased amount of disequilibrium or noise in relative prices manifesting itself in the labour market in increased unemployment and the increased amount of search activity also manifesting itself in the labour market in the form of an increase in measured unemployment. This conjecture is consistent with the analysis of the 'new microeconomics' school, particularly that of Mortensen [30] who notes that increased imperfection of information in the labour market results, in his model, in a reduction of the acceptance rate of job offers. More formally, the natural rate of unemployment in his model increases with the variance of the distribution of wage offers. We have just argued that, because of the cost of changing prices and the loss of information in posted prices, the variance in relative prices – including wages in specific firms – will typically rise with inflation even if the latter is perfectly expected in a stochastic sense.

Some of the major costs of inflation are, of course connected with unanticipated rather than expected inflation. These costs are extremely hard to express formally and even harder to measure. Some of them are discussed briefly in Genberg and Swoboda [14] and we will confine ourselves to a few brief remarks here.

A distinction may usefully be made here between an expected inflation that is anticipated in the sense that agents rearrange their transactions and asset-holding to take these expectations into account and one that is unanticipated in the sense that these rearrangements do not take place, presumably because of institutional or other constraints. In contrast unexpected inflation takes the public by surprise – though it can make provisions against such surprises, through indexation for instance.

The costs of inflation that loom large in most people's minds are those associated with the redistribution of income and wealth connected with unanticipated inflation. As economists, we are wont to confess our inability to evaluate such costs since we do not have a scientific criterion which enables us to assess whether the losers lose more than the gainers gain. Yet there must be some loss if the distribution of income was an optimal one before inflation started.

We are slightly more at ease with identifying costs that arise from constraints on the public's ability to anticipate inflation. Prominent among those constraints are regulations that prevent nominal contracts from reflecting the expected rate of inflation. They include ceilings on interest rates, regulation of mortgage terms, limitations on the range of assets particular institutions can hold, etc. The resulting costs should in principle be quantifiable by means of standard applied welfare analysis – at least to the extent that one can identify the degree to which distortions created by such regulations are related to a given increase in the rate of inflation. We suspect, for instance, that the current 'housing triangle' in the United Kingdom (due in good part to subsidised mortgage rates in the face of high expected inflation) may well be more important than the pure welfare cost of inflationary finance.

Finally, inflation brings in its wake serious political and social costs. Social tensions arise between those groups that are able to protect themselves against it and those that are not. Vested interests in its continuation are created and those groups that would lose most if it were stopped will carry the battle on in the political field. Such costs are difficult to measure precisely but their pervasive nature argues for more careful study and attention than economists have typically devoted to them. These costs are revealed in their starkest form in hyperinflation. It is a hard fact that no hyperinflation has ended without an extremely costly monetary reform and without the abandonment of liberal democracy and the introduction of some kind of authoritarianism. Whether an authoritarian political regime is regarded as a cost of hyperinflation is partly a matter of establishing whether or not such a regime inevitably follows hyperinflation and partly a matter of subjective evaluation of the desirablity or otherwise of such a regime. While it is clear that hyperinflation is not a necessary condition for an authoritarian regime the evidence suggests that it may well be a sufficient condition.

III. POLICIES TOWARDS INFLATION

First, there is a debate as to whether or not, once an economy has an inflation that is anticipated, it should take steps to eradicate that inflation or seek to minimise its disruptive effects and live with it. The 'cost-benefit' approach of Phelps [38] leads to the conclusion that in general it will pay to validate an ongoing expected inflation, rather than to suffer the temporary recession that would be the cost of eradicating it. However, the broader set of considerations concerning the costs of inflation itemised in the preceding section leads us to suspect that this conclusion will require modification when all the costs of inflation are adequately allowed for. Apart from re-emphasis of our discussion in the preceding section, we have nothing further at this stage to contribute to this debate and, in this section concentrate solely on the problem of designing policies to reduce rather than live with inflation. However, as part of that exercise we do examine the effects of indexation.

There are many alternative ways in which we could organise a discussion of the policy debate. We begin with a discussion of demand management and the assignment of demand management instruments to targets. We then examine indexation and finally direct controls and what may be termed 'natural rate reduction policies'.

The question of what constitutes the most appropriate (optimal) demand management regime is one of which there remains considerable disagreement. The disagreements centre partly on the degree of fine tuning which is appropriate, partly on the assignment of instruments to targets, and partly on the appropriate degree of domestic insulation to be sought from exchange rate variability.

The fine-tuning issue must be essentially empirical and one which turns on a judgement as to the length of the time-lags involved from pulling a particular policy lever to seeing its effects, relative to the length of the forecasting horizon, and on the capacity of the political process to produce policy responses of appropriate magnitude and timing. The first matter seems to us to be relatively settled. There is a large body of econometric literature (see Eckstein (ed.) (1972) for a recent survey for the United States) which could be broadly summarised as indicating that both fiscal and monetary policies matter in the sense that they both affect aggregate demand but that the lags on monetary policy are longer than those on fiscal policy. Against this, for most countries, fiscal policy is made by a political (including legislative) process which involves the legislature while monetary policy is made by the central bank with more or less co-ordination with the executive. Hence, the 'inside lags' are shorter for monetary policy than for fiscal policy. Formal analysis of the performance of an economy (the United States economy) controlled by a monetary rule compared with optimal control (optimal fine tuning) indicates that the rule can be beaten. However, a monetary rule wins when compared with the United States historical record. (See Fischer and Cooper [13]). This suggests (although by no means proves) that taking all the lags and likely misjudgements into account, simply from the point of view of stabilising demand, fine tuning is, in present circumstances, dominated by a rule.

The assignment problem has two dimensions, one associated with the dynamic stability in a non-stochastic environment and the other concerning asymptotic stochastic variability. The classic Mundell [31] assignment paper in which monetary policy was to be assigned to the achievement of the external balance and the fiscal policy to internal balance (in a fixed exchange-rate world) has many analogies in the context of both closed and open economies. The central analytical idea in Mundell's paper was to show that, under certain assumptions about the adjustment process, and given only qualitative information about aggregate economic relationships, a particular assignment produced a dynamically stable system. The same ideas can be applied to the question of the assignment of monetary and fiscal policy to real activity and price level goals in the context of a closed economy or of a flexible exchange-rate open economy. If there does not exist a long-run trade off between inflation and unemployment and if monetary policies are assigned to the attainment of full employment then, except by accident, the outcome will be an unemployment rate which is lower (or higher) than the equilibrium rate and a price level which continuously rises (or continuously falls).

If, alternatively, the monetary instrument is assigned to price level stability, but only indirectly via the pursuit of a stable growth rate for the money supply itself, then the inflation rate which will emerge in long-run equilibrium would be determined by the rate of monetary expansion, and the unemployment rate would be the so-called 'natural rate'. (We take up further below the problem of what might be done if the natural rate is politically and socially unacceptably high.) The key to the similarity between this analysis and the Mundell analysis is in terms of the dynamic stability (or instability) which results from pursuing the alternative policies. Shooting for a real target which is different from the 'natural unemployment rate' inevitably sets up a dynamically unstable price level process. Shooting for a price level target or a rate of inflation target inevitably sets up a dynamically stable process. In that respect it has direct analogies to the Mundell assignment of fiscal policies to internal and monetary policies to external equilibrium.

The second aspect of the assignment problem concerns the minimisation of the variance of real output or other macrotargets, as a weighted average of the variances of several targets, given *quantitative* knowledge of macrorelations. The pioneering article on this topic is that by Poole [39] although his analysis was conducted in the context of a fixed price level world. Specifically, Poole shows that whether one should use a money stock rule or an interest rate rule or a linear combination of the two depends on the relative stochastic variability of real expenditure as compared with the demand for money.

There is a natural extension of this analysis, although it has not yet been rigorously carried out, concerning the question of whether monetary and fiscal policy should be assigned to employment or price level stability. Presumably, by analogy from Poole's results, this will turn on the relative stability of the short-run Phillips-curve viewed as some kind of dynamic aggregate supply function and the short-run aggregate demand function which itself will depend upon the monetary and fiscal policy regime pursued. A pure fine-tuning regime could be viewed as setting a vertical or completely inelastic aggregate demand function, whilst a monetary rule could be viewed as setting an aggregate demand function which approximates a rectangular hyperbole with an elasticity of minus one. Which of these two alternatives will produce the greatest degree of stochastic stability in the unemployment and output levels would depend upon the nature of the stochastic variability in the short-run Phillip's-curve and aggregate demand function and the covariation between them.

Discussion of the degree of international insulation which should be sought from exchange rate flexibility is hampered by the lack of a well-developed theory of short-run adjustment under flexible rates (see previous section). It is clear that in long-run equilibrium in a world of stable prices, a fixed exchange rate will generate price stability regardless of domestic policy, whereas in a world of price level instability, fixed exchange-rate will produce unstable domestic prices regardless of domestic policy. Obviously therefore, the choice of exchange-rate regime will not be independent of the nature of the world environment in which the individual economy finds itself. However, there are major unresolved questions concerning the contribution of exchange-rate fixity to world price level stability and conversely the effects of exchange-rate flexibility on world average inflation (see Claassen [6]). Further, there are major unresolved questions concerning the capacity of an economy to provide itself with short-run insulation by adopting flexible rates.

A major question on demand management policies concerns the appropriate speed with which an established inflation should be squeezed out. There are basically two alternative procedures advocated. One may be called 'gradualism' and the other the 'big bang' approach. 'Gradualism' argues that no matter what policies are pursued, expectations adjust only slowly and therefore the rate at which the money supply growth rate is reduced in order to reduce the rate of inflation should be a moderate one in order that unemployment is not created on a massive scale during the period in which inflation expectations exceed the actual inflation rate. The alternative 'big bang' view works in the assumption that expectations are to some extent at least rational and that a visible and massive reduction in the rate of monetary expansion will immediately feed into inflationary expectations and reduce the actual rate of inflation independently of the state of excess supply in the economy. The resolution of this debate is clearly an empirical one and turns on the empirical viability of the rational expectations explanation of expectations formation.

In view of the painfulness of demand management policies as a means of reducing inflation many alternative procedures have been advocated. The one which is currently attracting a great deal of attention is the idea that cost of living indexation could not only make it easier to live with inflation while we have it but also make it less painful to squeeze out the inflation inducing a smaller than otherwise recession as part of the transitory cost of the inflation squeeze-out. Many questions concerning indexation are unresolved. A start has been made on the microeconomics of indexation, analysing its effects on the demand for bonds where index bonds are offered as part of the menu of choice and in particular examining the relative yields on indexed and non-indexed bonds and other assets (see Fischer [11]). Also, questions concerning the dynamic responsiveness of the inflation rate and the wage inflation rate and the level of real output and unemployment in an economy which is indexed are also now being analysed (see Fischer [12] and Parkin [37]).

A further set of policies, which if not widely popular amongst economists are very popular amongst politicians and which are advocated as a potential means of reducing inflation independently of recession creating excess supply, is that of direct wages and prices control. The effects of such policies have been widely investigated at an empirical level (see, for example, Parkin and Sumner [36]. The broad consensus of the results available to date is that direct controls have at best a minimal effect on the rate of inflation.

Finally, policies designed to make labour markets function more efficiently and reduce the equilibrium unemployment rate have been advocated by Holt [18]. These amount to policies designed to increase the state of accurate information available to employers and workers thereby reducing the amount of search unemployment.

The bulk of the preceding discussion of policy has been conducted as if the policy-making machine was a clinical instrument setting instruments to achieve economic targets free from the contamination of more explicitly political considerations. This stands in contrast to our discussion in Section I of the need for a political economy of inflation. In the absence of such a political economy there is little to be said about how or whether the political process is capable of delivering appropriate stabilisation policies. The key issue here concerns the relationship between political and economic institutions and the types of monetary and fiscal policies pursued. For example, is an independent central bank more likely to stabilise output and prices than a central bank which is completely controlled by the government? Or, at the world level, what kind of world monetary system and institution are likely to provide the most stable world monetary environment? What is the effect of the electoral system (in terms of frequency of elections and the like) on the inflationary attitude of policy? It is in this area of the policy debate that least progress has been and where, in our judgement, the payoff could be greatest.

REFERENCES

[1] Bank of England, 'The Importance of Money', *B.E.Q.B.*, Vol. 10 (2), pp. 159–198.
[2] R. J. Barro, 'Inflation, The Payments Period, and the Demand for Money', *JPE* Vol. 78, No. 6, (November/December 1970), pp. 1228–1263.
[3] W. Branson, 'International Transmission of Inflation: A Keynesian Approach', Mimeo, Brookings Conference on World Wide Inflation, (Washington, D.C., November 1974).
[4] K. Brunner and A. H. Meltzer, 'The Uses of Money: Money in the Theory of an Exchange Economy', A.E.R. Vol. LXI, No. 5, (December 1971), pp. 784–805.
[5] R. E. Caves and G. L. Reuber, *Canadian Economic Policy and the Importance of International Capital Flows*, (Toronto: University of Toronto Press, 1969).
[6] Emil-Maria Claassen, 'World Inflation Under Flexible Exchange Rates', Seminar of Flexible Exchange Rates and Stabilization Policy, Saltsjöbaden, 1975.
[7] Rudiger Dornbusch, 'International Transmission of Inflation: Some Comments', (Mimeo, 1974).
[8] Rudiger Dornbusch, 'The Theory of Flexible Exçhange Rate Regimes and Macro-economic Policy', presented at Seminar of Flexible Exchange Rates and Stabilization Policy, Saltsjöbaden, (1975*a*).
[9] Rudiger Dornbusch, 'Inflation, Unemployment and Growth: An Expository Framework', mimeo presented at Konstanz Conference, (1975*b*).
[10] E. L. Feige and Michael Parkin, 'The Optimum Quantity of Money, Bonds, Commodity Inventories and Capital,' *American Economic Review*, Vol. 61 (3), Part 1, 1971, pp. 335–49.
[11] Stanley Fischer, 'Demand for Indexed Bonds', MIT Working Paper 132, (May 1974).
[12] Stanley Fischer, 'Wage Indexation and Macroeconomic Stability', MIT mimeo presented at Conference on the Monetary Mechanism in Open Economies, Helsinki (1975).
[13] Stanley Fischer and J. Phillip Cooper, 'Stabilisation Policy and Lags', *Journal of Political Economy,* Vol. 81, July/August 1973.
[14] Irving Fisher, *The Purchasing Power of Money*, (London: Macmillan, 1911).
[15] H. Genberg and A. K. Swoboda, 'Inflation and Indexation; A Survey of the Issues', in *Indexation and Protection Against Inflation and Exchange Rate Risk,* (Stockholm, 1974).
[16] H. Genberg and H. Kierzkowski, 'Short-Run, Long Run and Dynamics of Adjustment Under Flexible Exchange Rates', mimeo, Graduate Institute, Geneva (1975).
[17] M. R. Gray and Michael Parkin, 'Discriminating Between Alternative Explanations of Inflation', Manchester Inflation Workshop Discussion Paper, 1974, forthcoming in Fratianni and Tavernia (eds.), *Proceedings of Conference on Money, K.U.L.,* (Louvain, Belgium, September 1974).
[18] C. C. Holt, 'How Can the Phillips Curve be Moved to Reduce both Inflation and Unemployment?' in Phelps (ed.), *The Microeconomic Foundations of Employment and Inflation Theory* (New York: Norton 1970).

[19] Harry G. Johnson, 'A Note on Seignorage and the Social Saving from Substituting Credit for Commodity Money' in R. A. Mundell and A. K. Swoboda (eds.) *Monetary Problems of the International Economy,* University of Chicago Press, 1969.
[20] P. D. Jonson, 'An Investigation of the U.K. Balance of Payments with Particular Emphasis on the Role of Monetary Disequilibrium Dynamics 1882–1970', University of London Ph.D. Thesis, (1974).
[21] H. Kierzkowski, 'A Model of Optimal Stabilization Policy', Queen's University mimeo (1973).
[22] M. Knight and C. R. Wymer, 'A Monetary Model of an Open Economy: An Application to U.K.', *AUTE*, 1975.
[23] Pieter Korteweg, 'Inflation and Economic Activity: The Dutch Experience', (Helsinki, 1975).
[24] David Laidler, *The Demand for Money: Theories and Evidence,* (Scranton, PA., 1969).
[25] David Laidler, 'The Influence of Money on Real Income and Inflation: A Simple Model with Some Empirical Tests for the United States, 1953–1972', *Manchester School*, Vol. 41 (4), pp. 367–95, (1973).
[26] David Laidler, 'Price and Output Fluctuations in an Open Economy' in *Essays in Money and Inflation*, (Manchester: Manchester University Press, 1975).
[27] David Laidler, 'Unemployment and Inflation: A British Commentary' in Friedman, *Unemployment and Inflation*, IEA (London, 1975).
[28] David Laidler, 'The Welfare Costs of Inflation in Neoclassical Theory – Some Unsettled Problems,' presented at IEA Conference on Inflation (1975), and forming chapter 12 of this book.
[29] Svend Laurensen and Lloyd Metzler, 'Flexible Exchange Rates and the Theory of Employment', *Review of Economic Statistics,* (February 1950).
[30] D. T. Mortensen, 'Job Search, The Duration of Unemployment and the Phillips Curve', American Economic Review, Vol. 60 (5), pp. 847–62, (1970).
[31] Robert A. Mundell, 'Capital Mobility and Stabilisation Policy Under Fixed and Flexible Exchange Rates', *CJE*, (November, 1963).
[32] R. A. Mundell and A. K. Swoboda, *Monetary Problems of the International Economy*, (Cambridge: Cambridge University Press, 1969).
[33] Robert A. Mundell, 'The Optimum Balance of Payments Deficit' in Claassen and Salin (eds.), *Stabilisation Policy in Interdependent Economics,* (Amsterdam: North-Holland, 1972).
[34] Michael Mussa, 'On The Inherent Stability of Rationally Adaptive Expectations', Rochester mimeo, 75–2, (1975).
[35] William Nordhaus, 'The Political Business Cycle', *Review of Economic Studies,* Vol. 42, April 1975.
[36] Michael Parkin and Michael Sumner, 'The Effects of Income Policy on the Rate of Inflation: A Survey of the Econometric Evidence', mimeo, University of Manchester, June 1972.
[37] Michael Parkin, 'Indexation and Monetary Stability', Manchester Inflation Workshop Discussion Paper, (1975).
[38] E. S. Phelps, *Inflation Policy and Unemployment Theory' The Cost-Benefit Approach to Monetary Planning*, (New York, 1972).
[39] William Poole, 'Optimal Choice of Monetary Policy Instruments in a Simple Stochastic Macro Model', *Quarterly Journal of Economics*, LXXXIV, (May 1970), pp. pp. 197–216.
[40] A. J. Schwartz, 'Six Episodes of Secular Price Change', *JMCB*, 1963.
[41] Larry Sjaastad, 'Why Steady Inflations Fail', in Parkin and Zis (eds.), *Inflation: The World Economy*, (Manchester: Manchester University Press, 1975).
[42] Alexander Swoboda, 'Monetary Approach to Transmission and Generation of Inflation', mimeo, presented at Brookings Conference on World-wide Inflation, November 1974, Washington.
[43] Knut Wicksell, *Interest and Prices,* Cass Reprint, (London, 1962) (first published 1898, first English translation 1936).

Discussion of the Paper by Michael Parkin and Alexander Swoboda

Professor Giersch opened the discussion. He said this was a fine co-operative paper which took account of all the recent literature, even including papers for this conference. The title might be: 'All about inflation in open and closed economies'.

The paper began by raising two semantic problems. The first was the definition of inflation. If there were an increase in the price level, which index should one use? The index of consumer prices, the G.N.P. deflator or even a more comprehensive index, including the prices of assets? He agreed with the authors that one should use a consumer price index, because this was in line with what both the public and the public authorities had in mind. He would be unhappy to use the G.N.P. deflator because no-one bought the G.N.P. At least, one would have to eliminate exports and include imports. This should have suggested itself in a paper that laid so much stress on an open economy.

The second problem was how far to go in looking at the causes of inflation. Perhaps the important issue here was how to draw demarcation lines between disciplines, and at some point economists might have to cede this subject to the political scientists or sociologists. The authors' view was that economists should concentrate on the money supply. Even so, they did not refrain from bringing in political models.

There were similar problems over the distinction between cost–push and demand–pull. The criterion here seemed to be why the money supply increased. Was there an active monetary policy? Or was the money supply adaptive in the face of aggressive social forces? Since the authors preferred a policy-orientated approach, it was surprising they had not carried this thinking through to their analysis. If the money supply increased at the same rate over a long period, so that actual and expected price increases were equal, the authors argued that one could then predict the inflation rate. One might call this a long-run equilibrium theory of inflation.

The question of the transmission mechanism was not settled. The authors had three hypotheses. The first two were based on a temporary money illusion and resulted in a temporary output effect, with expectations adjusting only slowly. One might call these the portfolio transmission theory and the Irving Fisher theory. For policy, it was unnecessary to distinguish between them.

The third hypothesis assumed rational expectations, in the sense of no money illusion. An increased money supply (an exogenous change) led to an increase in the expected rate of inflation and this carried through to the actual rate, so that there was no output effect. This model would hold if the rate of increase in the money supply were constant over a long period, or if the monetary authorities announced in advance the rate of increase in the money supply. The public could then deduce the implied rate of inflation.

The authors' discussion of international transmission under fixed exchange rates took account of commodity arbitrage and the monetary theory of the balance of payments. In a world of imperfect competition, commodity arbitrage would take time, and more time during a recession than during a boom. For example, in 1966–7 foreign firms had tried to sell at lower prices in Germany than elsewhere, in order to keep their German market share. Now,

Volkswagen was accused of underpricing its exports to the United States. It regarded the American slump as temporary and the maintenance of its United States market share in the long-run as worth a short-run loss. The one-price law could break down in a recession when foreign companies became more aware that they were marginal suppliers. They then showed greater price flexibility in foreign markets than in the domestic one.

The authors assumed common capital and goods markets, but not an integrated labour market. It did not surprise him that Michael Parkin, who was English, had ignored this. But he was surprised by Professor Swoboda, who came from a country which had experienced a good deal of immigration from neighbouring countries. When wages increased in the Federal Republic of Germany, the Dutch were pressed to increase wages in the Netherlands, otherwise substantial labour arbitrage would take place. The traditional theory of international trade had been based on the assumption that countries were islands, like Britain. On the continent, however, countries did have land borders. Moreover, co-ordinated international action by trade unions had recently developed, on industry lines, thus strengthening the tendencies towards wage equalisation.

With flexible exchange rates, one could consider several international transmission models in which changes in monetary policy led to delayed or overshooting reactions, so countries would not insulate themselves from outside inflation with flexible exchange rates *per se.* Professor Giersch would have been happier if the models could have been turned round. What strategy should a country with a floating exchange rate pursue to insulate itself? The answer was one of political economy. Some governments had introduced floating exchange rates and yet still blamed other countries for exporting inflation to them. The literature set out the issues, but politicians reading it might conclude that it did not help them. If economists could set out how a country could protect itself from imported inflation, they would make a more valuable contribution.

On the fiscal and monetary aspects of expansionary policies, the authors took a monetarist view. They stressed that the effects of fiscal policy were wholly allocative and redistributive. The outside lags of fiscal policy were shorter than those of monetary policy, but the decision lags of fiscal policy might be longer.

An important question was why we had monetary policies which led to rapidly increasing money supply. The authors gave three reasons: taxation; vote-seeking; and pressure groups.

The ideas about taxation were closely related to the Chicago theory of the optimal quantity of money. In an international context, say, under a dollar standard, the United States would tax the rest of the world by an inflow of resources to the United States, financed by an outflow of dollars. Other countries could avoid this 'taxation' only by adopting flexible exchange rates, and it had proved difficult to overcome traditional economic doctrines and resistance from vested interests. The authors argued that the international inflation tax argument was not very important because the United States had to pay interest on its dollar debt.

The question was whether interest rates were high enough to compensate for the loss of purchasing power. A near-monopoly like the American monetary system under the Bretton Woods arrangements would tend to break down if dollar prices were high, because American industry would then become uncompetitive. The world was now experiencing more competition among currencies and, of course, in private transactions. Competition among currencies might become a very relevant field of study for economists. From the government's point of view, the optimal rate of inflation tax within a country might vary. The government might want to fool the population by temporarily reducing inflation: hence the inflation tax. A new money illusion would then soon develop which could be exploited. So one had the successive creation and destruction of money illusion in a dynamic process.

Vote-seeking also led to instability. Perhaps the economic cycle had now been linked to the electoral cycle. One had expansion sufficiently long before an election and a fight against inflation in the rest of the period. The United States and Germany now had synchronised election dates, so we might soon see a perfect international synchronisation of the business cycle. Governments acted in this way to get credit for reducing unemployment. Keynes had said that economic policy was framed by those who had studied the textbooks of twenty-five years ago. The present generation of policy-makers was therefore devoted to the proposition that the rate of unemployment could be determined by demand management. This influence had been particularly great in the United States in the mid-1960s. Governments had tried to reduce the actual rate of unemployment below the 'natural' rate, by means of inflation. This was particularly important in periods when the natural rate of unemployment rose, due to accelerated structural change.

This led to the question of what was the long-run nature of the Phillips-curve. Perhaps the Phillips-curve was vertical in the long run, with no tradeoff between inflation and unemployment. Even then, accelerated inflation might reduce unemployment below the natural rate in the short run. The real issue was how short the short run actually was, and for how many people the money illusion had to be destroyed in order to deprive inflationary policy of its effect on employment.

The authors also suggested that governments sought to win *young* voters. In many countries, they were likely to be net debtors, not least because they had bought houses, and so wanted low real rates of interest. Inflation then became a mechanism to exploit the old to the benefit of the young. This meant that the age structure of the population became a major influence in determining government policy. However, in a country like Germany, where far more saving was carried out in advance of house purchase, this theory would perhaps be less applicable.

Trade unions as well as national or international cartels obviously aimed at redistribution. The question was whether the objective was to increase the share of the national income going to labour as a whole, or to a particular trade union. Inflation was a means of defeating attempts at redistribution.

As for the cost of inflation, the authors referred to Professor Laidler's paper.[1] Three propositions were relevant. First, a higher rate of inflation brought more variance in expectations, which frightened those members of the population who were risk-averters and led to a clear welfare loss. Second, there were the information costs of inflation that were dealt with by the new microeconomics or, more specifically, by the information theory of money. Inflation

[1] Chapter 12 in this book.

raised search costs and search employment. Third, there was the deterioration of money as a unit of account, which reduced the amount of information given by prices. It was no longer possible to deduce relative price changes from absolute ones.

The authors discussed both the political and social costs of inflation, and contended that no hyperinflation had ever ended without an extremely costly monetary reform and some kind of authoritarian government. As a German, Professor Giersch thought he had a right to point out that the *rentenmark* was introduced in 1923 within a democracy. An authoritarian government came only after a nine years' time-lag. Perhaps there was a connection between inflation and the rise of Hitler, but unemployment and deflation might be more important.

One might add that, with inflation, monetary assets were no longer as useful as a store of value, unless they could be indexed. In Germany there had been housing booms during recent inflationary periods. When the inflationary expectations declined, builders were left with unsold houses. This led to a slump in the building industry, followed by a further boom as inflation increased again. Professor Giersch considered this kind of situation typical of a country where indexed monetary assets were not available as substitutes for real assets.

On policy issues, the authors discussed the proposition, emanating especially from work by Professor Eckstein, that fine tuning was more likely to be effective if applied to fiscal rather than monetary policy, because the lags in fiscal policy were smaller. Professor Giersch wondered how relevant Professor Eckstein's results were. His model seemed to compare discretionary fiscal and monetary policies.

What conclusion would emerge if one compared discretionary fiscal policy with a monetary policy with preannounced targets? For example, in Germany, the central bank had announced the rate of increase in the monetary base for one calendar year. It might be even better to make the commitment for a longer period, fixing the target change in the monetary base for a particular phase of the business cycle rather than for a definite period of time. The announcement of such a strategy was important. As for fighting inflation, the authors distinguished between a 'big bang' theory and 'gradualism', which was, in principle, linked to adaptive expectations. They left out the possibility of announcements which influenced expectations.

This seemed to Professor Giersch to be the only potential advantage of an incomes policy. Where such a policy was introduced by force or moral persuasion it had not worked. Yet, in Germany, the social partners had taken account of and approved of the announced monetary targets. They hoped that, in the medium and long run, this would be a positive-sum game. Such a policy would only work if expectations were validated by government.

Adjusting expectations was one thing. Another possibility was to make them irrelevant. For example, it might be possible to induce people to make contracts in real terms. If the trade unions knew what increase in real wages they would get, whatever the rate of price increase, they would not need to make guesses about the inflation rate. In Germany, for example, the inflation rate assumed in wage contracts made for 1974 was 10 per cent. The actual rate of price increase had been 7 per cent. This had given an unintended increase in real wages – but only for the employed. So, one could either improve expectations through governments providing information to those operating in private markets, or one could, perhaps, make them irrelevant through indexation.

Professor Gordon wanted to talk about rational expectations. He thought the theories discussed in the paper by Parkin and Swoboda were weakened by the assumption of rational expectation.

This issue came up especially in the discussion of the three methods of transmission. The first two were essentially channels for getting money into expenditure, and, in the very short run, led to increased real output. After that, prices gradually increased because of excess demand. The other channel (perhaps operating simultaneously in other industries) represented a direct movement from the money supply to prices. Workers in firms voluntarily changed output.

One reason he was unhappy with the authors' distinction was that one could never tell which process was actually taking place. He thought this important because, if the first two channels were in operation, all supply decisions were voluntary. So, in a recession, all reductions in supply were voluntary, resulting from the reactions of people when they saw prices or wages below the level they expected. The other, he thought more realistic, theory was that prices were sticky. Then, if the money supply were reduced, output would fall. There was now a sales constraint, not a voluntary reduction in supply. If it were this channel in operation, an approach which assumed rational expectations would not to be correct.

He accepted that rational expectations came in at other places. First, there was the political business cycle. The idea, as explained by Professor Giersch, had been that governments would expand the economy just before elections and then contract if afterwards. Obviously, with rational expectations, governments could not follow such a policy for long. People would soon know that, after the election, prices would react to the earlier increase in the money supply. He did not know any example, in practice, of the political business cycle, but in theory it conflicted with rational expectations.

It also conflicted with the idea that the government should give a monetary rule. If output changed only because of misinformation, one would expect the announcement of a rule to lead to an instantaneous change in prices. One would get changes in output only if businessmen were taken by surprise.

If there were rational expectations, one would also be able easily to distinguish between a 'big bang' and a 'gradualist' approach. With rational expectations, the 'big bang' approach would be right, especially if it were an announced 'big bang'. Arthur Burns would be able to stand on the steps of the Federal Reserve Building and read out, from a parchment, to a television audience, what the new policy was to be. This certainly did not seem to have been happening in 1975, when everyone appeared confused about American monetary policy. The reality, Professor Gordon thought, was that we should assume irrational expectations.

Professor Bronfenbrenner proposed to discuss the welfare cost of inflation. Despite his Chicago training, he believed that the real welfare cost of inflation was mainly political, and wished that the paper had stressed these issues more.

There were two problems. First, individuals ascribed inflationary increases in their nominal income and wealth to real causes, but ascribed increases in their nominal costs to the inflation. The result was that the real cost of inflation was exaggerated and the recorded inflation rate incorporated in the propaganda of rival political and social systems. The result of this, in its turn, might be dictatorial tyranny, which promised to end inflation painlessly or claimed to have done so. The risk of such tyranny was the main real cost of inflation. Hitler might not really be a case in point, but Germany might have been lucky to escape a Hitler/Lüdendorff *putsch* in 1923.

Professor Lundberg suggested that behind the political problem must be either a view of welfare effects or superstition.

Professor Bronfenbrenner agreed that rational expectations were not the whole story. If Professor Lundberg meant that *any* move away from rationality was superstition, he (Bronfenbrenner) would disagree. He did not think he was superstitious himself, even when he departed from *ex post* rationality.

Professor Neumark wondered what we meant by expectations. We were always comparing our expectations of price changes with the actual behaviour of prices. He could see no way of defining expectations except: expectations are expectations are expectations, to paraphrase Gertude Stein.

We agreed that an expectation of price change must be an average, but of what? Was it a weighted average? One was bound to get a different answer according to the economic social group one was dealing with. Was it the government, or the central bank, or credit/borrowers, or wage earners, or entrepreneurs? In any event, he thought expectations were difficult to measure. We had high expectations of the success of this conference but he did not know how one could measure these.

Professor Machlup commented that while people had different expectations, we needed to be able to work in terms of a single figure to represent expectations. Perhaps we needed something Marshallian like representative expectations. The idea was not operational, any more than the idea of the representative firm was, but it might be helpful.

Professor Patinkin was not sure why Professor Gordon argued that if a firm reacted to a fall in demand by reducing its output rather than reducing its prices it was irrational.

Professor Lundberg wanted to ask Professor Gordon how money reached those who tried to adapt? Did people always start with money in their pocket?

Professor Gordon replied that he did not think a decision to reduce output rather than price irrational. But to reduce output certainly affected, and indeed made irrelevant, models in which rational expectations played a part. In all of these, output changed only because of misinformation. The supply function related the actual to the expected price of the national output. So it was the first channel money/output/price which raised questions about rational expectations.

Professor Patinkin responded that the model must also assume natural levels of inventory. One could hypothesise that a firm noticed that its inventories were increasing beyond these levels and reacted.

Professor Gordon emphasised that there was a mechanical view in Anglo-Saxon economics of the effects of money on nominal income and the relation of nominal income to prices. The issue was what percentage of change in nominal income resulted from a change in prices and what percentage from a change in real output. The question of how this was related to the way in which money came into the economic system had been little explored.

Professor Lindbeck wondered whether the problem was not that the adherents of the 'natural unemployment' theory had neglected the results of stickiness in prices and wages. This was a weakness of the Friedman tradition and led one to the analysis of unemployment as disequilibrium, as explained in chapter 13 of Professor Patinkin's book.

One could talk of rational expectation even if prices were sticky. So a change in unemployment would not always take place along a neoclassical demand curve for labour, but by way of a shift from a point to the left of the curve to a position closer to it.

Professor Lundberg reported that Swedish paper and pulp producers did not change prices as much as economic theory might suggest. They expected the next boom to be accompanied by scarcity and saw keeping prices stable as the best policy to pursue. It followed that price stability could be rational.

Professor Gordon replied that he was criticising the kind of model that neglected sticky prices. One could certainly have models that assumed both sticky prices and rationality.

Professor Laidler wanted to agree with both Professor Gordon and Professor Lindbeck. One should not overgeneralise from partial disequilibrium models of the labour market to the behaviour of the aggregate economy. Yet we were dealing with an aggregate economy in which each firm had price expectations and announced what its prices were to be. Firms set their own prices and did so in terms of expectations. We needed to combine the Phillips-curve with the Keynesian multiplier.

So, for example, a worker might study the labour market and decide to remain out of work. This would force him to cut current consumption, which would lead to a fall in the output sold and produced by firms. This might feed back to the labour market in the form of a reduction in wage offers. Later the worker might regret not having taken a job on terms available earlier. We could legitimately regard him as involuntarily unemployed. He was making a sensible decision at each point of time, given the information available to him at that point of time, but the constraints operating in the labour market had changed. He was certainly assuming that wages were flexible, but not flexible enough. The important thing was that we should link the partial and the general. Prices were set by business, not by public announcement.

Professor Frisch wanted to make a semantic remark. He often felt that one should talk about adaptive expectations, rational expectations and the rate of forgetfulness. Expectations were not independent of the past. In deciding how prices would change in the future, people were likely to take a weighted average of the past rate of inflation. These were adaptive expectations. Rationality would take all information available into account, so that an econometric model introducing rationality could use the reduced form equations. With rational expectations, for example, people would look at the increase in the money supply relative to the increase in G.N.P., and deduce price expectations from this.

The idea that people usually gave a constant weight to the past rate of inflation led to the idea of a rate of forgetfulness. The farther in the past a particular rate of inflation was, the more it was forgotten. The weights in this concept were not constant but functions of time.

Professor Parkin said that if one were using a model of inflation with a rate of inflationary expectations included, then one must be able to measure these expectations. In fact, one could do so. A paper by Carlson and himself had done this for the United Kingdom.[1] They had taken qualitative survey data, with two non-tested psychological assumptions, and converted this to obtain estimates of a mean inflation rate across individuals, as well as a standard deviation for those studied. They could not publish this information for confidential reasons but had samples for industries, firms and individuals. He agreed that one needed to work in terms of a set of expectations, but the problem of measurement had already been solved. In models, this information performed as one might hope. It was based on adaptive rather than rational measures. He thought it important to recognise that the length of time over which one was looking at expectations would depend on the problem in hand. If one were concerned with a three-year wage contract, one would need expectations over those three years. Someone investing in a one-month asset would need expectations for only one month. The information he had so far used in his model covered only a six-month period. However, one could use the same method to make longer predictions.

Professor Robinson wondered whether the model ran into difficulties if the expectations of workers were different from those of government and business. This could easily happen.

Professor Patinkin thought it difficult, in all cases to handle the expectations of governments. However, one could introduce different expectations for entrepreneurs and average citizens.

Professor Swoboda noted that in a recent study, Henryk Kierzkowski had built an inflation/unemployment model based on differing expectations by entrepreneurs and workers. On the basis of indirect measurement, it turned out that these expectations did seem to be different among the two groups, but perhaps less different than one might have expected.

Mr. Kaser referred to a study by Professor Hilda Behrend.[2] This was a survey of expectations about government anti-inflationary policies of managers, on the one hand, and trade union negotiators on the other. It revealed significantly different expectations influencing their respective bargaining positions. One might suggest that the enquiry could have gone farther, taking control groups with similar incomes and educational experience. This could have shown whether being put into a negotiating position altered the personal view of negotiators or whether their views were representative of wider social groups.

Professor Laidler insisted that the expectations for which one needed information depended on the problem being studied and the degree of aggregation being used, However, it was possible to get information about the government's

[1] 'Inflation Expectations' by J. M. Parkin and J. A. Carlson, *Economica* 42 (166) (May 1975).

[2] A. I. Glendon, D. P. Tweedle and H. Behrend, *Pay Negotiations and Incomes Policy: a Comparison of Views of Managers and Trade Union Pay Negotiators,* Dept. of Business Studies, University of Edinburgh, May 1975.

Here 9 per cent of managerial but 39 per cent of trade-union pay negotiators thought a social contract workable and 71 and 41 respectively considered it unworkable; 47 per cent of managers judged such a contract as intended 'to keep the Labour Government in power', but only 9 per cent of trade unionists.

expectations. The treasury made forecasts and the government explained what it thought should happen in particular fields.

Professor Lindbeck insisted that governments were very rarely likely to give accurate information about their expectations. They wanted to influence events by their statements, in particular, to be popular, etc.

Professor Bronfenbrenner wondered whether, in dealing with the German central bank, Professor Giersch had found that policies might be announced which some strong pressure group then said it would not permit to come into effect. Such 'politicoeconomic strikes' seem to have happened fairly frequently elsewhere.

Professor Giersch replied that when the German central bank had announced that the monetary base would increase by 8 per cent during 1975, no pressure had been brought on it to change its policy. This was because most of those concerned thought the policy fair. German trade unionists had reacted by reducing their wage claims to about 6 per cent.

Professor Gordon reported that a conference he had recently attended had come to the conclusion that economists might have to give up the attempt to determine why inflationary behaviour differed between countries. There were too many political and social issues involved. The interesting questions were not about the influence of money on prices but about what influences money. In recent months there had been rapid reductions in union wage demands in many countries. These would have brought envy from the British until perhaps a month or two ago, and he wondered whether there were any circumstances in which Mr. Wilson could get the same instantaneous co-operation as seemed to have been obtained in Germany.

As for whether what governments said was believed, one must remember why statements by American governments were always in doubt. First, Congress was independent. Second, the Federal Reserve System tended to lean against the wind in trying to stabilise interest rates. He thought it important to remember that the money supply could be influenced by major events, like the financial implications of the oil crisis.

Professor Patinkin thought members of the conference should recognise that there was no such thing as 'the' government. There were differences of approach even within a single-party government, and all the more so in a coalition government. The finance minister printed money to meet the total budgetary demands of all the ministers of the cabinet; this was how the system frequently worked. It was unrealistic simply to regard inflation as a tax on the public, levied on the basis of optimising decisions made by a government acting as an organic unity. To a significant extent inflation also served as a tax on the nominal budgetary allocations of each government ministry. It was a tax which ministers effectively levied on each other when they agreed to the inflationary deficit-financing of the sum total of their nominal budgetary demands. From this viewpoint, inflation served like an across-the-board real reduction in all these demands: the face-saving, non-discriminating kind of reduction to which it was easiest to get any group of strong individuals to agree.

People might retort that this was not rational behaviour but his response would be to ask the question: What is rationality? The rational procedure would be never to fight a war. Instead, conflicting governments would get together to work out how to distribute between themselves the payoff from not fighting. Unfortunately this was not the way things worked out in reality. We needed to remember J. M. Clark's saying, which Frank Knight always quoted, about our 'irrational passion for dispassionate rationality'.

Professor Lundberg suggested that people's expectations of price changes could not be taken seriously if people did not act on them. There was much wishful thinking, hope or fear. Dr. Parkin might say that his model worked, but there were many ways to explain what happened.

Since the 1950s, Sweden had had centralised wage bargaining, with those concerned deciding their expectations about export and import prices. They had to forecast productivity increase and thus the permissible wage increase. They also had to try to calculate the consequential effect of wage increases on prices. This was a short-run calculation, for a year, and it was based on quasi-rational statements of expectations. On top of this, was the responsibility of the government on policy, and especially its commitment to keep full employment. The government was usually able to do what it promised, but again this was based on its own expectations.

Firms were obviously concerned with their own prices, though one could aggregate what happened. The system was very complex and interdependent, resulting in the formation of opinions and perhaps the introduction of bias.

Professor Gordon noted the contrast between what happened in Sweden and what Professor Patinkin had said about the way government policy was formulated. Most countries would fit much more closely with Professor Patinkin's description. Professor Patinkin had described government ministers as competing for their share of tax revenue. There were many similar situations; unions competed; wages competed with capital; so did many other income earners. In most countries one could not bring them together for discussions. When one did, the outcome was usually changed.

Professor Nussbaumer thought it dangerous to suggest that one could always blame inflation for changes in income distribution. Professor Patinkin had pointed to the distribution between private and public funds, and an interesting question was why those concerned competed on some occasions more keenly than others. To answer this would take us a step back down the line, but perhaps it was a step worth taking.

Professor Parkin wanted to clarify the view which he and Professor Swoboda took on the role of the models of short-run price and output adjustment in their paper. They had seen these as being illustrative, rather than a definitive list of the possible alternatives. They had not presented models with more explicit quantitative constraints on choices, such as those developed by Clower, Barro or Grossman largely because those models did not focus on price adjustments but on quantity responses.

To Professor Gordon, Professor Parkin said he agreed that the nature of the transmission mechanism was important for some purposes and, in particular, for the question of the nature of unemployment. In the Irving Fisher analysis, unemployment was purely a voluntary matter, whilst in transmission mechanisms which made prices respond to excess demand, it could be involuntary. However, from the point of view of price level dynamics, the transmission mechanism became a matter of secondary importance.

He also found the notion of rational expectations unconvincing, except as a long-run proposition. If expectations were rational and if prices responded to excess demand and inflation expectations, then output fluctuations could not occur for monetary reasons.

He was glad that Professor Giersch had pointed to differences between the British and German situations as regards the structure of debt. Perhaps future work on the political and social origins of inflationary monetary policy should be based on international cross-section data, rather than time series data from individual countries. He also agreed with Professor Patinkin that government decision-making was not coherent, so that another need might be to look at the way in which different political systems solved their resource allocation problem.

He would like to soften what had perhaps been an overly strong statement in the paper concerning the inevitability of political authoritarianism following inflation. In deference to Professors Giersch and Bronfenbrenner, he would admit there did seem to be occasions when hyperinflation had not, itself, led to an authoritarian government. He was inclined to agree with Professor Bronfenbrenner that it would be more accurate to say that hyperinflations brought with them a very serious risk of authoritarianism.

Professor Parkin agreed with Professor Giersch that the costs of inflation which arose from people substituting into real assets had been understated in the paper. He suggested, however, that there was a real puzzle here as to why, in most economies, nominal interest rates usually failed to rise in line with the rise in the inflation rate. There were probably political restrictions on interest rates, but he wondered whether there was not also a constraint on the upward movement of interest rates, arising from the convention that money itself gave a zero nominal yield. This would, as it were, bolt down the interest rate structure at one end and perhaps prevent yields from adjusting fully. If so, even the introduction of indexed bonds would not necessarily solve the problem of resource misallocation unless, at the same time, money was also indexed.

Professor Lundberg had answered his own questions. However the emphasis in the reply might perhaps be changed to say that if a model did work, that might perhaps mean that the model was not wrong. It certainly would not mean that it was right.

Professor Swoboda began by thanking Professor Giersch for his valuable introduction which had served to highlight admirably the key points of his and Professor Parkin's paper. The paper's aim, however, had not been to write *all* about inflation but to point out the issues that seemed most worth discussing. In particular it made no claim to have surveyed the whole of the relevant literature.

He turned first to the discussion of the nature of expectations. Though neither an econometrician nor a statistician, he thought there was one very important point to be retained from the discussion of rational versus adaptive expectations. He was convinced that there were circumstances in which expectations simply could not be assumed to be adaptive, if only in the sense that people would use, in their forecasts, information other than the past behaviour of the variables they were trying to forecast. He thought it important to understand why, in the real world, one did not necessarily face the dilemma arising out of models that assumed rational expectations, namely, that monetary policy had no effect, even transitory, on real magnitudes. The main reason was that in theoretical models incorporating rational expectations there was typically nothing to stop all nominal variables from jumping immediately to their equilibrium values, except for lags in the expectation-forming mechanism. In fact, we might expect several such slowing-down mechanisms. For example, economic agents might be risk-averse so that they would tend to be typically 'slow movers'. Furthermore, there were adjustment costs, so that one would not expect variables to jump immediately to their equilibrium values.

Turning to the international transmission mechanism, he agreed with Professor Giersch's emphasis on the point that transmission would not be immediate in the absence of perfect competition. This was one more reason why, though one could expect reasonably complete transmission in the long run, one could not do so in the short run.

He agreed with Professor Giersch that it would be valuable to orient the discussion of the transmission of inflation and unemployment under flexible exchange rates towards policy issues. In particular, is should be directed towards the question how one could insulate oneself against imported inflation under flexible exchange rates. In this context, three points seemed worth noting. First, transmission under flexible rates, if it existed, would tend to be less than total in the short run and, probably, would fade away in the long run. This raised a difficult problem of 'fine tuning' for policy. Suppose, for instance, that macroeconomic policy became restrictive to mitigate a foreign inflationary impulse. As the latter's effects faded away with the gradual restoration of, say, purchasing power parity over time, must the restrictive policy be undone, and at what rate? Second, whatever transmission existed under flexible rates, it still remained true that this exchange-rate regime gave more freedom to authorities to use monetary policy for good or ill. Third, and this was related to the first point, what policy strategy was best suited to a regime of flexible rates – a monetary rule (and, if so, which?), automatic stabilisers, or discretionary fine tuning?

As to the question of whether real or nominal rates of interest were to be considered when analysing the seigniorage issue, this was an important question. However, the most important issue was the yield on alternative assets available to whoever paid seigniorage. In the short run, one could have a fairly good idea whether the yield, nominal or real, on assets that were alternatives to holdings of reserve-currency assets, had been higher or lower.

On the slope of the long-run Phillips-curve, he agreed that one might be able to squeeze out more employment by increasing inflation in the very short run. However, he and Professor Parkin held the opinion that, in the course of time, as expectations of inflation were incorporated into the public's anticipations, the short-run Phillips-curve would start moving up very quickly. This, in turn, might affect expectations and even lead to unemployment. Indeed, in the long run, the Phillips-curve might even slope 'backwards' from left to right.

Finally, he agreed very much with Professor Giersch's view of the role of incomes policy. Such a policy made sense only as part of a package which ensured that the rate of inflation actually fell. Thus, incomes policy might fail in a small open economy under fixed exchange rates where the actual rate of inflation was tied to the world rate. It might also fail when, as often happened, an attempt was made to use it as a substitute for, and not as a complement to, effective management of aggregate demand.

2 Recent Developments in the Theory of Inflation and Unemployment[1]

Robert J. Gordon

NORTHWESTERN UNIVERSITY, USA

'The writer on inflation is fortunate that his subject is generally well understood by economists' [85].

'La théorie de l'inflation est un des points les plus faibles de la pensée economique contemporaine' [13].

I. INTRODUCTION AND BACKGROUND

Theoretical and empirical research on the causes, costs, and cures of inflation and unemployment preoccupies a substantial portion of the economics profession. Any comprehensive survey of this body of work, while perhaps providing substantial revenue for the paper and ink industries, would be too indigestible to attract serious readers. Fortunately the restrictive word limit imposed on this paper prohibits an encyclopaedic review and requires a delimitation of scope. The paper takes a selective rather than comprehensive approach and is concerned with the causes of inflation and unemployment but not with their costs and cures; with theoretical developments but not with the results of empirical tests; and with papers written during the last decade but not those written earlier.[2] The paper's scope includes the causes of unemployment as well as inflation, because the most interesting recent papers have treated both phenomena as part of a single analytical problem, for instance, those which model the optimal adjustment by firms of employment and wage rates in response to unexpected changes in product demand.

The literature surveyed here spans the period since 1963, a starting point chosen not only because of the simultaneous appearance in that year of two inflation surveys by M. Bronfenbrenner and F. D. Holzman [16] and H. G.

[1] This research was supported by the National Science Foundation. I am grateful to S. Fischer and J. Frenkel for suggestions on the general issues to be surveyed, but neither has seen the actual paper and thus cannot be blamed for it.

[2] For a much more comprehensive approach, see the recent survey by Laidler and Parkin [57]. This paper differs from theirs in its greater emphasis on the causes of unemployment and on microeconomic models of labour-market behaviour and in its relative lack of attention to empirical results, to the detailed specification of econometric wage-price models, and to the costs of inflation. For a more general, shorter, and more readable introduction to the inflation literature, see Solow [87].

Johnson [53], but also because 1963 antedated the late-1960s acceleration which so greatly influenced current views of the nature of inflation, and also because the span of roughly a decade makes this paper a companion piece to S. Fischer's [27] recent survey of monetary theory.[1]

Novel theoretical contributions of the past decade can be most easily distinguished from those repeating earlier themes, if we examine the reactions of a hypothetical modern-day Rip Van Winkle who had become well acquainted with the earlier inflation literature but who only recently awoke from a decade-long nap. What were the major elements in the body of inflation theory which Rip had assimilated when he fell asleep after reading the Johnson and Bronfenbrenner–Holzman survey articles?

II. WHAT RIP VAN WINKLE KNEW WHEN HE WENT TO SLEEP

(1) DEMAND-PULL VERSUS COST-PUSH INFLATION

Theories of the causes of inflation were generally classified into two major groups, 'demand-pull' and 'cost-push', and can be distinguished with the aid of figure 2.1, where real output is plotted on the horizontal axis and an aggregate price index on the vertical. In each frame the aggregate demand curve DD is negatively sloped and represents those combinations of price and real output which clear *both* the commodity and money markets for a given level of the money supply, fiscal variables, and parameters in private spending functions. A higher price level reduces the real money supply and requires for money-market equilibrium a higher interest rate and hence lower level of real output to achieve a lower real demand for money.[2] An increase in the money supply or a fiscal stimulus, except in well-known extreme cases, shifts the DD curve rightward, for example, from D_0D_0 to D_1D_1. The aggregate supply curves S_0S_0 and S_1S_1 represent alternative assumptions about the combinations of real output and the price which keep factors of production (firms and workers) in equilibrium.

A 'demand-pull' inflation was initiated by some event, whether a monetary or fiscal policy change or a change in private spending behaviour, which shifted DD to the right. 'Demand-pull' theories were divided between the quantity theory, which emphasised the causative role of monetary changes, and Keynesian theories of inflation, which emphasised non-monetary impulses. The quantity theory differed, first, in its dynamic setting, which attributed a steady inflation to a continuous upward shift in DD fuelled by a continuous

[1] I must register here my own distaste for the widespread current practice in the American economics profession of defining as a separate field called 'monetary theory' a particular subset of topics within the general field of macroeconomic theory. Theoretical developments in investment behaviour or labour-market wage-setting behaviour may be just as important for the resolution of unsolved macroeconomic problems as are developments in the theory of money demand or supply or of financial markets.

[2] If the demand for real output is interest inelastic (the IS curve is vertical) then the DD curve will be vertical also. A complete development of the graphical apparatus is contained in Branson [15].

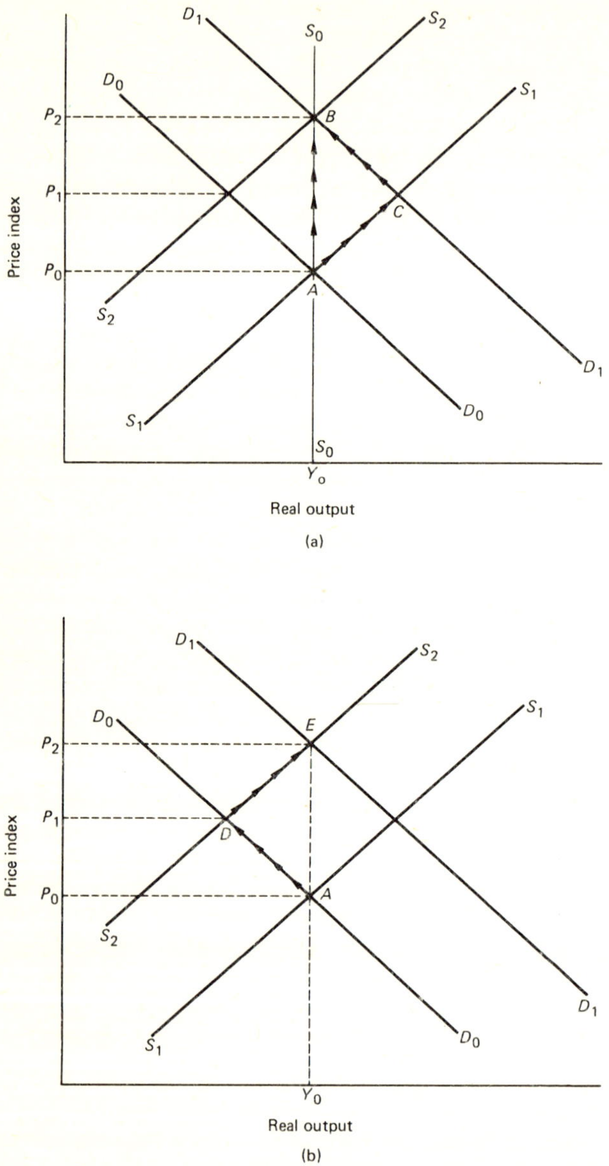

D1
S0
S2
D0
S1
P2
B
P1
C
Price index
P0
A
S2
D1
S1
D0
S0
Y0
Real output
(a)
D1
S2
S1
D0
E
P2
P1
D
Price index
P0
A
S2
D1
S1
D0
Y0
Real output
(b)

Fig 2.1

monetary injection. Keynesian inflation models, in contrast, could explain an increase in the price level from P_0 to P_1 or P_2 as initiated by fiscal or other non-monetary disturbances if the dynamic process were stable, and explosive inflation with unstable parameters, but could not explain a continuing inflation without the implicit assumption of an unlimited supply of idle money balances or a passive monetary accommodation.

A second difference was the quantity theory assumption of a vertical supply curve, which although not logically connected with the monetary source of the *DD* shift, had been part of the quantity theory tradition since Hume.[1] With the vertical supply curve S_0S_0, a continuous money-fuelled inflation shifted the economy in figure 2.1(a) from point *A* to *B* to further points directly north. The effect of a steady inflation on the real economy was limited to a redistribution from money holders to money issuers, especially the government, through the inflation tax. In contrast, Keynesian models emphasised shifts in the saving–investment balance as income was redistributed during the inflation process, through a wide variety of assumptions about the stickiness or constancy of some aspect of wage- or price-setting behaviour, for example, money illusion, lags, progressive taxation, differences in price-setting behaviour between sectors, etc.[2] Since the process of inflation generated real effects, a demand-induced price increase could be accompanied by an increase in real output, as along supply curve S_1S_1, in figure 2.1(a). Money illusion, for instance, might induce an increase in labour input as a result of an increase in the price level, and allow the economy to move from point *A* to *C*. If workers were allowed to 'learn', shifting the supply curve to S_2S_2, point *B* would eventually be reached, as in the quantity-theory approach.

'Cost-push' inflation was initiated in its various versions by a wage-push from small unions facing an inelastic demand curve for labour, rivalry among groups of unions, profit-push generated through administered pricing, or, more generally, a struggle for income shares among any set of subgroups in society. In figure 2.1(b) S_1S_1 shifted to S_2S_2 as a result of the spontaneous increase in costs and, as most writers recognised, caused a reduction in output and employment unless the push was ratified by monetary accomodation, which could maintain the original output level if the money supply were increased sufficiently to shift aggregate demand from D_0D_0 to D_1D_1.

The distinction between cost-push and demand-pull was largely spurious, because a one-shot spontaneous wage- or profit-push could only raise the *level* of prices not permanently increase their *rate of change*, unless accompanied by faster monetary growth. If there were an existing state of union of firm monopolies, but the *degree* of monopoly had not been increasing, monopoly power could not be a source of continuing inflation. Thus, in retrospect any

[1] See Friedman's [36] citations from Hume as precursors of the natural rate hypothesis.

[2] Sections II, C, and VI of the Bronfenbrenner–Holzman Survey [16], are all primarily devoted to innumerable assumptions which generate redistributions of income during an inflation.

sustained inflation became 'always and everywhere a monetary phenomenon'.[1] A demand-pull inflation initiated by a continuous monetary stimulus moved the economy from A to B to points further north in figure 2.1(a), while a cost-push inflation accomodated by monetary growth followed exactly the same path in figure 2.1(b) (*A* to *E* and points north). The two main types of inflation could be distinguished in retrospect only if adjustment speeds were slow. A demand inflation followed path *ACB* if lags or money illusion temporarily delayed the upward shift of supply curve S_1S_1 in figure 2.1(a), and a supply inflation followed path *ADE* in figure 2.1(b) if monetary accomodation were delayed.[2]

Ruling out as implausible and empirically unproved an infinitely elastic supply of idle balances, a Keynesian-demand inflation generated by shifts in fiscal policy or private spending propensities, or a cost-induced inflation generated by autonomous increases in wage or profit demands, had to be validated by the monetary authority. Could one therefore argue that a distinction should have been made *not* between demand-pull and cost-push inflation, but rather between inflations in which the role of money was active versus passive? Even this potential basis for classification became blurred when one recognised that, even in most classic wartime or postwar money-fuelled inflations and hyperinflations, the role of the monetary authority had been passively to finance deficits resulting from the unwillingness or inability of politicians to finance expenditures through conventional taxation.[3] Keynesian fiscal-induced money-accomodated inflation and quantity-theory money-initiated inflation had, in almost all actual cases, amounted to one and the same thing. Thus a more general view implicit in pre-1963 developments attributed inflation to the passivity of the monetary authority in the fact of pressures emanating from all groups in society – labour, management, and government. A notable feature of the pre-1963 literature, at least in the United States, was the disproportionate concern with unions and the bargaining process as the source of pressure, due presumably to the occurrence in the United States of the 1955–57 inflation inflation during a period of government surplus.

Within this more general framework the basic unsettled issues can be divided

[1] This phrase originated with Friedman [33, p. 18], albeit in the post-1963 period. As he pointed out, the 1933–37 period during which the N.R.A. and Wagner Act *raised* the level of firm and union monopoly power can be cited as an instance of cost-push inflation.

[2] Empirical tests by Seldon [83], Attiyeh [2], and Phelps [74] attempted to distinguish supply from demand-induced inflations along these lines but were generally inconclusive, as one might expect either if the supply curve shifted up rapidly following an initial demand shift, or vice versa. Far better opportunities for such empirical tests have been provided by events during the past decade, during which the 1964–66 acceleration in inflation was unambiguously accompanied by an increase in output, while the 1973–74 inflation was accompanied by a pronounced decrease in output.

[3] Among the few examples of monetary growth independent of government deficits were (1) 1919–20 in the United States when money expanded while the Federal budget was in surplus, and (2) 1929–33 when money contracted while the Federal budget was in deficit.

into two basic categories:

(1) Why do the pressures on the monetary authority from the private and public sectors differ across time within the same country, and differ across countries at any given time?

(2) What structural features of the economy influence the ability of the monetary authority to resist pressure? In particular, what fraction of a monetary contraction takes the form of a reduction in output as compared to a reduction in prices; in other words, what is the slope of the short-run supply curve (see, for example, S_1S_1 in figure 2.1 above) and when does the curve shift downward?

(2) WHERE THE PHILLIPS-CURVE FITTED IN

The Phillips-curve began as the result of an empirical investigation of United Kingdom wage behaviour by Phillips [80], was extended and put into a theoretical disequilibrium context by Lipsey [58], and was applied to the United States and popularised by Samuelson and Solow [81]. The relationship had originally been investigated by Irving Fisher thirty years previously in a long-neglected and recently rediscovered paper [31]. In Lipsey's version, the rate of change of wages in a single labour market was postively related to the excess demand for labour, and the unemployment rate was negatively related to the excess demand for labour. If one then aggregated and added the assumption that the price level was 'marked-up' over the wage rate by a relatively stable proportion, one obtained a negative relationship between the rate of inflation and the rate of unemployment. If by happy coincidence this negatively sloping Phillips-curve crossed the zero-inflation point (on the vertical axis) at an unemployment rate (on the horizontal axis) generally regarded as 'full', or 'optimal', no policy problem arose. If, however, full employment and price stability were not compatible, policy-makers were forced to choose some second-best point along the Phillips-curve. It was common in the United States for economic advisers to Democratic Presidents to recommend the choice of a point on the curve northwest of the target of Republican advisers.

As he fell asleep in 1963, Rip Van Winkle was puzzled at the failure of either survey author – Bronfenbrenner-Holzman or Johnson – to integrate the Phillips-curve with figure 2.1, where a higher aggregate price level could not induce a permanent increase in output once workers and firms in individual product markets had re-evaluated their higher wage offers and individual product prices in terms of the higher aggregate price level. Adjustment lags and/or money illusion were required in figure 2.1(a) for a demand shift to increase output permanently, so Rip wondered how higher output and an excess demand for labour could persist permanently as implied by the immobile Phillips-curve. He was also disturbed by the absence of any rigorous theory explaining the determinants of the zero-inflation unemployment rate. Why was the 'full-employment' unemployment rate so high, particularly in the United States, and why was the zero-inflation rate even higher than that?

III. RIP VAN WINKLE AWAKES AND VIEWS THE PAST DECADE

Immediately after awakening, Rip rushed to the nearest good library to bring himself up to date on the development of inflation and unemployment theory.[1] His reactions follow and emphasise primarily those developments which he found surprising, novel, and important: (1) the quantity theory resurgence (the natural rate hypothesis, the rise of monetarism, and the application of rational expectations to problems of monetary control; (2) the microeconomic theory of wage and employment adjustment (first as an explanation of voluntary unemployment, later as an explanation of layoffs and involuntary unemployment); and (3) the international transmission of inflation among open economies.

IV. REVIVAL AND EXTENSION OF THE QUANTITY THEORY APPROACH TO INFLATION THEORY

(1) THE NATURAL RATE HYPOTHESIS: IMPLICATIONS AND CRITIQUE

Early in the past decade, Rip was relieved to discover, the conflict between figure 2.1 and the Phillips-curve tradeoff was independently resolved by M. Friedman [33] and E. S. Phelps [75]. Friedman was the first clearly to state that 'there is no long-run, stable tradeoff between inflation and unemployment' [33, p. 60]. Friedman's labour-market analysis [34] differed from Lipsey's in its explicit assumption that both the demand for and supply of labour depended on the *real* wage rather than on the nominal wage. Since the nominal wage was evaluated in terms of the current actual product price by employers and in terms of the expected average consumer price level by workers, employment could only increase only as long as the expected price level lagged behind the actual level (thus simultaneously allowing a *lower* actual real wage to induce increased hiring by firms, and a *higher* expected real wage to induce a higher labour supply by workers). In equilibrium the expected and actual price level were equal, and so in equilibrium only one level of employment and output was possible. Friedman dubbed the associated unemployment rate (given population, technology, and labour-force participation) as the 'natural rate of unemployment'. The 'natural rate hypothesis' (N.R.H.) completely changes the framework of optimum stabilisation policy. Policy-maker indifference curves drawn on the inflation-unemployment axes, which had formerly allowed the choice of an optimum point on a stable Phillips-curve, were now irrelevant.[2] The Council of Economic Advisers was now to be divided into two independent branches, one group of labour economists which would tally up the costs and benefits of manpower programmes designed to shift the

[1] The library was indeed a good one, since it contained those unpublished papers cited below which were written as recently as July, 1975.

[2] 'Democratic' indifference curves were steep, with a point of tangency at a relatively high inflation rate and a low unemployment rate, whereas 'Republican' indifference curves were more gently sloped.

natural unemployment rate, on which monetary and fiscal policies by themselves had no effect, and a second group of monetary economists which determined the optimum rate of inflation as a function of the growth rate of real output and the interest rate paid on money (see Friedman [35]).

Phelps [78] pointed out, however, and Hall [49] later demonstrated in computer simulations, that this labour money policy dichotomy implicitly assumed a zero rate of time preference, implying that if the economy was presently operating at an inflation rate (p) above the optimum (p^*), a period of unemployment above the natural rate would be enjoyed temporarily, but that this transition cost had no bearing on the recommendation that p should be reduced to p^* for the infinite future. The policy-makers' utility function regained relevance, however, when their rate of time preference was positive. Even if initially $p = p^*$, the benefit of subnatural unemployment in the near future might outweigh the permanent legacy of $p > p^*$ in the far future. Similarly, a deliberate 1970-style recession might be rejected if the near-term social cost of extra unemployment was judged to exceed the long-term benefits of $p = p^*$.

The Friedman–Phelps N.R.H. was widely misunderstood and continously disputed during most of the decade. A basic misunderstanding was the belief that the N.R.H. had, in and of itself, revived the quantity-theory proposition that the rate of inflation (p) was determined by the rate of growth of the money supply (m). Consider the quantity identity.

$$p = m + v - q, \tag{1}$$

where lower-case letters represent proportional rates of growth, v is velocity growth, and q is real-output growth. Whether or not the Phillips-curve trade-off is stable, a fixed unemployment rate is associated with a given rate of growth of 'potential' output (the growth in the labour force plus technical progress). Assuming that velocity growth is exogenous (determined by the income elasticity of money demand and the rate of introduction of money substitutes at any given level of interest rates), the rate of inflation is fundamentally determined by the rate of monetary growth. This basic proposition was not altered in the slightest by the N.R.H., which was novel not by associating money with inflation, but rather in its claim that changes in the rate of monetary growth could not cause the rate of unemployment permanently to diverge from its 'natural rate' without a continuously accelerating inflation or deflation.

One line of criticism of the N.R.H. claimed that Friedman's model was logically invalid in a simple model based on Cagan-type adaptive expectations [18], in which the expected rate of inflation was mechanically extrapolated as a weighted average of past actual rates of inflation. After an acceleration of actual inflation, the expected rate would at first lag behind and then catch up. But the expected price *level* (the integral of past expected rates of inflation) would remain forever the actual level and thus allow the level of employment to stay forever above the natural rate. A simple Cagan-style formulation of adaptive expectations must, however, break down under steady inflation. As Nerlove [68] pointed out, the only way to justify adaptive expectations as 'rational' is in a model where price changes are thought by economic agents to be a generalisation of a random walk: a stochastic process whose increments have a mean of zero. If price changes are always above a certain positive constant for a considerable period, people will start adding a trend in their forecasts.

A second and more widespread group of critics essentially ignored the policy implications of N.R.H. on the empirical grounds that the United States data were inconsistent with it. In the following inflation equation

$$P_t = \alpha p_t^e + f(U_t - U_t^N), \tag{2}$$

p_t^e is the expected rate of inflation, expected at the beginning of period t, and U_t is the actual and U_t^N the natural rate of unemployment during that period. Equation (2) is consistent with the N.R.H., that is, $U_t \neq U_t^N$ implies $p_t \neq p_t^e$, only if $\alpha = 1$. Until 1971 published empirical tests for the United States, including those by Perry [72], [73], Solow [86], and Gordon [38], yielded estimates of α which were significantly less than unity. Two sets of influences gradually defused this line of criticism of N.R.H. First, the gradual acceleration of inflation during 1966–70 caused the computer to yield ever higher values of α as the passage of time provided additional observations, as demonstrated by Gordon [39], until finally tests with a sample period including early 1971 were unable to reject statistically the hypothises that $\alpha = 1$. Second, Lucas [59], [61] claimed that policy simulations with econometric models including fitted equations like (2) above could not provide guidance for policy decisions, because the fixed estimated parameters were based on the particular environment of the sample period, whereas the true parameters might vary with each alternative policy. (Lucas' point had been anticipated in Johnson's 1963 survey article in a brief speculation that the Phillips-curve might not prove to be stable 'if an attempt were made by economic policy to pin the economy to a point on it' [53, p. 133]). Both Eckstein and Brinner [24] and Gordon [39] developed models in which the α parameter was allowed to vary in response to changes in the inflationary environment.

A third criticism of the N.R.H. is its lack of validation in recession and depression episodes. According to equation (2), a period when the unemployment rate remains above the natural rate for a substantial period should be characterised by an accelerating decline in the first derivative of prices and eventually in an accelerating *deflation*. During the Depression the unemployment rate remained above 8·5 per cent for twelve straight years in the United States without the slightest sign of accelerating deflation.[1] The same story applies to the seven consecutive postwar years (1958–64) when the unemploy-

[1] Between 1934 and 1940 the United States G.N.P. deflator rested on a flat plateau, with a maximum deviation of only 2·5 per cent above and below the mean.

ment rate remained above 5 per cent during a period when the natural unemployment rate yielded by restrospective econometric estimates was well below 5 per cent. The failure of unemployment to decline during these episodes raises the possibility that wages and/or prices are less flexible downward than upward. In terms of equation (2), the N.R.H. simply states that $\alpha = 1$ without providing any information of the $f(\ )$ function – that is, on the shape or slope (given p_t^e) of the short-run Phillips-curve.

Finally, not only does symmetry require wages to be equally flexible in both directions in the main theoretical models incorporating N.R.H., but in addition all changes in employment result from the voluntary choices of workers without any role for layoffs or involuntary unemployment. In response to a decline in the expected real wage Friedman's [34] workers willingly reduce labour input by some combination of lower labour-force participation rates and fewer hours per week, and there is no mechanism to generate changes in unemployment. In the Lucas–Rapping model [62] increases in unemployment occur when workers regard rates at which they could currently be employed as temporarily low; workers quit their jobs and voluntarily choose to wait or search for improved conditions. Other models developed by Holt [51], Phelps [76], and Mortensen [65] in the tradition of the 'new microeconomics' both incorporate the N.R.H. and explain higher unemployment as the voluntary decision of workers to refuse job offers when falling product demand reduces wage offers relative to their 'acceptance' or 'refusal' wage.

In all of these models individual actors are induced to change their provision of labour input or output by prior changes in wages or prices relative to expectations. Unemployment and output fluctuations thus depend entirely on misinformation. This theoretical tradition based on the neoclassical price→output chain of causation has had a high fertility rate, spawning a literature on rational expectations which requires misinformation for output changes. But sceptics can point to the failure of such models to explain unemployment in the 1930s or in 1975 as evidence that misinformation may be only part of the story.[1] This theme recurs below when we examine the rational expectations literature in more detail.

(2) THE RISE OF MONETARISM AND STEPS TOWARDS POLITICAL THEORIES OF INFLATION

The popularisation of the N.R.H. and the rise of 'monetarism' occurred simultaneously in the late 1960s, and the two have occasionally been considered as

[1] Regarding 1975, see below. Regarding the 1930s, consider the failure of the Lucas–Rapping model to explain high unemployment rate after 1934: 'Whatever the cause, the expectations model we used implies that in 1934 the unemployment rate should have been at its 1929 or 1930 level, as opposed to the observed 22 per cent level. To make matters worse, our theory continues to 'miss' for the remainder of the depression years, accounting for the observed drift toward lower unemployment during this period but failing entirely to explain why this drift proceeded at so slow a pace' [63, p. 190]. Barro's empirical work [10] also fails to explain this period.

one and the same idea, partly as a result of Johnson's brilliant but misleading analysis [54] of the monetarist counter-revaluation, in which the success of monetarism is attributed to the acceleration of inflation in the late 1960s. Three separate statements must be distinguished:

(a) Monetary changes are the dominant cause of changes of nominal income, swamping the temporary and minor influence of fiscal changes.
(b) The N.R.H. is valid.
(c) Wages and prices are relatively flexible, so that the short-run Phillips-curve is relatively steep.

Statements (a) and (b) constitute the essence of monetarism. The rate of monetarism was not due just to the acceleration of inflation in the late 1960s, which helped win converts to (b), but was due also to the evidence resulting from the 1966 monetary squeeze and 1968 tax surcharge that monetary effects on nominal income dominated fiscal effects when the two were operating in opposite directions, which helped win converts to (a).

Johnson's analysis becomes particularly misleading when he claims that 'the triumph of monetarism has been short-lived . . . partly because . . . the monetarists vastly exaggerated the potency . . . of monetary restraint as a means of stopping inflation once inflation is well under way' [55, p. 63]. A rapid impact effect of a deceleration in monetary growth on the rate of inflation depends on the validity of proposition (c), which is logically separate from (a) and (b), and about which, as argued above, the original theoretical models incorporating N.R.H. provide no information. Thus the evidence from the 1970–71 episode of a sluggish downward response of wage rates to high unemployment has not prevented a continued conversion of the economics profession to (a) and (b).[1] Nevertheless, given the importance of (c) for their standard policy recommendations of monetary restriction to fight inflation, it is surprising that monetarist authors have done so little empirical research on the short-run dynamics of wage and price behaviour. As I have argued elsewhere [44], this lack of interest in (c) can be explained only by an extremely low rate of time preference among monetarists, so that in the Phelps-Hall optimum policy framework the benfits in the far future of reducing the rate of inflation to the optimum rate outweigh the near-term costs of recession, whatever the time duration of the latter.

[1] Regarding (a), a recent conference on monetarism (proceedings forthcoming in a conference volume edited by J. Stein) appeared to yield agreement by major monetarist authors that a change in government spending or tax rates could cause a one-time change in the level of velocity, and agreement by major non-monetarist authors that deficits induced by fiscal policy must be continuously financed (until the economy raises tax revenues enough to eliminate the deficit), requiring attention to stock effect of the continuous infection of money or bonds. Regarding (b), the leading non-monetarist author Modigliani has implicity adopted the validity of (b) in his recent use of the concept 'non-inflationary rate of unemployment' ('N.I.R.U.' [64].

In addition to their lack of interest in short-run adjustment, most monetarist authors have complacently reiterated the role of money as the basic determinant of income and price changes without any concern for the more fundamental underlying determinants of changes in money. The cost-push approach has been castigated and treated as a *contradiction* of the monetary approach particularly by Johnson [55], and Brunner [17], a clear step backward from the 1963 environment in which there was widespread recognition (as reflected in Bronfenbrenner and Holzman's survey [16], especially p. 614) that cost-push pressure causes a reduction in output unless accomodated by monetary expansion, and thus becomes a *determinant* of the rate of monetary expansion. Similarly, political pressures may force governments to finance large increases in expenditures during wars or other unusual circumstances by means of deficits, which in turn constitute a source of pressure for monetary expansion. Recently the political determinants of money-induced inflation have been analysed in two quite different (albeit complementary) frameworks. Nordhaus [70] and Sjaastad [84] have attributed unstable rates of monetary growth and inflation to the active, repeated, and implicitly successful attempts of governments to blow up the economy before elections and deflate it afterwards. I have analysed [45] the behaviour of a passive rather than active monetary authority which finances wars by monetary creation on the grounds that the inflation tax is part of an optimal tax package, and finances peacetime inflation to the extent necessary to avoid prolonged recession in the face of a relatively flat short-run Phillips-curve. In my own work I have regarded the slope of the short-run Phillips-curve as a basic constraint on the monetary authority and have treated labour unions, contract institutions, unemployment benefits, and other legacies of the Depression not as forces which push upward on wages by the same amount regardless of the state of demand, but rather as fundamental underlying behavioural determinants of the short-run Phillips-curve. In my view, in contrast to the opposing Johnson–Brunner–Laidler–Parkin position, a complete theory of inflation requires that the structural and institutional heritage of the 'cost-push' tradition be *merged with* rather than *juxtaposed against* the monetary approach.

(3) CAN THE IMPOTENT POLICYMAKER BE REJUVENATED? SEARCHING FOR THE LOOPHOLE IN RATIONAL EXPECTATIONS

While denying a permanent output-inflation tradeoff, the N.R.H. allows the monetary authority to cause *temporary* deviations in the unemployment rate from the natural rate if, according to equation (2) above, it causes the actual rate of inflation during a given period of time (p_t) to diverge from the rate which is generally anticipated at the beginning of that period (p_t^e). This can occur if expectations are mechanically extrapolated by a Cagan-type adaptive formula. Consider, however, an expectation which is 'rational' in the sense of Muth [67], that is, an unbiased predictor of actual inflation (p_t) given all the information available just before the period begins, say I_{t-1}

$$p_t^e = E(p_t | I_{t-1}), \tag{3}$$

where E is the expectations operator. This implies that p_t and p_t^e differ only by a random forecast error ϵ,

$$p_t - p_t^e = p_t - E(p_t | I_{t-1}) = \epsilon_t, \tag{4}$$

where ϵ_t is uncorrelated with everything known before the beginning of the period; any correlations which are present are part of I_{t-1} and can be exploited to improve the forecast value p_t^e. Substituting equations (3) into (2) and rearranging we obtain:

$$U = U^N + f^{-1}(\epsilon). \tag{5}$$

Now the monetary authority cannot cause even temporary changes in unemployment unless it does the unexpected; any feedback-type monetary policy rule which systematically incorporates past information becomes part of the information set I_{t-1}, is incorporated into p_t^e, and hence cannot cause the deviation of p_t from p_t^e which is necessary (according to N.R.H. in equation (2)) for unemployment to diverge from the natural rate. This rather dramatic attack on policy activism has recently attracted considerable attention, as a result of innovating papers by Lucas [60] and Sargent and Wallace [82], with recent extensions by Barro [8]. To put the point another way, the monetary authority can change output only if it can find some handle which moves p while not simultaneously moving p^e by the same amount; but if the public can predict how money will behave in reaction to previous history, and knows the structural connection between money and p, any predictable money change must simultaneously alter p, p^e, nominal income, the nominal interest rate, and other nominal magnitudes, and cannot alter unemployment, output, or other real magnitudes. Either the monetary authority can choose to follow Friedman's constant-growth-rate monetary rule, thus giving up the goal of controlling output, or it can choose to exercise its control in a totally unpredictable fashion (expanding money in reaction to some but not all increases in unemployment, chosen in a random fashion). What it cannot choose is a systematic derivative or proportional or 'formula flexibility' feedback rule which reacts to past deviations of target variables from their desired values, of the type analysed by Fischer and Cooper [30].

The amalgam of rational expectations (R.E.) and N.R.H. constitutes a major attack on policy activism, and a radical contribution to the theory of inflation and unemployment; any predictable change in the rate of monetary growth has 100 per cent of its effect on inflation, *even in the short run*, and zero per cent of its effect on unemployment. Where can one find loopholes in the powerful logic? An easy criticism of R.E. + N.R.H. is that a monetary feedback rule can affect real ouput if the monetary authority has superior information, so that its monetary changes in reaction to events unknown to individuals are treated by them as unexpected random events. But differential access to information is an implausibly weak reed upon which to rest a counter-attack against R.E. + N.R.H. in an economy like the United States in which government statistics are publicised in newspapers only a few days after they are compiled.

My own preferred line of criticism questions the assumption of perfect price flexibility and the associated chain of causation from prior price movements to subsequent output movements upon which most 'new microeconomic' models incorporating N.R.H., as well as the more recent Lucas–Sargent–Wallace–Barro contributions, have been based. The entire thrust of the R.E. + N.R.H. point requires that the effect of monetary changes reach real output by the route of changes in prices relative to expectations. Consider as an alternative extreme case a world of fixed wages and prices of the type analysed by Barro and Grossman [11], starting from an equilibrium position where firms and workers sell all they want, fix this wage and price level and reduce the money supply. Firms and workers now are able to sell less than they want at the going wage and price; they have been thrown off their voluntary 'notional' supply schedules onto 'effective' schedules constrained by the policy-imposed limit on sales. Any change in nominal income, whether engineered by monetary or fiscal policy, is completely reflected in a change in the sales constraint, output and employment. Once we discard the notional supply schedule relating output to the deviation of actual from expected prices, rational expectations become irrelevant to the output effect of systematic policy rules.

This criticism does not require the extreme assumption of completely rigid wages and prices, but is valid as long as wages and prices are less than perfectly flexible. Starting from an initial equilibrium set (W^*, P^*), a decline in the money supply requires a reduction to $(\hat{W}, \hat{P})$ if both firms and workers are to be able to sell all they want at that set of wages and prices. Any incomplete adjustment, for instance to (W', P') where $\hat{W} < W' < W^*$ and $\hat{P} < P' < P^*$ will once again impose a sales constraint on firms and workers and make rational expectations irrelevant.[1]

Faced with this criticism, the R.E. + N.R.H. group might counterattack by denying the possibility of incomplete price adjustment to a preannounced monetary change. Assume that the N.R.H. relationship takes the specific form:

$$P_t = p_t^e - a(U_t - U_t^N), \tag{6}$$

and allow the change in the actual unemployment rate from one period to the next to be determined by deviations in the actual rate of growth of the money supply (m_t) from the constant-unemployment monetary growth rate (m_t^*):

$$U_t = U_{t-1} - b(m_t - m_t^*). \tag{7}$$

[1] This line of criticism can be summarised in the phrase 'Barro schizophrenia', since the Barro–Grossman model of macroeconomic disequilibrium [11] implies the irrelevance of Barro's more recent theoretical work [8] on rational expectations.

where

$$m_t^* = p_t + q_t^* - v_t, \tag{8}$$

and q_t^* is the constant-unemployment rate of growth of 'potential' real output while velocity growth (v_t) is assumed and exogenous. Assuming that the economy starts in equilibrium with $U_{t-1} = U_{t-1}^N = U_t^N$, substitute equations (7) and (8) into equation (6) to obtain:

$$p_t = \frac{p_t^e + ab(m_t + v_t - q_t^*)}{1 + ab} \tag{9}$$

A typical United States quarterly econometric model with estimates of $a = \cdot 2$ and $b = \cdot 3$ would estimate a sluggish ·057 (=·06/1·06) per cent reduction in the rate of inflation in response to a one percentage-point reduction in the rate of growth of money, assuming that p_t^e is completely predetermined. The R.E. + N.R.H. group, however, would point out that expectations must incorporate all available information, including equation (9), Setting $p_t^e = p_t$ in (9) yields:

$$p_t = p_t^e = m_t + v_t - q_t^*, \tag{10}$$

in which a one percentage point reduction in monetary growth reduces the rate of inflation and hence m^* by a full one per cent, averting in equation (7) *any change in unemployment.*

Thus rational expectations implies that prices *out of logical necessity* must be perfectly flexible following preannounced monetary changes. But logic conflicts diametrically with the United States facts of 1934–40, 1958–64, and 1975–?, when high unemployment persisted in the face of a fully comprehended monetary policy.[1] Put another way, in the R.E. + N.R.H. world the unemployment rate can differ from its equilibrium value only by a serially uncorrelated random disturbance, but Hall [50] has shown that only 1·7 per cent of the quarterly variation in United States unemployment during 1954–74 remains unexplained in a simple two-quarter autoregression. Hall accepts the basic logic of R.E. + N.R.H. and concludes that 98·3 per cent of the variance of unemployment must have been due to shifts in the equilibrium unemployment rate (U^N), a position I find completely implausible.

The 1974–75 United States recession which followed the 1973–74 increases in food and oil prices provides an ideal test case which illustrates the limitations of the R.E. + N.R.H. approach. Could high unemployment in 1975 be fully attributed to a shortfall of prices below those anticipated by economic agents, due to their failure accurately to predict monetary growth? Apparently not, confesses Barro (one of the major proponents of R.E. + N.R.H.), in his empirical demonstration that the shortfall of monetary growth in 1974 below the R.E. prediction can account for 'only about one point out of the three point rise in the unemployment rate [in 1975] from the average of 1974' [10,

[1] Unanticipated monetary changes in 1937–38 and 1959 caused minor ripples of unemployment around a high average level.

p. 30]. The remainder of the increase in unemployment must then by definition have been due to an increase in the equilibrium unemployment rate U^N, the sources of which are 'beyond the scope' of Barro's paper.

It is not surprising that the R.E. + N.R.H. hypothesis cannot explain the 1975 increase in unemployment, because the latter should not have occurred under the key R.E. + N.R.H. assumption of perfect price and wage flexibility. As I have shown [41], any reduction in non-farm or non-oil employment following a crop failure or formation of an oil cartel must be purely voluntary when wages and prices are perfectly flexible. But when wages and prices adjust only partially, the external supply reduction has a multiplier effect which causes a recession and involuntary unemployment in the non-farm–non-oil sector. Following this approach, high 1975 unemployment is a disequilibrium rather than an equilibrium phenomenon. How then does one counter the point that the price adjustment coefficient (a in equation (6)) does not appear in the final reduced form (10)?

My own inclination is to reject the logic of R.E. entirely, specifically the transition from equations (9) to (10) above. The R.E. approach treats the problem of forming expectations as simply a matter of exploiting available information on the values of historical economic statistics available to policy-makers and private individuals alike. But the far more difficult information problem, determination of the true structure of the underlying economic model, is completely ignored. Why do real-life firms and workers fail to calculate reduced forms like equation(10)?

(a) Individuals do not know enough about the structure of the economy to estimate the market-clearing $\hat{P}$ and conservatively stick with adaptive expectations instead.

(b) As demonstrated by B. Friedman [32], if individuals gradually learn about the true structure of the economic system by a least-squares learning procedure, rational expectations closely approximate adaptive expectations.

(c) Even if individual A thinks he knows the structure, he may not believe that other individuals will form expectations rationally, and so A's expectation of some or all other prices may be set adaptively. This lack of confidence by A may not be illusory, but may reflect the prevalence of long-term contracts which insulate a substantial portion of wages and prices from current monetary changes and thereby justify an adaptive-type expectation which is a weighted average of the market-clearing $\hat{P}$ and previous actual levels of P.

As long as price expectations are at least partly based on an adaptive or history-based extrapolation, the full downward adjustment of expected prices to the market-clearing level ($\hat{P}$) is prevented, and this prevents in equation (6) a full downward adjustment of actual prices. If, for instance, expected inflation is a weighted average of past inflation and a rational expectation,

$$p_t^e = \lambda P_{t-1} + (1-\lambda)E(p_t | I_{t-1}) \tag{11}$$

then (9) is converted – in place of (10) – into the new more general reduced form:

$$p_t = \frac{\lambda p_{t-1} + ab(m_t + v_t - q_t^*)}{\lambda + ab} \qquad (12)$$

(12) becomes (9) when $\lambda = 1$ and becomes (10) when $\lambda = 0$. Output is once again determined by the Barro–Grossman sales constraint, and policy regains its short-run potency. The speed of adjustment of prices, and hence the persistence of unemployment, depends on the importance of long-term contracts and the average length of contracts (determinants of λ) and the slope of the short-run Phillips-curve (a).[1]

V. MICROECONOMIC MODELS OF VOLUNTARY UNEMPLOYMENT, LAYOFFS AND INDEXING

The preceding section reviewed first, the N.R.H. demonstration that the Phillips-curve is vertical in the long-run, and the amalgam with N.R.H. of rational expectations (R.E. + N.R.H.), which makes the Phillips-curve vertical even in the short run. This line of theoretical development was criticised on the grounds that sticky price adjustment throws economic agents off the voluntary output supply curves assumed in the R.E. + N.R.H. literature, and that the weight of the past on the present through long-term contracts makes agents guess the prices which will be set by others at least partly by means of an adaptive rather than an extrapolative procedure. How convincing are recent theoretical models of wage and employment adjustment as explanations of imperfect wage and price flexibility, and what role is played in them by long-term contracts?

(1) VOLUNTARY UNEMPLOYMENT IN THE 'NEW MICROECONOMICS'

Soon after he and Friedman had proclaimed the N.R.H., Phelps and others produced a remarkable group of essays [77] which appeared in book form in 1970 and collectively became known as the 'New Microeconomics' of inflation and employment theory.[2] With the single exception of Holt [51], the contributing authors build models of wage and price adjustment which incorporate N.R.H. Beyond exploring the implications of N.R.H., the authors are mainly concerned with the factors which (1) makes the natural unemployment rate greater than zero, and (2) explain the negative short-run Phillips-curve relationship between wage change and actual unemployment.

[1] Fischer [28], while accepting the flexible price framework of R.E. + N.R.H., has shown that if long-term, in other words, two-period, wage contracts, fix the wage rate one period ahead, the monetary authority can alter output by manipulating the price and through it the real wage which determined the voluntary notional supply decisions of firms. Phelps and Taylor [79] reach essentially the same result by assuming, less plausibly, that both the wage rate and price level are fixed one period in advance.

[2] Named after the title of Phelps' introduction to the volume.

Costly information and heterogeneous jobs and workers are sufficient to answer the first question. Workers sample comes from an array of job offers and firms sample from an array of workers. Both benefit by searching until it is no longer profitable to do so, where, for instance, workers apply the rule that wage offer is refused unless it exceeds the 'acceptance' wage, which in turn is set to equate the marginal cost of further search (costs of physical search plus foregone earnings net of unemployment benefits and taxes) with the marginal benefit of search (the expected value of further sampling from a known wage distribution).[1] Unemployment is a voluntary activity, but all voluntary unemployment is not necessarily socially beneficial; in fact only a small portion of unemployed time is spent in actual search, and government unemployment benefits tend to stretch out the interval between searches, imposing a social cost through the taxes levied on some to support the idleness of others.[2]

The new microeconomic papers by Holt [51], Phelps [76], and Mortensen [65] explain the second question, the causes of the relation between wage change and higher unemployment as the result of a rational tendency of workers to quit their jobs more frequently and take up search activity when firms cut their wages in response to a decline in product demand. As in the above discussion of rational expectations models, the chain of causation is explicitly from prior wage changes to subsequent quit decision and resulting increase in unemployment. The models strain reality by forcing all entry to unemployment through the mould of voluntary quit decisions, with no explanation for firing or layoffs.

The lack of reality in the standard 'new microeconomics' model is vividly illustrated in Phelps' well-known 'island parable' [77, pp. 6–7], in which individual firms are represented by separate islands lacking any inter-island communication links. Since an employee does not learn instantaneously of wage rates on other islands, but rather gains this information only after a slow trip by raft, individual firms face upward sloping rather than horizontal labour supply curves. When a firm suffers a decline in product demand during a recession, it reduces the wage rate to the level at which its demand for labour intersects its supply schedule. Some (but not all) employees quit on the assumption that the firm's behaviour is unique, boarding their rafts to sample wage offers on other islands. Only after several inter-island voyages do they realise that the recession-induced decline in demand is universal, and that they will be no better off in a new job than with the original firm.

Real-world employees are not nearly as mindless as the parable suggests. We live in a world of underground telephone cables between desert islands, in which almost any white-collar worker can search for an alternative job using a company telephone on company time and without any prior need to

[1] A clear and mercifully brief exposition of this approach is presented by Mortensen [66], who allows for differences in both wage offers and worker quality.

[2] Empirical estimates of time spent in search are contained in Appendix C of my work [40], and the adverse allocative effects of unemployment benefits have been most strongly criticised by Feldstein [25], [26].

quit. A blue-collar worker is only sightly less privileged and can substitute the neighbourhood bar for the company telephone, with ample opportunity to react to his wage cut by polling employees of other firms before he tenders his resignation. A cautious reaction is particularly probable when wages depend positively on seniority, for example, when employees through learning-by-doing accumulate firm-specific skills over time, since quitting to search for a new job then involves a reduction in the employee's wage rate. As evidence that employees are in a position to acquire information on employment conditions in other firms before they depart, voluntary quits in the United States actually *decline* during recessions, whereas the parable implies countercyclical fluctuations in quits.

During a recession layoffs increase, but neither the parable nor any of the detailed formal models of the 'new microeconomics' provide an economic explanation of layoffs. In these models economic booms and recessions are entirely symmetrical, in contrast to the real world where a firm has a single option in a boom, to attract more labour input by raising its wage offer, and two options in a recession, either to reduce the wage offer or to discharge employees.[1] The greater the extent to which firms elect to react by discharging employees, the less flexible wages will be in a downward direction as compared to their flexibility in an upward direction. Because the 'new microeconomic' models are symmetrical, they yield a second counterfactual implication, that the long-run Phillips-curve is vertical throughout, and hence a period when unemployment remains above the natural rate for a number of years will be characterised by an accelerating *deflation.*

The 'new microeconomics' labour market models are not identical. In the 'continuous auction market' models of Friedman [34] and Lucas–Rapping [62] a reduction in the wage rate relative to the expected price level causes an instantaneous withdrawal of workers from the labour force, whereas in the 'search' model of Mortensen [65], a reduction in the wage rate relative to the acceptance wage of workers causes an increased flow of quits into employment and a reduced flow of hires out of unemployment, in other words, an increase in both the number of unemployed and the duration of their unemployment. But there is no difference between the two approaches in their inability to explain layoffs and 'no help wanted' signs and in their implication that the long-run Phillips-curve is vertical throughout its range, and that the quit rate varies countercyclically. The major difference between the two approaches is in the ability of the search model rigorously to explain a positive rather than a zero 'natural rate' of unemployment.

[1] An additional choice, which is symmetrical in booms and recessions, must be made between changes in the number of employees and changes in hours worked per employee. It has been suggested that compulsory overtime is the reverse equivalent of layoffs in an economic boom, but the parallel is inexact because employees maintain the freedom to quit when compulsory overtime becomes objectionable, whereas in a recession there is no such alternative to an employee who is discharged. Compulsory overtime would be parallel to layoffs only in a society with slavery.

(2) THE 'NEW–NEW' MICROECONOMICS OF WAGE RIGIDITY AND LAYOFFS

Three simultaneously written but independent contributions by Azariadis [3], Baily [6], and D. F. Gordon [37] (A–B–G) provide an explanation of wage rigidity which does not rely on union regulations or institutional rigidities, but applies instead to a world of homogeneous employees and competitive firms facing stochastic fluctuations in demand. The first common assumption uniting A–B–G is a relative aversion to risk among employees as compared to their employers, partly because of the limits on diversification in human capital imposed by the prohibition of slavery and, more important, because entrepreneurs are self-selected individuals who are relatively indifferent toward (or actually lovers of) risk. Second, A–B–G analyse contractual arrangements between firms and employees which may be implicit and unwritten but which nevertheless constrain behaviour. Firms maximise profits by minimising the variability of income to their workers, who dislike variability, thus in effect providing a compensation package which consists partly of pecuniary wage payments and partly of insurance services.

Up to this point, however, the theory justifies only a fixed-income contract (tenure), whereas an explanation is needed for contracts which call for rigidity of wages together with variability in manhours, in contrast to the classical 'spot auction' labour market, in which wages are perfectly flexible and all variations in manhours, if any, are voluntary movements along notional supply curves. Firms find that workers are not indifferent between a fixed-wage–more-variable–manhour contract and the spot auction outcome even when total pecuniary income paid out by firms under both has the same mean and variance, if employees can earn some positive income during periods of reduced manhours which is not paid directly or indirectly by firms, particularly, the value of leisure (or the reduced disutility of work), and any unemployment benefits or welfare payments which are financed at least partly by general government revenues rather than by firm contributions based on their past unemployment experience.

As I pointed out in [42], the A–B–G theory as initially developed is incomplete. In the absence of government-financed payments, the superiority of the fixed-wage–more-variable–manhour policy compared to the spot auction outcome relies entirely on the value to employees of the extra leisure consumed during periods of low demand, a result which depends on an asymmetric analytical procedure in which demand can fail below normal but never rise above. When symmetric demand fluctuations are allowed, the hours of leisure foregone in high demand periods outweigh the less valuable hours gained in low demand periods and tilts the blaance back to a fixed-income (tenure) contract. Since the A–B–G theory cannot explain a fixed-wage contract without government payments, one can question its applicability to the period before the introduction of unemployment benefits in the late 1930s.

Two quite different considerations are capable of 'rescuing' the fixed-wage contract. Grossman [48], working within the A–B–G risk-aversion framework, argues that both agents entering into an implicit contract must weigh the risk of default by the other. A positive probability that a worker will default from a fixed income contract by shifting to the spot auction market during high demand periods will sufficiently reduce profits to force firms to eliminate from consideration the fixed-income option. The optimality of the fixed-wage contract as compared to the no-contract spot market alternative then depends positively on the degree of risk-aversion and the size of the default penalty. The appeal of Grossman's approach is its ability to explain why three different arrangements are observed in real-world labour markets–spot auction markets (when workers perceive a low default penalty and are only mildly risk averse) tenure fixed-income contracts (when the default penalty is high), and fixed-wage-rate contracts (in intermediate cases).

I have suggested [42] a second approach which is able to explain a fixed-wage policy without any consideration of risk aversion. Faced with the option of reducing wage rates or manhours when the demand for its product declines, a firm may prefer the certain reduction in its wage bill which can be achieved by a fixed-wage quantity-rationing policy. In contrast, a reduction in the wage rate may yield a highly uncertain reduction in the wage bill, because the number of employees who will quit depends on their subjective and unpredictable evaluation of alternative wage rates and employment opportunities open to them at the particular time.[1]

These initial modelling efforts measure labour input along a single dimension, manhours, and do not provide an explanation of the relative reliance on layoffs and reductions in hours per week when firms choose a fixed-wage policy. More recently both Baily [7] and Feldstein [26] have introduced hours per man and the number of men employed separately into firm production and worker utility functions; both illustrate the increased reliance of firms on layoffs as opposed to reductions in hours when there is an increase in unemployment benefits relative to the taxes a firm has to pay to finance benefits for its own employees.

The absence of any significant downward movement of wage rates during periods of high unemployment, for example, 1934–40, 1958–64, and 1970–71, together with the rather rapid response of wage change to periods of low unemployment, for example, 1955–57 and 1966–69, has stimulated interest in theoretical explanations of asymmetric wage adjustment. Tobin [89] developed a model in which the N.R.H. is valid only for downward departures of the unemployment rate below the natural rate, but his aggregate result depends on wage rigidity in individual microlabour markets which is assumed rather than deduced from maximising behaviour. Grossman [47] deduces asymmetry from the fact that in the spot market both manhours and the wage rate are high in booms, which makes its superiority over the fixed-wage contract in periods of above-average demand exceed its inferiority when

[1] Iwai [52] analyses the effects on wage-setting behaviour of uncertainty in a more general context.

demand is low, so that the alternative of the spot market places relatively greater pressure for revision of the fixed contractual wage during boom periods. Azariadis [4] emphasises the greater cost of default for employers than for employees as a source of asymmetry. While both papers are suggestive, a more essential element of asymmetry needs to be incorporated: in a recession firms deal with an *existing* group of employees under an implicit or explicit contract, but if demand increases sufficiently in a boom, the potential for raising labour input by higher overtime hours from existing employees must eventually be exhausted, requiring firms to go outside and attract new employees at sufficiently appealing terms to lure them away either from the spot market or from contracts at other firms.

(3) EFFECT OF WAGE INDEXING ON INFLATION AND UNEMPLOYMENT

In the A–B–G work on labour contracts under risk-aversion, firms sell insurance services to risk-averse employees. Since workers care about variance in real income, not just in nominal income, risk-neutral firms can profit by offering employees contracts which are 100 per cent indexed to changes in the consumer price level, a point recently made by Fischer [29] but not brought out in the original A–B–G papers. Full indexing would be optimal for the economy as a whole if prices were flexible and all disturbances were 'nominal', that is, caused by changes in the demand for commodities rather than the supply, leading wages and prices to change together but real output to remain unchanged following a disturbance. (The greater instability of prices in the indexed economy would have no adverse welfare consequences if indexing were extended not only to wages but to financial assets, the tax system, and accounting rules.) An indexed economy with flexible prices and nominal shocks is similar to a rational-expectations economy of the type described above; thus it is not surprising that Barro [9] found that indexing causes no effects on aggregate price or output behaviour in such an economy.

Full indexing, however, would increase the instability of real output if shocks were 'real', that is, changes in supply functions, since in that situation indexing would maintain a constant real wage instead of allowing the change in the real wage required to clear markets. If in 1974 United States wages had been totally indexed, the economy would have exhibited more inflation and greater unemployment in response to the food and oil supply shocks than actually occurred; as I showed in [41], a real 'indexing recession' can be avoided only by monetary accomodation of higher prices, leading to a very rapid inflation, the rate of which would depend on the lag in the indexing formula between the change in prices and the correction in wages. As Fischer points out, the payment of interest on money would amount to automatic monetary accomodation in this situation and would have to be counteracted by Central Bank open-market sales. If most real shocks tend to occur outside of the domestic non-farm part of the economy (in the foreign and farm sectors) the adverse effects of indexing could be eliminated if the wage-indexing formula were based on the domestic non-farm rather than the consumer price index.

(4) OTHER DEVELOPMENTS: MARK-UP PRICING AND TAXES

Most of the recent microeconomic theory reviewed above attempts to explain the wage-setting behaviour of competitive firms which are price *takers.* Very little innovative recent work has concerned the setting of prices.[1] Econometric models have typically pegged the price level to wage rates (adjusted for some mixture of actual and normal productivity) by a 'mark-up fraction' which in turn is a function of the excess demand for commodities. This is the 'running man wearing a raincoat' view of inflation – price change can never get very far from wage change, even though the relationship may wiggle around a bit in response to demand movements, just as a raincoat can never get very far from the running man who wears it, even though the coat may ripple a bit in the wind.

The most rigorous recent exposition of the mark-up approach to oligopolistic price behaviour is presented by deMenil [20], whose empirical work agrees with my conclusion [38], [39] that the price–wage relationship is quite stable, and that the direct effect of demand on prices, as opposed to the indirect effect of demand on prices through the wage–unemployment relation, is minor but nevertheless perceptible. The major difficulty with the mark-up pricing approach is its insecure theoretical base. In his comprehensive survey of the mark-up literature, Nordhaus [69] reached the surprising conclusion that mark-up pricing, which had been presumed to be justified only in non-competitive industries, was actually optimal only under conditions of perfect competition and constant returns to scale. In general, price should not be set as a simple mark-up over labour cost, but should be a weighted average of labour plus capital cost (plus the prices of raw materials, if any). Clearly more work is needed here and could begin by attempting to construct a single model to explain why mark-up pricing appears to characterise some markets (automobiles, new houses) but not others (copper, wheat, plywood).

In recent years the analysis of tax effects on inflation has become much more sophisticated, perhaps stimulated in part by the failure of the 1968 United States tax surcharge to stem inflation, by the introduction of the value-added tax in the United Kingdom and by the growing importance of payroll taxes in all countries. The essential point is that higher taxes are a two-edged sword, on the one hand reducing aggregate demand, and on the other hand increasing the 'wedge' between the market price of output and the after-tax income of factors of production. In principle all taxes–sales, excise, payroll, corporate income, and personal income – may be shifted forward in varying degrees to output prices, and the net effect of higher taxation may be inflationary

[1] An exception is Bewley's [12] study of transactions' costs as an explanation of discrete jumps in prices in a rather general context which does not analyse the source of determinants of the transactions' costs.

if after-tax wage rates are only partially flexible downward. The empirical contribution of higher tax rates to the late-1960s inflation was first pointed out by me in [38], and formal analytical models were used by Blinder [14] and Dernberg [21] to derive the conditions under which the effect on prices of a tax increase goes in the opposite direction from the standard textbook analysis. Parkin, Sumner and Ward [71] and I [43] have derived econometric wage and price equations from explicit labour market models where taxes of various types enter into both supply and demand behaviour. In the context of the first section of this paper, then, tax changes become another 'cost-push' element which, while unable by themselves to generate a continuous inflation, add to the pressures for a higher rate of monetary expansion.

VI. WORLD INFLATION AND THE TRANSMISSION MECHANISM

Almost all of the above literature, primarily developed by insular Americans, has concerned a closed economy. Three major questions immediately arise when one ventures beyond the national borders of the autarkic regime favoured by most United States macrotheorists. First, what determines the world rate of inflation; second, how are inflationary impulses transmitted from one open economy to another; and third, of what relevance for open economies is domestic inflation theory, in contrast to the opposing view that the domestic price level is simply pegged to that of the world outside?

Two major frameworks for the analysis of open-economy inflation have developed in the past decade, the monetary approach to balance-of-payments theory, which claims to have an answer for all three basic questions, and the 'Scandinavian' or Aukrust–E.F.O. approach, which only claims to deal with the second and third.[1] The monetary approach (M.A.) was developed primarily by R. Mundell and H. Johnson and their remarkable group of graduate students at the University of Chicago in the late 1960s. As summarised by Johnson [56], the M.A. answers the first question, the source of world inflation, essentially by repeating Friedman's dictum that 'inflation is always and everywhere a monetary phenomenon', at least when the open economies of the world are linked by fixed exchange rates. This straightforward quantity-theory view is subject to the same criticism as that directed above against domestic monetarism – most economists have long recognised that an inflation originating from any source must be ratified by monetary accommodation if it is to continue, so that a 'theory' which links world inflation to the growth rate of world money simply describes the symptoms of the disease rather than its causes and cure. A shallow response would attribute the increase in world money to the creation of an excess supply of dollars in the United States, together with the acceptance of those dollars by other nations in the form of international reserve accumulations in place of the inflation-fighting alternative of exchange-

[1] See Aukrust [5] and the E.F.O. volume", G. Edgren, K-O. Faxen, and C-E. Odhner, *Wage Formation and the Economy* (London, 1973).

rate appreciations. A deeper response would require the merging of the M.A. with the rudimentary theory of the politics of inflation, which accepts the basic premise of the quantity-theory approach as its point of departure and analyses the pressure on the monetary authority from public and private sources. An international extension of the political approach to those economies which do not have independent control over the domestic money supply would presumably examine the political power of exporters and import-competitors to resist revaluation. The political approach counters the facile M.A. recommendation of United States monetary restriction as a cure to world inflation by pointing to the real social costs of output reduction when wages are set according to slow-changing contractual arrangements, and when a positive political rate of time preference puts a positive weight on the near-term albeit temporary output loss (and, add the modellers of labour market asymmetry, 'temporary' may be a very long time).

Recent contributions on the international transmission mechanism are placed in perspective when contrasted with the alternative embedded in the large-scale econometric models of the mid-1960s, in which higher foreign demand reached the domestic price level by only two routes, the effect of higher exports on aggregate demand, both directly and via the Keynesian multiplier expansion, and through the appearance of import prices in the aggregate mark-up price equation. The M.A. added two additional channels, first by the assumption (at least in the simple Johnson version) that all goods are tradeable with prices set in world markets, and, second, by allowing domestic holdings of foreign reserves to increase (raising the domestic monetary base and money supply), not just as the direct result of the export surplus, but more generally because the higher price level raises the demand for money relative to the initial supply. The one-tradeable-good assumption focused attention on the neglect in previous econometric models of the direct effect of foreign prices on exports, and of the substitutability of domestic import-competing goods with imports. The critical contribution of the attention to money-market equilibrium was to focus on world capital markets rather than the trade surplus as the source of additional liquidity during an export-led expansion. Dornbusch [22] extended the one-good model by allowing for both traded and non-traded goods. In his version domestic non-traded goods prices are perfectly flexible and the labour market always clears, requiring in response to a foreign demand stimulus an initial increase in the single nominal wage rate and a drop in the relative price of non-traded goods. Eventually the inflow of reserves raises the domestic money supply by enough to finance an increase in the relative price of non-traded goods to the initial level. In the final equilibrium all nominal magnitudes, including the domestic supply of money, are increased by the same proportion as the increase in the world price level.

The transmission mechanism in the Scandinavian model is essentially a Dornbusch-type two-sector model without money. An initial increase in traded goods prices raises wages in that sector (the bargaining process maintains a constant rate of return in that sector), and non-traded sector wages rise in imitation, in turn pulling up non-traded sector prices (the latter are determined by a mark-up or are equal by definition to wages in many proprietor-owned service industries). In contrast to the Dornbusch monetary approach, there is no attention to the source of the extra money needed to finance the higher price level; it is implicitly provided as needed and its availability does not, as in the Dornbusch approach, constrain the speed at which non-traded goods prices can rise. A positive contribution, however, is made by the Scandinavian emphasis on differential productivity growth rates in the non-traded sector as sources of long-run differences in the growth of consumer price indexes across countries.

Turning to the third major question, both the Scandinavian and Dornbusch versions leave no room for the domestic Phillips-curve approach to wage determination, since excess labour-market demand and supply plays no role in the process of adjustment. Both models are uncomfortable hybrids; in the Dornbusch model, for instance, the process of monetary expansion is explicitly short run in nature, but the labour market is ruled by the long-run assumptions of perfect wage and price flexibility and full employment. Recent papers which attempt to merge together a short-run Phillips-curve with these long-run theories include Calmfors' [19] empirical demonstration that *both* the traded-goods price *and* excess labour demand determine Swedish wages in the short run, and my own theoretical analysis [43] which introduces imperfectly flexible price and wage adjustment and unemployment into the Dornbusch framework. But in the long run it is clear that the domestic Phillips-curve approach will not do. Any econometric simulation (for example, those regularly turned out by operation LINK) which yields a steady long-run divergence of domestic from world inflation rates when exchange rates are fixed (leaving aside differential non-traded-goods productivity growth rates) implicity depicts an economy which eventually reaches complete specialisation in traded or non-traded goods.

VII. RIP VAN WINKLE'S CONCLUSION

Rip, breathless from his fast trip through a decade's literature, was extremely impressed at the progress made since 1963. The revival of the quantity theory and its application to both domestic and international problems had brought with it important insights on the role of expectations, the preconditions for inflation, and the international transmission mechanism. Frictional unemployment had received a rigorous theoretical underpinning, and a healthy rigour had been evident in the increasing number of papers which had attempted to explain wage rigidity, layoffs, and asymmetric adjustment from microeconomic behavioural postulates.

The major remaining problems were, first, that the pendulum had swung too far toward a simple-minded monetarist view which required perfectly flexible prices for its validity. The extensive investment of resources in the flexible-price version of rational expectations had gone too far, and some government agency needed to encourage a conference at which the R.E. + N.R.H. group would be locked up in a room with the rigid-wage implicit-contract theorists and forced to re-examine their conclusions. Second, naive monetarism needed to be replaced by more attention to the economics of political behaviour, and more work needed to be done to determine why the rate of monetary expansion differed across time and space, and to test empirically the validity of the conjectural explanations which had thus far been provided.

REFERENCES

[1] A. A. Alchian, 'Information Costs, Pricing, and Resource Unemployment', in E. Phelps, ed., *Microeconomic Foundations of Employment and Foundation Theory* (New York: Norton, 1970).
[2] Y. Attiyeh, 'Wage-Price Spiral vs. Demand Inflation: U.S. 1949–57' unpublished Ph.D. dissertation, (University of Chicago, 1959).
[3] C. Azariadis, 'Implicit Contracts and Underemployment Equilibria', *Journal of Political Economy*, v. 83 (October, 1975).
[4] C. Azariadis, 'Asymmetric Wage Behaviour', presented at the Third Reisenburg Symposium, 'On the Stability of Contemporary Economic Systems', (July, 1975).
[5] O, Aukrust, 'Inflation in the Open Economy: The Norwegian Model', Central Bureau of Statistics of Norway, Working Paper 75/12, (March, 1975).
[6] M. N. Baily, 'Wages and Employment Under Uncertain Demand', *Review of Economic Studies*, v. 41 (January, 1974), pp. 37–50.
[7] M. N. Baily, 'On the Theory of Lay-offs and Unemployment', unpublished, (Yale University, June, 1975).
[8] R. J. Barro, 'Rational Expectations and the Role of Monetary Policy', unpublished, (University of Chicago, January, 1975).
[9] R. J. Barro 'Indexation in a Rational Expectations Model', unpublished, (University of Chicago, May, 1975).
[10] R. J. Barro, 'Unanticipated Money Growth and Unemployment in the United States', unpublished, (University of Rochester, July, 1975).
[11] R. J. Barro, and H. Grossman, 'A General Disequilibrium Model of Income and Employment', *American Economic Review*, v. 61 (March, 1971), pp. 82–93.
[12] T. Bewley, 'A Theoretical Study of Optimal Price Adjustment', unpublished, Harvard University, January, 1975).
[13] Pierre Biacabe, *Analyses contemporaines de l'inflation* (Paris, 1962).
[14] A. Blinder, 'Can Income Tax Increases Be Inflationary?' *National Tax Journal*, v. 26 (June, 1973), pp. 295–301.
[15] William Branson, *Macroeconomic Theory and Policy*, (New York: Harper and Row, 1972).
[16] Martin Bronfenbrenner and F. D. Holzman, 'Survey of Inflation Theory', *American Economic Review*, v. 53 (September, 1963), pp. 593–61.
[17] K. Brunner and A. Meltzer, eds., *The Phillips Curve and Public Policy*, (Amsterdam: North-Holland, 1975).
[18] P. Cagan, 'The Monetary Dynamics of Hyperinflation', in M. Friedman, ed., *Studies in The Quantity Theory of Money*, (Chicago: University of Chicago Press, 1956).
[19] Lars Calmfors, 'Swedish Inflation and International Price Influences', University of Stockholm, Institute for International Economic Studies, Seminar Paper 45, (March, 1975).
[20] George deMenil, 'Aggregate Price Dynamics', *Review of Economics and Statistics*, v. 51 (May, 1974), pp. 129–41.

[21] T. F. Dernberg, 'The Macroeconomic Implications of Wage Retaliation Against Higher Taxation', *International Monetary Fund Staff Papers*, v. 21 (November, 1974), pp. 758–88.
[22] R. Dornbusch, 'Devaluation, Money, and Nontraded Goods', *American Economic Review*, v. 53 (December, 1973), pp. 871–80.
[23] O. Eckstein, ed., *The Econometrics of Price Determination Conference*, (Washington: Federal Reserve Board, 1972).
[24] O. Eckstein and R. Brinner, *The Inflation Process in the United States,* A Study Prepared for the Use of the Joint Economic Committee, 92nd Congress, second session (Washington, 1972).
[25] M. S. Feldstein, 'Lowering the Permanent Rate of Unemployment', a Study Prepared for the Use of the Joint Economic Committee, 93rd Congress, first session (Washington, 1973).
[26] M. S. Feldstein, 'Temporary Layoffs in the Theory of Unemployment', unpublished, (Harvard University, July, 1975).
[27] S. Fischer, 'Recent Developments in Monetary Theory', *American Economic Review*, v. 65 (May, 1975), pp. 157–166.
[28] S. Fischer, 'Long-Term Contracts, Rational Expectations and the Optimal Money Supply Rule', unpublished, (Massachusetts Institute of Technology, June 1975).
[29] S. Fischer, 'Wage-Indexation and Macro-economic Stability', unpublished, Massachusetts Institute of Technology, June 1975).
[30] S. Fischer and J. P. Cooper, 'Stabilization Policy and Lags', *Journal of Political Economy*, v. 81 (July/August, 1973), pp. 847–77).
[31] I. Fisher, A Statistical Relation Between Unemployment and Price Changes', *International Labour Review*, v. 13 (June 1926), pp. 785–92. Reprinted in *Journal of Political Economy*, v. 81 (March/April 1973), pp. 496–502.
[32] B. Friedman, 'Rational Expectations are Really Adaptive After All', unpublished, (Harvard, February, 1975).
[33] M. Friedman, 'What Price Guideposts?', in G. P. Shultz and R. Z. Aliber, eds., *Guidelines: Informal Controls and the Market Place* (Chicago: University of Chicago Press, 1966), pp. 17–39 and 'Comments', pp. 55–61.
[34] M. Friedman, 'The Role of Monetary Policy', *American Economic Review*, v. 58 (March, 1968), pp. 1–17.
[35] M. Friedman, 'The Optimum Quantity of Money', in *The Optimum Quantity of Money and Other Essays* (Chicago: Aldine, 1969), pp. 1–50.
[36] M. Friedman 'Discussion' (of [27]), *American Economic Review*, v. 65 (May, 1975), pp. 176–179.
[37] D. F. Gordon, 'A Neo-Classical Theory of Keynesian Unemployment', *Economic Inquiry*, v. 12 (December, 1974), pp. 431–59.
[38] R. J. Gordon, 'Inflation in Recession and Recovery', *Brookings Papers on Economic Activity*, v. 2 (1971, No. 1), pp. 105–58.
[39] R. J. Gordon, 'Wage-Price Controls and the Shifting Phillips Curve', *Brooking Papers on Economic Activity,* v. 3 (1972, No. 2), pp. 385–421.
[40] R. J. Gordon, 'The Welfare Cost of Higher Unemployment', *Brookings Papers on Economic Activity*, v. 4 (1973, No. 1), pp. 133–95).
[41] R. J. Gordon, 'Alternative Responses of Policy to External Supply Shocks', *Brookings Papers on Economic Activity*, v. 6 (1975, No. 1), pp. 183–206.
[42] R. J. Gordon, 'Aspects of the Theory of Involuntary Unemployment', in Brunner and Meltzer (eds.) *The Phillips Curve and Public Policy*, (Amsterdam: North-Holland, 1975).
[43] R. J. Gordon, 'Interrelations Between Domestic and International Theories of Inflation', in R. Z. Aliber, *The Political Economy of Monetary Reform,* forthcoming.
[44] R. J. Gordon, 'Perspectives on Monetarism', in the Proceedings of a Conference on Monetarism held in Providence (November, 1974).

[45] R. J. Gordon, 'The Supply of and Demand for Inflation', in the forthcoming proceedings of a recent Universities-National Bureau Conference on the Economics of Political Behaviour held in Cambridge, Massachusetts (April, 1975).
[46] Jo Anna Gray, 'Wage Indexation: A Macroeconomic Approach', unpublished, (University of Chicago, April 1975).
[47] H. I. Grossman 'Is Wage Response Assymetrical?', presented at Conference on Inflation, Miami University (Oxford, Ohio, May, 1975).
[48] H. I. Grossman, 'The Nature of Optimal Labour Contracts; Towards a Theory of Wage and Employment Adjustment', presented at the Third Reisenburg Symposium, 'On the Stability of Contemporary Economic Systems', July, 1975.
[49] R. E. Hall, 'The Phillips Curve and Macroeconomic Policy', in Brunner and Meltzer (eds.) *The Phillips Curve and Public Policy* (Amsterdam: North-Holland, 1975).
[50] R. E. Hall, 'The Phillips Curve as an Explanation of Unemployment', to be presented at the Brookings Panel on Economic Activity, September 10–11, 1975.
[51] C. C. Holt, 'Job Search, Phillips Wage Relation, and Union Influence: Theory and Evidence', in *Microeconomic Foundations of Employment and Inflation Theory* (New York: Norton, 1970), pp. 53–123.
[52] K. Iwai, 'The Firm in Uncertain Markets and Its Price, Wage and Employment Adjustments', *Review of Economic Studies*, v. 41 (April, 1974), pp. 257–76.
[53] H. G. Johnson, 'A Survey of Theories of Inflation' in *Essays on Monetary Economics* (Cambridge: Harvard University Press, 1967), pp. 104–42. Originally published in the *Indian Economic Review*, v. 6 (August, 1963).
[54] H. G. Johnson, 'The Keynesian Revolution and the Monetarist Counter-Revolution', *American Economic Review*, v. 61 (May, 1971), pp. 1–14.
[55] H. G. Johnson, *Inflation and the Monetarist Controversy*, Professor Dr. F. De Vries Lectures (Amsterdam: North-Holland, 1972).
[56] H. G. Johnson, 'The Monetary Approach to Balance-of-Payments Theory', in *Further Essays in Monetary Economics* (London: George Allen and Unwin, 1972), pp. 229–49.
[57] D. Laidler and M. Parkin, 'Inflation: A Survey', *Economic Journal*, (December, 1975), pp. 741–809.
[58] Richard Lipsey, 'The Relation Between Unemployment and the Rate of Money Wage Rates in the United Kingdom, 1862–1957: A Further Analysis', *Economica*, v. 27 (February, 1960), pp. 1–31.
[59] R. E. Lucas, Jr., 'Testing the Natural Rate Hypothesis', in *The Econometrics of Price Determination Conference*, (Washington: Federal Reserve Board, 1972).
[60] R. E. Lucas, Jr., 'Expectations and the Neutrality of Money', *Journal of Economic Theory*, v. 4 (April, 1972), pp. 103–24.
[61] R. E. Lucas, Jr., 'Econometric Policy Evaluation: A Critique', in Brunner and Meltzer (eds.) *The Phillips Curve and Public Policy* (Amsterdam: North-Holland, 1975).
[62] R. E. Lucas, Jr., and L. A. Rapping, 'Real Wages, Employment, and Inflation', *Journal of Political Economy*, v. 77 (September/October 1969). Reprinted in *Microeconomic Foundations of Employment and Inflation Theory* (New York: Norton, 1970), pp. 257–305.
[63] R. E. Lucas Jr. and L. A. Rapping, 'Unemployment in the Great Depression: Is There a Full Explanation?', *Journal of Political Economy*, v. 80 (January/February, 1972), pp. 186–91.
[64] F. Modigliani and L. Papademos, 'Targets for Monetary Policy in the Coming Year', *Brookings Papers on Economic Activity*, v. 6, (1975, No. 1), pp. 141–163.
[65] D. T. Mortensen, 'A Theory of Wage and Employment Dynamics, in *Microeconomics Foundations of Employment and Inflation Theory* (New York: Norton, 1970).
[66] D. T. Mortensen, 'Job Search, The Duration of Unemployment and the Phillips Curve', *American Economic Review*, v. 60 (December, 1970), pp. 847–62.
[67] J. F. Muth, 'Rational Expectations and the Theory of Price Movements', *Econo-*

metrica, v. 29 (July, 1961), pp. 315–35.

[68] M. Nerlove, 'Distributed Lags and Unobserved Components in Economic Time Series', in W. Fellner, et al., *Ten Economic Studies in the Tradition of Irving Fisher* (New York: John Wiley, 1967), pp. 127–69.

[69] W. D. Nordhaus, 'Recent Developments in Price Dynamics' in *The Econometrics of Price Determination Conference* (Washington: Federal Reserve Board, 1972).

[70] W. D. Nordhaus, 'The Political Business Cycle', *The Review of Economic Studies*, v. 42 (April, 1975), pp. 169–90.

[71] J. M. Parkin, M. T. Sumner and R. Ward, 'The effects of Excess Demand, Generalised Expectations, and Wage-Price Controls on Wage Inflation in the U.K.', in K. Brunner and A. Meltzer, eds., proceedings of conference on controls held in Rochester (November 1973).

[72] G. L. Perry, *Unemployment, Money Wage Rates, and Inflation* (Cambridge: Massachusetts Institute of Technology Press, 1966).

[73] G. L. Perry, 'Changing Labour Markets and Inflation', *Brookings Papers on Economic Activity*, v. 1 (1970, No. 3), pp. 411–41.

[74] E. S. Phelps, 'A Test for the Presence of Cost Inflation in the United States, 1955-57', *Yale Economic Essays*, v. 1 (Spring, 1961), pp. 28–69.

[75] E. S. Phelps, 'Phillips Curves, Expectations of Inflation, and Optimal Unemployment Over Time', *Economica* (NS), v. 34 (August, 1967), pp. 254–81.

[76] E. S. Phelps, 'Money Wage Dynamics and Labour Market Equilibrium', in *Microeconomic Foundations of Employment and Inflation Theory* (New York: Norton, 1970) pp. 124–66.

[77] E. S. Phelps, *et al.*, *Microeconomic Foundations of Employment and Inflation Theory* (New York: Norton, 1970).

[78] E. S. Phelps, *Inflation Policy and Unemployment Theory* (New York: Norton, 1972).

[79] E. S. Phelps, and J. B. Taylor, 'Stabilizing Properties of Monetary Policy Under Rational Price Expectations', Discussion Paper 75-7607, (Columbia University, July, 1975).

[80] A. W. Phillips, 'The Relation Between Unemployment and the Rate of Change of Money Wage Rates in the United Kingdom, 1862–1957', *Economica*, v. 25 (November, 1958), pp. 283–99.

[81] P. A. Samuelson and R. M. Solow, 'Analytical Aspects of Anti-Inflationary Policy', *American Economic Review*, v. 50 (May, 1960), pp. 177–94.

[82] T. J. Sargent and N. Wallace, ' "Rational" Expectations, the Optimal Monetary Instrument, and the Optimal Money Supply Rule', *Journal of Political Economy*, v. 83 (April, 1975), pp. 241–57.

[83] R. T. Selden, 'Cost-Push is Demand-Pull Inflation, 1955-57', *Journal of Political Economy*, v. 67 (February, 1959), pp. 1–20.

[84] L. A. Sjaastad, 'Why Stable Inflations Fail', University of Chicago, in J. M. Parkin and G. Zis, eds., *Inflation in the World Economy*, (Manchester: Manchester University Press, 1975).

[85] A. Smithies, 'Behaviour of Money National Income Under Inflationary Conditions', *Quarterly Journal of Economics*, v. 56 (November, 1942), pp. 113–29.

[86] R. M. Solow, 'Recent Controversies in the Theory of Inflation', in S. Rousseas, ed., *Proceedings of a Symposium on Inflation*, (Wilton, Conn.: Kazanjias Economics Foundation, 1968).

[87] R. M. Solow, 'The Intelligent Citizen's Guide to Inflation', *The Public Interest*, (Winter, 1975), pp. 30–66.

[88] A. K. Swoboda, 'Monetary Approaches to the Transmission and Generation of Worldwide Inflation', in W. Salant, ed., proceedings of Brookings Conference on Worldwide Inflation held in Washington, D.C. (November, 1974).

[89] J. Tobin, 'Inflation and Unemployment', *American Economic Review*, v. 52 (March, 1972), pp. 1–18.

3 Causes and Origins of the Current Worldwide Inflation

Hans Genberg and Alexander K. Swoboda
GRADUATE INSTITUTE OF INTERNATIONAL STUDIES, GENEVA

I. INTRODUCTION

Inflation as a worldwide phenomenon is a popular topic for discussion and lament, even in the daily press, weeklies, and bar-rooms. Yet its origins and causes, the topic assigned to us for this conference, are the subject of much debate – especially in those bar-rooms where economists meet. The reader should be warned at the outset that this paper does not pretend to settle the issue. It only sketches one answer, but we believe a largely correct one, to the ambitious questions assigned to us.

In the next section, we begin by sketching briefly some of the characteristics of worldwide inflation and enquire into the meaning that can be attributed to that term. In the following section, we outline a few of the theories that have been offered in explanation. We then draw out some of the implications of our favoured theory, the so-called monetary approach to world inflation and the balance of payments. The resulting hypotheses are subjected to some tentative tests in the penultimate section of this essay. The tentative nature of our conclusions should serve as a reminder that what follows constitutes only a first report on the beginnings of research in progress.

II. THE EVOLUTION AND MEANING OF WORLDWIDE INFLATION

In the six episodes of secular price change, 1790–1934, studied by Anna Schwartz [17], the annual average rate of change of United States prices for subperiods (of 14 to 35 years) of inflation and deflation ranged from –4·1 per cent to +4·7 per cent.[1] The highest figure includes the first world war years; in the earlier inflationary episodes, 1790–1815 and 1850–73, prices rose at an annual average rate of 2·8 and 0·9 per cent respectively. Between 1950 and 1974, the United States consumer price index rose at an annual average rate of 3 per cent, a similar index constructed for ten major industrial countries at a

[1] It may be interesting to reproduce A. Schwartz's (see [17], p. 257) data concerning the United States price level here: 1790–1815: 2·8 per cent 1815–50: 2·2 per cent 1850–73: 0·9 per cent 1873–96: –1·7 per cent 1896–1920: 4·7 per cent 1920–34: –4·1 per cent. Note that over the period the price level returns almost to its original level.

3·5 per cent rate.[1] When set in historical perspective, current concern about inflation, and especially its recent acceleration, can readily be understood.

A closer look at current inflation also reveals its worldwide nature. Table 3.1 lists two alternative measures of world inflation. Column (1) gives the change from the preceding year of a weighted index of the national C.P.I.s of ten major industrial countries, the weights being 1963 nominal G.N.P.s converted into dollars at the 1963 exchange rate. Our 'world' thus consists of Belgium, Canada, France, Germany, Italy, Japan, the Netherlands, Switzerland, the United Kingdom, and the United States. Column (2) gives an average

TABLE 3.1
YEARLY RATES OF INFLATION 1950–1974

Year	(1) 'World' price index[1]	(2) Average inflation rate – ten countries[2]	(3) United States consumer price index	(4) Standard deviation[3]
1950	−1·2	0·5	−1·5	5·1
1951	7·9	7·5	7·9	8.4
1952	3·2	3·7	2·2	3·6
1953	0·7	0·7	0·7	2·7
1954	1·0	1·0	0·4	1·7
1955	0·4	1·0	−0·3	1·5
1956	2·1	2·5	1·5	1·4
1957	2·9	2·7	3·4	1·8
1958	3·4	3·5	2·8	4·0
1959	−0·2	1·1	0·9	1·7
1960	3·2	2·0	1·6	1·1
1961	1·6	2·2	0·9	1·3
1962	2·3	3·4	1·2	1·8
1963	2·5	3·8	1·2	2·2
1964	2·2	3·5	1·4	1·4
1965	2·7	3·8	1·6	1·5
1966	3·3	3·9	3·1	1·0
1967	2·8	3·1	2·8	0·7
1968	3·9	3·5	4·2	1·3
1969	4·9	4·5	5·4	1·7
1970	5·6	4·8	5·9	1·4
1971	5·1	5·7	4·3	1·8
1972	4·4	5·7	3·2	1·3
1973	7·3	8·4	6·2	1·7
1974	12·5	13·3	11·0	4·5

Notes: [1] Change over previous year of an index of ten countries' consumer price indices weighted by 1963 nominal G.N.P. Uncorrected for exchange-rate changes.
[2] Change over previous year of an unweighted average of the ten countries' individual year-to-year percentage change in consumer price indices.
[3] Standard deviation of inflation rates averaged in Column (2).

[1] These figures were calculated from *International Financial Statistics*. For a discussion and definition of the aggregate index, see the text below and the data appendix.

(unweighted) of the ten countries individual yearly rates of inflation, column (3) the yearly rate of inflation (measured by the consumer price index) in the United States whose weight in the 'world' index was some 56 per cent in 1963. The data indicate broad conformity between the trend of the two indicators of world inflation, with the usually lower rate of inflation in the United States being reflected in the fact that column (2) figures are usually above those in column (1).

A casual examination of table 3.1 confirms what we all know about the evolution of inflation after the second world war. The Korean war boom leads to a first surge in 1951–52, inflation rises again from 1956 to 1958, proceeds at a fairly steady pace of some 2·3 per cent per annum in the first half of the sixties and starts accelerating thereafter, with a 'dip' in 1972. It may be worth noting that, contrary to much of the earlier period, the United States inflation rate is higher than the average of column (2) for the 1968–1970 period. A summary record of postwar experience is given in table 3.1a below where the 1950–1974 period is broken down, somewhat arbitrarily, into five five-year sub-periods.

TABLE 3.1a.
TEN-COUNTRY AVERAGE ANNUAL RATES OF INFLATION

1950–55	1955–60	1960–65	1965–70	1969–74
2·6	2·3	2·3	4·1	6·9

In the preceding sketch of the historical record, we have somewhat casually talked of world-wide inflation. The average rate of inflation rose, but one may question the legitimacy of the averaging or of the construction of an aggregate price index for a number of countries. The argument for the aggregation is both practical – inflation rates have moved together – and theoretical – under fixed exchange rates we would expect them to do so. That they have moved together is borne out by the last column of table 3.1 which lists the standard deviation of the ten countries' yearly rate of inflation around their mean, as given in column (2). With the exception of 1950–1953, 1958, 1963, and 1974 these standard deviations remain in the 0·7–1·8 range. Remembering that, with exchange-rate margins of 1 per cent (or 0·75 per cent under E.M.A.) of any individual currency in terms of the dollar, the total range of fluctuation of any two non-United States currencies in terms of each other over time is 4 per cent (or 3 per cent under E.M.A.), temporary deviations of inflation rates from each other within that range are compatible with strict purchasing-power parity under fixed rates with margins. The standard deviations for 'normal' years are compatible with such a range since they imply roughly that 95 per cent of observed inflation rates fall within a band of 1·4 to 3·6 around the mean inflation rate. Furthermore, the deviant years are easily explained; 1950–53 was still a period of reconstruction and of high but changing trade and capital transactions restrictions; in addition, the Korean war and associated raw-materials boom created some abrupt changes in relative prices. The high 1958 standard deviation is largely the result of the French devaluations (bringing about a 15 per cent of inflation) for which the data was not corrected. The 1963 increase in dispersion, though not very substantial, is harder to explain.[1] The 1974 sharp increase in dispersion can of course be viewed as the consequence of the added degree of freedom given by flexible exchange rates for inflation rates to diverge. That this increase in dispersion did not occur before (say) 1971, when flexibility was already beginning to increase, is not hard to explain; suffice it to mention lags in the reaction of inflation rates to changes in rates of monetary and fiscal expansion and a common heritage of policy problems, and hence in policy reactions.

Variations of exchange rates (within margins or otherwise) are of course not the only source of divergences in inflation rates across countries. Among other sources we may mention here failure of arbitrage in traded goods, discrepancies in relative productivity growth or of growth of demand in the traded and non-traded goods sectors, and errors of measurement. The latter can take several forms: recording errors, discrepancies in the timing of collection of index components (for example, changes in housing rents are included monthly in some countries' indices, semi-annually in others), differences in the treatment of indirect taxes. Genberg [8], in a more detailed study, examines the behaviour of consumer prices in twenty-one OECD countries over the period 1955 to 1970. Using quarterly data and principal component analysis, he shows that the first principal component can explain 89·6 per cent of the covariation in price levels, but only 28·1 per cent of yearly rates of change. Taking the 1962–66 period during which there were no devaluations, these percentages rise to 97·5 and 38·2 per cent respectively. These figures compare favourably with those found by Hester in a recent study of yearly rates of change in twenty-one commodity classifications within the United States consumer price index. Furthermore, in a previous study, Genberg [9] compared the variance of inflation rates of regions (fifteen large United States cities) with that between sixteen OECD countries; on balance, the results indicated that the variation between countries was no greater than that within the United States.

The general conclusion to be drawn from this introductory sketch of inflationary experience is simply that it does not make sense to speak of a 'world' rate of inflation and that it is worth trying to explain inflation as a worldwide phenomenon, if only because of its increasing relevance as a policy problem over the last two decades.

III. ALTERNATIVE THEORIES OF WORLDWIDE INFLATION

A number of explanations have been provided for the simultaneous surge of inflation in the world economy. That surge has been accompanied by what

[1] In actual fact, it was due to spurts of inflation in Italy and Japan.

William Nordhaus [14] has called a 'worldwide wage explosion' and by an explosion of the number of special factors or 'theories' adduced to account for it. Nordhaus lists no less than ten of these. The most popular catalogue, these days, distinguishes among four main strands of analysis: Keynesian, Nordic (or Scandinavian), cost-push *cum* sociology, and monetary approaches.

A satisfactory theory of world wide inflation should be able to explain both its generation and its transmission from country to country. Of the four approaches mentioned above, only the last is capable of explaining both generation and transmission within a unified framework.

The sociological cost-push hypothesis does not have much to commend it – at least as long as no convincing theory (going beyond appeal to some vague international demonstration effect) is provided to explain why it should occur when it does, why it should take the particular magnitude it does, and how it should spread throughout the world. A coincidence of accidents may or may not be a contradiction in terms; it is, in any case, not a theory. Furthermore, wage explosions occurred in the second half of the sixties at quite different rates in different countries – and with some differences in timing. This did not prevent rates of inflation from staying within a fairly narrow band. If anything is to be rescued from this strand of reasoning, it is that disturbances in segments of the 'world' labour market may, to some extent, be transmitted to other segments through expectations, and so on. Why such disturbances should occur systematically remains, however, to be explained.

The 'Nordic' or Aukrust–E.F.O. model of inflation draws attention to an important element in the transmission process. In a small open economy the sector that produced goods that compete with similar products in the world market can, for most practical purposes, be regarded as a price-taker. The rate of change of prices in this 'competitive' or 'exposed' sector is determined by the rate of change of competitive goods prices in the world market. That rate of change is exogenous from the small country's point of view when the exchange rate is fixed. It serves as a peg to the rate of change of prices in the 'sheltered' or 'home' goods sector. The difference between the rates of inflation in the two sectors is related to different rates of growth of productivity, to labour shares and to wage-setting behaviour. Note, however, that logic would seem to require – once the rate of change of prices in the exposed sector and the rate of productivity change are given, and once full employment is assumed – that the rate of change in sheltered-goods prices be entirely determined and, with it, that of wages. As an explanation of inflation in the small open economy the Nordic model is but a version of the 'service-sector-augmented' version of the purchasing-power-parity theory developed by Béla Balassa [1] in 1964 – however useful it may be as a planning aid in the wage-bargaining process and as part of an explanation of income distribution. In the present context, the Nordic model suffers from two main defects. In the first place, the path of inflation is entirely determined by supply side considerations to the neglect of aggregate demand and monetary and fiscal policy (which are thus assumed to be entirely accommodating); in this respect, it is inferior to the recently developed general-equilibrium macroeconomic models that distinguish between traded (exposed) and non-traded (sheltered) goods while incorporating expenditure functions and a monetary mechanism of adjustment.[1] In the second place, the Nordic model leaves open the mechanism of generation of the world rate of inflation proxied by the exogenously given rate of change of the prices of the goods produced in the exposed sector.

There is no single all-encompassing prototype of the 'Keynesian' approach to worldwide inflation. Its main characteristic is perhaps emphasis on the role of expenditure on foreign goods and on trade multipliers in the transmission of economic disturbances. An increase in aggregate demand abroad is transmitted to the domestic economy through the effects on output, prices and employment of increased demand for the country's exports. Though domestic prices can temporarily diverge from world prices, repercussions through the balance of payments, capital markets and the money supply process will, in the more sophisticated versions of the approach, such as that developed by Branson [2], eventually lead to convergence of inflation rates. As a matter of fact, these more sophisticated versions share many of the characteristics of monetary approaches, at least with respect to the transmission if not the generation mechanism. The latter is left rather undefined in many 'Keynesian' writings; for some reason (monetary or fiscal policy, a struggle for income shares validated by authorities, some 'Phillips-curve' story) nominal expenditure increases abroad and spills over to the home country under fixed exchange rates.

The monetary approach to world inflation and the balance of payments starts with a methodological stance that is rather different from that of other approaches. In particular, it views the world rate of inflation as determined by the world rate of monetary expansion. To put the point heuristically – though not quite accurately – the monetary approach to a fixed exchange-rate world starts from a global point of view and then disaggregates down to countries (when dealing with individual balances of payments and deviations of national price and output levels from world trends) rather than the other way round. As an extensive survey of the approach has recently been provided by one of us [19], only a brief reminder of some of its main features will be given below.

Fixed exchange rates imply that, in some respects, analysis of the world economy can proceed in a manner analogous to that of a closed economy. Fixed exchange rates have two main implications. First, when coupled with the assumption of perfect arbitrage (the law of one price), they imply equalisation of the money price of traded goods expressed in a common national monetary unit up to transport cost and impediments to trade and also equalisation of their rates of change (a feature incorporated in the Nordic model).

[1] See Branson and Myhrman [4] for a critical evaluation of the Nordic model. The latter is evaluated in terms of the traded non-traded goods general equilibrium model by Kierzkowski [13]; the traded non-traded goods general equilibrium model has been used extensively by Dornbusch, for example in [6].

Second, the obligation of maintaining a fixed exchange rate implies that the rate of change of international reserves in the short run and of the money stock in the long run becomes an endogenous variable from the standpoint of any individual country in the system. The rate of change in traded goods prices provides the world inflation peg towards which the rates of change of non-traded goods prices, and hence national price levels, tend to adjust. The adjustment mechanism hinges on the substitution effects in both production and consumption brought about by a change in the relative price of traded and non-traded goods together with expenditure, liquidity, and balance-of-payments effects. In the long run national rates of inflation can differ only to the extent that productivity grows at different rates in the traded and non-traded goods sectors across countries (or that shares differ given similar productivity growth rates across countries).

This account leaves open the question of what determines the rate of growth of traded goods prices and eventually of 'the world price level' in general. The monetary answer is, of course, that inflation is the reflection of an adjustment of the price level to money creation in excess of money demand at the given price level. This explanation is simply transferred from the national to the fixed exchange-rate world. There, it is the growth of the world money stock that determines the growth of the world price level. This simple view, as stated, immediately raises three interrelated questions: over what run should we expect the simple proposition to hold, what is the exact nature of the transmission mechanism, and what determines the growth of the world money stock? We discuss these questions briefly below.

Many of the problems of macroeconomic analysis in the single country context arise also in the worldwide context – and then some. We know, for instance, that the relationship between money and prices is subject to long and variable lags and would expect this to hold at the world level. In the short run (say, with a lag of less than a year) we would expect close association between money income and the supply of money, the relationship between money growth and inflation being relevant to the longer run or to fairly long period averages – unless inflation has been high and accelerating and, hence more firmly built into the public's expectations. Better knowledge and predictability of the lags involved hinge on a better understanding and predictability of the exact channels through which monetary disturbances are transmitted to variations in output and prices. As recently stressed by Brainard and Cooper [2] in their brief assessment of our empirical knowledge of monetary macroeconomics, though various effects have been indentified and shown to be significant, much uncertainty remains as to the nature and stability of the links in the chain going from policy instruments of the central bank to high-powered money, to the money stock, to nominal income and to the division of the latter between output and price changes.

The chain is even more complex when studying monetary disturbances in an international context. Suppose one central bank in the system carries out an expansive open-market operation. One needs to assess not only how this policy affects the country's own interest rate, income level, and so forth, but also how it is transmitted abroad and the nature of the feedbacks to the domestic economy. The monetary approach to worldwide inflation is compatible with a wide variety of such transmission mechanisms and feedbacks – including those stressed by 'Keynesian' economists. In recent writings, however, much emphasis has been put on transmission through arbitrage in traded goods, capital movements, and the repercussions of real balance effects on the relation between income and absorption. The next section touches on some of the more specific aspects of this transmission mechanism. At this stage, it is, however, the strategic simplification of the approach that is of interest, namely, that it is the evolution of the world money stock (the sum of the money stocks in the hands of the public in various countries) which determines the evolution of world money income and, eventually, prices – whatever precise transmission mechanism is involved. Goods market integration insures that rates of inflation converge under fixed exchange rates; the pegging of the latter insures that the world aggregate money stock is distributed among countries – through the balance-of-payments adjustment mechanism – so as to satisfy the demand for money balances denominated in national currencies. Capital market integration serves to speed up the process of achieving an equilibrium distribution of the world money stock.

Unless it wants to leave a crucial question begging, the monetary approach must also analyse the determinants of the world money stock. This again raises problems that are familiar from closed economy theorising. It requires, first, that 'the world money stock' be defined. That aggregate can be defined as the sum of the money stocks held by the world's public. But what is money? In addition to the question of whether an M_1 or M_2 (or M_n) concept should be used, one would want to ask whether Eurocurrency deposits should be included. The answer, on an analytical level, is probably yes, at least if one uses an M_2 concept; on a practical level, it is more difficult since there is no good estimate of the net stock held by the public (and not banks). Second, all the familiar problems in relating the money stock to its determinants arise in the world context. They are made more difficult by the international reserve redistribution and creation or destruction that takes place in the wake of the adjustment process.

In domestic monetary analysis it is a conventional practice to model the money supply process by relating the monetary base to the money stock by a multiplier the value of which depends on policy parameters, the preferences of the public as to various forms of money holdings and of the banks as to asset holdings. Since these preferences are related to existing interest-rate patterns, so will the value of the multiplier. A world money supply function can be modelled in a similar manner under fixed exchange rates. Remembering that each country's money stock is related to its monetary base, the latter having both a domestic and foreign source component, the total world money stock should depend on the total of monetary bases, the latter being equal to the sum of the domestic sources of country bases plus the world total stock of international reserves. The relationship, however, is likely to be a complex one for a number of reasons. First, the world money stock will depend, at any point of time, not only on the total of international reserves but also on its distribution among countries to the extent that banking multipliers differ among countries. Second if there are any inside international reserves in the system (mainly foreign-exchange reserves of central banks), the total of international reserves cannot be taken as exogenously given. Swoboda [20] has suggested a theoretical solution to these problems. By postulating stable demands for money in various countries and given preference ratios of central banks, commercial banks and the public, he is able to relate the world money stock, the equilibrium distribution of international reserves, the stock of inside reserves, and the size of the Eurodollar market to two types of exogenous variables only, the domestic source components of national monetary bases and the stock of outside international reserves. Among the conclusions which emerge from the analysis, a number are relevant here.

The patterns of reserve holdings are quite important in determining the long-run effect of a change in domestic credit bases. Dividing the world into two regions, the United States and 'Europe', consider the effect of an expansive open-market operation of the same absolute amount in Europe and the United States; it can be shown that United States monetary policy thus defined results in a much more significant expansion in the world money stock than European policy. No empirical estimates exist, but Swoboda, using informed guesses as to the likely value of the parameters in his model and neglecting interest-rates effects, calculates that while a United States open-market purchase of 1 million dollars adds some 6 million dollars to the world money stock, a similar European purchase results in an increase of only some 3 to 4 million dollars to the world money stock. The main reason is the practice by European monetary authorities of keeping their foreign-exchange reserves in United States Treasury bills or with United States commercial banks. An expansive open-market operation in the United States creates a payments deficit for that country; this would, under an outside reserve system, lead to a loss of owned reserves and limit the expansion of the United States money stock. Under an inside reserve system, however, the expansion in European reserves (and the resulting increase in their money supply) occurs without a reduction in the United States money stock.

In addition, differential rates of money-income growth in Europe and the United States have repercussions on the world money stock that go beyond the combined effect of their sum, due to different income elasticities of the demand for money and to different bank multipliers in the two regions. Furthermore, shifts in asset preferences will change the value of the multiplier to be applied to a given world monetary base. For instance, any shift of money holdings towards the Eurodollar market, including an increased central bank propensity to hold their international reserves in that market, will tend to be expansionary. It is an open question whether such changes are largely autonomous in the short run or whether, as we suspect, they result from short-run changes in interest rates and exchange-rate expectations, themselves a function of fluctuations in rates of change of domestic credit expansion.

In short, the relationship between expansion in domestic credit, reserves, and the world money stock is a complex one, especially in the short run. We would nevertheless expect an identifiable relationship to hold over the longer run and United States monetary policy to play an important role in its determination. There are at least three reasons for this last contention. First, the sheer size of the United States gives its money stock a predominant weight in the world total stock (over 38 per cent of the total of ten industrial countries in 1973). This means that a 10 per cent expansion in the United States stock results, other things being equal, in an expansion of some 4 per cent in the ten industrial countries' total; in contrast, a 10 per cent expansion of the German money stock would result in only a 1·2 per cent in total M_2. Second, the asymmetry noted in the preceding paragraph does imply that an acceleration of domestic credit expansion in the United States will result in a more substantial change in the world money stock than similar expansion elsewhere. Finally, the nature of the international monetary system as it operated until recently, first as a gold-exchange standard, later as almost a pure dollar standard, does imply a much more severe reserve constraint on monetary expansion in countries outside the United States than in that country.

The preceding outline of the monetary theory of world inflation can be summarised in a few sentences. One would expect to find a close connection between aggregate monetary growth and the rate of change of money income in the short to intermediate run, between monetary growth and prices in the intermediate to long run. Fixed exchange rates make it meaningful to construct a world price index to be related to a world money stock. The growth of the latter is determined by both domestic credit expansion and the growth of world reserves and their distribution. The growth of world reserves plays a particularly important role under fixed exchange rates since they constrain the extent of domestic credit expansion in non-reserve-currency countries. The monetary policy of the reserve-currency countries play a particularly important role since it determines to a significant extent the growth in world reserves. All the relationships outlined above are of course subject to fluctuations and lags in the short run, some of which we have discussed, and to time trends in the long run.

Alternative theories of worldwide inflation should, of course, be subjected to empirical testing. Yet, empirical work on the subject is fairly scant. In a recent study John Pattison [16] has gathered much valuable information on inflation rates and some key relationships in OECD countries.[1] The only fairly complete study of the worldwide surge of inflation we are aware of is that of Nordhaus [14]. Nordhaus seeks to explain the wage explosion that occurred in 1968–71 in seven countries, the United States, Canada, France,

[1] We have seen too late for discussion here a reference to a study by Meiselman which, we gather, deals with a number of issues related to the ones we are raising below.

Germany, Japan, Sweden and the United Kingdom. He fits five different types of equations to 1956–1971 data for each of the seven countries separately. He finds that a naive monetary theory of wage determination works comparatively badly for all countries in the sample, that an expectations-augmented Phillips-curve fits the United States and Canadian case best, and that for the other countries (except France where no equation fits well), an export-constraint theory of wage movements (essentially a regression of wages and current and lagged import prices) is most adequate. His findings may seem discouraging for the monetary hypothesis; we do not find them to be so – on the contrary – for a number of reasons.

In the first place, we would apply the monetary theory to predict money income and the rate of change in prices – not that of wages (and, in any event, we would at least take changes in productivity into account). Nor would we expect velocity to stay constant over the business cycle. Second, as Nordhaus notes himself, good fit of an expectations-augmented Phillips-curve is consistent with a monetary view of the determinants of inflation. Moreover, one would expect that for smaller countries external factors would dominate price (including wage) developments, as Nordhaus finds and himself attributes to openness under fixed exchange rates. Finally, the monetary approach to worldwide inflation implies a methodology that is quite different from that adopted by Nordhaus: one would want to take a world rather than country approach as suggested above. Such a methodology has been applied with a fair amount of success in a number of studies of the inflation workshop at the University of Manchester.[1]

Eventually, then, we shall attempt to incorporate some of the major ideas of the monetary approach into one simple 'world' model. This appears to us to be the only way in which some of the lags and interactions involved can be estimated. The more limited aim of the remainder of this paper is to ask, first, whether the monetary theory is broadly consistent with (somewhat casual) empirical evidence.

IV. IMPLICATIONS OF THE MONETARY MODEL AND PRELIMINARY EMPIRICAL EVIDENCE

(1) MONEY, INCOME, PRICES, AND CAUSALITY IN THE WORLD ECONOMY

The monetary approach to aggregative analysis exploits a presumed strong relationship between money income and the supply of money. This relationship is postulated to hold for both closed and open economies, and derives from the existence of a stable income-velocity function. In other words, either the stock of money itself, or real income or prices, adjust so as to make the actual volume of money in circulation equal to what the public desires to hold. Which of the three variables will have to bear the brunt of the adjustment

[1] See, in particular, Cross and Laidler [5], Duck, Parkin, Rose and Zis [7], Parkin, Richards and Zis [15].

depends, we have argued crucially on whether the economy in question is closed or open, and on what time period we are considering.

In the extreme small open economy case and in a system of fixed exchange rates, prices and income will be determined essentially by factors other than the supply of money. Trade in goods and competition between domestic and foreign sources of supply will ensure that the price level adjusts rapidly towards purchasing power parity and capital mobility makes monetary policy unable to effect real income to any significant extent even in the short run. Flows of international reserves through the balance of payments will instead make the money stock adjust to keep it at a level compatible with what individuals want to hold, given their incomes. For a closed economy on the other hand, the nominal supply of money is essentially under the control of the central bank authorities, since there is no balance of payments constraint impinging on the monetary and financial markets in the economy. Portfolio decisions and spending behaviour of individuals will now determine real income and the price level.

There are strong reasons to believe that output in the long run will be independent of the quantity of money so that the price level will move in proportion to the money supply. While adjustment to monetary policy changes are taking place, however, and while expectations are being revised in view of new events there will in general be repercussions on output and employment as well as on prices. For a closed economy, then, we would expect that monetary policy would initially lead to changes in both output and prices but as time passes the latter effect should come to dominate.

Empirical evidence bearing on the money–income–price relationships has broadly tended to confirm the predictions of the monetary model as far as individual countries are concerned. For open economies, the strong international dependence of the price level and the limited scope of an autonomous monetary policy has been illustrated for a number of countries.[1] For an economy like the United States, which is large enough relative to the rest of the world to retain some closed economy attributes, there exists of course a large amount of empirical evidence relating to the role of money in the economy. The thrust of this evidence is, we believe, broadly consistent with the monetarists' propositions, although much controversy remains with regard to the exact channels of transmission of monetary impulses.

For the world as a whole, on the other hand, relatively little empirical evidence has been presented to date, even though the fact that it is the only truly closed economy ought to make it a good test case. In what follows we try to fill part of this gap by presenting some statistical material, designed both to check the monetary model's predictions against the data and to serve as guidance for the more ambitious model-building task we hope to undertake in the future.

In figure 3.1 we have plotted the world price level (solid line) and the world money stock (M_1, dashed line) series, as defined in the data appendix. Despite

[1] See for instance the studies of Genberg [9] and Zecher [21] for Sweden and Australia respectively, and the results for the United Kingdom in Jonson [12].

the growing gap between the series, which is the result of growth of real income, it is evident that world prices and world money have followed a roughly similar pattern throughout the entire postwar period. After the Korean war years, both series show relatively moderate growth rates during the rest of the 1950s. They accelerated throughout the next decade and, as we all know, both world prices and the world money stock have gone 'off the board' during the last several years.

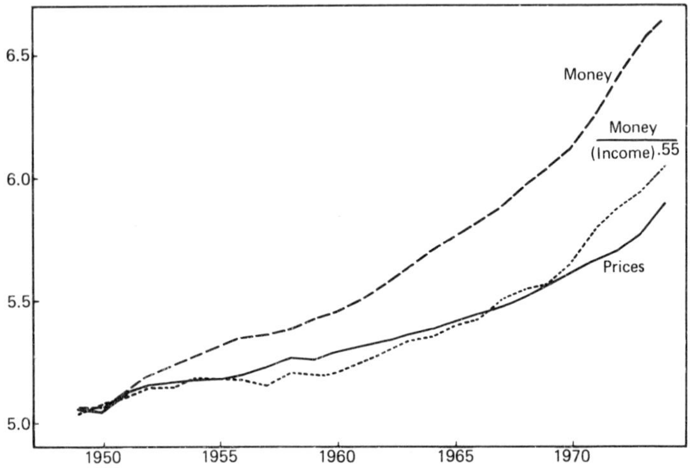

Fig. 3.1. World prices and the world money stock: logs of annual data

If we adjust the money series for the increased demand due to growing real income during the period we should get a more appropriate measure of what may be called excess world money creation. This measure should be more highly correlated with price movements if the monetary hypothesis is correct. Using the income elasticity estimate contained in the recent study of the world demand for money function by Gray, Ward and Zis [11], we divided the money stock series by our real income estimates raised to the power ·55.[1] The resulting variable is shown in logged form in figure 3.1 as the dotted line. We immediately note the improvement in the correlation with the price level. The relationship is indeed quite close up until the end of the 1960s when the price level again grows more slowly than predicted by the (adjusted) money series. This may be due to long lags (implausibly so in our view) in the adjustment of prices to excess money creation or to a change in the income elasticity of demand for money due for instance to distribution effects arising from changes in the relative sizes of the countries in our sample. It may also be the result of omitting some variable which has recently become important in the money demand function.

[1] Gray, Ward and Zis report a range of ·5 to ·6 for the income elasticity from which we chose the midpoint as the point estimate.

Leaving a detailed examination of these issues for future research, on the present level of simplicity is should be possible to argue that the excessive creation of world money has caused the price movements we have observed as far as the long-term trends are concerned. But we can be more specific than that. Looking at figure 3.2 where the money and price series are plotted as yearly rates of change it appears that changes in money have preceded changes in prices by one to two years starting in the mid-1950s. The relationship is of

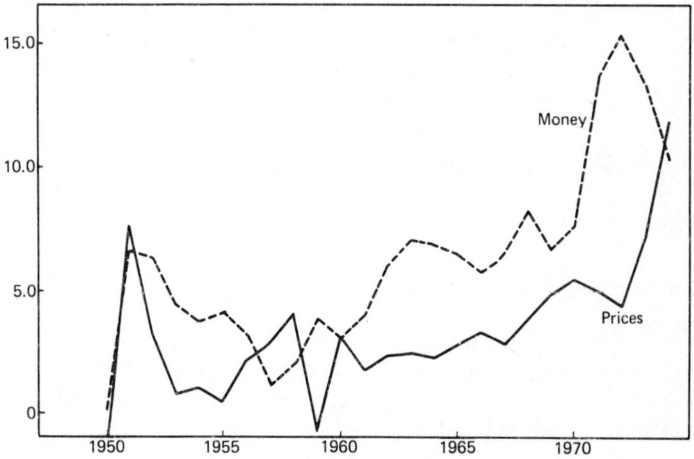

Fig. 3.2. World prices and the world money stock: Annual rates of change

course not perfect but it is nevertheless consistent with the monetary hypothesis. Before proceeding to some formal tests of the money-price level interaction, turn to figure 3.3 which shows yearly rates of change in nominal income and money. As implied by our framework this correlation should be closer than the one in figure 3.2 which it indeed is. By casually comparing turning points in the two series we observe a zero-to-one year lag which again can be interpreted as indicating that changes in the money supply have been the source of changes in money income during the past twenty years. But we do not have to rely on this rather subjective method to test the latter hypothesis. Recently Sims [18] has developed a test of causality which can readily be applied to our (ten-country) world economy once we move from yearly to quarterly data. The test which uses a concept of causality developed by Granger [10] essentially determines the temporal relationship between two variables and involves regressing prices on money plus future and lagged values of money. Sims' test implies that money changes cause price changes (in the Granger sense) if and only if the future values of money in this regression have coefficients which are zero as a group.

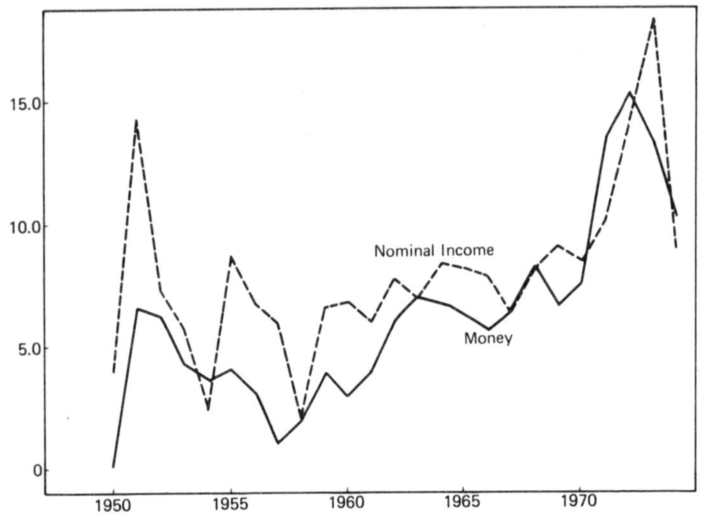

Fig. 3.3. World nominal income and the world money stock: annual rates of change

Tables 3.2 and 3.3 contain some regression results which we can use to sharpen our knowledge of the world economy. The first show that the relationship between *M* and *P* and *M* and *Y* are all highly significant. We can thus proceed to table 3.3 which reports the F-statistics we need for Sims' test.

TABLE 3.2
SUMMARY OF O.L.S. REGRESSIONS[a]

Equation	*F-statistic for independent variables*	$\bar{R}^2$
Y = f(M_1, 4 future, 4 past lags)	3·55*	·3595
Y = f(M_1, 4 past lags)	5·73*	·3344
Y = f(M_2, 4 future, 4 past lags)	4·23*	·4006
Y = f(M_2, 4 past lags)	8·49*	·3906
M_1 = f(Y, 4 future, 4 past lags)	10·97*	·6267
M_2 = f(Y, 4 future, 4 past lags)	10·68*	·6278
P = f(M_1, 4 future, 4 past lags)	12·21*	·6585
P = f(M_1, 4 past lags)	22·64*	·6309
P = f(M_2, 4 future, 4 past lags)	12·85*	·6698
P = f(M_2, 4 past lags)	22·17*	·6259
M_1 = f(P, 4 future, 4 past lags)	18·95*	·7495
M_2 = f(P, 4 future, 4 past lags)	16·57*	.7235

* Significant at ·01 level.

[a] The regressions were estimated for data covering the period 1957^{IV}–1974^{III}. Variables were expressed as first differences of logs of data series described in the Appendix. The reported F-statistic relates to the test of significance of all independent variables in each equation.

Note first that the future coefficients of money are always insignificantly different from zero as a group as they should be if money was a truly exogeneous variable. Income and prices, on the other hand, have highly significant future coefficients when they appear as the independent variable except in one case. With this one exception[1] we can thus tentatively draw the inference that money unidirectionally causes price and income movements.

TABLE 3.3
F-TESTS ON FOUR FUTURE QUARTERS' COEFFICIENTS[a]

Equation	*F-statistic*
Y on M_1	·52
Y on M_2	·22
M_1 on Y	5·92*
M_2 on Y	4·76*
P on M_1	1·07
P on M_2	1·77
M_1 on P	4·26*
M_2 on P	1·73

*Significant at ·01 level.
[a] The F-statistic relates to the test of significance of the *future* values of the independent variable in each equation which also contained the current value and four lagged values.

The tentative nature of these causality tests should be stressed and we should mention a few statistical matters which ought to be investigated before we can confidently accept our results. First of all we would like to test whether the residuals from each regression are white noise as they ought to be for the F-test to be strictly applicable. The Durbin–Watson statistic was very close to two in all regressions which used money as the independent variable, but some first-order serial correlation was detected in the reversed equations. There was no attempt made to check for higher-order autoregressive schemes. Closely related to the serial correlation issue is the choice of filter utilised to arrive at approximately stationary series for the regressions. For simplicity we used first differences in the logs of each variable but experimentation with alternative prefiltering rules is probably in order.

The third matter of concern is the estimated lag structure in the *Y* on *M* and *P* on *M* regressions, *a priori* one would expect to find a fairly smooth pattern in the lag coefficients but ours were rather more jagged. This may be due to seasonality problems or to multicollinearity between the explanatory variables or again to the particular method we used for prefiltering the variables. Including seasonal dummies and/or using different filter rules may again remove this problem, but this remains to be checked.

[1] In this case the first-future coefficient is by itself statistically significantly different from zero, however.

Finally there is the question of the contrast between the $M-Y$ relationship for a closed economy and for an open one. Unfortunately we do not yet have the result of Sims-type tests for each of our ten individual countries, but we hope to have some to present at the conference. Sims' own results for the United States indicate that it behaves on a closed economy, which could be taken to imply that United States monetary policy is a proximate cause of of variation in world income and prices. This last hypothesis is however, more properly discussed in connection with the determination of the world money stock, an issue to which we now turn.

(2) EVOLUTION OF THE WORLD MONEY STOCK

The world money stock has grown at an average annual rate of about 6½ per cent year for the last 25 years. As table 3.4 indicates, the growth rates for sub-periods have been rather different; note, in particular, the acceleration that takes place towards the end of the period. In looking for possible explanations of these movements we draw on the previous section where we discussed a world money supply model which implies a relationship between the total world supply of money and international reserves, on the one hand, and central bank domestic credit, on the other. Although, as noted above, the relationship between each one of these variables separately and the total money supply need not be a precise one in the short run, one implication of the model is that over longer periods it should be more predictable if the private sector acts according to stable behavioural functions *and* if central banks' actions reflect the balance of payments constraint they face.

A comparison of the two columns in table 3.4 broadly supports this conclusion. The growth of international reserves follows a similar pattern as that of money[1] especially with respect to the acceleration which took place in the middle to late 1960s. We may thus deduce that long-term movements in international reserve assets have lead to similar movements in total world money and together with the results from the tests performed in the previous subsection we can make a case for a causal relationship running from international

TABLE 3.4
AVERAGE ANNUAL PERCENTAGE GROWTH RATES

Period	*Money* (M_1)	*International reserves*
1950–55	5·00	2·16
1955–60	2·64	3·08
1960–65	6·18	2·14
1965–70	7·02	4·14
1970–74	13·23	14·75
1950–74	6·58	4·86

[1] The correlation coefficient between the two growth rates is ·79 which is statistically significant at the 90 per cent level.

reserves to money and ultimately to world prices. This relationship is most evident in the last ten years during which the correlation is quite high.

The model outlined in the previous section draws attention to the main reason why a simple causal relationship between international reserves and the world money stock should not necessarily be expected to hold and why, if a statistical association were found, it should be interpreted with great care. Under a gold-exchange standard (more generally in an inside-reserve system), the total of world reserves is itself determined by monetary policy since foreign-exchange reserves depend on domestic credit policies and on the behaviour of the public. Thus, an expansion of domestic credit in the reserve-currency country creates reserves and increases the world money stock, a contractionary monetary policy in the rest of the world also creates international reserves, other things equal, but *decreases* the world money stock. A more thorough discussion of the evidence would require us to relate the evolution of the domestic component of the base in various regions to both the world money stock *and* the foreign-exchange component of international reserves. We hope to provide some rough evidence on this issue in the revised version of this paper – after we will have managed to process data on domestic credit. More precise results, however, will have to await the construction of a more complete quantitative model of the world money-supply process.

Clearly not all, and, depending on the form of policy reaction functions and certain distributional issues to be discussed below, maybe not even the major part, of the long-term excess money creation can be ascribed to increasing international reserves. The last line in the table show that money has grown at an average of 1·7 per cent per annum higher than international reserves if we look as the whole period. This may be due to a trend in the multiplier which, considering the changing structure and increasing sophistication of financial markets, is not implausible. An alternative explanation would be that excessive domestic credit creation has been a major factor behind the growth in money at least up until 1970. This explanation would be consistent with the breakdown of the fixed exchange-rate system as the required monetary discipline was not observed, and it emphasises the point that a necessary condition for a stable fixed-rate system is as much that national monetary policies be held in check as that the creation of international reserves be non-excessive.

Turning briefly to some issues concerning the distribution and composition of reserves among countries, some interesting regularities emerge. First, we note the large increases in the proportions of international reserves made up of foreign exchange and, within the latter, of United States external liabilities (see table 3.5). This is no doubt a reflection of both the move towards a dollar standard with the consequent increasing demand for dollar balances on the part of non-United States central banks and of the supply of excess dollars arising from large money-financed deficits in the United States. Without a model with interaction between the United States and the rest of the world in terms of the distribution of reserves and monetary policy behaviour it is very

TABLE 3.5
MONEY MULTIPLIERS AND THE COMPOSITION OF INTERNATIONAL RESERVES

Year	*World*			*Non-United States world*		
	M/IR	*FE/IR*	*USEL/IR*	*M/IR*	*FE/IR*	*USEL/IR*
1950	4·7	·35		4·6	·35	
1955	5·3	·41		4·3	·41	
1960	5·2	·34	·29	3·5	·34	·50
1965	6·5	·30	·35	4·6	·31	·52
1970	7·6	·50	·42	5·1	·50	·54
1974	7·1	·65	·67	5·3	·65	·79

Definitions of symbols: M = Money (M_1)
IR = International Reserves
FE = Foreign Exchange
USEL = United States External Liabilities

difficult to sort out whether it is the supply or demand factors that have played the dominant role and whether one can put the blame on either the United States or some other set of countries for the excessive world money creation. Some indication may be obtained from looking at the evolution of reserve flows, relative rates of monetary expansion, and relative price levels as between the United States and the rest of the world. In a model where increases in the rate of growth in money lead to a higher domestic relative to foreign rate of inflation for some time, and where excessive credit creation also causes a balance of payments deficit, we should expect to find a positive correlation between a higher inflation rate in the United States and a United States deficit in the balance of payments when the United States is exporting inflation to the rest of the world, and vice versa. This implication can be used to explain the interaction between the United States and the rest of the world during the 1960s but it cannot be used to assign responsibility for the inflationary burst in the last few years. During the first three years of the period since 1960 the rate of monetary expansion in the non-United States world was far above average whereas in the United States it was relatively slow. The United States balance of payments deficit tended simultaneously to become smaller, and the United States relative rate of inflation fell. The reverse story is true for the latter part of the decade when the higher monetary growth rate in the United States caused both a deterioration in its balance of payments and a higher domestic rate of inflation, which in turn was followed by an acceleration in the world price level. The dynamics of the interaction is of course more complicated than this paragraph indicates, but the thrust of the monetary explanation of both the distribution of reserves and the rate of inflation comes through nevertheless.

The interaction during the first few years of the 1970s is more difficult to disentangle even though the relationship between money and prices is particularly evident here. The reason is that *both* United States and non-United States inflation rates and monetary growth rates have increased sharply, be it due to more highly integrated capital markets which spread shocks more evenly, or to coincidence in the thrust of policy which has achieved the same result.

Returning to the main theme of this subsection we must conclude, in perhaps a rather unsatisfactory manner, by stressing the need for more detailed research on the world money-supply function, taking acount not only of the evolution of total international reserves but also of changes in their distribution among countries, changes in asset perferences, the evolution of the Eurodollar market and the determination of domestic credit policy. Such research will undoubtedly add more detail and precision to the casual evidence presented here, but the main features will, we believe, continue to hold.

DATA APPENDIX

All data used in the paper were obtained from the International Monetary Fund's *International Financial Statistics* except for the real income series which were taken from OECD's *Main Economic Indicators.* The exact definitions were:

Spot Exchange Rate, end of period	line ae
Spot Exchange Rate, period average	line af
International Reserves	line 1
Foreign Exchange	line 1d
United States External Liabilities	line 9a
Money	line 34
Money and Quasi-money	lines 34 and 35
Consumer Price Index	line 64
Index of Industrial Production	line 66

The following ten industrial countries were taken to represent the world and all aggregate values refer to them:

Belguim	Japan
Canada	Netherlands
France	Switzerland
Germany	United Kingdom
Italy	United States

For the quarterly data used in section IV currency conversions of nominal variables were made using current spot exchange rates to represent all variables in units of United States dollars. Aggregations to get the world series were then simply performed by summing across countries except in the case of the consumer price index in which case current quarter nominal G.N.P. weights were employed. These G.N.P. series were obtained by multiplying the consumer price index by the real output series. Since only four countries (United States, United Kingdom, Canada and Japan) report quarterly G.N.P. figures, the remaining six series has to be estimated using yearly real G.N.P. figures as benchmarks and imposing the within-year variation in industrial production on them.

To get the proper dating of all variables for the lead-lag tests, the end of period stock variables were interpolated linearly between adjacent quarters.

REFERENCES

[1] B. Balassa, 'The Purchasing-power Parity Doctrine: A Reappraisal', *Journal of Political Economy* (December 1964).

[2] W. C. Brainard and R. N. Cooper, 'Empirical Monetary Macroeconomics: What Have We Learned in the Last 25 Years?', *American Economic Review* (May, 1975).

[3] W. H. Branson, 'International Transmission of Inflation: A Keynesian Approach', Paper presented at the Brookings Conference on Worldwide Inflation (November, 1974), *A.E.R.* 1975

[4] W. H. Branson and J. Myhrman, 'Inflation in Open Economics: Supply-determined Versus Demand determined Models', Seminar Paper No. 34, Institute for International Economic Studies (October, 1973).

[5] R. Cross and D. E. W. Laidler, 'Inflation, Excess Demand and Expectations in Fixed Exchange Rate Economies: Some Preliminary Empirical Results', Paper presented at the Manchester Conference on Inflation in the World Economy (July, 1974).

[6] R. Dornbusch, 'Devaluation, Money and Nontraded Goods', *American Economic Review* (December, 1973).

[7] N. Duck, M. Parkin, D. Rose and G. Zis, 'The Determination of Wages and Prices in the Fixed Exchange Rate World Economy, 1956–1970', University of Manchester, SSRC Research Programme on Inflation, Discussion Paper 7404 (Manchester, 1974).

[8] H. Genberg, 'The Concept and Measurement of the World Price Level and Rate of Inflation', Discussion Paper, GIIS–Ford Foundation International Monetary Research Project (Graduate Institute of International Studies, October, 1974).

[9] H. Genberg, 'Aspects of the Monetary Approach to Balance of Payments Theory: An Empirical Study of Sweden', in J. Frenkel and H. G. Johnson (eds.) *The Monetary Approach to the Balance of Payments* (London: Allen and Unwin, 1975).

[10] C. W. J. Granger, 'Investigating Causal Relations by Econometric Models and Cross-spectral Methods', *Econometrica*, XXXVII (July, 1969), 424–38.

[11] M. R. Gray, R. Ward and G. Zis, 'The World Demand for Money Function: Some Preliminary Results', Paper presented at the Manchester Conference on Inflation in the World Economy (July, 1974).

[12] P. D. Jonson. 'Money and Economic Activity in the Open Economy: The U.K. 1880–1970', Paper prepared for the 1975 Konstanz Seminar on Monetary Theory and Monetary Policy (May, 1975).

[13] H. I. Kierzkowski, 'Theoretical Foundations of the Scandinavian Model of Inflation', L.S.E.–S.S.R.C. International Monetary Research Programme Discussion Paper (September, 1974).

[14] W. D. Nordhaus, 'The Worldwide Wage Explosion', *Brookings Papers on Economic Activity*, 2, 1972.

[15] M. Parkin, I. Richards and G. Zis, 'The Determination and Control of the World Money Supply under Fixed Exchange Rates: 1961–1971', Paper presented at the Third Money Study Group Seminar (September, 1974).

[16] J. C. Pattison, 'International Inflation Linkages and the Recent Experience in Individual Countries', Paper presented at the Louvain Conference on 'Bank Credit, Money and Inflation in Open Economies (September, 1974).

[17] A. J. Schwartz, 'Secular Price Change in Historical Perspective', *Journal of Money, Credit and Banking* (February, 1973).

[18] C. Sims, 'Money, Income and Causality', *American Economic Review*, LXII (September, 1971), 540–52.

[19] A. K. Swoboda, 'Monetary Approaches to the Transmission and Generation of Worldwide Inflation', Discussion Paper, GIIS–Ford Foundation International Monetary Research Project, Graduate Institute of International Studies (October, 1974).

[20] A. K. Swoboda, 'Gold, Dollars, Eurodollars and the World Money Stock', Discussion Paper, GIIS–Ford Foundation International Monetary Research Project, Graduate Institute of International Studies (November, 1974).

[21] R. J. Zecker, 'Monetary Equilibrium and International Reserve Flows in Australia', in J. A. Frenkel and H. G. Johnson (eds.), *The Monetary Approach to the Balance of Payments* (London: Allen and Unwin, 1975).

Discussion of the Papers by Robert J. Gordon and by Hans Genberg and Alexander K. Swoboda

Professor Branson said that Professor Gordon's paper gave a survey of recent developments, using a modern-day Rip van Winkle. He fell asleep in 1964, having brought himself fully up to date on the literature on inflation, and woke up ten years later to discover what had happened in between. This enabled Professor Gordon to go through developments on the lines of the natural rate hypothesis (N.R.H.) and the rational expectations hypothesis, as well as to introduce a discussion of the new microeconomics of voluntary unemployment. Finally, the paper moved briefly to discuss world inflation.

Professor Branson had found little to disagree with in the paper, and wanted to go through it in order, adding his own interpretations.

The integration of the analysis of the Phillips-curve into the demand-pull and cost-push distinction could be seen from figure 2.1. This told the standard 1963 story in terms of an aggregate demand and aggregate supply curve, showing inflation in a static framework. However, one could think of things that would change the price level within that framework. For instance, each curve might move in the short run, or the demand curve might move continuously. The paper gave the impression that it was hard to reconcile the Phillips-curve and static approaches, and that the contribution of Friedman and Phelps was a breakthrough, reconciling figure 2.1 with the Phillips-curve. While it might not have been published in 1963, the reconciliation was well-known even then.

Professor Branson said that we could understand much of the subsequent analysis in terms of two equations. The first was a wage equation

$$\frac{\dot{W}}{W} = f(u) + a\left(\frac{\dot{P}}{P}\right)e \tag{1}$$

The second was a price equation, assuming a simple mark-up model of price formation.

$$\frac{\dot{P}}{P} = \frac{\dot{W}}{W} - \frac{\dot{q}}{q} \tag{2}$$

where q was output per worker. When Rip van Winkle went to sleep, it was known that the Phillips-curve of equation (1) and Gordon's figure 2.1 could be reconciled if demand and supply on the labour market were brought in. The second equation then showed how fast prices would increase with a given level of unemployment and of capital utilisation.

The solution was complete because one could then get a rate of growth of nominal output to be matched by a growth of demand which would hold unemployment at a given level. For nominal demand growth one had

$$\frac{\dot{Y}}{Y} = \frac{\dot{P}}{P} + \frac{\dot{Q}}{Q}\,. \tag{3}$$

With potential output growth given and $\dot{P}/P$ determined by equation (2), equation (3) gave demand growth, holding u constant. Rip van Winkle should have seen no conflict between the Phillips-curve and figure 2.1. Similarly, the foregoing analysis enables us to distinguish cost-push from demand-pull when Rip fell asleep.

Professor Branson explained that equation (3) gave a rate of growth of nominal demand required to maintain a given level of unemployment, in terms of a rate of price increase. A demand-pull situation was shown where demand increased more rapidly than output, pulling prices up faster than indicated by equation (2). There was a cost-push impulse in the system if the growth of nominal demand required to maintain the target unemployment rate was increased. For example, an increase in oil prices independent of wage-push, would change the nominal G.N.P. necessary for a given level of unemployment.

The tone of the paper denied to some extent the distinction between cost-push and demand-pull. However, the distinction was useful, because one knew the prescription for a simple demand-pull situation, as in the United States in the mid-1960s. One simply stopped the demand expansion. If prices were increasing and unemployment rising at the same time, because of the cost situation, then one had a true dilemma. Changing demand now made one variable better at the cost of worsening the other. There was no mystery here. One knew precisely why unemployment rose when inflation increased, the problem being what to do about it. This was contrary to the suggestions made recently in the American press that economists could not explain what was happening.

Friedman and Phelps asserted that, in the long run, the value of coefficient '*a*' in equation (1) was around 1. If the expected rate of price increase was equal to the actual rate, then one obtained from equations (1) and (2) the natural rate of unemployment. According to Professor Gordon, Friedman and Phelps reconciled the Phillips-curve with figure 2.1. Professor Branson wanted to say that the natural rate hypothesis simply gave a polar value for '*a*'. In the middle 1960s, research had shown that it probably lay between 0 and 1. In saying that the value of '*a*' was 1, Friedman and Phelps were concerned with this polar case.

In considering empirical validation, Professor Gordon cited the rise in estimates of '*a*' as more work had been done since the mid-1960s. He suggested that '*a*' should depend on the rate of inflation, and that this dependence should make '*a*' equal 1. While it was plausible, Professor Branson did not see the logic in this inference. If the rate of inflation was, say, between 0 per cent and 6 per cent, as before the late 1960s, '*a*' would not necessarily be 1. He could see why '*a*' would rise with a rising rate of inflation, but not why it should be 1.

As for policy, the N.R.H. was logically irrelevant. It was taken as a long-run hypothesis, and in most models the long run was an infinitely long run. So, if the unemployment rate was below the natural rate, it would return to it in the long run. But most models said that it did so asymptotically, and this meant remaining below the natural rate for a long period. The definition of the long-run natural rate must relate to a period of at least a few years, during which policy could keep the natural rate away from the actual rate.

An additional problem was that the N.R.H. hypothesis was a long-run one and hard to test with short-run data. To do so would require finely specified equations and Professor Branson was not yet convinced of its validity.

On rational expectations, he did not have much to add to Professor Gordon's objections. Even with rational expectations at the macro-level, there was still the usual aggregation problem for macro-policy. It was an interesting and clear hypothesis, but he did not feel that anyone should 'buy it' just because of that.

On the new macroeconomic theory, Professor Gordon leaned too much on the fact that in booms firms made new hirings rather than raising wages, but took various actions in slumps. He thought there was more symmetry than Professor Gordon suggested. For example, during booms firms would pay higher wages for overtime. There was a good paper in *Econometrica* by Black and Kelejian which modelled this problem rather well. Professor Gordon thought this problem should be investigated; but Professor Branson argued that these authors has already done so satisfactorily.

On world inflation, one should look first at the transmission mechanism and at the monetary approach to the balance of payments. Professor Gordon described three transmission mechanisms: Keynesian; Scandinavian (Aukrust); and balance of payments effects on the money supply. Any reasonable model must include all three. One could perhaps add migration, where results obtained by Helliwell might be generalised.

Professor Gordon talked of the monetary approach. The heart of this issue was that a surplus or deficit on the balance of payments must alter the money supply. If the balance of payments was zero and the country devalued, this would lead to a surplus. However, the money supply would then increase, so that prices and output would both rise. The balance of payments would return to balance, leaving the country in the same position, except with increased reserves. One needed to pay attention to the monetary equilibrium argument.

A final point which bothered Professor Branson was the impact of the massive increase in world liquidity since 1970 on inflation. Since the United States had abandoned a fixed exchange rate in 1971, there had been a change in the world velocity of circulation because of a change in the payments mechanism. If one moved from a fixed to a floating exchange rate system, one probably needed a planned extinction of reserves. This had not happened since 1971; quite the opposite, in fact. So, from a monetary point of view, the world had recently increased prices to bring real reserves back to equilibrium. Excessive reserves tended to remove the balance-of-payments constraint and led to an increase in prices and output. This was probably an important element in the 1972–73 boom. There was now the growing view among macroeconomists that we were seeing a political business cycle, and that this was why there had been so strong a boom in 1972–73. What he had just said implied that there might be a much more economic explanation. So he would himself hesitate before accepting that we now had a new phenomenon – the political business cycle.

Professor Malinvaud said that in introducing the paper by Genberg and Swoboda, he laid himself open to a high risk of being in error. This was particularly so because he was happier with normative than with positive economics.

He did not want to comment at all on the first part of the paper, concerning wage inflation in the last 25 years, but would endorse its conclusions. It did make sense to speak of a world rate of inflation, and this rate had been increasing since the mid-1960s.

The second part of the paper looked at alternative theories. Perhaps the title was over-ambitious because the authors disposed of three theories in two pages and then devoted six pages to the monetary explanation. They told us that the sociological cost-push hypothesis did not have much to commend it.

The sociological side of the hypothesis was not the object of precise theorising, from which it seemed to follow, according to the authors, that sociology had nothing to do with facts. Moreover the rates of inflation in all countries appeared to move together, whereas sociology which was supposed to be concerned with erratic accidents, according to the authors, should have played quite different roles in various countries.

The second hypothesis, that of the 'Nordic model', was rightly dismissed in the present context because it looked at individual countries and took the price of internationally traded goods as given. The Keynesian model, like the Nordic one, could not explain the generation of worldwide inflation, the authors claimed, unless money were brought in. So one was left with the monetarist explanation.

However, he wanted to point out that the chain of causation set out was a complex one. There was a very interesting and clear explanation on the way in which the world money stock had been formed, at least in the conditions of the 1960s. The authors discussed the accumulation of foreign exchange reserves, and in particular the role of the United States. They also said that they were working on a model which would quantify the mechanism, and he would follow the developments here with interest.

The authors then gave their empirical evidence. This took the form of regressions of the quarterly rates of variation in prices and the money stock between 1957 and 1974. One of these regressions showed price in a particular quarter as related to the variation of the money stock in the four preceding and the four following quarters. So one really had nine explanatory variables – namely the rate of variation in the money stock in nine quarters around the quarter in question. The authors obtained the interesting result that one could erase the terms relating to what had not yet happened. A variation in the price level tended to follow a variation in the money supply, which meant that the latter was probably the explanation of the variation in the price level.

Turning to discuss the expansion of the money supply, the authors suggested that the creation of international reserves had not been the main element in world inflation but that national monetary policy was important too. They asked whether the United States had a major impact. Professor Malinvaud agreed with the authors that more research was necessary on the causes of changes in the world money supply. Today, the question was whether we could accept a change in the money supply as *the* cause of world inflation.

As for the regression results, the r^2 coefficient which characterised the regression was only 0·63. This was not bad, but still left room to identify other variables influencing the rate of inflation, which he would label z_1, z_2, etc; hence an eclectic economist could still hold the position that inflation had many causes. But behind this regression there was still a risk of a spurious correlation. During the period the authors had studied, there had been an upward trend in the world money stock, with four cycles. The rate of inflation also had an increasing trend, with rough cyclical variations lagging behind the money supply. It was well known from business cycle theory that one could get such lags even between exogenous variables and he thought it possible to have this lag even if the cause of world inflation had nothing to do with monetary policy.

To make the argument more concrete, he wanted to take, as an example, the well-known sociological troubles in France in 1968. These had led to a big increase in wages. To avoid putting firms into financial difficulties, the monetary authorities had decided to expand the money supply significantly in late 1968. So the increase in wages and in the money stock had both led the increase in prices. But how did one then characterise the cause of the French inflation of 1969? Was it cost-push cum sociology? Or money cum sociology?

Had it been possible, Swoboda and Genberg should have read the paper by Parkin and Swoboda! In the first few pages of the latter paper there was a good discussion of causality and two interesting ideas. First, any explanation must contain an analysis of how prices were set. Second, a complete causal explanation was not only not available, it was not necessary. The relevant question was: what would happen to the rate of inflation if some well-defined policy measures were taken?

In the Parkin–Swoboda paper there was an equation given as an example of what the adjustment process could be.

$$\Delta p = \Delta p^e + \delta(y - y^*)$$

Behind $y - y^*$, were monetary impulses as well as fiscal and autonomous implications of the kind used in short-run business cycle analysis. Econometricians would want to use other terms (other zs) into the equation. What could these be? One could be a cost-push element, for example, an oil price increase or a wage increase; or on might have factors affecting the mark-up on costs. He mentioned this because many European economists seemed to think that inflation had a good deal to do with changes in mark-up margins, the argument being that this had been made necessary by capital accumulation. It was thought that excessive capital accumulation in the late 1960s and early 1970s might be partly responsible for the inflation of the recent period. If so, one ought to find a mark-up element in this sort of equation.

So if one had found the correct equation, various policy measures could be studied, including those affecting costs and mark-up. Even the Swoboda–Parkin paper gave us reason to be eclectic.

Professor Malinvaud wanted, however, to recognise the difficulty of reconciling fully the complex process of short-run adjustment with the necessary parallelism between trend rates for prices and the money stock. Certainly, there was room here for a serious study. He would point out that the paper under discussion did not concentrate only on the long run. The equation he had quoted dealt with only four quarters, from which it followed that the authors considered the monetary explanation as applying in particular for the relatively short run.

Professor Liviatan wanted to expand on the point Professor Gordon had made about the idea of a short-run effect of an increase in the money supply on output. The monetarist theory was that the effect would be first on output and then on price, because of short-run price rigidity. He did not think this approach well founded. When one had an adjustment process, in the familiar Marshall analysis, one got prices increasing in the short-run and output in the long-run. Even if everyone had complete information, the situation would be the same, because of increasing short-run marginal cost curves.

If one started with the level of unemployment at the natural rate, the long-run result would be a rate of inflation equal to the rate of growth of the money stock. But what were the adjustment costs that stopped this happening? He could see no satisfactory answer.

Professor Liviatan wanted to suggest why the effect of an increase in the money supply might not be expressed in changes in output. He would make two assumptions. First, he would assume, along with the monetarists, that some law by which short-run output increased as a result of an increase in the money supply was true. Second, he assumed that it must be known to everyone. This was weaker than the assumption of rational expectations. The assumption was not now about events, but about a known law. If the law were always true, everyone must know it. And if all did know it, was there not an incentive to act so as to change the situation? If everyone knew that in the short-run prices would not rise, but that in the long-run they would, this gave an incentive for speculation. It would pay people to buy now in order to profit, which should raise prices immediately if sufficient people behaved in this way. Indeed, if everyone behaved in this way, prices now would be equal to the expected price a year hence minus the net carrying charge. Thus the effect of an increase in the money stock would be expressed in prices and not in a change in output.

Professor Lindbeck wanted to go behind the equation Professor Malinvaud had quoted from the paper by Swoboda and Genberg, where the increase in money supply and prices was correlated. Another possibility would have been to explore the relationship, on a global level, between unused capacity and prices. If one did this, one found a very close correlation between the two with about a one-year lag. So, it might be reasonable first to relate prices to excess demand (capacity utilisation), and then to relate excess demand to monetary policy, etc.

To Professor Liviatan, he would say that in reality the rate of price increase went up *after* output increased. The maximum increase in prices was often found twelve to eighteen months after the boom had come to an end. However, the heated discussion of the problem recently might lead businessmen to act sooner. Perhaps, in the United States, the fact that economists were talking of a new inflation within a year of two could hasten price increases so that, next time, they came earlier in the boom.

If Professor Branson were right, and if moving towards flexible exchange rates led to an excess supply of money, one should conclude that it was dangerous after a while to shift back to fixed exchange rates. This would lead to recession in the world. The argument also led to a recommendation for keeping the same exchange rate system.

Professor Bajt believed that Professors Swoboda and Genberg were right to insist on transmission mechanisms. Therefore, without a convincing theory of how cost-push cum sociology inflation might spread across the world, one could postpone its acceptance at world level.

However, an exact description of the transmission mechanism was also needed for the monetarist interpretation of world inflation. He wondered whether this could be done at all with yearly data. The same would apply to the paper by Professors Parkin and Swoboda. The authors there argued that using quarterly or monthly data imported too much 'noise'. He thought such data imported more information, and that more information was needed to identify causal relationships. He did not think it was enough to know that there was a lag. One wanted to know the direct impulse-giving/impulse-receiving links. To do this, he thought one wanted much more data which meant both more frequent data – perhaps even weekly data -- and data on transmitting variables.

Professor Gordon's mark-up could be taken as an example, in Yugoslavia there were quarterly and monthly figures about this. Quarterly information showed the results Professor Gordon would expect – prices determined by labour cost. Once one moved to monthly data one found that the impact of the costs weakened and that the influence of excess demand became strongest. He was therefore glad, that, at the end of their paper, Swoboda and Genberg did use quarterly data, although they did so only because they applied the Sims test. He was unconvinced by their findings. This was not so much because of the low R^2, suggested by Professor Malinvaud, but because they proved only the time sequence of the rough yearly data. This was suggestive, of the cause/effect relationships, *only* under very restrictive assumptions, linearity and a direct linkage between money and activity.

Professor Machlup said that volumes had been written on the issue of 'cause'. Perhaps it was better to talk of necessary and sufficient conditions. If he took Professor Malinvaud's example about what happened in France in May 1968, surely one wanted to ask what triggered the situation. Was it sociology or politics? Or one could start from a shift in demand, an increase in the oil price, and get an increase in the money supply which caused inflation.

But none of these initial changes were necessary or sufficient for creating inflation. The increase in the money supply was. He knew of no example of a sustained price increase without an increase in the money stock sustained over a period. So an increase in the money supply was not necessarily the cause of inflation, but it was a necessary and sufficient condition.

Professor Bronfenbrenner noted that no-one had asked who had put Rip van Winkle to sleep. So far as he could remember, Rip had spied on some gnomes, not in Zurich but in upstate New York, when they were playing a skittle game.

Professor Gordon's paper had quoted three such gnomes – Bronfenbrenner, Holzman and Johnson. Since the others were not here, Bronfenbrenner would speak for all three. He and Holzman had indeed assumed that changes in price levels *could* affect unemployment permanently. They had only used the natural rate of unemployment as a polar case. As for the reconciliation of the Phillips-curve with the real world, he had at first been optimistic but had since changed his mind. He had also believed that an increase in aggregate demand could simultaneously reduce unemployment and increase prices.

Professor Bronfenbrenner thought that perhaps the Gordon paper was too cavalier in eliminating monopoly power and cost push. It was not only the *fact* of monopoly power but the threat of its use that might be important. For instance, monopoly power was not important only as an element on the cost side of the market. It was also something which might react in either direction, to government anti-inflationary policy.

Mr. Plessz considered how worldwide inflation worked. It was certain that in the last up-turn a major role had been played by the asymmetrical impact of commodity speculation on prices, linked to the case of financing under monetary conditions in 1972–73.

To the extent that increases in primary commodity prices were incorporated into final product prices, they increased the cost of living and wages. But when commodity prices fell again, little happened. If an increase in commodity prices was fed by speculation, a rise in the quantity of money was certainly a necessary condition for the original increase; but when speculation unfolded, there was not much impact on the price level.

There was a rapid learning process here and there had recently been a speculative bubble. This was not the result of an increase in final demand but, as Professor Liviatan said, of knowing that prices would rise soon and being able to buy easily into the market.

Professor Patinkin commented that the monetarist position was supported in the Swoboda–Genberg paper by statistics showing the correlation between money and prices. This was hardly the monetarist position. It was not a question of whether there was a correlation. If prices rose significantly, there *must* be more money about, for the price of a good was the number of units of money that one had to supply in exchange for it.

The historical debate on the quantity theory was not on whether prices and money were correlated, but over whether money was the cause of the price increase. The debate in the mid-nineteenth century between the banking school and the currency school was on whether the increase in the money supply led to to the price increase or vice versa – on which was the exogenous variable. He did not think anyone had ever denied that with full employment an increase in the money supply would increase prices. If they had, he had not seen the denial.

He wanted to remind Professor Machlup that if x was a necessary and sufficient condition for y, then x was identical with y. It therefore could not be designated as the explanation of y.

After the increase in oil prices, there would have been no subsequent increase in the general price level of any specific country unless it had had a prior monetary expansion. Hence the real question was: what determined whether or not the monetary authorities would decide to expand the money stock? Similarly, the real question was why so many western countries in the last decade had simultaneously decided greatly to expand their respective money supplies? For the situation was not like that which prevailed in Europe during the price revolution of the sixteenth century. Then, in the absence of monetary management, the inflow of gold from the New World automatically and simultaneously generated inflation in the various countries. Answers to questions like that might give us insights into the ultimate causes of inflation. Correlations did not.

He would agree that it helped if one could show that future changes were not important. But the important thing was the change in money supply resulting from past price increases.

Patinkin's Law of Regression was that for every regression there existed another saying the opposite.

Professor Machlup replied that he did not consider money and price as an identity. The question was whether there were possible exceptions to be pointed out to those who said that money was a cause, or a necessary and sufficient condition, of inflation. One was variation in the velocity of circulation. This was why he had referred to a sustained period – perhaps of two to three years. He did not think that velocity could increase for more than about three years. After that, there would have to be an increase in the money supply.

The other question was whether money was the dependent variable. Where it was, then he was wrong. His point was that money was controllable but not always controlled. This was a matter of politics. If the politicians wished to control money, and could do so, then one had to explain why they did, or did not, do so.

Professor Frisch noted that the paper by Swoboda and Genberg was related to one by van Rijckeghem (Brussels) on why inflation rates differed between countries. Rijckeghem distinguished three explanations. The first was the monetary hypothesis, the second the Phillips-curve, the third the Aukrust–E.F.O. model.

The monetarists would say that the differences in the rates of inflation depended on differences in the increase in the money supply. The Phillips-curve related international differences to differences in the unemployment rate. The Aukrust–E.F.O. argument would be that the rate of inflation depended on productivity differences between the exposed and the sheltered sectors of the economy. The paper showed that one could not discriminate statistically between the three hypotheses so that we were back to our prejudices and biases. He thought an analysis of the same problem by Swoboda and Genberg would show the same result.

Professor Parkin replied to Professor Patinkin. He thought there were two questions: first, what had generated monetary policy historically? Second, what increase in prices and variations income would one get if one controlled money in a well-defined way? He wanted to know more about whether the equation Professor Malinvaud had used had further *z*s independent of both excess demand and inflationary expectations. If one focused on this one could learn more.

What did he think had been learned already? Professors Swoboda and Genberg referred to work in Manchester. One of these studies spelled out the transmission process from money to prices. For ten countries it got equations like those of Professor Malinvaud, but with adaptive expectations. It explained about 75 per cent of the quarter-by-quarter variation of world prices and had clean residuals.

Another paper studied the evolution of demand. This started from the demand for money. It was not necessary to go further because the worldwide demand for money was very simple, with a variation of velocity from partial adjustment. The model fitted the facts well. This was not to say that no other factors affected inflation. All he could say that there was no evidence of other variation in the United Kingdom. The evidence was not overwhelming, but it was certainly very powerful.

It did seem to confirm to many economists the natural rate hypothesis. If there were others who were not convinced, he would like to ask what further evidence the doubters would require.

Since it appeared that the Phillips-curve was nearly vertical, one could not say that the long-run had been ignored. After all, 1975 was the long-run from the view of the early 1960s.

Professor Frisch's idea that the three explanations were equally good was not a good way to assess whether there was an inflationary price increase.

Professor Parkin said he wanted to add that the price expectations found in his model changed when the United Kingdom devalued.

Professor Malinvaud referred to experience in France. Where other variables were bought in, like the minimum legal wage rate, these improved the fit for prices and in wages.

Professor Laidler referred to the natural rate hypothesis. Even if the relationship was asymptotic, it might be important for short-run policy, since it gave a level of employment above which one had accelerating rates of inflation. There was some reason to believe that the natural rate varied over time, which implied that attempting to gear monetary and fiscal policy to pursue an unemployment target assumed more knowledge than we actually had. Perhaps it would be better to look at the desired rate of price increase as a target and to use more direct labour-market policies to control unemployment.

To Professor Liviatan, Professor Laidler pointed out that while the logic of his argument was correct, there was a body of knowledge which tried to explain why output increased before prices. This included the work of Clower and Leijonhufvud. When demand varied, firms were unable to decide how permanent, general or sustained the change would be. This led to stickiness of prices.

To Professor Patinkin, he would say that the most famous recent British quotation came from the Radcliffe Report: velocity is a mere statistic varying without upper limit. Lord Kaldor said that velocity would change to accommodate any change in money income. Sir Alec Cairncross said that the way the government financed its deficit was irrelevant to the time path of money income. These ideas were alive and well in the United Kingdom, even if not elsewhere.

Professor Polaczek explained that socialist countries were interested in currents of thinking on problems of inflation. Non-socialist inflationary policies did affect socialist countries. So he would like to come back to what Professor Branson had said – that he was in agreement with the general line of the paper, but not on its details. His own view was the exact opposite. He would be ready to agree on details, but not on the general line of the paper.

Monetary policy was effective in normal times: it was an obviously insufficient tool now. The current inflation was not just the result of short-run fluctuations in monetary policy, but of major economic errors accumulated over a long period. He did not think one should put too much weight on what had happened in 1972 and 1973. The mistakes during that period were not significant compared with what had happened earlier. Even without these recent mistakes, there would still be disproportions in economic development.

If he could use the analogy of the motor car. On the road one found big and small cars. Small cars had little effect on traffic jams, but big cars did and for different reasons. The British car, for some time now, usually needed a general overhaul: the American car had lost some of its shape on the roads of Vietnam: the Japanese car was attractive but was expensive and needed good road conditions. Thus an extraordinary situation, like the present one, needed extraordinary measures. Traditional monetary policy would not help. It was necessary to integrate anti-inflation policy measures and to develop a package of different policies, including social policy, income policy and price policy

– including price controls.

It was clear that the situation must be extraordinary when the figures in the paper by Mr. Fleming showed a set of leading industrial countries with zero growth of G.N.P. and a 12 per cent price increase in 1974.

Professor Duesenberry thought that the reason there had been so little discussion of Professor Gordon's paper itself was that it covered an enormous field so well.

He thought the discussion of the new microeconomics was a most important development. It tried to explain phenomena observed by labour economists. Here, if there were a fall in demand, firms bought off the labour force by keeping its wages fixed, or even increasing them. Professor Gordon set out possible motivations for entrepreneurs, but claimed that the issue was rather mysterious. The paper argued that the labour force had to trade off wages against terms of employment. But most employees who were permanently in the labour force got a combination of the two, because firms had systems of seniority, etc. After a time, a worker would keep his employment permanently unless there were a severe slump. If one asked employers which was the best contract to offer, they did not see a choice between whether to fix wages or terms of employment. Few firms, especially in oligopolistic industries, would believe that if they reduced their wages they could maintain employment. They did not think their competitors would do the same and did not believe that market elasticity of demand was all that high. Because of this, one got variability in wages from new hiring. Firms had classification systems and hired at or above the minimum possible wage, depending on the market situation. In the secondary labour market, there would be more flexibility.

A major problem with economists was that they wanted to have theories which applied to a homogeneous world. This might be entertaining, but if they wanted to explain the real world, they simply had to allow for trade unions and for firms which were big enough to have elaborate personnel policies. We were not dealing simply with an industrial bazaar.

Professor Modigliani recalled that Professor Machlup had argued that an increase in the money stock was necessary and sufficient for inflation, and therefore its cause. Surely Professor Machlup did not quite mean what he said. He meant that if the increase in the money supply were greater than the increase in output then prices would rise. This would happen provided velocity was constant, which was quite plausible in the long-run. So, all that Professor Machlup was saying was that, in the longest run, money was neutral, that it had no real effect on the economy. The only question was how long was the long run?

On the same basis, Professor Machlup would have to say that wage increases caused inflation because they were a necessary and sufficient condition for price increases. This was exactly the same argument as the previous one. One could imagine a system where the central bank set the real rate of interest to clear the commodity market, so that wages determined prices.

It followed that one could not fall back on the concept of 'necessary and sufficient,' but had to look at the facts. Then things were not so simple. Some times an expansionary monetary and fiscal policy led to wage increases. There were other factors too. For example, in the United States in the short run, increases in raw material and import prices had a definite effect on the price level. In fact, once one allowed for unemployment, raw material prices and import prices, money was not necessary to explain inflation in the United States.

Professor Laidler had argued that the money supply should be allowed to eventually run at a constant rate, and that the economy would adjust, reaching a natural rate of unemployment. This again raised the question, how long was the long run in this context? Here, Professor Modigliani felt there was a basic disagreement with Milton Friedman, and many monetarists. For Professor Modigliani, the short run was a matter of years; for them, but a brief interlude.

Professor Liviatan had turned to the question of rigidity of prices. The assumption that firms would let output vary was perhaps true of microeconomic changes. Macroeconomic changes would rapidly be transmitted to prices.

Professor Laidler wanted an explanation of short-run output changes. A pure monetary expansion would not lead to a change in output in the short-run. If the money supply increased and government expenditure increased, then one could get an output change, because this would pass the consistency test of expectations.

Professor Laidler replied that the individual economic agent could not separate aggregate from random factors. He would probably recognise that there had been a change but would not quickly be able to determine how permanent it was.

Professor Duesenberry thought the issue depended on relative variability for the firm, the sector and the whole economy. The kinds of event caused by the Korean War meant that Professor Liviatan's argument would hold. But if one was arguing over a difference between a 5 per cent or 6 per cent increase in the money supply, its results would almost certainly be very small for the individual firms. However, there must be a break point between these two extremes.

Professor Lindbeck said Professor Modigliani had explained why what Professor Machlup has said was not very helpful. He wanted to add that we lived in a world with disturbances from various sources. It was perhaps best to counteract these disturbances at their source. If so, one needed to know where they did occur. Perhaps one should offer premiums to investors and deal with wage-push when disturbances occurred in these sectors, rather than say that we would stop their consequences by influencing the money supply. He could not believe that we denied a partial relationship between the state of the labour market and wage increases. If we did, we simply threw out the baby with the bath water. We should accept structural equations with more than one explanatory variable!

Professor Patinkin pointed to an example of a neutral change in the money supply. In 1960, in France, when 100 old francs became one new franc, prices immediately fell to 1 per cent of what they had been on the previous day; in that case there had been no problem because everyone had perfect information. That explained why an economy never adjusted perfectly on other occasions.

Professor Bronfenbrenner held that one of our difficulties was that the Phillips-curve flopped around too much. The fact that variables such as Phillips-curve slopes kept the same sign was obviously not very much help.

Professor Gordon wanted to clarify some points in his paper and so clarify the discussion.

He believed the monetarists had taken us backwards since 1963. In 1963 we accepted that wage-push, adminstered prices etc. were part of a fight for relative shares in national income, and led to changes in the money supply. He wanted to agree with Professor Patinkin and Malinvaud that nothing was accomplished by those who showed correlations between money and prices. Rip van Winkle would not have been in the least surprised by these correlations, either in 1963 or 1973. Of course changes in money and prices were correlated in the medium and long-run.

He had tried to pull things together. It might be optimal for the government to increase the money supply as a tax. It might want to buy votes, or it might fear unemployment. These were the real reasons why the money supply was affected. The right question to ask about France in 1968 was: Would the money supply have increased towards the end of that year without the sociological changes? The correct explanation was sociology cum money. The monetarist approach was not an integrated one. There was no rigorous statement about the natural rate of unemployment, which represented a reintroduction of the monetary approach but made no statement to that effect.

To Professors Frisch and Lindbeck, he would say that he did think that the relationship between the natural rate of unemployment and capacity utilisation was well summed-up in the equation quoted by Professor Malinvaud. The short-run Phillips-curve of 1963 had related price increases to changes in excess demand. In this equation, Professor Bronfenbrenner did not think that changes in price expectations should be left out, thinking these linked with $(y - y^*)$. Professor Gordon thought the natural rate hypothesis was correct in arguing that, in the long-run, the monetary authorities had no permanent effect on, for example, output and unemployment.

He had explained in his paper that the Aukrust model encompassed work in monetary theory. He said so because the model did represent a hypothesis about the transmission process.

Professor Gordon did not think Professor Frisch's three theories were all-inclusive. There were other things there. There was no contradiction here with what Professor Parkin had said because Professor Parkin had not taken his analysis past 1974. Wages and prices were not perfectly flexible. Relative price increases etc. could lead to an increase in the price level with an increase in the money supply because other commodity prices were not perfectly flexible downwards. Other factors *were* there. But how long an inflation would go on depended on the behaviour of other prices.

Professor Liviatan had started from rational expectations. If one knew the price level would increase in the medium run, then it would increase now, but this ignored the point of Professor Gordon's paper. There were many reasons why individual actors would not think in this way. Nor could people agree on forecasts of what would happen. Moreover, while this argument might hold for commodities, it would not hold with, for example, consumer durables. In the United States, General Motors had announced that the price of their cars would increase in September. Americans had bought more cars in July and output had increased, but speculators had not accumulated stocks of cars.

Professor Gordon agreed with Professor Duesenberry that we needed a theory including oligopolistic firms and trade unions, but he first wanted to understand a much simpler world.

As for excise taxes, they did affect prices and profit margins. It would have been possible to use tax changes to offset the O.P.E.C. increases in oil prices, but this had not been done. Nevertheless, there had been a revival of fiscal policy in the American economy.

Professor Genberg wanted to thank Professor Malinvaud. His introduction illustrated the importance of lead-lag relationships. The authors would have profited from reading the Swoboda–Parkin paper, but since they had finished theirs before the Swoboda–Parkin one was completed, the direction of causation could only have gone in the opposite direction.

To Professor Bajt, he wanted to emphasise that the lead-lag relation did not necessarily say anything about the direction of influence. A third variable might cause both, and one would need a more complete model to test this hypothesis. Such a model would, however, have to explain the observed temporal relationship between changes in money and prices on a world scale, in order to be credible.

On causality, the Sims test in the paper was supposed to show which were the exogenous and which the endogenous elements. So it was appropriate here. He believed that what the test showed was only that the timing of the movements in money, income and prices was consistent with the story set out at the start of the paper. This would be useful for future work on a more complete model of world developments.

Professor Swoboda agreed with Professor Malinvaud that the reference in the title of the second section of his and Professor Genberg's paper to 'alternative theories' was misleading in the sense that he and Genberg had concentrated on monetary theory and dismissed alternative theories rather casually. There was an important point there all the same. Any theory of worldwide inflation must explain simultaneously both the transmission and generation of inflation, and only the monetary theory passed this test. It was developed, of course, under the hypothesis that there were fixed exchange rates which made it possible to deal with one world. This approach was very much in the spirit of the papers mentioned by Professor Parkin. The final objective was to construct a more structural model. In particular, he and Professor Genberg were trying to pay greater attention to the structural nature of the evolution of the world money stock.

The paper had been written on an assigned title. In particular, the authors had not insisted, probably wrongly, on leaving out the word 'cause' from that title. Had they done so, they would have written a paper more in the spirit of the Swoboda–Parkin argument. The authors had looked at data on a very aggregate basis; this they had done mainly as a first check, to see whether a more structural model could be expected to be of any use, They believed that first results indicated that such would indeed be the case and, in further work, the kind of model suggested by Professor Lindbeck would be of help.

He agreed with Professor Polaczek that extraordinary situations should indeed lead to extraordinary policy measures. However, he questioned that the 'situation' of worldwide inflation was all that extraordinary. He did not agree that it was extraordinary, in the sense that each particular inflationary event needed a particular theory. The paper had not been concerned with unemployment in a particular country at a particular point in time, but with what had happened in the world as a whole over an extended period. To take one example: of course, what had happened in France in 1968 was of interest. But, until exchange rates had altered, prices in France did not increase by the full amount of the wage increase. This international parallelism in prices, rather than the 'extraordinary' event of 1968, had been his and Professor Genberg's concern. To this, he wished to add that though they had been concerned with long-run parallelism, they had also used short-run data to show developments over time.

Professor Frisch wanted the transmission mechanism looked at in greater detail. In this respect, the Aukrust theory combined with a more detailed specification of the money and expenditure sector, seemed to be a very useful and promising starting point. One could certainly expect it to hold for small countries. There, and on the whole, one would expect the temporal process to run from income to money rather than from money to income. This implied that, in looking at one small part of the world, a simple monetary theory as developed for a closed economy would be an inappropriate starting point.

4 The Role of Money in the Inflation Analysis[1]

Helmut Frisch

TECHNICAL UNIVERSITY OF VIENNA

I. INTRODUCTION

In this paper I propose to discuss the role of money in a process of inflation, not by analysing empirical data but rather by discussing the more important contributions of the so called 'monetarists'. I shall be dealing primarily with the recent contributions by Friedman [14] to [20], Allais [1], Brunner and Meltzer [6] to [11], Stein [33] and [34] and Laidler [24]. As the monetarists are not a homogeneous group, it is not easy to analyse their models so as to get precise information about the multiple role of the quantity of money and its rate of change in relation to the inflationary process. We find agreement only with respect to two assertions

(1) inflation is a monetary phenomenon for the explanation of which the quantity of money is fundamental

(2) the ruling Keynesian theory has failed in the field of inflation problems.

Spokesmen for all monetarism, especially for the anti-Keynesian atmosphere in which monetarist theory has been formulated, are Brunner's paper 'The Monetarist Revolution in Monetary Theory' [4] and Johnson's lectures 'Inflation and the Monetarists' Controversy' [23] in which both topics are treated with great vigour. Before the Keynesian revolution Hayek [21] presented a very well developed monetarist economic cycle and inflation theory which may be compared with the present American monetarism. I shall try to organise the discussion about the role of money in the inflation analysis in terms of five hypotheses which are formulated in the various lines of thought of monetarism (often with varying emphasis). The propositions are the following

(1) the acceleration theorem;
(2) the temporariness (of monetary impulses);
(3) endogenous expectations;
(4) the financing theorem (money or bonds);

[1] Editorial note: This paper has been considerably revised since it was presented and discussed by the conference.

(5) the crowding-out effect;

(6) a sixth topic may be added, inflation and the capital–labour ratio, which is not essentially a monetarist proposition, but is a central problem in the consideration of the role of money in the inflationary process.

II. ACCELERATION, TEMPORARINESS AND ENDOGENOUS EXPECTATIONS

The acceleration theorem (M1) implies that only an acceleration or deceleration of the rate of growth of money produces any real effects, for example, employment and output effects, while a constant rate of growth of the quantity of money determines the rate of inflation. Using Laidler's formulation: 'The effects of a change in the rate of change of money supply are felt initially on the level of real income and on the rate of inflation, but in the long run it is *only* the rate of inflation that is affected' [24].

In Friedman's [14], [15], Stein's [36] and Laidlers' [24] work, as well as in Hayek's work [21], the acceleration theorem appears in connection with a further conjecture, that an acceleration (or deceleration) of the growth of quantity of money has only a temporary effect on the real economy. Brunner's formulation of the *temporariness theorem* (M2) reads as follows: 'The impact of monetary acceleration (or deceleration) on output and employment is essentially temporary' [4], page 14.

Both conjectures, according to which an acceleration of the expansion of the quantity of money produces production and employment effects, but these disappear after a certain interval, play a central role in Friedman's, Stein's and Brunner's as well as in Hayek's theories. Both propositions can be found in a particularly simple formulation in Friedman's models. Summarising both his theoretical models [14], [15] the following theoretical outline is obtained[1]

$$\pi = \pi^* + \alpha(y - y^*) + \gamma(\log X - \log X^*) \tag{1}$$

$$x = x^* + (1 - \alpha)(y - y^*) - \gamma(\log X - \log X^*) \tag{2}$$

$$y = y^* + \frac{1}{1 - s\beta}(m - y^*) \tag{3}$$

This system of linear differential equations (1) (2) (3) expresses the acceleration theorem very clearly. If in (3) the exogenous rate of growth of the quantity of money increases compared to the *expected* rate of growth of nominal income ($m > y^*$) there will be a positive difference ($y - y^*$).

[1] Lower case letters signify rates of growth, i.e. $\pi = \frac{dp}{dt} \cdot \frac{1}{p}$ $\quad y = \frac{dY}{dt} \cdot \frac{1}{Y}$ $\quad m = \frac{dM}{dt} \cdot \frac{1}{M}$ etc., $\quad s = \frac{1}{V} \cdot \frac{dV}{di}$ . . . rate of change of the velocity of money as a function of the interest rate, β is an expectations' adjustment coefficient, X signifies the level of real income.

Equation (1) and equation (2) show how a deviation of the actual rate of growth from the expected, affects the rate of inflation π through equation (1) and the rate of growth of real income X through equation (2). The parameter α, and $(1 - \alpha)$ can be interpreted as price and production elasticities. The system demonstrates a causal direction: an increase of the growth rate of the quantity of money ($m > y^*$) produces real effects via equations (1) and (2), the magnitude of which are set by the ratio $\frac{\alpha}{1 - \alpha}$.

An expectations adjustment process increases y^* in the state of disequilibrium until $y = y^* = m$. In the new steady state the effects of an increase of the growth rate of the quantity of money on the real variables have disappeared and all actual rates of growth are equal to the anticipated. If it is intended to produce real effects again, m must be raised again. A permanent effect on the real system can only be made possible by a permanent acceleration of the growth of the quantity of money.

In the above-quoted works of the monetarists (except Hayek) the acceleration theorem and the temporariness assumption are in general used together with the concept of *endogenous inflation expectations* (M3).

Currently there are three rival hypotheses to explain how endogenous expectations are formed

(1) adaptive expectations
(2) the rate of forgetfulness
(3) rational expectations.

The concept implied by 'adaptive expectations' is that the expected rate of inflation is a function of the rates of inflation observed in the past. Deviations of the observed variables from those expected lead to corrections of the error by a certain percentage. This expectations-formation is comparable with an error-learning process.

According to Allais [1], economic agents use a backwards discount as expressed in the 'rate of forgetfulness'. 'More specifically, the effect of the past on the present is assumed to be reduced by forgetfulness in the same way as the discounting process reduces the influence of the future on the present', [1], page 42.

Allais' 'rate of forgetfulness' belongs to the class of adaptive expectations in a wider sense. The difference being that he uses variable and not constant weights in the expectations formation process.

The 'rational expectations' hypothesis is that all economic agents know the model and use all the information available immediately before the period begins. The expectations of economic agents are assumed to be the same as the predictions of the model in which they are assumed to be actors, [7] page 162. Rational expectations as developed by Sargent and Wallace [31], exclude non-neutral monetary policy in the sense of influencing the real economy. They are not consistent with the acceleration theorem and are not assumed by the monetarists. The monetarist models assume in general an adaptive-expectations mechanism.

(1) M1, M2, M3 IN THE STEIN MODEL

The combination of these three hypotheses into a theoretical unity shows that an acceleration of the quantity of money leads to real effects, but these disappear again due to the endogenous expectations' adjustments process. The application of M1, M2 and M3 is very clearly expressed in the Stein's models [35], [36]. Stein uses a Patinkin type of macroeconomic model including a labour market, a bonds market and a goods market. As a substitute for the money market there is an equation for the change in real balances. Further included is an expectations' adjustment equation and a definition of the budget deficit. A budget deficit leads to either an increase in the quantity of money or in bonds, or to an increase in both respectively. The unemployment rate, the rate of inflation, the expected rate of inflation, the real wage rate, the real balances, the nominal rate of interest, and the ratio of bonds to the money supply θ are endogenous variables. Stein discusses two problems in the framework of this model: first, an increase of government expenditure (ΔG) financed through the sale of bonds; and second an increase of ΔG financed through an increase of monetary expansion.

Both, a budget deficit financed by bonds, and equally by creation of money, have expansive effects in the sense that (in the short run) the rate of unemployment will be reduced *below* equilibrium level (natural rate of unemployment). An additional distinction now has to be introduced. If ΔG is financed by the sale of bonds, the ratio of bonds to money θ will increase and this implies an increase of the market rate of interest. According to Stein we have to consider the following principal difference

$$\frac{\partial \pi}{\partial \theta} < 0 \text{ (non-positive)} \qquad \text{Monetarists}$$

$$\frac{\partial \pi}{\partial \theta} > 0 \qquad \text{Neo-Keynesians}$$

This difference will be discussed in more detail in M4 – the financing theorem, and in M5 – the crowding-out effect. Assuming that $\frac{\partial \pi}{\partial \theta} = 0$ (the monetarist position) an increase of ΔG, financed by an acceleration of the money supply, will produce a real expansive effect. Real balances per worker start to rise and the excess-demand is increased. The increased rate of inflation reduces the real wages (or the growth of real wages) and decreases the rate of unemployment. If the increase of government expenditure levels off ($\Delta G = 0$) but monetary expansion remains at the higher rate, the unemployment rate (U) will increase, but stay below the equilibrium level. If the expectation of future inflation catches up, $\pi^*(t) = \pi(t)$, money wages will rise again and the system converges to the natural rate of unemployment but at a higher rate of inflation corresponding to the higher rate of monetary expansion. One can hence conclude (1) that a monetary impulse can only reduce the rate of unemployment temporarily, and (2) the rate of unemployment can only be reduced below its equilibrium level when the rate of growth of money expansion is continuously increased.

If ΔG is financed by sale of bonds, the impact effect becomes expansive (i.e. U drops below U^*). When government expenditures stabilise at the higher level ($\Delta G = 0$) the system will return to the preceding values of the rate of inflation and unemployment (π, U), even when the expectations of inflation remain stable. The explanation of this phenomenon is the 'crowding-out' effect. The increase of the nominal rate of interest causes investment to recede $\left(\frac{\partial I}{\partial i}\frac{\partial i}{\partial \theta} < 0\right)$ thus compensating the increase in consumption $\frac{\partial C}{\partial \theta}$ exactly.

(2) M1, M2, M3 IN THE BRUNNER–MELTZER-MODEL

The Brunner and Meltzer model contains an output market, two asset markets, a credit market and a money market, as well as an explicit formulation of the government sector. Disturbances in the system set off four adjustment processes in respect of which the short-run, the intermediate run and the long-run need to be distinguished

(1) short-run flow adjustments include the response of the commodity market to changes in the asset markets;

(2) an intermediate adjustment is determined by interaction of the asset market, the commodity market and the government budget;

(3) a longer-run adjustment of employment and the labour and output markets;

(4) a long-run adjustment of capital and wealth.

Despite the fact that the Brunner and Meltzer model is extremely elaborate, its essential features can be expressed by means of a simple diagram to facilitate our discussion.

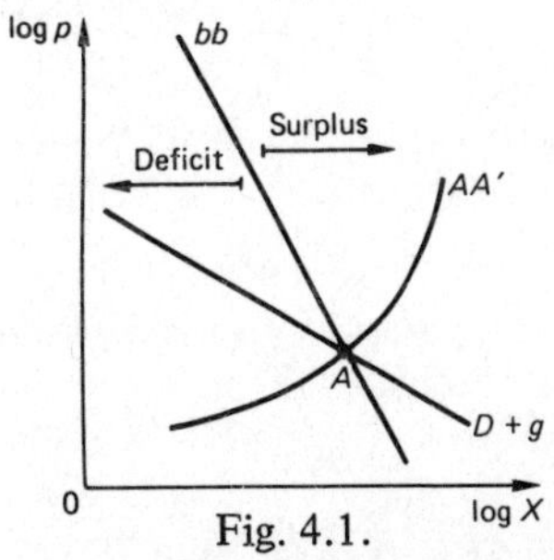

Fig. 4.1.

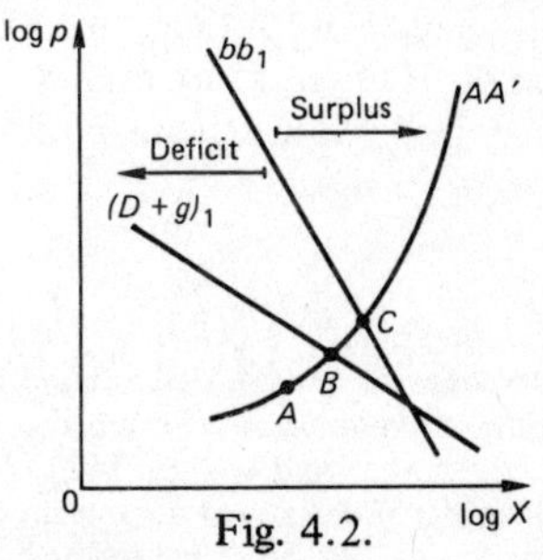

Fig. 4.2.

Essential features of the Brunner and Meltzer model.

$D + g$ represents demand. Private demand $D(\underset{-}{p}, \underset{+}{H})$ is a function of the price-level p and private wealth H, consisting of base-money B and the value of securities $v(i)S$.[1] The supply curve AA' is only valid under the assumption of given money wages W and given price level expectations p^*. An increase of W and p^* shifts $A(\underset{+}{p}, \underset{+}{p^*}, \underset{+}{W})$ upwards. The important feature of the Brunner and Meltzer model is the introduction of the budget equation bb.

This curve is the locus of all combinations (p, X) that satisfy the asset market equilibrium. The following equation represents the bb curve:

$$p \cdot g + I(i)S - t(p, X) = 0.$$

Total nominal government expenditure $p{\cdot}g$ plus the expenditure for the interest payment $I(i)S$ are equal to the tax revenue.[2] In a diagram in the (p, X) plane, with given taxes, given real government spending and the stock of securities, the budget schedule is negatively sloped, since an increase in the price level raises real taxes, while it lowers real government outlays by reducing the real value of interest payments. The bb line divides the positive orthant into three sets of points. To the right of bb are positions of budget surplus (the money stock and the stock of securities are reduced). Left of the bb schedule are positions of deficit, asset-market and budget equilibrium.

To compare the Brunner and Meltzer model with the Stein model let us carry out two mental experiments. Government expenditure is increased and the deficit is financed in the one case by money creation and in the other case by issuing securities. In both cases the impact effect of an increase in g raises both the $D + g$ and the bb curve. The latter shifts to the right, since budget balance requires higher real taxes to match the higher level of government spending.

Because of the corresponding elasticities the shift of the bb curve always exceeds the shift of the $D + g$ line (see figure 4.2 on page 113)[3]. The output market is cleared at the new flow equilibrium at point B, but a budget deficit exists. If the deficit is financed by money creation, the increase of money balances raises aggregate demand even further until the intermediate-run equilibrium is reached.[4]

The conclusion is that, for given money wages, the stock/flow equilibrium lies at a higher output and higher prices after the adjustment to an increase in real demand financed by money creation. But this intermediate equilibrium can only be temporary, since the real wages were lowered through an non-anticipated inflation.

[1] S = outstanding stock of government debt at face value; $v(i)$ = price per dollar of S; g represents real government expenditure.

[2] For an explanation of the bb curve, see Appendix 1, page 126. See [10].

[3] See Brunner and Meltzer [10].

[4] Brunner and Meltzer prove that the elasticity $(p, B/bb) < 0$, i.e. an increase in base money B shifts the bb curve to the left. The rising $D + g$ curve will meet the bb curve between points B and C (see Appendix 1).

If the increase in the government demand is financed by issuing securities, the impact effect of increased spending is identical with the former situation (shift of the $D + g$ curve and the *bb* curve). The difference arises with respect to the *bb* curve. Contrariwise to the former case the *bb* curve also moves to the right (since the increased debt raises government expenditure). Convergence requires that the *bb* schedule moves less than the $D + g$ line. Otherwise the deficit continues, the stock of government bonds would increase without limits and inflation would exist forever. In the Brunner and Meltzer model there exists a critical 'mix' of a combined securities–money financing of the debt, where the position of the *bb* curve remains fixed. Since the debt component of the deficit financing shifts the *bb* curve to the right, we can conclude that the price level is higher the higher the share of debt issued in a budget financing process.

The propositions M1, M2 and M3 cannot be adequately applied to the Brenner and Meltzer model. Since their model is formulated in 'levels' M1 can only be applied in an extended sense. A monetary impulse means, therefore, not a change in the rate of expansion of money supply but a change in the quantity of money. Furthermore for the developed part of their model, for the 'intermediate run' the expectations are not endogenous but given as a parameter (in other words M3 is not valid). This means in addition that M2 (the temporariness proposition) which is related to endogenous expectations is not integrated into their model. It is obvious that the interesting results of the Brunner and Meltzer model of an intermediate stock-flow equilibrium were obtained by explicitly not introducing an expectations adjustment mechanism into the supply-function. A surprising result of this analysis is that the Brunner and Meltzer model has a special position, and when viewed from the standpoint of the first three propositions M1, M2, M3 cannot be called 'monetarist'.

(3) M1, M2, M3 IN HAYEK'S MODEL

Hayek's model contains explicitly the acceleration theorem and the temporariness hypothesis, as opposed to present American monetarism; the concept of endogenous expectations is, however, missing. In contrast to contemporary monetarism the temporariness of a monetary impulse is not effected through a lack of the adjustment of money wages (which happens immediately), but through an insufficient voluntary propensity to save. The beginning of Hayek's story is the original sin of additional creation of money by means of bank credit. The increase in the rate of monetary expansion lowers the nominal market rate of interest (liquidity effect).[1] The decrease of the market rate of interest disturbs monetary equilibrium which, according to Wicksell and

[1] A short but careful exposition of Hayek's model is given by Machlup [26]. Hayek is not explicit as to whether by a credit expansion only the quantity of money or the rate of expansion of money supply is supposedly changed. The latter interpretation is not consistent with Hayek's business cycle model.

Hayek, consists essentially of an equality of the 'natural rate of interest' (composed of the real marginal product of capital $r(z)$, where $z = \frac{K}{N}$ and the expected rate of inflation π^* and the market rate of interest i. This brings about a rentability difference $r(z) + \pi^* - i > 0$, leading to an excess demand for investment goods.

The rise of the rate of monetary expansion explicitly leads to a 'first round effect'. The additional money is spent for the purchase of investment goods and relative prices P_I/P_C will increase. If the creation of money is effected during a condition of full employment, workers and 'non-specific' means of production will be removed from their current use and will be 'invested' in stages of production further removed from consumer goods products. The change in the allocation of labour between the consumer goods sector and the capital goods sector leads to a (relative) decrease of consumer goods production, or in Hayek's claim an absolute decrease. But this raises the consumer goods prices P_C. The excess demand for consumer goods, and hence π_C, become more accentuated, as a consequence of the increases in monetary wages in connection with the reallocation of labour from the consumer goods sector to the investment sector. The Wicksell and Hayek process definitely becomes critical at this point.[1] If the propensity to save does not increase – as Hayek assumes – then the market rate of interest i will increase. Undoubtedly a further rise in the rate of monetary expansion, an acceleration of the rate of supply of money would become necessary. Hayek is very clear about this point. The essential quotation is: 'All this must mean a return to shorter or less roundabout methods of production if the increase in the demand for consumer goods is not compensated by a further proportional injection of money by new bank loans granted to producers. And at first this is possible. The rise of the prices of consumer goods will offer prospects of temporary extra profits to entrepreneurs. They will be more ready to borrow at the prevailing rate of interest. And, as long as the banks are going on *progressively* increasing their loans it will, therefore, be possible to continue the prolonged methods of production or perhaps even to extend them still further. But for obvious reasons, banks cannot continue indefinitely to extend credits, and even if they could, the other effects of a rapid and continous rise of prices would, after a while, make it necessary to stop this process of inflation' [21], page 80.[2]

As soon as the additional supply of money ceases, the market rate of interest begins to go up again until it reaches its original level. But this makes the

[1] As Hicks remarks, the propensity to save would have to increase: 'A further increase in the saving propensity will be necessary if the "boom" (as he would call it) is to be maintained. If this increase is not forthcoming, there will be a "crisis" [22] page 212.

[2] Why can 'banks not continue indefinitely to extend credits'? In his interpretation of Hayek's model Machlup says: 'This, however, cannot happen, either because the banks find it impossible or too risky to go on expanding at an increasing rate, or because investors find it too risky to go on borrowing and investing' [26], page 502.

rentability difference negative $i > r(Z) + \pi^*$ and a cumulative downward process is triggered again, resulting in a restructuring process which reduces existing excess capacity and lowers the capital coefficient. At the end of this process the system has again reached a point with a lower capital-output ratio, lower real wages and a higher 'natural' rate of interest.

If we consider M1, M2 and M3 as a theoretical unit and if we try to look inside the 'monetarist black box' we find that the acceleration of the growth rate of money supply induces real effects only when a non-anticipated inflation results. If expectations do adjust, so that $\pi^* = \pi$ the positive employment and quantity effects successively disappear and the system again reaches the equilibrium unemployment rate, although at a higher rate of inflation. The faster the economic agents learn to adjust their expectations, the weaker are the real effects of an increase in the supply of money. It is not the acceleration of the growth of the supply of money that produces real effects but the lack of anticipations of a starting inflation. The acceleration theorem and the temporarity theorem were well known in macroeconomic theory before Keynes, as the analysis of Hayek's *Prices and Production* shows. The contribution of the monetarists to an improved analysis of the monetary process lies in the reformulation of both of these theorems and in having connected both of these with the concept of endogenous expectations.

III. MONEY CREATION, DEBT AND THE RATE OF INFLATION

A second set of problems that characterise the monetarists can be brought together under the headings of the 'financing theorem' and the 'crowding-out' effect.

(1) THE FINANCING THEOREM (DEBT OR MONEY) (M4)

This hypothesis deals with the question as to what effects different ways of financing a budget deficit have, namely creation of money or borrowing from the public. 'Whether a deficit produces inflation depends on how it is financed. If, as so often happens, it is financed by creating money, it unquestionably does produce an inflationary pressure. If it is financed by borrowing from the public, at whatever interest rates are necessary, they may still exert some minor inflationary pressure. However, their major effect will be to make interest rates higher than they would otherwise be', [20] page 915. Looking at this proposition in the framework of the *IS–LM* model, which is also used by Friedman, one sees that in the case of a deficit financed by borrowing the *IS* curve moves to the right (where the *LM* curve remains fixed), thus producing an increase in the rate of interest, the velocity of money and a higher level of spending. In the case of a deficit financed by means of creation of money both the *IS* and the *LM* curve shift to the right. The shift of the *LM* curve continues as long as the nominal stock of money continues to grow. If however, the price level begins to rise, the shift of the *LM* curve to the right is offset. As soon as real balances (M^r) decrease, the *LM* curve moves back. Real income may return to its initial level, but nominal income will stay at a higher level.

(2) THE CROWDING-OUT EFFECT (M5)

Using the Hicksian *IS–LM* schedule one can conclude that the increase of government expenditure at a constant quantity of money *M* will raise the market rate of interest because of the additional borrowing by the government to finance the deficit. This will crowd out some private expenditure. This crowding-out effect is specially emphasised by Anderson and Carlson [3], the econometricians of the St. Louis model, as well as by Milton Friedman. A clear formulation reads as follows: 'Monetarists generally hold that fiscal actions in the absence of accommodative monetary actions, exert little net influence on output and the price level. Government spending unaccompanied by accommodative monetary expansion, that is, financed by taxes or borrowing from the public results in a crowding out of private expenditures with little if any net increase in total spending'. [14], page 8.

According to Stein the acceptance or rejection of the financing theorem is the point of difference between the 'Monetarists' and the 'Neo-Keynesian School'. Let us use a simplified exposition of Stein's model [19], 1974, in the form of two equations, which resemble the *IS–LM* model (compare Appendix 2).

$$E(U, \pi^*, M^r, i, G, \theta) = 0$$

$$i = g(U, \pi^*, M^r, \theta)$$

The excess-demand function $E(\, .. \,) = 0$ is the locus of all combinations (i, M^r) that satisfy the commodity market equilibrium. The unemployment rate U, the rate of expected inflation π^*, the level of government expenditure G and the ratio between interest-bearing bonds and money θ are considered as parameters. This represents the *IS* curve in the (i, M^r) plane. Equation (2), the BB' curve is the set of pairs (i, M^r), where the bonds market is in equilibrium. The *IS* curve is upwards-sloping. A rise in real balance M^r would raise excess-demand and must be compensated by an increase in the nominal rate of interest. The BB' curve is negatively sloped. A rise in real balances induces a rise in the demand for bonds and has to be compensated by a decline of the market rate of interest. Suppose that the government reduces taxes and finances the deficit through the sale of bonds. Thereby the ratio $\theta = \frac{\text{Bonds}}{\text{Money}}$ increases, i.e. $d\theta > 0$.

The increase of the wealth relation shifts the *IS* as well as the *BB* curve. The shift of the *IS* curve is measured by:

$$di(IS) = -\frac{E_\theta}{E_i} \, d\theta^*$$

$$^*E_\theta = \frac{\partial E}{\partial \theta}, \quad E_i = \frac{\partial E}{\partial i} \text{ etc.}$$

i.e., the *IS* curve shifts upwards in figure 4.3. The budget-deficit raises private wealth, and consumption is stimulated by $E_\theta \cdot d\theta$, but the shift is weaker, when an increase of the rate of interest results in reduced private expenditures.

$(E_i < 0)$.

Since the budget-deficit raises the bond–money ratio the bond market can only be in equilibrium at the given M^r if the nominal rate of interest rises by $g_\theta \cdot d\theta$. This shift of the BB' curve as a consequence of $d\theta > 0$ is/$di(BB') = g_\theta \cdot d\theta$. The vertical shift of the *IS* curve minus the shift of the *BB* curve is

$$di(IS) - di(BB') = \frac{[E_\theta + g_\theta E_i]}{-E_i} \cdot d\theta = \frac{P_\theta}{-E_i} \cdot d\theta$$

It is important to note, that we can derive P_θ directly from equations (1) and (2), if we consider the effect of an increase of θ upon the expenditure function. Let us further assume, that $\pi = \lambda \cdot E(\ldots)$.

Differentiating with respect to θ we get

$$\frac{\partial \pi}{P\theta.} = \lambda(E_i \cdot g_\theta + E_\theta) = \lambda \left[\frac{\partial E}{\partial i}\frac{\partial i}{\partial \theta} + \frac{\partial E}{\partial \theta}\right] = P_\theta$$

The impact of an increase in the bond–money ratio on the rate of inflation consists of two opposite effects. The negative'crowding-out' effect of a rise in the rate on interest and the positive private wealth effect on private expenditure

$\frac{\partial E}{\partial i} \cdot \frac{\partial i}{\partial \theta} < 0$ crowding-out effect

$\frac{\partial E}{\partial \theta} > 0$ wealth effect

These two opposite effects signify the difference between montarists and neo-Keynesians according to Stein [35] . We have the following differences:

$\frac{\partial \pi}{\partial \theta} < 0$ monetarist

$\frac{\partial \pi}{\partial \theta} > 0$ neo-Keynesian

Reducing the problem in such a way, the differences between both schools can be described by the following three diagrams. Compatible with the monetarist position are figure 4.3 (see page 120) and figure 4.4, whereas figure 4.5 shows the neo-Keynesian position.

In the case of figure 4.3 we have $E_\theta + g_\theta \cdot E_i = 0$, i.e. the positive wealth effect is exactly compensated by the negative 'crowding-out' effect, the interest rate rises, but the price level, the real balance and the real wages remain constant. The financing of the deficit leads only to a substitution of private by public expenditures.

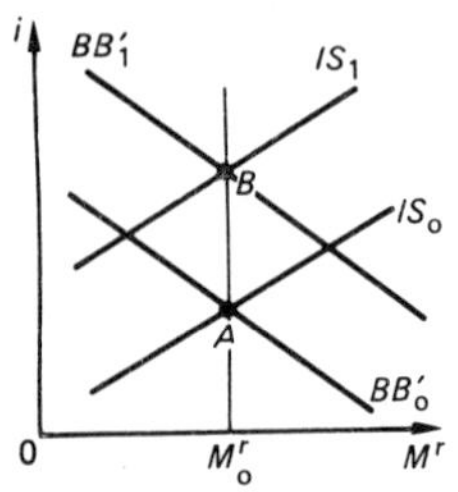

Fig. 4.3.

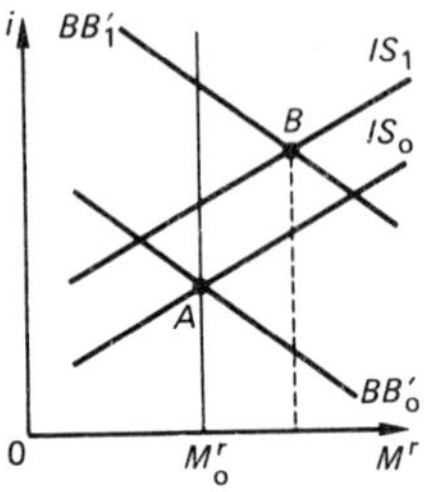

Fig. 4.4.

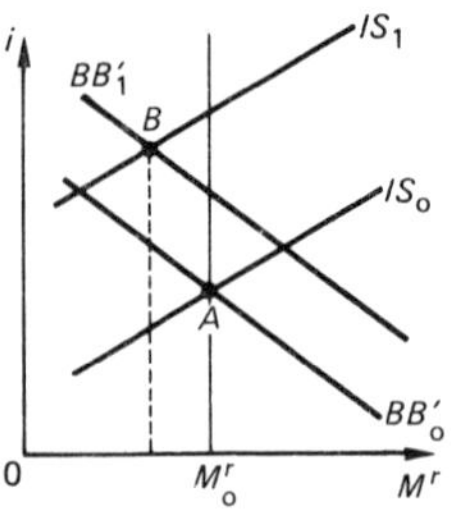

Fig. 4.5.

In figure 4.4, P_θ is negative, the BB' curve rises relative to the IS curve. The interest rate rises, but the goods market can only remain in equilibrium if real balances increase. (For given M this means that the price level would have to fall.) Real wages would increase and unemployment would rise.

The neo-Keynesian system assumed $P_\theta > 0$ (figure 4.5). This means that the IS curve shifts relative to the BB' curve. In the new equilibrium at point B real balances have declined (for given M the price level has increased). Real wages decrease and tend to reduce the rate of unemployment. The situation in figure 4.3 and figure 4.4 is based on the fact that the crowding-out effect either exactly offsets, or even more than offsets the positive wealth effect, thus triggering a deflationary effect (M^r increases). In the neo-Keynesian regime the positive wealth effect overcompensates the crowding-out effect, so that an inflationary impulse is caused (M^r decreases). The 'financing theorem' is adopted by Friedman, Anderson and Carlson, and Stein.

In direct opposition to the financing theorem is the result of the Brunner and Meltzer model. Here the final equilibrium depends on the mix of the financial assets B (= base money) and S (= securities). The debt component of the deficit financing shifts the bb schedule to the right (in the $\log p, \log X$ plane), so we can conclude that the higher the share of debt issued in a budget-financing process, the higher the price level.

With a higher share of money creation the system will find a final equilibrium with a smaller real income and a smaller rate of inflation (or level of prices). The explanation for this effect, in the Brunner and Meltzer model, is the absence of the *crowding-out* effect in the short-run and intermediate run. Certainly, deficits financed by bonds raise the market rate of interest, the level of prices and exert a partial 'crowding-out' effect on the expenditure function. But the contractive effects are overcompensated for by the expansive impact effect and by the wealth effect ($\Delta i \cdot \Delta S$). So far as the financing theorem is concerned (M4) and (M5) we can characterise the Brunner and Meltzer model as 'neo-Keynesian'.

Can anything be said about the macroeconomic significance of the crowding out which is emphasised by Friedman, Anderson and Carlson and Stein, but rejected by Brunner and Meltzer? Modigliani and Ando [27] point out, that as a consequence of a 'monetary impulse' the crowding-out effect is only one of several effects. Financing ΔG through issuing debt will produce the following effects

(1) an impact effect (direct effect $\Delta G \rightarrow \Delta X$);
(2) an induced consumption effect ($\Delta X - \Delta C$);
(3) the accelerator effect (inventories);
(4) price effects;
(5) a wealth effect;
(6) the crowding-out effect;
(7) the real balance effect (Pigou–Patinkin effect).

According to Modigliani and Ando we can assume that effects (3), (7) and (5) are empirically negligible for the short-run. Of the other effects, (1) and (2) are expansive and (6) is contractive. Empirical evidence suggests that the contractive mechanism tends to work more slowly than the major expansive one. One can argue that first real income will increase, but because of the crowding-out effect (to a lesser extent through the real balance effect) in the intermediate run the system moves back to the initial situation.

IV. MONEY, INFLATION AND THE CAPITAL–LABOUR RATIO

Can the capital–labour ratio (K/N) be raised by an increase in the rate of monetary expansion? The question is central to Hayek's model and is also answered by the neoclassical school (Tobin [37], [38], Sidrauski [32], Mundell [28], Patinkin [30], Stein [34]). The answer of the neoclassical theory and of Hayek's model is an unambigous 'yes'. It is true that the Tobin–Mundell result only holds for the steady state, whereas Hayek's model refers to a disequilibrium state of the economy.

The neoclassical result can be broken up into two partial results

(1) *Short run:* A rise in the rate of monetary expansion unambigously lowers the holding of the real balances.
(2) *Long run:* The decline of real balances increases the rate of real savings and as a consequence the capital–labour ratio.

The neoclassical argument rests on three basic assumptions:

(1) real balances are not an argument of the production function;
(2) the money supply is exogenous to the private sector;
(3) supply and demand for real balances are equal in every t.

A rise in the rate of monetary expansion raises the equilibrium rate of inflation. In a steady state the expected rate of inflation π^* must be equal to the actual rate of inflation. Thus at a higher expected rate of inflation the demand for real balances decreases. It follows, since the money market equilibrium must prevail, that the actual stock of real balances held by the non-bank public must also decline. An aletrnative formulation would be that in the new steady state the desired income–money ratio (the velocity of circulation) has increased.

The second part of the story is about the long-run implication of reduced real balances for the capital–labour ratio. There are two variations of the argument. In the Mundell variant – as a consequence of the real balance effect – real savings are negatively related to real balances: when real balances are reduced real savings will rise.[1] In the Tobin variant savings means accumulation of real balances or 'physical' capital, with the restriction that the overall rate of savings is constant. A higher expected rate of inflation changes the composition of savings in favour of a larger proportion of 'physical' capital. It follows – in both variants – that the decline in real balances raises the capital intensity of the economy.

This result holds only for the steady state. As soon as we depart from the steady state the uniqueness of the neoclassical result is completely lost. In the state of disequilibrium the result depends on the choice of the expectations and price-adjustment pattern, as Fischer [13] correctly emphasises. An increase in the rate of monetary expansion initially raises real balances per unit of capital above their equilibrium level. If we now consider the effect of an increase in the real balances on the capital–labour ratio we find (in contrast to the steady state) two compensating effects on the capital–labour ratio: planned savings will decrease (the real balance effect); this lowers capital intensity, but the rise in the expected rate of inflation stimulates investment and thereby tends to raise capital intensity. We cannot say *a priori* which effect will predominate. A plausible hypothesis for the rate of capital formation if market disequilibrium prevails, is[2]

$$\frac{\dot{K}}{K}=\frac{S}{K}+\frac{\alpha(I-S)}{K};0<\alpha<1.$$

The parameter α is an institutional one that indicates the extent to which firms are able to finance an excess demand $(I-S)$ by additional bank credits. If α is very small (firms cannot expand their investment plans beyond planned savings due to the lack of means of financing), the rate of capital formation is determined by the rate of planned savings and the capital–labour ratio will decline (the reverse of the neoclassical result). If α is large then the rate of growth of capital is determined by planned investment, capital will grow and raise capital intensity. This is the neoclassical conclusion, although real balances have increased (and not declined) in the case. For the disequilibrium

[1] Mathematically we have $S = S(r, m \cdot A)$ where r is the interest rate, m is real balances and A the value of assets. The partial derivatives $\frac{\partial S}{\partial m}$, $\frac{\partial S}{\partial A}$ and $\frac{\partial S}{\partial(m+A)}$ can be referred to as the real balances effect, the asset effect and the wealth effect; all are assumed to be negative [28], page 6.

[2] This formula for the rate of growth of the actual capital-stock in a disequilibrium situation is used by Stein [34], p. 75.

state of the economy the uniqueness of the neoclassical result is completely lost. An acceleration of the money expansion can raise capital intensity as well as lower it.

One can say that the question whether the capital–labour ratio can be increased by additional creation of money constitutes the central problem of Hayek's theory as set out in *Prices and Production.*[1] Hayek answered this question positively (as does neoclassical theory) that although capital deepening is brought about by 'forced savings' which can only be stabilised by a permanent increase of the creation of money (acceleration theorem) or by an increase of voluntary savings. Without worrying about details, Hayek's account has the following features.

A rise in the rate of monetary expansion lowers the market rate of interest below the natural rate of interest. But this implies an excess demand for investment goods $I - S > 0$, which results in an increase of the rate of growth of capital stock by the rate of forced savings, over and above the rate of planned savings. We have the same formula as above:

$$\frac{\dot{K}}{K} = \frac{S}{K} + \alpha\left(\frac{I}{K} - \frac{S}{K}\right)$$

if $\alpha > 0$, (if, that is to say, it is predominantly the entrepreneurs who have access to the new credits and the households are excluded from additional credits), then the capital accumulation changes in the way indicated and the capital–output ratio increases. At the new equilibrium the real rate of interest (= the natural rate of interest) has in fact decreased (via the higher capital coefficient) and the real wages have risen. But this equilibrium is only temporary. In order to stabilise the lower rate of interest, either planned savings have to rise or additional creation of money must occur. There are hence only two methods to raise the capital–output ratio

(1) without inflation: to increase voluntary savings;

(2) with inflation: by continuous progressive creation of money permanently suppressing the market rate of interest below the natural rate of interest.

The neoclassical theorem, that a rise in the rate of monetary expansion lowers the holding of real balances, increases the rate of real savings and the capital–labour ratio, is only valid under the condition of full price flexibility and complete anticipation of all endogenous variables (in other words, only in

[1] Our discussion of Hayek's model is based on his *Prices and Production* [21]. In a latter essay 'Profits, Interest and Investment' (1939) Hayek used exactly the opposite argument. He claims there that an inflation induced by money creation lowers the capital–labour ratio, because of the 'Ricardo-effects' introduced by Hayek. This inconsistency in Hayek's theory was emphasised and criticised by Professor Kaldor in 'Professor Hayek and the concertina effect', (1942) in his *Essays on Economic Stability and Growth* (1960). Hayek has never subsequently attempted to refute this criticism.

equilibrium). It loses its uniqueness properties if we depart from the steady state and consider disequilibrium states. Capital intensity can increase or decrease as a consequence of additional money creation. The neoclassical theorem is hence not 'robust' with respect to slight modification of its assumptions. Finally, an additional money creation leads to a cumulative process in Hayek's model increasing the capital–labour ratio via 'forced savings'. The permanent increase of the capital–output ratio however, requires an increase in the propensity to save or a continuous acceleration of the rate of money supply to stabilise the market rate of interest below the natural rate (the acceleration theorem).

V. CONCLUSIONS

The *acceleration* theorem together with the *temporarity* theorem and the concept of *endogenous expectations* form a theoretical unit and the most relevant contribution to the development of the post-Keynesian macro-economic theory. In the monetarist models, an acceleration (or deceleration) of the rate of growth of the money supply produces real effects, if as a result of this process an unexpected acceleration of the rate of inflation occurs. As soon as a full anticipation of the rate of inflation occurs, as a result of an expectation adjustment process the real effects disappear, and the system returns to the previous situation, but with a higher rate of inflation. The acceleration and the temporarity theorem were well known in the macro-economic theory before Keynes, as the analysis of Hayek's *Prices and Production* shows. The contribution of contemporary monetarism to an improved analysis of the monetary process lies in the reformulation of both of these with the concept of endogenous expectations.

The second set of problems that characterised the role of money in the inflationary analysis has been brought together in this paper under the heading of the '*financing theorem*' and the '*crowding-out effect*'. An argument can be developed that the acceptance or rejection of the financing theorem is the point of difference between the 'monetarist' and the 'neo-Keynesian' schools. The financing theorem implies that a budget deficit, if financed by creating money, will increase the rate of inflation; if financed by issuing debt it will have its major effect on an increase in the rate of interest (with some inflationary effects). This theorem is understandable only when we consider the operation of the crowding-out effect. The rise in the interest rate will 'crowd out' so much private expenditure that the rate of production and the rate of inflation will again go down and the rate of unemployment will increase. If, on the other hand, the budget deficit is financed through creation of money, the rate of inflation will (after temporary real effects) be permanently higher, according to the higher rate of money expansion.

Is it possible by accelerating the rate of growth of money supply to increase the capital–labour ratio? The neoclassical theorem as developed by Tobin, Sidrauski and Mundell answers this question with an unambiguous 'yes'. An increase in the rate of money supply raises inflationary expectations; this reduces real balances and stimulates planned savings. As soon as we leave behind us the realm of the steady state this theorem loses its firmness. The acceleration of money supply can raise or lower the capital–labour ratio. In the Hayek model the increase in money supply can raise the capital–labour ratio, although via a process of 'forced savings'. If the propensity to save does not increase (Hayek's conjecture) an acceleration of the rate of monetary expansion is necessary in order to stabilise the rate of 'forced savings'.

The topics in this paper in no way consider all the possibilities involved in the role of money in inflationary analysis. At least two important points have been neglected: the long-run positive relation of the rate of money supply, the rate of interest and the rate of inflation and the problem of stability or instability of a monetary economy as extensively discussed by Brunner and Meltzer, Johnson and others.

APPENDIX 1

The Brunner and Meltzer model is, compared with other macroeconomic models, rather elaborate.[1] The model consists of an output-market, two asset-markets (one for money, one for securities) and a government sector. Important for the working of the model is the government budget-equation: $g \cdot p + WN_g + I(i)S - t(p, X) = dB + dS$. Government expenditure consists of the nominal value of the purchase of goods ($g \cdot p$), of labour services (WN_g) and of interest payments for government debt $[I(i)S]$. The tax-revenue function $t(p, X)$ depends on the price level p and real income X. The budget deficit $G - t$ is financed either by an increase of base-money (dB) or an increase of securities (dS). Let μ be the proportion of the deficit (surplus) financed by issuing (or withdrawing) base-money and let v be the amount of base-money issued (withdrawn) by open market operations, we have:

$$dB = \mu(G - t) + v$$

$$dS = (1 - \mu)(G - t) - v$$

To obtain the *bb* curve, one has to substitute the solution of i from the asset-market into the balanced budget: $i = i(X, p, S, B)$

$$bb\colon p \cdot g + WN_g + I(i)S - t(p, X) = 0$$

The position of the *bb* curve depends on fiscal and monetary policy. An increase in B (= base-money) lowers the *bb* line (the elasticity $\epsilon(p, B/bb) < 0$) whereas an increase in S (= securities) raises the line [the elasticity $\epsilon(p, S/bb) > 0$].

APPENDIX 2

Stein's model[2] consists of seven behavioural equations. One each for the labour-market, the bonds-market, for real balances, for the rate of unemployment, for the price changes, for adaptive expectations and a government balance equation. The rate of price change consists of two components

a labour cost-push element: $\pi^* + h(U)$,
π^* is the expected inflation and
$h(U)$ a Phillips-curve

a demand pull element: $E(\ldots\ldots)$

$$\pi = \pi^* + h(U) + \lambda E(.\ \ ) \tag{1}$$

The excess demand equation is defined as follows:

$$E = E(U, M^r, g(U, \pi^*, M^r, \theta), G, \theta) \tag{2}$$

[1] See Brunner and Meltzer, [8] 1972 and [10] 1974.
[2] See Stein [35] 1974.

Excess demand is a function of the rate of unemployment U, real balances M^r,
the nominal rate of interest $i = g(U, \pi^*, M^r, \theta)$,
real government expenditure G, and
the ratio between bonds and money θ.
E is, of course, defined as $E = C + I + G - X$

The partial derivative of equation (1) with respect to θ is:

$$\frac{\partial \pi}{\partial \theta} = \lambda \left[\frac{\partial E}{\partial i}\frac{\partial i}{\partial \theta} + \frac{\partial E}{\partial \theta}\right] = \lambda \left[\frac{\partial I}{\partial i}\frac{\partial i}{\partial \theta} + \frac{\partial C}{\partial \theta}\right], \tag{3}$$

if we assume

$$E = C(U, M^r, \theta) + I(U, \pi^*, i) + G - X(U)$$

For equilibrium, Stein's model can be expressed by two equations:

$$E(U_e, \pi_e, M^r, i, G, \theta) = 0 \tag{4}$$

$$i = g(U_e, \pi_e, M^r, \theta) \tag{5}$$

The slope of the modified IS curve is (given M^r and G):

$$di(IS) = -\frac{E_\theta}{E_i}\, d\theta$$

The slope of the asset market curve (BB curve) given (M^r and G) is:

$$di(BB') = g_\theta \cdot d\theta$$

In the (i, M^r) diagram, the change of equilibrium real balances depends on the difference of the vertical shift of IS less the shift of the BB' curve.

$$di(IS) - di(BB) = \frac{[E_\theta + g_\theta E_i]}{-E_i}\, d\theta \tag{6}$$

Stein's model and his conclusions rest on the fact that the expression in the brackets in (3) is equal to the numerator of equation (6).

REFERENCES

[1] M. Allais, 'Forgetfulness and Interest', *JMCB* (1972).

[2] M. Allais, 'The Psychological Rate of Interest', *JMCB* (1974).

[3] L. C. Anderson and K. M. Carlson, 'A Monetarist Model for Economic Stabilisation', Federal Reserve Banks, St. Louis (1970).

[4] K. Brunner, 'The Monetarist Revolution in Monetary Theory', *Weltwirtschaftliches Archiv*, Vol. 105 (1970).

[5] K. Brunner, 'A Survey of Selected Issues in Monetary Theory', *Schweizer Zeitschrift für Volkswirtschaft und Statistik* (1971).

[6] K. Brunner and A. Meltzer, 'Friedman's Monetary Theory', in M. Friedman's *Monetary Framework*, p. 63–89 (1974).

[7] K. Brunner and A. Meltzer, 'Money, Debt and Economic Activity', *Journal of Political Economy* (1972).
[8] K. Brunner and A. Meltzer, 'A Monetarist Framework for Aggregative Analysis', *Kredit und Kapital 1* (1972).
[9] K. Brunner and A. Meltzer, 'Monetary and Fiscal Policy in Open, Interdependent Economies with Fixed Exchange Rates', Paris-Dauphine Conference (1974).
[10] K. Brunner and A. Meltzer, 'An Aggregative Theory for a Closed Economy', Conference on Monetary Economy, Brown University (1974).
[11] K. Brunner and A. Meltzer, 'Mr Hicks and the "Monetarists",' *Economica* (1973).
[12] D. Fand, 'A Monetarist Model of the Monetary Process', JoF (1970).
[13] S. Fischer, 'Recent Developments in Monetary Theory', *American Economic Review* (Papers and Proceedings, 1975).
[14] M. Friedman, 'A Theoretical Framework of Monetary Analysis', *Journal of Political Economy* (1970).
[15] M. Friedman 'A Monetary Theory of Nominal Income', *Journal of Political Economy* (1971).
[16] M. Friedman, 'The Role of Monetary Policy', *American Economic Review* (1968), reprinted in M. Friedman (1969).
[17] M. Friedman, *The Optimum Quantity of Money and other Essays*, London (1969).
[18] M. Friedman, 'The Monetary Studies of the National Bureau', Annual Report of the National Bureau of Economic Research (1964).
[19] M. Friedman, 'The Lag in the Effect of Monetary Policy', *Journal of Political Economy* (1961).
[20] M. Friedman, 'Comments on the Critics', *Journal of Political Economy* (1972).
[21] F. Hayek, *Prices and Production*, London (1932).
[22] J. Hicks, *Critical Essays in Monetary Theory* ('The Hayek Story'), (Oxford, 1967).
[23] H. G. Johnson, *Inflation and the Monetarist Controversy*, (Amsterdam–London, 1972).
[24] D. Laidler, 'An Elementary Monetarist Model of Simultaneous Fluctuations in Prices and Output', in H. Frisch, ed. *Inflation in Small Countries* (1976).
[25] D. Levhari and D. Patinkin, 'The Role of Money in a Simple Growth Model', *American Economic Review* (1968).
[26] F. Machlup, 'Friedrich von Hayek's Contribution to Economics', *The Swedish Journal of Economics* (1974).
[27] F. Modigliani and A. Ando, 'Impacts of Fiscal Actions on Aggregate Income and the Monetarist Controversy: Theory and Evidence', Brown University (1974).
[28] R. Mundell, *Monetary Theory* (*Inflation, Interest and Growth in the World Economy*) (Pacific Palisades, 1971).
[29] D. Patinkin, *Money, Interest and Prices*, New York (1965).
[30] D. Patinkin, 'Friedman on the Quantity Theory of Money and Keynesian Economics', *Journal of Political Economy* (1972).
[31] D. Patinkin, 'Money and Growth in a Keynesian Full-employment Model', in *Studies in Monetary Economics*, (New York, 1972, ch. 10).
[32] T. J. Sargent and N. Wallace, ' "Rational" Expectations, the Optimal Monetary Instrument, and the Optimal Money Supply Rule', *Journal of Political Economy* (1975).
[33] M. Sidrauski, 'Inflation and Economic Growth', *Journal of Political Economy* (1967).
[34] J. Stein, *Money and Capacity Growth* (New York, 1971).
[35] J. Stein, 'Unemployment, Inflation and Monetarism', *American Economic Review* (1974).
[36] J. Stein, 'Inside the Monetarist Black Box', Conference on Monetary Economics, (Brown University, 1974.)
[37] J. Tobin, 'Money and Economic Growth', *Econometrica* (1965).

[38] J. Tobin, 'The Neutrality of Money in Growth Models: A Comment', *Economica* (1967).
[39] J. Tobin, 'Money and Income: Post hoc ergo propter hoc', *Quarterly Journal of Economics* (1970).
[40] J. Tobin, 'Friedman's Theoretical Framework', *Journal of Political Economy* (1972).

Discussion of the paper by Helmut Frisch

Professor Patinkin remarked that the paper took several growth models of money, some more formal than others. It looked at similarities and differences in terms of three subgroups of criteria. In the first group were the acceleration theorem; the temporariness of change; and exogenous change. In the second were the financing theorem, and the crowding-out effect. In the third was the effect of a variation in the rate of inflation on the capital–labour ratio.

Professor Patinkin saw a great deal of similarity between the models Professor Frisch discussed, which far outweighed the differences. For example, Professor Frisch contended that, in Friedman's model, changes in the rate of inflation did not affect the economy once expectations and reality came into line again. Professor Patinkin thought the statement exaggerated, because he was sure that Friedman said this only in relation to the degree of unemployment and not to other factors. After all, the theory of the optimal quantity of money took the view that a different rate of inflation generated a different quantity of real money balances.

Professor Patinkin wanted to concentrate on putting the paper into the framework of the whole conference, and the differences which were claimed to exist between neo-Keynesians and monetarists. He thought this had now become a religious debate with extreme positions defended, although they were held by perhaps only one or two in each camp.

He wanted to begin by saying that he felt uncomfortable in using the term Keynesian to describe an analysis of inflation. After all, Keynes's *General Theory* was mainly about a world where there was a great deal of unemployment. Keynes' distinctions were not formulated for the case of inflation. However, some people seemed to have a deep psychological need to prove that Keynes, if he were writing today at an age of over 90, would agree with them. All this seemed to him a meaningless exercise.

Most of the models in the paper dealt with long-run steady states with different rates of inflation. But the conference was concerned with more short-run phenomena, though the short run could often be rather long. Everyone knew Keynes's remark that 'in the long run, we are all dead'. It should, perhaps, be pointed out that this appeared, not in the *General Theory*, but in the *Tract on Monetary Reform* and that Keynes made the remark about the quantity theory of money at a time when he accepted it. Nor were policy questions concerned with long-run steady states.

As for the distinction between Keynesians and non-Keynesians, there were missing names in the paper. Tobin was mentioned, it was true, but his major contribution was not discussed. This was his extremely important paper on 'Money and Economic Growth'.[1] There was also the basic work by Duncan Foley and Miguel Sidrauski on *Monetary and Fiscal Policy in a Growing Economy* (1971).

Tobin distinguished two kinds of neutrality. The first was the neutrality of the stock of money. The second was neutrality in the rate of change of money. Most models had neutrality relative to the money stock, whether they were Keynesian or non-Keynesian. This was found both in the *General Theory* and in criticisms of the *General Theory*. However, there were

[1] *Econometrica*, 1965.

differences of view on neutrality with respect to the rate of change of the money supply. But even these were not related to the distinction between Keynesians and non-Keynesians.

He next wanted to talk about the crowding out effect – what in British economic history of the 1920s was called 'the Treasury view'. If one took the usual *IS–LM* diagram, an extreme Keynesian, though not Keynes himself, would have a liquidity trap – that is, a horizontal *LL*. If the money supply increased, nothing would change because of the liquidity trap. This was the picture that most textbooks wrongly attributed to Keynes.

The Treasury view could be interpreted as stipulating a vertical *LL* curve. The excess demand for money was then not responsive to changes in the rate of interest. If government expenditure increased, the rate of interest would rise and there would be no increase in real national income. The government would borrow more in order to increase government expenditure. However, since there was no increase in the amount of money, the rate of interest would rise and real output would not change. The Treasury view was that saving was constant. If the government spent more on public works, fewer resources would be available for private investment.

The Keynesian theory, as in the general case, showed that reality was not a matter of comparing black with white. If one had an economy in equilibrium, and if government expenditure increased with an increase in the money supply, both the *IS* and *LM* curves would move to the right. With full employment, the excess of the 'equilibrium' level of income (at which *IS* and *LM* intersected) over that of full employment would give a measure of inflationary pressure.

If the increase in government expenditure were financed, not by an increase in the money supply but by an issue of government bonds, there would be expansion, but it would be less than with an increase in the money stock. So, in Keynes, money did matter. There was also a qualitative distinction in that an increase in money was more inflationary than an increase in bonds in Keynesian theory too. So, once again, one could not distinguish between Keynesians and non-Keynesians here.

Nor was there any distinction with respect to endogenous expectations. The chapter in the *General Theory* on expectations also dealt with endogenous expectations.

The paper claimed that in Hayek's *Prices and Production* one found a large number of propositions on acceleration, etc. However, Professor Patinkin wanted to check that Hayek fitted in with a discussion on growth, since Hayek had written more in the context of unemployment. He would be hesitant to transfer Hayek to a world of growth models.

Professor Machlup said that the word 'growth' certainly did not appear in *Prices and Production*, or indeed the word 'model'. The book dealt with the deepening of the capital structure. To that extent, it concentrated on an important element of growth. Hicks had recently said that Hayek's contribution was more to the theory of growth than to that of the business cycle. The reason was that Hayek went on to show that, with voluntary savings, one could lengthen the production period only for a limited time, after which there would be retrenchment during a downswing. The relationship to growth models came from the application of Hayek's ideas to other writings on growth theory.

Professor Nussbaumer felt that, in discussing whether the term Keynesian was correct, one had to distinguish two elements in growth – aggregate demand and aggregate supply. There was also the structure of demand and supply. Since, in economics, structural questions often seemed to be regarded as neoclassical, he wondered whether Professor Frisch had anything especially Keynesian in mind. Or was he simply concerned to exclude structural effects of so-called basic inflation?

Professor Frisch replied to Professor Patinkin. He had not given emphasis to contrasting neoclassical with Keynesian economics. He had done this only in one part of his paper. There he had shown that if deficit financing of the budget was obtained by the issuing of bonds, the rate of interest would increase. So the effects could be deflationary, or lead to no change in the rate of inflation. This would imply a strong crowding-out effect. But if inflation accelerated as a consequence of issuing bonds, the result was neo-Keynesian. This might be a semantic point. Professor Frisch did not, in his paper, have a relationship between real output and the rate of interest, but one between real balances and the rate of interest. One should not compare directly what Professor Patinkin had said with his own view.

What he thought a monetarist would say was this. Assume an increase in investment brought about by an increase in the money supply. Then both the *IS* and *LM* curves would shift to the right. But that was not the end of the story. If the price level began to rise, real balances would fall and then the *LM* curve would move backwards to the left to offset, at least in part, the rightward shift in the *IS* curve. So a monetarist would say that there was only a temporary real effect caused by an increase of money supply.

Professor Patinkin suggested that a Keynesian would say the same.

Professor Laidler wanted to clarify the argument. It was important to realise that the *IS–LM* diagram was very badly adapted to studying inflation. Everything of significance went on behind the diagram. Also, it was important to specify whether the increase in government expenditure was of a one-shot nature, or whether government expenditure increased by a given amount and continued at the higher level. If one were concerned with the latter case, there would be continuous increases in the stocks of either money or bonds, or both. He thought no-one in the conference, and few elsewhere, would argue that a one-shot increase in government expenditure, financed by a once-for-all increase in the money supply, would lead to continuing inflation. If one were dealing with a system which in the end got back to full employment, then, in full equilibrium, one could have a continuing increase in both the money supply and the price level with no excess demand. That was to be explained by the role of expectations in the price-setting process. Inflation became a self-fulfilling prophecy. Again, this matter had little to do with Keynesians *versus* non-Keynesians. It was not what the *General Theory* was about. He would add that the distinction between cost-pull and demand-push did not mean anything in this kind of world either.

Professor Patinkin agreed that the *IS–LM* curve analysis was not the correct way to proceed in an analysis of inflation, and he used it for simplicity only. However, one could adapt the diagram to an analysis of inflation, as had been done more fully elsewhere by Mundell, Foley and Sidrauski, as well as by himself. All he was saying was that one got the same conclusions as from a more complex diagram.

Professor Bronfenbrenner noted that some of his colleagues would say that it was illegitimate and contrary to Keynes to use the *IS–LM* analysis in this context. But he advocated going along anyway and not worrying about doctrinal purity.

Professor Mussa saw no fundamental differences between Keynesians and non-Keynesians on the issue of crowding out. The issue could usefully be divided into three parts. First, in the short run, an increase in government expenditure financed by debt issue would be expected to increase output; crowding out would not be complete, even in the view of the Federal Reserve Bank of St. Louis. Second, in the longer run, when output would be expected to be at its normal level, an increase in government expenditure would require an equal reduction in private expenditure. Given the level of output, if the government took more, someone else would have to take less, and in this sense, crowding out would be complete. Third, in the long run, there was the issue of whether debt-financed government expenditure led to excess crowding out because of the burden of the debt. Specifically, if holdings of government debt were a substitute for holdings of real capital, an increase in government debt would be expected to reduce the capital stock and, hence, reduce the normal level of output. However, recent work by Barro, published in the *Journal of Political Economy*, had shown that this conclusion of excess crowding out was not necessary. The result depended on the motivation for household saving, and particularly the motivation for bequests to future generations.

Professor Patinkin recalled that there was another old question – anything over ten years being old. This was whether government debt was a net asset to the private sector, because it implied a future tax liability. If the government represented the people, then increasing the government debt had a neutral effect.

Professor Laidler pointed out that, in general, if the electorate voted to increase taxes and debt-holding, this would mean that they saw some kind of gain. At the margin, debt might be neutral but not necessarily on average.

Professor Bronfenbrenner emphasised that the whole notion of the natural rate of unemployment was not orthodox Keynesianism, so Keynesians would object.

Professor Fischer agreed with Professor Patinkin on the uselessness, at this stage, of the Keynesian–non-Keynesian distinction. Professor Bronfenbrenner was fortunate to find himself with colleagues on the two extremes.

The crowding-out issue was the major outstanding point of disagreement, and analysis of that was straightforward. If there were a one-time increase in government expenditure, financed by borrowing, with government expenditure thereafter returning to its original level, there would be a once-for-all increase in government debt. Assume one started and ended with full employment. The question could then be posed by asking whether the price level would be higher than it had been originally. Alternatively, would the rate of interest be higher? Most theories of portfolio balance implied there would be an effect on the price level, unless the demand for money were interest-inelastic. One therefore came back to the equation of whether the *LM* curve was vertical; there was little evidence that it was, and much that it was not. Accordingly, one should not expect full crowding-out, even in a full-employment world.

Professor Frisch replied to the discussion. He said that if one looked at the role of money in the inflation process one could adopt different viewpoints. He had tried to discuss the most recent and important contributions of the so called 'monetarists', and he had tried to get their models under the same hat, using three propositions: the acceleration theorem, the temporariness of a monetary impulse and the concept of endogenous expectations. He was glad if the conference thought he had reconciled them.

In the second part of the discussion of the financing theorem and the crowding-out effect, he had used the idea of starting from equilibrium and assuming a tax cut financed by issuing bonds. People felt richer with more bonds and so spent more. An increase in bond-holding then led to an increase in nominal wealth and increased spending, and so affected the commodity market. However, an increase in the rate of interest led simultaneously to a crowding-out effect on private expenditure. Such an increase in the supply of bonds raised the price level, and this was probably neo-Keynesian. Professor Frisch thought that an increase in the ratio of bonds to money must have either no effect on the price level, or a deflationary one.

Professor Patinkin had made a comparison with Hayek's *Prices and Production.* The important issue in Hayek was very similar to Tobin's problem. If there were a steady state, with a given capital–output ratio, and if the money supply increased and there were rational expectations, inflationary expectations would increase. So there would be a fall in real balances and, with a constant savings ratio, a shift from real balances to physical capital. The real stock of capital would also increase.

This was also the Hayek problem, but Hayek had another model. If one started from equilibrium, an increase in money supply, by which he meant more money supply to investors, would induce a fall in the market rate of interest which would move away from the natural rate. This would stimulate investment, which would increase the capital–labour ratio. Hayek saw the situation as unstable. Once the increase in the money supply ceased, there would be a cumulative process in reverse. Hayek argued that one could stabilise the situation only through an increase in voluntary savings, or a continuous acceleration in the money supply to keep down the market rate of interest. But then there would be hyperinflation, and that would also upset people. Information about some recent developments could be obtained from Hayek's ideas, and had been rediscovered by Friedman.

5 Some Problems of Current Price Movements

Revold Entov

INSTITUTE OF THE WORLD ECONOMY AND INTERNATIONAL RELATIONS, MOSCOW

I. INTRODUCTION

There have been a number of peculiar features that can characterise the development of the contemporary inflation process. In the past few years a slump in production and a rise in unemployment rates in a number of the capitalist countries have been accompanied by a further rise in prices that has made still more acute the economic and social problems facing those countries. These events have been the logical result of the deepening of contradictions imbedded in such economic growth. The ruling class has done its utmost to transfer the burden of declining production and accelerating inflation onto the working people.

This paper deals with: the possible role of institutional changes in the economic structure of the developed capitalist countries as one of the factors affecting the steady and irreversible price rise (sections II and III of the paper). It then examines some mechanisms that may have contributed to the current acceleration of the inflation process (section IV).

II. MONOPOLISTIC AND OLIGOPOLISTIC PRICE FORMATION AND ITS CONTRIBUTION TO INFLATION

It is well known that short-run price rises may be caused by numerous factors, and in the past decade one could trace the especially intricate interplay of such forces. The steep rise in government expenditures caused by the escalation of warfare in Southeast Asia gave impetus to a faster rise in prices in the United States. In the development of inflationary trends at a later stage one can also try to single out some elements of influence of the excessive money demand-pull, cost-push and profit-push pressures, shift in price expectations and changes in the structure of aggregate demand. Contractions of aggregate demand in two recessions during the first half of the 1970s in the United States and some other countries failed to lead to a fall in prices in an unusually large number of industries (similar tendencies could also be traced in earlier postwar recessions, though they were not so conspicuous).

There is undeniably a temptation to explain price rises during recessions within the framework of traditional competitive concepts and to attribute such movements of prices to the contraction of supply connected, say, with changes in weather conditions, beyond the control of producers (agricultural prices) or with a steep rise in external costs (import prices). But a more detailed analysis of production price and cost movements in industries with rising or stable prices during periods of considerable contraction of the aggregate demand (taking account of inevitable lags in this process) must, to my mind, lead to the conclusion that the traditional competitive interpretation is inadequate.[1] The divergence between the movements of prices and market demand appears to indicate that today one cannot consider movements of prices as the sole source of information. This is true at least in respect to industries with a relatively high level of concentration.

This consideration again poses the question of the appropriateness of some of the traditional neoclassical concepts for the theoretical interpretation of contemporary inflation. An understanding of inflation probably requires a more profound insight into the dynamic processes of price formation at the microeconomic level and the identification of mechanisms of price increases in various economic structures. In this connection I should like to emphasise the importance of certain factors that have undermined earlier forms of price competition.

Can monopoly (it is of no importance whether we have in mind here a single monopolistic firm or effective collusion by several big companies) be a source of steady price rise? This question had been widely discussed in economic literature. At an earlier conference of the International Economic Association dealing with the inflation problem, the view was expressed that the emergence of a business monopoly can entail only a once-and-for-all price rise and cannot be a source of continuous inflation (see [7]).

There are, however, two aspects of this problem. No doubt, a monopoly can *per se* generate price movements only to a limited extent; the degree of monopoly power and the limits to it essentially depend on the place of the given monopoly in the whole system of production and market distribution, including all monopolistic and competitive relationships, which conflict with each other and limit each other. But the existence of such limits does not mean that effective concerted pursuit of production and price policies in key industries cannot play an important role in the mechanism of modern inflation. No doubt, the majority of primary impulses to price movements are usually generated by decentralised changes in production and market demand. However, as the impulses become effective in the new relationship between supply and demand, they can be – and in many cases are – modified in consequence of the independent actions of a number of producers.

[1] This certainly does not mean that prices are completely immune say, from the cyclical demand movements. Econometric calculation dealing with aggregated and – much more important – disaggregated price indexes show a considerable, though not always stable, relationship between them and capacity utilisation, volume of new orders, etc.

Putting aside the numerous technical details, we can maintain that under monopolistic (oligopolistic) competition participants more often than not strive to restrain open price rivalry, especially under declining demand (when such rivalry seems to be most dangerous); but they do not appear to be so often concerned with restraining upward price movement when demand is increasing, especially under inflationary expectations. And the largest producers in key industries – to all appearances – now possess a sufficient share of market supply and financial power to exert considerable influence on the movement of market price.

Some authors, having in mind the discontinuity of a firm's demand curve (see, for example, [17]), conclude from this that prices in the oligopolistic sectors are likely to be especially stable. But such an approach is rather static; it is of little use for analysis of the inflation process. But if one introduces into such a model the factors that determine the basic level of price, one can see that changes in costs and market demand may modify the strategy of price-setting. Thus, considerable price rises in factor markets or the rapid accumulation of unfilled orders may not only encourage large firms to raise their prices, but also act as an accepted signal for a concerted price rise greater than is necessary to compensate for the corresponding cost increase (for example with target-return price-fixation).

In contrast to the case of price reduction, an increase of a firm's price does not imply a serious threat to other oligopolistic firms (as a matter of fact this consideration is an essential factor in the kinked demand-curve models). But in turning to the dynamic aspects of such price behaviour one can identify various asymmetrical features: when there is predominance of deflationary expectations, big firms become interested in the stabilisation of their prices; but under the influence of inflationary expectations each producer can test out the advantages of a possible price rise. Traditional kinked demand-curve models do not take into account the additional opportunities they provide for participants – opportunities that can be created in the process of gradual experiment and from the rising importance of collusive decision-making. Co-ordination of market strategies is most clearly expressed in the practice of price leadership, while results of several empirical studies [8], [15] confirm the conclusion that the mechanism of effective leading is rather more suited to the raising of prices than to price-cutting.

A concentrated sector's reaction to changes of demand is likely to differ from that of atomistic industries both in the frequency of price changes and in their amounts.[1] On the basis of this assumption, some authors [19], are inclined to regard large firms as a kind of shield against the inflationary

[1] During a cyclical boom, for example, one finds the steepest rises of prices in a number of relatively less concentrated industries. Such a rise may express not only the more direct dependence of atomistic production on market demand, but also the derived nature of the demand and a lower price elasticity of demand for some industrial materials, less flexibility of market supply, very active speculation on the raw materials markets, and similar factors.

tendencies. To my mind such an appraisal of the role of 'big business' is, to say the least, one-sided. A number of empirical studies [10], [11], [20] among others, show that during the 1950s and 1960s concentrated industries in the United States and in some other countries managed to shift the rise of the factor prices onto the consumer.

The assertion that concentrated industries provide a dampening effect on the rate of inflation appears to be based on the differences in price dynamics during cyclical upswings; it does not take into account the subsequent price movements during recessions. But under contractions of aggregate demand, the prices in concentrated industries were more often than not less flexible than prices in atomistic industries. Since prices in many key industries had not fallen considerably during recessions, an earlier price increase in these industries could form the pivot of an irreversible price increase.

Thus the changes in the economic structure of the developed capitalist countries during the twentieth century would appear to have promoted certain 'distortions' of the usual path of a price movement. The concentration of production and capital has changed the competitive relationships. As Lenin has remarked 'the rise of monopolies, as the result of the concentration of production, is a general and fundamental law of the present stage of development of capitalism'. At the same time he stressed that capitalist monopoly has grown out of capitalism and exists in the general environment of capitalism, commodity production and competition and remains in permanent and insoluble contradiction to this general environment.[1] A changed institutional framework may favour the propagation of impulses to price rises and in other cases guard against subsequent falls in prices. The changed economic structure makes it possible for the biggest companies to act in a way similar to that of an electric valve which has conductance in a given direction several times higher than in the opposite direction. Within certain limits imposed by modern competition they can 'rectify' diverse impulses and thus contribute to a progressive price rise.

But the movement of the general price level is always a kind of resultant, subject to the influence of many forces. Thus the development of the relevant trend is always modified by a number of different factors, including the historically derived features of the institutional framework, the peculiar combination of cyclical forces, the stage reached in the inflation process, government policies, and similar factors. Through comparison of price movements in different industries it can be seen that such a trend is also affected by the peculiarities of the production process, by the fixed-cost/variable-cost ratio, the degree of remoteness of the industries concerned from the point of satisfaction of final demand, and other such factors.

In order to verify the hypotheses outlined above an attempt has been made to define some of them in a stricter form and to carry out some empirical

[1] See V. I. Lenin. *Collected Works.* Vol. XIX, International Publishers, New York, 1942, pp. 96, 169–170.

analysis. It may be appropriate to describe briefly some of the preliminary results of these investigations.

Certain comparisons can be based on the published data of the BLS detailed survey of wholesale price movements in the United States during the fifties [5]. The rank correlation (Spearman) coefficient between the degree of concentration[1] and the share of commodities which experienced a considerable (5 per cent and more) price decline is about – three-quarters and the rank correlation between the degree of concentration and the share of commodities which experienced a considerable (5 per cent and more) price increase is about + two-thirds.

The majority of our calculations have been based on the regularly published United States wholesale price indexes. The most frequent quarterly price declines occurred in atomistic industries (in agriculture above all) and, in various industries in which technical progress has been leading to exceptionally great cost reductions (for instance household appliances and some similar industries). Commodity groups in which quarterly price reductions occurred comparatively seldom can be subdivided into : (1) a variety of industries with moderate concentration in which intensive technical progress generated an expanding demand for their products (for example certain types of machinery and equipment); and (2) industries with a high concentration (such as metal containers, steel mill products). In some cases (for instance agricultural machinery and equipment) a combination of both factors can be found. It is noteworthy that the relation of the standard deviation of prices to the standard deviation of production appears to be consistently less in the more concentrated industries.

Regularly published price data were used to construct two quarterly wholesale price indexes (with fixed weights) including in one of them prices in the atomistic industries and in the other prices in the more concentrated industries. The latter demonstrated a more stable growth, showing price falls for about one-fifth of the twenty-year period (1952–1971), while the first index showed price falls for about two-fifths of the whole period. At the same time the mean range of quarterly price fall for concentrated price industries was only about one-third of that in the atomistic industries.

An attempt was made to develop econometric models which could explain the movement of both indexes. The equation specifications adopted were tested for the stability of coefficients over the whole period (Chow test) and the stability hypothesis was rejected. In the best equations describing price movements during the second sub-period (mainly the 1960s), market demand variables exerted more influence on the prices of atomistic industries, while variable costs regressors were less significant and exerted somewhat weaker

[1] Unfortunately, there were only available the aggregated data published in [5]; such classifications provide no possibility of using 4-firm or similar concentration ratios. Thus in this case (and in some other studies which will be mentioned later) we used a somewhat less satisfactory concentration index – the share of value added that is produced by the largest enterprises.

influence on these prices. We also tested the movements of the indexes described for their behaviour with respect of two different demand proxies (expansion and contraction of demand). Strong aggregate demand exerted more influence on the prices of atomistic industries. During the second half of the 1960s and the early 1970s one could trace the tendency for compensatory pricing ($\frac{\partial P}{\partial D} < 0$, where P is the price index and D one of the demand variables), and this tendency was more pronounced in the concentrated industries.

Most of the available information deals with quoted prices; this is why the results of the study of transaction prices, made in the United States by Stigler and Kindahl [16], are of particular interest. The variation of transaction prices of course exceeds that of quoted prices. But it is remarkable that in the regression equations, describing the variance of transaction prices, coefficients of the concentration variable proved to be negative and statistically significant; in other words, the price variance is, *ceteris paribus*, smaller in the concentrated industries.

From data published in [16] it follows that, in those industries in which the four-firm concentration ratio was less than 25 per cent, prices of all the commodities surveyed were falling in recessions; meanwhile in the industries in which the 4-firm concentration ratio was 50 per cent and more, prices of approximately one-quarter of all commodities remained stable, and prices of another quarter of all commodities were actually increased during recessions.[1]

III. MONETARY EXPANSION AND INFLATION

The rise of the general level of prices could not take place without a corresponding monetary expansion (the rise of MV) and any consideration of price dynamics, of course, cannot disregard this absolutely essential element in the inflation process. A number of papers dealing with the role of money in the inflation process are presented to this conference and I shall confine myself to one repeatedly discussed institutional aspect which has bearing on the subject.

A substantial increase in the economic power both of the largest firms in key industries and of the state in the developed capitalist countries has undermined the efficacy of various forms of internal money circulation based on the 'pure' gold standard. In the new situation when the mechanism of automatic control of the money circulation and credit flows does not exercise its functions to the full and credit expansions become more intensive and more protracted, monetary growth is becoming almost irreversible (at least in nominal values).

The immense increase of militarism, combined with increases of other government activities during peacetime, have inevitably led to the piling up

[1] The steel industry can again serve as a classical example: during ten years the transaction prices of carbon steel were reduced only once – by 0·2 per cent.

of state borrowings, including especially rapid accumulation of short-term debts. The development of this extensive credit infrastructure and the growth of specialised financial intermediaries have also contributed to the increase of liquid assets; during recent decades liquid assets have been rising more rapidly than total financial assets.[1] Accumulation of liquid assets has exerted increasing pressure upon the monetary system and has widened the possibility of the contribution of excess liquidity to money demand expansion.

The processes of conversion of some part of liquid assets into money are, it is true, under the influence of monetary authorities. But the range of the state's policy objectives has been gradually widening and the 'national priority' required to keep stable the purchasing power of money has quite often been sacrificed. At the same time the expansion of the financial activities of the government, and in particular the increasing need to re-finance the public debt, has made additional breaches in the system of control over the money supply and widened the areas of possible conflict between the treasury and the central bank. It is not at all easy to find examples showing that fiscal and monetary authorities have been successful in maintaining balanced economic growth and stable price levels over a long period.

It may be added that when monetary authorities have turned to deflationary policies, their restrictions have entailed higher interest rates, contributing to the increased velocity of money. The role of these processes has become especially evident during periods when the growth of money supply has been reduced but the increase of the velocity of money has permitted a further rise of the price level (for instance the cyclical upswing after the recession of 1953–54).

IV. THE CUMULATIVE MECHANISMS OF INFLATION

Some of the factors that have contributed to the unusual extent and duration of the recent price rise appear to emphasise the cumulative characteristics of the inflation process. One usually has in mind the following cumulative mechanisms of inflation: (1) the interaction between price rise and income velocity, and (2) the interaction between money incomes and prices (these two mechanisms are evidently 'partly overlapping' and their merging can make for an acceleration of the price rise).

To set in motion a cumulative process a certain threshold has apparently to be crossed. The existence of such a threshold seems to be associated first of all with certain settled behavioural stereotypes of the economic agents concerned, and secondly their lack of response might be explained within the framework of economic rationality (the absence of any money illusion presupposes a steep increase in costs of information and its processing).

In the postwar years one could observe the growing interest of most

[1] In 1929, the total of private liquid assets held by American non-financial investors (excluding the money aggregate M_1) accounted approximately for one-fifteenth, and now accounts for more than one-seventh of the total of financial assets.

economic agents in current and future changes of the purchasing power of money. The process of overcoming the money illusion appeared to be very uneven as between various social groups.[1] The burden of adjustment to frequent price increases proves to be especially heavy among the lower income and less wealthy sections of the population, the groups with lower educational level.

In the United States, the population's confidence in a future price fall, according to some surveys [9], had already begun to wane in the 1950s. But the consumer's judgement about buying conditions remained more closely associated, as Juster has shown, with such factors as recent changes in liquid assets and income, income expectations and expectations about general business conditions. American businessmen at the beginning of the 1960s appeared to display greater interest in expected changes in prices [18].

Regularly published price expectations (diffusion indexes) show that in the second half of the 1960s for the first time an overwhelming majority of American businessmen and most American consumers were expecting higher prices. 'Shocks' caused by abrupt consumer price rises in recent years may well strengthen these tendencies.

Certainly, it would be quite wrong to consider recent inflation in the United States and West European countries to be a spontaneous self-generating process, accompanied by an accelerating mass 'flight from money'. Awareness of the inevitability of a future rise of prices is a necessary but not sufficient condition for the 'flight from money'. Econometric studies [1], [3] show that even during periods of hyperinflation there have remained a number of factors that have restrained the untwisting of the 'flight from money' spirals. Numerous estimates of the demand for money functions have shown that the influence of price rises on the aggregate demand for cash balances in developed capitalist countries appears to be relatively weak even today.[2]

In the future the interaction between prices and various functional forms of income may play a more important role. With growing inflationary expectations some forms of this interaction can contribute to the acceleration of a price rise.

Thus a continuous price rise induces one to re-examine the rates and book values of capital depreciation. Let us assume, for example, that the technical characteristics of the equipment during its life cycle remain constant and the rate of the price increase for the equipment is equal to the general price rise; it is not difficult to show that under such assumptions a businessman has to increase sooner or later the allocation to capital depreciation (a kind of expression of the accelerator relationships).[3] At the same time changes in

[1] A number of examples based on German Federal Republic data are presented in Schmölders' studies (see, for example, [12], [13]).

[2] Nevertheless, it may be significant that an increasing proportion of investment funds are now searching for inflationary hedges.

[3] This process can be further accelerated by any long-term increase in the relative prices of investment goods.

United States tax legislation have provided rather wide possibilities for raising allowable writeoffs up (see [21]).

Inflationary processes can contribute to an accelerated increase of interest rates – interest payments have to cover capital losses, resulting from depreciation of loan-money and, other things being equal, to increase the money income in accordance with the general price rise.[1]

Increases of capital depreciation, interest payments and other costs, as well as cumulative pressures, increased by target-return price-formation, exert influence upon the movement of wholesale and retail prices.

During recent years attention has been focused especially on the movement of prices of primary commodities. Describing the peculiar features of the 'commodity inflation' some authors have pointed to its discontinuity; they believe that 'commodity inflation' comes in the form of a one-stage discrete price rise, which is then followed by a slump in prices. There is no doubt that the specific character of many primary commodity markets and the influence of some institutional and political factors have caused from time to time intensive commodity booms and dramatic price rises. But there is another side of the problem. Recent price increases of fuels and other raw materials reflect a profound crisis in a longstanding inequitable division of labour between non-socialist countries. The new situation which is emerging in some primary commodity markets makes possible a more continuous and, under certain conditions, a more acute interaction of the inflation process in the industrialised countries, involving a rise in prices of some of their important raw materials.[2]

The accelerating rise in prices cannot leave workers indifferent. The unexpected and dramatic increase of the cost of living reinforced by their already difficult financial position, clearly demonstrate the socioeconomic class character of the inflation process. The persistent struggle for increases in wage rates becoming especially active at present is to all intents and purposes the defensive reaction of the working class warding off unceasing attacks against incomes fixed by wage bargains.[3]

Simultaneous econometric analysis of price and wage equations covering various subperiods seems to show that the elasticity of wages with respect to price expectations has increased during recent years. Some results of our

[1] The sum of net interest paid by United States non-financial corporations increased during the twenty-five postwar years by more than twenty times; during eight years (1965–1973) net interest cost per unit of gross product of non-financial corporations (when the product is calculated at constant prices) more than doubled.

[2] The very low industrial growth rates between 1974 and the first half of 1975 have exerted appreciable influence on commodity prices. But distinct from price movements following the commodity boom of 1950–1951 (from 1950 to 1970 the ratio of primary commodity prices to prices of manufactured goods exports had dropped more than one-third, it is doubtful whether the relative prices of primary commodities will decline rapidly during the next few decades.

[3] Baumol points out that: 'A voluntary abstention from wage-raise demands by one particular union will do little to relieve the overall inflationary pressure and will indeed put its members completely at the mercy of rising prices' ([2], p. 141).

calculations correspond with the conclusions to the question raised in [4], [6].

Some part in the development of the inflation process may be played by the cumulative interaction between uneven price increases and changes in the structure of aggregate demand. It is well-known that, with imperfect flexibility of the 'key' prices and a changing structure of aggregate demand, there can develop additional inflationary pressures (see [14]). On the other hand, an uneven and steep rise in prices exerts different effects on the demand for various commodity groups, making the movements more irregular and spasmodic and contributing to the rise of a specific demand for 'hedges'. These assumptions are consistent with some of the results of price dispersion analysis. An attempt has been made to compute wholesale price dispersion indexes based on United States data which cover more than 70 commodity groups. The coefficients of variation $\frac{\sigma}{I}$ and $\frac{\sigma}{I}$ (where σ is the standard deviation of the quarter-to-quarter rates of growth of prices and I is the wholesale price index), which since the recession of 1957–58 had experienced irregular fluctuations, displayed at the end of the 1960s the tendency to rise. Since the second quarter of 1972 a dramatic increase of price dispersion can be traced. I have calculated also the coefficients of variation of the quarter-to-quarter increases in the production of the 24 United States manufacturing and mining industries. These coefficients showed irregular fluctuations during the cyclical boom of the 1960s; drastic rises in values of this coefficient can be traced at the beginning of the 1970s. In this respect the swift industrial growth of the second half, 1972–73, had rather more in common with the boom of 1955–57 than, say, with the cyclical upswing of 1963–66. The subsequent sharp rise in prices of a fairly narrow commodity group (crude oil, agricultural raw materials and food) further promoted this trend.

The problem of accurately appraising the roles of all these various cumulative mechanisms in contemporary inflation is highly complicated. Obviously, such an appraisal demands a more profound theoretical and empirical analysis. But nevertheless the following hypothesis seems to be valid. Protracted inflation will gradually activate a number of cumulative mechanisms of price increase. As a consequence the inflationary process tends to gather momentum, worsening the factors unfavourable to economic performance and reducing the efficacy of centralised control of price movements.

A sudden rise in the inflation rate has intensified the redistribution of the national income, slowing down the growth of real wages, and in a number of cases leading to a fall. Further development of inflationary trends will lead to the deepening of social conflicts. The rising movement of the working class is tending to shake the very foundations of the capitalist society.

REFERENCES

[1] M. Allais, 'A Restatement of the Quantity Theory of Money', *American Economic Review* (December 1966).

[2] W. Baumol, *Welfare Economics and the Theory of the State*, (Cambridge (Mass.): Harvard University Press, 1965).

[3] P. Cagan, 'The Monetary Dynamics of Hyperinflation', in *Studies in the Quantity Theory of Money*, M. Friedman (ed.) (Chicago University Press, 1963).

[4] O. Eckstein and R. Brinner, *The Inflation Process in the United States.* A Study Prepared for the Use of the Joint Economic Committee. U.S. Congress, (Washington, Government Printing Office, 1972).

[5] *Frequency in Change in Wholesale Prices. A Study of Price Flexibility.* A Study Prepared for the Joint Economic Committee by the US Department of Labour, Bureau of Labour Statistics (Washington, 1959).

[6] R. Gordon. 'Inflation in Recession and Recovery', *Brookings Papers on Economic Activity* (1971) N 1.

[7] G. Haberler, 'Internal Factors Causing and Propagating Inflation' in *Inflation. Proceedings of a Conference Held by the I.E.A.* ed. by D. Hague (London, 1962).

[8] R. Lanzilotti, 'Competitive Price Leadership – a Critique of Price Leadership Models', *Review of Economics and Statistics* (February, 1957).

[9] E. Mueller, 'Consumer Reactions to Inflation', *Quarterly Journal of Economics* (May, 1959).

[10] E. Nevin, 'The Cost Structure of British Manufacturing', *Economic Journal* (December, 1963).

[11] F. Ripley and L. Segal, 'Price Determination in 395 Manufacturing Industries', *Review of Economics and Statistics* (August, 1973).

[12] G. Schmölders, *Psychologie des Geldes*, Reinbek bei Hamburg, (1966).

[13] G. Schmölders, *Der Umgang mit Geld in privaten Haushalt*, (Berlin, 1969).

[14] C. Schultze, 'Recent Inflation in the United States. Study Paper I in *Study of Employment, Growth and Price Levels* (Washington, 1959).

[15] G. Stigler, 'The Kinky Oligopoly Demand Curve and Rigid Prices'. *Journal of Political Economy* (October, 1947).

[16] G. Stigler and J. Kindahl, *The Behaviour of Industrial Prices*, The National Bureau of Economic Research (New York, 1970).

[17] P. Sweezy, 'Demand Under Conditions of Oligopoly'. *Journal of Political Economy* (August, 1939).

[18] S. Turnovsky, 'Empirical Evidence on the Formation of Price Expectations'. *Journal of the American Statistical Association* (December, 1970).

[19] F. Weston, 'Large Firms and Economic Performance', in *Impact of Large Firms on the US Economy* ed. by F. Weston, S. Ornstein (Lexington (Mass.), 1973).

[20] W. Yordon, Jr., 'Industrial Concentration and Price Flexibility in Inflation: Price Response Rates in Fourteen Industries, 1947–1958'. *Review of Economics and Statistics* (August, 1961).

[21] A. Young, 'Alternative Estimates of Corporate Depreciation and Profits'. Part II. *Survey of Current Business* (May, 1968).

Discussion of Paper by Revold Entov

Mr Kaser introduced the paper by Professor Entov. Among the many interpretations of the inflationary process put to the conference – monetarist, Keynesian, fiscalist, structuralist, sociological, and others – no-one would have expected a Leninist hypothesis, particularly one that was constructive, as opposed to destructive. Professor Entov had formulated such a theory, marshalling an impressive survey of relevant Western literature in its support. All too often, it must be said, Marxist economists from Eastern Europe neglected both the analytical tools of Western economics and the books and journals in which those instruments were applied. Professor Entov formulated his hypothesis in terms assimilable in the conference.

A brief exchange had begun earlier from a comment by Professor Stahl on Lenin's view of the destructive power of inflation. Mention might be made of the interpretation that the policy makers of Soviet 'War Communism' (1918–21) saw inflation as destroying the market. This relied on Marx's theory of alienation, in so far as the market veild the mode of production and hence facilitated reification and exploitation. The attack on the stability of money was one on market fetishism, which, once dispersed, enabled the proletariat to perceive its true class interests. This was the 'ancient view' of stable value and the market to which Professor Mussa had referred.

Mr Kaser wanted to stress that Professor Entov derived his interpretation from earlier work by Lenin. He gave no reference in this part of his paper, though it would doubtless be in part to Lenin's *Development of Capitalism in Russia.* The causes and effects of entrepreneurial concentration as perceived by Lenin were keenly debated by Russian Marxists at the time; by Tugan-Baranovsky and Struve on industrial concentration and by Chayanov on agricultural concentration. Professor Entov selected one that had been shared by recent Western economists and developed it himself.

Professor Entov's paper, like Professor Duesenberry's, placed importance on cost rigidities; but while Professor Duesenberry selected wages, Professor Entov took all cost movements, reflected as input prices of producers' goods, as stickier downwards in fluctuations, and the stickier the greater the imperfection of the market. Short-run price changes had tended to be more numerous in the past decade, as Professor Entov pointed out, and more poorly related to macromovements of cyclical activity in concentrated industries than in competitive ones.

This argument could easily be interpreted as requiring that the degree of oligopoly would have to increase to make prices stickier, and consequently to increase inflation beyond the limits normal at a previous, higher stage of competition. This would be aligned with the standard argument that decreasing competition made for a once-and-for-all increment in the price level, to which Professor Entov referred, noting the I.E.A.'s earlier conference on inflation. Professor Entov's point did not require any change in competitiveness, but only a sizeable share of oligopoly. This was because he attributed to existing monopolists a learning process which improved their ability to be rigid over price declines and to 'sound out' the scope for price increases – a process facilitated once inflation started and easier the quicker the price rise. Moreover, as Professor Entov added, price leadership had institutionally increased and it communicated rigidity to the less concentrated sectors of the economy. As he said, price leadership was more suited to price rises than price cuts, so that a vicious spiral affected this particular element in his argument.

Professor Entov reported a high positive correlation between the level of oligopoly in United States industries over the period 1952–71and the share of commodities showing considerable price rises (R - 0·66) and high negative correlation with the share of considerable price falls (R = −0·75). One might add that his industrial data related only to horizontal integrations. Both vertical integrations and conglomerates could well intensify the stickiness. Vertical integration might do so because intracorporation transfer prices were likely to be more rigid downward than market-formed transaction prices. Conglomerates might do so because intracorporation profit transfers could postpone price cuts or other defences to demand change. This latter would be consistent with such corporate policy as was described in Marris's *Managerial Capitalism*, and Professor Entov fortified his position by target-return pricing.

He introduced target returns in the further context of his cost-push analysis, better termed, perhaps, 'value-added push'. This had two additional constituents. First, there was upward pressure on depreciation charges as interest rates and replacement values rose. Second, there were wage pushes which, under other eyes, had been called 'collusive', where a concentrated industry monopsonised unionised labour. Professor Entov took a Marxist line, seeing wage push as a defensive class struggle. Wages, he added, were mobile with price rise expectations. He could have strengthened his theory by reference to the frequency of wage negotiations increasing under expectations eroding the money illusion.

He reiterated this frequency concept by reference to 'shocks' – abrupt consumer price changes – on the cost-push side. This correlation of demand variation with a degree of concentration (the price dispersion results) was part of his earlier argument on stickiness, but one enlarged by reference to the exogenous effects of the increasing power of large firms, and the state when military budgets were rising fast. All these were further cases of the 'upward ratchet' which was at the centre of Professor Entov's arguments. There was congruence to the mark-up margin generated by capital accumulation, to which Professor Malinvaud had referred in his discussion of the paper by Professor Genberg and Swoboda.

Mr Kaser ended by noting that Professor Entov's paper was titled 'Some Problems of Current Price Movements', in contrast to the originally announced designation 'Problems of Price Dynamics in Different Countries'. When invited to act as discussant, Mr Kaser had thought that these 'different countries' would include socialist countries and not be mainly restricted to the United States as an imperfect market. Had Professor Entov extended his cover, Mr Kaser would have wanted him to consider the international transmission mechanism and perhaps especially his own group of economies. Mr Kaser had prepared tables 5.1 and 5.2 in expectation of such coverage. But instead they complemented the paper by Professor Csikós-Nagy.[1] Mr Kaser

[1] Printed as Chapter 16, page 417 ff. Dr Entov's paper was discussed in the same session as that of Professor Csikós-Nagy. Reference may be made to the discussion of that paper, pages 431–44.

TABLE 5.1
RETAIL SALES AND PRICES IN COMECON
1960 = 100

	Index of Retail sales at current prices		*Volume index*		*Price index*		*Annual rate*[a]	
	Food	*Non-food*	*Food*	*Non-food*	*Food*	*Non-food*	*Food*	*Non-food*
Bulgaria[b]								
1970	226·7	235·3	188·7	227·3	120·1	103·5	1·8	0·3
1973	276·4	294·9	228·3	286·4	121·1	103·0	0·3	–0·1
Czechoslovakia								
1970	157·6	191·3	149·3	172·4	105·6	111·0	0·5	1·1
1973	179·2	230·0	170·1	208·6	105·3	110·3	–0·1	–0·2
German Democratic Republic								
1970	144·8	140·2	144·9	137·0	99·9	102·3	–0·0	0·2
1973	159·1	172·8	160·9	166·0	98·9	104·1	–0·3	0.6
Hungary								
1970	204·4	204·6	188·7	204·1	108·3	100·2	0·8	0·0
1973	259·7	260·3	217·0	242·9	119·7	107·2	3·4	2·3
Mongolia								
1970	216·5	152·1	212·8	135·1	101·7	112·6	0·2	1·2
1973	260·9	180·9	255·3	160·8	102·2	112·5	0·2	–0·0
Poland								
1970	191·8	206·1	163·9	185·2	117·0	111·9	1·6	1·1
1973	258·9	291·3	219·7	268·5	117·8	108·5	0·2	–1·0
Romania[a]								
1970	260·2	211·9	238·1	238·1	109·3	89·0	0·9	–1·1
1973	332·6	260·8	297·6	295·2	111·8	88·3	0·7	–0·3
USSR								
1970	201·5	192·8	192·3	204·1	104·8	94·5	0·5	–0·5
1973	236·6	236·0	225·0	253·1	105·2	93·2	0·1	–0·1

[a] 1960 to 1970 and 1970 to 1973 respectively

[b] Indices based on 1960 figures excluding private commerce, whereas 1970 and 1973 data include a very small volume of private commerce.

FOREIGN TRADE AND UNIT-VALUES IN COMECON

Indices 1960 = 100

	Current prices		*Constant prices*		*Unit-values*		*Annual rate*[a]	
	Imports	*Exports*	*Imports*	*Exports*	*Imports*	*Exports*	*Imports*	*Exports*
Bulgaria								
1970	350·7	289·5	371·4	300·5	94·4	96·3	–0·6	–0·4
1973	478·7	428·6	490·7	426·9	97·5	100·4	1·0	1·4
1974	621·3	561·3	532·6	516·1	116·7	108·8	19·7	8·4
Czechoslovakia								
1970	203·5	196·6	202·8	195·7	100·3	100·5	0·0	0·0
1973	273·9	254·3	245·4	236·6	111·6	107·5	3·6	2·3
German Democratic Republic								
1970	220·9	207·5	230·2	215·8	96·0	96·2	–0·4	–0·4
1972	247·9	258·1	252·7	266·4	98·1	96·9	0·7	0·2
Hungary								
1970	257	265	270	301	95	102	–0·5	0·2
1972	298	347	261	335	99	104	1·3	0·6
Poland								
1970	241·3	267·6	245·7	266·2	98·2	100·5	–0·2	0·0
1973	436·5	402·8	418·8	362·6	104·3	111·1	2·1	3·4
1974	582·3	521·0	478·7	400·5	121·6	130·1	16·6	17·1
USSR								
1970	208·4	230·1	180·6	244·2	115·4	94·2	1·5	–0·6
1973	306·9	315·6	257·2	296·4	119·3	106·5	1·1	4·2
1974	371·8	414·2	288·1	362·4	129·1	129·1	8·2	7·3

[a] 1960 to 1970, 1970 to 1973, (1972 for German Democratic Republic and Hungary) and 1973 to 1974 respectively

Source: Bulgaria: *Statisticheski izvestiya*, No. 1, 1964, pages 44–5, No. 2 1975, page 35; Czechoslovakia: *Statistická ročenka ČSSR 1974*, Prague 1974, pages 426–7; German Democratic Republic: *Statistisches Jahrbuch der DDR 1974*, Berlin 1974 pages 281–2; Hungary: *Külkereskedelmi statisztikai évkönyv 1972*, Budapest, 1973, page 10; Poland: *Maly rocznik statystyczny 1975*, Warsaw, 1975, page 184; USSR: *Vneshnyaya torgovlya SSSR za 1974 god*, Moscow, 1975, pages 12 and 19 and *Vneshnyaya torgovlya SSSR* 1918–1, 66, Moscow, 1967, page 63.

NOTE: World unit-value index 1960 = 100; Imports 1970 – 111; 1973 – 115, 1974 – 221; exports 1970 – 114; 1973 – 159, 1974 – 224 (*UN Monthly Bulletin of Statistics*, July 1975 pages xx–xxii).

drew attention to the paradox that rates of domestic inflation in socialist countries (table 5.1) were higher when their foreign trade unit value increments (table 5.2) were low (1960–70) and lower when these unit values were rising (1970–73). Of course, this was as a consequence of world inflation on that part of trade conducted outside the more constant prices of Comecon. The fact that trade within Comecon was, from 1975, being conducted on prices based on world levels (a three-year average being used to lag the impact of inflation) meant that the transmission of world pricing was now on the point of having a significant effect on Comecon domestic economies. As Professor Csikós-Nagy's discussion on subsidisation (as equivalent to exchange revaluation) pointed out, the difficulty came only when the terms of trade changed radically.

Table 5.2 showed some of those changes, when net importers of raw materials were adversely affected by the late-1973 oil and materials price explosion. In Hungary in 1973, import prices with non-socialist states rose 40 per cent while export prices gained only 25 per cent. The swing then went the other way. Thus in Czechoslovakia in 1974, export prices rose 32 per cent with non-socialist states, and accounted for almost 90 per cent of the increase in exports; import prices rose 25 per cent and accounted for over 80 per cent of the rise in imports.[1] If there were a permanent shift in the terms of trade, a realignment of domestic prices would be required, at least for the more trade-dependent economies. This topic appeared to be the link between the two papers by Professors Csikós-Nagy and Entov.

[1] K. Kudlák, *Rude Pravo*, 25.2.75

Part 2

International Aspects of Inflation

6 International Aspects of Inflation

J Marcus Fleming*

INTERNATIONAL MONETARY FUND
WASHINGTON, D.C.

* To the very great regret not only of all participants but also of all his many friends Marcus Fleming died very shortly after the Conference. We believe this represents his last published contribution to economics.

I. INTRODUCTION

My object in this paper is to indicate some of the ways in which inflation in general and contemporary world inflation in particular are influenced by the fact that the world is divided into separate political units.

But first, I should perhaps say a word about inflation, or rising prices in a closed economy (such as the world). I take the commonplace view of this as being attributable to an interweaving of demand-pull and cost-push factors. More precisely, but still very crudely, I think of output as determined by money flows and supply prices, of the rate of price inflation as determined proximately, in the main, by the inflation of costs, and of the latter as determined in part by the level of employment and output in relation to capacity and in part by past rates of inflation. The short-term Phillips-curve I take to be such that inflation becomes increasingly responsive to output increases, as employment and output approach their physical limits; moreover, the response of inflation to accelerations of past inflation also increases the longer inflation persists and the higher its rate. This description of the inflationary mechanism applies strictly only to imperfectly competitive sectors of the economy. In some sectors, particularly agricultural, conditions are more competitive and prices respond promptly to changes in money demand and to exogenous changes in supply. A characteristic pattern of inflation is one in which rising money flows and industrial output drive up competitive primary product prices, and these in turn react on wages, on industrial and commercial price margins, and on inventory investment.

I have spoken in terms of money flows. But of course – and here again my views are very banal – I regard money flows as determined after a time lag by monetary policies, budgetary policies, and the various Keynesian propensities and incentives, including price inflation itself on the incentive to invest.

The course of world inflation over the last quarter century does not fit too badly into this schematism. From 1948 to 1959, though prices in industrial countries rose every year, there was no perceptible upward trend in the rate of inflation, which was generally around $2\frac{1}{2}$ per cent per annum (see table 6.1 and figure 6.1). There was, however, a short period from 1950 to 1951 when

G.N.P. deflators rose almost as fast as they have been rising recently. This followed, with a short time lag, an expansion in output, the strongest in the postwar period, which took place in 1950 before and after the outbreak of the Korean War and which was associated with a very sharp rise in primary product prices and a deterioration in the terms of trade of most industrial countries. Later in the 1950s, the rapid but short-lived expansion of 1954–55

TABLE 6.1
Industrial Countries[1] – Percentage Changes from Previous Year

	Consumer prices[2]	*GNP deflator*[3]	*Real GNP*[3]	*Nominal GNP*[3]	*Money*[4]
1949	–0·2	2·0	3·3	5·3	
1950	1·7	1·6	8·9	10·7	5·4
1951	8·9	8·4	7·3	16·2	7·4
1952	3·7	4·0	3·5	7·6	7·5
1953	1·0	1·2	4·7	6·0	4·8
1954	1·3	1·6	0·8	2·4	4·3
1955	0·5	1·8	7·3	9·2	5·4
1956	2·2	3·9	3·2	7·2	4·4
1957	2·8	3·7	2·7	6·5	3·3
1958	3·4	3·2	0·4	3·6	4·5
1959	1·3	1·9	5·9	7·9	6·5
1960	2·0	2·0	4·3	6·4	5·3
1961	2·0	2·3	3·8	6·2	6·4
1962	2·7	2·4	5·7	8·3	6·7
1963	2·8	2·6	4·6	7·3	7·5
1964	2·5	2·7	6·2	9·0	7·9
1965	3·0	3·0	5·4	8·6	7·2
1966	3·4	3·4	5·8	9·4	6·1
1967	3·0	3·2	3·6	6·9	7·2
1968	3·9	3·7	5·7	9·6	9·1
1969	4·9	4·8	4·7	9·7	7·5
1970	5·6	5·9	2·6	8·7	7·7
1971	5·1	5·4	3·7	9·4	10·7
1972	4·5	4·8	5·7	10·7	12·2
1973	7·6	7·0	6·2	13·9	10·2
1974	12·5	11·7	–0·2	11·4	7·9

[1] United States, United Kingdom, Austria, Belgium, Denmark, France, Germany, Italy, Netherlands, Norway, Sweden, Switzerland, Canada and Japan.

[2] Individual country changes in the annual average index weighted by 1970 G.D.P. in dollars.

[3] Individual country changes weighted by preceding year's G.N.P. in dollars.

[4] Individual country changes weighted by 1970 G.D.P. in dollars. Changes in averages of beginning and end year stocks. Money is defined as currency plus demand deposits.

Source: International Monetary Fund, Research Department calculations based on I.F.S. data.

was followed by a few years of relatively rapid price increases, not, however, exceeding 4 per cent per annum. From 1959 to 1968 there took place a gradual but rather steady acceleration in the pace of inflation in industrial countries, from 2 per cent to almost 4 per cent, reflecting perhaps a gradually increasing aggressiveness of labour under conditions of generally higher employment and capacity utilisation. Then, the resumption, from 1967 to 1969, of a rate of output growth which had been maintained without untoward consequences earlier in the 1960s, but which was now accompanied

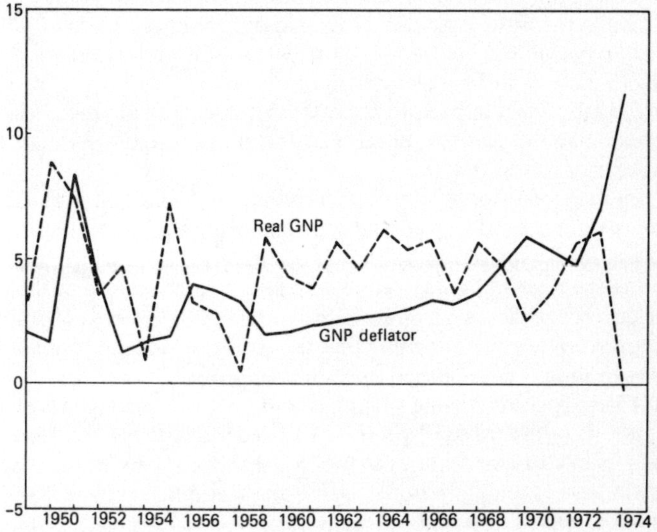

Fig. 6.1 G.N.P. deflators and real G.N.P. of industrial countries – percentage changes from previous year

by an increase in primary product prices, led, from 1968 to 1970, to an acceleration of general price inflation to approximately 6 per cent per annum. In the latter stages of this inflation restrictive financial policies brought about a slowing down of growth. This episode, a low key rehearsal of our current ordeal, gave currency to the term 'stagflation', signifying a coincidence of price inflation and output recession, though a very similar development had occurred in 1956–58.

The present inflation, beginning in 1972 and still in progress, has been of exceptional length and severity. From 1972 to 1974 G.N.P. deflators in industrial countries rose by almost 20 per cent and are expected to rise another 10 per cent in 1975. Outside the industrial countries, prices have been rising even faster. There is nothing obscure about the genesis of this inflation. Its seeds lay in the monetary and fiscal expansion which took place from 1970 to 1972. This led to a strong expansion of industrial output from 1971 to 1973, accompanied and followed by very rapid increases in primary product prices from 1971 to 1974, which in turn led to a steep increase in general prices from 1972. As we know, the subsequent stages of the inflation, from 1973 onwards, have accompanied the most severe recession in the post-war period, marked by declining output and rapidly rising unemployment. This 'stagflation' is an indication that cost-push influences have taken over. If we ask why these influences have been so strong on this occasion and why inflation has taken on a totally new dimension, the main answer is probably to be found in the quite exceptional escalation of primary product prices which accompanied the boom of 1971 to 1973, followed by the oil price increase effective in 1974. The escalation of primary product prices, in turn, was itself attributable, in part, to the rather strong and widespread character of that boom, and in part to a number of fortuitous supply shortages, notably in the sphere of foodstuffs.

The rise in primary product prices, including oil,[1] amounting to almost 155 per cent in terms of United States dollars, from the fourth quarter of 1971 to the fourth quarter of 1974 – as against a maximum increase of 50 per cent during the Korean boom – entailed a severe deterioration in the terms of trade of the industrial sector, and a radical arrest in the growth of real wages in many countries. It is not surprising that the workers' attempt to restore real wage growth should have pushed up industrial prices.

What I have been discussing so far has to do with inflation in its *global* aspects, not its *international* aspects, as I have defined them. With the exception of one or two features to which I shall recur, the whole development could have taken place just as well if the world had constituted a single political unit. What I now wish to examine are the various ways in which the division of the world into sovereign states affects the inflationary process. These include the effects of the national exercise of demand management, the existence of reserve currencies, the existence of xenocurrency banking, the variability of national exchange rates, the existence of international cartels, and the existence of national controls over prices and incomes.

II. NATIONAL EXERCISE OF DEMAND MANAGEMENT

The demand management function in our world is exercised by national monetary and budgetary authorities. If these authorities administered a set of national economies that were hermetically sealed off from each other with respect both to trade and to capital flows, there is no reason to assume that their policies would on average be more or less expansionary than those of a hypothetical world authority. In open economies with fixed exchange rates

[1] The increase in the price of primary commodities excluding oil amounted to over 100 per cent.

and free trade, national authorities have limited power to influence the degree of inflation and the level of activity within their borders. They must accept, broadly speaking, the degree of inflation that prevails in the world as a whole, adjusted to allow for differences among countries in relative productivity growth in tradeables and non-tradeables output and for changes in the terms of trade. Each country has, however, a certain ability to diverge at least temporarily from the rate of world inflation, as thus adjusted, to the extent that it is able and willing to use up or to accumulate reserves, or to the extent that it can attract or repel capital. And by exercising this leeway in the direction of demand expansion or contraction, countries collectively will increase or reduce the rate of world inflation.

So far as reserves are concerned, there is a well-known asymmetry between deficit and surplus countries. In theory, it is technically possible for surplus countries to accumulate reserves indefinitely and offset their expansionary effects on money stocks and flows, whereas the physical limit on the running down of reserves may force deficit countries into contraction so long as fixity of exchange rates is regarded as overriding. This is the famous 'balance of payments discipline' for which those who fear inflation more than unemployment praise the fixed rate system in general and the gold standard in particular. Prima facie, this would seem to imply that, given fixed exchange rates, the division of the demand management function among national units would tend to reduce world inflation. While in most historical circumstances this has probably been the case, the argument is not watertight. For one thing, much depends on the level of world reserves and on the possibility of covering balance of payments deficits by borrowing. Under modern conditions, where the mobility of capital is very high, expansion of domestic expenditure will often lead, at least in the short run, to an inflow rather than to an outflow of reserves. This is quite likely to happen if the expansion is generated by an increase in the propensity to consume or in the incentive to invest or by an increase in the budget deficit. In these circumstances, if the supply of money is not too elastic, interest may rise sufficiently to attract more capital from abroad than is required to offset the deterioration in the current account. Even if the enhanced level of activity leads to a rate of price inflation markedly higher than prevails abroad, the overall balance of payments may continue favourable for a surprisingly long time, partly because the deterioration in the trade balance takes time to develop, and partly because the inflation itself further enhances the interest rate and the marginal incentive to invest, and sucks in investible funds from abroad.

If each country could tap an unlimited supply of foreign capital at the world interest rate, so that it had no reserve constraint at all, in the strict sense, would anything remain of balance of payments discipline? That discipline would certainly remain so far as monetary policy is concerned. Indeed, in the circumstances assumed, expansionary action would be impossible and contractionary action ineffective. But would fiscal policy be less expansionary (more contractionary) in an open economy than in a closed one?

The answer would seem to depend on whether the situation in the average country is one in which the government is acting to stimulate or to restrain demand. Government expenditure in an open economy differs from that in a closed economy in that some proportion of it, at the margin, has to be financed by an increased inflow, or reduced outflow, of capital. The incentive to expand government expenditure will therefore be less in an open than in a closed economy if the return on publicly financed investment is lower, or the return on public saving higher, than would correspond to the world interest rate; in the opposite case, the incentive to spend will be higher in an open than in a closed economy. In other words, governments will tend to carry neither expansionary nor contractionary budgetary policies as far in an open as in a closed economy. However, the total effect on demand depends not only on governments' incentive, but also their ability, to control expenditure. In a world of open economies, if the main deficit countries are not subject to reserve constraints while surplus countries may be forced to permit greater demand expansion than they desire, demand in the world as a whole may be higher than would be the case in closed economies, or than would be desirable.

III. FOREIGN EXCHANGE RESERVES AND LIABILITY FINANCING[1]

As we have seen, international mobility of private capital and the ability of monetary authorities to 'borrow' reserves from the private market and from each other blunts the 'discipline' exercised by the fixed exchange rate system over expansionary national policies. The use of the currencies of certain countries in the reserves of other countries, particularly in the centralised form in which we have known it throughout the postwar period in which a single country, the United States, was directly and indirectly the ultimate reserve centre for the rest of the world, can relax that discipline to the vanishing point, so far as the ultimate reserve centre itself is concerned. This was particularly true of the United States after the virtual suspension of convertibility in 1968, but even before that it could count on the major part of any payments deficits being financed automatically by the accumulation of reserve liabilities. In such a situation the United States was largely free to pursue not only an independent fiscal policy, but also an independent monetary policy.

This argument would seem to lead straight into the familiar proposition that the United States took advantage of this necessity for balance of payments discipline to pursue unduly expansionary policies, thus creating an enormous balance of payments deficit which, by expanding the reserves of other countries and forcing an expansion of money, exported and almost imposed inflation on the outside world. This comfortable European myth is, however, seriously misleading in a number of respects.

[1]On the questions arising in this section, see also Heller, 'International Reserves and World-Wide Inflation', DM/75/63.

(1) Not only has the rate of expansion of M_1 throughout the postwar period been considerably lower and the level of unemployment considerably higher in the United States than in other industrial countries, but the rate of price inflation also, except for a period from 1967 to 1969, has been substantially lower in the United States than in other industrial countries. The enormous United States payments deficit which appeared in calendar 1970, 1971, and 1972, so far as it occurred in the current account, was evidence of a decline in the demand for United States products relative to those of other countries. To the much more important extent to which it occurred in the capital account, it had much more to do with the United States recession of 1969 and 1970, and the consequential decline in interest rates and the demand for money there, than with any excessive expansion in the money supply. The biggest factor of all, of course, was the movement of funds out of the dollar into other currencies in anticipation of dollar devaluation.

(2) The enormous increase in the reserves of industrial countries other than the United States which took place from end-1969 to end-1972 was undoubtedly partly responsible for the expansion in money supply in these countries over the same period (see figure 6.2). But the very fact that the latter was proportionately so much smaller than the former (22 per cent per annum as against 35 per cent) shows that these countries had considerable ability to offset the effects of the influx of central bank reserves on commercial bank reserves and hence on money supply. This ability to offset by means of open market sales, government market borrowing, raising of reserve

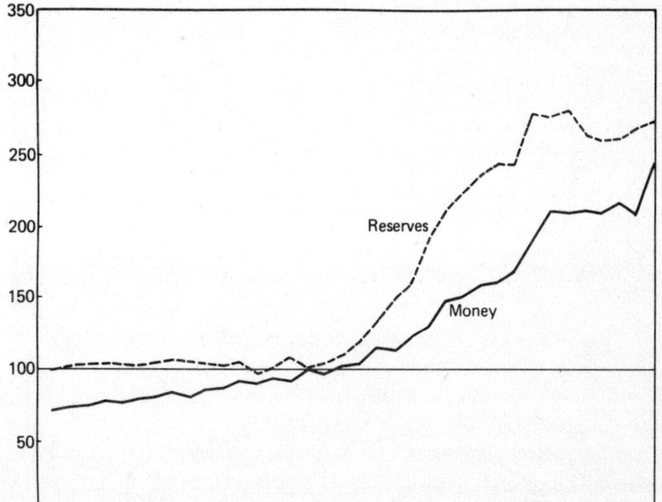

Fig. 6.2 Reserves and money (M_1) of industrial countries except the United States – Index of United States dollar stocks

requirements, etc., is greater in some countries than in others. But only in countries like Germany that were particularly the focus of inflows, and these only in the later stages of the influx, could it be said to have been nearly impossible to maintain control over the money supply.

(3) Finally, the theory that international reserve arrangements were responsible for the present inflation rests primarily on a monetarist view as to the genesis of such inflation. We must all agree that monetary expansion is a necessary condition for any sizeable increase in monetary demand. But is it typically the initiating cause? Unfortunately we lack 'full employment' budgetary data that might enable us to indicate, for industrial countries as a whole, the aggregate effect of changes in budgetary policy, whereas we do have data on monetary expansion. These data are cited by monetarists to show that variations in money expansion tend to lead variations in real G.N.P. growth by one year and variations in price inflation by two years. Figures 6.3

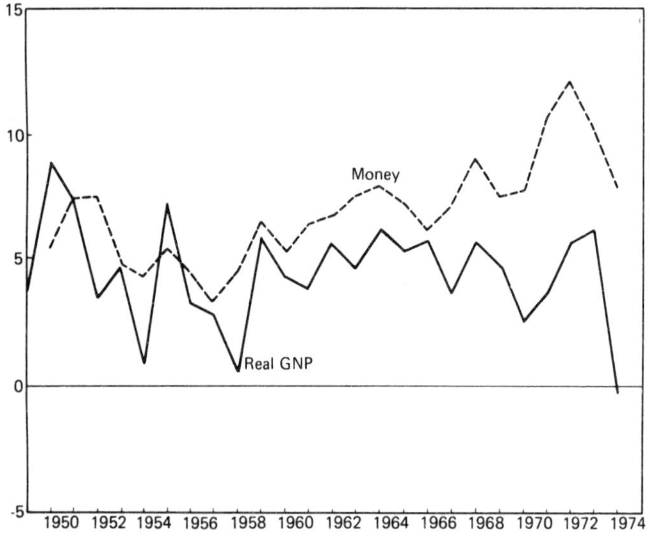

Fig. 6.3 Real G.N.P. and money of industrial countries – percentage changes from previous year

and 6.4 would seem to indicate that these relationships did indeed manifest themselves in the industrial countries as a group from about 1963–64 onwards, but not before. From 1949–50 to 1956–57 there appears to have been a more or less synchronised relationship between money, output, and price, while from 1956–57 to 1963–64 money expansion leads output expansion by one year, but neither appears to exercise any influence on price inflation.

It is interesting to note (see Figure 6.4) that from 1956–57 onwards to the present a synchronised but inverse relationship appears to have prevailed between price inflation and money growth, showing presumably that monetary policy is itself a function of current inflation, and it may well be that the two-year lead of money expansion over inflation, which begins about the same time, is effect as well as cause of a four-year cycle in output and prices.

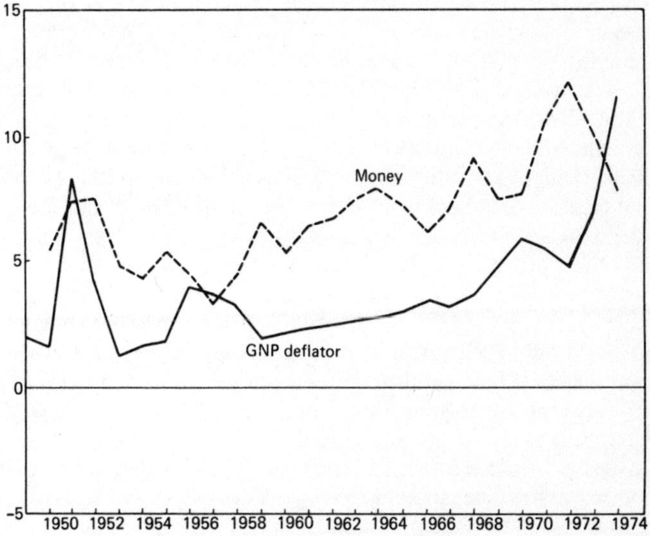

Fig. 6.4 G.N.P. deflators and money of industrial countries – percentage changes from previous year

I have wandered somewhat far afield in considering the effects of liability financing by the reserve centre on expansionary policies. If such liability financing had not been open to the United States, it would almost certainly have devalued the dollar in 1970 rather than abandon its recovery policies. However, if we stick to our provisional assumption that exchange rates are fixed,[1] the United States like any other deficit country would have had to adopt a contractionary monetary policy in 1970, thus accentuating its recession but helping to cool down the expansion in the surplus countries. In this sense I would agree with Professor Triffin and others that the exchange standard reserve system bears some responsibility for accentuating the monetary expansion of those years.

[1] See p. 156 above.

IV. XENOCURRENCY MARKETS

The division of responsibility for monetary policy in the world has the further consequence that certain sectors of world banking – the so-called Euro-currency or xenocurrency markets – escape the control of any of the national monetary authorities. The characteristics of Eurobanks are that they borrow and lend in currencies other than those of the host country, that they are competitive, and that they deal in small margins and large amounts.

The host countries are loath to regulate them because most of their business is with foreigners, much of it with transnational enterprises, and is thought liable, if regulated too severely, to migrate to another centre. Besides, national governments do not feel that the foreign currency liabilities of banks on their soil constitute part of *their* money supply, threatening *them* with excess demand and price inflation and therefore requiring to be subjected to reserve requirements and other controls. And they may be largely right. The additional transactions these liabilities facilitate may occur, and the domestic money deposits for which they are substitutes might have been held, in countries other than those in which the xenobanks are established.

Since they are generally not subjected to reserve requirements and deal in large amounts, the xenobanks can afford to operate on very low margins, and the volume of liquid claims held in xenocurrencies has expanded very much faster than the more conventional forms of money or quasi-money in the world. For example, over the period, from end-1969 to end-1972, during which M_1 rose fastest, world money stocks rose from \$524 billion to \$784 billion, or some 14 per cent per annum. Over the same period, the external foreign currency liabilities of banks in eight European countries rose from \$56·4 billion to \$131·9 billion, or almost 33 per cent per annum.

It may be questioned whether xenocurrency deposits are, strictly speaking, money. But they are certainly substitutable for liquid balances held in domestic currency and, since xenobanks hold no base-money, their existence substantially increases the superstructure of liquid assets that can be erected on a given volume of base-money. So that the accumulation of xenocurrency balances has probably increased to a significant extent the amount of private liquidity in the world. This supplement to liquidity growth was greatest when world money was itself expanding fastest. In 1974 when monetary expansion subsided to a more normal level the expansion of the Eurodollar market was also checked, largely because restraints on the export of United States banking funds were removed and partly because of the presumed weakness of some Eurobanks. However, by that time, as we have seen, demand inflation had receded and cost-push had taken over as the main engine of inflation.

The xenocurrency market plays a role, not only in the expansion of private liquidity, but also in the growth of world reserves. World currency reserves tend to rise, under fixed exchange rates and even to some extent under managed floating, whenever private individuals or monetary authorities transfer balances from the United States to other countries which, in their turn, acquire dollar reserves to prevent their exchange rates from rising. The xenocurrency markets foster this kind of switch in two different ways. First of all they attract deposits in dollars which would otherwise have been held in the United States, and then lend the dollars to other countries, both industrial and less developed. Secondly, they offer facilities for holding balances in the strong currencies of countries, such as Germany, which do not welcome the direct holding of official balances in their own banks or money markets. In both of these ways they foster an expansion of reserves as well as a geographical diversification, and to some extent a currency diversification, of reserves. The amount of reserve creation resulting from reserve diversification is thought to have amounted to over $11 billion both in 1972 and 1973.

Though the expansion of the xenocurrency market slackened off in 1974 to something like 14 per cent in Europe and 19 per cent in the world as a whole, its role in promoting reserve diversification has been particularly marked since the oil price increase. OPEC countries have been somewhat shy of holding too large a proportion of their reserve accumulations in the United States and have probably put over $20 billion-worth of funds into the Euro-markets: on the other hand, many countries, including some important industrial countries, apprehensive about their oil deficits, have borrowed from the market either directly or through public enterprises. The resultant expansion in world reserves has been criticised as perpetuating the inflationary expansion of reserves and base money which in earlier years resulted primarily from the United States deficit. However, it has undoubtedly played a very constructive role in preventing the reserve stringency which would otherwise have resulted from the accumulation and – at least temporarily – sterilisation of reserves in the vast 'reserve sink' constituted by the OPEC countries.

V. EXCHANGE RATE VARIABILITY

The most important characteristic of the international monetary system differentiating it from a world monetary system is of course the existence of separate currencies, the relative values of which are liable to vary, and indeed, since the recent demise of the par value system, have varied quite a lot. In what way does the variability of exchange rates affect the inflationary process and problems?

In principle, variability of exchange rates can take the form of substantial par value changes at longish intervals, of frequent small step changes, or of continuous changes achieved through more or less managed floating. In practice, given the high mobility of capital under modern conditions, floating tends more and more to become the only form of exchange rate variability that is able to cope with the massive capital flows engendered by discrepant rates of inflation, discrepant interest rate policies, and the speculation associated with exchange variability itself.

What, then, are the effects on inflation of exchange rate variability of the type that now prevails, namely, floating subject to a greater or lesser degree of exchange market intervention and other forms of management? We shall assume, as appears to be the case, that exchange management results in a type of behaviour intermediate between that characteristic of a par value system and completely free floating.

Effects on inflation may be considered under three heads: (1) effects on real demand, (2) effects on real costs, and (3) effects on the relationship between inflation and real demand.

(1) EFFECTS ON AGGREGATE DEMAND IN REAL TERMS

The effect of exchange rate variability on real demand depends primarily on the extent to which it weakens the constraints on demand management which the balance of payments would exercise under fixed rates, but also on the extent to which it substitutes other constraints, and on how it affects demand variations arising spontaneously from within the private economy.

We recall that balance of payments constraints on demand policy, though generally thought of as imposing a discipline and forcing governments to put up with lower levels of demand than they would like, sometimes, in the case of surplus countries that have exhausted the possibilities of offsetting, force them to permit higher levels of demand than they would like.

Now, in both would-be expansionary countries and would-be contractionary ones, given the spontaneous tendencies of the private economy, the option of allowing the exchange rate to vary should make it possible to get closer to officially desired demand levels. In the case of countries which have to tolerate undesirably low demand because reserves are threatening to run out or because foreign indebtedness is increasing or because rising costs are threatening to make the country increasingly uncompetitive, the option of exchange depreciation offers a possibility of expanding the level of demand while at the same time checking the outflow of reserves, reducing borrowing from abroad, and checking the decline in competitiveness. On the other hand, the option to allow the exchange rate to depreciate cannot be exercised without considerable cost to the countries in question, in the form of a stimulus to inflation over and above that resulting from the demand and output effects of any improvement in the current balance of payments. This stimulus would come from a rise in the cost of imports or marking up of the prices of importables and exportables, a consequential increase in the cost of living, and, through the desire to maintain real and relative incomes, a rise in wages and prices generally. This, as we have seen in the last years in countries such as Italy and the United Kingdom and, for a time, Japan, may constitute a serious deterrent to the free use of the exchange rate instrument. Of course, deficit countries are not *obliged* to allow the exchange rate to depreciate. Under managed floating they are free to employ the same techniques to defend the exchange rate as they would employ under a fixed rate system.

In the case of countries that under fixed rates would have to endure undesirably high demand levels because of the technical difficulties in offsetting the effect of reserve increases on base money and the money supply, or because they would otherwise have to provide increasing quantities of real resources in exchange for inadequately remunerated claims on the outside world, floating effectively facilitates a contraction of demand by putting a stop to the influx of reserves and, after a lag, promises a curtailment of demand pressures arising from the foreign sector. Appreciation of the currency will evoke equilibrating speculation, and the mere fact that the currency is capable of falling as well as rising may discourage any net capital inflows. The incentive to curtail demand in such a way as to raise the rate will be enhanced by the price effects. The fall in the price of imports and other tradeables will help not only to restrict demand but also to damp down cost-push inflation. A country whose currency is tending to appreciate is, of course, free to limit the appreciation by purchasing foreign exchange or by relying rather on budgetary than on monetary contraction. The principal reason for doing this, apart from a desire to prevent speculative overshooting in the short run, would probably be concern for the situation in particular foreign trade industries.

Since, as we have seen, the price effects of depreciation are adverse, those of appreciation favourable, these price effects systematically discourage demand expansion, which leads to depreciation, and encourage demand restraint, which leads to appreciation. In this sense exchange rate flexibility imposes its own built-in constraint on expansionary policies, at least during periods when inflation is a problem.

The main effect of the option to vary the rate of exchange, however, is to enable governments to get closer to their demand targets. This motivation was very clear in 1973. Whether the net effect is on balance expansionary or the reverse will depend on the international payments and liquidity situation, in other words, whether at fixed rates deficit countries would be suffering more from imported underemployment than surplus countries from imported overheating, or the reverse. In most circumstances the adoption of floating rates would probably release a net tendency towards expansion and hence inflation. But in the circumstances in which generalised floating took hold in 1971 and 1973 there is little doubt that the effect was to encourage or facilitate contraction. Thanks to the existence of a structural dollar deficit, the fixed rate system in 1971 and 1972 was definitely generating more expansion than countries desired. The fact that cyclical expansion had got out of control meant that most countries wanted to curtail demand; therefore, in 1973, the countries whose currencies tended to appreciate allowed them to do so while the countries whose currencies tended to decline mostly intervened with the aim of limiting that decline. The effect was to limit the expansion of reserves and money. It is significant that the growth in the money supply of industrial countries reached its maximum in 1972, a year of mostly fixed rates, and declined substantially in 1973 and sharply in 1974.

While exchange variability gives governments, within limits, an extra instrument for controlling demand pressures that are transmitted internationally, it might be argued that if the rate is allowed to vary with any degree of freedom this will make it more difficult for governments to cope with expansionary demand pressures arising from the private economy at home. If, as used to be assumed, an increase in the propensity to consume or in the incentive to invest, leading to an increase in domestic absorption, tends, under floating rates, to depress the foreign exchange value of the currency, this depreciation will, after a short time lag, tend to prevent or reduce the deterioration in the current balance that would otherwise have taken place. The expansionary influence will then be reflected back on the home economy, making it more difficult for the authorities to contain excess demand. I have argued elsewhere,[1] however, that under modern conditions of high capital mobility, and given a reasonably inelastic supply of money, the unfavourable effect exercised by these expansionary influences on the current balance of payments may well be offset, or more than offset, by their favourable effect on the capital account, so that the currency of a country in which such influences arise is as likely to appreciate as to depreciate. In these circumstances, expansionary influences arising in one particular country are as likely to be dissipated over the face of the earth – in the form of direct income stimulus – under a floating as under a fixed rate system. Only if the expansionary tendencies in the domestic economy are allowed to push up domestic costs and prices relative to those in other countries does it become inevitable that the currency will sooner or later depreciate, thus reinforcing inflation at home. Some empirical work done in the Fund by Duncan Ripley and others leads to results not inconsistent with this impressionistic analysis. First of all, we find that a relatively strong cyclical position in a country, though associated with a deterioration in its current account, is not associated with any particular tendency in its overall balance of payments: which means that under floating rates there is no systematic tendency for a strong cyclical position to be associated with depreciation. Moreover, examination of the year-to-year percentage growth of real G.N.P. shows no increase in dispersion across countries in 1972–73 and 1973–74, as one might expect, if floating had a tendency to prevent the diffusion of demand pressures (see table 6.2). Indeed, the dispersion of cyclical positions seems to have been particularly low in calendar 1973, though it was restored to a more normal level in 1974 (table 6.3). There does, however, appear to be some increase in the dispersion of percentage growth rates of money supply and of prices in 1973–74, which is, I think, what one would expect under floating rates. In this connection it is interesting to note that over the two-year period from the first quarter of 1973 to the first quarter of 1975 exchange rates have moved broadly in parallel with the movement in relative national price levels for manufactured goods.

[1] In 'International Monetary Reform and the Stabilisation Problem', a paper included in *International Aspects of Stabilization Policies* ed. Ando, Herring, and Marston, Conference Series No. 12, The Federal Reserve Bank of Boston and The International Seminar in Public Economics.

TABLE 6.2
Standard Deviations of the Individual Industrial Countries Percentage Changes from Previous Year

TABLE 6.3
Standard Deviation of the Individual Industrial Countries Percentage Differences Between Actual and Trend Industrial Production

	G.N.P. deflators	*Real G.N.P.*	*Nominal G.N.P.*	*Money*[1]	Table 6.3: Actual and Trend Industrial Production
1951	6·4	3·3	7·4	7·5	3·9
1952	4·3	3·1	4·2	4·2	2·3
1953	2·3	1·6	3·0	4·7	3·1
1954	1·6	2·8	3·6	6·2	2·6
1955	1·4	3·2	2·9	5·1	3·6
1956	1·5	2·2	2·3	4·8	2·1
1957	1·4	2·1	2·7	4·2	2·4
1958	3·2	2·1	3·7	4·3	3·6
1959	2·1	2·1	2·4	5·3	1·9
1960	2·7	2·9	5·4	4·8	2·6
1961	2·3	3·2	5·1	5·1	3·9
1962	1·6	1·7	2·3	6·0	2·6
1963	1·9	2·0	3·1	7·3	2·5
1964	1·7	2·4	3·1	2·3	1·7
1965	1·5	1·1	1·6	4·4	3·1
1966	1·4	2·2	2·2	4·2	3·1
1967	1·1	3·1	3·6	3·7	3·9
1968	1·1	2·6	2·9	4·4	3·3
1969	1·2	2·5	2·9	7·3	2·3
1970	1·8	2·6	2·9	5·8	3·5
1971	1·7	1·7	1·8	6·6	2·4
1972	1·7	1·6	2·2	5·6	2·2
1973	1·8	1·7	3·3	5·7	1·3
1974	4·2	2·5	4·1	7·2	3·2

[1] End year stocks

Source: International Monetary Fund, Research Department calculations based on I.F.S. data.

My conclusions as regards the effects of exchange rate variability on real demand and output over the past two years would be that it has probably made very little difference to the United States; that in countries, such as the United Kingdom and Italy, where exchange rates have declined, it probably facilitated for a time the maintenance of demand through the avoidance of exchange crises, though later official demand management reacted negatively to the inflationary price effects of depreciation; but that in most of the 'snake' countries it has assisted, despite the momentum of a surprisingly strong current account, in the process of curtailing demand and output. If anything, the net effect on the level of real demand in the world as a whole may have been contractionary.

(2) INCREASED REAL COSTS

The exchange rate instability associated with floating rates may be expected to give rise to increased real costs in international transactions, and also to increased instability of employment and uncertainty of investment in tradeable goods production. Day-to-day and week-to-week instability of exchange rates has been somewhat greater than might have been expected from experience with the Canadian dollar. For example, in the third quarter of 1973 daily variations in the United States dollar rates for some 'snake' currencies averaged over 0·8 of 1 per cent and they were not much lower in the first quarter of 1974. Weekly variations of 4, 5, or even 6 per cent have sometimes been experienced. The explanation doubtless lies in the paucity of official intervention in these cases and in the fact that private bank speculation, as certain well-known bank failures showed, was sometimes of the 'bandwagon' rather than the equilibrating variety. There have also been swings in both directions, lasting from three to six months on the average, on effective exchange rates of the United States dollar on the one hand and some of the currencies in or associated with the 'snake' on the other. These cyclical movements, often resulting from changes in relative interest rates, have sometimes been of the order of 10 per cent or even more, though, despite the disturbed conditions arising out of the oil price increase, they have shown some tendency to decline. It is difficult to say what effect, if any, these fluctuations have had on the proportion of goods traded internationally or on the volume of international capital flows. The excess of the percentage growth of imports of industrial countries over the percentage growth of their output increased a little in volume terms in the first half of 1973, then fell to a negative figure in the second half of 1973 and in 1974. But this may well have been due to recession, which normally leads to wider fluctuations of imports than of output. The effect on international capital flows is even more difficult to decipher. There was probably some decline in such flows in 1973 – measured net by country but aggregated irrespective of sign – though the developing countries, under the stimulus of the commodity boom, managed to attract more of the available funds to themselves. Developments in 1974 were so much influenced by the emergence of OPEC countries as a great new source of investible funds, and by the enhanced importance of official borrowing operations, as to throw little light on the influence of exchange rate variability on the volume of international capital flows. The spreads between buying and selling rates in the foreign exchange market have doubled, tripled, or quadrupled as compared to fixed exchange rate days but the additional cost involved, for transactions other than tourism, is negligible. No evidence is available regarding profit margins in international trade, but it seems highly unlikely that the costs of which I have been speaking have made any significant contribution to the inflationary pressures in the world.

(3) EFFECTS ON THE RELATIONSHIP BETWEEN REAL DEMAND AND COST INFLATION

Apart from the effect of exchange flexibility on the incentive to adopt expansionary demand policies and the effect of exchange rate uncertainty on the costs of international transactions, there is a third possible channel through which the exchange rate regime might influence the rate of inflation, namely, through its effect on the tradeoff between inflation and real demand or output.

In a paper written some years ago[1] I argued that a regime of rigid fixed rates would compel either deficit countries or surplus countries or both to have a level of real demand other than that which represented their ideal compromise between inflation and unemployment. I added that this was likely to result in a less favourable world Phillips-curve and thus either more unemployment or more inflation than if exchange rates could move in such a way as to eliminate international disequilibria.

This analysis, however, takes national Phillips-curves as given and does not take account of the effects of exchange rate changes on import prices, on price anticipations, and hence on wage inflation. These effects may alter national Phillips-curves in one direction or another.[2] I have already noted the fact that depreciation is apt to give an impetus to a country's cost-push inflation, and that the fear of this could be a deterrent to expansion, and has in fact made many countries reluctant to allow their exchange rates to decline. However, for analogous reasons exchange rate appreciation can be assumed to have a favourable effect on the countries whose currencies appreciate. And since one currency's depreciation is another's appreciation, the question that

[1] 'On Exchange Rate Unification', *Economic Journal*, Vol. 81, September 1971.

[2] I am here using 'Phillips-curve' in the sense of the relationship between wage inflation and employment, in abstraction from any indirect effects increased employment and output may have on inflation via their effects on productivity and terms of trade – effects which must depend on the *composition* of the increased employment and output.

arises is whether exchange rate variation has any net effect on cost-push inflation in one direction or the other.

Three mechanisms may be taken into account in considering whether these net effects would be inflationary or otherwise. First is the mechanism whereby the prices of a country's foreign trade goods tend to respond to movements in the prices of competing foreign trade goods produced abroad. Second is the mechanism whereby wages in the sheltered sector of a country respond to changes in wages in the foreign trade sector. And finally there is the mechanism whereby wages in general tend to respond to changes in the cost of living resulting from the changes in prices of imports and domestic foreign trade goods.

All of these mechanisms may show some asymmetries. From work that has been done in the Fund by Michael Deppler it would appear that in most countries, after due allowance is made for domestic factors affecting export prices, these respond proportionately more to upward than to downward changes in competitors' prices. The latter, of course, are affected by factors other than exchange rate changes, but there is some supporting evidence, though as yet statistically somewhat inconclusive, of an asymmetrical response to changes in effective exchange rates considered in isolation.

As regards the other two factors, it appears plausible and consonant with human nature that wages in the sheltered industries would respond more strongly to acceleration than to deceleration of wage growth in the foreign trade sector and that wages in general would respond more strongly to acceleration than to deceleration of cost of living increases, whether due to import price changes or anything else. At least such an assumption would appear plausible so long as the rate of inflation is within a threshold zone over which money illusion is falling – and sensitivity to cost of living increases rising – as inflation itself increases. It may be that this particular asymmetry is present in some degree at all times, but I should doubt that it is very marked when inflation itself is as high as it has been in recent years.

If one considers in conjunction all the mechanisms that have been referred to, it seems likely that variations in exchange rates have to some extent reinforced inflationary price trends, but hardly to an extent that would justify references to exchange rate fluctuations as 'an inflation machine'. There is some hope, too, that the more clearly such fluctuations are recognised as being of a temporary character, the less effect they will have on prices. However, there is no reason for complacency. In some currencies, such as the DM, the Swiss franc, and the United States dollar, effective exchange rates have fluctuated over periods of several quarters to an unnecessary extent owing to the inadequacy of official action to limit the swings in the rate and prevent it from diverging unduly from its longer-term trend. In other cases, however, there has been resistance to a downward trend in the value of the currency – which, though doubtful from the standpoint of adjustment, may have helped to damp down inflationary pressures.

VI. OTHER ASPECTS OF NATIONAL SOVEREIGNTY

There are two further aspects of the division of the world into separate sovereignties which perhaps deserve a brief mention for their bearing on the inflation problem; one of them tends to aggravate inflation, the other, at least potentially, to bridle it. In the first aspect, I am thinking of the indispensable role played by the national state in fostering cartel action, particularly in the sphere of primary products. In this sphere, few effective worldwide cartels have been organised without the backing of governments in the producing countries. In the case of oil, we have seen how much more effective a cartel can be when it is organised by governments than when it is organised by even very large commercial companies. Such cartel actions always tend to have a cost-inflationary effect, but rarely if ever can there have been such a powerful one as that exercised by OPEC in 1974. The really unique feature of that experience, however, was that while from the cost side it was inflationary, its effect on the redistribution of world income, and hence on demand, was decidedly deflationary, whereas most cartel action in the raw material field is probably neutral or expansionary in its effect on demand in that the propensity to spend of the producers is at least as great as that of the consumers. The action of OPEC clearly served to intensify the stagflation from which the world had already begun to suffer in 1973.

A relatively favourable aspect of the political fragmentation of the world comes to light when we consider the feasibility of wage and price control as an anti-inflationary weapon. Opinion among economists is very divided on this issue. Some of us think that a more or less permanent structure of such controls is a necessity of modern economic life, if inflation and underemployment are both to be kept down to tolerable dimensions, and we are hopeful that in time countries will learn to apply such policies in a way that takes adequate account of the need to equilibrate demand and supply for the different types of labour and product, at least in the longer run. Others, feeling that this is impracticable and perhaps dangerous to political liberty, have reconciled themselves to what they call the natural level of unemployment as the price of containing inflation. Whatever side one takes on this issue, it cannot escape any observer that up to now cases of relatively successful application of incomes policies have been largely confined to small political units, such as the Netherlands, the Scandinavian countries, Austria, New Zealand, and Australia.

VII. CONCLUSION

I have interpreted the topic – 'international aspects of inflation' in a somewhat idiosyncratic way in the hope of getting a few new angles on the problem from the shift in perspective. I am not too sure the experiment has been worthwhile and I would not quarrel with anyone who contended that it has not been. There is no reason to expect that the splitting up of economic functions among national entities would tend unambiguously either to promote or to restrain inflation, and it would be tedious to try to draw up a balance sheet on these lines. I will only conclude by expressing a general prejudice that a regime of national states and open economies, partly by reducing the domain over which governmental functions are exercised, and partly by adding a few new instruments of policy, tainted as some of them are by beggar-thy-neighbour potentialities, makes it easier for peoples to do what they want – either to control inflation or to give way to it.

Discussion of the Paper by J. Marcus Fleming

Professor Machlup introduced the paper. He said that Mr Fleming's approach was original and interesting, especially to those with a theoretical, somewhat speculative, bent. Unlike a more pedestrian analyst, Mr Fleming did not select for discussion those aspects of price inflation which either were effects of, or had effects on, international phenomena. Instead, he asked a novel question: What difference did it make to worldwide increases in price that the world was not a single, closed economy, but was divided into separate political units?

This question was not pragmatic; we had no choice; the world would stay divided into political units whether we liked it or not, at least for the lifetime of everybody at this conference. Thus, if we were to decide that a universal world state would be less or more vulnerable to inflationary policies, this would hardly affect actions or dreams. Even if Robert Mundell were to pronounce the whole world the optimum currency area, one would expect no great rush of central bank governors petitioning for jobs as managers of branch offices of the World Clearing House, or heads of state asking to become provincial administrators.

Mr Fleming's exercise, though disguised as a fictional comparison, was not without pragmatic value. For he dealt with timely questions, debated by economists as well as men of affairs, which did affect current policy. His analysis threw light on: the principles of national demand management, reserve-currency practices, xenocurrency banking, variability of exchange rates, the influence of international cartels and national wage-and-price controls. That he placed his study of these issues in the setting of his main theme – the single world state versus the multistate world – did not detract from the analysis but added an intellectually or aesthetically pleasing frame.

Mr Fleming first presented the major propositions for an analytical model of causal interrelations. (1) Output is determined by money flows [aggregate demand for goods and services] and supply prices. [$Q = MV/P$, not $P = MV/Q$.] (2) The rate of price increase is determined, approximately and chiefly, by the rate of cost increase. (3) The rate of cost increase is determined (a) partly by the level of unemployment and excess capacity and (b) partly by past rates of price increase [evidently working through expectations of future rates of price increase]. (4) Money flows [MV or aggregate demand] are determined by monetary policies and budgetary policies and the usual set of propensities, including the influence of price increases on the incentive to invest. Professor Machlup thought this somewhat eclectic set of relationships quite workable, although some might prefer a reduced form, even if a streamlined model would not seriously affect the outcome of arguments in which it was employed. With these tools, Mr Fleming tackled his questions, not forgetting his ambition to make comparisons with his fictional, undivided world state.

In the polar case of 'open economies with fixed rates and free trade', the national exercise of demand management – in contrast with demand management by a world monetary authority – operated under constraints limiting the power of national authorities 'to influence the degree of inflation and the level of activity within their borders'. Their ability to diverge temporarily from the rate of world price inflation depended, among other things, on the willingness to use or accumulate reserves or on the ability to attract or repel foreign capital. The famous asymmetry of the reserve constraint received its due recognition: there was a definite limit to the use of reserves – they ran out – but no limit to the ability to accumulate reserves. The effect would be anti-expansionary, on balance. However, where deficit countries issued currencies that were used as reserves by surplus countries, this constraint disappeared, and fixed exchange rates served as part of an effective mechanism transmitting any monetary expansion occurring in the reserve-currency countries. Thus, the presumption of a constraint holding back expansion gave place to the presumption of one aiding it.

Professor Machlup could not help injecting doubt about the relevance of the discussion, if it really was meant to apply to a world of countries with fixed exchange rates. If Mr Fleming meant perpetually fixed rates for all currencies, such a world was no less imaginary than a world with only one country. To make some allowance for reality, how long must an exchange rate be maintained unaltered to be called fixed? If less than ten years, neither the constraints nor the inducements to monetary expansion might be effective. We knew instances where countries, desiring to expand, devalued to a level that permitted them to go on increasing their money stocks relatively rapidly for ten or more years, when they had to refix the exchange rate. Would Fleming say that France was constrained by a fixed rate between 1914 and 1974? Where was the borderline between a truly fixed and truly variable rate? If we took all countries that had existed for 25 years and calculated the average number of variations in their exchange rates, Mr Fleming's treatment did not seem relevant – except as a lesson for those who loved to speak of a 'return' to a fixed-rate system but had not yet learned what it would imply – if it existed.

Mr Fleming turned next to 'foreign-exchange reserves and liability financing'. He effectively debunked the 'European Myth', according to which expansionary policies in the United States had taken undue advantage of the reserve-currency status of the dollar and forced Europe to import American-made price inflation. This charge must be rejected, at least for the years before 1971. Professor Machlup would himself add that, if the countries had promptly started to pay less for the clearly overvalued dollar or altogether stopped buying dollars, there would not have been the dollar flood of the early 1970s. Of course, the large accumulation of dollar reserves by central banks actually expanded their monetary base and invited an inordinately large creation of money in many countries.

In this section, Mr Fleming dealt with the monetarist view that increases in money stocks regularly caused – not merely enabled, but actually initiated – increases in monetary demand. His observations in figures 6.3 and 6.4 struck Professor Machlup as somewhat peculiar. In figure 6.4, the rate of increase of the money stock was positive in every year from 1949 to 1973, as was the rate of increase in the G.N.P. deflator. Again, from 1959 on, both these series had shown some *acceleration* – from an annual increase of 5 per cent or less to one of 7 per cent or more. He would never have expected a parallel acceleration of the two rates of increase year after year. It would not have surprised him to see the rate of money creation fall during one or two years – say, from 7 to 5 per cent – while the rate of price increase was rising – say, from 3 to 4 per cent, or vice versa.

As he understood the monetarist position, it did not include belief in any consistently parallel accelerations or decelerations, synchronised or lagged, of the two series. Monetarists would expect an increase in the money stock to produce a lagged increase in money G.N.P., but did not predict how it could be divided between output and prices. So they would not be puzzled by a lack of parallelism in the acceleration rates of money creation and price index.

Mr Fleming, however, had observed the lack of parallelism and, from 1956–57 onwards, a 'synchronised but inverse relationship' between the rates of acceleration of annual money creation of annual price increase. This suggested to Mr Fleming the possibility that 'monetary policy is itself a function of current inflation'. Why should this surprise anybody? If a group of policymakers with a strong sense of responsibility for preventing accelerating price inflation found the price index moving up faster, would they not quickly step on the brake and try to slow down the money-printing press? In modern terminology, they would have tried to 'lean against the wind'; in earlier periods – pre-Keynesian – we would have called them a bunch of inflationists if they had allowed the money stock to increase at all. Obversely, if the policymakers made the printing press run faster as soon as price inflation slowed down, we should not be surprised at that either. He would simply see them as regular fellows with the normal present-day schizophrenia, trying to keep their balance between attempts to create more employment and attempts to avoid more inflation. Whenever the rate of price increase became less frightening, they rushed forward with more expansionary policies to create employment.

There was yet another type of monetary policymaker, for whom the 'inverse relationship' would not hold. He would characterise them as inflationary fools of a higher degree, suffering from the Helfferich syndrome. Helfferich was the Governor of the German Reichsbank who believed it was his duty to print more money faster because prices were rising so fast that the real value of the total money stock was falling. Professor Machlup understood that this syndrome still existed; those afflicted by it denounced a central banker who allowed the rise in the price level to run ahead of the increase in money stock as a 'deflationist'. In neither case would he see anything puzzling in Mr Fleming's discovery that monetary policy might itself have become a function of current price inflation. This was true neither of the maniac who wanted to restore the real money stock to its level before prices rocketed, nor of the paragon of monetary virtue who wanted to slow down the increase in money stock when he saw price inflation gathering speed.

Indeed, lawmakers and governments who had given to money policymakers the obligation to attain three objectives at once – price stability, full employment, and foreign balance – had imposed on them the policy Mr Fleming thought he had observed: a stop–go policy. The monetary authorities, anxious to maintain high employment, switched to *GO* whenever the rate of price increase seemed to subside; they switched to *STOP* whenever price inflation accelerated. This would probably go on until the monetarist counter-revolution removed the schizophrenic rules for demand management.

In discussing the effects of xenocurrency markets, Mr Fleming gave a perfect account of the two sources of expansion of xeno-currency stocks:

(1) the creation of xenocurrency deposits through loans by commercial banks, and (2) the creation of official foreign-exchange reserves by central banks placing currency reserves in xenocurrency markets. These contributions to worldwide money inflation is a divided world with divided monetary control and separate currencies was sometimes overestimated, sometimes underestimated. Mr Fleming had the right sense of proportion.

On the controversial issue of exchange-rate variability, Professor Machlup was glad to note another agreement with Mr Fleming, who stated that 'floating tends more and more to become the only form of exchange rate variability that is able to cope with the massive capital flows engendered by discrepant rates of inflation, discrepant interest-rate policies, and the speculation associated with exchange variability itself'.

Although we had, at present, no practical alternative to managed floating, Mr Fleming asked whether we should credit it with having reduced, or increased, the rate of price inflation. He analysed this in three steps: (1) effects on aggregate demand in real terms, (2) effects on real cost, and (3) effects on the relationship between real demand and cost inflation. The first question was whether actual and/or expected fluctuations of exchange rates caused the demand for credit and the supply of bank loans and money to be greater or smaller, and monetary policy to be looser or tighter, than under some fictitious alternative. It could be answered only by a one-armed (and closed-minded) economist. For other economists, if they understood their craft, this was a matter of 'on the one hand' and 'on the other hand'. Mr Fleming manipulated his hands like a skilled handicraftsman. On the one hand, the monetary authorities, under managed floating, could do as they pleased, either intervening or leaving the rate to the currents of the market. On the other hand, floating reduced speculative capital flows and, hence, stopped inflows of foreign exchange much faster than with pegged rates. Consequently, there was less expansion in the receiving countries.

Moreover, since the direct price effects of currency depreciation were known to speed up price inflation, there would be greater aversion to depreciation and, hence, a reduced propensity to expand effective demand. Likewise, since currency appreciation helped to combat price inflation, and a demand constraint might bring currency appreciation, the propensity to restrain an expansion of demand was again reduced. On the other hand – one really needed several pairs of hands to go through a small fraction of the possible outcomes – the adoption of flexible rates 'probably releases a net tendency towards expansion and hence inflation' though, on the next hand, this had not been the case in 1971 to 1973, when the net effect was contractionary.

He was not making fun of Mr Fleming, who did precisely what an honest scholar ought to do: go through the possibilities for which the probabilities looked relatively good. Even if one selected the most plausible, one still ended with several that pointed in one direction and others that pointed in the opposite direction. Mr Fleming's conclusion was that, for the world as a whole, it seemed doubtful whether the adoption of exchange-rate variability 'has had any significant net effect on the level of real demand'.

The second question raised by floating rates was their possible effect on 'increased real costs'. The phrase was misleading. To Professor Machlup real cost meant the use of factors of production to produce particular outputs. What Mr Fleming had in mind was the transfer of income from those who payed for bigger spreads between bidding and asking prices in the exchange market to those who collected them – to exchange dealers. But this was not really a serious question. Mr Fleming, who evidently regarded the spread as a payment for uncertainty bearing, and the bearing of uncertainty by private parties as a real cost, estimated this effect of exchange variability upon price inflation as negligible. This was good to know, because the advocates of the nationalisation of risks and uncertainty usually asserted that the effect was substantial.

The third channel through which the exchange-rate regime might influence the rate of price inflation was its effect on the tradeoff [he would add: *supposed* tradeoff] between real demand and cost inflation. Since one currency's depreciation was another appreciation, there was a question whether exchange-rate variation had any net effect at all.

In analysing this question, Mr Fleming distinguished three mechanisms: (1) direct price effects, (2) wage-boost imitation, and (3) wage escalation with consequent increases in consumer prices.

Had these effects been symmetrical for appreciations and depreciations, the net effect would have tended to be zero. Unfortunately, they worked asymmetrically, pushing prices up, but never down. The mechanisms were usually discussed with the analogy of 'ratchet effects': what went up did not come down, because of monopolistic market power.

Under 'other aspects of national sovereignty', Mr Fleming discussed first the effect of price cartels. With the oil-price increase by the OPEC cartel, Mr Fleming found the effects on costs inflationary but those on demand through redistributing income from quick spenders to slow spenders and non-spenders – deflationary. Mr Fleming did not mention that the money which consumers of oil products had to hand over to producers in higher prices was, in several countries, restored to them in higher wages or subsidies. For the whole world, however, it might be true that consumers were left with less to spend on things other than oil.

To link this discussion to his broader theme, Mr Fleming speculated about the probability of cartels acquiring strong and enduring market power. He argued that most cartels flourished only with government backing, which was only likely to be forthcoming in nation states. He also speculated about the effectiveness of anti-inflationary controls of wages and prices. Only small political units had thus far had any success with them.

The big question – whether the average rate of price inflation would be greater or smaller in a single world state than in a world divided into separate political units – remained unanswered. But in his undertaking Mr Fleming had explored many important problems. If he arrived at few conclusive answers, he did point to ways to approach them.

Mr Fleming noted that Professor Machlup had criticised him for not being clearer about the time period he had in mind in speaking about fixed exchange rates. He wanted to make it clear that when he said fixed he meant immutable for all time, opposing a fixed rate to a fully floating rate. He had thought that the analysis would be easier if one contrasted the situations at the two ends of the spectrum.

Professor Machlup had made some gentle fun of the multiplicity of 'hands' which he had employed in looking at the effect of flexible exchange rates on demand. He would now perhaps conclude that flexible exchange rates on balance tended to damp down inflation.

The main issue was this. With fixed exchange rates, would more of the important countries be forced to deflate or would they inflate more than they liked? Flexible exchange rates certainly gave more national control over demand management. In the early 1970s, he thought that many countries had been forced to be more inflationary than they would have wished. One way to look at it was that the main deficit country, the United States, was strong enough as a reserve centre to refuse to accept the constraints which would have been imposed on it by a fixed exchange rate system and other countries were flooded with purchases. More recently, flexible exchange rates had allowed countries to be more restrictive than they otherwise would have been.

On the Phillips-curve, Mr Fleming agreed, in general, that such asymmetry as existed worked in an inflationary direction. If exchange rates diverged, prices in the depreciating country were more likely to rise, and in the appreciating country to fall, which, on balance, would probably be inflationary. If world prices were reasonably constant, deficit countries would have difficulty in reducing costs. With all countries inflating, the difficulty of making adjustments between countries whose prices were increasing more or less slowly would be less important.

To the comment that one could not have permanently fixed exchange rates, Mr Fleming said that to have tackled the problem differently would have called for even more 'hands'. For example, he would have had to show how far, and for what reasons, countries were sticking to overvalued and undervalued currencies for too long. His own approach had been more analytical and made it easier to show the effects of national sovereignty under fixed exchange rates.

Professor Bronfenbrenner wanted some elucidation of the problem of the xenocurrency. Although the dollar had recently fallen in value relative to the yen and the deutschmark, no Americo-yen or Americo-mark had emerged. He had heard that the reason was that if a loan was made in yen or deutschmarks in the United States, those making it would have to report to the monetary authorities. The administrative costs of doing so would be big enough to prevent them proceeding. Was this true of other countries? If not, why not? It might be desirable for invididual countries to consider introducing such rules (as the American) to prevent the spread of xenocurrency systems.

Mr Fleming thought Professor Bronfenbrenner might be right for those dealing with marginal amounts of foreign currency in countries with no reserve requirements. But it was the absence of these reserve requirements that constituted the main advantage of the xenocurrency market. This was what was offered by centres like London, Zurich, Singapore, etc. The thought of exerting greater control over xenocurrencies was not absent from the IMF but one must remember that these funds had provided a useful buffer during the oil crisis.

There might well be big difficulties in instituting reserve requirements.

First, would all conceivable places in which such markets might develop agree to introduce the same requirements? Second, would a centre like London require deposits with the Bank of England or with the central bank of the country in which the parent of the branch was located? Again, the insistence on reserve requirements generally meant that the central bank was required to provide assistance if other banks got into difficulties. Yet the Bank of England would probably not be prepared to bail out all foreign banks operating in London. The fear in London might be that imposing such controls might lead overseas banks to move elsewhere.

Professor Aukrust asked whether the world would be less inflation-prone if there were fewer national units. If there were less division, might there, for example, be more synchronisation of cycles and, consequently, wider swings. Recently, unemployment in Europe had been 2 per cent to 3 per cent. With synchronisation, it might well have been around 5 per cent.

Mr Fleming explained that tables 6.2 and 6.3 in his paper both gave information about synchronisation. It interested him that in table 6.3 the synchronisation of cyclical movements in different countries was actually very low in 1973, the first year of generalised exchange floating. This was the opposite of what a good deal of theorising suggested. It was true that, with the oil crisis, discrepancies reappeared in 1974, but even these were not very great.

There were reasons why floating exchange rates should not hamper the transmission of demand. For example, spontaneous moves to expansion in one country were more likely to lead to an improved, rather than a worsened, balance of payments. Recently, it had been found that effect of expansion on capital account was likely to outweigh any worsening on current account. With floating exchange rates, the currency might well appreciate rather than depreciate with, perhaps, a bigger spillover of demand into other countries. Appreciation should lead to benefits overseas, so that income effects might be bigger than with fixed exchange rates.

Professor Aukrust replied that he was not considering whether exchange rates were fixed or floating, but wanted to know the effect of national versus international action on a country's cyclical policy. If the Phillips-curve was such that problems did not arise with 5 per cent unemployment, but did if unemployment were in the range 0 per cent to 2 per cent, then he thought that synchronisation of the cycle might have inflationary effects. There might be, on the whole, more unemployment and yet more inflation with larger, integrated economies.

Mr Fleming agreed that synchronisation might lead to more inflation. But he was not sure whether more-centralised control would lead to more inflation. Admittedly, if, in the EEC, one had a single monetary policy and a few countries were in recession, he would expect pressures for general expansion in the EEC. This might well push other countries into boom.

Professor Duesenberry suggested that one could get information about this problem by observing what had happened in the United States. Off the cuff, he would say that the correlation of cyclical movements was greater within the United States than within the EEC. He saw this as a result of the fact that the United States had only a single monetary policy, but he would agree that overall integration was needed to get that degree of common policy.

He had sometimes wondered whether the United States might have a less satisfactory Phillips-curve than most of Europe, so that it was differences in the European economies which restrained inflation. Did the United States have a less satisfactory tradeoff between unemployment and price increases?

Professor Lundberg suggested that one reason why the Phillips-curve in the United States seemed to have moved to the right was the dispersion of unemployment, industrially and regionally.

Professor Duesenberry thought there were two elements. First, there might be disparities resulting from underlying differences in the development of industry in different locations. The remainder of the dispersion might result from the way common policy had developed.

Professor Swoboda said that he and Professor Genberg had not read the paper by Mr Fleming before writing their own, or revising it. They had done this deliberately so as not to be influenced by Mr Fleming's views. Now that he had read Mr Fleming's paper, he found that many figures in it were the same as the ones he and Genberg used, but that Fleming's paper reached rather different conclusions from this same set of figures.

For instance, the evidence on the relationship between monetary expansion and world inflation was much firmer than suggested in Fleming's paper. One could probably attribute a good deal of world inflation after 1968 to the sharp increase in the rate of monetary expansion in the United States, though this relationship was certainly much less clear for earlier periods.

He then raised two questions. First, he addressed himself to the relationship between the sharing of the burden of adjustment between deficit and surplus countries and the extent of world inflation. On one hand, the relationship was not a simple one; it required one to know what caused the deficit in the first place. On the other hand, it might be true that surplus countries could more easily sterilise the increase in their reserves than deficit countries could neutralise their exchange losses. Yet in some countries, for example Germany, it had been very difficult to sterilise the inflow of reserves, because instruments to carry out open-market operations were inadequate. So, the money supply had tended to increase significantly.

Second, he questioned Mr Fleming's argument that in 1971–72, the United States had been forced to abandon fixed exchange rates because of its structural balance-of-payments deficit. To hold such a view required spelling out what these structural difficulties were. It also raised the question whether the structural deficit had gone now, and if so, how and why?

Mr Fleming agreed that it was hard to sterilise funds under fixed exchange rates but, over longish periods, he thought Germany had been reasonably successful. Other countries had cried 'wolf' too soon.

He saw the United States deficit as largely due to structural factors, and did not see much room for European complaints. The rest of the world, especially Europe, had progressively caught up with American methods of manufacture and productivity levels, while foreign goods had become more acceptable in the United States. Whether the depreciation of the dollar would create conditions for eliminating this structural shift was harder to say.

Professor Swoboda replied that he could agree that the dollar was, in some sense, overvalued in 1971–72 relative to policies and developments in other countries. However, he was not sure that the cause of this overvaluation was of a structural nature, rooted in the structure of the United States balance of payments, rather than resulting from divergent trends in macroeconomic policies and the nature of the system. With floating exchange rates, the deficit had, by definition, disappeared. Yet there was little evidence of fundamental structural change. After all, why should devaluation help to alter structure in the long run, unless accompanied by other policy measures?

Professor Machlup pointed out that structural change could mean a change either in flows of goods and services or in capital. If the change was simply in goods, he would point out that the United States had a trade surplus of 8 billion dollars in 1964. By 1971–72, it had a small deficit. With the dollar devalued, there was not a small surplus again. If that did not represent structural change, he did not know what structural change was.

Professor Neumark thought there might be some connection between the United States deficit in the late 1960s and the profound change in the method of financing the federal budget, especially from 1966.

Professor Machlup replied that this was what he meant. The dollar was overvalued because of the deficit of the federal government.

Professor Malinvaud was afraid that readers of this record would not understand what Mr Fleming was saying when he referred to the European myth. The European myth was that the American government's policy of 'benign neglect' with respect to the balance of payments deficit of the United States had made the fight against inflation harder. If so, what Mr Fleming said did not contradict the myth. With the dollar overvalued, the policy of the American government aimed at bringing about equilibrium would have required the elimination of excess demand. This would have increased unemployment in the United States by more than elsewhere to give a lower rate of inflation. Even though some move in this direction had occurred, it had been too weak to eliminate the structural deficit, which had only more or less disappeared after the dollar had been devalued.

The European myth was not really a myth at all, but a statement of fact.

Professor Machlup explained that the phrase 'benign neglect' had been used by Professor Haberler as advice to the United States government, which had repudiated it. What was meant was that because the dollar was overvalued the United States could not solve its balance of payments problems by demand management. The degree of deflation required would have been too severe for the rest of the world.

The only correct reaction was therefore devaluation. Benign neglect only meant postponing devaluation, which in any case at that stage had been opposed by Europeans. The 1971 moves were therefore intended to give a big enough shock to Europe to persuade it to accept an American devaluation.

The myth was that the United States had an inflationary problem and was not prepared to take the steps required to eliminate it.

Professor Malinvaud disputed this. The European myth meant that the United States had a responsibility to act and had not done so.

Professor Machlup wanted to know why the United States needed to act when there had been no rapid price inflation in the United States relative to Europe.

Professor Swoboda pointed out that American inflation had *not* been slower in 1968–70. It was true that the increase in the United States money supply in 1970 and at the beginning of 1971 had been relatively slow, but afterwards there had been a rapid acceleration in monetary expansion.

Professor Machlup recalled that he had written attacking the European myth in his Wicksell Lectures in 1965, under the title of *Involuntary Foreign Lending*. He would draw particular attention to the section on 'The Complaints of the Surplus Countries', pages 60–69.

Professor Duesenberry reminded participants that one had to remember that, by 1971, the United States had been begging some European countries to appreciate for a number of years. Its government did not feel that the United States, acting alone, could achieve a satisfactory reduction in the exchange value of the dollar.

On benign neglect, for some years before 1968 the United States had used a number of devices to reduce its balance of payments deficit. The real contention of benign neglect was that the United States could not go on for long taking more and more such steps. In the end, it would have to accept a devaluation of the dollar. After 1968, exchange-rate adjustment became inevitable. The question was simply how to do it. The European countries complained about their own surpluses but would not accept the costs implied in allowing their exchange rates to appreciate. The policies pursued had not matched the economics of the situation, until the trade surplus for Europe as a whole had become huge.

The war in Vietnam meant that Europe had either to accept even larger surpluses or pay the price of revaluation. In that sense, it was true that the United States did make things increasingly difficult for Europe, but Europe always had a choice.

Mr Fleming replied to the discussion. His paper had been disparate, and the discussion equally so. He would be interested in the later discussion of Professor Swoboda's paper, including Professor Swoboda's attempt to validate the proposition that monetary expansion gave rise to increases in output and prices after a lag. It was not that he did not believe that this happened, he had simply not observed it happening at all times, and especially not in the early postwar period.

In his paper, he had noted an inverse relation between an increase in the money supply and in prices. He did think that, where this happened, it was easy to make a false correlation. For example, fiscal expansion could lead to an increase in output and in prices. Later it would be necessary for monetary policy to react inversely. Perhaps a cyclical movement could develop, as a result of fiscal action, but it could appear to result from monetary action. This would be because of the lag between the change in fiscal policy and its effect on prices. The monetarists seemed too ready to assume that evidence from the early postwar period supported their views.

7 Policy Autonomy of Small Countries[1]

Hans Genberg

GRADUATE INSTITUTE OF INTERNATIONAL STUDIES, GENEVA

I. INTRODUCTION

As the title indicates, this paper deals with policy autonomy of small countries in the world economy. In keeping with the subject of the conference, I shall narrow the topic down to treat only policy autonomy with respect to the rate of inflation. This also suggests that I should limit the analysis to the case of fixed exchange rate economies. Under a flexible exchange rate regime a country may independently choose its own long-run rate of inflation, so the autonomy issue becomes uninteresting. In the shorter run even a flexible exchange rate will transmit inflationary impulses between countries, so the topic would remain relevant, but an analysis of this case will, for the sake of brevity, be left for another occasion.

Within the overall topic my aim is first of all to discover the sources of autonomy and the possible means available to policy authorities for achieving it. Section II sets out the simple analytical framework which I will use throughout the paper, and it also defines what I will take to be the definition of a 'small country'; the existence of a set of goods whose prices are externally given to the country in question.

The external and internal constraints which determine the scope for policy independence are discussed in the subsequent two sections. Section III is concerned with what I call long-run autonomy which essentially means the possibility of affecting the general trend in prices without running into balance-of-payments difficulties. Shorter-run autonomy which allows for the financing of inflationary policies by running down international reserves is discussed in section IV. Both these sections are also geared towards the second aim of the paper, namely to discover the likely *quantitative* extent of policy autonomy in the open economy. Some of the parameters which are crucial for this question are identified and plausible guesses as to their values help give indicative answers. The quantitative aspects are pursued further in sections V and VI where I present some regression and simulation results. The former are

[1] This paper contains ideas developed in connection with a research project on 'National Economic Policy and the International Monetary System' at the Graduate Institute of International Studies under a grant from the Ford Foundation. The author would like to thank P. D. Jonson and H. Kierzkowsky for helpful comments on the previous draft.

intended to give a broad picture of what have been the actual relationships between some major countries' rates of inflation in the postwar period, and they can be interpreted as showing that very little autonomy has been possible without changing the exchange rate. The simulation results of section VI are based on an econometric model of the United Kingdom economy and give more detailed information on the consequences of policies which aim at a different rate of inflation than that dictated by the rest of the world.

The third goal of the paper is finally approached in the last section which contains some observations concerning the proper role of inflation policies in open economies.

II. THE ANALYTICAL FRAMEWORK

In what follows I shall deal exclusively with policy autonomy of a *small country*, where by 'small' I mean that there exists a class of goods, produced and consumed in the country, whose prices are determined on world markets independently of supply and demand conditions in the home country. This class of goods need not include all importables and all exportables but for simplicity I shall assume that it does. Furthermore I shall not concern myself with changes in the terms of trade and consequently I shall be able to aggregate exportables and importables into a single traded goods category which I shall contrast with a non-traded goods category. The latter are assumed not to be tradeable at current relative prices due to, for instance, high transport costs relative to their domestic prices. Although it will not be introduced into the analysis, the possibility that some non-traded good becomes imported or exported as its relative price changes sufficiently should be kept in mind.

By the domestic rate of inflation I shall mean the relative rate of change in a price level index which contains the prices of both traded and non-traded goods.

$$P = I(P_T, P_N) \qquad I_1, I_2 > 0 \tag{1}$$

and

$$\pi \equiv \frac{1}{P}\frac{dP}{dt} \tag{2}$$

where

P = the home country price level
P_T = the domestic currency price of traded goods
P_N = the domestic currency price of non-traded goods
π = the home country rate of inflation

Begging many questions dealing with the proper construction of price indexes, I will finally assume for convenience that the index in equation (1) has fixed exponential weights, summing to unity, attached to the two components. This allows me to write the overall rate of inflation in terms of the rates of change in the prices of traded and non-traded goods, π_T and π_N

respectively, as in equation (3).

$$\pi = \pi_T + w(\pi_N - \pi_T) \tag{3}$$

Taking equation (3) as a point of departure, we can define policy autonomy on the part of the domestic economy as being able to make π differ from π_T by using policy tools. This is an appropriate definition in my framework since I have assumed π_T to be given exogenously. Thus we see that policy autonomy depends on the policymakers' ability to change the *relative price* of non-traded goods. This proposition has some important implications for what we should expect from economic policy. In particular we should expect that policies which in a closed economy setting do not have real effects should be incapable of influencing the nominal rate of inflation in a small open economy. General monetary policy comes to mind as a case in point, but certain types of neutral fiscal policy will also be impotent as will be shown presently. To put the point in a slightly different way, we should expect to be able to achieve autonomy only with policies which have a differential impact on the two goods markets.

The need to change relative prices in order to affect the price level in a small country also draws attention to two important analytical considerations which must be kept in mind. One is the distinction between equilibrium (sustainable) inflation rate autonomy and quasi-equilibrium (short-run) autonomy. Sections III and IV deal with each of these concepts separately. The second consideration which will appear frequently is the distinction between a *once-and-for-all* relative price change and *continuous* relative price changes.

III. POLICY AUTONOMY IN LONG-RUN EQUILIBRIUM

Restricting the analysis of this section to states of long-run equilibrium I shall work explicitly within a framework of full employment where balance of payments equilibrium is maintained through the usual automatic adjustment mechanism. In a static model those conditions must be met in full equilibrium. In a dynamic context where growth of income takes place through factor accumulation or technical progress or where policy succeeds in continuously altering relative prices, the balance of payments equilibrium condition must be relaxed to allow for the surpluses necessary to provide the economy with the liquidity needed to support higher incomes and demands for money. To simplify the diagrammatic exposition I will avoid this complication by assuming that the necessary liquidity is supplied entirely by the domestic monetary authorities. This should be viewed as a simplifying device *only* and should not alter the basic quantitative conclusions.[1]

[1] I shall also exclude the capital account of the balance of payments from the discussion of this section. The justification is that capital mobility has been shown to affect only the speed of adjustment towards equilibrium but not its location (see, for instance, A. Swoboda, 'Equilibrium, Quasi-Equilibrium and Macroeconomic Policy under Fixed Exchange Rates', *Quarterly Journal of Economics*, Vol. LXXXVI (February 1972) pp. 162–71). In long-run analysis therefore capital mobility need not be taken explicitly into account.

The standard two-sector international trade model, appropriately converted into the traded–non-traded framework, can now be seen to provide a convenient analytical base for determining what kind of economic policies are needed to secure equilibrium inflation autonomy. As I pointed out above this involves searching for policies which can alter the price of non-traded goods *relative* to that of traded goods.

It will be instructive first to review some of the reasons why relative prices may change irrespective of government policy. With reference to figure 7.1 these may be divided into production effects and consumption effects.

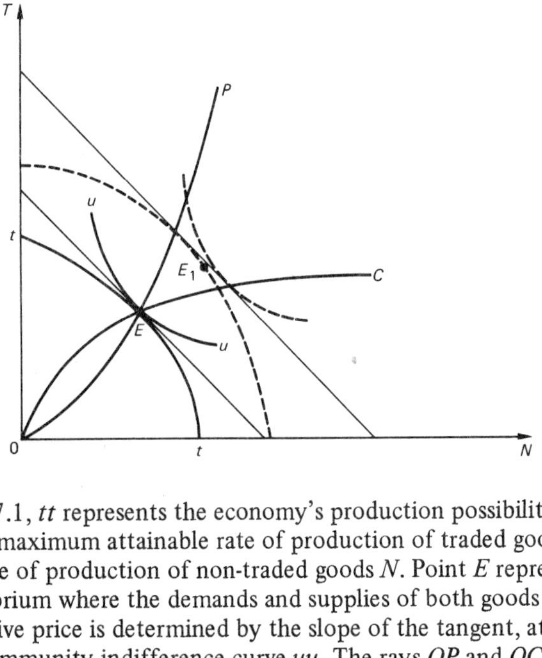

Fig. 7.1

In figure 7.1, *tt* represents the economy's production possibility frontier, showing the maximum attainable rate of production of traded goods, *T*, for any given rate of production of non-traded goods *N*. Point *E* represents the initial equilibrium where the demands and supplies of both goods are equal and the relative price is determined by the slope of the tangent, at *E*, to both *tt* and the community indifference curve *uu*. The rays *OP* and *OC* indicate how the production and consumption mix would change over time if relative prices were held constant as the economy grew. In the figure it is assumed that production increases are biased towards traded goods. This bias may stem from a particular pattern of factor endowment growth together with differing factor intensities in the two sectors. Alternatively, and in keeping with some recent theoretical and empirical work on inflation in small economies, we may assume that the bias is due to more rapid technical progress in the *T* sector as compared with the *N* sector.[1]

[1] See B. Bàlassa, 'The Purchasing-power Parity Doctrine: a Reappraisal', *Journal of Political Economy*, Vol. 72, 1964, pages 584–96; G. Edgren, K. O. Faxen, C. E. Odhner, *Wage Formation and the Economy*, London, 1973, and O. Aukrust, 'Inflation in the Open Economy: The Norwegian Model', Working Paper from the Central Bureau of Statistics of Norway, March 1975.

The consumption ray *OC* is drawn to reflect the also commonly held view that services (identified as a large component of non-traded goods) are income elastic in demand.

The assumptions underlying figure 7.1 imply that as the economy grows over time, the equilibrium production and consumption mixes will be described by points such as E and E_1 which in turn imply that the relative price of non-traded goods will increase as time passes. We may get an idea of the approximate magnitudes involved by specifying the demand and supply functions of non-traded goods and determining the relative price change necessary to maintain equilibrium in the fact of growth. The resulting expression can be reduced to

$$\frac{dP_N}{P_N} - \frac{dP_T}{P_T} = \frac{\eta_y - \epsilon_y}{\epsilon_p - \eta_p} \frac{dy}{y} \tag{4}$$

where

η_y = the elasticity of demand for N with respect to y
ϵ_y = the elasticity of supply of N with respect to y
η_p = the elasticity of demand for N with respect to the relative price
ϵ_p = the elasticity of supply of N with respect to the relative price

and where y should be thought of as the endowment of resources available to the economy.[1]

The expression makes explicit the well-known result that the higher the elasticities of substitution in both consumption and production (quantities related to η_p and ϵ_p respectively) the smaller will be the relative price changes for a given size disturbance to the demand or supply functions. It also brings out the roles of the output demand and supply elasticities. Finally we note that for a given (positive) value of the elasticity ratio in equation (4), the relative price change will be greater for a country which grows relatively rapidly than for a slow-growing country.

As I have already mentioned, the last two propositions have been subjected to empirical tests which seem to corroborate the arguments.

Returning to the question of the impact of governmental policies it should now be clear that general expenditure-reducing or expenditure-increasing policies will not work in a long-run equilibrium setting because the full employment and balance of payments equilibrium conditions are consistent with only one level of aggregate demand. The reason of course is that a difference between expenditures and full employment income implies a balance of trade deficit or surplus which can not be sustained indefinitely. To affect relative prices then, the government policy must be of the switching type either working on supply curves or expenditures. It is in this case the

[1] A similar expression has been derived by H. G. Johnson for the effect on the terms of trade of growth in a two-country model. See H. G. Johnson, 'Economic Development and International Trade', in H. G. Johnson, *Money, Trade and Economic Growth* (Cambridge (Mass.): Harvard University Press, 1962), p. 97.

distinction between once-and-for-all and continuous relative price changes becomes important. Consider for example a production subsidy to non-traded goods producers financed from general tax revenues. This will increase the supply of non-traded goods which implies that the relative price facing consumers has to fall in order for the new equilibrium to be established. The result will be a once-and-for-all fall in the general price level but the rate of inflation will not be affected.[1] A continuously increasing subsidy is needed to achieve the latter.

The same principle applies to tax financed government expenditures which have a different mix than private expenditures. Suppose for simplicity that government expenditures fall predominantly on non-traded goods and that the private choice between N and T is not affected by the government policy other than by the general income tax. Then the equilibrium relative price will depend positively on the rate of government expenditures and an increasing relative price can only come about if the government sector is *expanding*[2] (see figure 7.2).

As a final type of government policy, consider a scheme which encourages biased-growth in the economy. In terms of equation (4) we can think of this policy as affecting the output elasticity ϵ_y and it may take a variety of forms such as subsidising research and development, promoting increased labour productivity or encouraging capital accumulation in a particular sector. In terms of the figure, the effect would be to shift the production possibility frontier non-uniformly outwards and to alter equilibrium relative prices. So long as the differential growth incentives are in effect we should observe continuous changes in relative prices with corresponding effects on the general rate of inflation.

Before we try to assess the scope of policy autonomy from a quantitative point of view it is useful to relate our arguments to the type of theory advanced in the so-called Scandinavian, Aukrust, or E.F.O. models of inflation. These models have the same commodity classification as we have used above, but while we stress both supply and demand considerations in the determination of relative prices, they concentrate almost exclusively on supply factors.[3]

[1] It might appear that I am belabouring a rather obvious point but I feel that it needs emphasising in view of statements often made to the effect that, for instance, indirect tax increases, currency devaluations and oil price increases create inflation.

[2] Casual observations of the United Kingdom economy seem to support this proposition in that both relatively high rates of inflation and a rapid expansion of the government sector has occurred during the postwar period. In fact, recent empirical evidence indicates that increasing government expenditures exert strong pressure on domestic prices. (See P. D. Jonson, 'Money and Economic Activity in the Open Economy: The UK, 1880–1970', International Monetary Research Programme Discussion paper, London School of Economics, July 1975.) As I illustrate in section VI, however, the relative high rate of inflation as it relates to government expenditures is best interpreted as a *disequilibrium* phenomenon which is not sustainable.

[3] See W. Branson and J. Myhrman, 'Inflation in Open Economies: Supply-Determined versus Demand-Determined Models', Seminar Paper No. 34, Institute for International Economic Studies (October, 1973) for a further discussion of this point.

Combining a particular theory of wage bargaining with mark-up pricing, the Scandinavian model implies that relative price changes depend on relative

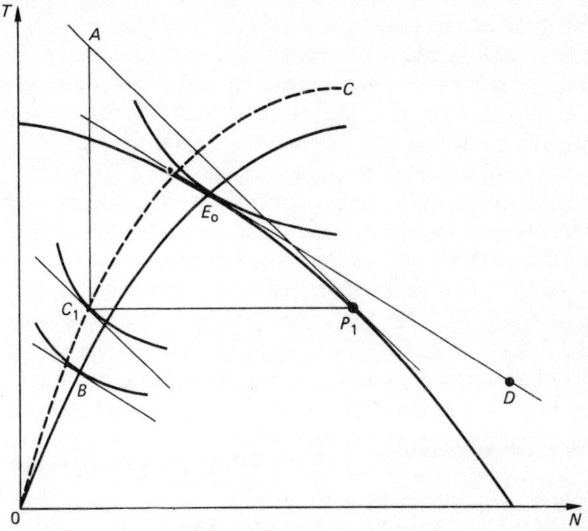

Fig. 7.2

Note on Figure: Initial equilibrium without expenditures or taxes occurs at E_0 where the excess demands for both traded and non-traded goods are zero. Holding relative prices constant, a tax, with real value in terms of T equal to AC_1, used to finance an equal-valued purchase of N would move the private sector consumption point to B and the total demand for non-traded goods to D leaving a net excess demand. This will be eliminated by a higher relative price of N increasing production to P_1. The private consumption point is C_1 and the government consumes C_1P_1 units of N. Increasing government taxes and expenditures would move P_1 further away from E_0 and lead to a higher price of non-traded goods.

rates of productivity growth in the two sectors. More specifically

$$\frac{dP_N}{P_N} - \frac{dP_T}{P_T} = \rho_T - \rho_N \tag{5}$$

where ρ_T and ρ_N represent the rates of technical progress in the traded goods and non-traded goods industries respectively.[1]

The apparent success this model has had in empirical work on inflation in

[1] Equation (5) can be interpreted in terms of our more general expression (4) by noting that $\rho_T - \rho_N$ can be related to ϵ_y and that the Scandinavian model abstracts from relative price effects on supplies and all demand factors which are captured by the other three elasticities in equation (4).

several countries[1] justifies some further examination of its properties and a possible alternative interpretation of the statistical results.

Although derived from a partial equilibrium view of the economy, the basic implication of the Scandinavian model (equation (5)) can be shown to be consistent with long-run predictions of a commonly used general equilibrium model if income and price elasticities of demand are unity and technical progress is Hicks neutral.[2] These conditions are quite stringent and it is often assumed that they are in fact not fulfilled, as far as the private sector's behavioural equations are concerned. This is the case particularly for the restriction on the income demand elasticities. To explain the empirical success of the Scandinavian model in some countries, it thus remains to look at government sector expenditures and I shall propose one rationalisation based on an assumed labour market oriented policy.

Suppose that for some reason the government considers the existing distribution of labour between the sectors of the economy as being in some sense optimal. This may be for reasons connected with regional, industrial or social stability but may simply reflect the government's view that movements of labour between sectors should be avoided on the grounds that it creates frictional problems and temporary unemployment. If the government backs up this view by policies to ensure that no labour movements occur then the result in equation (5) follows from the assumption of a homogeneous labour market employed in the Scandinavian model. This can be shown by using the condition that the wage rate is equal to the value of the marginal products of labour in the two sectors

$$w = P_N MPL_N = P_T MPL_T \tag{6}$$

The assumption of constant labour employment in each sector implies that the marginal products can only change if there is technical progress.[3] Denoting the percentage changes in the marginal products of labour in the two sectors ρ_N and ρ_T equation (6) immediately yields

$$\frac{dP_N}{P_N} - \frac{dP_T}{P_T} = \rho_T - \rho_N \tag{7}$$

which is identical to equation (5).

[1] See L. Calmfors, 'Swedish Inflation and International Price Influences', Seminar Paper No. 45, Institute for International Economic Studies, March 1975, for a study of Sweden; and O. Aukrust, *op. cit.*, for a description of work done on the Scandinavian model. Note however also the results of Branson and Myhrman, *op. cit.*, which imply that a simple Phillips-curve model outperforms the Scandinavian model on a mean square prediction error criterion in the case of Sweden.

[2] See H. Kierzkowski, 'Theoretical Foundations of the Scandinavian Model of Inflation', International Monetary Research Programme Discussion Paper, London School of Economics (September, 1974).

[3] This assumes that the other factors used in production, for example capital, are also held fixed. This is probably not a bad approximation to reality as far as short- to medium-run analysis is concerned.

If this argument is correct then the implication for testing of the Scandinavian model as far as its theoretical underpinnings are concerned is that we cannot use a single equation model, instead we have to estimate a system of equations one of which is a government policy function.[1] The reason is both that simultaneous equation biases might otherwise affect the estimates and that we cannot be sure whether we are estimating a structural relationship of the private sector or a policy reaction function. The latter uncertainty is of course particularly troublesome if we want to try and use the model for predictions of the effects of *changes* in the government policy behaviour.

Finally, the dependence of the derivation of (7) on a particular government policy may explain why statistical estimates show some countries to be less well described by the Scandinavian model than others. It seems then that more traditional models of aggregate price behaviour cannot yet be ruled out, and a combination of the commodity classification of the Scandinavian model with a more developed demand structure as attempted here may prove to be useful.

Returning to the main theme of this section the reader may recall that I have argued that by suitable expenditure or output switching policies a country may under certain conditions achieve some autonomy without giving up the full employment and balance of payments equilibrium targets.[2] Whether or not this autonomy is worth using depends of course on its costs and benefits but also on the *quantitative* effects likely to be achieved. It might be that what has been described in this section are second order of small effects. At this point in the analysis it is thus necessary to form some quantitative estimates of the likely effect to governmental inflation policies in long-run equilibrium.

Consider again relation (4) which describes the equilibrium rate of change in the relative price of non-traded goods in a growing economy. Suppose, for lack of any empirical evidence on these parameters, that both supply and demand price elasticities are unity and that the income elasticity of demand is 1·25. The assumption that non-traded goods are income elastic in demand has often been made in the literature together with the assertion that growth is mainly associated with the traded goods sector. To give a specific example, assume that half of the economy's production constitutes non-traded goods and that the output elasticity in the traded goods sector is three times as large

[1] The fact that government policy may become endogenous in the Scandinavian model is pointed out in the Branson–Myhrman and Aukrust papers, although these authors use different policy objectives than those employed here. They also do not pursue the implications this has for testing and policy analysis.

[2] It should be pointed out that these policies can not strictly be carried out indefinitely either because the government would eventually absorb all of the economy's G.N.P., or because the economy would end up specialising in either traded or non-traded goods, or because non-traded goods would become traded at some relative price. The proposition in the text is thus not about the steady state growth path of the economy.

as in the non-traded sector. Then ϵ_y will be 0·5 and the equilibrium rate of relative price change will be three-eighths $\frac{dy}{y}$, that is 1·5 per cent per year if the annual rate of growth of output is 4 per cent. This relative price change would occur in the absence of any governmental policy.

Suppose now that the government succeeded in bringing about an increase in the growth of the non-traded sector to the extent that the output elasticity of the T sector was made only twice as large as in the N sector. Then ϵ_y would be two-thirds and the new equilibrium relative price change seven-twenty-fourths $\frac{dy}{y}$. The change due to the government policy would be one-twelfth $\frac{dy}{y}$ or three tenths of 1 per cent per year on the same assumption as above with respect to real growth. Using equation (3) we note that the impact on the overall rate of inflation would be 0·15 per cent per year, a figure which certainly does not seem substantial.

Turning to the effect of government expenditures of the type discussed above and in figure 7.2, similar calculations carried out on the assumption that the government's share in total income is 25 per cent indicate that an increase in the *rate of growth* of government expenditures from being equal to the rate of growth in output to being twice as large as the latter would alter the rate of inflation as measured in equation (3) by about four-tenths of 1 per cent per year. Anticipating the discussion in section VII, it does not seem plausible that this small effect on the overall rate of inflation by a relatively drastic policy change would make the pursuit of an independent long-run rate of inflation a worthwhile objective in a small open economy. Short-run stabilisation possibilities may still be substantial, however, depending on the size of certain elasticities and speed of adjustment parameters in the private sector's behavioural functions. This issue will be taken up in the next section after a brief discussion of the implication of my analysis for comparisons of inflation rates across countries.

Each small member country in the world economy will in equilibrium experience an inflation rate which can be described by equations (3) and (4). Comparing any two countries we then see that differences between them stem from either of three sources. They can first of all be due to a different degree of openness between the countries as measured by the size of the non-traded sector in aggregate output and expenditures. Secondly, the elasticities making up the ratio on the right hand side of equation (4) may vary across countries. Different production technology and tastes may make one economy more price sensitive than the other, and growth need not be biased in the same direction in each economy. Finally equation (4) tells us that the real growth rates of countries will influence their relative inflation rates.

If we confine the analysis to the western industrial countries, the quantitative estimates above suggest that we should not observe substantially different inflation rates among countries and in particular that government policies will only have relatively small impacts. If we then add to that the equalising force provided by factor mobility among nations, we should not be surprised at some recent empirical findings suggesting very close relationships between OECD country inflation rates. In two related papers[1] I have argued that comparisons of price indexes across countries is complicated because of differences in index construction between them. These differences may be as large as the variability introduced by the other factors discussed above, including government policies, so that observed discrepancies in published statistics are not necessarily a measure of autonomy. This argument finally leads to the idea that we can treat countries as if they were regions in an integrated world economy and that in an analysis of the causes of inflation we should put more emphasis on worldwide developments rather than country-specific factors.

IV. AUTONOMY IN THE SHORT RUN

In the previous section I have argued that the ability of a small economy to affects its long-run rate of inflation is very limited. This conclusion is, I submit, extremely important not only because it implies a very definite constraint within which long-term government inflation policy has to operate. It also implies that short-run policy has to be conducted so as to be consistent with the longer-run possibilities, or rather lack thereof. In other words, the policies pursued must aim *only* at short-run stabilisation if they are not to be destabilising in the long run.

Two questions have to be dealt with in this context: What are the constraints and limitations (other than long-run consistency) which operate in the short run? How long is the short run? In this section I shall discuss these questions from a theoretical point of view. Some statistical results bearing on the same issues will be provided subsequently.

The first long-run constraint which will be relaxed is the requirement of balance of payments equilibrium. As will be shown, this has the effect of rendering general monetary and fiscal policies successful in influencing domestic price trends. The mechanism by which prices are affected in the short run can be illustrated in the basic figure used above, if we modify it to take account of divergencies between income and expenditures of the economy as a whole caused by government policy. Figure 7.3 is drawn for an expansionary monetary or fiscal policy assumed not to alter private individuals' spending patterns. In initial equilibrium income equals expenditures and trade balances at E_0. In terms of traded goods, income (and expenditures) is measured by the distance OY_0. An expansionary policy which, again in terms

[1] Hans Genberg, 'A Note on Inflation Rates Under Fixed Exchange Rates', Graduate Institute of International Studies, May 1974; and Hans Genberg, 'The Concept and Measurement of the World Price Level and Rate of Inflation', Discussion Paper, G.I.I.S.-Ford Foundation International Monetary Research Project (Graduate Institute of International Studies, October 1974).

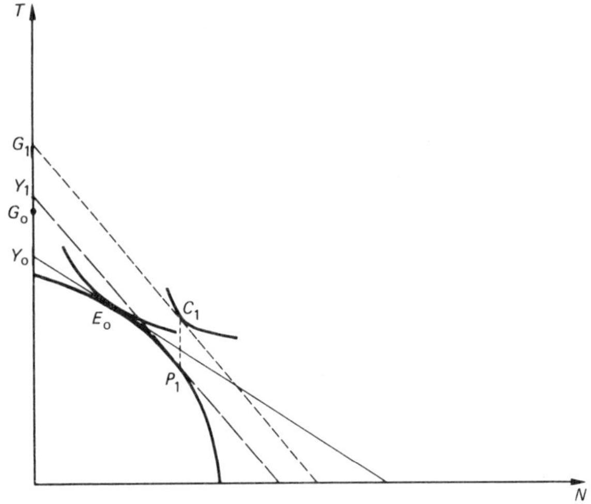

Fig. 7.3

of traded goods, would increase aggregate demand by Y_0G_0 would at the original relative prices create an excess demand for non-traded goods and thus drive their relative price up. Short-run equilibrium will be attained at P_1 as far as production is concerned and C_1 in terms of the consumption mix. Income from production is now OY_1 and total expenditures OG_1 where Y_1G_1 (= Y_0G_0) represents the policy-induced excess of total spending over receipts for the economy as a whole. The same distance also represents the balance of trade deficit of our country which eventually will bring the economy back to E_0. The movement from E_0 to P_1 has brought about an increased relative price of non-traded goods and implies some policy control over domestic inflation during the adjustment process. Comparing one (short-run) equilibrium point with another, however, shows that the expansionary policy only creates a once-and-for-all change in P_N and thus the price level. The rate of inflation at P_1 is not affected by the expansionary policy but remains equal to the world average.

Noting that equilibrium points like C_1, P_1 also entail a balance of payments deficit we can show the short-run trade-off between relative prices (and the price level) and the balance of payments in figure 7.4.[1] The location of this tradeoff locus depends in general on the structure and parameters describing the whole economy, but its slope will be determined mainly by an expression, like the ratio on the right hand side of equation (4), involving price elasticities of demand and supply and expenditure elasticities of demand.

[1] Rudiger Dornbusch has developed and used similar figures in analysing devaluations. See, for instance, R. Dornbusch, 'Real and Monetary Aspects of the Effects of Exchange Rate Changes', in Robert Z. Aliber (ed.) *National Monetary Policies and the International Financial System* (Chicago: The University of Chicago Press, 1974), pp. 64–81.

Two important propositions are implicit in this tradeoff. The first is that the policy authorities have to pursue *increasingly* tight or expansionary policies in order to affect the rate of inflation and not merely the price level.[1] The increasingly severe policies will also bring about *increasing* deficits or surpluses in the balance of payments, as the case may be, the effects of which become harder and harder to sterilise and sooner or later forcing the policies to be abandoned.[2] The second point implied by figure 7.4 is that the relative rate of inflation between the country and the rest of the world need not be associated with a particular balance of payments position. A movement along the tradeoff locus from E_0 to E_1 would entail a higher rate of inflation than the rest of the world and at the same time a balance of payments deficit.

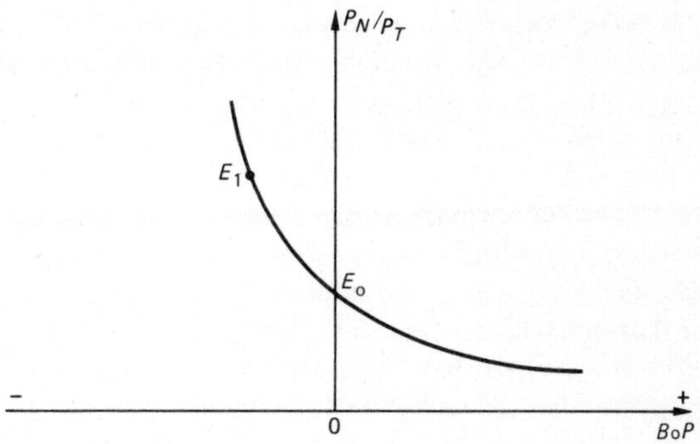

Fig. 7.4

During the reverse movement we would still observe a deficit but a slower rate of inflation than elsewhere. The correlation we should expect from figure 7.4 is between differential rates of inflation and *increasing* deficits in the balance of payments.

Once we move from qualitative statements about the degree of policy autonomy enjoyed by a small country to more detailed and quantitative questions dealing with the exact dynamic paths followed by the variables in the system the answers become more and more dependent on the particular model we operate with. This is particularly true if we are interested in getting estimates of the length of the time lags in the economy which determine the span of time over which short-run policy is effective.

[1] This statement refers to states of short-run equilibrium such as points E_0 and E_1 in figure 7.4. The movement from E_0 to E_1 due to an expansionary policy is regarded here as an adjustment of the price level to its new (quasi-) equilibrium level. It may be interpreted as a temporary surge of inflation if there are adjustment lags in the economic system.

[2] The problem of sterilisation and the related issue of capital mobility is discussed below in the context of the speed of adjustment to policy actions.

In a class of money and goods models which has become widely used in macroeconomic theorising about small open economies,[1] the duration of policy effects depends, apart from the demand and supply elasticities already mentioned, on the strength of the real balance effect in the aggregate expenditure function. With the latter often claimed to be fairly weak[2] it has been concluded that the short run is in fact quite long. This neglects, however, the crucial role played by the degree of capital mobility in determining the speed of the balance of payments adjustment mechanism and in delimiting the scope of sterilisation policies. Several empirical studies suggest that financial integration among western industrialised economies is strong enough to rob monetary policy at least of most of its effectiveness within a quarter or two after its introduction.

Leaving the world of full employment, the task of generalising about the dynamics of policy response becomes even more difficult as the number of possible models now becomes overwhelming.[3] It is certainly possible to add a Phillips type tradeoff to the balance of payments defined in figure 7.4 and thus get dynamic interaction between inflation unemployment and the balance of payments. This exercise would be far from trivial however if we are to keep the traded–non-traded goods classification employed in this paper which I feel is an important part of modelling small open economies. A promising route seems to be the introduction of price and wage expectations into labour market behavioural functions; but rather than pursuing this further we now turn to some very simple empirical evidence designed more to raise questions than to provide answers.

V. SOME SIMPLE REGRESSION RESULTS

Tables 7.1 and 7.2 contain ordinary least squares estimates from equations (8) and (9) respectively

$$\log P_i = \alpha_0 + \alpha_1 \log P_e + u_i \qquad (8)$$

$$\Delta \log P_i = \beta_0 + \beta_1 \, \Delta \log P_e + v_i \qquad (9)$$

where P_i and P_e stand for the price level in country i and in Europe as a whole respectively.

[1] See, among others, M. Parkin, 'Inflation, the Balance of Payments, Domestic Credit Expansion, and Exchange Rate Adjustments', in Robert Z. Aliber (ed.) *National Monetary Policies and International Financial System*, Chicago: The University of Chicago Press, 1972, pp. 49–63.

[2] Many attempts to isolate a real balance effect empirically have indeed failed, but it can be argued that this is due to the use of misspecified models. In an expenditure function which incorporates the real balance effect more correctly, P. D. Jonson, *op. cit.*, finds a strong and significant relationship between excess money holdings and expenditures in the United Kingdom.

[3] One generalisation which still seems to come through is the long-run impotency of monetary policy and the role of capital mobility in defining the short run (see A. Swoboda, *op. cit.*).

TABLE 7.1
O.L.S. estimation of $\log P_i = \alpha_0 + \alpha_1 \log P_e + u_i$

P_i	P_e	α_0	α_1	R^2	$D-W$
Austria	Europe	0·10 (0·15)	0·98 (0·03)	0·98	0·80
Belgium	Europe	0·99 (0·12)	0·79 (0·03)	0·98	0·57
Germany	Europe	0·16 (0·19)	0·96 (0·04)	0·97	1·25
Italy	Europe	0·36 (0·20)	1·07 (0·04)	0·98	0·54
Luxembourg	Europe	1·51 (0·11)	0·68 (0·02)	0·98	0·92
Netherlands	Europe	−1·28 (0·14)	1·28 (0·03)	0·99	1·42
Norway	Europe	−0·51 (0·09)	1·11 (0·02)	1·00	2·19
Portugal	Europe	0·44 (0·26)	1·10 (0·06)	0·97	0·41
Sweden	Europe	−0·69 (0·13)	1·15 (0·03)	0·99	0·80
Switzerland	Europe	0·53 (0·10)	0·88 (0·02)	0·99	0·75
United States	Europe	1·54 (0·19)	0·67 (0·04)	0·95	0·40

Notes: The price levels were measured by yearly observations covering 1955–1970 on consumer price indexes obtained from O.E.C.D. *Main Economic Indicators; Historical Statistics.* The sample of countries was chosen so as to avoid some of the problems posed by large exchange rate changes. The European Index was constructed as a weighted average of the ten European countries in the sample. For a justification for using these ten countries and for a discussion of the weights used in the average, see Hans Genberg, 'The Concept and Measurement of the World Price Level and Rate of Inflation'.

Figures in parentheses are standard errors and the column headed D–W contains Durbin–Watson statistics.

The implication of the theory in the previous sections is that, in an open economy, the domestic price level is determined in part by foreign prices adjusted for exchange rate changes and in part by policy affecting relative prices of home and foreign goods. In general we would expect policy to be conducted with an attempt to affect this price ratio during an extended period of time as well as to be effective only after some time lag. Since we have put all policy influences into the error terms of equations (8) and (9) we should thus expect the u_is to be serially correlated if the policy variables have an impact on the domestic *price level* covering several periods.

Similarly we should observe serial correlation in the v_is if governments can and do affect their *inflation rates* for several successive periods. As illustrated in figure 7.4 the difference between a general policy aimed at the price level and one aimed at the rate of inflation is that the former will produce a con-

TABLE 7.2
O.L.S. estimation of $\Delta \log P_i = \beta_0 + \beta_1 \Delta \log P_e + v_i$

P_i	P_e	β_0	β_1	R^2	$D\text{–}W$
Austria	Europe	0·00	0·88	0·33	2·60
		(0·01)	(0·31)		
Belgium	Europe	0·00	0·74	0·40	1·55
		(0·01)	(0·23)		
Germany	Europe	–0·02	1·54	0·41	1·75
		(0·02)	(0·47)		
Italy	Europe	–0·00	1·08	0·39	1·37
		(0·01)	(0·34)		
Luxembourg	Europe	0·00	0·63	0·24	2·56
		(0·01)	(0·27)		
Netherlands	Europe	0·01	0·89	0·23	2·52
		(0·01)	(0·39)		
Norway	Europe	0·00	1·07	0·46	2·47
		(0·01)	(0·30)		
Portugal	Europe	–0·01	1·30	0·43	1·19
		(0·01)	(0·38)		
Sweden	Europe	0·00	1·05	0·47	1·41
		(0·01)	(0·29)		
Switzerland	Europe	–0·00	0·81	0·50	1·08
		(0·01)	(0·21)		
United States	Europe	0·00	0·72	0·28	0·74
		(0·01)	(0·28)		

Notes: See table 7.1

stant balance of payments deficit or surplus whereas the latter results in an increasing one. If these balance of payments consequences are quantitatively large and rapid, a price level policy may be feasible while an inflation policy is not.

Looking first at the coefficient estimates and the R^2, it is evident that the level regressions have produced what we expected them to in this regard given the trend in the variables. The rate of change figures in table 7.2 are more interesting in that the foreign inflation rate still exerts a strong influence on individual countries[1] and explain a substantial proportion of the variation in the dependent variables. This relatively good performance suggests that one use of the model might be as a benchmark against which more sophisticated models can be compared and evaluated.[2]

[1] *t*-ratios appropriate for the hypothesis that $\beta = 0$ are all greater than 2·25, and the hypothesis that $\beta = 1$ cannot be rejected for any of the ten European countries.

[2] The first that come to mind are the country models specified and estimated in R. Cross and D. Laidler, 'Inflation, Excess Demand and Expectations in Fixed Exchange Rate Open Economies: Some Preliminary Empirical Results', from the proceedings of a conference on Inflation in the World Economy at the University of Manchester, July 17–19, 1974. Note that this comparison is somewhat complicated by the fact that sample periods differ, and that Cross and Laidler use a world rather than a European index as the independent variable.

Turning to the Durbin–Watson statistic, it is interesting to note the difference between the level and rate of change regressions. In the former, seven out of the ten European countries show definite serial correlation in the residuals[1] whereas for the latter none of them do. Portugal and Switzerland are in the indeterminate region of the test statistic, and for the rest of the countries the serial correlation hypothesis can be rejected at the 95 per cent level. An extreme conclusion from these findings would be that while countries do have some control over their price level, their rate of inflation is essentially determined from abroad (except for periods shorter than a year) if they want to stick to a fixed exchange rate. The alternative conclusions would be that the apparent lack of autonomy reflects a choice of policy makers not to attempt to pursue an independent inflation policy and is thus the result of policy co-ordination rather than lack of autonomy. More research, and in particular research aimed at identifying and estimating the lags imbedded in the structure of open economies, is clearly needed to choose between these two explanations. It is hoped that the above results will serve as a challenge in this respect.

The last line in tables 7.1 and 7.2 is included as another challenge. Here the United States price level and rate of inflation are regressed against the corresponding European ones. Even though the coefficient estimates and the R^2s are reasonably good, the Durbin–Watson statistic indicates the presence of serial correlation in the residuals of both equations. This may be the result of substantially greater autonomy between the two continents than within each, and it directs attention to the need of discovering the transmission mechanisms which are at work both between Europe as a whole and the United States, and between individual European countries.

VI. POLICY AUTONOMY IN THE UNITED KINGDOM: SOME SIMULATION RESULTS

The thrust of my arguments in this paper has been that a small country with a fixed exchange rate has negligible power to affect its price level in the long run and that the rigidity of the balance of payments constraint will define the shorter-run bounds of policy autonomy. The empirical evidence I have presented seems to indicate that even these bounds are quite narrow in the sense that inflation rates in the major industrial countries have not deviated from each other for significant lengths of time in the postwar period. Of course, many interpretations can be given to the kind of single equation estimates contained in table 7.2, so an empirically satisfactory treatment of the issue must be cast in a structural model framework.

Any model attempting to answer the questions dealt with in this paper should, as a minimum, be able to explain four endogenous variables: the general price level, the balance of payments, and the two major monetary and

[1] For fifteen observations, the upper and lower 95 per cent confidence points are 1·36 and 1·08 respectively. The corresponding 99 per cent points are 1·07 and 0·81.

fiscal policy tools; for instance the rate of government expenditures and the rate of domestic credit creation. The price level being the main variable of interest must of course be endogenous. The balance of payments must also be taken into account since it is one of the external constraints facing the open economy. Policy tools are usually assumed exogenous in macro-econometric models but, as I have argued above, they ought to be endogenised in order for the estimates of the structural parameters in the model to be free of biases. In addition to these main variables it may be useful and necessary to include other relationships in a model of a particular country to get a satisfactory representation of its economy. Since the issue of policy autonomy is furthermore closely tied up with time lags and adjustment processes, the models we specify should finally be capable of estimating and explaining how long these processes take to work themselves through the economic system.

Research on the scale required for this kind of model building is clearly beyond the scope of the present paper, but I shall make use of recent advances in this direction to illustrate some of the theoretical points. Specifically I shall provide some simulation results designed to discover the degree of policy autonomy enjoyed by a particular country, the United Kingdom. I believe that the results will be shown to be generally indicative of conditions prevailing in other countries as well once the appropriate models become available.

The model of the United Kingdom economy that will be used for the simulation exercises is one recently developed by P. D. Jonson at the London School of Economics.[1] This model, which to my mind is one of the best specified and most consistently estimated open economy econometric model available, explains twelve of the major macroeconomic variables,[2] among them the four mentioned above. The model was also designed to capture both the time lags and the balance of payments constraints operating in the United Kingdom economy which makes it particularly useful for our purposes.

We shall report the results from four simulations (see table 7.3) containing two expansionary (fiscal) policies and two contractionary (monetary) policies and compare them with the control solution generated by the model when all exogenous variables were allowed to take on their actual values during the period 1954–74.

The tables that follow contain some of the more interesting results from these simulations which give a few clues as to the possibility of pursuing an independent inflation policy in an open economy, and the consequences thereof.

[1] See P. D. Jonson, *op. cit.*, and the same author's recent Ph.D. thesis at the London School of Economics. A brief description of the model is given below in an Appendix.

[2] The endogenous variables are: the stock of money, the stock of bonds, the general price level, export prices, exports, total domestic spending, imports, total output, bank rate, domestic credit, international reserves, and total government taxes.

TABLE 7.3
Types of Simulation

Control	All exogenous variables at historical values.
Simulation 1	Real government spending was allowed to grow 2 per cent per annum faster than it actually did historically.
Simulation 2	Real government spending was allowed to increase by 37·5 per cent over the actual value in period 1 and was held that much over the historical value for the rest of the simulation.
Simulation 3	The authorities' target interest rate[1] was raised by 60 per cent above the control solution target.
Simulation 4	Same as simulation 3 plus a reduction in the forward discount on the sterling by approximately the same amount.

[1] The model has a policy reaction function for Bank Rate which implies that this formulation involving the target bank rate is the appropriate monetary policy.

TABLE 7.4
Simulation results: log *P*

Period	*Control*	*Simulation 1*	*Simulation 2*	*Simulation 3*	*Simulation 4*
0	0·851	0·851	0·851	0·851	0·851
1	0·908	0·910	0·938	0·907	0·907
5	1·096	1·119	1·209	1·084	1·084
10	1·285	1·354	1·447	1·241	1·240
15	1·510	1·633	1·688	1·427	1·427
20	1·794	1·973	1·970	1·673	1·674

TABLE 7.5
Simulation results: Average annual compounded rates of inflation

Period	*Control*	*Simulation 1*	*Simulation 2*	*Simulation 3*	*Simulation 4*
0– 1	5·9	6·0	9·1	5·8	5·8
0– 5	5·0	5·5	7·4	4·8	4·8
5–10	3·9	4·8	4·9	3·2	3·2
10–15	4·6	5·7	4·9	3·8	3·8
15–20	5·8	7·0	5·8	5·0	5·0
0–20	4·8	5·8	5·8	4·2	4·2

TABLE 7.6
Simulation results: the stock of international reserves

Period	*Control*	*Simulation 1*	*Simulation 2*	*Simulation 3*	*Simulation 4*
0	983	983	983	983	983
1	935	923	836	936	941
5	999	920	672	1021	1050
10	1281	987	640	1288	1333
15	1525	887	548	1422	1500
20	534	212	141	454	486

TABLE 7.7
Simulation results: international reserves, difference between control and simulated values as a percentage of the control values

Period	*Simulation 1*	*Simulation 2*	*Simulation 3*	*Simulation 4*
0	0	0	0	0
1	−1·3	−10·6	0·1	0·6
5	−8·0	−32·7	0·3	5·1
10	−23·0	−50·1	0·5	4·0
15	−41·9	−64·1	−6·8	−1·6
20	−60·3	−73·6	−15·0	−9·0

TABLE 7.8
Simulation results: domestic credit

Period	*Control*	*Simulation 1*	*Simulation 2*	*Simulation 3*	*Simulation 4*
0	8434	8434	8434	8434	8434
1	8866	8866	9228	8778	8778
5	11048	11384	13494	10199	10097
10	15063	17327	22248	12965	12836
15	23861	31888	40538	19535	19149
20	37798	61084	70969	29437	29144
Average annual percentage change	7·8	10·4	11·2	6·4	6·4

TABLE 7.9
Simulation results: ratio of real government expenditures to real G.N.P.

Period	*Control*	*Simulation 1*	*Simulation 2*	*Simulation 3*	*Simulation 4*
1	16·6	17·0	22·6	16·6	16·6
5	15·8	17·3	21·3		
10	18·1	21·9	25·0		
15	20·0	27·1	28·4		
20	23·1	35·0	33·0	25·8	25·8

TABLE 7.10
Simulation results: bank rate

Period	*Control*	*Simulation 1*	*Simulation 2*	*Simulation 3*	*Simulation 4*
0	3·03	3·03	3·03	3·03	3·03
1	4·65	4·65	4·65	6·06	6·06
20	9·46	10·76	12·16	17·57	17·24

The first significant proposition which the tables illustrate is that in the long-term the ability to alter the rate of inflation by domestic policies is very limited, quite apart from the question of whether such policies can be carried out considering their side effects. The long-run rate of inflation is changed by less than 1 per cent per annum in each of the simulations even though all policies pursued are quite radical as measured by the ratio of government spending to real output for fiscal policy and the rate of interest for monetary policy. In cases 1 and 2 with the expansionary policy, the percentage of real output absorbed by the government more than doubles in the simulation runs whereas in the control solution it increases by less than 50 per cent. The rate of interest produced by the restrictive monetary policies increases to over 17 per cent by the twentieth period as compared to the control value of about 9·5 per cent. These policy shocks are quite large and it is likely that other goals set by the government necessitate changes in them.

Another way of illustrating the constraint imposed by the openness of the economy is by comparing the rate of inflation that would have been generated had the economy been closed with the actual rate of inflation produced in the simulations. If we for simplicity take the rate of credit creation over the twenty periods as an indication of the closed economy rate of inflation then the difference of 2·6 per cent per annum (see table 7.7, last line) in this rate between simulation 1 and the control solution should have created a difference in the inflation rates by the same amount. The actual difference of 1 per cent suggests that only about 38 per cent of the closed economy policy effect is retained. For the other simulations the corresponding figures are 29, 43 and

43 per cent. This measure of the reduced policy effect *does not take into account the adverse balance of payments consequences* of the policies.

The second proposition the tables bring out is that a country cannot pursue policies which significantly alter their inflation rate without also causing severe balance of payments difficulties. Tables 7.6 and 7.7 show that for the expansionary policies the average balance of payments deficit is roughly doubled and the stock of international reserves is reduced by 60 and 73 per cent respectively compared to the control solution at the end of the twenty years. Keeping in mind the balance of payments difficulties suffered by the United Kingdom in the postwar period, this additional burden is unlikely to have been endured with a fixed sterling exchange rate. As predicted by the theory, the payments consequences of an expansionary policy are seen to be *increasingly* severe when a differential inflation rate policy is pursued.

A third point we can extract from the tables is that fiscal policy seems to have a larger impact on the price level and rate of inflation than does monetary policy,[1] although the comparison is complicated both because of difficulties in defining the appropriate unit policy shock and by the interdependence between monetary and fiscal policy implied by the government budget constraint. The result is nevertheless interesting since it confirms what, following Mundell, has become the standard theoretical proposition regarding the relative efficacy of monetary and fiscal policy in fixed exchange-rate economies.

Turning finally to more short-run considerations, it appears that the *possibility* for policy-induced deviations from purchasing power parity is larger in the short-run provided the necessary amount of foreign exchange reserves can be absorbed or disposed of to finance the induced international payments flows, and provided that the government is willing to take very drastic policy actions. The massive expansion of the government sector produced in simulation 2 manages to alter the rate of inflation by an average of 2·4 per cent per annum during the first five years of the policy. This does not however seem to be a substantial figure considering the price paid in terms of the size of the policy shock and the balance of payments consequences it generates which for the same first five years imply that the stock of reserves falls by about one-third compared to either the control and the initial values. It is unlikely that flows of this scale could be kept from generating speculative capital flows forcing the abandonment of the policy or the fixed exchange rate.

[1] To get this result, take the difference in the twenty-period annual rate of inflation between the control and simulated solution for each of the simulations. Divide this number by the change in the policy tool measured as the difference between the control and simulated annual rate of change in the policy variable over the same period. The ratio so obtained is one measure of the relative effectiveness of the policy tools, and for the simulations discussed here it takes the values 0·5, 1·0, 0·2 and 0·2 respectively. Fiscal policy has the higher ratios and is thus more effective on this criterion.

To summarise what we have found from the simulation runs in this section, we note first of all that policies aimed at affecting the rate of inflation in an open economy must be quite drastic if they are to have a noticeable impact. Fixed exchange rates do in fact limit the scope for policy autonomy to a large extent even in the short run so that only a small fraction of the closed economy policy effect is retained. Secondly we have found that the size of the balance of payments consequences of the policies is such that it is unlikely that the fixed exchange rate could have been maintained together with the other policies. This finding is extremely important for two reasons when we interpret our simulation results. First of all it makes it clear that the policy simulations carried out here were aimed at checking what were the *possible* deviations from purchasing power parity given the structure of the underlying model, not whether these policies could or should be carried out considering the preferences of policy makers and the likely reaction of the private sector to large and persistent balance of payments disequilibria. Secondly, the large balance of payments deficits in simulations 1 and 2 should make it clear that we cannot argue from our results that it is after all not so worrying if the government sector expands much more rapidly than it has, because it does not affect the rate of inflation very much. The point is that the balance of payments deficits generated by too rapid government sector expansion not financed by increasing taxes will eventually force a devaluation, which in turn makes room for the necessary price increases. So in this more fundamental sense, a too rapid government expenditure expansion, or any other inflationary policy, will eventually generate price increases coupled with a depreciating exchange rate.

VII. IMPLICATIONS FOR INFLATION POLICIES IN SMALL COUNTRIES

In the introduction to this paper I set three goals for the analysis. The first was to determine what kinds of policies would be able to affect the rate of inflation in a small open economy, and to assess the quantitative importance of the implied policy autonomy. The previous sections have provided enough information on these questions for us now to be able to proceed to the third goal, namely to determine what proper attitude the authorities in a small country should have with the respect to inflation-control policies.

Suppose the government authorities have a set of goals in mind, one of which is a particular value of the country's rate of inflation. If that value is different from the one prevailing in the rest of the world, the government will in general have to give up some other policy aim in order to maintain the preferred inflation rate. Whether this is desirable or not depends obviously on both the benefits and costs of the policies, and it is here that the above analysis and evidence fit in. I have not discussed the benefits derivable from an inflation rate which is different from the world rate, but I have shown that the costs of obtaining even a very small differential inflation rate in the long run are quite large in terms of the size of the required policy measure, and therefore in terms of the sacrifice of other policy goals. The required policy measures were shown to be quite drastic even for shorter-run inflation objectives, and the balance of payments was in addition found to be a severe constraint.

Besides the commonplace conclusion that small countries committed to a fixed exchange rate should not try to alter their long-run rate of inflation but should rather set policies consistent with maintaining the world rate, the above arguments suggest that even in the short run a country should not aim at deviating from the rest of the world. The costs of doing so both in terms of the balance of payments and, more importantly, the sacrifice of other policy objectives is unlikely to be outweighed by the benefits from the small deviations which are actually possible to obtain.

If we do not consider the possibility of a floating exchange rate, it may be possible to argue that an appropriate strategy to follow would be to increase international goods market integration such that the country's price level becomes even more dependent on the world's price level. Closer ties with the rest of the world would, if they lead to a closer relationship between inflation rates, avoid the presumably disruptive *relative* price oscillations produced when the country's price level periodically rose above and fell below the world price level.

Alternatively, if the authorities placed a very heavy weight on being able to determine their own rate of inflation, they could opt for a flexible exchange rate. As always in equations relating to the optimum currency area issue, however, the major source (internal or external) of price fluctuations would have to be located before we could determine whether this move would make for greater domestic stability.

APPENDIX[1]

In this appendix I will describe briefly Jonson's model of the United Kingdom economy which I used in the simulation exercises in section VI of the main text. As mentioned there, the model explains twelve macroeconomic variables. The behavioural functions are generally specified as differential adjustment equations where the actual value of a variable is adjusted over time towards a long run or desired value. This allows the estimation of adjustment lags in the system. The long-run or desired functions are of fairly standard form with the major addition being that monetary disequilibrium is allowed to play an important role.

Apart from the partial adjustment mechanism, domestic expenditure on domestic output is determined by disposable income, the rate of interest and the discrepancy between actual and desired money balances. Imports depend on relative prices and total domestic sales, exports on relative prices and foreign income, and output is essentially demand determined.

Both export prices and domestic output prices incorporate partial adjustment towards purchasing power parity and demand pressure measured by the deviation of real government expenditures and private domestic expenditures from their steady state growth paths.

The asset side of the model include demand functions for money and government bonds which are of the fairly standard stock adjustment variety relating the desired change in asset holdings to the difference between the actual and desired level of the asset, the latter being determined by the relevant income and interest rate variables.

Together with introducing the real balance effect into the expenditure function, the model is novel in that it uses a government policy reaction function to determine the rate of interest and bank rate. The government authorities are assumed to adjust bank rate in order to achieve targets relating to the price level, the stock of foreign reserves, the rate of unemployment and the level of output. The government is also represented by a tax function.

A budget constraint and a balance of payments identity finally help determine the rate of domestic credit expansion and the flow of reserves.

The model was originally estimated with data spanning 1880–1970 using the Full Information Maximum Likelihood technique for estimating differential equation systems recently developed by C. R. Wymer.[2] Without going into the details of the result it may be useful to point out that Jonson shows that his model outperforms a 'conventional alternative model' in terms of explaining major macroeconomic variables.

Relating to the simulations performed here it should be pointed out that

[1] This appendix was added after the Conference at the request of several of the participants.

[2] See C. R. Wymer, 'Econometric Estimation of Stochastic Differential Equation Systems', *Econometrica* (1972).

real government expenditures is exogenous in the model which makes simulations 1 and 2 particularly simple to perform. Since bank rate is determined by a policy reaction function a change in monetary policy is most conveniently introduced by altering the target rate at which the authorities are aiming (simulation 3). Finally, the forward discount on sterling (exogenous in the model) was changed in the last simulation together with the change in the target bank rate in order to introduce interest rate parity and short-term capital flow responses into the model.

8 Inflation and the Exchange Rate Regime[1]

W. M. Corden
NUFFIELD COLLEGE, OXFORD

I. INTRODUCTION

The purpose of this paper is to sort out the relationship between inflation and the exchange rate regime. Are fixed or flexible rates more conducive to inflation? The focus is not on the well-known subject of the international inflation transmission process in the fixed rate system, nor on analysing the consequences of *given* monetary expansions in different countries (a matter much discussed by 'monetarists') but rather on the outcome of policy adjustments by fiscal and monetary authorities which are designed to bring about whatever transmission of, or insulation from, external inflation these authorities desire. The aim is also to show how the various inflation rates are determined in a fixed rate system when there are many different monetary authorities interacting on the rates chosen by different countries.[2]

The polar systems of rigidly fixed rates and perfectly flexible rates will be compared here. In fact the world has moved along the continuum between these limits in the flexible direction. Governments feel freer to alter their exchange rates under the managed floating system than under the Bretton Woods system. But most felt they had a little, occasional, freedom even under the old regime and some still do not feel complete freedom now. The polar analysis to follow would thus need to be modified if one wanted to compare the actual regimes of which we have recent experience.

II. THE FIXED RATE SYSTEM WITH IMBALANCES: THE INFLATION PRONE COUNTRY

We begin by considering the point of view of one country which is sufficiently

[1] This is a revised version of a paper presented both to the 'Seminar on Flexible Exchange Rates and Stabilisation Policy' organised by the Institute for International Economic Studies of the University of Stockholm, and to the Economic Association Conference. It is being published in the *Scandinavian Journal of Economics*, No. 2, 1976, as well as in this volume. I am indebted to valuable comments on an earlier draft from Herbert Grubel and John Martin.

[2] The main paper dealing with aspects of this subject (and anticipating some of the points in the present paper) is Fried[3]. See also Mundell [6]. On the international transmission process, see Caves [2], Turnovsky and Kapura [7], Branson [1], and various papers – notably those by Aukrust, Branson, Salant and Swoboda – in Krause and Salant [4].

small that it cannot significantly affect the rate of inflation in other countries. Figure 8.1 refers to this country. The vertical axis shows an index of national welfare (U_N) as perceived by its monetary authorities. The horizontal axis shows its domestic rate of price inflation.

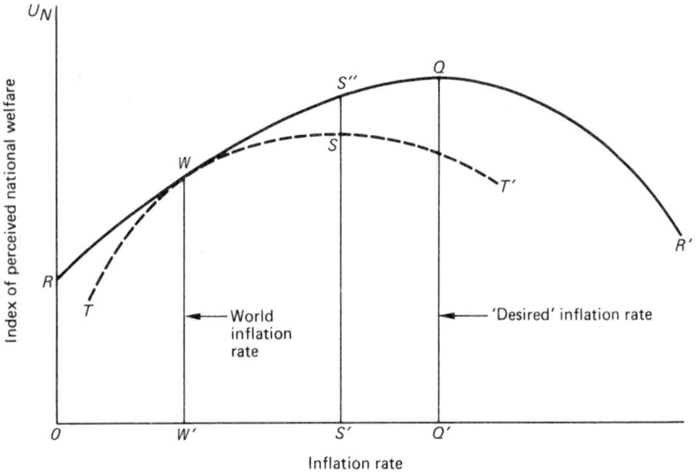

Fig. 8.1

If the exchange rate is flexible, the monetary authorities can choose their own inflation rate, irrespective of what this rate is in the rest of the world. This is the well-known point that a flexible rate can insulate a country from external inflation or deflation. The curve RR' is the curve of *inflation benefit* in the flexible rate system. The benefit is maximised at an inflation rate of OQ', this being what we shall call the *desired inflation rate.*

Alternatively, the exchange rate may be fixed. The world rate of inflation – namely OW' – then becomes relevant. If the authorities do not wish the country to run a balance of payments deficit the domestic rate of inflation must then be equal to the given world rate – at least, provided there are not structural changes (which we shall assume away) that would make a different rate of inflation compatible with absence of payments imbalance. Balance of payments equilibrium is here defined as absence of 'accommodating' capital movements or undesired reserve changes. With this externally determined rate of inflation the perceived welfare level to the country is $W'W$.

We are assuming that this particular country is an *inflation-prone* country, namely a country (such as Britain) that chooses to have a higher rate of inflation than the given world rate when it is a free agent, that is, when it has a flexible rate. It is to be contrasted with an *inflation-shy* country (such as Germany) that chooses a lower inflation rate than the world rate when it has a flexible rate regime. We shall come back to the inflation-shy country later.

What is the nature of the *inflation benefit*? It is the benefit perceived by the government and monetary authorities from domestic inflation and what goes with it – that is, from increased monetary demand for domestically produced goods and services. This benefit may consist of an expected reduction in unemployment or avoidance of an increase (which may only be a short-run benefit) and of a desired income redistribution towards the public sector and within the private sector. One could count the various efficiency and uncertainty costs of inflation as negative benefits here. The curve refers only to *perceived* or expected benefit. The inflation benefit curve could – but need not be – derived from an orthodox short-run Phillips-curve tradeoff and preference map.

The curve RR' will change over time. If a given level of employment can only be maintained with accelerating inflation it is likely that the welfare level attainable at the *desired inflation rate* would fall over time, while the *desired rate* itself might rise. In any case, our approach here is short-run, so we keep the curve constant. We shall look more closely at the meaning of this curve in the next section.

Figure 8.1 shows that in the fixed rate system with no imbalances the government has an 'excess demand' for inflation of $W'Q'$. It can satisfy some or all of this 'excess demand' by running a deficit. It could, perhaps, run a deficit sufficient to bring its domestic inflation rate up to the *desired rate* OQ'. The perceived welfare level that would then be attained would differ from that attained with the same inflation rate in the flexible rate system. For this time the country is running down its reserves or is borrowing, and in doing so is obtaining extra resources. Thus there is a cost as well as an additional benefit. Possible elements in the cost are the real rate of interest paid on borrowed funds, the interest foregone on funds otherwise invested abroad, an increased sense of insecurity owing to reduced owned reserves, and a political cost incurred in order to finance the deficit. The benefit is that the deficit makes available real resources to the country, absorption exceeding national output.

Now we come to an important stage in the argument. What is the *net* benefit from the deficit, excluding its effect on the inflation benefit? Suppose that before the deficit is incurred the country is borrowing abroad at an optimal rate. The real resource gain at the margin is then equal to the real rate of interest. We can include not only private borrowing but also 'autonomous' public borrowing here. Any extra borrowing will be 'accommodating', being the byproduct of choosing an inflation rate above the world rate. There must then be a net loss on any 'accommodating' borrowing, since it means borrowing above the optimum. Further, it also seems to follow that the greater the deficit and hence the greater the inflation rate, the greater the net loss.

This is represented in figure 8.1. The net loss is subtracted from the *flexible rate* inflation benefit curve RR' to yield the *fixed rate* benefit curve of WT'. The net loss increases with the rate of inflation because the deficit increases with the rate of inflation. The curve has also been continued to the left of W, to TW, to represent the idea that a surplus would also yield a net loss since foreign lending would be above the optimum. The curve TT' must also change over time. If the domestic inflation rate exceeds the world rate by a constant amount the deficit must be steadily increasing, so that TT' must be steadily falling (but always tangential to RR' at W), gradually approaching the vertical line WW'. This is because an increasing deficit (and possibly even a constant deficit) will only be capable of being financed at an increasing real rate of interest.

If the authorities do indeed perceive the effects of payments imbalances in this way we can conclude that they will choose an inflation rate of OS' in the fixed rate system, thus getting closer to, but not actually attaining, the *desired inflation rate* of OQ'. In fact, they will have 'bought' some extra inflation ($W'S'$) at a cost of what appears to be 'excess' borrowing, this cost being represented by SS''. But given the fixed exchange rate constraint it is not really excess borrowing. It is excess only in relation to the optimal borrowing rate in the flexible system.

There may be constraints on the ability to borrow. In that case the curve will turn sharply down at some point, in the extreme case becoming vertical, and thus setting a clear limit to the inflation rate. But the inflation rate that maximises the perceived welfare level may be below this constraint level.

It has been supposed here that in the fixed rate system it is possible for a country to choose its own inflation rate and so to run its economy at an inflation rate different from that of the world rate, the only limitation being the cost of excess borrowing or lending abroad. This involves two assumptions.

Firstly, there have to be a reasonable number of non-traded goods. Since the domestic prices of traded goods, strictly defined, must rise with their world prices under the fixed rate regime, some goods and services have to be *non*-traded in the sense that their prices are not wholly set in world markets. This, clearly, is a reasonable assumption.

Secondly, we are assuming that international capital mobility does not prevent a country from determining its own inflation rate. If there were perfect capital mobility, any one country could only bring about its desired inflation rate through fiscal policy, since monetary policy could not affect aggregate monetary demand for domestic goods and services. But in the absence of such perfect mobility, either monetary or fiscal policy, or some combination of them, could be used.[1]

[1] The various models of the international inflation transmission process show to what extent an external inflation is transmitted *automatically* to the domestic economy. The models attain their precision by making specific assumptions about monetary policy (constant interest rate or constant domestic credit creation), about rigidity of money wages or real wages, and so on. Here we are concerned with the outcome of *policy* adjustments that may offset or supplement the automatic processes, and that are designed finally to bring about whatever transmission of, or insulation from, external inflation the government and monetary authorities desire. We assume that the monetary authorities or governments of countries actually *succeed* in putting their countries on

Finally, it can be noted here that, conceivably, foreign borrowing may initially be below the optimum, or at least may be perceived to be. For some reason there may be a net *gain* from 'accommodating' borrowing. But this raises a question about the definition of 'autonomous' and 'accommodating' borrowing and why the borrowing did not take place 'autonomously', perhaps by the government, if there was a gain to be obtained. We shall come back to the general point of a net gain from accommodating borrowing when discussing the position of the reserve currency country, but here it need only be observed that the possibility exists and can be analysed in terms of our diagram (as is done in figure 8.3 later).

III. THE INFLATION BENEFIT CURVE FURTHER EXAMINED

Let us look a little more closely at the *inflation benefit curve* before going on with our main analysis. There are all sorts of difficulties about this simple curve, these difficulties raising all the problems of closed-economy inflation theory which are not the main concern of this paper.

If one believed in a stable Phillips-curve and a government welfare function with unemployment and the rate of inflation as arguments, there would be no problem. Indeed, one could even believe that inflation does not affect the rate of unemployment but has certain redistributive effects, and put the latter effects, rather than employment, into the welfare function. It is the instability over time of the tradeoffs that is the problem. The *desired inflation rate* may maximise short-term perceived utility, but may carry within it the seeds of utility losses later, perhaps through the expectations that are generated.

Perhaps one should then redefine the inflation benefit curve as referring to the present value of discounted perceived utility resulting from various short-run rates of price inflation. This would take into account not only possible short-run employment gains from a high rate of inflation but also the unemployment to which it may give rise later.

Furthermore, the following difficulty in the analysis of the previous section has been evaded so far. The resources provided to a country by an external deficit may in the short run improve its inflation-benefit curve.

We have supposed that the inflation-benefit curve depends on the *domestic* tradeoff between inflation, unemployment, income distribution, etc., and that this tradeoff is itself invariant to the exchange rate regime and whether or not there is foreign borrowing. At the same time the net loss from a *given* accommodating payments deficit has been assumed independent of the rate of inflation, even though the amount of the deficit depends on this rate. Hence we have simply subtracted the net loss from the given inflation benefit curve. Now the point is that they *may* be related.

---

that point of the inflation benefit curve where they want their countries to be; thus they are able to sterilise monetary inflows or to avoid deficits or surpluses that they do not want.

Suppose that the external deficit is matched by a public sector deficit and that some part of this is used not for investment but to subsidise wage-goods (for example, food), this in turn improving the short-run Phillips-curve trade-off. A fixed rate with a deficit then makes more real resources for consumption available in the short-run than a flexible rate system does. On the other hand, if we hold investment constant for this purpose, eventually consumption would have to fall relative to what would have happened without this deficit, since the deficit represents a foreign loan, not a gift. Hence in the long-run the tradeoff may be worsened. On balance one cannot assume that the inflation-benefit curve – which embodies both short-run and expected long-run effects – will move in a particular way. Hence one may be justified in keeping the benefit curve constant.

There is yet another complication. World inflation – and especially changes in the rate of world inflation – may be associated with changing *relative* prices. Thus a rise in the world inflation rate may, at least temporarily, raise prices of primary commodities relative to prices of manufactures. And such relative price effects may, in turn, affect the short-run Phillips-curve tradeoff and hence our RR' curve. One might argue that *any* significant relative price change will increase the rate of inflation for given unemployment (worsen the tradeoff), or alternatively that only a rise in the prices of commodities relative to manufactures will have this effect. In any case, this complication is not explicitly incorporated in our analysis, though no doubt it could be.

IV. THE INFLATION-SHY COUNTRY AND DOWNWARD WAGE RIGIDITY

Clearly, the whole analysis could be applied to a small inflation-shy country. This case is represented in figure 8.2. The desired inflation rate with flexible rates, OQ', is below the given world inflation rate OW', and once the possibility of a surplus is introduced, the country will 'buy' a reduction in inflation of $S'W'$ with such a surplus.

In this inflation-shy case there is an additional complication. In the fixed rate system the prices of traded goods must rise at the world inflation rate OW'. The domestic inflation rate which the government perceives to be optimal is OS'. This latter rate is a weighted average of the rate of inflation of the prices of traded goods and non-traded goods. The prices of non-traded goods must then rise slowly enough for this average to be attained given the constraint on the prices of traded goods. This may not present a problem when the share of non-traded goods in the relevant domestic price index is high. Also, it does not present a problem when – as now – the world rate of inflation is high. But if the share of non-traded goods in the index is low and the world rate of inflation is moderate, it might then be necessary for the prices of non-traded goods to fall absolutely to achieve the desired result. And this presents a new constraint. If non-traded goods prices can rise, but not fall, in response to demand management policies there will then be a lower limit to the attainable domestic inflation rate in the fixed rate system, given the world inflation rate. The downward rigidity of non-traded goods may be derived from the downward rigidity of money wages. It may of course not be absolute: at a cost of sufficient unemployment it may be possible to force non-traded prices down over a range.

In figure 8.2 we could interpret the curve TT' broadly to trace out the maximum perceived welfare attainable under the fixed rate system at various inflation rates. The curve will then turn down more sharply as one moves to the left along it from W, and the optimal inflation rate OS' could (but does

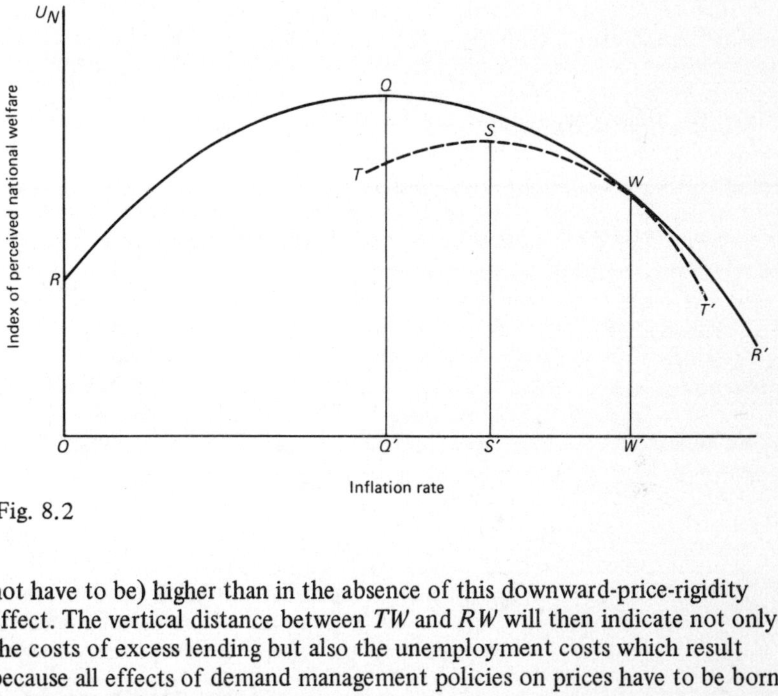

Fig. 8.2

not have to be) higher than in the absence of this downward-price-rigidity effect. The vertical distance between TW and RW will then indicate not only the costs of excess lending but also the unemployment costs which result because all effects of demand management policies on prices have to be borne in the non-traded sector.

V. FIXED RATES WITH IMBALANCES: THE WHOLE SYSTEM

Let us now look at 'equilibrium' in a fixed exchange rate world of many countries, some inflation prone and some inflation shy. (The term 'equilibrium' is perhaps not quite accurate since the analysis is short term and the relevant curves must shift endogenously over time.) Since the reserve currency country might be a special case, let us postpone consideration of it. We thus suppose that there is a given quantity of reserve assets – gold and S.D.R.s – and that there is no reserve currency country.

We start with a given uniform rate of inflation throughout the world, however determined, with optimal autonomous capital movements for all countries, and no accommodating capital movements. Now the inflation-prone countries seek to buy the opportunity of raising their inflation rates closer to their desired rates by 'selling' deficits, while the inflation-shy countries similarly seek to sell surpluses (buy deficits). There is a sort of market. If many countries are inflation prone in relation to the initial world inflation rate or if some very large country is inflation prone, the average world inflation rate facing the typical country will rise. Thus OW' in figure 8.1 will shift to the right and less borrowing for some countries will be necessary than if the world inflation rate were given at its original level. The equilibrating factors in this market will be the inflation rates in the various countries, the rate of interest on accommodating capital movements and also any non-pecuniary elements affecting this type of capital movement.

It is clear enough that a large country will have a bigger effect on the average world inflation rate facing a particular other country than will any smaller country. And since every country will end up with an inflation rate that is somewhere between this world rate and its own *desired rate* – and may in the long run be quite close to the former – it is true that the large country to some extent 'exports' its rate of inflation to the others.

But beyond this one cannot really go. One cannot say that the world rate of inflation will be determined by the inflation shy rather than the inflation prone or vice versa. It used to be a popular argument in Britain that the inflation shy – the excessive deflators – determine the rate of inflation for others (that is, force deflation on them) because they can and do impose absolute constraints on foreign borrowing by the inflation prone. The shy can then vary their inflation rates at choice, running surpluses if they wished, while the prone are constrained. When the prone try to run inflation rates closer to their desired rates they find that their foreign exchange reserves run out, it becomes harder to borrow, and the potential lenders exert political pressure. The objection to this argument is that increasing real resource losses by the surplus countries in return for low rates of interest *do* present some constraint on continued surpluses, so that they have incentives to reduce their surpluses by inflation.

The alternative, similarly extreme, view, popular at one time in Germany, is that the inflation prone determine the rate of inflation for the inflation shy. In this view the inflation shy are compelled to accept any surplus imposed on them by the inflation prone at a given rate of interest. But the weapon of the inflation shy is presumably the rate of interest. If they do not want to run surpluses nor to raise their inflation rates to eliminate these surpluses they can raise interest rates charged to the inflation prone, hence discouraging the latter from running deficits and forcing them to cut their inflation rates.

In fact, neither the inflation shy alone nor the inflation prone alone determine the world equilibrium. Both blades of the scissors play their part.

Looking at the world of inflation prone and inflation shy countries together we can see that the possibility of trade imbalances brings mutual gains – in fact 'gains from trade'. Each can get closer to its desired inflation rate, which is the one it would choose in a flexible rate system. Each gains somewhat more freedom from the opportunity to run imbalances. But assuming that foreign borrowing and lending were originally close to optimal, neither group will actually go as far as it would in a flexible rate system. The inflation-prone country will still inflate less than in the flexible rate system and the inflation-shy country will still inflate more.

It must be stressed that at this stage we are accepting the various governments' social welfare functions. One might well take the view that increasing the freedom of inflation-prone governments to inflate may not really yield gains to countries. But that is another matter, to which we shall return at the end of this paper.

VI. THE RESERVE CURRENCY COUNTRY

The reserve currency country is a large country. Therefore, in the fixed rate regime it will have a bigger influence on the world rate of inflation facing other countries than most countries have. Countries that do not wish to 'import' the large country's rate of inflation can insulate themselves from it, but only by running surpluses. But these surpluses involve net costs (assuming that foreign lending was initially optimal), so these inflation-shy countries will choose a higher rate of inflation than their *desired* one, this choice being the byproduct of the inflation preferences of the large country.

It is a separate question whether even in the short run it is technically possible for the inflation-shy countries to insulate themselves from world inflation in a fixed exchange rate regime. This has been much discussed, especially with respect to Germany. In the presence of high international capital mobility insulation through monetary policy may be difficult, so fiscal policy has to be sufficiently flexible. But the point here is that even though full insulation may be *possible* only partial insulation may be perceived by the monetary authorities as being *optimal.*

Is there anything special about the reserve currency country other than that it is an exceptionally large country? One might argue – and this has been a fashionable argument – that the borrowing which it does in its reserve currency capacity is at an exceptionally low rate of interest, lower than the world market rate applying to autonomous capital movements. The net benefit is seigniorage. Thus, given that it can borrow at such a low rate when it practises its reserve currency role, its borrowing is initially – in the absence of the deficit and thus of its reserve currency activities – below the optimum. Even if autonomous borrowing were at the optimum there may then be a net gain from accommodating borrowing. This represents the popular view that the United States has been able to obtain real resources from other countries exceptionally cheaply because she was the reserve currency country.

This case, where there is a net gain from a deficit, was referred to earlier and is represented in figure 8.3. The inflation-benefit curve with a flexible rate system is RR', as before, and the rest-of-the-world rate of inflation is OW'. The benefit curve with a fixed rate system and with the opportunity to run deficits or surpluses is TWT'. This time TT' cuts RR' at W, instead of being tangential to it, the vertical distance between WR and WT' indicating the net gain from accommodating borrowing, i.e. from seigniorage. The optimal inflation rate under the fixed rate regime, OS', is now actually higher than the desired rate under the flexible regime.

There is an implicit assumption in this approach. It is that the reserve currency status of this country is *given*, being quite independent of its rate of inflation. We shall come back to this assumption later.

Given this assumption, the United States authorities have then an incentive to engage in monetary and fiscal expansion sufficient to achieve a domestic price inflation rate above the one that would be desired with flexible rates. When there is a net *gain* from a deficit it pays to accept some 'excess' price inflation. This means that the possibility of running deficits yields *two* reasons for greater United States monetary expansion compared with a flexible rate regime. (We are comparing points S and Q in figure 8.3 here.) Firstly, the extra monetary expansion is needed to produce the payments deficit with the given desired inflation rate OQ', and secondly it is needed to produce the greater rate of domestic price inflation OS'.

If the assumption of a net gain to the United States from her deficits is correct we get the interesting result that even when her desired inflation rate under a flexible rate system might have been quite low, she would rationally have chosen a higher inflation rate under a fixed rate regime. For under such a regime she benefits from the reserve currency role and has an opportunity to obtain real resources cheaply from the rest of the world. And since she is a very large economy her own inflation rate will then have a big effect in pulling up the rest of the world's. It is even possible that she pulls up the world rate of inflation above the desired rate which most countries would choose if exchange rates were flexible. In that special case the fixed rate system could be said to be more inflationary from a world point of view than the flexible rate one. But no claim is made here that this was actually so. It has been shown only that popular arguments that world inflation was generated or encouraged by the consequences of the United States reserve currency role in the fixed rate system *could* be fitted into the framework of the general model presented here.

Finally, let us come back to the assumption implicit in this analysis that the reserve currency status of the country is given. Presumably the willingness of other countries to hold interest-free deposits of dollars will be reduced by American inflation, but once interest payments are allowed, a rise in the nominal rate of interest can always compensate for expected United States inflation. Thus it is not obvious that United States inflation must endanger the reserve currency role nor that the real rate of interest she must pay need change because of the inflation. It is true that the continuance of a deficit and accumulation of foreign liabilities faster than general world growth will have this sort of effect (steadily moving the WT' curve in figure 8.3 down over time), but it would not be the result of inflation *per se*, but only of continuous deficits *per se.*

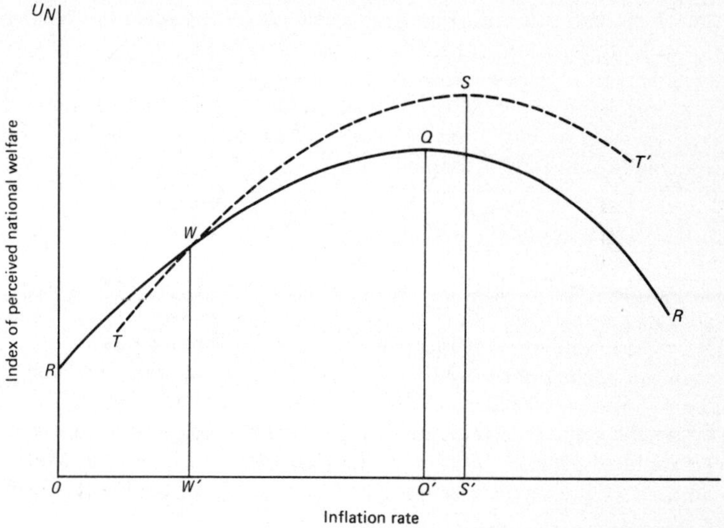

Fig. 8.3

Nevertheless, perhaps one should allow for some kind of rigidity or lags affecting nominal rates, perhaps because market expectations lag behind reality, so that the real rate of interest at which the reserve currency country is borrowing falls the more she inflates. Two conclusions then follow. Firstly, given the reserve currency role, the gains to the United States from it will be greater the more she inflates, since she will be borrowing more cheaply in real terms. Secondly, the reserve currency role itself will be endangered by her inflation. The first effect will cause curve WT' in figure 8.3 to be higher, encouraging United States inflation, while the second effect, if it operates as a threshold effect, may cause the curve suddenly to turn down at some inflation level. The latter effect could operate above or below the desired rate OQ', so that the effect of the reserve currency role could, after all, be to moderate rather than to increase the inflation rate which the United States would aim at otherwise. Thus this threshold effect could completely reverse the conclusion above that the United States authorities have an incentive to engage in monetary and fiscal expansion sufficient to achieve a domestic price inflation rate above that desired with a flexible rate.[1]

VII. SUMMARY SO FAR

Can anything be said in summary so far as answer to the principal question posed at the beginning? Are fixed or flexible rates more conducive to inflation? It is clear that the answers are opposite for the inflation-prone and the inflation-shy countries and that this remains true even when one allows countries to have payments imbalances in the fixed rate system. Nothing in general can be said for the world as a whole. But the reserve currency country could conceivably be a special case. It seems possible that it would choose a higher rate of inflation in the fixed rate than in the flexible rate system even though it may be relatively inflation prone.

VIII. WHICH REGIME IS TO BE PREFERRED?

Finally, it seems useful to classify various common views about the relative desirability of the fixed and the flexible regime. This discussion applies also, of course, to the more relevant issue of whether it would be desirable to move along the continuum within these limits, back towards the movable peg, where alterations in exchange rates are reluctant, or forward to more flexibility in the management of the floating system. The position of various observers seems to depend crucially on the view they take about the wisdom of governments and monetary authorities. What follows is, no doubt, a rather obvious classification.

(1) If one is a Fabian and believes that governments know best (or, at least, that they are amenable to good advice) then the flexible system is best. It gives governments maximum freedom. Governments can still borrow and lend, but they can also choose their own inflation rates without having to engage in (otherwise) non-optimal foreign borrowing or lending.[2] A qualifica-

[1] In Mundell [5] there is an elegant analysis of the relationship between inflation in the reserve currency country and holdings of its currency by other countries. The analysis is along the lines of this paragraph. United States inflation (actual and expected) lowers the real value of, and real return on, dollar balances held abroad, and this inflation tax affects the demand for these balances and hence the United States deficit. Mundell assumes that dollar balances earn a zero nominal rate for their holders. From this point of view (but ignoring the other considerations stressed in the present paper) there will be an optimum rate for United States inflation designed to maximise its seigniorage. The argument is also expounded thoroughly in Mundell [6] where account is taken of the domestic costs of inflation, which the reserve currency country then balances against the seigniorage gain to determine the optimum inflation rate.

[2] Why do governments ever commit themselves (or say that they might commit themselves in the future) to a fixed rate regime, since in terms of their perceptions the constraint of a fixed rate seems to reduce national welfare? It is clear from our diagrams that the point Q (the best point attained with a flexible rate) always represents a higher welfare

tion to this is that the fixed rate system may be best for the country that benefits in that system from the reserve currency role – assuming that there is significant seigniorage to be derived by it.

(2) If one believes that governments (or the parliaments that push them) generally have an excessive inflation-bias – a view common in Germany – then the fixed rate system is best for the inflation-prone countries and the flexible rate system best for the inflation-shy countries. In particular, the fixed rate system acts as a discipline for the inflation-prone countries.

(3) Similarly, if one believes that governments have an excessive *de*flation-bias – a view that used to be common in Britain – then the flexible rate system is best for the inflation-prone and the fixed rate system for the inflation-*shy* countries. The fixed rate system then forces some inflation on the *shy* countries.

(4) One might broadmindedly believe that the governments of the *prone* countries have an excessive inflation-bias while the governments of the *shy* countries have an excessive deflation-bias. In each case it is excessive from their own points of view. In that case a fixed rate system might be best since it forces each to move in the direction of the other. Of course, one of them might be forced to move too far in the other direction, since we cannot assume that the world inflation that would emerge in the fixed rate system would be just the right one.

(5) If one is an internationalist and prefers international collective decisions, explicit or implicit, the fixed rate system *may* be best. Each individual government is constrained, at least in the longer run, but the collective governments are not. This view clearly depends on how inflation rates are determined in the fixed rate system, and is particularly relevant when there are some explicit attempts by the main governments to influence each other's policies through O.E.C.D.-style discussions. One might even hope that the system would lead to some explicit and formalised collective decision-making process. This thinking underlies some arguments for European monetary integration, the motive there, of course, being not internationalism but Europeanism.

(6) If the common inflation rate towards which the system tends in the fixed rate system is essentially determined by a very large, or *the* reserve currency country, then one's view must depend on whether one regards the government of that country to have an excessive inflation or deflation-bias. If one feels that it has just the right bias, then presumably the flexible system

---

level than the point *S* (the best point attainable with a fixed rate) – except possibly in the reserve currency country case. Perhaps the commitments of governments to exchange rate fixity are never absolute for this very reason. Perhaps official advocates of fixed rate regimes do not see the issues clearly. Perhaps some politicians or officials are trying to impose constraints on other politicians or officials, even in their own country. And, of course, there are sectional interests within a country that may at times benefit from exchange rate rigidity.

would be worse for all other countries, but if the large country has the 'wrong' bias, then the flexible system would be better for some and worse for others.

POSTSCRIPT SUBSEQUENT TO THE CONFERENCE

Some time after completing this paper I realised (thanks to John Black, and after reading R. I. McKinnon, *Private and Official International Money: The Case for the Dollar*, Princeton Essay in International Finance, 1969) that there may be an unjustified implication in one of the arguments, namely that the United States reserve currency role goes with a fixed rate system but disappears with flexible rates. But this is clearly not so: we are now in a world of managed floating, and the dollar is as popular an international asset as ever. The main argument is simply that *given the reserve currency role* the United States may have an incentive to get other countries to accumulate dollars because of the supposed seigniorage effect, and in a fixed rate system, but not a flexible rate one, the United States can encourage this by more domestic inflation.

REFERENCES

[1] William H. Branson, 'Monetarist and Keynesian Models of the Transmission of Inflation', *American Economic Review, Papers and Proceedings*, Vol. LXV, No. 2 (May, 1975) pp. 115–119.

[2] Richard E. Caves, 'Looking at Inflation in the Open Economy', Harvard Institute of Economic Research Discussion Paper No. 286 (March, 1973).

[3] Joel Fried, 'Inflation–Unemployment Trade-offs under Fixed and Floating Exchange Rates', *Canadian Journal of Economics*, Vol. VI, No. 1, (February, 1973), pp. 43–52.

[4] L. Krause and W. Salant, (eds.), *Worldwide Inflation*, Brookings Institution, Washington.

[5] Robert A. Mundell, *Monetary Theory*, (Pacific Palisades: Goodyear Publishing Co., 1971).

[6] Robert A. Mundell, 'The Optimum Balance of Payments Deficit', in E. Claassen and P. Salin, (eds.), *Stabilization Policies in Interdependent Economies*, (Amsterdam: North-Holland Publishing Co., 1972).

[7] S. J. Turnovsky and A. Kaspura, 'An Analysis of Imported Inflation in a Short-Run Macro-economic Model', *Canadian Journal of Economics*, Vol. VII, No. 3 (August, 1974), pp. 355–380.

Discussion of the Papers by Hans Genberg and W. M. Corden

Professor Aukrust said Professor Genberg's subject was important to all small countries and, in some degree, all countries were small except the United States. This was a tightly argued and scholarly paper. The theoretical part was based on reasoning not often found in his own bureau, and he hoped he would be forgiven if he proved to be not very familiar with it.

Professor Genberg dealt with three topics: the sources of policy autonomy; the degree of autonomy; and policies to follow. Professor Genberg limited the paper to dealing with a situation where there were fixed exchange rates and small, open economies. He defined small as meaning that there existed a class of goods, produced and consumed in the country whose prices were determined on world markets independent of supply and demand conditions in the home economy. One therefore had a two-commodity country with traded and non-traded goods. Professor Genberg defined the national price level by an unusual formula, which was transformed to a rate of change basis in equation (3). Professor Aukrust gave his own version of this equation, as:

$$P = P_T^{1-w} \times P_n^w \qquad (3^*)$$

Here, changes in the national price level depended on (1) exogenous changes in traded commodity prices, and (2) changes in relative prices. One could therefore reason wholly in terms of relative commodity prices, and what policy-makers could do to influence them.

In table 7.1 of the paper, one had, in traded and non-traded space, a production possibility line *tt*. One also had the community indifference curve *uu* and rays *OP* and *OC* which gave production and consumption mixes. The paper showed how the situation changed if there were relative price constraints as the economy grew. Initially, the economy was in equilibrium at point *E*, with the relative prices of commodities depending on the slope of the joint tangent at *E* of *tt* and *uu*. Later, at E_1, one again had consumption equilibrium. However, the joint tangent of *pp* and *uu* was now likely to have a different slope. An analytical explanation of the situation was shown in the elasticities of equation (4) of the paper.

So, Professor Genberg showed what happened if there was no government intervention. The rate of inflation depended on: first, the exogenous price of the traded good and, second, the relative prices resulting from the elasticities in equation (4). The economy had a price trend forced on it by world prices, and by the supply and demand elasticities of the economy itself.

The authorities could influence this price trend only by altering relative prices. There were two possibilities. First, they might shift the slope off the *tt* curve, for example, by influencing productivity in particular sectors. Or they might shift the equilibrium point *along* the curve by changing the consumption mix of the economy, for example, by government expenditure which had a different product mix from that of the rest of the economy.

In his paper, Professor Genberg tried to suggest reasonable magnitudes for critical variables and this gave him relative prices and possible inflation rates. His analysis led Professor Genberg to the conclusion that the government could not affect the inflation rate much. In this part of the paper there was a short digression on the Scandinavian inflation model, a basic assumption of which was set out in equation (5). In its long-run version, the Scandinavian model relied entirely on supply conditions. Professor Genberg showed that equation (5) in the paper was a special case of models which included demand. Professor Aukrust wanted to point out that, in his thinking, he found the justification for equation (5) in the Marshallian analysis showing the long-run prices of commodities to vary in proportion to costs.

Professor Genberg used his analytical framework to consider the autonomy of policy authorities in the short run, showing that when one relaxed the long-run equilibrium constraints there were more points of choice – possible sets of relative prices. So one could influence the rate of inflation more in the short run than in the long run. Professor Aukrust had not found this part of the paper very interesting. He did not think it very useful, in analysing this problem, to use a model working entirely in commodity prices. We all knew that, over two or three years, relative prices might vary a great deal, without this necessarily being reflected in the national price level. However, Professor Genberg knew the shortcomings of his models, as the paper showed. Moreover, he went on to show that if one relaxed the full employment condition, generalisation was even harder. In the short run, almost anything could happen.

The second part of the paper was empirical. Professor Genberg used regression analysis to see whether, during the period 1955–70, prices in ten European countries behaved as the model would predict. He got a price index for these ten countries and set out to see what happened to prices relative to prices in the United States. His two formulae were in his equations (8) and (9). Professor Aukrust had tried to see how they were derived, and had arrived at the following equations; which he would describe as (8*) and (9*)

$$P_i = \alpha_0 \; P_e^{\alpha i} \tag{8*}$$

$$\log P_i = \text{const} + \beta_0 t + \beta_1 \; \log P_e$$

$$\delta_0 \; P_i = \text{const} \; e^{\beta_0 t} \cdot P_e^{\beta_1} \tag{9*}$$

It might have been useful if Professor Genberg had explained why these forms of the equations had been chosen. In table 7.1 of the paper, one would expect equation (8) to give estimates of α' approximately equal to unity, implying a stable relationship between the country's own price level and the European one. One would also expect a small α_0, deviating somewhat from zero, as a result of structural differences between countries, and causing deviations in national price trends. In table 7.2, based on equation (9), one would expect β_1 to be close to 1 and β_0 to be small.

By and large, this was what one did find. However, while one had large deviations from 1 in β_1 in, for example, West Germany, one also got a big negative estimate for β_0. It followed that if the European price level increased by 3 per cent, the term β_1 implied that Germany would have $4\frac{1}{2}$ per cent inflation, corrected downwards by 2 per cent for β_0. So the formula said that the price increase for West Germany would be $2\frac{1}{2}$ per cent when the European rate was 3 per cent.

Professor Genberg believed the calculations confirmed that in the long run national price levels moved together. Since he was no econometrician,

Professor Aukrust could not judge whether this conclusion was justified, and would leave it to those more competent to do so.

The paper went on to an interesting attempt to test Professor Genberg's hypothesis by simulation analysis. One could pick an econometric model into which one fed alternative policies to simulate what might be achieved. The particular model was for the United Kingdom, and Professor Genberg gave the results of four simulations plus a control run, choosing simulations to represent big deviations. Indeed, these were so large that they would have had intolerable side effects on government expenditure and foreign currency reserves. Even so, the apparent effects on inflation were limited.

One might wonder with Professor Genberg whether the ability to alter the rate of inflation by domestic policies was limited, irrespective of side effects. Perhaps one could not alter the rate of inflation in the United Kingdom without balance of payments effects. Perhaps fiscal policy was more potent than monetary policy.

Professor Aukrust added a word of warning. One ought to treat simulation with caution. No simulation was better than the model it used and the classification of factors in the model as exogenous or endogenous. A model would always tell one that changes in endogenous variables were caused by changes in exogenous ones. Professor Aukrust was doubtful here, because he did not know which were Professor Genberg's exogenous variables. He wondered whether the wage level was a variable in the model. If so, it appeared to be an exogenous variable because it was not in the list of endogenous ones. If wages were exogenous, then it might have been interesting to run the model with different wage trends.

It was quite clear that a different model would have given different simulation results. Therefore, the outcome of the simulation should be interpreted with some reserve. However, he would like, in general, to see more use of simulation models, though he would want them used very carefully.

Professor Aukrust suggested the following topics for discussion. First, technical comments would be welcome, since he found the model clear and original. Second, he would like a discussion both of how to interpret the regression results and of the statistical/technical problems involved in them. Third, he wondered whether participants would agree that the interest of the simulation was not so much the particular findings in the paper as the general problems of using simulation as an analytical tool. Fourth, he would like to see a discussion of policy strategy, which the author touched on only briefly. Finally, and outside Professor Genberg's paper but in line with the basic subject of the conference, what autonomy did participants think small countries actually had?

Professor Driehuis introduced Dr Corden's paper. The analysis of the links between inflation and the exchange rate system took place in a world where structural changes in the demand for foreign goods, and in income elasticities etc., were absent. In the short term, then, differences in inflation rates between countries might occur in a system of fixed exchange rates, once countries were prepared and able to run payments deficits, or, to be more precise, increasing deficits.

The analysis dealt with the polar systems of rigidly fixed exchange rates and perfectly flexible ones. A fundamental concept in the paper was the so-called inflation–benefit curve. This showed the relation between an index of national welfare, as conceived by the monetary authorities, and the rate of price inflation. More national welfare could be obtained at the cost of a higher rate of inflation up to a certain maximum, where a higher inflation rate reduced national welfare. What was the benefit? In Dr Corden's view, it was the benefit received by the government and the monetary authorities where inflation resulted from increased monetary demand for goods and services. It might consist of an expected reduction in unemployment or an expected net benefit for the government arising from distributional effects, both within the public sector, and between it and the private sector.

There were two types of inflation benefit curve, one under flexible and one under fixed exchange rates. Apart from reserve currency countries, to which he would return, the fixed exchange rate benefit curve lay below the flexible exchange rate benefit curve. This could be explained as follows: assume flexible exchange rates; a country could then choose the optimal exchange rate, the one which provided it with the optimum inflation benefit. This situation could be reached without accommodating capital movements so that it also implied an optimal capital account structure, so to say. If a country, for one reason or another, wanted to choose a higher inflation rate than the world inflation rate under fixed exchange rates, it should in principle strive for the optimal inflation rate under flexible rates. However, this optimum could not be reached under fixed rates because the country could only obtain a higher rate of inflation than the world rate by running a deficit, that is, by borrowing. Since this borrowing would represent a less-than-optimal situation, there would be a net loss of welfare. Under fixed rates, the inflation-benefit curve was therefore below the one for flexible rates.

Dr Corden described a country choosing a higher rate of inflation than the given world rate, under a system of flexible rates, as inflation prone. Dr Corden mentioned Britain here, to contrast it with an inflation-shy country, like Germany, which chose a lower inflation rate under a flexible exchange rate system. So inflation-prone countries might 'sell' inflation by deficit, and inflation-shy countries 'buy' it through a reduction of the inflation rate with a surplus.

The main point was that inflation-prone countries were likely to choose a lower rate of inflation under fixed rates than under flexible rates. For the shy countries, the reverse would be the case.

Dr Corden concluded that both inflation-prone and inflation-shy countries determined the world rate of inflation, and not one or other group. The world inflation rate would depend on the relative strength of the countries and the position they chose on their benefit curves. This would determine whether there would be a net increase of world inflation under fixed, as compared with flexible, rates.

Ultimately, a sort of equilibrium would be reached as a result of the 'selling' of deficits and the 'buying' of surpluses. So no definite answer could be given as to whether fixed or flexible rates were more conducive to inflation.

The foregoing discussion left out the existence of reserve currency countries, mostly large ones with a relatively bigger influence on the world rate of inflation under fixed rates. Apart from that, Dr Corden argued that a reserve currency country did not have a higher inflation-benefit curve under fixed rates than under flexible ones. The reason was that reserve currency countries would be able to borrow at a lower rate of interest than the world market rate. This would mean a net gain from the deficit which would shift the inflation curve upwards.

Dr Corden was of the opinion that inflation and the exchange rate system had been discussed too much, but that much of this discussion had been piecemeal. Although he did not arrive at radically new results, he claimed to have developed a coherent framework for analysing or re-analysing the problem.

Professor Driehuis argued that Dr Corden's conclusions nevertheless did not differ very much from what had been written in the textbooks on this issue, remaining as inconclusive as ever. What was interesting was the sort of general equilibrium framework Dr Corden was applying, instead of looking at the matter from the point of view of the individual country.

Even so, one would like to see the international general equilibrium model worked out more fully, since it was not quite clear from the paper how the equilibrium was reached. Dr Corden made it difficult for anyone to introduce his paper since he himself paid so much attention to the deficiencies, and rather strong assumptions, in his theory – especially the fact that the benefit curves were not as stable as one might wish. Professor Driehuis wondered whether Dr Corden was right in neglecting the role of the transmission process and in concentrating on the outcome of policy adjustments. The papers by Parkin and Swoboda and by Fleming suggested that the transmission process was, at least, of some importance.

One could also argue that the inflation-benefit curve did not exist at all in the minds of policymakers, and that the whole analysis was less relevant than Dr Corden seemed to believe. Professor Driehuis had serious doubts about the existence of an inflation-benefit curve. There was more to the issue than the fact that governments should enjoy the redistributive effects of inflation, which he did not believe to be very important. Experience in his own country showed, for instance, that the policymakers currently expected higher unemployment, especially structural unemployment, when inflation was higher. Whether the Phillips-curve actually existed was, as Dr Corden argued, irrelevant.

In a final remark, Professor Driehuis wondered if it was true that a reserve currency country, like the United States, behaved according to Dr Corden's theory and ran a higher rate of inflation than the rest of the world. Why did this not happen? Or was the assumption about seigniorage unrealistic?

Professor Patinkin wondered about the relationship between the two papers. An important question seemed to be, what was the general framework in the Genberg paper? It seemed self-evident that with fixed exchange rates the rate of inflation was likely to be the same in all countries.

Inflation was concerned with movements in a price index and Professor Genberg assumed a two-commodity world with traded and non-traded goods. For traded goods the price must be the same in all countries. So to get different inflation rates, there must be differential price increases in non-traded goods. This presumably implied an increase in the ratio of traded to non-traded goods in the price index. For this to happen, one would need all sorts of governmental contortions. Why was it so important for a country to have its own inflation rate that the government wanted to go through all the difficulties that this implied? It might be easier to get one's own inflation rate by moving to a flexible exchange rate. He therefore wondered what was this class of country which wanted its own inflation rate, fixed exchange rates and yet contained very small countries. Wanting one's own inflation rate implied that one wanted to move to flexible exchange rates.

He also wanted to make a comment on Dr Corden's paper. The exchange rate regime could not be treated as an exogenous factor. If there were benefits from having one's own inflation rate, these would be benefits that the government sought. Such a government would accept a flexible exchange rate, and, indeed, all policy measures necessary to achieve its own rate of inflation. So a major question was not on the analysis but on the specification of the problem.

Professor Lundberg suggested that this implied that to get a different inflation rate, one needed a shift in production from traded to non-traded goods. This was not necessary in the Scandinavian model. If one had a steadily increasing differential in productivity the process could continue, though no actual shift could be so significant.

Professor Genberg was not sure whether the emphasis in his paper had come out as he had intended. His point was precisely that to get one's own rate of inflation would mean distortions. The case for pursuing an independent inflation policy must be strong enough to justify accepting these distortions.

Professor Nussbaumer argued that if a country had a high rate of inflation, then one would expect technical progress to be more rapid in the open sectors. But if the export sector was large, the fact that a country had a lower rate of inflation did not help, but would add to the problem. One then ran into the complication Professor Patinkin had mentioned.

Professor Patinkin felt that the implication of the discussion so far was that if a country had a different rate of productivity increase it could have its own rate of inflation. He did not see how this process worked. The paper showed how difficult it was to get a differential inflation rate, but how important was the elasticity of substitution, on the demand side, between the non-traded and traded goods? If it was significant, then that reduced the degree of freedom of the government.

Professor Parkin felt the position was clear on technical progress; indeed, the paper explained this. Some rate of inflation was given by the rate of increase in world prices for traded goods. Given the rate of technical progress, this gave a unique rate of inflation for non-traded goods. This in turn gave a unique rate of inflation for each country under full employment. To alter the rate of inflation, one would then need contortions. Perhaps no countries were at present in this particular box, whereas in the 1960s, almost all countries had been. So this was a valid exercise, showing the inconsistencies of policies pursued in the 1960s.

Professor Malinvaud said that if one went back to figure 7.1, in the Genberg paper, with traded and non-traded goods, one might suppose that the *tt* frontier was a straight line, in which case prices would be determined from production conditions alone. If the line *tt* shifted to $t_1 t_1$, as in his, one would then get different relative prices, which meant that there was no freedom for the individual country. Under fixed exchange rates, it would experience the world rate of inflation modified by its own productivity increase. There would be choice only if the *tt* line were bent a little.

Professor Aukrust pointed out that other countries might have slightly different *tt* curves and, for this reason, slightly different rates of inflation.

Professor Patinkin replied to Professor Parkin that this was not the world of the 1960s. What Professor Parkin had said applied to certain European countries and a few others, but not to the postwar world as a whole.

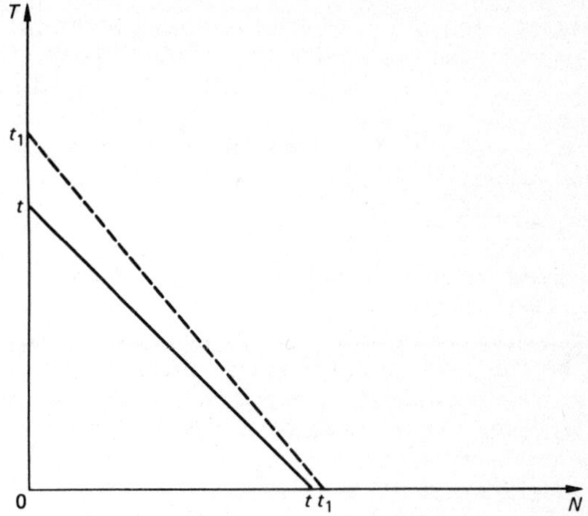

Fig. 8.4.

Professor Swoboda wanted to point out something that Professor Genberg had shown in his paper. Though there might be significant differences in intersectoral productivity growth or income elasticity of demand, and in government expenditure patterns among sectors, these would result in less difference in intercountry inflation rates than one would have expected.

On the general question of policy autonomy, he would make much the same statements as Professor Patinkin, but this was just what Professor Genberg himself was saying. Governments did try to have different inflation rates. The issue, however, was this: with fixed exchange rates, what was the cost of such differential inflation in, for example, restrictions on the permitted range of fiscal policies, the implied share of government expenditure in national income, the stock of exchange reserves, etc. The paper showed that the cost of achieving even minor deviations in inflation rates were quite high under fixed rates, and this might well have been what led several countries to adopt flexible exchange rates.

On Genberg's general framework, it was worth noting that the only autonomy he considered was with respect to the price level. In fact, countries attempted to gain independence with respect to inflation in order, also and for example, to gain added leverage on the level of unemployment. Thus, though this was not covered in the paper, government policies towards non-traded goods were sometimes not aimed at the rate of inflation but at the level of employment. To summarise, with fixed exchange rates, the essential question was what degree of autonomy a government had.

As for the discussion of reserve-currency countries, Corden had stated that the gains for reserve-currency countries were best studied in a model where rates of inflation across countries did not differ or differed only because of structural factors. This had the advantage of putting the seignorage issue in stark relief. Professor Mundell had produced a paper on this issue (published in the proceedings of the 1971 Paris–Dauphine conference), reaching similar conclusions to those of Dr Corden.

Professor Patinkin thought it seemed to come down to this. One had a rate of productivity increase in the manufacture of traded goods. If one wanted one's own rate of inflation, all one had to do was to be inefficient in the non-traded sector.

Professor Frisch said one could give a formal statement of the problem in the following equation:

$$P = P_e + \alpha(q_c - q_s)$$

This was the Aukrust model. With fixed exchange rates, the rate of inflation was the world rate of inflation (P_e) plus the difference in productivity increase between the traded goods sector (q_c) and the non-traded goods sector (q_s); α showed the weight of the non-traded goods sector. A slow productivity increase for non-traded goods did lead to a rate of inflation higher than that in the rest of the world. But in the short run, α was constant, and one could not change technical progress much. The only way out was then a managed floating of the exchange rates.

Professor Nussbaumer found the Genberg model useful because making models using unrealistic assumptions helped one to show policy implications. For example, the Genberg model showed that those wanting more stable exchange rates, and involved considerably in foreign trade, must change their exchange rate. Relying on technical progress was a solution if the rate of inflation was higher. It was not a solution if the rate of inflation was lower, because technical progress might well be faster in the open sector.

So, in the short run, if there were fluctuations, one could balance them by the government borrowing or repaying abroad. In the short run, if one wanted a different exchange rate, one could balance this through the capital market. In the long run, there was no way out. Then, in order to have a lower rate of inflation, one must adopt flexible exchange rates as a measure which called for least intervention by government.

Mr Oppenheimer suggested to Professor Patinkin that if one relied on increasing inefficiency in the production of non-traded goods to establish one's own rate of inflation, then, in the long run, the non-trading sector would become very small. So this was only a pseudosolution.

Professor Patinkin maintained he had not suggested it as a solution. It was simply a *reductio ad absurdum.*

Professor Patinkin wondered whether it was helpful to speak of non-traded goods. If one did the analysis in terms of specific factors of production, one then got either unemployment or reduced rents.

Professor Frisch told Dr Corden that it was not clear whether anti-inflationary policy was easier with fixed or flexible exchange rates. He thought the answer was flexible rates. With fixed exchange rates, there was always imported inflation. With flexible rates, one could have totally home-made inflation.

Professor De Wolff noted that in his statistical section, Professor Genberg had used a weighted average of the home price levels of ten European countries as an indicator for the foreign price level confronting these countries. He then had run correlations between the individual indices and the average index to measure the elasticities of the impact of the foreign prices on internal ones. However, it did not seem correct to derive an index for internationally traded goods from home price levels. The latter were strongly influenced by prices which were entirely irrelevant to foreign trade. On the other hand, they gave too little weight to raw material prices which, in the past, apart from the most recent years, had risen much less than consumer prices. He therefore doubted much of what Professor Genberg had been doing as well as many of the conclusions at which he had arrived.

Professor Kleiman suggested that in Dr Corden's paper, what was important was that it queried the conventional wisdom, that under fixed exchange rates governments lost their economic sovereignty. He admitted that one still taught this in introductory courses. Dr Corden showed that even under flexible exchange rates there would be checks and balances on the internal policies pursued. This was an important moral in the papers by Dr Corden and Professor Claassen, but there was an extra check which needed to be mentioned. Professor Kleiman drew figure 8.5. As in Dr Corden's figure 8.1, one had a y-axis which represented an index of government utility, and an x-axis which showed the rate of inflation. There was some relation, like *OR*, showing the marginal utility of inflation to government, which first increased and then decreased. The curve *OR* should best be regarded as describing inflationary benefits when there were no balance of payments constraints. Under a fixed exchange rate, W^1 was the domestic rate of inflation at which the rate of interest was compatible with the structure of the economy so that there were no balance of payments troubles.

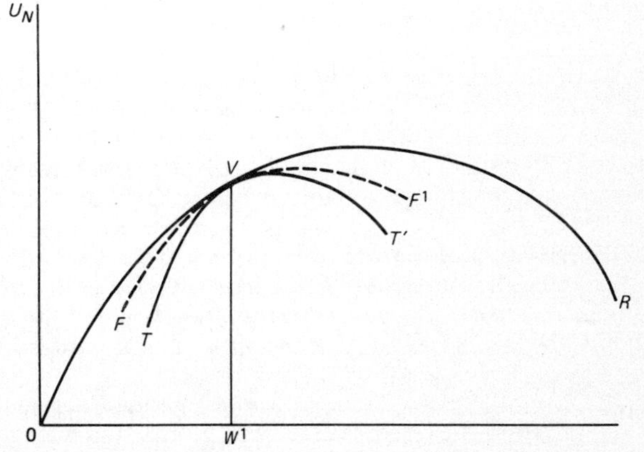

Fig. 8.5

If, under a fixed exchange rate, a country inflated more, it had to borrow abroad and so increase the rate of interest on overseas borrowing. If one deducted the cost of overseas borrowing, one got the curve TT^1 as in Dr Corden's diagram.

However, with flexible exchange rates, the further one was from the point W^1, the more exchange rate depreciation there was. This had internal effects, on income distribution among other things, which a government might regard as undesirable. For example, successive United Kingdom governments believed there were negative effects from currency depreciation and so kept fixed exchange rates. So the flexible exchange rate curve was not OR in the diagram, but some lower one, call it FF^1, passing between OR and TT^1. There were stronger checks under flexible exchange rates than Dr Corden suggested.

In the case of a reserve-currency country, described in Dr Corden's figure 8.3, there was the further problem of seignorage. But here one should take into consideration the expected value to the reserve country of losing its seignorage profits when other countries became fed up with its rate of inflation. In this case, the TT^1 curve would ultimately intersect the OR curve. So, again, the difference between the policies pursued under the two exchange rate regimes turned out to be smaller than they first seemed to be.

Professor Parkin thought the Genberg paper valuable because it almost represented an overkill. It killed off policies followed by many European countries in the 1960s. He would like to have seen a split between the current and capital account on the balance of payments. His own conjecture was that one would have had substantial current account deficit with a high rate of inflation, leading to a high bank rate. It would also be interesting to break out of the policy reaction function and find what would be an acceptable policy. He wondered if Professor Genberg had done this.

Professor Parkin was unhappy about the simulation of an invisible model – this one was in an unpublished Ph.D. thesis. Perhaps it might be possible to give an appendix to the printed paper showing which model had been used.

He had one detailed question. What were the initial conditions for the simulation? What was real time?

Professor Genberg replied that the model had dealt with the period 1955–75.

Professor Swoboda asked about policy reaction functions in the model.

Professor Genberg replied that the model had been built by P. D. Jonson. The endogenous variables had been listed in a footnote in his (Genberg's) paper. As to the determination of the policy variables, government expenditures were assumed to be truly exogenous, whereas bank rate was determined by a policy reaction function containing, as arguments, the world rate of interest and the deviation of the rate of inflation and the unemployment rate from their desired levels. The policy simulations included both monetary and fiscal policy, but because of the policy reaction function and the government's budget restraint, the two were interrelated so that a clear-cut distinction could not be made.

Professor Malinvaud explained that he would hate the Conference to use the expression 'inflation shy', because the costs of inflation were usually understated. The term 'inflation shy' implied the rather pejorative implication that Germany had no personality and a strange behaviour relationship towards inflation. France was certainly not such a country!

He wanted to refer to Professor Kleiman's diagram. One must not forget that countries were in a different environment if they had fixed rather than flexible exchange rates. He could see a reason for the dotted line showing the marginal utility of the government under flexible exchange rates being brought down further throughout its length. Uncertainty over the exchange rate had a cost for the country in terms of productivity, so that it would be better off if it had fixed rather than flexible exchange rates. We all knew firms which faced big fluctuations in export prices under flexible exchange rates. This had a real cost. So, despite what Professor Kleiman said, we should not use this diagram too freely in our classrooms.

Professor Duesenberry felt there was too much enthusiasm for seeing the Aukrust model as a special case of the Genberg one. The Aukrust model had wages determined by an internal distribution process concerned with firms in the open sector, influenced by world prices, wages, productivity etc. This was an internal labour arbitrage model, while Professor Genberg's was a commodity arbitrage model. There was an argument that it was hard for a country which could have had a slower rate of wage increase if it had been isolated, when it became trapped in a world inflation because of its trade in some goods. While some goods did have uniform prices, there were classes of good in which there was a wide spread between countries and yet no enormous swings in trade. In the United States, Japanese steel producers had driven American steel firms out of the production of certain products altogether.

There were some products where the elasticity of demand for given firm's products was not all that high. We were all too glib in assuming that all commodities were of the same type as grain. If this were so, it would make economic theory even harder. In practice, firms could vary their prices without this leading to too much variability in output.

Professor Fischer argued that part of the discussion had overlooked the familiar distinction between positive and normative analysis. It was interesting to ask why governments did or did not inflate. It was also important to ask whether there were benefits from inflation. At best, the Phillips-curve was a delicate instrument and the benefit of choosing one's own rate of inflation was less than many people had thought five years ago. There was still room for further analysis of the attraction of being independent on inflation rates.

One might wonder whether governments wanted to impose constraints on themselves. The answer was clearly that they did in some cases. Certainly constitutions did. If the benefits of having one's own rate of inflation were small, then the case for fixed exchange rates became stronger. Dr Corden seemed to say that we might want to tell inflation-prone governments that it would be a good thing to tie one hand behind their backs by moving to fixed exchange rates so that they would behave better. He agreed with this as a general possibility but wondered whether the paper supported that implication.

Professor Claassen wondered about the demand side of the Genberg model. The income elasticity of non-traded goods was greater than 1. One therefore wanted to see the tables arranged in another way, with some countries growing faster than others. For example, in the 1960s Western Germany, Austria and other countries had grown faster than others. The model led to different inflation rates if one country grew faster than another, since the former then had higher prices for non-traded goods. An analysis of this problem had been carried out by McKinnon.

Dr Corden's argument supposed that, with a deficit, a country would borrow at once. In practice, borrowing was the last thing it would do. Normally, it would first reduce its reserves and only borrow just before there was a balance of payments crisis. This point was very important if the costs of running down reserves and of borrowing were different.

Dr Corden wanted to explain how his paper related to a large literature. He felt he had nothing to add on the automatic inflation transmission process in the fixed exchange rate system. He was talking about government policy adjustments to world inflation. There might even be little automatic transmission, but if a country acquired a balance of payments surplus, because of inflation in other countries, its policymakers might ask themselves whether they wanted that surplus. For example, one could take the case of Japan. He had read a paper about this written by Professor Komiya for a recent Brookings conference on worldwide inflation. American inflation had not, in the main, been automatically transmitted to Japan. Japan had developed a large balance of payments surplus partly because of United States inflation, and therefore undertook domestic expansion. It was mainly this, and not a process of direct transfer, that transmitted world inflation to Japan, though the end result was the same.

How did his paper relate to Professor Genberg's paper? In a full employment situation, a country might want to choose its own rate of inflation, different from the rate in other countries, and at the same time maintain a fixed exchange rate. If so, there were two consequences. First, there would be continuous switching between traded and non-traded goods within the country, induced by a continuous relative price change. Second, the country's balance of payments would get out of balance. Professor Genberg focused on the cost of switching and stressed that a country could not switch for ever. His own paper focused on the costs of excess borrowing or lending, resulting from balance of payments disequilibrium. He had not referred to the cost of switching.

Was there an inflation-benefit curve? There might not be a Phillips-curve, but governments behaved as if there was. The situation was similar with an inflation-benefit curve.

On normative versus positive issues, Professor Patinkin had asked why one should bother to move to a fixed exchange rate if it constrained the government of one's country. The answer was that introducing a flexible rate regime had indeed shifted the constraint curve outwards, and this appeared to be beneficial for any one country, as seen by its government. Nevertheless, there were international discussions of whether there should be joint imposition of new constraints in the form of agreement to a fixed rate regime. It was a fact that this was proposed. Perhaps some civil servants or economists might want constraints imposed on their politicians. He had considered the perceived welfare function of the government and, at the end of the paper, brought in his own views. Which regime was desirable depended to some extent on one's confidence in governments.

Professor Frisch had remarked that with flexible exchange rates inflation stayed at home so that one could not blame foreigners for it. Hence, flexible exchange rates were anti-inflationary. But an essential point of Dr Corden's own paper was that this argument only applied to 'inflation-shy' countries. By contrast, in the case of 'inflation-prone' countries, flexible exchange rates moved the constraint outwards and were likely to lead to more inflation.

He agreed with Mr Oppenheimer that there were differences between the short and the long run. Clearly in the short run one could allow reserves to fall or borrow 'accommodating capital'. But this could not go on for ever. For the long run, the answers were the same as in the Genberg paper. A country could not go on for an indefinite period switching between the production of traded and non-traded goods and engaging in accommodating borrowing.

Mr Kaser said that the criticism levelled at Professor Genberg's use of domestic consumer prices for prices of internationally traded goods could be readily substantiated from table 7.5 of Professor Genberg's paper, and from the second table which he had circulated during the discussion of the Csikós-Nagy and Entov papers. Between 1959 and 1969 (Genberg's years 5–15) the eleven-country mean (in national currencies) rose by just over 4 per cent annually. On the other hand, the world unit values of imports (converted into dollars) rose only 1 per cent between 1960 and 1970. From 1969–74, Professor Genberg's index rose by nearly 6 per cent per annum, whereas world unit values rose by no less than 17 per cent annually, a figure deflated for dollar depreciation.

This called for separate indices of traded and non-traded goods, as the model conceptually required. It had been suggested in the discussion that the distinction should be between the factor prices of traded and non-traded goods respectively. But Professor Genberg was surely right, because the same goods might at times be traded and at other times non-traded. Mr Shore's appeal to 'Buy British' was a stage in making British cars into a non-traded good. Factor markets were the transmission, and possibly equilibrating, mechanism between traded and non-traded goods but should not be used as surrogates for the transaction prices themselves. Changes in technical progress affected factor markets but were reflected in the ratio between traded and non-traded goods only to the extent that they caused substitution among their respective inputs.

Professor Aukrust said that the Nordic model was intended to determine the rate of wage increase. In the very long run, say, periods of five to fifteen years, the model suggested that trends in national wages and prices were determined by international trends, modified by productivity and exchange rate changes. If the model were correct, it was impossible for national prices, measured in international currency units, to move differently from world market prices.

In the short run, say, over periods of one to two years, lasting from the conclusion of one round of wage negotiation until the conclusion of the next, a short-run variant of the model suggested that the ability of national authorities to influence price developments was very limited. The outcome of wage negotiations would determine the course of wages (apart from wage drift), and hence prices, for a future period. What the policy authorities could do in these circumstances was very limited. They might try to slow down wage drift through a policy of demand management or monetary policy, or to counter price increases triggered off by the wage increases by resorting to the use of subsidies, price controls or similar devices. This would delay but could not hold back indefinitely the price increases to be expected as a result of the wage settlement.

However, in the medium run, over periods of, say, two to five years, the scope for a national price policy should be considerable. It seemed perfectly possible for wages over such a period to rise more or less steeply, depending partly on the outcome of wage negotiations taking place during the period and partly on the size of wage drift. The outcome of wage negotiations and the size of wage drift presumably depended somewhat on the general economic climate. So it should be possible for policy authorities to influence wage and price developments in the medium run through a policy of demand management or monetary policy, perhaps supplemented by income policy. However, we should observe that the scope for such a policy was limited by the need for actual wages always to remain within boundaries laid down by international trends.

Professor Genberg explained that the introduction by Professor Aukrust had brought out most of the ideas he wanted to stress. He wanted to show where the sources of autonomy in small countries lay. He also wanted to give a rough quantitative idea of the importance of these sources. On this basis, he wanted to go on to see what should be the appropriate inflation policy for a small country. The discussion of policy autonomy for any country led to a distinction between the long and short run. It was clear that, in a model like the one presented in the paper, there was not much autonomy at all in the long run. So why did we observe differences between countries? For example, had the lower average rate of inflation in Germany resulted from a contractionary policy followed over a considerable period? He had wanted to show that the Nordic model implied that there could be long-run divergences of inflation rates, which were not due to policy measures. What difference could policy measures make? The answer was: not very much.

As for the short run analysis, he thought that Professor Aukrust might have misunderstood what he wanted to get across. He had not meant that one did not know what went on. He had tried to spell out the short-run implications for the balance of payments of attempts at policy autonomy. There was difficulty, however, in determining what happened in the short run to unemployment. Professors Parkin and Swoboda pointed out in their paper that Phillips-curve models for an open economy could become very difficult to handle. One had to deal not just with the aggregate demand for labour but also with sectoral demand, and this was not a well-developed area in the literature. On short-run autonomy, this was largely an empirical question of what were the values of the relevant parameters.

The regression results were perhaps provocative. It was not his aim to test traded-good arbitrage. His equations should be interpreted more as a reduced form of price equations.

There was a good case for viewing inflation as a world phenomenon under fixed exchange rates. He had wanted to take this argument and see how each country's inflation rate varied. If one looked at the paper one found that one country's rate of inflation was the world rate of inflation plus an error term.

Equation (9) introduced a time trend. One could interpret the coefficient β_0 as pointing up differences in productivity growth between sectors. He argued that to affect the price level, policies had to be pursued for a considerable time. One would therefore expect serial correlation in equation (8). In equation (9), one would also expect serial correlation of the residuals. α_1 and β_1 would both equal 1 if each country had the same rate of inflation. If the productivity growth argument were important for differences between countries, one would then expect β_0 to be very different from zero. The results were roughly consistent with the model and these *a priori* expectations.

Professor Duesenberry's comment on American and European inflation was important, because it showed that there was more independence between Europe and the United States than between each individual country within Europe. So perhaps the analysis of world inflation should be carried out in a two-region model.

On the distinction between traded and non-traded goods, his aim had been to get an analytical handle on the problem. Even if there were little arbitrage in the short run, the long-run homogeneity of the system implied that the rate of inflation would be equalised across countries.

In the long run, the very high cost to a country of pursuing its own inflation policy would become evident. Perhaps even in the short run there was not much policy autonomy, and very high costs of seeking it. He wondered whether a country should try to pursue an independent policy in this case. Might it not be better either to have a flexible exchange rate, or to tie oneself even more closely to the world rate of inflation? To deal with unemployment or income distribution issues, one could use more specific measures than general monetary and fiscal policy.

9 World Inflation under Flexible Exchange Rates

Emil-Maria Claassen
UNIVERSITY OF PARIS-DAUPHINE

I. INTRODUCTION: THE WORLD INFLATION RATE AND THE NATIONAL INFLATION RATE

Under a system of fixed exchange rates the phenomenon of inflation is a world phenomenon. This statement is derived from price-theoretical considerations with respect to the price formation of tradeable goods in the world goods market and it is independent of any explanation of inflation. whether it is Keynesian or monetarist, of a sociological or of any other type.

All inflation theories – relevant or irrelevant -- must have the explanation of world inflation as their target of analysis. The 'national weight' in the determination of the world inflation rate is related proportionally to the relative size of the country concerned within the world economy. Consequently, inflationary impulses originating in a relatively big country have a more important impact on world inflation than those which happen in a small country. Furthermore, if the big country is simultaneously a key-currency country suffering from no external reserve constraint, it can be said that this country can – but not necessarily must – constitute the main source of world inflation.

It is known that nearly all inflation theories ignore the worldwide aspect of fixed exchange rates. Haberler argues that the construction of an inflation theory for a closed economy is already a rather difficult attempt so that one has to abstract first of all from any 'international complications'. This holds for 'monetarists', 'fiscalists', advocates of a Phillips-curve approach, for those who distinguish between demand-pull (buyers) and cost-push (sellers) inflation as well as those who deny the validity of this distinction, [5], page 179. However, these theoreticians will find use again for their models when there is a system of flexible exchange rates, because in such a system the phenomenon of inflation is fundamentally a national phenomenon. The world inflation rate is no longer equal to a common national rate, but it becomes now the weighted average of the national inflation rates. The relevant 'closed' economy is no longer the world economy but the national economy. There is still the 'law of one price' for a good within the world economy, but differences in price levels (inflation rates) between countries can be maintained permanently because they are corrected by a corresponding (continuous) change in the exchange rate.

If the world inflation rate under flexible exchange rates can be explained so easily, there is no need to discuss this subject any further. However, the challenge comes from the empirical side where we observe a higher world inflation rate since the introduction of floating exchange rates at the beginning of the 1970s, even though with increasing differences between the national inflation rates. Without being accused of the fallacious argument of *post hoc ergo propter hoc*, there is nothing astonishing about its explanation, because we know that floating exchange rates *can* be more inflationary than fixed exchange rates in the same way as they *can* be less or equally inflationary. If they can be more inflationary and if they can be also less inflationary, nothing precisely can be said so that we are left again with the explanation of the subject of world inflation under flexible exchange rates.

However, there are some arguments which indicate the higher probability of a higher inflation bias with a system of flexible exchange rates and which we shall examine critically in the following two sections. The first argument is that of a country's lower inflationary discipline when it has adopted a floating exchange rate; the second argument is concerned either with price rigidities which become virulent because of the system of flexible exchange rates, or with certain automatic world-price level increases following the introduction of floating exchange rates. Because we shall use the monetary hypothesis from among the various inflation theories, the above arguments can be reformulated as follows. A higher growth rate of the world quantity of money could arise from the regime of floating exchange rates if there is some systematic propensity for a higher growth rate of the national quantity of money in certain countries (section II) or/and if there is some automatic worldwide tendency of a higher growth rate of the money supply (section III).

II. THE ARGUMENT FROM LOWER NATIONAL MONETARY DISCIPLINE UNDER FLEXIBLE EXCHANGE RATES

According to the 'traditional' formulation of this argument, a country's pursuit of a higher inflation rate, exceeding the world inflation rate, will be 'punished' more severely under a system of fixed exchange rates because it will be accompanied by reserve losses and a possible balance of payments 'crisis', whereas a system of floating rates will only produce a depreciation. Whatsoever may be the strength of the argument, the question of a higher or lower discipline is only concerned with the discipline towards the deviation of the national inflation rate from the world inflation rate while the latter can be on any level. Furthermore, the statement of a greater monetary discipline imposed by fixed exchange rates is based on the implicit assumption that a depreciation is less harmful for an economy than a potential monetary 'crisis'.

Even if the external constraint is less imperative with an autonomous monetary policy – in the sense of a lower monetary discipline as well as of a higher monetary discipline – in a system of flexible exchange rates, the argument should be reformulated in terms of the specific conditions under which a country opts for a higher inflation propensity which has been made possible 'technically' by the regime of flexible exchange rates. Among various conditions we have found two plausible cases. The first one results from the freedom to choose any point on the Phillips-curve and the second one arises from a special type of an interest-rate orientated monetary policy.

(1) A LOWER MONETARY DISCIPLINE FOR THE PURPOSE OF AN IMPROVEMENT IN THE EMPLOYMENT RATE

The essential assumption of this case is not the existence or non-existence of a Phillips-curve, but the belief of the monetary authorities (or of the government) in the relationships portrayed in the Phillips-curve. Suppose that in the mind of the central banker there is a 'short-run' and a 'long-run' Phillips-curve represented by lines *I* and *F*, respectively, in figure 9.1. Contrary to the

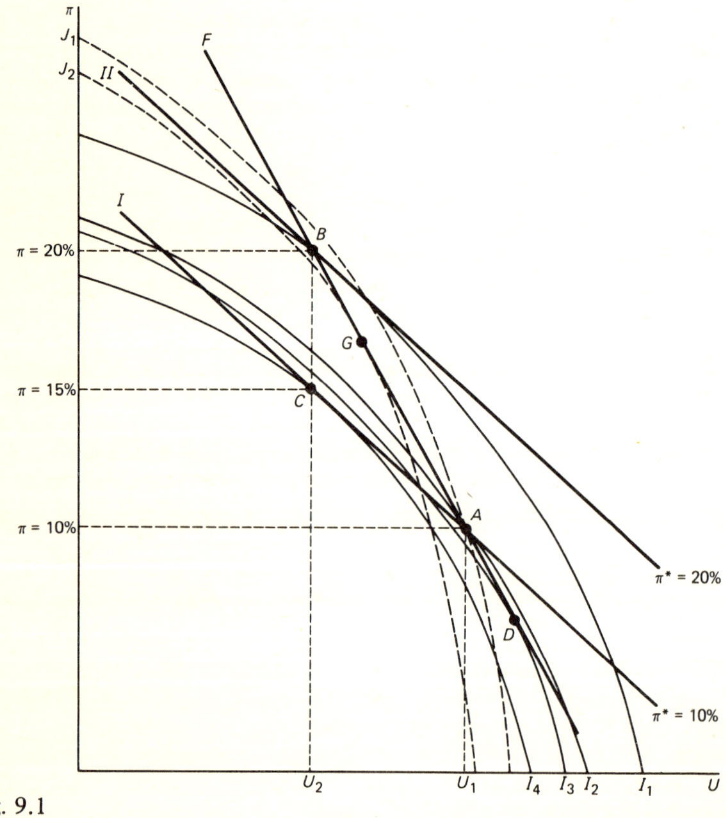

Fig. 9.1

traditional distinction made in Phillips-curve discussions between the short run and the long run in terms of inflation expectations, I shall reserve this distinction for an *open* economy where the length of the short period is inversely related to the degree of openness, the latter being defined in terms of the ratio of tradeable to non-tradeable goods.

Suppose that the foreign or (world) inflation rate (π^*) is 10 per cent and that the country's inflation rate (π) is also 10 per cent so that it is on its Phillips-curve at point A with an unemployment rate of U_1.

Suppose that the country wants to reduce the unemployment rate from U_1 to U_2. It will move on its short-term Phillips-curve from A to C when it pursues an inflation policy of $\pi = 14$ per cent. In a system of fixed exchange rates it has to abandon this autonomous monetary policy after a certain while because it can only temporarily maintain a relatively higher price level of nontradeable goods and it must go back to point A because this is the only permanent point it can 'choose' on its Phillips-curve for a world inflation rate of $\pi^* = 10$ per cent. With a system of flexible exchange rates, it could choose any point on its long-run Phillips-curve F. If the country still wants to reduce the unemployment rate to U_2, it has to realise an inflation policy of $\pi = 20$ per cent in order to stay at point B. Under fixed rates this long-run position will only be conceivable if the world inflation is $\pi^* = 20$ per cent while under flexible rates the country's exchange rate will continuously depreciate at the rate of $\pi - \pi^*$.[1]

By comparing the country's inflation rate for a system of fixed versus flexible exchange rates, one can argue that flexible rates are more inflationary if the country wants *absolutely* the lower unemployment rate U_2 which it can achieve only temporarily under fixed exchange rates. However, this choice is not necessarily consistent with its 'subjective' tradeoff between the two 'evils', inflation and unemployment, represented by the indifference curves I_1, I_2, I_3, I_4 in figure 9.1. Under fixed rates the country was forced to point A at which the long-run Phillips-curve intersects the indifference curve I_2; during the short run it could have attained the 'lower' indifference curve I_4 which is tangent to the short-run Phillips-curve I at point C. However, if the system of indifference curves remains the same under flexible exchange rates, the country will choose a lower inflation rate at point D where the Phillips-curve F is tangent to the indifference curve I_3; the choice of point B would be inconsistent because the country would be on the indifference curve I_1 (compare [4], pages 48–49).

Consequently, the introduction of flexible exchange rates may be less inflationary. But it can also be more inflationary if one assumes the system of indifference curves J_1, J_2 under which the country will improve its welfare when it moves from A (fixed exchange rate) to G (flexible exchange rate). It

[1] The Phillips-curve F is also a long-run relationship for the regime of flexible exchange rates, since in such a system a divergence between the national and foreign inflation rate does not need to be corrected *immediately* by a change in the exchange rate because of the existence of nontradable goods.

follows that, regarded from the aspect of an improvement in the *optimal* tradeoff choice between inflation and unemployment as a consequence of a regime of flexible exchange rates, a higher inflation propensity is a plausible case, but not necessarily a strong case.[1]

(2) A LOWER MONETARY DISCIPLINE AS A RESULT OF AN INTEREST-RATE ORIENTED MONETARY POLICY

Another possible case of an increased inflation propensity of a country when it adopts a floating exchange rate has been suggested by Melitz [9]. He assumes a special behaviour of central bankers with respect to the conduct of monetary policy. Their target variable is neither the inflation rate nor the growth rate of the money stock, it is exclusively the interest rate. But this is not all. They propose to fix the interest rate at the level of the international (or foreign) interest rate. Thus if, for instance, foreign countries pursue a higher inflation policy, with a resulting higher nominal interest rate, the concerned country will imitate the same policy in order to have the same interest-rate level. Such a behaviour of central bankers – for some economists a highly irrational behaviour – may arise either from a misunderstanding of the functioning of flexible exchange rates or from the solidarity conduct of interest-rate conscious governors who behave in a similar way to consumers under the relative income hypothesis. However, this special behaviour does not fully explain a higher inflation rate under flexible exchange rates because central bankers behave, at least with respect to the interest rate on tradeable financial assets, exactly as if they were in a system of fixed exchange rates.[2]

[1] The system of indifference curves in figure 9.1 is a static system because it does not shift during time (in the same way as the Phillips-curve *F* is assumed to be static). There is certainly the possibility of an upward shift because people become more familiar with inflation such that they attribute a lower disutility to inflation. The result would be a higher inflation rate in comparison to point *D* or *G*. But this phenomenon could also take place in a system of fixed exchange rates in which the world inflation rate moves smoothly upwards due to a changing inflation mentality within the main countries of the world economy.

[2] 'If the monetary authorities do not really understand the economics of using a floating rate to achieve domestic price stability, and in particular a domestic price trend sharply at variance with other countries inflationary domestic price trends, they will in fact simply have a fixed rate system with a little cushion of extra flexibility in the form of movements of the rate; they will therefore have pretty much the same inflationary trend as everyone else; and this in turn will build into the system expectations of continuing inflation and conventional responses to them that will make the transitions to a genuinely independent policy employing the full flexibility of rate movements a painful and prolonged process, because the public as well as the authorities will have to learn a new set of rules and a new framework for forming expectations .... It means that the monetary authority of the price-stabilising country must expect and accept as natural a nominal interest-rate differential in favour of the other country' (Johnson [6], pp. 178 and 182).

An additional hypothesis has to be made concerning the adjustment process of the internal interest rate towards the higher international level. A central bank which pursues an interest-rate guided monetary policy has to adjust also to the temporary interest-rate fluctuations which take place constantly in an economy. If on the other hand the higher international interest-rate level fluctuates also, it is conceivable that the central bank, as a result of time-lags and of errors of forecasts of present and future economic activity, may overshoot its target level so that it arrives at a higher nominal interest rate than the international one. And if the central bank does not revise this higher level downwards, the country concerned will have a higher inflation rate than under fixed rates. It can be seen that it is only by a variety of specific assumptions regarding central bankers' behaviour and regarding the stochastic performance of an economy that one can construct a case – and certainly not a strong case – for a country having higher inflationary bias under a regime of flexible exchange rates.

However, for the hypothesis of an interest-rate guided monetary policy, I think I have found a more plausible case than that proposed by Melitz for the transmission of inflation from one country to another. Suppose that a country – for instance the foreign country in the two country case – opts for a higher inflation rate under a regime of floating exchange rates because, for instance, of an 'optimal' lower unemployment rate as described in the last section. A higher inflation rate signifies a higher nominal interest rate after the inflationary expectations have kept up with the ruling rate of inflation. A higher nominal interest rate reduces the desired holdings of real-cash balances with the consequence of a higher expansion path of the price level and of lower real-cash balances by which the existing wealth is reduced. In order to restore their previous wealth level, individuals will increase their savings rate, with the result of a lower real rate of interest by which the additional savings will be absorbed by an additional investment. The downward pressure on the real interest rate will be worldwide because a difference of *real* interest rates, at least for tradeable financial assets, is not conceivable in a world of integrated capital markets, either under a system of fixed exchange rates or under a system of flexible exchange rates; the latter system allows only a difference of national nominal interest rates reflecting a difference in national inflation rates. The worldwide reduction of the real interest rate affects equally the home country. If the latter pursues an unchanged inflation policy, its nominal interest rate will fall. If, however, the home country seeks to maintain its nominal interest rate at the previous level – a more plausible version of an interest-rate oriented monetary policy – it has to inflate (more) at an (additional) rate which corresponds to the difference between the previous and the current real interest rates.

Figure 9.2 illustrates this case. In figure 9.2a the equilibrium condition in the world goods market is given by the $S_W I_W$ line. For certain combinations of the real interest rate which must be the same in all countries (r_W) and the real world quantity of money (m_W) there is an equality between world

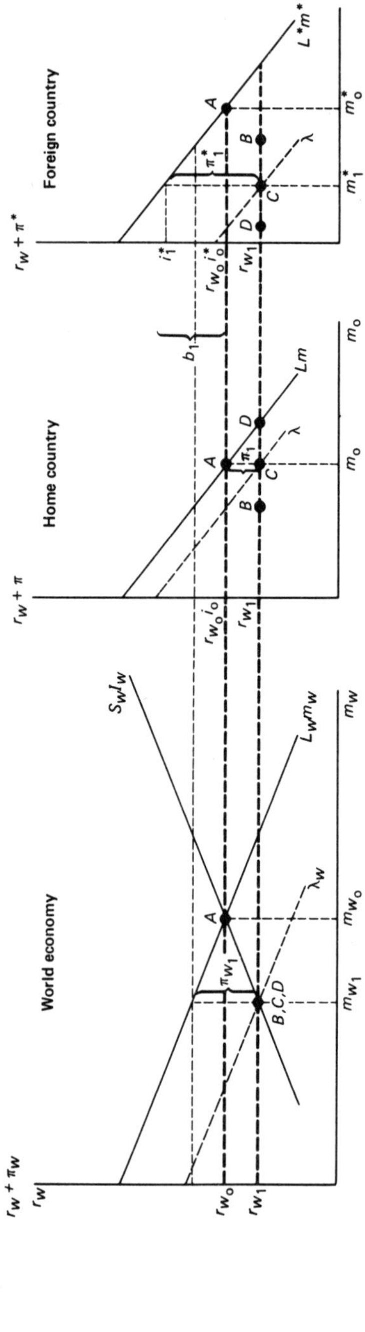
World economy
Home country
Foreign country
(a)
(b)
(c)
$r_w + \pi_w$
r_w
r_{w_0}
r_{w_1}
$S_w I_w$
$L_w m_w$
λ_w
m_{w_0}
m_{w_1}
m_w
π_{w_1}
B,C,D
A
$r_w + \pi$
$r_{w_0} i_0$
r_{w_1}
Lm
λ
m_0
π_1
b_1
B
C
D
$r_w + \pi^*$
i_1^*
$r_{w_0} i_0^*$
$L^* m^*$
π_1^*
m_0^*
m_1^*

Fig. 9.2

savings (S_w) and world investment (I_w)

$$S_w(r_w, m_w) = I_w(r_w) \tag{1}$$

where S_w and I_w are, respectively, the sum of national savings and the sum of national investments. A similar procedure can be applied for the equilibrium condition in the world money market

$$L_w(r_w + \pi_w) = m_w \tag{2}$$

represented by the $L_w m_w$ line in figure 9.2a where π_w is the world inflation rate and $r_w + \pi_w$ the nominal world interest rate. For sake of simplicity we assume stationary economies. For the special case of a zero growth rate of the world quantity of money ($\lambda_w = 0$), the equilibrium in the world goods market and in the world money market is situated at point A producing the equilibrium values r_{wo} and m_{wo}. A certain growth rate in the world quantity of money where

$$\lambda_w = \gamma\lambda + \gamma^*\lambda^* \tag{3}$$

implies a world inflation rate of

$$\pi_w = \lambda_w \tag{4}$$

such that the real world interest rate falls to r_{w1} and the nominal world interest rate rises to $r_{w1} + \pi_{w1}$; the coefficients γ and γ^* represent the relative size of the home country and of the foreign country, respectively, within the world economy and $\lambda(\lambda^*)$ is the growth rate of the money stock in the home (foreign) country.

This representation is applicable for the system of fixed exchange rates as well as for the system of floating rates. The difference between the two regimes consists in the interpretation of π_w, λ_w and $r_w + \pi_w$. In a system of fixed exchange rates, π_w must be identical to the home inflation rate (π) and to the foreign inflation rate (π^*): $\pi_w = \pi = \pi^*$; the same is valid for $\lambda_w = \lambda = \lambda^*$ (under the assumption of stationary economies) and for $r_w + \pi_w = r + \pi = r^* + \pi^*$. Under floating rates these rates are *weighted averages of national rates* as it is indicated for λ_w in equation (3) and as it can be written for

$$\pi_w = \gamma\pi + \gamma^*\pi^* \tag{5}$$

Differences in national inflation rates are corrected by continuous changes in the exchange rate according to the purchasing power parity

$$\rho = \pi - \pi^* \tag{6}$$

where ρ represents the rate of change in the exchange rate.

The equilibrium condition in the national money markets is represented by the Lm line in figure 9.2b for the home country and by the L^*m^* line in figure 9.2c for the foreign country. For instance, the equilibrium in the home national market is

$$L(r_w + \pi) = m \tag{7}$$

where

$$\pi = \lambda \tag{8}$$

There is still required another equation which defines the real world quantity of money as

$$m_w = m + m^* \tag{9}$$

With these nine equations we can determine the nine variables $r_w, \pi_w, m_w, \lambda_w, \pi, \pi^*, m, m^*, \rho$. Equations (1)–(4) determine the equilibrium levels for r_w, π_w, m_w and λ_w for a given λ and λ^*. Knowing r_w equations (7) and (8) determine π and m. The remaining variables are obtained by equation (5) for π^*, by (6) for ρ and by (9) for m^*.

This equilibrium system for the world economy and for the national economies must be interpreted, first of all, for the inflationary equilibrium in a system of fixed exchange rates ($\rho = 0$) represented by point *B* in the three panels of figure 9.2. The vertical distance between *B* and the corresponding point on the money-market equilibrium line indicates that $\pi_w = \pi = \pi^* = \lambda_w = \lambda = \lambda^*$ and that $r_w + \pi_w = r_w + \pi = r_w + \pi^*$. The real-world quantity of money has fallen from m_{wo} to m_{w1} because of the reduction in the real national quantities of money in each country from *A* to *B*.

Under a system of floating exchange rates and for a given value of λ_w, many equilibrium positions are conceivable in the home and foreign country depending on the value of λ or of λ^*. We shall examine two situations illustrated by points *C* and *D*, respectively.

C represents the special case we had in mind when the home country pursues an interest-rate oriented policy *and* when it wants to maintain a certain nominal interest rate (i_o in figure 9.2b) whatever may happen in the rest of the world. Suppose that the foreign country moves from *A* to *C* because of its money expansion rate λ^* (see the λ^* line in figure 9.2c). The real-world quantity of money is reduced by $m_o^* m_1^* = m_{wo} m_{w1}$ with the subsequent fall of r_w to r_{w1}. In order to maintain the nominal interest rate at i_o, the home country has to inflate by λ (see the λ line in figure 9.2b and of which the λ_w line in figure 9.2a has already taken into account). Consequently, due to this special interest-rate policy, there is a 'transmission' of the foreign inflation rate (π_1^*) to the home country (by π_1) by means of the lower real world interest rate (r_{w1}) and because of the interest target of the home country (i_o); the annual appreciation rate of the home currency is ρ_1. However, this case is only one conceivable case among many others. If, for instance, the home country does not pursue an interest-rate policy and wants a zero rate of inflation, it will be at point *D* (figure 9.2b) while the whole expansion of the world quantity of money originates in the foreign country.

In summarising the results of the argument regarding lower national monetary discipline under a regime of flexible exchange rates, we can conclude that neither the (Keynesian) belief in the existence of a Phillips-curve nor a (Keynesian) interest-rate guided monetary policy leads *necessarily* to a higher inflation rate than the inflation rate under fixed exchange rates. The opposite is equally possible. Thus the system of flexible exchange rates is neither *inherently* more inflationary nor *inherently* less inflationary.

III. THE ARGUMENT FROM ASYMMETRICAL AND INFLATIONARY PRICE EFFECTS OF A FLEXIBLE-EXCHANGE-RATE SYSTEM

This argument is more concerned with a worldwide view in terms of the world quantity of money, than with the national view last described, in terms of the quantity of money of various individual countries, even though the world quantity of money is the sum of the national quantities of money.[1] Furthermore, I shall confine myself to the possible link between flexible exchange rates on the one hand and world inflation on the other hand without discussing the opposite – and more probable – link of a higher world inflation leading to the introduction of a flexible-exchange-rate system; this latter question is important for the explanation of the existence of flexible exchange rates and it has to be differentiated according to the type of higher world inflation under fixed exchange rates, in other words, whether it is due to a common 'inflationary' shock in terms of an increase of the relative prices of certain goods with price stability of other goods (for example, the increase in food prices in 1972–73 and in oil prices in 1974) or whether it is due to inflationary shocks originating in certain large countries through a particular expansionary monetary policy. Thus, by looking only at the possible causal relationship between flexible exchange rates and a *higher* world inflation rate, we have discovered two possible cases. The first, attributed in the press to Mundell and Laffer (compare [10] even though it is not clear that they would fully subscribe to 'their' argument), concludes that flexible exchange rates lead to a higher world quantity of money to the extent that there are price rigidities in the economies involved. The second case is concerned with the possibility of an excess supply of international reserves as a consequence of the transition from a system of fixed exchange rates to a system of (controlled) flexible exchange rates.

(1) THE ASYMMETRICAL PRICE EFFECT OF CHANGES IN THE EXCHANGE RATE

The so-called 'Mundell–Laffer argument' can be summarised as follows. If the system of flexible exchange rates produces a greater number of depreciations

[1] Plus the outstanding amount of Eurocurrencies which we do not analyse in this paper since we do not see any specific relationship according to which the amount of Eurocurrencies should increase or decrease as a consequence of the existence of floating exchange rates (with the exception of a possible link between reserve holdings and the volume of Eurocurrencies).

than of appreciations, there will be an increase in the world quantity of money provided that the latter is expressed in terms of the currency unit of the depreciating countries. On the other hand, a change in the exchange rate causes an upward price pressure in the depreciating country and a downward price pressure in the appreciating country; if there is a price rigidity in the latter country (the so-called ratchet effect), it will pursue an expansionary monetary policy in order to avoid unemployment – a behaviour which gives rise to another increase in the world quantity of money.

This argument regarding an increase in the world quantity of money as a consequence of a change in the exchange rate can be illustrated by figure 9.3. Even though this model, presented by Dornbusch [3] and concerned with the devaluation effect of a country under principally fixed exchange rates, will turn out to be irrelevant to our problem, it is sometimes useful to analyse relevant cases by irrelevant models. The world economy is assumed to consist of two countries of equal size which are stationary and with full-employment income (y and y^*). There are only tradeable goods so that the exchange rate (e) is equal to the ratio between the internal price level (P) and the foreign price level (P^*) (see figure 9.3c). Both countries have the same liquidity preferences (k and k^*) so that their demand-for-money functions (M^d and M^{d*}) are identical (see figure 9.3b and 9.3d). The world quantity of money is given and shown by the line $\overline{M}_w\overline{M}_w{}^*$ in figure 9.3a. It is the sum of the quantities of money at home (M) and abroad (M^*) and it can be expressed in the currency unit of the home country ($\overline{M}_w = M + eM^*$) or in the currency unit of the foreign country ($M_w{}^* = M/e + M^*$). The equilibrium in the national money market is at point A; at B, for instance, the national money markets would be in disequilibrium for the price levels P_1 and P_1^* because there is an excess supply in the home money market (BC) and a corresponding excess demand in the foreign money market (CA).

Suppose that the home country devalues from e_1 to e_2, which is equivalent to a revaluation in the foreign country; see the dotted lines in figure 9.3a and 9.3c. The world quantity of money increases (by M_1^*de) when it is evaluated in the home currency and it decreases (by $M_1 d\left(\frac{1}{e}\right) = -M_1\left(\frac{1}{e^2}\right)$ when it is expressed by the foreign currency unit. The new equilibrium will be at D with a higher home price level (P_2) and a lower foreign price level ($P_2{}^*$). The 'formal' reason for this result is that de/e must be equal to $dP/P - dP^*/P^*$. The economic interpretation of this result is as follows.

Suppose that the home country is very small in relation to the foreign country and that the impact effect of the devaluation is $de/e = dP/P$ where $dP^*/P^* = 0$, eliminating any relative price effect. Due to the price increase in the home country there will be a (stock) excess demand for money (the so-called real-balance effect). The (flow) excess demand for money corresponds to an excess supply in the home goods market and because the home goods market is a part of the world goods market, there will be a corresponding excess supply on the world goods market with the consequence of a price fall

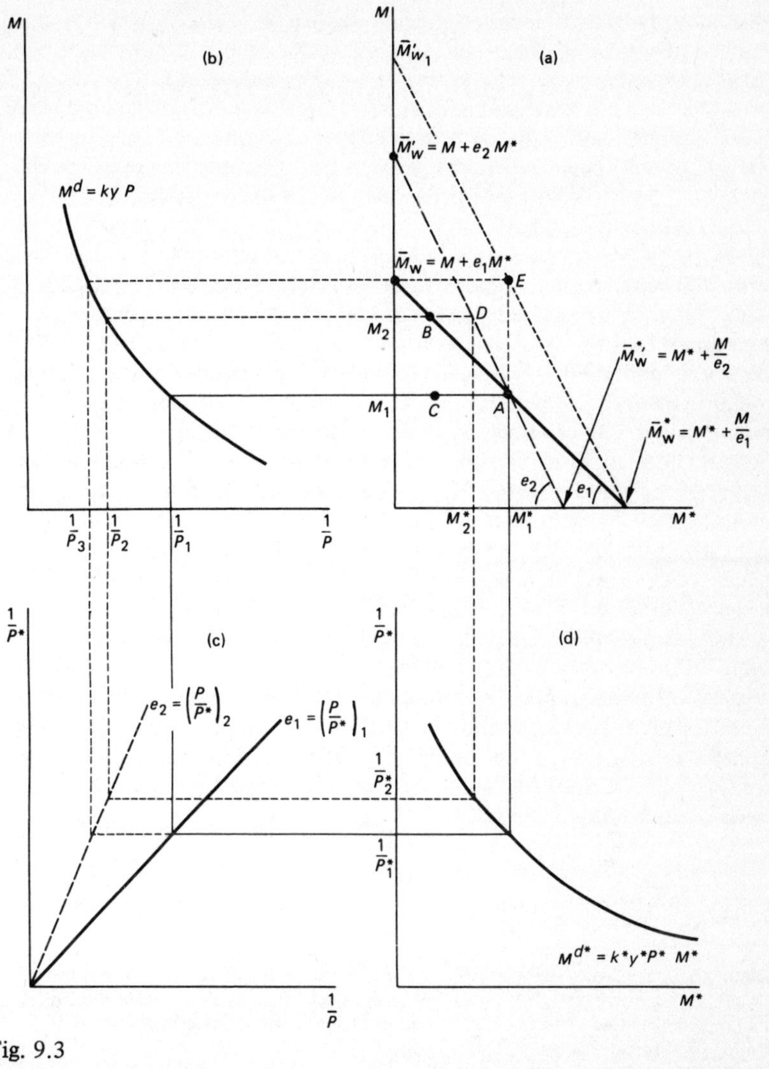

Fig. 9.3

on this market, giving rise to an excess supply in the foreign money market and a temporary balance of payments deficit in the foreign country and a temporary surplus in the home country.[1] Because the home country was assumed to be very small, its excess supply of goods is extremely small in

[1] A (flow) excess demand for money can correspond to an excess supply of goods *and* to a (flow) excess supply of securities. In our simplified reasoning we have abstracted from this latter possibility and, by this, from temporary interest-rate fluctuations. Cf. Claassen [2].

relation to the world supply of goods so that there will be only a very small decrease in the foreign price level whereas the home price level will be insignificantly below its price level which had increased initially by the devaluation rate. If on the other hand the home country is a very big country, the main price-level adjustment (in the downward sense) will take place in the foreign country. However, in all cases, the world price level as a *weighted* average of the two countries price levels will remain unchanged.[1]

With this simplified two-country model we can give some answers to the question whether changes in parities are inflationary or not. The first aspect of the 'Mundell–Laffer' argument refers to an increased world quantity of money when it is evaluated by the currency of the devaluing country. There is no doubt that this is a fallacy because the nominal quantity of money in the world economy has remained constant and so has equally the world price level. Furthermore, depending on the relative size of the devaluing country, the world quantity of money in terms of the devaluing currency may increase, decrease or remain constant if one takes into account the opposite change in the world quantity of money, now evaluated in the currency of the revaluing country. For instance, if the devaluing country is a very small economy in which there is only a very small fraction of the total world quantity of money, there will be an enormous increase in the world quantity of money in terms of the devalued currency. This increase is only partly compensated by the decrease in the world quantity of money expressed in terms of the currency of the revaluing country, because the latter is extremely large by assumption. A complete compensation only takes place if both countries are of equal size, and an overall decrease in the world quantity of money will arise only if the devaluing country is bigger than the revaluing country. Nevertheless, the 'numeraire' aspect of the 'Mundell–Laffer' argument remains fallacious.[2]

[1] According to Dornbusch [3], page 874, it can be shown that

$$\frac{dP}{P} = \gamma^* \frac{de}{e} \text{ and } \frac{dP^*}{P^*} = -\gamma \frac{de}{e}$$

where $\gamma(\gamma^*)$ represents the relative size of the home (foreign) country within the world economy and where $\gamma + \gamma^* = 1$. Consequently, the variation of the world price level (P_W) as the weighted average of the variation of the national price levels will be:

$$\frac{dPw}{Pw} = \gamma \frac{dP}{P} + \gamma^* \frac{dP^*}{P^*} = \gamma\gamma^* \frac{de}{e} - \gamma^*\gamma \frac{de}{e} = 0.$$

[2] However, the nominal world quantity of money will increase if the devaluing country increases its money supply at the amount of the accounting gains in its initial stock of reserves. Under this aspect of the evaluation of reserves, our two-country model has to be differentiated according to the criterion if one or both countries is a key-currency country or not. If there is a key-currency country and if the other country is the devaluing country, then there is the above possibility of a higher nominal world quantity of money. On the contrary, if the key-currency country is the 'devaluing' country, there will be no accounting gains because the 'reserves' of the key-currency country are equal to its own quantity of money. According to the usual intervention

The second part of this argument is related to the ratchet effect which maintains that the price rigidity in the revaluing country involves an expansionary monetary policy and, through this, an increase in the world quantity of money in order to avoid unemployment. This would mean in terms of figure 9.3 that the foreign price level remains unchanged at $P_1{}^*$, which is only possible if the world quantity of money increases by $\bar{M}_W{}^{*\prime}\bar{M}_W{}^*$ or by $\bar{M}'_W\bar{M}'_{W1}$ (see the dotted line $\bar{M}_W{}^*\bar{M}'_{W1}$ in figure 9.3a and the new equilibrium point E). Consequently, the foreign money supply has to be increased by more than $M_2{}^*M_1{}^*$, that is by more than the rate of the hypothetical price fall $P_1{}^*P_2{}^*$. The reason for this is that in our model of two countries of equal size a devaluation of 10 per cent in the home country would lead to a 5 per cent increase in the home price level and to a 5 per cent decrease in the foreign price level. If the foreign price level should remain constant, there will be a 10 per cent increase in the home price level such that the world quantity of money has to be increased by 5 per cent, which could be realised, for instance, by a 10 per cent increase in the foreign money supply. This numerical example is important, particularly for the case of a very big country which devalues, because in such a case the foreign country has to increase its money supply considerably and the world price level will increase almost by the devaluation rate as a consequence of the size of the devaluing country.

Even though the ratchet-effect argument is completely valid so far as concerns the world price level increasing effect of parity changes, three restrictions have to be stated which turn this argument into a completely irrelevant case. Firstly, in an inflationary world the absolute price rigidity becomes a relative price rigidity, which is less probable because in the revaluing country the prices have only to rise less rapidly. Secondly, the ratchet effect explains a once-and-for-all increase in the world price level and not a continuous increase, and thus does not explain a continuing world inflation *rate*; the latter can only be explained with the help of the ratchet effect if there is a continuous devaluation, or if there is a cyclical devaluation and revaluation. This last point leads us to the third and decisive restriction which takes the form of asking the question *why* the country concerned devalues. Our two-country model assumed an external equilibrium and a constant quantity of money before the country concerned devalued. Consequently, the reasons for this devaluation could only be either an increase in the stock of reserves or/and an

---

rules, it is not the key-currency country (the nth country) which devalues, but the other country (the $n-1$ countries) which revalues and which will have an accounting loss in its initial reserve stock; if its monetary policy maintains a direct and unchanged relationship between its outstanding money supply and its reserve stock (evaluated in its own currency), there will be a decrease in its money supply and, by this, in the world quantity of money.

In the case that both countries are not key-currency countries (the case of the gold standard or of a special drawing rights standard), there would only be an upvaluation of the initial reserve stock in the devaluing country (because of the existence of $n+1$ currencies).

increase in the internal price level; this latter case of a higher internal price level by the means of a devaluation could only be relevant for those countries which are not able, from the point of view of the technical control of the money supply, to increase the monetary base by its domestic component, that is by domestic credit. This is certainly a very limited case so that in all other cases the reason for a devaluation is just the opposite of our two-country model: instead of a devaluation which leads to a higher internal price level and to a higher nominal quantity of money in the devaluing country, it is first of all its quantity of money which increases with the consequences of a higher internal price level which causes a devaluation. However, this 'normal' causal link of a devaluation does not at all affect the foreign price level to the extent that the devaluation rate is equal to the expansion rate of the money supply in the devaluing country.[1]

Consequently, our two-country model turns out to be completely irrelevant for the reality of parity changes. It is also irrelevant for another reason. In a world of (pure) flexible exchange rates there cannot be devaluation or revaluation. The central bank has an influence on the exchange rate only indirectly through its monetary policy so that the only relevant cause of a 'devaluation' or of a 'revaluation' in a system of flexible exchange rates is the case of a more expansionary or of a more restrictive monetary policy. And with this typical reason for a *depreciating* or an *appreciating* exchange rate we are back again at the argument of the national monetary discipline for the explanation of world inflation under flexible exchange rates.

(2) THE INFLATIONARY PRICE EFFECT OF AN EXCESS SUPPLY OF RESERVES

The second argument regarding a higher world quantity of money through flexible exchange rates is derived from the possibility of an excess supply of reserves as the consequence of the introduction of flexible exchange rates. This excess supply can be created by a reduced need for international reserves, the latter being zero in the extreme case of a 'purely' floating system, whereas it will be reduced less under a system of controlled flexibility.[2] With such a system an external disequilibrium is partly financed by reserves and partly eliminated by the exchange-rate flexibility (and possibly by other internal adjustment policies).

Figure 9.4a shows this tradeoff relationship between real reserve holdings (R/P) and the degree of flexibility (β) by the line P_1P_1. This policy combina-

[1] It should be mentioned that the above argument of the reasons for a devaluation was related to our two-country model in which both were stationary and in which no capital movements took place. It is evident that an external disequilibrium and a following parity change do not need to be caused only by a different evolution of the price levels. They can also be caused by different real growth rates or by capital movements.

[2] Machlup [8] shows that the interventions of central banks in the foreign exchange market were even more frequent during the last years of flexibility.

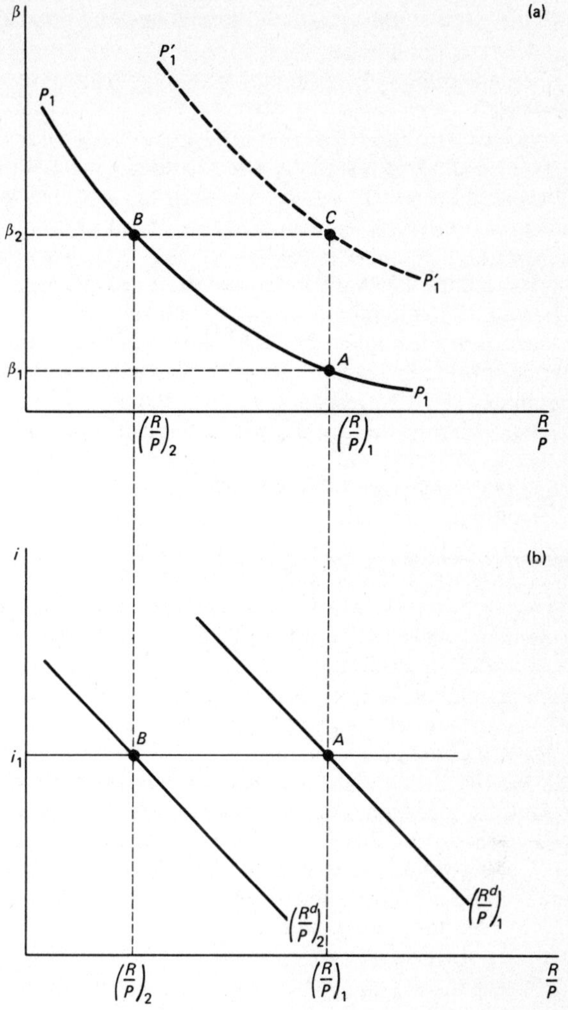

Fig. 9.4

tion guarantees a certain degree of external liquidity (P_1). At point *A* the economy is under a fixed exchange rate which allows a certain flexibility, β_1, around the par-value; the desired holding of real reserves is $(R/P)_1$ for a given level of its opportunity cost, i_1, which is equal to the nominal interest rate minus the interest rate received on reserves. The demand for reserves is a decreasing function of the opportunity cost as it is shown by the demand curve $(R^d/P)_1$ in figure 9.4b (compare Claassen [1]). If the country abandons the system of fixed exchange rates and opts for the degree of flexibility β_2 by maintaining external liquidity of type P_1, it will move to point B (figure 9.4a) with the result of a lower demand curve for real reserves, $(R^d/P)_2$ (figure 9.4b); for an unchanged opportunity cost i_1 its desired stock of real reserves is reduced to $(R/P)_2$.

The question we now have to answer is by what means a country can reduce its effective stock of real reserves to the desired level. We shall suppose a two-country model in which one country is the key-currency country and the other country – the country with which we are concerned with a reduced demand for reserves – constitutes the 'rest of the world'. There are two possible ways to reduce the stock of reserves to its desired level: either in real terms (an increased P) or in nominal terms (a reduced R).

The first case is not realisable. The central bank increases its money supply and, by this, provokes an increase in its price level with a subsequent depreciation of its currency *and* a corresponding gain in the book value of its reserves without affecting their real value (and without any change in the variables of the foreign country).

The second case implies that the central bank sells the unwanted part of its reserves on the foreign exchange market which involves, *ceteris paribus*, a corresponding decrease of its monetary base. The resulting appreciation of the currency, provoking a fall in the book value of the reserves of the concerned country, and the downward price movement taking place during the same period, would not affect the real amount of reserves if one did not take into account that part of excessive reserves which had been sold on the foreign exchange market. It is this part of the excessive reserves which has reduced the real amount of reserves of the country concerned. But the other country – the key-currency country – will encounter a corresponding increase in its money supply because there will be a real transfer of goods from the key-currency country to the domestic country against the acquisition of its own currency (the excessive reserves of the domestic country). Consequently, the world level of prices will not have changed. The reason for this is the trivial fact that the world quantity of money has not changed and, because of this, the world price level and the real world quantity of money have remained constant.[1]

[1] There is another possibility of an excess supply of reserves which is caused by an increase in the supply of reserves. Suppose again a two-country model. One of the two countries should be the key-currency country. The latter increases its money supply, that is the potential reserves for the other country. The result will be a higher price level and a subsequent depreciation of the key currency with the result that the nominal and real amount of reserves remain unchanged in the other country. On the other hand, if the additional supply of reserves consists of special drawing rights or of an increase in the price of gold, there will be an excess supply of reserves in *both* countries which can only be eliminated by a money expansion and, by this, by an increase of the price levels in both countries without affecting necessarily the exchange rate. However, these cases of an excess supply of reserves via an additional supply of reserves can happen in a system of fixed exchanged rates as well as under floating rates.

With the description of the first case (the illusionary reduction of non-desired reserves via an increased national price level) we have shown in this paper a third 'national' motivation for a lower national monetary discipline with a system of flexible exchange rates. The first concerned the possibility of reducing the unemployment rate by a higher inflation rate to the extent that the central bank believed in the existence of a Phillips-curve and believed that the optimum choice on this tradeoff line was a higher inflation rate. The second was related to a very special hypothetical behaviour of a central banker who is assumed to pursue a monetary policy by aligning the country's nominal interest rate to the foreign nominal interest rate, and to the extent that foreign countries were more inflationary and that the central banker overshot the foreign-interest-rate target level, he might produce a higher inflation rate. The third motivation for a lower national monetary discipline is the reduction in desired reserve holdings during a *transition* period from a system of fixed exchange rates towards a system of flexible exchange rates. However, the illusionary reduction in desired reserve holdings produces only a *once-and-for-all* increase in the world price level. On the other hand, it is conceivable that a lower demand for reserves because of flexible exchange rates may be offset by other factors which in their turn increase this demand (take, for instance, the energy crisis which coincided with the beginning of floating rates). Such a case is illustrated in figure 9.4a. The probability of a higher variability of international payments shifts the line P_1P_1 towards $P'_1P'_1$ in order to maintain the same degree of external liquidity (P_1); in this particular case the demand curve for international reserves, $(R^d/P)_1$, remains unchanged (figure 9.4b).

It is left to the reader to find other reasons for a lower national monetary (or inflationary) discipline – but also, to be just, for a higher national monetary (or inflationary) discipline – under a regime of flexible exchange rates. This task is comparatively easy because he has only to forget the whole of monetary inflation theory and to open the Pandora box which contains all other national inflation theories.

IV. CONCLUDING REMARKS: FUTURE OUTLOOK

My main concern has been to show that flexible exchange rates are neither inherently more inflationary nor inherently less inflationary than fixed exchange rates. They can be more inflationary and they can be less inflationary. But the main responsibility for a possible higher world inflation rate (as the weighted sum of the national inflation rates) has now shifted to individual national monetary policies and, by consequence, to the degree of monetary discipline exercised by these individual countries. The relatively short period of flexible exchange rates during the last few years has shown the possibility of a higher world inflation rate, even though this empirical argument is not completely conclusive because we do not know what would have happened to the world inflation rate if the previous system of fixed exchange rates had been maintained. On the other hand, for the future, one cannot exclude the alternative possibility of a lower world inflation rate than that of the late 1960s, and one could even envisage the possibility of a zero world inflation, as Harry Johnson [7] does: '. . . floating rates are a consequence, and not a cause, of our 'stagflation' problem. And it may even appear in hindsight that floating rates, by bottling up inflations within the borders of the inflating countries, have sufficiently stiffened national anti-inflationary resolve – in particular in the United States – to get us back to 1920s stability by the 1980s.'

REFERENCES

[1] Emil-Maria Claassen, (1975), 'Demand for International Reserves and the Optimum Mix and Speed of Adjustment Policies', *American Economic Review*, (June, 1975).

[2] Emil-Maria Classen, (1976), 'The Role of Economic Size in the Determination and Transmission of World Inflation', in Helmut Frisch (ed.), *Inflation in Small Countries* (1976).

[3] Rudiger Dornbusch, (1973), 'Devaluation, Money, and Nontraded Goods', *American Economic Review* (December, 1973).

[4] Joel Fried, (1973), 'Inflation-Unemployment Trade-Offs under Fixed and Floating Exchange Rates', *Canadian Journal of Economics* (February, 1973).

[5] Gottfried Haberler, (1974), 'Inflation as a Worldwide Phenomenon: An Overview', *Weltwirtschaftliches Archiv*, vol. 110, No 2 (1974).

[6] Harry G. Johnson, (1975a), 'Inflation, Unemployment, and the Floating Rate', *Canadian Public Policy* (Spring, 1975).

[7] Harry G. Johnson, (1975b), 'Have Floating Rates Worked so Badly?', *Bulletin de l'Institut Economique de Paris* (July–August, 1975).

[8] Fritz Machlup, (1975), 'Recent Experiences with Floating Currencies', in Emil-Maria Claassen and Pascal Salin (ed.), *Recent Issues in International Monetary Economics*, (North-Holland, Amsterdam, 1975).

[9] Jacques Melitz, (1975), 'On the International Transmission of Inflation under Floating Exchange Rates', paper for the Konstanz Seminar on Monetary Theory and Monetary Policy (June, 1975).

[10] Jude Wanniski, (1974), 'The Case for Fixed Exchange Rates', *Wall Street Journal*, (June 14, 1974).

Discussion of the Paper by Emil-Maria Claassen

Professor Liviatan explained that the paper looked at the relationship between fixed and flexible exchange rates and world inflation. It moved from exchange rates to world inflation, but one could perhaps move in the opposite direction too, asking what kind of exchange rate system would be best with what kind of world inflation. He did not believe one could hold any exchange rate system against strong world forces. Perhaps the author's way of looking at the problem was correct in the short run, though it might not be in the long run.

Could one find any bias in one system rather than the other? Professor Claassen said one could not, and he agreed. Other authors seemed to think the same. Professor Claassen tried to look at inflationary bias and decided it was impossible to reach a conclusive result. For example, with floating exchange rates, one country could insulate itself and have its 'own' inflationary policy, perhaps to reduce unemployment. The question then was whether it wanted more or less inflation than the rest of the world.

Professor Claassen considered the hypothesis that there was a tendency to keep the same nominal rate of interest as in other countries – or at least to keep one's own nominal rate of interest constant. Professor Liviatan asked why this was. Why nominal rather than real rates? One would expect market forces to equalise *real* interest rates. In any case, suppose one had a flexible exchange rate and the rest of the world inflated. Then if one wanted to keep the same nominal interest rate, one would have to inflate too. This could be described in the following equation:

$$i_{\text{nom}} = \pi + r$$

where π represented the rate of inflation and r the real rate of interest. This meant that, with a given nominal interest rate, an increase in the average money supply for the world would reduce the real interest rate. Since real interest rates were equalised across the world, this would in the end affect one's own country. To be passive, a country with a nominal interest rate illusion would have to inflate more highly than it originally intended. He did not know many bankers, but the ones he did know did not suffer from this kind of illusion.

Another reason was the effect of devaluation. Some simple monetarist models showed that if a country devalued, with a constant nominal world stock of money, this would increase its price level. If the inflationary country devalued, other countries should reduce their prices. If, because of rigidities, they could not do this, the inflationary country would inflate more and this would lead to a bias. In an inflationary world, it was difficult to reduce one's absolute price level, but a reduction in other countries' inflations would follow if a country devalued. Unfortunately, it was often hard to reduce even the relative rate of inflation.

Professor Claassen's point was that this was not how the steps occurred. Devaluation did not appear out of the blue. If there were an increase in one's own money supply, then to devalue after this would mean that there was no transmission of inflation.

When a country moved from fixed to floating exchange rates, all its reserves would no longer be necessary. On some assumptions, the world velocity of circulation would increase. This would lead to higher world inflation, though it was a once-and-for-all process. One could not infer from the exchange rate system whether it would contribute more or less to inflation.

Professor Liviatan thought it important to recognise that when one spoke of a fixed exchange rate one was not referring to the gold standard. If all countries inflated, with an increase in the price level, then a gold standard with a fixed nominal gold price would mean that reserves were not enough for the whole world. There would be a need to increase the price of gold. So this was not a problem simply of fixed exchange rates but one of simultaneous devaluation.

A theoretical question which bothered Professor Liviatan was how a world rate of inflation was determined. With flexible exchange rates, a country could isolate itself, the world rate of inflation was the weighted average of the rate in all countries. With fixed exchange rates, the situation was more complicated. With small countries, no one country would have much effect on the world inflation rate. To know how much it could inflate, it would have to keep in line with that rate, which meant that the country would have to guess what the world inflation rate would be. If everyone were playing the same guessing game, then whatever rate of inflation they expected would materialise. Expectations would be self-fulfilling. The difficulty was that this left all inflation rates hanging in the air, each country waiting for others to decide. There was an inherent instability in such a system, and he wondered what pinned it down. Perhaps it was the fact that some large countries were price leaders. They decided what rate of inflation they would like and others had to follow. What determined the result would then be the interests of the large blocs of countries which would act as price leaders.

These large blocs could determine their own rates of inflation, whether exchange rates were fixed or floating, simply because they were big. They thereby determined the world rate of inflation and enabled one to conclude which exchange rate system was more inducive to inflation. It was possible that under flexible exchange rates small countries might be more able and willing to inflate faster than under fixed rates. The key issue was therefore whether small countries were more inflation-prone than big ones. If there were two large blocs – like the United States and the EEC – then this would lead to an oligopolist system, this, however, was an issue which he preferred to avoid.

Dr Corden said the paper reached the same conclusions as he did in his own paper, on those topics which they had in common. In the first part of the paper, Professor Claassen disposed of a number of unsound arguments. The most interesting part of the paper was the last. If a country moved from fixed to floating rates it required less reserves, though it had a choice about how to achieve this. It could either appreciate its exchange rate or increase the prices of domestic products. If all countries appreciated their currencies for this reason, this would lower the real value of reserves and thus achieve the desired result. Alternatively, the countries could increase their domestic price levels. This would again reduce the real value of world reserves, but this time it would cause an inflationary process. Since the latter was only one of two possible processes, it was not inevitable that a fall in the real value of world reserves would be inflationary.

Professor Duesenberry felt Professor Liviatan was arguing that the choice between fixed and floating rates, if made, had to be made for a long time. However, if a country had large reserves, this gave it time to collect information on other countries' intentions and see how things worked out. This might make it possible to converge to a position where all countries found what their desired rate of inflation was. Whether they then converged or not depended on the spread of intentions.

He wanted to make two related points. The first was on capital movements. It had been suggested that there was no reason why a central bank would want to stick to a given nominal rate of interest. He felt there were good reasons. First, the whole past set of rates and institutions was built round a particular nominal rate. It would take a long time to adapt. This was a good reason for trying to stick to a given pattern of nominal rates.

Second, it was possible to have the same rate of inflation but different targets for the real rate of interest. This meant that a major issue was how far a country could have its own inflation rate and its own economic policies. This would not be true if monetary policy were the only policy instrument. Then, if the nominal rate of interest were out of line, there would be capital movements and exchange-rate problems. Many countries did have other policy instruments, but to be able to control their own fate needed substitutes for monetary policy in the shape of an array of credits and taxes. These were rarely deliberately integrated with monetary policy.

Professor Duesenberry thought that too much of the argument assumed a world where one had flows of goods but not of capital. In the United States fluctuations in the dollar exchange rate were only incidentally the result of relative prices or trade flows. The dollar was most heavily influenced by capital movements. This was not just rate of interest arbitrage, but genuine speculation. It meant that a country wanting to devalue had more, and less easily manageable, problems than much of the discussion suggested.

Dr Corden contended that some problems *were* sorted out. For example, suppose there were an increase in demand, with flexible exchange rates and high capital mobility. The interest rate would fall, capital would move out and the exchange rate would fall. This would switch demand away from overseas goods and increase demand for domestic goods. This effect would not operate if there were capital mobility with fixed exchange rates.

Mr Plessz thought the paper disposed too easily of the arguments of Professor Mundell. According to these, large fluctuations in exchange rates had a mechanical price-raising effect on all countries because of a downward rigidity of domestic price levels. Actually, the events of the last few years had provided a textbook example of this thesis. Exchange rate changes were much bigger than could be justified by relative price movements, because of the size of short-term capital movements and anticipations. As for the main depreciating currency – the dollar – there had been a reversal of the trend in 1975, and if the appreciation continued it could have a strong inflationary impact on other countries. Thus, the world might go back to something like the Smithsonian exchange rate structure, meanwhile there was a significant increase in the trend rate of inflation and in inflationary expectations.

Recent experience suggested that the move to more flexible exchange rates resulted in a kind of paradox. For reasons mentioned earlier, the direct price effect had been clearly inflationary. At the same time, demand management, and notably the monetary policies of the various countries had, on balance, become more restrictive. This was partly as a reaction to a more inflationary environment and partly because governments recognised that by currency depreciation they were running the risk of a cumulative acceleration of domestic inflation. On the whole, there had been a tendency for currency appreciation or depreciation to overcompensate for relative price movements, at least in the short run. This had led monetary authorities to intervene in foreign exchange markets.

There was no doubt that floating reduced the need for reserves. In practice, however, the maldistribution of foreign reserves was such that it reinforced the tendency for the appreciation of some currencies.

Professor Nussbaumer did not agree with Professor Liviatan on small and large countries. Which big country did one select to follow in one's policy? Austria might follow Germany, but it might equally follow Italy or the United Kingdom. The small countries in the world were not completely tied to any particular big bloc, but had a good degree of freedom.

In addition, small countries could choose to appreciate their currencies. They did not necessarily choose more inflation than other countries, but might choose less, especially if they hoped to improve their export chances. If they tried to appreciate the currency, they might then meet opposition from these export industries. There was a positive effect on competitiveness and exchange reserves.

Professor Nussbaumer agreed with Professor Duesenberry that one should not mix models which assumed the movement of goods with those assuming capital movements. If one did, the outcome was open. Goods might move because of capital inflows, or capital might move because goods had done so. One should stick to one model. If one did, and if one dealt only with capital, he thought there was a case for saying that central banks did try to keep nominal interest rates constant. If they did not, there were increases or decreases in bond values, which was something that monetary authorities and stock exchanges tried to avoid.

Where did capital come from? Experience showed that if the real rate of interest fell below 2 to 2½ per cent, inflation had an effect on net savings. However, this effect was not important so long as the rate of inflation was between 3 and 5 per cent. Austrian banks found they could then adhere to a fixed rate of interest.

Both arguments explained why central banks wanted fixed exchange rates and no offsetting policy measures. It was because this imposed an extra constraint on monetary authorities. If inflation meant depreciation of the exchange rate, one would have a lower interest rate and a higher rate of inflation because of exchange rate changes. With fixed exchange rates, one could ignore the fact that an interest rate was really a rate of interest plus a repayment of capital. But fixing the nominal rate of interest, and moving to flexible exchange rates, meant that inflation had an automatic effect both on the nominal rate of interest and on the volume of foreign assets in a country. It was likely to lead to capital outflows and currency depreciation, as had been seen recently. With flexible exchange rates in Europe, countries with appreciating currencies had to oppose capital movements.

Professor Giersch commented on what Mr Plessz had said. If the OECD conclusion was that the move from fixed to flexible exchange rates was on balance inflationary, he wanted to ask what alternative there was. Was it a Smithsonian system, based on OECD calculations, or on figures hurriedly worked out on the backs of envelopes during a conference? The system had broken down either because different countries had different views of their Phillips-curves or because they wished to be on them at different points. While there might be no Phillips-curve at all, except in the shortest of short runs, governments believed that there was. So the system would not work.

In the past, it had produced distortions in industrial structure. For example, in Germany undervaluation of the currency had led to an increase in foreign exchange reserves, and excessive bias towards export orientation which had been hard to remove.

On the other hand, countries like Germany whose currencies had appreciated had experienced reductions in import prices that had helped to stabilise domestic price levels. In an inflationary world, a fall in import prices was one factor working against the one-sided operation of the price ratchet.

Professor Claassen explained that before writing the paper he had been excited about the subject. Now he was less excited, because he had reached very traditional conclusions. In other words, flexible exchange rates could be more or less inflationary according to circumstances. It was even possible that a country could insulate itself wholly from foreign inflation. If one allowed for capital movements, one got some transmission of other countries' inflation to a particular country.

This did not mean that all countries had to have the same rate of inflation. One could argue that in the long run the purchasing power parity theory held, while in the short run it did not. If one stuck to purchasing power parity, this still did not say anything about short-run foreign exchange rate movements. To the extent that expectations about the exchange rate were sticky – for example, depending on expectations linked to current and past exchange rates – the exchange rate would not reflect the purchasing power parity. This might mean, for instance, that capital moved out of a country, leading to a depreciation of its currency and a higher domestic price level.

In the foreign countries, it would lead to an appreciation. So the price level would tend to fall and the ratchet effect would come in. The ratchet effect had to be considered in two different aspects. The first was one where the exchange rate did not reflect purchasing power parity. It would then be dominated by capital movements, which would lead to effects on the domestic and foreign price levels. With price rigidities, this would lead to higher wages and prices. The second aspect was one of a long-run model, where the theory of purchasing power parity prevailed. This was not so relevant, because the main reason for changes in exchange rates was monetary policy. If the money supply increased, prices would increase with a subsequent devaluation, and this would have no effect of foreign prices.

He agreed very much with Professor Liviatan on the question of which exchange rate system was more inflationary. With fixed exchange rates, the world could inflate at any rate. Much would depend on the type of international monetary order. For example, the position of the dollar had been different since 1965. Before that, the whole set of exchange rates was fixed because one currency was linked to gold. The gold/dollar price therefore gave *one* fixed point to the system, and, in this sense, the world could not do what it liked. Only with no convertibility between the dollar and gold could the world choose its own inflation rate. The period since 1968 was a relatively short one in monetary history, and perhaps there would be a return to convertibility.

Professor Liviatan had argued that the world was asymmetrical, with big countries, small countries and super powers. In such a world the big countries could determine their own inflation rates. However, in the real world, one had monetary blocs. He did not agree with Professor Nussbaumer that Austria could join whichever major country she wanted. She was likely to choose one with similar inflationary policies.

Professor Claassen, while underlining what Professor Giersch had said, said that Professor Liviatan had argued that he (Claassen) had looked at the problem only from one point of view. Professor Liviatan had also wanted him to say which kind of world inflation led to flexible exchange rates. It was true that he had not done this, but one could not tackle the problem by *a priori* reasoning. Looking at the recent past, one could say that rapid world inflation had led to flexible exchange rates. Now it was hard to make comparisons. One could not say that because inflation in the 1970s had been more rapid than in the 1960s, flexible exchange rates were more inflationary than fixed. With the latter, it was quite possible that there would have been even more inflation.

Dr Corden had commented that a move from fixed to flexible exchange rates could lead to an excessive supply of world reserves. In a world of $n - 1$ non-key currencies, where excess reserves were dollars, the world would get rid of these reserves by appreciation. The currency would appreciate, the central bank would sell foreign currency, and domestic prices and the domestic money supply would fall because of open market operations in reserves. This process would lead to lower real reserves and was a sensible one, because if one reduced one's money supply, there would be a transfer of real reserves against goods from the nth country.

Part 3

The Effects of Inflation

10 Inflation and Income Distribution

James Duesenberry
HARVARD UNIVERSITY

I. INTRODUCTION

It has for a long time been recognised that inflation, and especially unanticipated inflation, causes changes in income distribution. In particular, it has often been pointed out how, in an unanticipated inflation, holders of assets demoninated in nominal terms will suffer. Other groups, especially pensioners, whose nominal incomes are fixed, also lose in times of inflation. Other discussions centre on the lag structure of wage and price responses, which can produce shifts in the income distribution as between wages and profits. More recently attention has been directed toward the distributional effects of tax systems with progressive rate structures stated in nominal terms. When such a tax system is operative, inflation can produce income losses to groups paying the higher marginal tax rates. The distribution of the offsetting gain depends, of course, on the actions of the government whose revenue has been increased.

I have no quarrel with those observations and not much to add. I would like to look at the relation between inflation and distribution from a somewhat different point of view. Instead of discussing inflation as something which causes distributional problems, I want to consider inflation as a phenomenon which is caused *by* distributional problems. Moreover, I shall argue that under our present institutional arrangements, inflation may be a necessary part of the process by which certain redistributions required by market forces are brought about.

That is not, of course, an entirely new thought. One may consider major war inflations as efforts by the government to transfer a larger share of income to itself by printing money and then allowing the rise in prices to extract income and wealth from various groups. Indeed, that process has received most attention in the distributional discussions alluded to above.

Secondly, when cost-push inflation became a popular concept it was generally thought to result from efforts by trade unions and oligopolists to increase their share of total income. I have no doubt that that kind of cost-push inflation has its importance at times. New monopolies and newly organised or strengthened unions can certainly generate inflationary pressures. The large wage increases obtained by public employee unions in the United States provide an example. But well-established unions or industrial monopolies should long ago have pushed their relative wages and prices as far up as they can profitably go even from their own point of view.[1] If nothing else were happening cost-push inflation would not be so important.

While positive or offensive efforts to shift the income distribution toward a particular group may have been exaggerated at times, the significance of defensive efforts to maintain incomes in the face of adverse market forces has been somewhat neglected. In the United States at least there has been some disposition for politically and economically powerful groups to accept the *status quo* in income distribution provided that each got its share of rising output, while vigorously resisting any loss of absolute or relative position. There has not been enough popular support to push through a major tax reform to increase the effective progressivity of the income tax or of estate and gift taxes.[2]

But this political truce does not by any means solve all the problems of income distribution. It is in the nature of a market economy that relative prices and wages are constantly shifting so as to reallocate resources in response to changes and technology, capital accumulation, demographic shifts, and natural resource availability. Unfortunately those relative price and wage changes also imply changes in income distribution.

Moreover, in spite of what may be said in textbooks about the beauties of free markets, hardly anyone believes that market forces should be allowed to cause a deterioration in his absolute or relative income position. People may more or less passively accept the inequalities of the *status quo* but that does not imply an ideological acceptance of the idea that the distribution dictated by the market is the right one. That becomes apparent when the market requires a change. Those observations might only imply that market-induced changes in income distribution would generate a lot of complaint and perhaps some political action. They do, of course, generate various types of political action which results in protectionist legislation in favour of industries with declining markets. In addition, however, it turns out that most groups in our society have enough market power to resist downward pressures on their wages and prices. This resistance applies first of all to nominal wages and prices but also applies in less degree to real wages and also to relative wages. The result, as I shall argue below, is that some inflation and some unemployment are both required to bring about the relative price changes required by a dynamic economy.

That view is, of course, inconsistent with the neoclassical view which lays all the blame for inflation on the demand side. In a neoclassical model, with flexible prices and a level of aggregate money expenditure which is independent of the price level, relative price changes occur without inflation. Shifts in

[1] Of course there may be times when emotional or ideological factors cause unions to completely ignore market realities and in that case old unions may generate a wage price spiral. Recent events in the United Kingdom may be a case in point. I shall discuss the market restraints on trade union action in a later section.

[2] Revenues from the basic tax system plus increases in social security taxes have financed large increases in transfer payments which have served to offset the tendency toward increasing inequality of family income distributed from an increased proportion of families with females or aged heads.

the composition of demand cause some prices to rise and others to fall thus inducing the appropriate shift of resources from one sector to another. Technological progress causes reductions in the prices of commodities where factor productivity increases relatively rapidly, and increases in those with slow progress, while money wages rise at the average rate of productivity increase (assuming that aggregate money expenditure is made to grow at the rate of growth of real potential output).

A proper neoclassical world should, in principle, have digested the increase in oil prices by the OPEC cartel without inflation. The increase in oil prices could have been offset by price and wage reductions elsewhere.

To the extent that prices and wages *do* respond sensitively and symmetrically to excess demand or supply, inflation can be prevented by maintaining a growth rate of aggregate money expenditure equal to the growth rate of real potential output. And the policy which prevents inflation should hold unemployment to the frictional minimum. But the fact is that wage and price do not respond sensitively and symmetrically to excess demand and supply on the market.

Keynes long ago argued that money wages do not readily move down under the pressure of unemployment. That proposition is generally accepted. But it does not go far enough. There is also resistance to any reduction in real wages, and there are strong forces tending to maintain the structure of relative wages against market pressure. Prices are not as rigid as wages, but there are many areas in which prices rise more readily under the pressure of cost increase or excess demand than they fall under pressure of falling cost or excess supply.

To put it briefly there is a great deal of resistance to the redistributions of income which market processes tend to produce. Nonetheless if resources are fully employed, or nearly so, relative prices must change. I shall argue that in those circumstances a certain amount of inflation is required to bring about the necessary adjustments, and that at the same time a certain amount of slack in the system will also be required.

I shall first elaborate a little on the rigidities in real and money wages and on the linkages among wages. I shall then try to outline the implications of those observations. I will try to show that they create an inflationary bias in the sense that prices tend to rise at less than full employment even under conditions of steady growth. Next I shall argue that those same considerations make the United States economy vulnerable to accelerating inflation whenever any force tends to drive up the cost of living. Finally, I shall maintain that our vulnerability to inflation results from the fact that we are trying to make the market solve distributional problems which are essentially political in character.

In making this argument I am not, of course, denying that if the monetary and fiscal authorities rigidly held the growth rate of aggregate money expenditure to the growth rate of potential output they could prevent inflation. What I am arguing is that they can only do so by creating unemployment. One way of putting it is to say that

(1) market forces make certain redistributions necessary,

(2) in view of the rigidities in the wage structure these redistributions will lead to inflation if resources are fully utilised,

(3) the inflation can only be checked and the necessary redistribution completed if there is a considerable amount of unemployment,

(4) the unemployment is not acceptable until after a period of inflation. In that sense the distributional shifts and resistances to them cause both the unemployment and the inflation.

II. WAGE RIGIDITIES AND LINKAGES

In this section I shall make some assertions about the behaviour of wages under various conditions. I shall make no attempt to prove them empirically. On the whole, I do not think they are very controversial at least among labour economists.

I shall make three main assertions:

(1) wages rise more readily in markets with a labour shortage than they fall in markets with a labour surplus;

(2) when the cost of living rises, workers tend to get at least partial compensation;

(3) wage increases in one market have a positive influence (linkage) on wage changes in other markets.

(1) DOWNWARD RIGIDITY OF NOMINAL WAGES

It is hardly necessary to argue that nominal wage reductions for workers already employed on a specific job occur only under unusual circumstances. Since there is very considerable turnover that is not the whole story. But it is equally true that employers with organised personnel systems to not shift their pay schedules down for new workers even when there is a labour surplus. At most, new hires come in at the bottom of the schedule when the market is 'easy' and above it when it is tight. This provides very limited downward flexibility. Small scale employers are not bound by rigid wage systems but it is they who are most often affected by minimum wage legislation and by the opportunity cost factors of welfare and unemployment compensation.

On the other hand there is no particular inhibition on raising wages except the employers' recognition that old employees must have increases if new ones are hired at rates above those previously ruling. On the whole then, it seems fair to say that wages are rigid downward and flexible upward though the crude statement may slightly oversimplify things.

(2) RIGIDITY IN REAL WAGES

The more controversial and less certain proposition is that real wages cannot readily be reduced. Trade unions, of course, often cite a rising cost of living as a part for wage increases. That may be only rationalisation. But any substantial or prolonged decline in real wages is bound to influence the emotional attitude of trade union members and increase their willingness to take a long strike to recover their losses.[1] Increased willingness to strike increases the effective bargaining power of unions.

Sensitivity to the cost of living and resistance to real wage reductions is by no means confined to organised labour. Most employers recognise that a decline in real wages will create poor morale and stimulate their best qualified employees to look elsewhere for higher pay. In my own observation employers seem to take it for granted that they must give at least partial compensation for a rising cost of living.

Of course, resistance to reductions in real wages cannot be absolute. The willingness of employers to grant wage increases in response to strike threats or their fear of loss of productivity due to low morale or high turnover will obviously depend on the level of employment and the strength of the product market. But a rise in living costs can generate wage increases in circumstances in which the supply and demand balance in the labour market would not do so.

(3) WAGE LINKAGES

The concept of wage linkage is not so common in aggregate economics though it is frequently used by labour economists. It has been given great emphasis by my colleague John T. Dunlop. The notion of wage linkages makes no sense in a purely competitive world with perfect knowledge and no transactions costs. In reality, however, trade union bargains contain arbitrary elements partly because of uncertain knowledge of the effect of wage changes on employment and profits, partly because bargaining is affected by willingness of the parties to bear costs to attain their objectives. The outcome of one settlement may, therefore, be affected by the fact that a trade union's leadership or membership believes that it should have parity with another union. Union settlements are also, of course, linked to other wages through market processes.

In addition, I shall argue that wage and salary administration in the non-union sector is also somewhat arbitrary so that the concept of comparability can play a significant role.

In the union sector two types of linkages may be distinguished. First there are positive linkages between union settlements which arise partly from the internal politics of unions and the fact that there are arbitrary or indeterminate elements in the bargaining process. Most labour economists are convinced that the settlement obtained by the Steelworkers in their negotiations with the Can and Aluminium companies will have a very substantial effect on the steel settlement and that steel and auto settlements affect one another. In the

[1] It may be noted that income losses from reductions in over-time or increased taxes may provide the same response as a reduction in real wages due to price increases in excess of wage increases.

fragmented craft unions in the building trades, settlements in one trade affect those in the same trade in adjacent areas. Building trades settlements are also alleged to have an impact on industrial settlements in the same area. These positive linkages and the political pressures within unions force the leadership of one union to attempt to keep up with the performance of related unions even though the objective economic situation may be different. In the short run at least, there is always an area of indeterminancy in settlements. The outcome will depend in part on the willingness of union leadership to take a strike. Their willingness to do so will depend in part on the pressure for performance from their own membership.

Second, there are market constraints on the wage gains of any one union. In spite of their ability to extract wage increases by the strike threat, union power is limited by market forces working through non-union competition, foreign competition, substitute products and mechanisation. As a union's relative wage increases, competitive forces restrict employment and, by forcing employers with a choice between a profit squeeze and a price increase which reduces volume, increases employer resistance. In a static situation one might expect that a union once organised would push up wages by a limited amount and then stop. But in a dynamic world some wage increases are always occurring. Wage changes elsewhere move the constraint on any particular union which can then demand and obtain wage increases so that in that sense wage movements are linked.

Linkages among wages extend far beyond the trade union sector. First most employers whose blue-collar workers are unionised raise the wages of their non-union employees when they negotiate a wage increase with the union.

Second, most large non-union employers have elaborate systems of job classification and a structure of pay grades similar to those used in civil service. Differentials between these grades are usually determined on the basis of long term considerations and change slowly. When rates are increased the whole structure moves up at once. (Most private employers use a range for each pay grade which permits some flexibility for merit increases and differential responses to supply problems. However, the use of ranges permits only limited flexibility.) In arriving at decisions in regard to changes in wage levels and differentials personnel administrators are strongly influenced by considerations of 'comparability' between the wages of their own employees and those of other firms. The widespread use of wage surveys in the decision process introduces a strong 'follow the leader' component into wage determination.

III. IMPLICATIONS

The rigidities and linkages described above create an inflationary bias in the system in the sense that inflation will occur at a level of aggregate demand well below the potential output of the economy. Moreover, those same factors make the system vulnerable to a persisting inflationary process in response to any shock which raises prices or wages in any section of the economy. In effect the system can only accomplish the shifts in relative income required by market forces by using inflation as a mechanism of redistribution.

Let us consider first an economy growing steadily and maintaining a constant ratio of vacancies and unemployment to labour force in the aggregate but with a considerable dispersion in the supply and demand balance among labour markets. In some markets (defined by area and occupation) vacancies exceed unemployment while the reverse is true in others. Migration, and job training will tend to remove any particular inbalance but new ones will constantly appear.

In a neoclassical flexible-price, model, wages should tend to rise in markets in which vacancies exceed unemployment and fall in the reverse case. If, in the aggregate, vacancies and unemployment are equal, the resulting relative wage shifts should cause relative price shifts leading to expansion of output in the labour surplus markets and a decline in the shortage markets. At the same time they will induce migration of workers and plants in the appropriate direction, cause adaptation in production methods, and lead workers to change training or accept a different type of job. Thus relative price and wage changes serve to speed up the adjustments which would occur anyway in response to shortages and surpluses as such. If the aggregate vacancies and unemployment are in balance these adjustments could take place without any change in the overall price level. On the other hand a net excess of vacancies or unemployment would raise the average wage level and vice versa. In the neoclassical model net excess demand for labour is required to produce wage inflation.

If, however, nominal wages do not decline at all the adjustment of relative wages is one sided. Wages rise in the shortage markets and do not fall in the surplus ones. It follows, of course, that average wages will rise even when vacancies and unemployment are equal. Indeed if there is sufficient dispersion of supply-demand balances among markets there can be a significant increase in the average wage level even when unemployment exceeds vacancies by a substantial amount. The likelihood that that will be the case is considerably increased by the linkage among wages noted above. Market-induced wage increases will pull up other wages through application of the comparability doctrine. An increase in wages in one market will reduce the constraints on trade unions on other markets. Those responses dilute the effect of the initial market-induced wage change so that a greater amount of absolute wage change is required to produce a given relative wage change. The result then, is an upward drift of wages even when there is an excess of unemployment over vacancies.

The average rate of wage increase will, of course, tend to be higher the lower the unemployment rate (or more properly the higher the vacancy rate). At some level of unemployment the average rate of wage increase will just equal the average rate of productivity increase so that prices will be stable (assuming of course no notable rise in profit margins, food and raw material prices or other import prices). At that level of unemployment the necessary relative wage change and the required redistribution of income occur with labour in the surplus markets getting a constant real and money wage while workers in the shortage markets (or benefitting from the linkage factor) get all of the productivity gain.

At a lower level of unemployment, however, even without aggregate excess demand for labour, the rate of money wage increase induced by the process described above would exceed the rate of productivity increase. If there were no further reaction the result would be a reduction of real wages in the labour surplus markets. In fact, however, for the reasons given above workers in the surplus markets are likely to get at least partial compensation for the cost of living increase even though the market would not permit a wage increase in the absence of the cost of living increase. To the extent that nominal wages rise in the surplus sectors the average rate of wage and price increase is stepped up. A new set of linkage factors comes into play, the constraints on trade unions are further relaxed and the relative wage increases in the shortage sectors are further diluted so that an additional acceleration in wage and price inflation occurs. This, of course, again leads to real wage reductions in the surplus sector so that the process repeats.

If there were full compensation for any decline in real wages the rate of inflation might be expected to accelerate indefinitely until demand condition (in real terms) changed. In fact, however, at moderate levels of unemployment those groups in the weakest labour markets (or without strong organisation) will bear some real wage loss. The relative wage changes and the corresponding income redistribution required by the market will therefore take place gradually through the fact that workers in the weakest markets do not share in productivity benefits and actually lose some real income.

In that event the inflation need not accelerate. It need only go fast enough to produce the necessary relative wage changes. How fast that is, depends on the strength of wage linkages and on the attachment of workers and employers to maintenance of real wages as well as on the overall tightness of the labour market, the dispersion of balance between vacancies and unemployment among markets, and the average rate of productivity increase.

It should be noted, however, that the role of productivity increase is ambiguous. A uniform rate of productivity increase should serve to offset the bias toward wage inflation in the system. On the other hand differences in the rate of productivity growth may tend to cause inflationary pressures. If an industry has above-average productivity growth, managements can give way to union wage demands without having to reduce profits or increase the relative price of their product. They need not suffer a profit squeeze or lose market share though they lose the opportunity to increase market share. If the wage increases in the high productivity growth industries work to pull up wages elsewhere prices will be inflated in the sectors with relatively low productivity growth. In this process the benefits of high productivity growth are distributed through the system with the workers in the sectors with highest productivity growth getting real wage increases which are less than their own productivity increase. Workers in other sectors get real wage gains in excess of their own productivity increase.

Thus economies such as those of Japan, Germany and Sweden with high average productivity increases concentrated in the export sectors may tend to have chronic inflation in the non-manufacturing sector. At the same time this inflation may go on without accelerating because all sectors are getting substantial increases in real wages.

I have described a somewhat hypothetical process though the description does bear some resemblance to the situation in the United States in the early 1960s when there was a modest price rise even though unemployment remained over 5 per cent for several years and inflationary expectations were apparently dormant. The argument given above is clearly related to familiar discussions of the Phillips-curve and in that way contains little that is surprising. My point, however, is to emphasise that inflationary processes of the type described arise out of distribution issues. The market tends to produce certain types of redistribution of income which are not considered acceptable by workers or even by their employers. A certain measure of inflation and a certain measure of unemployment have been required to induce acceptance of those redistributions through the back door of rising money wages with falling real wages.[1]

The distribution aspect of inflation comes out more clearly when we consider the impact of a cost of living increase from some source other than wage increases, for example, a rise in food or raw materials prices. Suppose we limit the rate of wage increase to the rate of productivity increase so that the price level is on average stable. Food or raw materials now rise sharply and the cost of living rises. A transfer of income to food or materials producers must be made. For the moment suppose that aggregate money demand is managed so as to maintain a constant rate of unemployment. In the sectors where money wages were not rising or rising slowly workers will get compensation for at least a large proportion of the cost of living increase which will, of course, lead to a further cost of living increase. Moreover, as before, linkage effects and a reduction in the constraint on unions will lead to still further wage and price increases.

Before the episode is over prices must rise by a multiple of the initial increase. Meanwhile someone must bear the burden of the transfer of income to the food and raw materials sector so long as the relative prices of those products remain at their new level. Temporarily, the lags in the adjustment of wages to prices will permit the burden to be shared on a turn-taking basis; first one group then another will lose real income because it is one jump behind in the adjustment process. But, as expectations adjust to the experience of inflation, wage adjustments will take the price rise into account and prices will have to rise faster and faster to accomplish the transfer. If, however, the workers in the weakest markets cannot obtain full compensation for cost of living increases the transfer can be accomplished by a rise in prices which exceeds the

[1] If such a process were to go on for a long time inflationary expectations would be built into the adjustment process so that a further acceleration of the rate of inflation would take place.

rise in wages in the weak markets by enough to affect the rise in the cost of food and raw materials. Since the transfer through that process may take some time inflationary expectations may build up so that price increases go on for a time after the initial causes are removed.

One can envisage a variety of outcomes depending on the precise specification of the formation of expectations, the structure of labour and product markets, and the distribution of supply and demand in the submarkets. A simple resort to the interaction of aggregate unemployment and inflation expectations does not provide much insight into the underlying problem. Whatever the details of a model the basic problem is that the burden of the transfer must be borne by someone. The transfer can be achieved with a limited amount of inflation and no rise in unemployment if there are groups who find themselves unable to obtain (even with a lag) full compensation for the cost of living rise. If not, there must either be accelerating inflation, with the transfer burden shared on a temporary basis through lags, or there must be a rise in unemployment sufficient to force some groups to absorb the transfer.

Obviously the outcome must depend in part on the movement of aggregate demand. For expositional purposes, I have assumed thus far that the movement of real demand is controlled in such a way as to maintain a fixed rate of unemployment regardless of the inflation rate. This implies that *money* demand grows at the rate of growth of potential output plus the rate of price increase, and that monetary and fiscal policy are adjusted continuously to bring that about. At the opposite extreme one might suppose that aggregate money demand grows at the potential output growth rate regardless of the inflation rate. Again the monetary and fiscal authorities would have to make continuous adjustments. In that case an initial rise in raw material or food prices would reduce aggregate real demand and increase unemployment. The initial rise in unemployment would slow the rate of increase in prices and unemployment would have to continue to rise until the inflation stopped. Thereafter, with unemployment above equilibrium, wages would rise by less than productivity, prices would fall slowly and employment would gradually rise. In the end the price level would have to be the same as at the start (or a little higher to allow for the loss of supply which started the whole thing).

Thus we cannot, strictly speaking, say that the wage rigidities and linkages I have been discussing cause inflation (except temporarily). Rather they ease a collision between the goals of high employment and of price stability. Wage rigidities raise the unemployment level required to maintain stable prices under steady growth conditions. Increasing raw material and food prices raise the rate of unemployment consistent with price stability still further. On the other hand declining raw material and food prices may lower the level of unemployment required for price stability. Inflation arises, then, because the levels of unemployment consistent with price stability are unacceptably high (at least until the public has experienced the inflation for a while).

The scenarios for the steady growth case and the raw materials price rise case were artificially constructed for expositional purposes. The real history of inflation is, of course, far more complex but those artificial scenarios do reflect some of the major features of the real situation. In the United States there are four cases of marked acceleration of inflation after the initial adjustments following the Second World War: the Korean War, the mid-1950s, the Vietnam war, and the 1973–74 explosion of inflation. Each of these cases was marked by a sharp acceleration in demand and a significant reduction in unemployment. Even if nothing else had been involved the reduction in unemployment would have implied a higher rate of inflation. The overall reduction in unemployment receives a great deal of weight in the extended Phillips-curve explanations but other factors may have been of greater importance. In the rapid expansion of the 1965–66 market pressures on wages were most marked in the non-union sector. At the bottom, in the lower wage manufacturing sectors – textiles, shoes, furniture – and in low wage service industries workers moved to higher paying manufacturing jobs. The result was labour shortage and wage increases in the low wage sector.

At the top the general expansion generated greater competition for the services of managerial, technical and professional workers. These wage increases, of course, had the expected effect on other wages. Union wages lagged for a time and then regained their relative position. In 1955 on the other hand the automobile boom led to an unusually large settlement for the auto workers. That settlement became the basis for a 'round' of large wage increases in other durable industries. In all four cases increases in food and raw material prices played a significant role in raising the cost of living and thereby accelerating the general inflation. The general expansion of demand played a major role in raising food and raw material prices but adverse supply factors were also involved in some cases.

The acceleration of inflation from 1972 onward brings out the income distribution aspects of the inflation problem more clearly than any of the other cases. First, because the rise in food, raw materials and finally energy prices played such a dominant and obvious role in setting off the inflation it seems fairly obvious that the inflation occurred because no other means were available to assign the distribution of the burden of the transfer. Second, the inflation has persisted everywhere in the face of very high unemployment. In the United States with unemployment at 9 per cent the G.N.P. deflator is still rising at 5 per cent and is likely to accelerate again as soon as capacity utilisation improves. Third, there was, for the first time, some public discussion of the use of political means to separate the change in relative prices from the income transfer. It has been proposed for example that domestic oil prices be allowed to rise while at the same time a 'windfall tax' would be imposed on oil producers and the proceeds distributed to the public through adjustment of other taxes. The price of 'old oil' remains relatively low and no generally acceptable arrangement for raising it has been found. Everyone, rightly or wrongly, seems to be convinced that a further rise of oil prices will result in an acceleration of inflation by much more than the price increase directly involved. In other words it is expected that everyone will resist paying his share of the burden and try to push it off onto someone else.

In effect the sequence of events since 1972 reveals more sharply than ever the consequences of the simultaneous use of the price system to allocate resources and to distribute income. Economists have long recognised that a competitive equilibrium may be Pareto optimal but produce an unsatisfactory income distribution. They also recognise that there is no ethical presumption in favour of the distribution of income produced by the market and so accept the use of taxes and transfers to modify the distribution produced by the market. To the extent that work incentives are adversely affected by taxes and transfers their use involves a loss of efficiency which must be balanced against the assumed benefits from redistribution. Economists have tended to argue that distribution is essentially a political matter – except to the extent that one method of redistribution causes more loss of efficiency than another.

In fact it appears that the political process in the United States has failed and in doing so created a whole set of economic problems. It can hardly be said that there is a consensus in favour of the present distribution, but there is no consensus in favour of any alternatives. Such redistribution (from the market distribution base) as we do achieve is done in a somewhat left-handed way. The increase in income tax rates achieved in the Second World War has been left largely intact (with sufficient loopholes to limit attacks on the rate structure) and generates enough revenue to permit transfer payments – welfare, food stamps, housing and medical subsidies. A limited and unpublicised redistribution occurs through social security (taking advantage of the free ride for each generation resulting from the growth of population and income). But no proposal for a substantial redistribution has proved politically attractive. Many individual subgroups seek to improve their own position but they do so by seeking protection from market pressures or piecemeal tax adjustments without ever raising the question of who will pay – the other side of the distributional coin. And even those who are not very active or successful in pushing for improvements in their position resist very strongly when faced with a loss of income or even a worsening of their relative positions.

In these circumstances our society is in no position to deal with the income distribution problem when market forces tend to generate any significant change in distribution. If there were any consensus on the characteristics of a desirable distribution it would be natural to seek a response to any new event which would move the distribution in the desired direction or at least minimise movement in the wrong direction. In the case of rising prices for food and raw materials or energy this might involve the use of taxes and subsidies to adjust the level of the transfer in the desired direction. In the case of changes in the supply and demand balance among labour markets a more active supply policy, such as training programmes and labour mobility programmes and an active policy with respect to industrial location, could obviate the necessity for undesired changes in relative wages.

Lacking such a consensus, inflation and unemployment together bring about redistribution of income without the direct use of the political process.

They do so however at a heavy cost in terms of economic cost and social and political friction even when as often happens very little net redistribution occurs. In the OPEC case there is presumably a permanent redistribution in favour of the energy producers to be made. The transfer will ultimately occur when there is a sufficient decline in the real income of the groups in the weakest markets and the least effective organisation. It will take some time for that to be accomplished. Meanwhile the burden of the transfer will be borne temporarily by many groups whose incomes do not adjust quickly to rising prices. Each group which falls behind will in time catch up and push the burden off on someone else. In these circumstances everyone feels injured by the process and seeks someone to blame. Moreover, though the political process is not used to solve the basic problem it has to be used to adjust the wages of public employees, welfare and public pension payments, tax rates and the regulated prices such as electricity rates and transit fares. All of these decisions produce political and social strains. Finally, of course, we have to pay the social and economic costs of the unemployment which is necessary to bring the process to an end.

In a case like the OPEC we can at least say that a necessary (given the existence of the cartel) transfer is accomplished by the long painful inflationary process. In most of the other cases of accelerating inflation the shifts in relative prices, for example, increases in raw material prices, were only temporary and were reversed after a relatively short time. That is also probably true of most of the relative wage shifts. In those cases temporary redistributions of income generated a great deal of friction with no useful result.

Discussion of the Paper by James Duesenberry

Professor Bronfenbrenner introduced the paper. He had expected Professor Duesenberry to summarise and extend empirical studies, carried out in the United States and elsewhere, on the effects of contemporary inflation on income distribution. The usual procedure was to compare the results with a hypothetical anti-inflationary policy. He had expected Professor Duesenberry to show how this affected some beneficiaries, and what were the distributional effects resulting from macroinflation, or from certain specific microinflationary accompaniments of inflation. He had therefore prepared stories about how one hypothetical inflation A helped the poor and a different inflation B helped labour costs or the rich. The answer would depend on who bore the inflation tax, or rather the mix of inflation tax and inflation subsidy.

Actually, Professor Duesenberry had restated and expanded a distributional theory of the *causes* of inflation – distinguishing them from crude cost-push theories that he (Bronfenbrenner) did not agree were discredited.

Professor Bronfenbrenner referred to a diagram derived from a distributional theory by Professor M. W. Reder, in the *Canadian Journal of Economics*, 1948. This diagram, figure 10.1, had the price level on the x-axis and money claims on the y-axis. If one allowed real output to vary, one could rotate the radius vector between x and y.

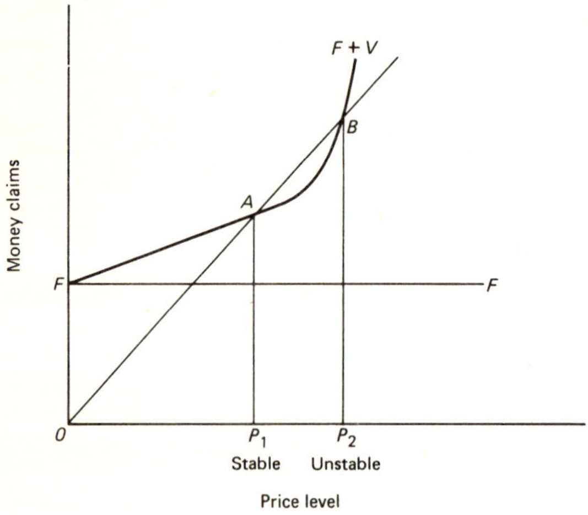

Fig. 10.1.

Fixed income receivers obtained OF (measured on the y-axis) while variable income receivers obtained the amount indicated by a curve $(F + V)$. Two intersections, at A and B, related to two price levels, P_1 and P_2. At P_1, with a great deal of money illusion, equilibrium was stable. At P_2 there was no money illusion, and 'super-rational' expectations. This equilibrium was unstable. Far enough beyond P_2, one 'went to hell in a (hyperinflation) basket'.

This was not *the*, but *a*, distributional theory, and he did not know whether Professor Duesenberry would accept it.

According to Professor Duesenberry's own theory, no organised group would accept a significant fall in real income without putting up resistance. Most would not even accept a proportional shift of real income in favour of other groups, especially where those other groups received rent or unearned increment. This resistance ordinarily involved inflationary claims for sufficient increases in income to overcome any control measures which forced some unemployment on the group. This feature enabled Professor Duesenberry to explain stagflation *with* unemployment. Professor Duesenberry argued that, in a pressure-group economy, some increase in unemployment would be the normal accompaniment of inflation, especially if there were inflationary controls. To Professor Duesenberry, such cost-push seemed inconsistent with standard economics. If a group had economic power now, why had it not used it previously? Professor Duesenberry distinguished distributional and cost-push theory sharply on this basis.

This dual construct was highly plausible, but it might be incomplete on historical grounds. To take an American example, why was the Korean inflation sloughed off more easily than the Vietnamese? No doubt Professor Duesenberry would regard his (Bronfenbrenner's) modification as a step backward, but he favoured recombining distributional and cost-push theories.

Ordinary cost-push was a market process usually directed at a given set of consumers or employers. There was probably also a second type of cost-push in operation, directed not against the other side of the market so much as at the anti-inflationary policies of the government itself. This Professor Duesenberry had omitted.

There might or might not be a distributional motivation here. If there were, it might be an offensive one: 'We want to increase our share'. Or it might be defensive: 'We want to keep pace with certain others'. Or it might be to prevent those others receiving 'unearned increment'. Such a neo-cost-push argument could be both collusive and redistributional, with a round of wage increases after a round of price increases. Again, one might have industries with labour and management in collusion, threatening government with defeat at the polls unless it introduced acceptable monetary and fiscal policies. Price increases and wage increases might never be rescinded even if they were superoptimal. (The government might be threatened instead.)

Such a policy would not make sense against an anti-inflationary government headed by a popular father figure and disorganised opposition. It would not make sense unless the pressure groups combined *de facto*. Perhaps one should compare this with the Boxer Rebellion, with its 'ten million harmonious fists'. In the economic case, the harmonious fists against anti-inflation policies would represent labour, business and agricultural interests.

Such a policy would make sense only after some social/psychological learning process had gone far enough. Then the pressure groups could unite, as a government with shaky backing and which scorned economic advice was trying to secure full employment now and put off inflation until after an election.

Conference participants might see here a comparison between the Eisenhower regime and the Nixon/Ford one. Professor Bronfenbrenner was not sure how relevant such an analogy would be for Europe or Asia. He had, however, attempted a more generalised distributional theory than Professor Duesenberry's, intended for capitalist countries with strong pressure groups. It also made a bow towards introducing social/psychological theories of combination and learning.

Professor Duesenberry wondered whether he should apologise for turning the subject round, but his paper would not have come to much if he had left it as it was. All he could have done then would be a 'hand' job, and he did have things to say.

He thought it important not to get hung up on the pure cost-push issue, and would not draw a distinction so sharply as Professor Bronfenbrenner had suggested. He wanted to emphasise the peculiarities of the dynamic process involved in distribution.

Professor De Wolff found a number of points in this paper that were relevant to the Netherlands. There too, a large number of defensive groups had been active in recent years, including not only trade unions and employers' organisations but also professional groups.

A factor pointing in the same direction had been the strong tendency in centralised negotiations over wages to improve the relative position of the low paid and the young. The cost-push resulting from such adaptations could have been eliminated if the position of the wage earners in the higher-income brackets had been improved correspondingly less, either through negotiations or appropriate monetary or other policies. However, these groups could usually defend their position successfully.

During the years of rapid growth such developments had hardly had any effect on employment but mainly worked out in increased inflationary pressure. These examples supported the thesis put forward by Professor Duesenberry.

Professor Lundberg thought there was a similar position in Sweden. There had been strong pressure for increased incomes from those with low pay. Others, in a strong demand position, had gained much back which had led to running inflation, because of successive pushes from the low-paid. This was a dynamic process not explicitly mentioned in Professor Duesenberry's paper.

In Sweden, the situation was aggravated by high marginal tax rates. If the marginal rate was 60 per cent and the average 30 per cent, a strong multiplier process could be set up if everyone tried to maintain his post-tax income. This was not mentioned in the paper, perhaps because of the low rate of tax in the United States! But one should remember it.

One should remember the problem of the relationship between wages and profits. The attempt to increase the share of wages in G.N.P. was an ongoing fight, along old lines. In 1974, with high profits, Swedish trade unions had said they had to rectify the situation by a wage push. Then the cycle had turned, taking wage costs above the normal level, and profits below those needed in the international competitive situation. Professor Lundberg thought it important to remember that Keynes had made much of the distinction between profit- and price-inflation.

Full employment policy was also important. When there was full employment, in a boom, the cost of increasing the firm's labour costs was high. Labour mobility led to expensive retraining, etc. This had a high marginal cost, but in inflationary times it could be recovered, thus leading to an inflation rate above the normal one.

Professor Nussbaumer pointed out that the low-income groups were usually well organised collectively, and often had government support as well, which offset their low individual 'waiting' capacity. The result was a shift in income to them, though those with high incomes were not necessarily at a disadvantage. The latter often had superior individual bargaining power, certainly greater financial reserves, and could therefore afford to 'wait' longer. So one had wage push at low income levels and wage drift at higher ones.

There was also a contradiction of aims. The government wanted a more equal income distribution, which could lead to inflation because of the low savings ratio of low-paid workers. Governments also feared that greater equality of income distribution would lead to inflation. So they compensated, for example, by various kinds of investment relief. They did this even if to do so meant making deductions from personal incomes, and even if it led to inflation.

Professor Bajt saw wage linkages as representing the main impetus to inflation in Yugoslavia, where he had studied the interindustry mechanism of wage inflation. Yugoslav institutions allowed workers to decide on their incomes, and wages were roughly proportional to the enterprise income per worker. So actual wages in some enterprises (per unit of the equilibrium wage) were lower than in others. The same was true between whole branches. This was an unstable situation and one would expect a movement of workers from the lower to the higher-paid sectors, but it did not happen.

The reason was that, in general, the branches with the highest incomes were monopolistic, and those with the lowest competitive. In the long run, the wages of both groups were increasing more quickly. However, during business cycles economic conditions changed differently for different branches. Low-income – low-wage – industries were particularly hard hit by slumps, so that during slow growth, wages in the low-wage branches rose more slowly. In a boom, the situation was reversed, with the biggest increases in the low-wage branches.

The whole mechanism had been tested econometrically. It could be taken as an illustration of Professor Duesenberry's wage linkages, though it came from a non-capitalist economy.

Professor Stahl suggested that while most economists had the expertise necessary to help them to study these problems, perhaps macroeconomics was too non-political. Many of those engaged in the game were organisations operating on majority decision rules, rather than following traditional maximisation policies. Economists were reluctant to incorporate such behaviour into economic theory.

However, bankers, for example, did not take a monetarist view. Perhaps this was because they acted on different premises. They were not dictators trained in monetarism, but were trying to reconcile different points of view.

For example, participants had been asking why bankers did not alter nominal interest rates more than they did. He thought this, again, was because a decision on the nominal rate was governed by a majority decision rule, which made it possible to explain monetary policy. This was why monetary authorities behaved the way they did, and the same kind of argument would be true about indexed loans. A rational political man would find it hard to organise a movement in their support. High inflation triggered off a lot of political movements to recompensate losers, but the index bond lobby was too weak to succeed.

Dr Corden found it interesting that the real wage of the young, the unskilled, and women had increased in some countries, for example Sweden, the Netherlands, and Australia. Unemployment then increased above the previous level, but this increase in unemployment led to additional monetary expansion.

What were the reasons for pressures for increases in real wages, especially of the young and the unskilled? He would suggest a few, some of a 'sociological' nature. First, monetary expansion led to a boom and high employment, and this increased left-wing tendencies because people felt secure enough to exert industrial pressure. Second, monetary expansion led to land and property booms – and hence large, apparently unearned, profits – which in turn led to further calls for egalitarianism. Third, there might be a demographic factor. Perhaps the increase in the number of young in recent years had increased their political power. Fourth, perhaps in some countries a reduction in immigration had helped, by reducing the inflow of the lower paid members of the labour force. But, in the last case, the higher wage would not be associated with higher unemployment in the immigration country.

Mr Plessz said that while Professor Duesenberry looked at the macroeconomic side of the problem, he wanted to extend the argument to the microeconomic sode. Microeconomic effects hit households in a roughly random way.

In most countries there were cumbersome mechanisms, redistributing income in favour of large families or the unemployed. Inflation played havoc with such schemes, because price increases coupled with higher marginal taxes skimmed off the benefits. To offset this, it was necessary to increase gross transfer payments constantly. Admittedly, these netted out, but one had to finance them either through tax or through inflation. This gave a steady increase in the ratio of transfer payments to the national income, with very strong inflationary effects.

Professor Rehn had seen nothing in the papers about the fact that a net increase of the number of workers in a firm implied much more than a proportional increase in the wage bill. To the costs of search, induction, training and wage drift had to be added especially high turnover among newly hired people, particularly in a near-to-full-employment economy. Expansionist demand management, therefore, led to hardly any increase in employment until there was a price increase to compensate for the over-proportional increase in labour costs. These extra costs were temporary, like any other one-shot expenditure connected with an expansion; but the difference was that one could not mortgage the investment one had made in the training of a worker who had left.

One method of fighting inflation, therefore, might be to introduce a subsidy (or an inter-enterprise clearing system) whereby this threshold of cost could be eliminated from entrepreneurial calculations. A reduction of unit costs was usually achieved in a slightly longer run, thanks to scale effects, when production and employment were increased. This could help to stabilise prices without being offset by the ratchet effect connected with climbing the 'threshold'. Governments in several countries had begun to discover the logic of this reasoning. Sweden and Finland had introduced systems of 'employment increase premiums', of between 15 per cent and 40 per cent of wages, that were paid for a couple of years when there was a net increase of employment in manufacturing firms in low-employment areas. Many other countries applied incentives to the hiring of members of disadvantaged groups.

On the other hand, restrictive demand management tended especially to hit 'green' youngsters, women wanting to leave the kitchen for income-earning work, older workers and handicapped persons. Precisely these groups had the smallest influence on the price-wage spiral (cf. Perry's article, 'Changing Labor Markets and Inflation', *Brookings Papers on Economic Activity*, No. 3, 1970).

As was noted in Professor Gordon's paper, one would expect female wages to fall if more women went to work – as they did nowadays. At the same time, their growing importance in the labour market increased their political and organisational power to press for a true, but inflationary, realisation of the equal-pay principle.

Professor Gordon replied that this assumed that women were imperfect substitutes for men, and implied a fall in relative wages which often did not occur. There had been some fall in women's wages in the United States though not in the wages of young people because they were protected by minimum wage arrangements.

Professor Laidler was puzzled by this approach. He saw competition for share of the national income as an old problem. There had been acute difficulties, for example, during the nineteenth century, when hand-loom weavers in Britain had suffered from the introduction of power looms. He wondered whether this kind of analysis really suggested that the natural rate of unemployment had gone up, or whether inflation was undermining the efficiency of markets. Or was there a quite different problem? What facts should he study to see whether he agreed with what was being said?

Professor Duesenberry had tried to explain why the natural rate of unemployment and the short-run Phillips-curve were higher than one would expect. He thought he had said the right things about the macrodemand side, but admitted that the relationships were very complex.

Professor Bronfenbrenner wondered whether his own comments had helped. He had tried to give a distributional explanation which would also apply to wage drift.

Professor Neumark wanted to see more emphasis on the impact of inflation on the taxation of income and profits. If taxation were not indexed, the real rate of tax went up rapidly because of inflation. In Germany, the share of workers' wage tax in the absolute sum of income and corporation tax levied had doubled in the last five years. On profits, there was a flat-rate tax, while profits were also favoured by tax relief on investment to help entrepreneurs.

He thought it quite possible that workers would try to increase their wage claims to offset this, seeking a bigger increase in nominal incomes than if there were no such perverse inflationary tax effects.

Professor Kleiman wondered whether there might be too many alternative theories of inflation at the moment. For example, he had listened during the conference to the generation gap theory; the sex theory; and the women's liberation theory; there was also the tax theory. We should perhaps try to do justice to Colin Clark, who had said that there was a set limit on the acceptable proportion of tax to national income. Beyond that, the public defended itself through inflationary pressures. So there was not just a loss of money illusion but of tax illusion too. People did care about post-tax incomes and therefore tried to shift the tax burden, probably mainly to prices. An increased share of tax in national income led to increased pressure for forward tax shifting.

Professor Patinkin pointed out inflation itself was another kind of tax.

Professor Kleiman agreed, but thought the public was not so aware of this as of taxation itself: an individual economic agent could not prevent the decline in the purchasing power of money by abstaining from raising the price of his own output.

Professor Duesenberry replied to the discussion. In a way, he had got his approach to the paper by looking at transfers from the mass of the population via, for example, the oil price increase. Everyone was trying to push the effects away from himself. It was not a question of illusion. People didn't care about the collective national income, but about their individual standards of living. So unemployment caused a loss to come to rest – in this case on the unemployed. Similarly, professors bore part of the burden because they could not increase their salaries sufficiently. These were spectacular examples of market-induced shifts, but there were smaller ones too.

To Professor Rehn, Professor Duesenberry said that in a labour force with high turnover, one had to recognise that the net marginal productivity of an additional worker to the firm could even be negative. So one needed social investment to help. This had policy implications, but he had ignored them.

The paper had been written mainly on the basis of American experience and others had brought out European experience. The main point was that there was a lot of illusion – and of false generosity, for example, transfer payments, private expenditure on ecology, and the manipulation of income distribution through the wage structure. But this kind of one-sided generosity did not explain who paid, for example, for ecological improvements. That was left to the market process.

Professor Duesenberry hoped that the paper contained a balanced approach to trade union issues. He thought the conference must include a number of neoclassical economists, because he had found that monetarism was often highly correlated with neoclassicism. He was therefore surprised that there had not been more criticism of what he had said about linkages.

11 The Welfare Implications of Uneven Inflation[1]

Dwight Jaffee
PRINCETON UNIVERSITY
and Ephraim Kleiman
HEBREW UNIVERSITY

I. INTRODUCTION

The assumption of 'steady' inflation has proven to be a common starting point for most welfare analysis of inflation. As defined, steady inflation has three basic properties

(1) it is perfectly foreseen, so that the expected inflation rate, which alone influences behaviour, is in fact the inflation rate actually realised;
(2) market institutions adjust sufficiently to accommodate the inflation; one example of such an adjustment would be the use of price-indexed contracts; other examples will be given below;
(3) the effects of inflation are uniform over all commodity groups; that is, inflation causes no changes in relative prices.

Given such a definition, welfare effects of steady inflation are shown to result only from the role of inflation as a tax on cash balances.[2] The key point is that the three properties of steady inflation insure that the price (or interest rate) on each nominally denominated contract, except for cash, fully reflects the inflation that will occur over the life of the contract. A cash balance is unique in that its nominal interest return is fixed at zero. Consequently, there is a holding cost for cash balances equal to the nominal interest rate (real rate plus inflation), and inflation acts as a selective excise tax where real cash balances are the commodity and the rate of inflation is the tax rate. The welfare costs of steady inflation can thus be evaluated in terms of the excess burden created when individuals attempt to economise on their cash balances.

[1] The major work on this paper was completed at the Institute for International Economic Studies, University of Stockholm. We are grateful for the discussion and comments of our colleagues there, and for the support provided by the Institute. We thank Professors Stanley Fisher, Jacob Frenkel and Robert Gordon, and also Jan Haggstrom and Anita Blaustwin who carried out the calculations.

[2] See Barro [1] and Foster [5] for recent studies and citations to the large literature. The motion of a cash balance tax effect has been expanded up in the contribution by David Laidler to this conference 'The Welfare Costs of Inflation in Neoclassical Theory – Some Unsettled Issues' (Chapter 12).

Indeed, given that the social costs of creating cash balances is zero, empirical quantification of the welfare cost is simplified and may be based, with appropriate assumptions, on the area under the demand curve alone.

A frequent conclusion drawn from such analysis is that the welfare costs of steady inflation are quite minor. For example, if inflation is instigated directly for its taxation effect, then it is argued that the excess burden of the inflation tax may compare favourably with other possible taxes, at least over some range of inflation rates. Alternatively, if the source of inflation is some other exogenous or policy factor, then it may be argued that the quantitative magnitude of the excess burden is simply small. This conclusion is reinforced, moreover, to the extent that a yield is paid on demand deposit balances, so that if the yield varies with inflation, then there is no tax effect on this component of money balances.[1] Whichever the case, it is clear that the conclusion, that the welfare costs of steady inflation are minor, will have important implications when applied to policy questions involving inflation.

It is tempting, therefore, to apply the welfare results of steady inflation to the real world. It is immediately apparent, however, that the conditions of steady inflation have generally not characterised observed inflationary processes. First, actual inflations are *sporadic*, in that the amount of inflation varies over time. Second, actual inflations may be dispersed, since inflation may have differential effects over commodity groups. *Steady* inflation may then be contrasted with *uneven* inflation, where the latter means the inflation is either sporadic or dispersed.

Steady inflation and uneven inflation do not necessarily have different welfare implications. In particular, they would have the same welfare implications if the three properties listed above for steady inflation were equally valid or even approximately valid for uneven inflation. In fact, however, the effects of steady and uneven inflation have been clearly distinguished in terms of their income redistribution impacts. Following the standard exposition, an individual is conceived of as forming a point estimate for the rate of inflation, and then fully adjusting his behaviour to this estimate. Then, given that individuals have formed different estimates, the realised inflation rate will cause a series of windfall losses and gains for individuals depending on whether they underestimated or overestimated the inflation rate. Under steady inflation, of course, such redistributions will not occur, since – by force of property (1) above – all individuals will anticipate the same inflation rate, and this, in fact, will be the realised rate. But under uneven inflation, it would appear likely that there will be divergent expectations, and hence unexpected outcomes will result.

Whether uneven inflation has an additional welfare cost due to this source, depends, of course, on the costs associated with the income redistribution. One approach is to assume that we begin with a socially optimal income distribution, and that the social preference function is concave in the utility or

[1] Conceptually, the government could also pay a competitive return to its currency issues. In this case there should be no excess burden from steady inflation.

income levels of individuals. Then, it is true that even a random series of gains and losses will push the distribution away from the optimum, although the magnitude of cost associated with this change is not clear. An alternative, and more common, approach is to assume that the initial distribution is not sufficiently equitable, and that the series of gains and losses caused by inflation, rather than being random, tend systematically to exaggerate the inequities of the income distribution. Again, however, the available empirical evidence is quite ambiguous as to whether observed inflation redistributions actually do exaggerate the inequity of the income distributions.[1]

Thus, to summarise, our survey of the literature indicates an emphasis on two basic points. First, the available theory distinguishes two sources for the welfare costs of inflation. The cash balance tax burden is the only welfare cost associated with steady inflation. The income redistribution effect is then an additional cost associated with uneven, that is sporadic, inflation. Second, in terms of empirical magnitudes, there is at least some evidence that the welfare costs from either of these sources is relatively minor. Or, to put the empirical evaluation in relative terms, it appears that both the professional literature and the general professional view tend to evaluate the welfare costs of inflation at a much lower value than is the 'popular' estimate as voiced, say, by politicians or in the press.

This suggests the possibility that the models used to analyse the welfare costs of inflation have not, in fact, identified all the relevant costs. This question, indeed, was approached in a pair of interesting and companion papers by Okun [11] and Gordon [7]. Okun, in particular, argued that the welfare cost of actual (uneven) inflation significantly exceeds the cost that would be associated with an idealised steady inflation. It appears, however, that both Okun and Gordon follow the literature in assuming the three properties of inflation given above, albeit with a weaker form for (1); also, as indicated below, we have reservations concerning Okun's interpretation of the historical data. Our approach, in contrast, is to start directly with the case of uneven inflation, and to make assumptions that appear realistic in such a setting. The result is that we are able to identify several potentially important types of welfare costs, other than tax and redistribution effects, that appear only with uneven inflation.

The remainder of the paper is separated into four sections. In section II, we attempt a systematic approach to analysing the welfare costs of sporadic inflation. In section III, the same techniques are applied to dispersed inflation. In section IV, we consider the empirical properties of uneven inflations, using simple regression analysis of inflation across countries, time, and commodity groups. A main question here is the relationship between the average rate of inflation and the degree to which it is uneven. In section V, the conclusions of the study are developed by combining the results of the previous sections.

[1] Foster [5] surveys this literature. The critical question appears to be whether labour income, in fact, adjusts rapidly to the inflation rate. This adjustment could come through either the nominal wage rate or an increase in employment.

II. THE WELFARE COSTS OF SPORADIC INFLATION

We consider an individual who treats inflation as a stochastic process, and who forms a subjective evaluation (prior) for the probability distribution $f(X)$ for the inflation rate X. Assuming, for simplicity, that the distribution is normal, or that the individual's utility function is quadratic in real wealth, the relevant features of the distribution are its mean value E and its standard deviation Σ.[1] Although this framework is standard for problems involving decision-making under uncertainty, it generally has not been applied to the welfare costs of an uncertain inflation. Instead, as indicated above, it has generally been assumed that individuals form point estimates of the inflation rate, and then fully adjust their behaviour to this estimate. Both of these assumptions – point estimates and full adjustment – appear inappropriate when inflation is intrinsically uneven.

To proceed now, we distinguish between the *ex ante* and the *ex post* costs of inflation. *Ex ante* costs occur whenever inflation is expected and individuals are affected or change their behaviour on this account. Thus, as long as inflation is expected, *ex ante* costs will occur regardless of whether the inflation actually takes place. Similarly, when inflation is a surprise, then there will be no *ex ante* costs. The excess burden of the inflation tax on cash balances is a clear case of *ex ante* costs. *Ex post* costs of inflation, in contrast, arise when the realised inflation rate differs from the anticipated rate. Thus, *ex post* costs can arise either because the prior probability distribution was wrong, or, even if the distribution were right, because individuals did not take actions to anticipate its effects.[2] An undesired income redistribution resulting from an unanticipated inflation is a clear example of *ex post* costs.

A model of individual adjustment to inflation should help to make clear the role of *ex ante* costs and the difference between *ex ante* and *ex post* costs. Consider an individual holding a portfolio consisting initially of real and nominal assets, R_0 and N_0 respectively. To simplify matters, let the nominal return on the two types of assets be the same, but let the end of period real value of the nominal asset be decreased by inflation while the end of period real value of the real asset is invariant to inflation. Finally, assume the individual can exchange nominal assets for real assets in the amounts of ΔN and ΔR

[1] Formally, we should consider an individual who enters into nominal contracts in the amount W (for wages or wealth), but derives utility from the real amount W/P where P is the price level at the time of consumption. Consequently, it is the prior distribution on $1/P$, not the inflation rate X, that is relevant. Our theoretical analysis could be carried out in terms of $1/P$ without difficulty. It is more common, however, to approximate real consumption by $W(1-X)$ for empirical purposes, and then the distribution of X is the relevant function. Care should be taken, however, in interpreting empirical results based on this approximation.

[2] We distinguish in our terminology between *expected* inflation and *anticipated* inflation. *Expected* inflation refers to cases in which the mean value of the prior distribution exists and is positive. *Anticipated* inflation refers to cases in which inflation is expected *and* individuals change their behaviour on this account.

respectively. The individual's end of period real wealth is then given by

$$W = R_0 + \Delta R + \frac{N_0 + \Delta N}{1 + X}, \tag{1}$$

subject to the wealth constraint

$$\Delta R + \Delta N = 0. \tag{2}$$

The inflation rate X is assumed for the moment to be non-stochastic.

Next consider the costs of switching from nominal assets to real assets. The costs (C) can be specified as a function of the amount of real assets purchased (ΔR)

$$C = C[\Delta R]; \; C'[\cdot] > 0; \; C''[\cdot] > 0. \tag{3}$$

Thus the marginal cost of purchases is positive, and the marginal cost is itself an increasing function of the size of the purchase. Indeed, the marginal cost might approach infinitely if it is interpreted, for example, as the cost of doing without any cash balances.

The optimisation problem for the individual consists of maximising his wealth net of transactions costs, that is $W - C$, subject to the wealth constraint in equation (2). Maximising this criterion with respect to ΔR, yields the first order condition

$$\frac{X}{1 + X} = C'[\Delta R]. \tag{4}$$

That is, portfolio shifts are carried out until the marginal cost of further shifts equals the relative inflation rate.

The optimisation problem is illustrated also in figure 11.1. Both end of period real wealth (W) and transactions costs (C) are graphed against the amount of adjustment (ΔR). $W_0 = R_0 + \dfrac{N_0}{1 + x}$ is the individuals end-of-period

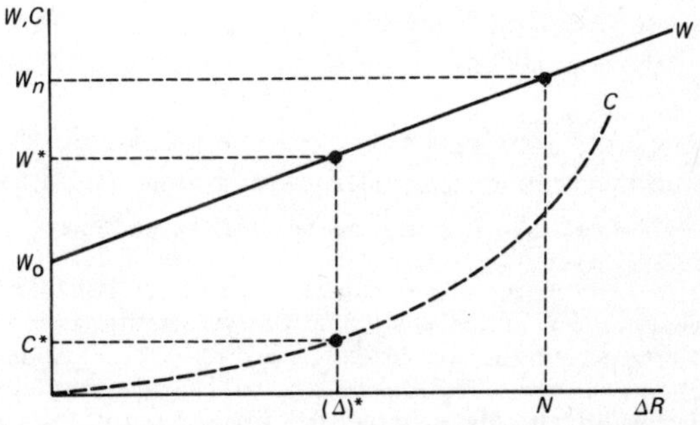

Fig. 11.1

real wealth if he abstains from any anticipatory action. The slope of the real wealth curve is $X/(1+X)$ (see equation (1)) and the slope of the cost curve is $C'[\cdot]$, so the optimality condition is to pick that ΔR at which the slopes are equal; this is (ΔR^*) in the figure. At this point the individual has protected his wealth position by the amount $W^* - W_0$, but at a cost of C^*, leaving a net gain of $W^* - W_0 - C^*$. The individual could have fully protected his position against inflation by selling all his nominal assets (the point $\Delta R = N_0$ in the figure), but this is not warranted due to the rising marginal cost of such transactions.

Figure 11.1 demonstrates the distinction between expected and anticipated inflation. The *expected* loss due to inflation is $W_N - W_0$; that is the difference between a fully protected position and the initial position. Of this amount, $W^* - W_0$ is anticipated, by spending C^* on purchasing protected real assets, leaving $W_N - W^*$ as the foreseen loss which the individual is willing to take because the cost of additional transactions is too high. If the inflationary expectation materialises, then the anticipated loss, $W_N - W^*$ will become an *ex post* loss. On the other hand, the cost of anticipating the expected inflation, that is C^*, is incurred independently of whether or not the expectations are fulfilled.

Consider next the effect of an increase in the expected inflation rate X. It is reasonable to assume the cost function is invariant to the amount of inflation, and thus in figure 11.1 the C function is unchanged. The real wealth function, on the other hand, has a slope of $X/(1+X)$ and thus it will rotate upward as X rises. It is thus apparent that greater amounts of protection will be purchased as X rises.

This model can easily handle the case where the inflation is stochastic. As above, let E and Σ be the expected value and standard deviation of the individual's subjective probability distribution. Were the individual risk neutral, then the expected value of $X/(1+X)$ would appear in equation (4), but otherwise the analysis would be unchanged; (see also footnote 1 on page 288). A risk-averse individual, on the other hand, would put a higher premium on a more fully protected (and therefore more certain) position. Consequently, a risk-averse individual would spend more on protection (a higher C^*) and obtain a more fully protected position (a higher W^*) than the risk-neutral type. Moreover, the greater the standard deviation Σ, the more protection the risk averter would buy.[1]

Finally it is useful to anticipate the case where the inflation is not uniform, but may vary among commodities. Specifically, assume that the individual

[1] Some degree of imperfection in capital markets may be a necessary assumption for this result. Otherwise, if capital markets were perfect, then individuals – even risk averse individuals – might ignore the dispersion of outcomes. In years with inflation higher than expected, they would borrow to maintain the flow of real consumption. In years with inflation lower than expected, they would lend or pay off past borrowing. Once capital markets are imperfect, however, a higher than expected inflation would translate directly into reduced real consumption. And even though a windfall gain of real consumption might be obtained later, the sporadic flow of consumption would by itself create a lower utility level.

knows the average inflation rate X with certainty, but that some commodity prices will rise by more or by less than others. This increases the marginal cost of purchasing protection: it is not enough any longer just to switch from nominal to real assets; one has also to allocate the resources among specific real assets. In terms of the analysis of figure 11.1 the wealth curve W is not affected by this consideration, since it is only a function of the average inflation rate. The cost curve, however, will be more steeply sloped, and thus the amount of protection purchased will be reduced. Moreover, the shift of the cost function will be positively related to the amount of dispersion across commodities (S), and thus the greater this dispersion the smaller the amount of protection.

To summarise, an individual's protective outlays on anticipatory action will:

(1) increase with E, the expected rate of inflation (or with X the actual inflation rate when inflation is non-stochastic).

(2) increase with Σ, the standard deviation of the subjective inflation distribution (given the individual is risk averse);

(3) decrease with S, the standard deviation of expected inflation across commodity groups.

The total *ex ante* welfare losses due to inflationary expectations then consist of two components: the protection costs as just described; and the foreseen but unanticipated loss that results from obtaining less than full protection. And finally, the *ex post* costs of inflation will consist both of the foreseen but unanticipated loss just noted and any losses due to the fact that the prior evaluation of the probability distribution was itself in error.

(1) THE *EX ANTE* COSTS OF SPORADIC INFLATION: EXAMPLES

With this basic model of the welfare costs of sporadic inflation developed, it is now useful to consider some more specific and concrete applications of the principle.

THE LEVEL OF EXPECTED INFLATION E

We begin with examples of how changes in the expected inflation rate can create *ex ante* costs beyond the well-recognised cash balance tax effect.

(1) Mundell [10], and the later literature on the non-neutrality of money in growth models, developed the proposition that the real rate of interest will decline as expected inflation rises. The decline in the real rate of interest in such models is the result of a shift from nominal assets to real assets as the expectation of inflation rises. The necessity of shifting portfolio allocations at the point of transition will obviously involve transactions costs. Moreover, once past the transition, a greater proportion of each portfolio will be allocated to real assets, involving both higher costs of management and additional trans-

actions costs as each individual follows his life cycle of accumulation and retirement consumption.

(2) Along similar lines, one finds institutional rigidities in the financial markets such that the structure of real interest rates, as well as the average level of real rates, is affected by expected inflation. A good example in almost all countries is the tendency for the spread between short-term capital market rates and short-term time deposit rates to widen with inflation. A common reason for this is that depository institutions suffer capital losses on their assets as rates rise, and this limits their ability to bid for new funds. Individuals with a preference for deposit-like assets thus have the costly dilemma either of accepting a reduced real rate of interest or of entering the markets for primary securities or real capital in which the transaction costs and risks are much greater.

(3) In labour markets, employees will want to negotiate nominal wages that include an allocation for the expected rate of inflation. Among firms, however, there may be a divergent set of expectations. Firms with expectations of high inflation will view nominal wages based on average expectations as equivalent to reduced real wages, and such firms will expand. Similarly, firms with expectations of low inflation will interpret the new nominal wages as the equivalent of higher real wages, and such firms will contract. Since the expansion and contraction of firms is based on divergent expectations, not all of which can be right, a welfare loss through the misallocation of resources is implied. In addition, the transition costs for employees and other resources shifting between firms are socially unproductive since, in following periods, the misallocation will be revealed, and the process will be reversed.

The main lesson from these examples is that 'steady inflation', as defined at the beginning of the paper, is a tightly structured and logically consistent system in which nothing can go wrong, except for the noted case of cash balances. Sporadic inflation, on the other hand, is fully consistent with (1) imperfect and divergent price expectations, (2) incomplete institutional adjustments, and (3) dispersed inflation over commodity groups. The properties of sporadic inflation are loose in this sense, and thus they are consistent with a wide variety of allocational mistakes. Taken together with the costs of search, transactions, and risk-bearing, it appears clear that the welfare costs of sporadic inflation are potentially very great.

It may be replied, of course, that if expectations for inflation are maintained long enough at some constant level E, then the mistakes and misallocations of the system will work themselves out. In other words, in this sense our examples are based on transitory effects. This is generally true, and indicates that if E remains constant long enough, then sporadic inflation may acquire the properties of steady inflation. What is really at stake then, however, is the empirical question of whether constant expected inflation or steady inflation can be attained, and, if so, what is given up in the process. We return to this question in the last two sections of the paper.

THE STANDARD DEVIATION OF INFLATION Σ

We next consider specific examples of how the standard deviation of inflation expectations can create welfare costs. It is important to stress again that these costs are *ex ante* in either the sense that they are the result of transactions costs resulting from attempts to anticipate inflation, or they are the costs of maintaining a fixed position when the effects of inflation are foreseen, but transactions costs are too high to allow anticipatory action.

(1) Some contracts, such as wage agreements, are currently indexed or escalated in part. To the extent that escalation shifts risk onto the firm, escalation protection presumably has a cost in terms of a lower real wage offer from the firm. For example, consider some firm i that sells the quantity Q_i at the price P_i and had nominal production costs as a function of the nominal wage W_i in the form $W_iF[Q_i]$. Assume as one possible case that the firm sets its price P_i at the beginning of the period on a non-stochastic basis as some function of the overall expected price level. If the average price level is P, the firm's real profits in terms of P are

$$\Pi_i = (1/P)(P_iQ_i - W_iF[Q_i]. \tag{5}$$

Since P is the only stochastic variable, the variance of real profits is the product of $VAR\ (1/P)$ and the square of nominal *net income* (the second term in parentheses). Alternatively, if a real wage w_i is negotiated through indexing such that real production costs are $w_iF[Q_i]$, then real profits are given by

$$\Pi_i = (1/P)\,(P_iQ_i) - w_iF[Q_i]. \tag{6}$$

Now the variance of real profits is the product of $VAR\ (1/P)$ and the square of nominal *gross income* (the second term in parentheses). Since gross income necessarily exceeds net income, the variance of real profits will be greater when wages are set in real terms (indexed). This result depends, of course, on our assumption that P_i is a non-stochastic variable and therefore is uncorrelated with P. Indeed, at the opposite extreme, P_i and P may be perfectly correlated, in which case the firm's real profits are invariant to the final price level under indexing. The point, however, is that there is a range of correlation between P_i and P over which the firm would prefer nominal to indexed wage-setting, and therefore over this range employees will have to pay a price to induce the firm to participate in indexed wage contracts.

(2) Equity securities and other claims against real capital would generally provide nominal returns that are highly correlated with inflation (or, equivalently, real returns almost independent of inflation). However, a variety of costs are involved in maintaining a portfolio of equities, rather than, say, fixed debt instruments. Most importantly, there are risks both on the level of the individual firm and for the economy as a whole (if a diversified portfolio is held). In addition, the transaction costs of purchasing equities are generally

higher than for debt claims, and these costs would rise with the degree of diversification (and fragmentation) of the portfolio.[1]

(3) Investments in inventories of real goods, where the price is expected to move with inflation, provide for protection of real values. Again, however, the risk of changes in relative prices, and the transactions costs, make the cost of such protection potentially high. Moreover, if the demand for such inventories has the effect of shifting real resources from productive to non-productive use, then this is an additional cost, both privately and socially.

To summarise, the risks created by an uncertain inflation can create welfare costs in two main ways. First, if individuals do nothing to offset the risks, then the private levels of welfare will be reduced, although there will be no changes in the real allocation of resources. Second, attempts by individuals to avoid the risks of inflation will increase transaction costs (which are not socially productive) and may distort the allocation of real resources (as through the holding of non-productive inventories). Now it is true, as with the level of expected inflation E, that if Σ remains at a high value over time, then it becomes more likely that the economy will be restructured so as to reduce the costs of protection; full price-indexing, in fact, is a possible solution in this sense. But, as can be confirmed for the examples just presented, as long as market institutions do not adjust, the welfare costs will continue over time. That is, the welfare *costs are not simply the costs* of adjusting to a new value for Σ.

CHANGES IN E AND Σ

We have illustrated how the welfare costs of sporadic inflation will be positively related to the level of E and Σ, even when these prior parameters remain constant over some time. The costs are transitory only in that market institutions may be caused to change on account of the values of E and Σ. It should be clear, therefore, that additional welfare costs will result if E and Σ also tend to vary over time. In particular, additional transactions costs will result as asset portfolios are adjusted, and transition costs will result as the allocation of real resources shifts.

(2) THE *EX POST* COSTS OF SPORADIC INFLATION

Assuming now that the *ex ante* decisions in anticipation of inflation have been made, we now turn to the *ex post* costs of realised inflation. The main set of costs are associated with the realised inflation rate X, and in particular with its value relative to the expected inflation rate E. In addition, costs may be associ-

[1] It is worth stressing that the costs of investing in a portfolio of equity securities will continue as a flow over time even if Σ is constant. For example, even if the portfolio is fixed once and for all, the additional exposure to firm or economy risk will still continue to flow over time. Also given that households tend to accumulate and spend savings over a life cycle, the higher transaction cost of equity portfolios will continue.

ated with the variations in X over time, as might be measured by the standard deviation σ.[1]

With regard to the spread between X and E, the welfare costs are primarily the redistributional effects described in section I. In particular, a high rate of inflation X will create losses for individuals that either (1) expected a low rate in terms of E, or (2) did not protect themselves against high rates because of the cost of protection. Now, if there is little correlation between the income of individuals and the likelihood that they meet the conditions of (1) and (2), then the amount of income redistribution will depend primarily on how widely divergent were the expectations of individuals. The level of X then serves only to determine who gains and who loses. On the other hand, it is intuitively appealing, if not empirically verified, that lower income individuals are more likely to meet the conditions of (1) and (2). In this case, high levels of X relative to the average E directly cause the income distribution to become more skewed. Consequently, divergence in the value of E for individuals is a necessary condition for *ex post* redistribution effects, while a correlation between low incomes and lack of anticipation of inflation is sufficient for the redistribution effect to depend on the level of X.

It is more difficult to relate the redistributional impact of inflation to σ, the amount of variation in inflation over time. For example, assume that it is lower income individuals that systematically do not anticipate inflation. If σ is low, then this would imply that low-income individuals suffer a loss year in and year out. On the other hand, if σ is large, then low-income individuals would suffer large losses in some years, but small losses in other years. The average loss, however, will be the same for the two cases, since the average depends on X and E, but it is independent of σ.

Indirectly, of course, there may be a variety of mechanisms through which *ex post* variations in the inflation rate affect income distribution and other welfare costs of inflation. For example, the observed values for σ will no doubt be major determinants of the prior value for Σ. Also, the amount of *ex post* variation may affect the amount of institutional adjustment to inflation that does occur. Similar remarks hold, of course, for the realised rate X as well. We return to these issues in the concluding section.

III. THE WELFARE COSTS OF DISPERSED INFLATION

We can consider the welfare costs of inflation in terms of the variation in inflation rates across different commodity groups. It should be noted first, however, that differential inflation rates may be simply a reflection of changes in

[1] It is important to be clear on the distinctions made in our notation; E and Σ are respectively the mean and standard deviation of an individual's prior probability distribution for the stochastic inflation rate X; S is also the standard deviation of a prior distribution, but referring to the dispersion of inflation across commodity groups; σ, in contrast, is the actual standard deviation of observed inflation rates over time. And, finally, below we shall denote as $\overline{X}$ the actual average over time of observed inflation rates.

relative prices owing to factors other than inflation. In this case there would be no welfare costs causally related to inflation. Or the causation could be simply reversed if inflation is the result of relative price changes, as, for example, when relative prices change and there is downward price change rigidity. We are concerned, clearly, only in cases in which inflation is itself the causal source of the differential inflation rates, or in which there is some common source for both the average inflation rate and the differentials between commodity groups. We shall discuss in section IV the grounds for causal relationships from average inflation to differential inflation, but for the moment we simply assume this is the case.

The welfare costs of dispersed inflation can be analysed with the same framework as used above for sporadic inflation. Thus, we now assume that individuals have prior probability distributions for the rate of inflation for each of the major commodity groups. From these distributions, the expected average rate of inflation over all commodity groups can be derived; and from the co-variances of the components, a measure of the prior dispersion of the inflation, for example the standard deviation across commodity groups, can be derived. We will denote the prior mean and standard deviation as E and S respectively.

The welfare costs associated with the expected average rate of inflation E are unchanged from the case of sporadic inflation, since the variable is essentially the same in both cases. With respect to the welfare costs associated with S under dispersed inflation, however, the situation is fundamentally different. It is tempting to argue, in analogy with sporadic inflation, that inflation dispersed across commodity groups creates a welfare loss simply because of the uncertainty that is created. This, in fact, is wrong, and the error is that uncertainty is not necessarily created. For example, suppose one used a supermarket with a fixed average price level, but on successive trips found that the relative prices of goods varied randomly. Clearly different baskets of goods would be purchased on each trip. But, if the average price level were properly weighted, then each basket would still have the same utility, and there would be no uncertainty in terms of utility. Consequently, the fact of dispersed expectations on relative prices does not by itself create a welfare loss.[1]

While the supermarket example eliminates one source of welfare loss from consideration it equally well demonstrates at least three grounds on which there would be a welfare loss. First, a direct effect of fluctuating relative prices is that individuals must spend more resources in terms of search and information gathering. In the supermarket, you should make two passes – the first to gather information and the second to gather goods. This point was also noted in the model at the beginning of section II above. Second, to the extent that the purchase of durable goods is involved, there is a question not only of what to buy, but also when to buy it. In this case, dispersed inflation does create

[1] This is analogous to the effect, discussed in footnote 1 on page 290, whereby perfect capital markets may eliminate the welfare loss due to uncertainty in the inflation rate over time.

uncertainty, and an *ex ante* welfare cost does result. Third, again in terms of durable goods, the *ex post* pattern of demand under dispersed inflation will not be the same as the pattern that would have resulted had the expected value of the relative price distribution been observed as a constant over time. A variety of resource misallocations can result from this. As one example, assume that firms expand or contract on the basis of the market signals given by the distribution of observed demand across products. The demand signals, however, are wrong in that they are based on relative prices which include the random fluctuations due to inflation. Consequently, the resource allocations based on these demands are inefficient, or, at the least, unnecessary transaction costs are incurred as mistakes are corrected.

IV. THE EMPIRICAL EVIDENCE

In the preceding section the welfare cost of uneven inflation was shown to be an increasing function of both the expected inflation rate and of the expected dispersion of inflation rates over time and over commodities. This referred to the individual's prior subjective estimates of these parameters. But such subjective estimates should be strongly influenced by actual experience. We now turn, therefore, to examine the empirical evidence regarding the *ex post* relationship between these variables.

(1) VARIABILITY OF INFLATION RATE OVER TIME

In the paper referred to earlier, Okun [11] examined the standard deviation of the annual rates of inflation from their 1951–68 average for each of seventeen OECD countries. He expected variability in the annual inflation rates to be greater the higher the average rate for the period, as a whole, and theorised about the type of policies reflected by it. To facilitate comparisons with samples of other countries and other periods, it is convenient to summarise the relationship by a linear regression equation

$$\sigma_i = a + b\overline{X}_i \tag{7}$$

where $\overline{X}_i$ is the ith country's average rate of inflation for the whole period, and σ_i the corresponding standard deviation of the annual observations. Throughout this section, we use summary measures of the rate of inflation, rather than summary measures of the rate of change of the purchasing power of money (which of course is the correct measure), so as to retain comparability with the tests of earlier investigators.[1] The regression equation estimated from Okun's data is presented in the first row of table 11.1. As neither the intercept of the regression line is significantly different from zero, nor the regression coefficient from one, it suggests variability to be proportionate to the average inflation rate. Okun provided also observations on five more OECD coun-

[1] See footnote 1, page 288.

tries, which were excluded from his comparisons because of their extreme values or because they related to substantially shorter time periods than did the rest of his sample. But, as can be seen from line 2 of table 11.1 their inclusion would not have significantly affected his findings.

Okun measured inflation by changes in the implicit G.N.P. price deflator. It may be argued that some of the prices constituting this deflator are irrelevant to the decisions of inflation-anticipating individuals – for example, the prices of public services. As an alternative, we have experimented with the implicit price deflator of a narrower bundle of goods, the final private expenditure on consumption, extending the period covered up to 1971. The results, which are presented in line 3(i) of the table, are almost identical with those obtained from the Okun data.

The OECD sample is restricted to countries with a relatively mild inflationary experience. For the whole period covered, the average annual change in the price level varied, in the case of the G.N.P. deflator, from 2·1 in the United States to 7·9 in Turkey (or to only 4·7, in France, if we ignore the countries excluded by Okun). OECD findings need not, therefore, be reproducible under more strongly inflationary conditions. To test their generality we utilised the data recently published by Vogel [12] for sixteen Latin American countries for the years 1950–69. These data use changes in the consumer's price index as a measure of inflation, and range from an average rate of 0·3 per cent per annum in E1 Salvador to 43·0 per cent in Uruguay. The results obtained from Vogel's data, which are summarised in line 4 of table 11.1 are strikingly similar to those obtained for the OECD countries. They all tend to indicate that fluctuations in the annual inflation rates are proportionate to their central value, the coefficient of variation, $V = \sigma/\bar{X}$, being on the whole the same in high- and low-inflation countries.

Okun identifies the correspondence between high variability over time and high average inflation rates with 'stop and go' policies. The model he seems to have had in mind is illustrated in figure 11.2a, where the annual rate of inflation is traced over a time sequence. The two sinusoidal lines describe two different types of inflation, one with a high, and one with a low, dispersion of

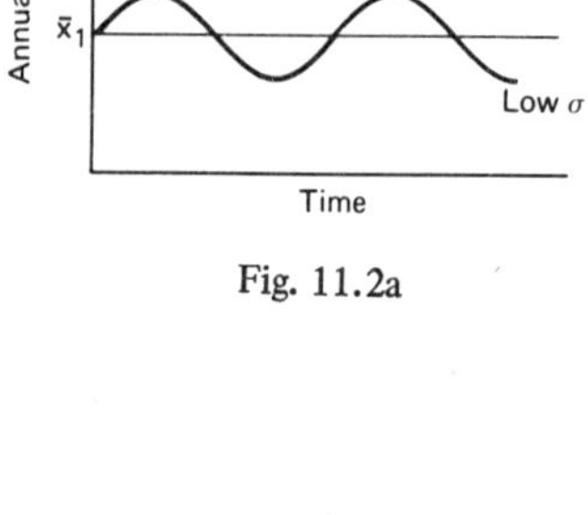

Fig. 11.2a

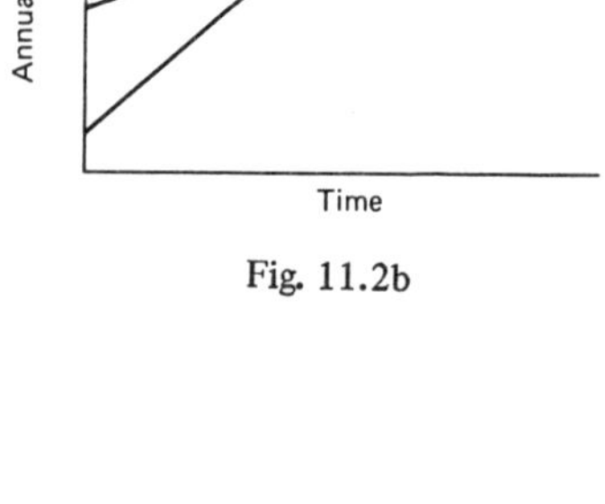

Fig. 11.2b

REGRESSION OF STANDARD DEVIATION OF ACTUAL ANNUAL INFLATION RATES ON PERIOD AVERAGE – INTERNATIONAL CROSS-SECTIONS

Number	*Source*	*Number of countries*	*Period*	*Price index*	*Range of average inflation rates (per cent)* *Lowest*	*Highest*	*Regression equation*	R^2
				(a) OECD countries				
1. (i)	Okun		1951–63	Implicit G.N.P. deflator	2·1	4·7	$\sigma = -0{\cdot}81 + 0{\cdot}87\overline{X}$ (0·73) (0·20)	0·554*
(ii)	Gordon	17[1]	1951–59		n.a.		n.a.	0·81*
(iii)	Gordon		1960–68		n.a.		n.a.	0·16
2.	Okun	22[2]	1951–68		2·1	7·9	$\sigma = 0{\cdot}39 + 0{\cdot}54\overline{X}$ (0·35) (0·20)	0·691*
3. (i)			1951–71	Implicit deflator of private consumption	2·3	4·4	$\sigma = -0{\cdot}79 + 0{\cdot}96\overline{X}$ (1·00) (0·26)	0·457*
(ii)		17[3]	1951–59		1·5	6·6	$\sigma = -0{\cdot}50 + 1{\cdot}09\overline{X}$ (0·69) (0·17)	0·728*
(iii)			1960–71		2·1	5·5	$\sigma = 0{\cdot}71 + 0{\cdot}22\overline{X}$ (0·46) (0·12)	0·176
				(b) Latin American Countries				
4. (i)	Vogel		1950–69	Consumer price index	0·3	43·0	$\sigma = 0{\cdot}95 + 0{\cdot}87\overline{X}$ (5·54) (0·16)	0·803*
(ii)		16[4]	1951–59		1·1	75·6	$\sigma = 1{\cdot}18 + 0{\cdot}72\overline{X}$ (1·65) (0·06)	0·899*
(iii)			1960–69		0·5	46·4	$\sigma = 1{\cdot}00 + 0{\cdot}57\overline{X}$ (1·10) (0·06)	0·876*

[1] Canada, United States, Japan (1952 ff), Austria, Belgium (1953 ff), Denmark, Finland, France, Germany, Greece, Ireland (1951–67), Italy, Netherlands, Norway (1954–67), Sweden, Switzerland, United Kingdom.

[2] Including also (period specified in parentheses): Luxembourg (1960–67), Iceland, Portugal (1956–68), Spain (1958–68), and Turkey.

[3] As in one. The period covered starts with 1952 for Italy and Norway, 1953 for Japan, and 1954 for Belgium, and it ends in 1969 for Switzerland and 1970 for Greece.

[4] Uruguay, Bolivia, Brazil, Chile, Argentina, Paraguay (excluding 1962–63), Colombia, Peru, Mexico, Nicaragua (excluding 1968–69), Equador, Honduras, Costa Rica, Guatemala, Venezuela, El Salvador.

* Significant at the 1 per cent level.

the annual rates. Okun's contention was that 'stop and go' policies would result in raising the average rate, so that the more wavy line must, on the average, lie above the less wavy one.

However, differences in σ may also occur when inflation rates vary monotonically over time. Thus, in figure 11.2b, differences in the acceleration of the inflation rate result in differences in the standard deviation of the annual rates, though $\bar{X}$, the average rate, is the same in both cases. The same result may, of course, be due to differences in deceleration. Thus σ is not a statistic that can act as an indicator of the policies pursued.

Gordon [7] has also criticised Okun's interpretation of the data, although for a somewhat different reason. Gordon found that when the period examined by Okun is broken up into two subperiods, 1951–59 and 1960–68, a positive association between σ and $\bar{X}$ is found to have existed in the earlier subperiod, but not in the later one. The fits reported by Gordon are shown in lines 1(ii) and 1(iii) of table 11.1 and full regressions using our data are shown in lines 3(ii) and 3(iii) of the table. These results clearly confirm Gordon's position that the relationship is different in the two periods. Gordon, however, explains the better fit in the earlier period on the basis of the aftermath of the Korean War and because of the adjustment to wartime dislocations. This may be correct, but it seems beside the main point. In our view, the key point is that inflation rates were high and widely dispersed in 1951 (perhaps due to the Korean War), but then they all decelerated to a more homogeneous rate by the end of the decade.[1]

Similar tests were performed for the Latin American sample, and they are shown in lines 4(ii) and 4(iii) of the table. The results show a slightly weaker relationship in the later subperiod, but basically there is a strong and positive relationship in both periods. This may appear consistent with Gordon's interpretation, in that the role of the Korean War in the inflations of the Latin American countries was relatively minor. But Gordon should then expect a weak relationship in both periods, whereas, in fact, just the opposite holds. Indeed, in this way the results might seem to support Okun. More careful examination, however, indicates that the high values for σ in Latin American countries are also the result, in greater part, of inflationary and deflationary trends, rather than of oscillations about some constant rate. It happens, though, that the intervals of acceleration and deceleration occurred in the countries at different times, and thus there is no simple decade-like split in the sample that reveals it.[2]

Thus, to summarise, the question is whether countries that have experienced

[1] In other words, across countries, the rate of inflation, say, in 1951 is highly correlated with the variation in inflation rates 1951–59. In fact, for the thirteen countries for which data were available for 1951, the rank correlation coefficient was 0·84; and rose to 0·97 when the extreme observation of Greece was excluded.

[2] Thus, for example, Bolivia experienced an acceleration of inflation between 1951 and 1957, while in Paraguay inflation may be said to have decelerated throughout the whole period considered here.

higher rates of inflation on average have also experienced more variable rates of inflation. The data, unfortunately, appear to give no clearcut answer once the technical effect of acceleration and deceleration trends is recognised. In particular, these data at least provide no justification for Okun's emphatic claim that 'if the United States would accept a higher inflation rate, Americans would have an excellent basis from world experience to expect a more variable inflation rate in the future' (Okun [11], page 485).

There does exist another source of data in the form of direct surveys of the inflation expectations of individuals. These data have been infrequently used both because of limited availability and because of concern with their accuracy. Recently, however, interesting results have been obtained with such data collected by the Survey Research Center at the University of Michigan; see de Menil and Bhalla [3], de Menil [2], and Juster [8]. Indeed, the data appear doubly attractive for our purposes since they directly measure the prior expectations and they are available on a time series basis for both the expected inflation rate E and the standard deviation Σ. The results of a simple linear regression are[1]

$$\underset{}{\Sigma = \underset{(0{\cdot}09)}{1{\cdot}38} + \underset{(0{\cdot}03)}{0{\cdot}31}E} \tag{8}$$

$R^2 = 0{\cdot}58$; Sample = 1955:2 to 1971:2; standard errors in parentheses. Taken at face value, equation (8) indicates a strong and positive relationship between the expected value of inflation and the prior dispersion associated with this expectation. If valid, equation (8), much more than the time series of actual inflation, strongly confirms Okun's position. That is, it would appear that at least one cost of a high expected inflation is that prior expectations are then also highly dispersed. At this point, however, equation (8) probably raises more questions than it answers. For example, as noted in footnote 1 page 288, the (E, Σ) data can be derived in alternative ways, and the Σ measure is formally the dispersion between individuals, not the prior dispersion of a single individual. Also, it is possible that E and Σ are being generated jointly by underlying factors, in which case the interpretation of equation (8) depends very much on the nature of these factors. Further work along these lines is thus clearly called for.

(2) VARIABILITY OF INFLATION RATES AMONG COMMODITIES

An attempt to examine the overall effects of inflation on relative prices has

[1] We are grateful to Professor George de Menil of Princeton for his assistance and for providing us with his data. The raw data, from the Survey Research Center, is in the form of survey responses that inflation will 'go up', 'stay the same', or 'go down'. Consequently, several techniques are available for determining the parameters E and Σ. The results shown are based on data described in de Menil [2]. It should also be noted that Σ is directly the standard deviation of expectations across the sample of respondents, whereas we interpret it as the standard deviation of the prior distribution of a representative individual. The same type of correspondence has been assumed in a paper by Juster [8].

been made by Glejser [6]. To measure the change in the relative price of a commodity group, Glejser compared the average value, for the years 1953–59, of this group's price index with an average of the values of the whole consumer price index. Distinguishing between seven main-commodity groups, he then computed the standard deviation of the thus defined relative price changes for each one of fifteen OECD countries. This standard deviation he found to be positively associated, as across countries, with the average annual increase in the consumer price index. Using his data we estimated the regression equation as

$$\sigma = \underset{(0{\cdot}21)}{0{\cdot}65} + \underset{(0{\cdot}07)}{0{\cdot}25}\bar{X};$$

$$R^2 = 0{\cdot}503; \quad \text{standard errors in parentheses.} \qquad (9)$$

However, Glejser's interest in his paper was different from ours, and his computations are not quite satisfactory for our purpose. His investigation does not not allow a distinction between the year-to-year effects of changes in relative prices and the cumulative effects of these changes. And the association between variability and the average inflation represents a cross-section of different national experiences, rather than developments over time in any one given country. In fact, when Glejser compared the experience of a single country, France, in two different periods, he found the standard deviation of relative prices to have fallen as the inflation rate rose.[1]

To establish the relationship between relative prices and inflation we investigated it separately for a number of individual countries. The choice of the sample was determined, on the whole, by the accessibility of sufficiently detailed breakdowns of the consumer price index for a reasonable length of time. In ten of the countries examined we were able to distinguish between eight and thirteen commodity groups. Three other countries with less detailed data were included because of their special inflationary histories. The periods covered vary in length, but in no case do they fall short of eight years. For each year we calculated the standard deviation of the per cent increases in the prices of the main commodity groups over their levels in the preceding year. These standard deviations were then related to the corresponding changes in the general price level. The resultant scatter-diagrams varied considerably from one country to another. In all the cases examined here, however, the coefficient of variation, $V = \sigma/\bar{X}$, decreased with $\bar{X}$. As can be seen from table 11.2 the observations follow very closely a hyperbolic function of the form:[2]

[1] Glejser [6], page 77. The standard deviation in this case was calculated for 40 commodity groups, and the (partly overlapping) periods compared were 1950–56 and 1950–60.

[2] Data sources are given in Appendix [6]. Only the absolute values of the inflation rates were used, on the assumption that it is the magnitude of the price change, and not its sign, which is associated with dispersion. This need not be so, but negative observations were, in any case, rare. It should be stressed that the coefficient of variation is equivalent to the standard deviation of the relative prices from unity.

$$V = a + b\bar{X}^{-1}. \tag{10}$$

As the degree of commodity aggregation varies from one country to another, the regressions of table 11.2 are not strictly comparable (though this is somewhat ameliorated by the standard deviations being weighted by the various groups' mid-period weights in consumption). But they leave no place for any doubt as to the shape of the relationship. As in the majority of cases the regression constant is not significantly different from zero, the findings of table 11.2 suggest that the absolute dispersion of the specific inflation rates is invariant to the overall rate of inflation.[1]

An explanation for this result can be based on the adjustment costs of making finely tuned price adjustments in an inflationary situation. For example, it could be that discreteness in the monetary unit and in weights and measures, as well as a preference for round numbers, leads to indivisibilities and thresholds in price changes. The results would suggest, moreover, that the resulting dispersion in price changes is proportionate to the price level, not to the rate of inflation. In other words, one would find the same dispersion around an inflation rate of 10 per cent (say 8 per cent to 12 per cent) as around an inflation rate of 20 per cent (say 18 per cent to 22 per cent).

The data of table 11.2 enable us also to see to what extent intercountry comparisons do diverge from the experience of individual countries over time. Were all regression constants equal to zero, differences in the regression coefficients would have represented differences in the country averages of the standard deviations. As it is, this correspondence is not complete. We compared, therefore, the actual averages of the annual standard deviations with the corresponding countries' average inflation rates in the periods examined, both of which are shown in table 11.2. Despite the variations in the number of commodity groups distinguished and in their definitions, and in the lengths of the periods, a positive association was found to exist between the two variables.[2]

The completely different results obtained from the examination of time series for individual countries and from international cross-section analysis of period averages, points out how misleading the findings of the latter may be when applied to any one individual country. They also show how seemingly contrasting relationships, such as that established by Glejser and that reported

[1] Multiplying both sides of $\sigma/X = bX^{-1}$ by X, the equation reduces to $\sigma = b$. For very high rates of inflation one would then expect the observations to be approximated by a straight line of a very low slope. And in fact, the linear relationship was almost as good as the hyperbolic one in the case of Brazil, while in Chile the observations seemed to form a straight line parallel to the horizontal axis. It should, however, be pointed out that in his contribution to this conference, Revold Entov reports that the coefficient of variation, for a high disaggregation of the relative prices of the United States wholesale price index, rose in the late 1960s as average inflation rates rose; see R. Entov, 'Some Problems of General Price Movements', Chapter 5 in this volume).

[2] The correlation coefficient for all the thirteen countries of table 11.2 was 0·92. And even when the three Latin American countries, with their high average inflation levels, were excluded, the estimated relationship, $\sigma = 0{\cdot}72 + 0{\cdot}68X$, was significant at the 1 per cent level with $R = 0{\cdot}73$.

TABLE 11.2
REGRESSION OF COEFFICIENT OF VARIATION OF RELATIVE PRICES ON RATE OF INFLATION – COUNTRY TIME SERIES

Country	*Period*	*Commodity groups*	*Observations*	*Average inflation*	*Dispersion*	*Regression equation*	R^2
Argentina	1951–66	5	14[a]	24·1	8·0	$V = 0{\cdot}04 + 6{\cdot}40\bar{X}^{-1}$ (0·03) (0·56)	0·916*
Finland	1952–71	5	20	4·8	3·0	$V = -0{\cdot}58 + 5{\cdot}21\bar{X}^{-1}$ (0·43) (0·99)	0·607*
Brazil	1962–70	10	9	46·2	8·4	$V = 0{\cdot}09 + 4{\cdot}60\bar{X}^{-1}$ (0·24) (1·50)	0·573**
West Germany	1963–72	9	10	3·2	1·5	$V = -0{\cdot}45 + 2{\cdot}84\bar{X}^{-1}$ (0·09) (0·21)	0·957*
Japan	1954–72	10	19	5·9	4·3	$V = 0{\cdot}36 + 2{\cdot}15\bar{X}^{-1}$ (0·18) (0·39)	0·639*
Sweden	1954–72	10	19	4·0	2·6	$V = 0{\cdot}11 + 1{\cdot}73\bar{X}^{-1}$ (0·05) (0·10)	0·948*
Norway	1965–72	9	8	5·2	1·4	$V = -0{\cdot}02 + 1{\cdot}43\bar{X}^{-1}$ (0·07) (0·13)	0·653**
United Kingdom	1965–72	10	17	3·8	1·9	$V = 0{\cdot}12 + 1{\cdot}34\bar{X}^{-1}$ (0·07) (0·13)	0·873*
France	1963–70	8	8	4·0	1·6	$V = 0{\cdot}07 + 1{\cdot}32\bar{X}^{-1}$ (0·19)	0·463***
Denmark	1958–72	13	14	5·2	2·2	$V = 0{\cdot}19 + 1{\cdot}27\bar{X}^{-1}$ (0·02)	0·972*
Israel	1956–72	10	17	5·9	3·3	$V = 0{\cdot}37 + 1{\cdot}25\bar{X}^{-1}$ (0·11) (0·23)	0·653***

Chile	1951–68	4	18	32·5	7·4	$V = 0{\cdot}21 + 1{\cdot}11\bar{X}^{-1}$ $(0{\cdot}06)\ (1{\cdot}15)$	0·055
United States	1958–71	9	14	2·7	1·2	$V = 0{\cdot}10 + 0{\cdot}91\bar{X}^{-1}$ $(0{\cdot}20)\ (0{\cdot}32)$	0·402***

* Significant at the 1 per cent level ** Significant at the 1 per cent level *** Significant at the 2 per cent level
[a] Excluding 1954 (where $X = 0$) and 1959

Data Sources for Table 11.2 – dispersion of inflation rates among commodity groups

Argentina (Buenos Aires) Brazil (Sao Paulo) Chile (Santiago)	Statistisches Bundesamt, Wiesbaden, *Allgemeine Statistik des Auslandes*
Germany	Statistisches Bundesamt, Wiesbaden, *Statistisches Jahrbuch für die Bundesrepublik Deutschland*
France	Institut national de la statistique et des études économiques, *Annuaire statistique de la France*
Denmark	Danmarks Statist Kobenhavn, *Statistisk Årbog*
Norway	Statistisk Sentralbyrå Oslo, *Statistisk Årsbok*
Sweden	Statistiska Centralbyrån, *Statistisk Årsbok för Sverige*
Finland	Statistikcentralen, *Statistsk Årsbok for Finland*
Israel	Central Bureau of Statistics, *Statistical Abstract of Israel*
United States	United States Department of Commerce, *Statistical Abstract of the United States*
Japan (Tokyo)	Japanese Bureau of Statistics, *Statistical Yearbook*
United Kingdom	United Kingdom Central Statistical Office, *Annual Abstract of Statistics*

here, may be reconciled. In particular, they indicate that though countries characterised by high rates of inflation were also characterised by a high variability of relative prices, changes in the rate of inflation *within* any given country were not accompanied by systematic changes in this variability. These results are consistent, instead, with a situation in which, as structural change becomes stronger and prices more rigid downward, the economy may expect in the long run a higher rate of inflation. But while the average σ may be an index of a country's structural change or downward price rigidity, year to year changes in σ need not, and in fact do not, represent variations in the strength of either of these phenomena within the country.

V. CONCLUSIONS

In sections II and III of this paper, we hope to have demonstrated that a wide variety of welfare costs can be associated with inflation once it is recognised that inflations tend to be uneven. In particular, we have tried to go beyond the 'standard' cash balance tax effect of steady inflation and the income redistribution effect of unanticipated inflation. Also it is important to stress that the welfare costs of uneven inflation are not necessarily transitory; that is, they do not necessarily vanish even if the prior parameters for inflation remain constant over extended periods. They are transitory, however, in the sense that inflationary experience may create basic structural changes in the economy and may eliminate the divergence in inflationary anticipations between individuals, so that the welfare costs in large part are eliminated.

Our analysis does, therefore, have the standard implication that a steady inflation should be preferred to an uneven inflation, given that the criterion is simply to minimise the gross welfare cost of inflation (unemployment aside). In practical terms, however, it must be recognised that a policy of strictly steady inflation is not likely to be feasible. Rather, a situation, in which the prior probability distribution of inflation is constant, would appear the most that could be hoped for. But then, at least within the current institutional setting, gross welfare costs will be minimised by policies that minimise the expected value of the prior distribution. Moreover, in this sense we can fully agree with Okun's descriptive phrase that to promise a relatively costless steady inflation is to promise something of a 'mirage'.

The case for low expected inflation rates is made stronger, of course, if it is true that the dispersion of expectations is also a function of the expected inflation rate or some average of historically observed inflation rates. Our analysis in section III of the data for inflation over time indicated, however, only a very weak relationship between the average inflation rate of a country and the fluctuations around this average. The most promising results, in fact, were based on survey data of inflation expectations, and this would appear worth pursuing in more detail. In a similar vein, our analysis in section IV of the dispersion of inflation across commodity groups indicated that the dispersion was actually independent of the average inflation rate. It is true that across countries one finds high inflation rates are correlated with high dispersion between commodities, but this seems to be the result of more fundamental structural changes and downward price rigidities in the countries.

Finally, while we have focused almost solely on the welfare costs of inflation, it should be added that there are potentially certain benefits from inflation. One point, illustrated in our results of section IV, is that if there is downward price rigidity, then the relative dispersion of price changes across commodity groups may be inversely related to the rate of inflation. And perhaps a more important effect, at least on the macroeconomic level, is the possibility that inflation rates may influence unemployment rates. For example, if one believes in a short-run, non-vertical, tradeoff curve between inflation and unemployment, and, in particular, if this tradeoff curve shifts through time, then there may be benefits from allowing or instigating an uneven inflation rate through time. These benefits, of course, would have to be weighed against the welfare costs of the inflation.

REFERENCES

[1] Robert J. Barro, 'Inflationary Finance and the Welfare Cost of Inflation', *Journal of Political Economy* (September/October, 1972).

[2] George de Menil, 'Rationality in Popular Price Expectations', mimeo (1974).

[3] George de Menil and Surjit Bhalla, 'Direct Measurement of Popular Price Expectations', *American Economic Review* (March, 1975).

[4] Revold Entov, 'Some Problems of General Price Movements', chapter 5 in this volume.

[5] Edward Foster, 'Costs and Benefits of Inflation', Studies in Monetary Economics #1, Federal Reserve Bank of Minneapolis (1972).

[6] H. Glejser, 'Inflation, Productivity, and Relative Prices – A Statistical Study', *Review of Economics and Statistics* (1965).

[7] Robert J. Gordon, 'Steady Anticipated Inflation: Mirage or Oasis?', *Brookings Economic Papers* (1971: 2).

[8] F. Thomas Juster, 'Savings Behavior, Uncertainty and Price Expectations', paper prepared for the Conference on the Economic Outlook, Ann Arbor (November 15–16, 1973).

[9] David Laidler, 'The Welfare Costs of Inflation in Neoclassical Theory – Some Unsettled Issues', chapter 12 in this volume.

[10] Robert Mundell, 'Inflation and Real Interest', *Journal of Political Economy* (June, 1963).

[11] Arthur M. Okun, 'The Mirage of Steady Inflation', *Brookings Economic Papers* (1971:2).

[12] Robert C. Vogel, 'The Dynamics of Inflation in Latin America, 1950–1969'. *American Economic Review* (March, 1974).

Discussion of the Paper by Dwight Jaffee and Ephraim Kleiman

Professor Stahl introduced the paper. He recalled that Lenin had said that perhaps the best way to destroy capitalism was to destroy its currency. This might be the best point from which to start a discussion of the paper, because it tried to go from neoclassical real balances to more important effects. Pure distribution effects had been discussed in this conference in the Duesenberry paper, and real balances were discussed in Professor Laidler's paper, chapter 12.

Professor Stahl wanted first to say something about the terminology in the Kleiman and Jaffee paper. The authors had discussed the causes of inflation, making the usual distinction between exogenous and endogenous factors. Here one found inflation as an endogenous variable, and that made for methodological problems. One could begin with uneven excess demand, or the social costs of bad monetary policy. He did not want to go farther into this but simply to emphasise that it would simplify the logical issues if one worked on these lines.

The authors looked at two types of inflation – sporadic and dispersed, seeing sporadic inflation as a kind of stochastic process. At the end of the paper, one had a relationship where the average value of inflation was linear

$$\alpha = a + bx$$

There was a different rate of inflation for each different group, and one was looking at a stochastic process. If one considered there was a shift of pattern, with more inflation. Higher inflation gave the distribution a higher average value and a larger standard deviation. This was the distribution of expected inflation for an individual, with zero or negative inflation as the lower limit.

With adaptive expectations, one would have the situation now found in Sweden. This gave a widening of the distribution, though it would have the same lower limit. One would then get the kind of statistical results one had in the paper. It was important, however, to distinguish the costs of inflation and the widening of inflationary expectations, and it was not quite clear which the paper was considering.

On sporadic inflation, it was essential to distinguish two concepts implicit in the paper. First, there were divergent expectations, which created specific costs. Second, there was uncertainty, which led to costs of a risk character.

Divergent expectations led to discriminatory pricing systems and so had some allocative effect. For example, suppose that one had a marginal efficiency of capital function, with given rates of return associated with given levels of investment. If, in the market, one had only a nominal rate of interest, the real rate of interest the firm expected to pay was the nominal rate less the expectation of inflation. This gave an expected real rate and pessimistic businesses would therefore invest less. This was nothing to do with risk: it resulted simply from different estimates of future inflation. The result was to destroy the competitive price system, because it became hard to relate behaviour rationally to basic factors.

The uncertainty effects of the model were not fully fledged, but one could use a simpler model and still keep the risk elements. Wealth for the individual could depend on the inflation rate, being a stochastic variable in real terms.

One could assume that wealth included all future income, which would make it possible to use a utility function of wealth. The risk argument in the paper was that if there were no inflation, so that one expected given wealth, one would expect given income too. Inflation introduced uncertainty. The expected value of wealth might be the same as the original given level, but there was now variability in the possible outcomes, so that the utility value decreased. With given expected wealth, utility fell with greater variability in outcome. This was the main argument in the paper.

The fall could perhaps be overcome by hedging. For example, one could go into stamp or art collection – but at a real cost to the individual, who would give up wealth to reduce the dispersion of utility. This led to problems in *ex post* and *ex ante* analyses.

A major issue was whether a sample of one unit belonged to this distribution. Professor Stahl could see the logic of the analysis but it was not operational for the individual, though it might be possible to formulate expectations in the market. Indeed, one strong argument for indexed loans was that it would lead to a market view on the future inflation rate.

Professor De Wolff agreed that wrong expectations of the uneven inflationary movements which occurred in reality could lead to a social loss. The problem, however, was not so much that relative prices moved differently as that the expectations of these movements were incorrect. It was clear that if one assumed that this fact might contribute to the explanation of an increasing rate of inflation, it would be necessary to prove that the amount of mis-specification was dependent on the rate of inflation. He would like to ask if the authors had evidence of a relation of this kind.

Secondly, there was the remark about 'a constant prior probability distribution appearing the most that could be hoped for' in the concluding paragraph of the paper. He would like to remark that even with a constant rate of inflation it would take a rather long time before such a stable distribution could be obtained.

Professor Lundberg emphasised that when one spoke of inflationary expectations, one was always taking the existing view. Everyone had such a view, but some were more active in acquiring it than others. Writers in the United Kingdom suggested a distinction between 'sharpies' and the 'suckers'. The latter adapted slowly and largely lost. A major phenomenon was the skill with which the sharpies used inflation. How wonderful it would have been for Kruger, the famous Swedish businessman. There were lots of Krugers now, buying up firms, building up liquidity, and making large gains. What they did also altered the allocation of resources.

Perhaps one should abandon a passive way of looking at expectations. There was a great deal of collection and analysis of gossip and information in some circles, though the suckers were outside these.

He wanted to raise a minor point, on the discussion of *ex ante* issues. One had equities and other claims, but perhaps it was a new phenomenon that equities were no longer a good escape if inflation were a consistent phenomenon. In Sweden, if one looked at the internal rate of return on equities in the whole Swedish market, it had been 5 per cent before tax in recent years. For owners of stocks it had been as low as 1 per cent to 2 per cent. The real internal rate of return was therefore about −6 per cent or −7 per cent. Keeping one's money in bonds and banks would have been much better.

In addition, as Professor Stahl had already mentioned, one saw private individuals shifting from stocks to other things. This was a new phenomenon. Looking at the harbour outside the conference room, he could see that at least some people had been selling stocks and buying ships. He wondered whether this was an international phenomenon.

Professor Modigliani suggested that it was a question of blue ships *versus* blue chips.

Professor Stahl agreed about the real costs of guessing. However, he had already explained that this was because there was no market test. There would be if one could compare the performance of indexed and non-indexed bonds.

Professor Duesenberry told Professor Lundberg that John Lintner had presented a paper to the American Finance Association which dealt with equity performance. It showed, *inter alia*, that poor performance after the beginning of a period of inflation was not new. For instance, it had taken some time for equity markets to adjust after the Second World War. Lintner had explained the phenomenon.

On indexation, his own observation on term structures was that they might measure expectations but were usually wrong. So that was not much help.

Professor Entov had some reservations. The authors had interesting analyses of the relationship between uncertainty and the utility of a commodity basket during a period of inflation. But perhaps they understated the real cost of price uncertainty. For example, in the case of a supermarket with random prices, the existence of a welfare loss crucially depended on the nature of individual utility functions.

From their empirical results, the authors suggested there were reasons why it was unlikely that the dispersion of commodity prices would be the same with faster inflation. He did not exclude this possibility, but the results were not wholly convincing. Perhaps the disaggregation was not always sufficient. He also wondered whether cyclical movements influenced price dispersion. If so, the analysis was rather inadequate.

Most important, the number of degrees of freedom in the regression analysis was too small.

He had tried to calculate price dispersion in the United States. While this work was not directly comparable with the paper, his main suggestion was that price dispersion rose quickly with an acceleration in inflation.

To Professor Stahl, he wanted to say that he did not know when Lenin made the remark that the best way to destroy capitalism was to destroy its currency. He would certainly like to see this quotation, but was sure he could find a similar quotation in the earlier works of J. M. Keynes.

Mr Kaser explained that there had been a dispute over this issue in the London *Times*. A verifiable quotation was that of Lenin's minister of finance, Sokolnikov, on the expansion of the quantity of money in inflation. He said that 'the printing press is the machine gun of the proletariat, mowing down the moneyed classes'.

Professor Gordon wanted to return to the correlation of the mean and standard deviation of inflationary expectations, and to congratulate the authors on bringing the argument back to simple terms. The original discussion of this problem was concerned not with whether we should start from a zero rate of inflation, but was in terms of steady fully expected inflation. Early in 1971, when United States inflation was around 5 per cent, it had largely been anticipated. The question was, should one live with it and adjust one's behaviour? Or should one force an economic recession? In fact, price controls had been introduced and different answers found.

He reminded participants that some *ex ante* costs of inflation were merely the costs of transition to a higher rate. What were the costs of inflation? First, there were the inherent and continuing costs of zero inflation. Second, there were the inherent and continuing costs of 5 per cent to 10 per cent inflation, continuing at the same rate. Either way, inflation could be interrupted, for example, by an oil crisis. In each case, the question was whether the monetary authorities would accommodate the 'real' shock.

Regression analyses included both countries with passive, accommodating monetary policies, and those where the monetary authorities chose to administer shocks. He was therefore suspicious of spurious correlations between the means and standard deviations of inflation in different countries. However, one could still advocate the acceptance of a steady rate of inflation, since one would then know the dispersion round the mean. One could use indices to show this but to do so would point to the danger of the indexation of wages which had real welfare costs and was not a first-best situation. If shocks were emanating from the real part of the economy, one had to make things work. This would give a higher standard deviation both for investment and unemployment.

Professor Duesenberry thought there were some illusions on indexing. When he was in Cambridge, he had learned that Professor Reddaway was going to Sierra Leone to quell a riot! This had been over the way the cost of living index in that country was being computed. If one had a high rate of inflation and used indexation, major problems arose over exactly what the price index contained. Costs then returned, though of a different kind. Widespread indexing would not necessarily do the trick.

While there were individual welfare costs with inflation, the real frictions were social and arose from lags. One must clearly recognise the existence of distributional conflict among groups and this was the greatest social cost of inflation. Issues arose which had not arisen before, causing groups in society to clash. The social and political costs of inflation were much more important than the personal problems.

Professor Modigliani suggested that Professor Duesenberry should remember that if absolute prices rose, it was easier to make some needed adjustment in relative prices. Up to a point, inflation was a kind of lubricant.

To Professor Gordon, he wanted to say that the way he presented the problem was misleading; 5 per cent inflation for two years was not the same as 5 per cent inflation for ever, both in the past and the future. For example, many contracts would be left over from the previous situation. If all knew there would be 5 per cent inflation from now on, the rate of interest would adjust, but this would still lead to capital gains and losses which would be distributed in a capricious way.

There was also a difference between indexing loans and wages. One did the former to reduce uncertainty in the rate of return. The indexation of wages was a problem of dynamic stability. However, one could get the same result if one had a capital market where most assets were paid floating shortrun interest rates and there was no interference. The rate of interest would then match the inflation rate.

Mr Plessz argued that firms were not interested in prices *per se* but in the prices of their inputs, the prices of what they sold, and the quantities sold. The return was what mattered. The effects of price uncertainty were especially important for enterprises with a great deal of risk capital and high amortisation, for example, essentially basic material industries. For these, sales prices were more volatile than the global price level. Because their costs were mainly capital costs, their rentability calculations were bound to assign special importance to prospects or uncertainties of sales prices. Consequently, a period of high prices could lead to substantial overinvestment, as after the Korean boom. Persistent weakness in prices could provoke substantial underinvestment, as there had been in the late 1950s and early 1960s. Currently, price uncertainties were a major factor reducing investment in basic industries. Enterprises traditionally operating in this sector had tended to shift to shorter-term, and thus less uncertain, investments. This represented a genuine misallocation of resources.

Professor Frisch asked Professor Stahl whether he meant that if the rate of inflation were a stochastic variable, the wealth owner had a straight-line expected value. With a concave utility function, there would be risk-aversion; on a straight line, risk would be neutral. One had to remember that Professor Gordon said that the 'new–new microeconomics' assumed risk neutrality. It was therefore possible to exploit workers because they were more risk-averse. The answer depended on the degree of risk-aversion.

Professor Stahl replied that revealed preference analysis showed that people were risk-averse.

Mr Plessz pointed out that some portfolio analyses had shown that in an inflationary period any holder of a stable portfolio was a net loser. Paradoxically, the best way to limit losses on one's savings was to put them into a savings bank. Of course, if one had constantly switched one's portfolio during the inflation, one could have made a great deal of money.

Professor Kleiman explained that the paper resulted from the authors' dissatisfaction with the emphasis which the existing analyses put on the *ex post* of inflation. They wanted to look at the problems of anticipation. If one expected inflation, but did not act, one lost. But there was no social loss, only redistribution. The authors had been trying to stress that if individuals tried to protect themselves from private loss, the individual costs were also social costs. They also wanted to establish that, with risk-aversion, these costs would be greater the more rapid the inflation and the greater the variability in price increases. Professor Lundberg had made the point that trying to estimate inflation was part of the cost of inflation. People spent money on trying to foresee what the inflation rate would be, and on taking appropriate action.

In their empirical work, the authors had wanted a reference point, which was why they had looked at the problem as they had. The correct variables were not the inflation rate, but the expected decrease in the value of money and its dispersion. Perhaps they should recalculate the data on this basis.

To Professors de Wolff and Entov, he wanted to say that he was surprised how few studies there had been of the behaviour of relative prices under inflation. He agreed that he and his co-author had based their analysis on too few observations, and that there was too much aggregation. He would like to see the analysis reported in Professor Entov's paper, which was more disaggregated.

The usual argument of businessmen against indexation was that one's own firm's prices might go up more slowly than the index in general.

Professor Jaffee thought that the discussion showed general agreement on the main points. He emphasised the distinction between the *ex ante* and *ex post* costs of inflation, illustrating it with the example of automobile insurance. The *ex ante* costs of automobile accidents were revealed in direct and indirect expenditures on automobile insurance. The *ex post* costs of an actual accident then arose when the optimum insurance coverage was less than complete. Indexation provided a means for eliminating the uncertainty of different inflation rates. He was pleased that the discussion had brought out the fact that the absence of indexation was evidence of a market failure. The paper by Professor Fischer brought this point out clearly.

On the relationship between the average inflation rate and the dispersion of inflation, the literature accepted the contention that countries with high rates of inflation also showed greater variability in price increases. He stressed that this correlation was less clear with objective inflation data, once trends in inflation rates were removed. However, the contention could be confirmed from data based on individuals' subjective expectations of inflation rates and dispersion. Naturally, one then needed to know the relationship between expected inflation and actual inflation to give the full picture.

On the shift into real assets, he stressed that this was the primary means by which individuals obtained inflation protection. In part, real asset investment became important because the interest rate on financial contracts was frequently not allowed to adjust fully for inflation. This was unfortunate, since an investment in real assets that were not productive (sailboats, second homes, gold), and not optimum in terms of consumption allocation, had a social cost that rose with the rate of inflation.

Professor Modigliani pointed out that in the calculation at the end of the paper the authors were comparing average inflation rates with the dispersion of inflation. He thought the argument confused. What mattered was the dispersion of relative prices, one should be consistent and carry out an analysis, not for one country, but for a cross-section. Perhaps the authors should re-run their regressions on this basis.

12 The Welfare Costs of Inflation in Neoclassical Theory—Some Unsettled Problems[1]

David Laidler
UNIVERSITY OF WESTERN ONTARIO

I. INTRODUCTION

The worldwide inflation of recent years has slackened off markedly in most countries over the last twelve months. However, even in such low inflation countries as Germany, it is still running at a rate which, a decade ago, would have been regarded as intolerably high. Moreover, the recent reduction in inflation rates has been achieved only at the cost of unemployment levels unprecedented in the postward period. It is far from clear that the current recession will anywhere be permitted to last long enough to bring inflation back to the levels of the early 1960s; indeed there are good reasons for believing that recovery from the current recession will be accompanied by an acceleration of inflation as demand is permitted to expand before the inflationary expectations generated over the last five years are completely removed from the system.

Because inflation is difficult and painful to cure, there is a plausible case to be made for learning to live with it instead. It is widely agreed that inflation is at its most socially destructive when it is not anticipated. However, unanticipated inflation is also relatively costless to cure; depression and unemployment become a necessary accompaniment to slowing down the inflation rate only when inflationary expectations have become embedded in the price setting and wage bargaining processes. On the other hand, the more fully adjusted is the economy to the presence of inflation, the less socially disruptive is its continuation. Neoclassical monetary theory would have it that, in the limit, when inflation is fully anticipated, the only costs it imposes are those associated with the community's attempts to economise on non-interest-bearing money balances. This limiting case is precisely the one in which the costs of reducing inflation in terms of unemployment – not to mention in terms of

[1] I have benefited greatly from discussions of the issues dealt with in this paper with Reuven Brenner, Alan Coddington, Laurence Copeland, Stanley Fischer, David Levhari, Alvin Marty, Michael Parkin and George Zis. Since several of those whom I have implicated have not had the opportunity of reading and commenting on a draft of this paper before it was presented, the usual disclaimer, that any errors and omissions it might contain are the author's sole responsibility, is to be taken particularly seriously.

the other phenomena such as the disruption of debtor-creditor relationships that would accompany an unanticipated reduction in the inflation rate – are maximised.

Given that this is what contemporary economics tells us about the policy options when inflationary expectations are deeply embedded in the economy, it is hardly surprising that many find the case for trying to live with inflation, rather than attempting to cure it, a strong one. I shall examine one aspect of this case in this essay: namely neoclassical analysis of the welfare costs of anticipated inflation. I shall argue that conventional theory underestimates those costs and that it does so because it concentrates on money's role as a store of value for the individual economic agent to the exclusion of considering the effects of anticipated inflation on money's roles as a means of exchange and a unit of account. My arguments strengthen the case against living with inflation, but they by no means make that case. The most appealing feature of the application of Marshallian welfare analysis to inflation is that it appears to permit quantification of its resource costs, and I shall not here suggest means of quantifying the extra costs, associated with anticipated inflation, which the following arguments suggest should be taken into account.

This admission is not fatal in the current context. The costs involved in bringing down the inflation rate below its anticipated level are not quantifiable either in terms analogous to the welfare measures that we use in dealing with anticipated inflation. The latter measure utility foregone as a result of misallocating a stock of fully utilised resources. Part of the cost of bringing down the inflation rate involves leaving some resources unutilised, albeit temporarily. To be sure, certain contemporary approaches to the theory of unemployment would have it that such resources are simply misallocated in the direction of search activity rather than being totally unused, but there is no solution to our problem along these lines. Even if we relabel 'unemployed' resources as 'misallocated', the misallocation in question is not of the type that orthodox welfare analysis deals with.[1]

It is of the essence of orthodox analysis that agents act in response to incentives and achieve the expected outcome of their decisions. Misallocations arise because private incentives do not accurately reflect social constraints. Unemployment arises (or a shift of resources towards search activity takes place) because individuals act on the basis of expectations which are not, in the event, fulfilled. The *ex post* outcome of actions differs from that expected *ex ante*, and we have no welfare economics of the consequences of mistaken decisions. The same argument applies to our ability to assess the importance of that other consequence of unanticipated changes in the inflation rate, the disruption of debtor–creditor relationships (in favour of creditors, be it noted, when the inflation rate is slowing down). Orthodox welfare economics has little to say about distributional effects that arise from privately appropriate

[1] For analysis of unemployment as search activity, see for example Alchian [1]. I have dealt with this approach to unemployment in more detail in Laidler [13].

responses to changed constraints, let alone about those which arise from erroneous decisions.

In short, we do not know how to quantify the costs associated with unexpected variations in the inflation rate, and it is the burden of this paper that we know less than might have been thought about the nature of the costs involved in living with perfectly anticipated inflation, though all the arguments I shall present suggest that these are greater than conventional neoclassical analysis would have them.[1] In the next few pages I will first set out a version of that conventional analysis before submitting it to what I hope will be judged constructive criticism.

II. A SKETCH OF NEOCLASSICAL ANALYSIS OF THE WELFARE COSTS OF ANTICIPATED INFLATION

I shall present the conventional analysis of the effects of fully anticipated inflation on economic welfare in terms of a simple one-sector neoclassical growth model of the type widely employed in work on the long-run neutrality of money. Such a model is open to criticism for begging important questions about the role of money in the economy; I use it here not because I regard criticism of it as invalid but because it seems to me to be a useful starting point for raising the questions which I wish to take up in this essay.

Figure 12.1 sets out a particular version of the model in question. It depicts an economy with one output, produced by two inputs, 'capital' and 'labour', the capital input being transformable from and into the single output costlessly and in fixed proportions.[2] The population grows at a constant, exogenously determined rate, and the supply of labour is proportional to the population. The production function in this economy displays constant returns to scale and diminishing returns to each factor. Thus output per head of the population is a unique function of capital per head of the population. With pure rates of flow measured on the vertical axis, and capital per head on the horizontal, the downward sloping curve in panel (a) of figure 12.1 depicts the marginal product of capital as a function of capital per head.

There are many ways of characterising savings behaviour in a model like this one, and here we follow the lead of Sidrauski [18] : the capital stock per head is always maintained by savings at a level k_0 at which the marginal product of capital – a pure rate of flow because of our ability to measure capital and output in the same units – is equal to the rate of time preference. For present purposes this rate of time preference is assumed to be constant and equal to the rate of growth of the population. Thus, our economy's long-run

[1] But note that the paper by Jaffee and Kleiman, given at this conference (see chapter 11) does attempt to analyse such problems, and is complementary to this one.

[2] To analyse the role of money with a model of an economy producing one good is, to put it mildly, dubious. This has been a much-criticised characteristic of the type of analysis discussed here. See for example Clower [6]. I shall take up some of the issues below pp. 326–7.

equilibrium growth path has the following properties: saving as a proportion of national income is equal to profits; consumption is equal to labour income; in terms of figure 12.1(a), the area ABC is consumed while O_kCBD is saved in order to maintain the capital labour ratio constant as the population grows.

Money is introduced in panel b of figure 12.1. It is an asset produced at zero marginal social cost, but which bears no interest. It makes no difference to the following analysis whether money is thought of as the liability of the government or of a privately owned banking system, and the reader may take his choice here.[1] The demand for real money balances per head is independent of the population and of the price level, and is measured from right to left in figure 12.1(b). The demand for real balances per head is assumed to depend inversely on the nominal rate of interest, this variable in turn being given by the sum of the marginal product of capital and the expected rate of inflation.

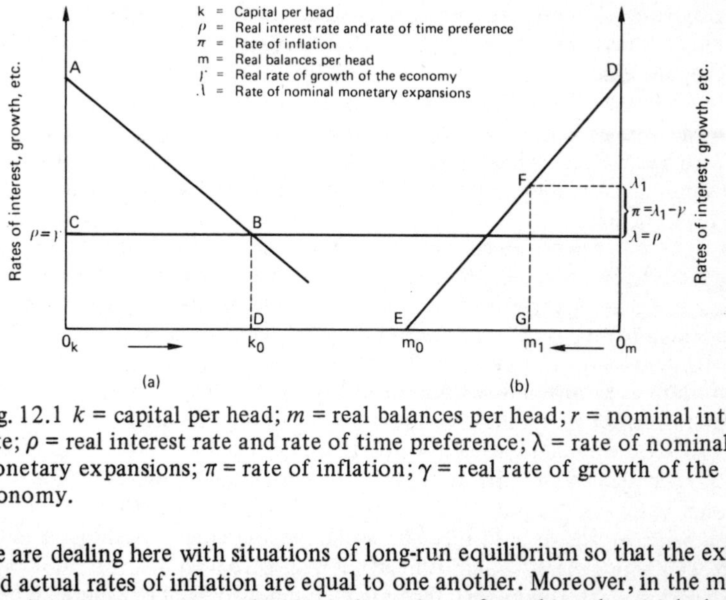

Fig. 12.1 k = capital per head; m = real balances per head; r = nominal interest rate; ρ = real interest rate and rate of time preference; λ = rate of nominal monetary expansions; π = rate of inflation; γ = real rate of growth of the economy.

We are dealing here with situations of long-run equilibrium so that the expected and actual rates of inflation are equal to one another. Moreover, in the model as constructed, output per head is independent of anything that might happen in the money market – indeed it is constant – so there is no need to complicate the analysis with awkward questions about the relationship between the demand for real balances and national income per head.

In this economy, if the quantity of nominal money balances is held constant over time, then there will of course be a negative inflation rate just equal

[1] I have gone into this issue in terms of the model used here in another paper (Laidler [14]) where I have also extended the analysis to non-golden age and non-neutral money cases. Nothing in the present paper hinges upon the special assumptions made here. Their role is purely a simplifying one.

in absolute value to the economy's rate of growth γ. Because we have assumed equality of the rates of time preference and population growth, the rate of growth and the real rate of return on capital are equal to one another. Hence, with a zero rate of nominal monetary expansion the nominal rate of interest will be zero and real balances per head of m_o will be held. The standard welfare analysis of money tells us that the amenity yield of money per head is given by the area under the demand curve for it, O_mDE in this case; that same analysis tells us that a situation of Pareto optimality exists in the money market because the private and social marginal opportunity costs of real balances are equal at zero. In a model such as this one, any positive rate of monetary expansion generates suboptimal money holdings; a rate of monetary expansion such as λ_1 in excess of the economy's growth rate will, for example, generate a rate of inflation π equal to $\lambda_1 - \gamma$, a nominal interest rate of $\rho + \pi$, and a demand for real balances per head equal to m_1. As compared to the zero monetary expansion case, the amenity yield on money is reduced by *EFG*, this being the loss in economic welfare associated with a fully anticipated inflation rate of π.

Now there are of course many awkward questions that can be raised about treating an area such as EFG under any demand curve let alone under a demand curve for real balances, as a measure of economic welfare. Consumer's surplus only has a unique value given by the area under the individual's demand curve for a particular good on the quite stringent assumptions that the marginal utility of all other goods to the individual is constant and independent of the quantity being consumed of the good under analysis. Such problems are sidestepped in the foregoing exercise because the model we have chosen to use is one in which money is neutral; there is no question of variations in the inflation rate affecting the quantities of real output produced and consumed and of these variations in turn influencing the utility of money's services. In a model with non-neutral money, the consequences of varying the rate of nominal monetary expansion, and hence the inflation rate, would involve shifts of, as well as movements along, the demand for money function, unless we made the patently false assumption that the per head income elasticity of demand for real balances was zero. In this case welfare measurement would have to be undertaken with general equilibrium rather than partial equilibrium tools. Quite apart from this problem concerning the uniqueness of our measure of welfare, we are here dealing not with the economic welfare of an individual but with what purports to be a measure of aggregate economic welfare. There are many who would question the propriety of discussing welfare in the aggregate without taking account of distributional factors, while others would go so far as to question the meaning of any such aggregate measure, distributionally weighted or otherwise.[1]

Problems such as these are common to any application of welfare economics and though they are certainly relevant to the seriousness with which we take

[1] The *locus classicus* for the case against making interpersonal utility comparisons is, of course, Robbins [17].

orthodox analysis of the welfare costs of inflation, they are not central to the issues that I wish to raise in this paper. The latter arise from taking a closer than usual look at the nature of money and the amenity flow that it provides. The analysis which was sketched out above has its origins in the work of Bailey [2] and represents an application to a normative, rather than positive, problem of Friedman's [10] restatement of the quantity theory as a theory of the demand for money.[1] In his essay, Friedman has very little to say about the role that money plays in the economic system. He is far more concerned with analysing the factors that influence the amount of money people will hold than in explaining why money is held. He refers to money as a 'temporary abode of purchasing power' and proceeds to analyse the factors determining the demand for it as if it were essentially the same as any durable good that provides a flow of services to its owner. He treats the theory of the demand for money as a special case of his permanent income hypothesis of consumption, and in emphasising his theory's predictions about behaviour rather than in paying attention to producing a set of precise and descriptively accurate assumptions to underpin it, Friedman is simply putting into practice his own methodology of positive economics (cf. Friedman [9]).

Now there can be no doubt that, in treating money as if it were a consumer-durable good, and in applying to the analysis of the demand for it the tools of Fisherian capital theory, Friedman and his associates laid the foundations of an enormous advance in our understanding of the interaction of money and economic activity. The modern quantity theory is surely a prime example of the power of the 'as if' methodology applied to positive economics. But here we are dealing with an application of this analysis to a different set of questions. A simplifying assumption that is powerful and fruitful in one application of a theory may be dangerously misleading in another application.[2]

The ease with which the costs of inflation illustrated in the foregoing analysis can be removed suggest that some such problem might be present here. If the monetary authorities were to pay the equilibrium nominal interest rate available on other assets on money balances, the opportunity cost of holding the latter would be zero and the economy would be in a state of Pareto optimality at any rate of inflation. In the special case which I have explicitly

[1] In referring to this application to welfare economics as 'normative' I am following what I believe is common usage. Note, however, that, at least at the level of the individual, propositions about the effects of particular changes on consumer's surplus are in principle testable. One can conceive of offering a subject the choice between positive or negative compensation and a change on the one hand, and neither compensation nor change on the other, and observe the outcome. The main point in the present context is not that this application to welfare economics is normative, but that it involves an area beyond the empirical scope of the theoretical framework as originally conceived.

[2] Friedman's methodology is the methodology of a practitioner, rather than of a detached observer of economics, as Alan Coddington has stressed to me. But the pragmatism that rightly leads one to the view that the behaviour of an expert billiard player at the billiard table can usefully be predicted by analysing it as if he were an expert mathematician can cause trouble if it also leads one to predict the same billiard player's performance in a mathematics examination on a similar basis.

analysed, it would suffice that newly printed nominal balances found their way into circulation as interest payments on existing money balances to ensure that inflation had no costs. In general this means of financing interest payments on money would not do, of course, but other methods are not hard to devise.[1] If we take the foregoing analysis seriously as an account of the social damage done by anticipated inflation, any economy which has long undergone inflation at a more or less stable rate can avoid damage from letting inflation continue simply by paying interest on its money stock at the appropriate rate. Though we might find widespread agreement that such a step would help matters, it is hard to believe that there are many who would think that such a step would make inflation irrelevant.

Now some of the scepticism about the ease with which the above analysis suggests the costs of inflation can be removed arises from the fact that a model such as we have been considering starts from a situation in which everything except the rate of return on real balances is already adjusted to inflation. Implicitly it deals with an economy in which taxes and transfers are fully indexed and in which the rates of return on all other nominal assets are fully adjusted to inflation. For the latter condition to hold, term structure of accurate inflationary expectations must be built into the term structure of nominal interest rates, and have been built into it for sufficiently long that no holder of a maturing or soon to mature long-term asset will receive *ex post* a real return that differs in any way from that which he expected to receive *ex ante* when he purchased the asset. To meet these conditions is a tall order and it is clear why proposals for widespread indexation must be a necessary accompaniment to any proposal for living with inflation that rests on the proposition that the welfare loss associated with a less than optimal quantity of money is the only cost of living with inflation. Even so, there are other problems here to which I now turn in more detail.

III. AN ALTERNATIVE VIEW OF THE ROLE OF MONEY AND ITS IMPLICATIONS FOR THE NEOCLASSICAL ANALYSIS

As we have seen, the analysis of the welfare costs of anticipated inflation is based on a theory that, in treating money as a 'temporary abode of purchasing power', emphasises its traditional properties in a store of value role. It views money as a durable good that yields an undefined amenity flow to its owner in a way that makes money exactly parallel to a refrigerator or a piece of sculpture. There is no doubt that this approach has proved extremely fruitful in generating useful predictions about aggregate demand for money functions of the type used in short run macroeconomic models. However, consider the archetypical isolated economic agent Robinson Crusoe: he might obtain a flow

[1] Indeed it would only do in a golden age. In other cases we can think of interest payments being financed out of the receipts of lump sum taxes, or out of revenue generated for the monetary authorities by productive assets which they may, in the past, have purchased with newly created money.

of services from a refrigerator or from a piece of sculpture and hence demand one, but not from a 'temporary abode of purchasing power'. It would be absurd to postulate that he would demand real balances because they yielded him an amenity flow. Money's desirability as a store of value derives from its role as a means of exchange and exchange requires more than one agent in the economy. Even two agents would gain nothing from abandoning barter. It is only when indirect trade becomes a possibility that there is any gain to be had from adopting one particular item as a generally accepted means of exchange.

Money is inherently a social phenomenon, and yet the monetary theory on which our welfare analysis of inflation is based treats it as if money holding were a purely private affair. In dealing with money holding and the welfare it generates on a per head basis, we implicitly take it for granted that the economic welfare generated for any individual agent by his own money holdings is the only welfare produced by them, that the social product of the money stock is simply the sum of the private products accruing to the individual holders of its components. I would suggest, to the contrary, that there is something of the nature of a public good about money, and that we should be wary indeed of treating the sum of its private products as its social product. In order to develop further the conjecture that there are externalities in the consumption of money's services, let us look at those theories of the demand for money that emphasise its means of exchange role, theories of the transactions and precautionary demand for money.

The most popular transactions demand model, the so-called Baumol–Tobin inventory approach, is not helpful here. Appealing though it is at the level of the individual agent, this analysis makes little sense at an aggregate level.[1] A more useful approach to the problem is to be found in the work of Brunner and Meltzer [5] and Patinkin [16]. The former analyse the social productivity of money, showing that the existence of a universally accepted means of exchange enables those involved in a market economy to realise the gains from trade at less resource cost than in its absence. They argue that, by holding an inventory of money balances, the individual provides himself with a buffer stock of a readily tradeable commodity that enables him to carry out his market ac-

[1] Though this analysis deals with money holding as a means of reducing transactions costs, the costs in question are those that arise in trading between money itself and interest bearing assets, and not in trading among goods. In the aggregate this approach would have half the economy making continuous payments and receiving receipts at discrete intervals, and vice versa for the other half. To get the whole money stock continuously held, the continuous receivers would have to take cash to the bank to exchange for bonds at the same moment that the continuous payers took bonds to the bank in exchange for money. The economy could, in short, dispense with the bank, and having done that could achieve a further resource saving by adopting interest-earning bonds as its means of exchange. Baumol–Tobin 'money' has no social role to play and those approaches to the analysis of the welfare economics of a money economy such as Barro [3] or Feige and Parkin [8] that are based on this theory do not seem to be any more soundly based than those which take Friedman's analysis of the demand for money as their starting point.

tivity on the basis of less information about the structure of prices than he would require in its absence. Such information is costly to generate, and money holding enables the individual to economise on its acquisition.[1]

Now clearly when there is uncertainty about the behaviour of trading partners, about what goods are going to be available when and at what prices, there is going to be a stochastic element to the timing of any individual's pattern of payments and receipts. Patinkin makes such a stochastic element the basis of his theory of the demand for money by arguing that inability to make a payment when it is called for imposes costs in terms of embarrassment on the individual. To this we may add that running out of cash unexpectedly is not only embarrassing but costly in other ways as well. It can lead to the unexpected cancellation of transactions plans that would have generated gains had they been followed through, and/or to costly sales of less liquid assets to replenish money holdings.[2]

To approach the analysis of the demand for money along these lines makes it easy enough to see where externalities may arise from money holding. The random element that is present in any one individual's pattern of payments and receipts must arise from the decisions and actions of other agents. The more real balances other agents hold on average, the less likely is it that they will be unable to make a purchase that they would normally have undertaken, or that they will delay in handing over cash when presented with a bill. Moreover, the less likely is it that they will unexpectedly present a bill of their own, or perhaps call in a debt, to replenish an unexpected shortfall in their own cash balances. Thus any one agent, holding cash balances of a given average size, is less likely to incur the costs of temporarily running out of cash, the larger are the average balances of those with whom he trades. Any one agent's cash balances produce services not just for himself then, but for all other agents with whom his market activities might bring him into contact.

On the foregoing argument, the social productivity of the money stock is higher than its private productivity and it is of course changes in the social productivity of money that are important as far as the assessment of the welfare costs of inflation is concerned. The conventional neoclassical analysis of those costs, set out in the previous section of this paper, deals only with the effects of inflation on the private productivity of the money stock and therefore underestimates the welfare costs of anticipated inflation. This is not the only way in which it does so, as we shall now see.

The conventional analysis developed earlier takes it for granted that the number of economic agents in the economy is exogenously given, but the term economic agent is vague to the point of ambiguity. Much of the literature on

[1] I have gone into this analysis in much more detail in Laidler [14].

[2] Patinkin does not add these riders because, in his analysis, trade among goods takes place, at equilibrium prices, before agents settle up in terms of money. Models of the demand for money based on a stochastic element in the pattern of payments and receipts have, of course, received much development since Patinkin's work. A survey of more recent work is to be found in Orr [15].

money and economic welfare deals with the determination of output per head, and analyses the determinants of the demand for money per head; in doing so it unquestioningly identifies the biological individual as the relevant economic agent. From the point of view of monetary theory this will hardly do.[1] It is firms and households whose activities are co-ordinated through markets in which money functions as a means of exchange. The activities of individuals within those institutions are co-ordinated on a different basis. In a market economy individuals voluntarily join firms, households and other institutions and it is now four decades since Coase [7] pointed out that the question as to whether particular activities would be co-ordinated within an institution – specifically a firm in his case – on a command basis, or between institutions or institutions and individuals on a market basis, would depend upon the relative costs and benefits associated with these alternative means of organisation.

Now clearly, one of the costs associated with co-ordinating activities through markets rather than within institutions is the cost of holding money. If inflation, even fully and correctly anticipated inflation, increases those costs, then it is to be expected that, on the margin, some activities which from the social point of view would be better co-ordinated through markets, will instead be organised on some other basis, either within larger firms than might otherwise exist, or within cartel arrangements, or by resort to one form or another of government planning. Thus it is not only that, in the presence of inflation, existing agents will receive a smaller amenity flow from their cash balances and will have to spend more time and trouble planning their economic activities; it is also likely that there will be fewer agents participating in market activities. Thus there is a further potential loss of economic welfare arising from anticipated inflation that results from society's devoting real resources to the organisation of economic activity within institutions, activities that would, in the absence of inflation, be more cheaply organised on a market basis. This again is a matter of which neoclassical monetary theory takes no

[1] Subsequent work and discussion with colleagues has convinced me that this conclusion is at least too hastily drawn and at worst misleading. If the foregoing discussion of the nature of the demand for money function is correct, then it would be the case that, as the rate of inflation increased, any one agent would both move up his demand for money function, and experience it shifting out to the right as all other agents reduced their demand for money. The observed change in his money holdings would be the combined result of these two effects. Thus the estimated aggregate demand for money function that is used in obtaining empirical estimates of the welfare costs of inflation would presumably reflect the effects of interdependence between agents in the consumption of money's services discussed above. The question still arises, however, as to the relationship between the area under a portion of such an aggregate demand for money function, and the Marshallian consumer surplus concept, that would permit us to interpret this area as giving a quantitative estimate of the welfare cost of inflation.

I am grateful to David Burton, Jo Anna Gray and Milton Friedman for discussion of this point.

account in attempting to measure the resource costs of anticipated inflation.[1]

The potential effects of anticipated inflation on the efficiency of the monetary system which we have been considering so far all arise from anticipated inflation making it more expensive to hold real balances. Our analysis has money becoming less productive overall as a result of inflation because the economy uses less money and not because anticipated inflation actually impairs its productivity. Thus the damage to the monetary system that we have been discussing in the last few pages, though additional to the costs of anticipated inflation upon which conventional monetary theory focuses, may nevertheless presumably be avoided by the conventional remedy of paying interest at an appropriate rate on money balances. Now it is widely recognised that inflation, which is less than perfectly anticipated, undermines money's social productivity by making it a less efficient substitute for devoting resources to the generation of information upon which plans can be based. Even in a state of perfectly anticipated inflation, however, there seems to be scope for such an effect, for there to occur shifts of, as well as movements along, what might be termed the marginal social product of real balances schedule. The problem here is best seen by focusing on money's role as a unit of account.

Money is the item universally acceptable in exchange for any commodity, and it is economic for all traders to state the price of the goods they have to sell, or wish to purchase, relative to money, the item they intend to exchange them for. Thus money's unit of account function is closely related to its role as a means of exchange. I would argue that inflation makes money less productive because it makes less reliable and more difficult to interpret the information about *relative* prices contained in the array of *money* prices about which any agent may have information. To say this, of course, is in some sense to call into question the very notion of 'perfectly anticipated' inflation upon which conventional analysis is based and which has underlain our discussion so far in this paper.

It is customary to discuss 'the general price level' when talking about inflation, and the analysis with which we began this essay treats that concept as if it were the price in terms of money of a single good; but of course it is not, it is an index number. By 'perfectly anticipated inflation' we must mean that the rate of change of that index number is correctly foreseen over every relevant time horizon and that this foresight is acted upon. In an economy in which there were no reasons for relative prices to change over time, a continuous upward change in the money price of each good at an equal rate would be consistent with a fully anticipated inflation, as would continuous changes at different rates in the money prices of goods, holding the rate of change of the price index constant, in an economy in which relative prices were changing.

[1] And although I have stressed only the economic aspects of the above arguments, they clearly have strong political overtones. In their light, it is not difficult to understand why it is that those who have most faith in the market mechanism as a desirable form of socioeconomic organisation also seem to have the strongest objections to inflation.

The analysis we have carried out so far of the consequences of inflation would be adequate to deal with cases such as these.

But what about the resource costs of changing prices, and of disseminating information about their having changed? If such costs did not exist then the view of money's social role which underlies this essay would tell us that money would not exist, and without money there could hardly be inflation. Thus it is difficult to defend ignoring these costs on the grounds of analytic simplicity when dealing with inflation, but that is what we have, in effect, been doing.[1]

Part of the appropriate response to this problem is to note that economic agents do in fact have to devote real resources to changing prices and to disseminating and collecting information about them, and that, to the extent that there are more changes in money prices during inflation, the extra costs associated with making them are part of the overall cost of inflation. However, the matter goes a little deeper than this. The costs of changing a price and of spreading information about such a change do not depend upon the size of the price change in question. Barro [3] has shown that, in such conditions, the present-value maximising firm will vary the price of its output in discrete steps in response to a continuous shift in the demand curve facing it. This would imply that, during an inflation, firms will change their output prices discretely and also perhaps that input prices will rise in discrete steps. There is no reason to suppose that the timing of such price changes will be co-ordinated across firms and industries.

It is thus perfectly possible that the overall value of an economy's general price index can change at a continuous and perfectly foreseen rate while the pattern of relative prices underlying it fluctuates as different firms and industries change their output prices at different moments. Such inflation induced fluctuation in the pattern of relative prices would both reduce the amount of information about relative prices to be generated from any particular sampling of money prices, and it would also open up incentives for the devotion of resources to speculative activity that would not exist in the absence of inflation.[2] The social productivity of the monetary mechanism as a means of co-ordinating economic activity is thus potentially further reduced by inflation in yet another way that is overlooked by conventional analysis and there are further incentives implicit here towards the organisation of economic activity

[1] Resource costs of obtaining and disseminating information about prices lie at the root of Brunner and Meltzer's analysis of the productivity of money. I have gone into this matter in much more detail in Laidler [13]. Note that Genberg and Swoboda [11] deal with the implications of these and related matters in the context of the debate over indexation.

[2] Of course speculative activity would tend to reduce such fluctuations in relative prices, but at a real resource cost. Uncertainties about the time path of prices are recognised to lie at the root of much of the damage that so-called unanticipated inflation can do. The above arguments, in suggesting that they might be present even when the time path of the overall price index is fully anticipated, perhaps provide a basis for a closer integration than we have previously seen of the analysis.

by non-market mechanisms.[1] Moreover, the costs in question here are not such as can be avoided by paying interest on money in an otherwise fully indexed economy. Indeed the resource costs of indexing taxes and transfers, the scope for tax avoidance and such that would be opened up by changes in tax rates inevitably being made at discrete intervals, not to mention the difficulties of devising means whereby interest could effectively be paid on money, particularly on currency, are particular examples of the types of costs we have just been discussing. In an inflationary economy it might be preferable to incur these costs than not to do so, but the absence of inflation would be a still more preferable state of affairs.

IV. SOME CONCLUSIONS

It now remains to summarise the arguments presented in this paper. Inflation has now become deeply embedded in the economic system, and there seems little prospect of ridding ourselves of it without generating significant unemployment for a substantial period of time. In the light of this, the alternative of living with inflation is certainly worth considering and is not without its advocates. No-one suggests that living with inflation would be costless, but there is a large body of literature whose principal conclusion is that, once inflation has become fully anticipated, its only costs arise from the inefficiency in the monetary mechanism which the incentives to economy in holding real balances, inherent in anticipated inflation, lead to. This literature also suggests that these costs may be measured in terms of the appropriate area under the aggregate demand for real balances function.

It has been the burden of this essay to argue that this approach to assessing the costs of living with anticipated inflation misses many aspects of these costs and that it does so because it overstretches the applicability of the assumption that the role of money in the economic system may be analysed as if money was simply a durable good yielding a flow of services to those who hold it. This assumption is powerful in generating predictions about what arguments belong in the demand for money function, and in organising analysis of the role of the quantity of money in short-run stabilisation policy, but is potentially misleading in the present application. Consideration of analysis which pays more explicit attention to the specific functions of money in the economic system points to at least three aspects of the potential costs of anticipated inflation that orthodox neoclassical analysis overlooks. First there is reason to believe that there are externalities in the consumption of money's services: that the social losses from individual agent's economising on cash balances in the face of inflation are greater than the sum of the private losses. Second, a market mechanism that uses money is by no means universal as a way of co-ordinating the economic activities of individuals. The more costly is money to use, the more aspects of economic activity are likely to be organ-

[1] Again, therefore, there are political overtones to these arguments, cf. footnote 1 on p. 319.

ised on some more costly alternative, non-market basis. This tendency also arises in the context of the third potential problem with inflation raised in this paper – namely the possibility that relative prices fluctuate as a result of inflation itself, even if the overall rate of inflation is completely stable and predictable. Such fluctuations would also tend to undermine the effectiveness of market mechanisms based on the use of money as a means of organising economic activity.

Now it should go without saying that the above arguments are tentative. I have presented no evidence which would enable anyone to judge their quantitative significance. However, although the ideas in question are not sufficiently developed in this paper immediately to be susceptible to empirical tests of their importance, there is no reason why they cannot be so developed. They do, after all, potentially have implications about merger activity and its relationship to inflation, about the behaviour of relative prices during inflation, and so on.

With further work, we ought to be able both to derive such implications more precisely and subject them to test. The only excuse for not doing so here can be that one can only accomplish so much in one paper. Nevertheless, if this essay convinces the reader that the ideas contained in it are worth further development so that their empirical importance can better be assessed, and that, pending such further development, he should be wary indeed of accepting orthodox neoclassical measures of the welfare costs of anticipated inflation as being well founded or in any way comprehensive, it has fulfilled its purpose.

REFERENCES

[1] A. A. Alchian, 'Information Costs, Pricing and Resource Unemployment' in E. S. Phelps *et al.*, *The Microeconomic Foundations of Employment and Inflation Theory* (New York: Norton, 1970).

[2] M. J. Bailey, 'The Welfare Cost of Inflationary Finance', *Journal of Political Economy*, Vol. 64, pp. 93–110 (1956).

[3] R. J. Barro, 'A Theory of Monopolistic Price Adjustment', *Review of Economic Studies*, Vol. 39, pp. 17–26 (1972).

[4] R. J. Barro, 'Inflationary Finance and the Welfare Cost of Inflation', *Journal of Political Economy*, Vol. 80, pp. 978–1001 (1972).

[5] K. Brunner and A. H. Meltzer, 'The Uses of Money – Money in the Theory of an Exchange Economy', *American Economic Review*, Vol. 61, pp. 784–805 (1971).

[6] R. W. Clower, 'Reconsideration of the Microfoundations of Monetary Theory', *Western Economic Journal*, Vol. 6, pp. 1–8 (1967).

[7] R. Coase, 'The Nature of the Firm' in A.E.A. *Readings in Price Theory* (Homewood, Ill.: Richard D. Irwin, 1972) (First published *Economica*, 1937).

[8] E. Feige and J. M. Parkin, 'The Optimal Quantity of Money, Bonds, Commodity Inventories and Capital', *American Economic Review*, Vol. 61, pp. 335–49 (1971).

[9] M. Friedman, 'The Methodology of Positive Economics' in M. Friedman (ed.), *Essays in Positive Economics* (Chicago: University of Chicago Press, 1953).

[10] M. Friedman, 'The Quantity Theory of Money – A Restatement' in M. Friedman (ed.), *Studies in the Quantity Theory of Money* (Chicago: University of Chicago Press, 1967).

[11] H. Genberg and A. K. Swoboda, 'Inflation and Indexation: A Survey of the Issues', in *Indexation and Protection against Inflation and Exchange Rate Risk,* Stockholm, 1974

[12] D. Jaffee and E. Kleiman, 'The Welfare Costs of Variable Inflation', Paper given at the I.E.A. Conference on Inflation Theory and Anti-Inflation Policy, Saltsjöbaden Sweden (August–September, 1975) (see Chapter 11 of this book).

[13] D. Laidler, 'Information, Money, and the Macroeconomics of Inflation', *Swedish Economic Journal*, Vol. 76, pp. 26–41 (1974).

[14] D. Laidler, 'Monetary Expansion and the Revenue of the Monetary Authority A Geometric Exposition', University of Manchester Inflation Workshop Discussion Paper 7510 (mimeo).

[15] D. Orr, *Cash Management and the Demand for Money* (Pall Mall Press, 1971).

[16] D. Patinkin, *Money, Interest and Prices* (Evanston, Ill.: Row Peterssen, 1956) (2nd ed., New York: Harper and Row, 1965).

[17] L. C. Robbins, *An Essay on the Nature and Significance of Economic Science*, 2nd ed. (London: Macmillan, 1935).

[18] M. Sidrauski, 'Rational Choice and Patterns of Growth in a Monetary Economy', *American Economic Review*, Vol. 57, pp. 534–44 (1967).

Discussion of the Paper by David Laidler

Mr Brenner said the paper continued the theme of the Kleiman–Jaffee paper. In the first part, Professor Laidler defined his aim as to argue that the neoclassical analysis of the welfare costs of anticipated inflation underestimated those costs. It did so because it concentrated on money's role as a means of exchange and a unit of account. There were two further costs, not taken into consideration – which Professor Laidler did not take into consideration either. These were: (1) the cost of eliminating inflation, which included misallocation of resources (unemployment, for example); and (2) the cost associated with unexpected and unanticipated inflation.

The second part of the paper gave a brief summary of the neoclassical theory. The author emphasised that this theory treated money as a 'temporary abode of purchasing power', so that it was this role which caused the welfare costs associated with inflation. This served as Professor Laidler's point of departure.

His first argument was this. One agent's cash balances produced services not only for himself but for all other agents. Consequently, any attempt to economise on real money balances during inflationary periods might cause an unexpected cancellation of transactions. One consequence of this was that the social productivity of money was higher than its private productivity. So, even if inflation was correctly anticipated (which was the case in neoclassical theory) the increasing costs of holding money might cause organisational changes. Larger firms might set up cartel arrangements, or there might be governmental intervention in an attempt to save those unnecessary costs by returning to a barter system in some markets (but this again had its costs).

Professor Laidler's second point was his assumption that inflation itself caused perpetual change in relative prices. Though he did not explain why this process happened, Professor Laidler pointed out that it undermined the effectiveness of money as a means of organising economic activity.

Mr Brenner wished to begin the discussion by making the following comments:

(1) The paper attempted to provide a basis for introducing money into welfare analysis. However, the model was not well defined. Money had a meaning in the context either of uncertainty or of transaction costs, but Professor Laidler treated neither of them.

(2) In the neoclassical model as Professor Laidler described it, output was independent of anything that might happen in the money market. The question was thus, what was the cost of inflation?

(3) One way Professor Laidler proposed to live with inflation was by paying a nominal interest rate on money equal to the rate of inflation. This meant indexation, but again the problem was not fully analysed. The following quotations from the paper were examples of what Mr Brenner had in mind:

(a) 'unanticipated inflation is also relatively costless to cure'. Indexation was the treatment for such an inflation, but the very fact that it did not appear in free markets meant that it was not costless.

(b) 'an economy can avoid damage from letting inflation continue, simply by paying interest on its money stock at the appropriate rate'. The meaning of this was that everything would be indexed, so that inflation was meaningless.

Professor Laidler did not seem to notice that this scheme of indexation would be appropriate for an economy in which no real changes were taking place. The problem was that such changes were occurring together with monetary ones. So again, the source of the change in relative prices was not clear. Perhaps Professor Laidler could clarify these points.

Professor Laidler replied that greater subtlety had been attributed to what he had written than he had intended. He was dealing only with expectations in the Phillips-curve context. One had to take control of inflation before expectations got built into the wage and price-fixing processes. If one did so, one could then reduce inflation with less unemployment than otherwise.

There was an undertone to the paper that Chicago monetary theory was out of its depth on welfare issues. This related to the 'as if' methodology used in such work.

Professor Liviatan commented that when one spoke of welfare losses, some of these were not attributable to inflation as such. For example, while one might use inflation as a tax to transfer resources from the public to the private sector, this was not a welfare loss but taxation. A welfare loss must be a different phenomenon. Loss from miscalculation was part of the more general idea that inflation led to uncertainty and that people could not adjust to it at once.

Perhaps one could look at the matter in this way, and say that the welfare loss was an unintended loss for the public. If the government wanted to confuse the public as much as possible, one then had a game problem between the public and the government. For example, suppose there was a random change in the money supply. What could the public do to defend itself? The problem of adjustment was a public loss, but some theory, for example a paper by Samuelson in the *Quarterly Journal of Economics*, argued that introducing randomness was a bad thing. What Professor Laidler said about the transaction problem was similar. Once inflation had gone on for some time, the public adjusted to it more and more.

Professor Patinkin noted that the paper argued that though the theory emphasised the loss on money as a store of value, this was not equally true for money used for transaction purposes. Most discussions of welfare losses came to exactly the opposite conclusion. There were many substitutes for money as a store of value and the more characteristic function of money was as a medium of exchange.

Professor Laidler talked of integrated firms as a new example. Professor Patinkin thought that this was the kind of thing that various writers had in mind when they discussed the shoe-leather cost of inflation: in other words, the extra efforts required to effect transactions as a consequence of economising on the holding of cash balances.[1]

Professor Patinkin had been brought up to fear consumer surplus and its related triangles, unless applied to an analysis of unimportant goods. He therefore wondered about the validity of using the triangles for such an important good as money.

Professor Laidler claimed that consumer surplus had a unique value given

[1] Cf. for example, Milton Friedman, *The Optimum Quantity of Money and Other Essays* (Aldine Press: Chicago, 1969), page 14; also D. Levhari and D. Patinkin, 'The Role of Money in a Simple Growth Model', *American Economic Review*, LVIII (1968), page 737–38.

by the area under the individual's demand curve for a particular good. But this was so only on the quite stringent assumptions that the marginal utility of all other goods to the individual was constant, and that it was also independent of the quantity of the good under analysis being consumed. In the next sentence, Professor Laidler said this problem did not arise in the exercise in his paper because the model he had chosen to use was one in which money was neutral. So there was no question of variations in the inflation rate affecting the quantities of real output produced and consumed, and hence influencing the utility of money's services. Where, then, was the welfare loss of inflation? If real output was not affected, what was the paper about?

Professor Laidler argued that this was a purely semantic point. He agreed that there was room for differences about the use of consumer surplus in relation to money. All he meant here was that the use of partial equilibrium analysis swept this problem under the table. With general equilibrium analysis, there were problems over what happened if money was not neutral. He had left all this out in order to simplify the paper. His model had argued that consumer surplus could be looked at in terms of behaviour on the margin of substitution between leisure and trading.

Professor Patinkin replied that this was not a semantic point. In inflation one had perhaps to work an eight-hour day and then spend several additional hours using up shoe leather in order to effect transactions.

Professor Laidler replied that this did affect consumer surplus.

Professor Patinkin felt that it invalidated the whole triangle.

Professor Fischer was not sure what the externality was in holding money. Suppose there were no uncertainty and that one was working in the context of the demand for money, as in the Baumol–Tobin analysis.[1] In these circumstances, no-one ran out of money. They simply went to the bank more often. So what was the externality?

With a well-developed capital market, the economy would not necessarily be unstable with indexation, because the monetary authority could undertake offsetting open market operations.

Mr Brenner argued that if one went to the bank more often, someone else was holding more money. As for relative prices, Professor Laidler argued that inflation should be defined in terms of relative prices.

Professor Swoboda noted that the argument seemed to be that the more money other people held, the greater was the social productivity of money. But, against this must be set off the fact that the more money was held, the more likely it was that someone else would make a claim on one's own resources, thus reducing one's future wealth. How could the two things be squared?

Professor Laidler asked how much of the welfare loss had been captured by neoclassical theory. He removed one assumption – that the actual and expected inflation rates were equal. But, even if actual and expected rates were equal, economic agents still could not hedge fully against variance. This incapacity was also not accounted for by the standard analysis. How would Professor Laidler see the relative costs of the two phenomena?

Professor Claassen wondered whether one should perhaps conceive of money as a production factor. He was not arguing that it should be conceived

[1] W. J. Baumol, *Quarterly Journal of Economics* (1952).

of as the third or fourth factor of production, but that it should be seen as having indirect productivity. Perhaps one should divide the economy into production and transaction activities. With more money to hold, there would be less bank-visiting to do. If his own cash balances were increased, he would need less input of labour into the transaction activity, and the labour released could go either into leisure or into productive activity. Consequently, the wage rate must be one argument in the demand for money. A higher actual and expected inflation rate implied that the desired real balances would fall, so that the individual must put more input into transactions. Money became less productive.

Professor Mussa thought that the important question in dealing with the welfare cost of inflation was not whether the triangle was relevant, but rather which triangle? He suggested that there were at least five important costs which the usual triangle under the demand curve for money left out.

First, money functioned as the standard of value and the unit of account in many kinds of contracts and implicit understandings. As such, it played an important role in the way markets functioned and tended to destroy the usefulness of money in playing this role. Second, inflation almost inevitably led to social discord. Someone was always blamed for raising prices or wages and social and economic relationships became more acrimonious. Third, there were frequently attempts to stop inflation by deflationary macroeconomic policies, which often led to increased unemployment and hence to pressure for more inflationary policies. As a result, the economy went on a roller coaster ride. Fourth, inflation frequently led to price controls and wage controls which interfered with adjustments of relative prices and distorted the allocation of resources. Fifth, various institutional arrangements such as maximum interest rates on mortgages and progressive tax rates set in nominal terms were usually not adapted to an inflationary environment, or at least not adapted very rapidly. In the presence of rapid inflation, these institutional arrangements led to important misallocations such as the collapse of housing credit in the United States and the virtual destruction of the capital market in some Latin American countries.

Professor Patinkin wanted empirical evidence to show that capital markets in Latin America had been destroyed. He wondered whether developed markets of this kind had ever existed there.

Professor Duesenberry thought one ought to be quite clear what game one was talking about. He thought Professor Laidler had been looking at the hypothetical question: What loss would there be if there were pure expected inflation? He also thought that Professor Laidler wanted to distinguish this aspect from the rest of the problem.

Professor Duesenberry asked the question: What would happen if the amount of currency were negligible, and banks paid interest on demand deposits? If the rate of interest then adjusted to inflation, the bank depositor would be protected against that loss. It was not clear why anyone should make excessive efforts to economise on money, because he got his protection against inflation by operating a bank account.

Professor Laidler replied that he did give an answer in terms of three things not usually caught in welfare triangles. Two of these would be taken care of by the payment of interest on demand deposits. But on the third issue, where individual prices were moving at different times, the costs of inflation thus generated would not be taken care of by paying interest on money.

Professor Kleiman asked what situations one should compare. A given rate of inflation with a perfectly certain zero inflation? Or was it an expectations mean of zero inflation with some expected positive value of inflation? Any uncertainty had some effect on the capital market and on money as a store of value. The question was whether the uncertainty increased with the positive or negative change in the value of money.

Professor Swoboda pointed out that the information content of prices was lowered as soon as inflation was positive or negative. Hence, the hypothesis was that people found it harder to carry out economic activities with either positive or negative inflation.

Professor Liviatan thought one had to suppose that inflation was necessary to achieve some particular result. If so, one could not look at the welfare loss unless one compared the actual with some alternative policy. If one took a revealed preference approach, society wanted to solve some problems by inflation. There was thus a *prima facie* case for arguing that the gain was greater than the loss. It might be better if we had a clearer view of the alternatives.

Professor Giersch emphasised that any society with a legal order had built this order on the implicit or explicit assumption of a constant standard of value. Divergences of reality from this assumption would create a misallocation of resources and an arbitrary redistribution of income. Even society itself might disintegrate.

Professor Fischer suggested that since the aim of the conference was to understand inflation, what Professor Liviatan had said meant that we should perhaps reconsider everything we had so far discussed.

He would, however, like to point out that Professor Phelps, in a *Swedish Journal* article (1973), had already considered the inflation tax as one among potential sources of government revenue.

Professor Bronfenbrenner suggested that the effectiveness of inflation in achieving desired aims had to be seen as an offset to its costs. Inflation acted as a shock or a deviation from what was expected. One might well find that the optimal rate was positive, but certainly not as high as the current rate.

Professor Stahl thought one had to be very careful in introducing externalities. In Professor Laidler's paper, the examples were production units that were effectively examples of public industry, like electricity. This had network costs but low marginal costs of operation. Hence the optimal solution was a two-part tariff for taking part in the monetary system.

Professor Laidler thought there was a good analogy with the telephone system, which was a public good on the consumption side and therefore had similarities with money. Professor Stahl and he could talk on the telephone only if they both had telephones. The externality here was therefore important, but he was not sure how one could quantify it. However, one could not look at the problem in this way if one took money as a durable good yielding only private returns, à la Friedman, or as in the Baumol–Tobin model.

He agreed with Professor Patinkin on the danger of applying consumer surplus analysis to a generally used good like money, but there were also externalities in the use of other goods which were not captured by welfare triangles.

Professor Malinvaud reported that the International Economic Association had recently held a conference on the microfoundations of macroeconomics. Big questions arose on the cost and consequences of inflation. An important paper was given by A. Leijonhufvud on 'Costs and Consequences of Inflation'. This paper would in some ways have been more appropriate in the present conference. It looked at inflation and its legal-cum-social and political consequences. It argued that the costs of inflation were social and political as well as economic. Indeed, we might be missing something if we forced ourselves to stick to the economic cost of inflation.

Concerning social and political consequences, there were two important ideas. First, being effective at the production of real goods was less important in inflation. One had also to spend time on forecasting and coping with inflation, in ways suggested in the Kleiman–Jaffee paper. Second, inflation led people to rely less on private contracts and more on political compacts in trying to ensure for themselves a reliable frame for their economic lives.

Professor Frisch pointed out that the shoe-leather theory saw money as a standard of value, but money was not useful for transactions if there was serious inflation. One was then back to barter, which led to enormous calculation costs. In the shoe-leather model, inflation had no effect on the economy, but if one were driven back to barter, huge disadvantages would arise.

Professor Polaczek pointed out that people wanted a stable unit of account as consumers. The same was true as businessmen. If there were no stable standard of value, there would be misallocation of resources due to deviations of relative prices.

Professor Bajt felt that people might think a zero inflation rate was best, but while we might prefer this as buyers, we did not as sellers.

Professor Nussbaumer noted that money performed a specific function. If one did not have price stability, one did not know that true relative price changes had been. Anything blurring the price signals in the economy – as inflation did – hampered effective resource allocation. That must reduce welfare unless there was a negative effect on production because of the positive welfare effect on distribution, and that would be hard to prove.

Professor Mussa saw circumstances in which an increase in uncertainty concerning relative prices, due to an increase in the rate of inflation, could lead to an increase in the demand for money. But, it would be incorrect to conclude from such a circumstance that welfare had increased. For instance, one might want to carry enough cash on a trip to cover the cost of gasoline purchases. Increased uncertainty of gasoline prices would lead to larger cash holdings but not to higher welfare.

Professor Laidler thought this was a relatively simple issue. The big problem was that one could not measure consumer surplus by a triangle if the demand curve shifted. One had to remember that while decisions were taken in the present, commitments entered into were for the future. This complicated welfare measurement. With many goods and shifting prices, even if one could predict the future value of money, one might get less information from a sample of relative prices than if the price level were stable.

Professor Laidler went on to sum up the discussion at this stage. A lot of it had been on issues not emphased in the paper. The paper had tried to cover: the general question of methodology in monetary economics; different monetary theories; and the question of the welfare costs of *fully anticipated* inflation.

There was a well-developed analysis of the welfare cost of inflationary finance. It had been argued that if inflation was fully anticipated, these costs were the only ones imposed. This analysis made the costs of raising extra revenue by increasing the inflation rate look large relative to the benefits. But these same costs could be made to look small if one already had steady inflation at, say, 5 per cent per annum and was considering reducing it. It might seem better if one stayed with this inflation rate.

He would accept that the achievement of full equilibrium took a very long time and the paper set all these lags aside. The question then was whether the triangle measured what one thought was the full cost of a monetary change. The essay by Milton Friedman on *The Quantity Theory of Money* had been deliberately designed to provide a framework for empirical analysis. One could not necessarily apply this analysis immediately to welfare questions. There was a different and longstanding strand in monetary theory in the work of various people, including Hayek, that in modern terms was concerned with the precautionary demand for money holdings as a hedge against stochastic elements in the pattern of receipts and payments.

A further problem was that when one carried out conventional analysis, one spoke of demand for money per head. The question was knowing what unit one should use for the analysis. The number of economic agents was endogenous, varying with the costs of transactions in various institutional settings. Conventional neoclassical analysis did not cope with this.

Both the problems implicit here vanished if banks paid interest on cash balances, but this still left a final problem. It was not quite a question of menu costs; menus were also changed discontinuously. At any moment, when people took decisions for the future, they got less information per look at the menu than with zero inflation, because menu changes were not synchronised. This was analogous to Keynes's argument on the lack of synchronisation of wage cuts. Perhaps a command economy could cope with such a problem, but not a market one.

There were two views on the worthwhileness of attempting to quantify welfare costs. Even if one did not know quite how to do it, the problems raised in the paper might still be of interest. He had flown a kite, though some people in the conference appeared to think he should have flown a different one.

Mr Brenner wanted to note one problem on zero inflation. It was not so much that one needed a zero inflation rate as that one needed a stable rate of price increase. If one had a stable inflation rate, there was no need for indexed bonds. Why, then, should one separate out the zero inflation rate for special analysis?

Professor Laidler agreed that unanticipated inflation was worse than anticipated inflation, but even if we could predict the rate of inflation, we could still have trouble over relative prices.

Professor Neumark noted that Mr Brenner said that with a stable rate of inflation there was no need for indexation. But indexation of what?

Mr Brenner replied that he meant indexation of wages, taxation, pensions, etc.

Professor Neumark pointed out that with a progressive tax system, even a stable rate of inflation would distort the distribution of tax burdens.

Professor Laidler took the view that the real problem was that expected and anticipated inflation were not synonymous. Anticipated inflation was both expected and fully adjusted to. So an economy with fully anticipated inflation must be one where all elements except money holdings were indexed.

Professor Bronfenbrenner wondered whether a simple diagram (figure 12.2) would help. On the horizontal axis one had the difference between the actual and expected inflation rate. On the vertical axis, one had some proxy – whatever it might be – for social conflict. There was a wide range where people could be mollified if there was disagreement on what was offered, allowing for some illusions. But it was more likely that a wide divergence between the actual and expected inflation rate would exacerbate conflicts. One could consider these two cases in the same diagram.

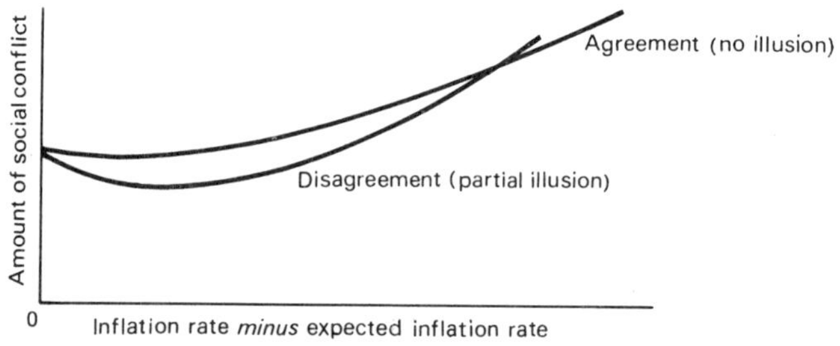

Fig. 12.2

Professor Duesenberry wanted to look at the comparison between zero and positive inflation rates, but in terms of the anticipated rate of inflation. With a positive rate of inflation, the social cost was the menu cost because the average cost of printing was higher. If printing had to adapt to relative and absolute price changes, relative changes might be delayed with positive inflation. The social cost was the menu one – which got greater information from more recent relative prices. But even a stable rate of inflation called for more arithmetic, because one had to multiply current prices by one-point-something to find out what would happen next week.

Professor Bronfenbrenner thought that much of the discussion brought us back to the distinction which Professor Lundberg had mentioned between the 'sharpies' and the 'suckers'. We disliked the sharpies most.

Professor Rehn stressed that inflation drew intellectual and economic resources away from productive use to the generation of income and wealth for some individuals in all classes, at the cost of others. The numerous resulting inequities and injustices undermined the moral foundations of the social system. Western societies might have to suffer from the consequences during an indeterminate future period. 'Hate inflation' remained a valid slogan.

Professor Parkin talked about the cost of anticipated inflation. With a zero expected inflation rate, an economy which was continuously shocked by random events would still have no clear relative price structure. If one tried to calculate the dispersion of this distribution, differences could not be the result of changes in the speed of inflation. Real factors changed relative prices.

If one had a positive expected rate of inflation, but it was costly to print menus, perhaps the dispersion of prices would be bigger. Then there was an incentive to change prices less frequently and in bigger jumps. If more dispersion led to more search effort, this was a cost of fully expected inflation.

Professor Laidler emphasised that he was not necessarily implying that one printed more menus. Each individual firm printed one menu, and consumers had to sample them. There was no social co-ordination of menu printing. 'Sharpies' were too valuable to be given this job.

13 Effects of Inflation on Public Revenue and Expenditure

F. Neumark

J. W. GOETHE – UNIVERSITY, FRANKFURT/MAIN

I. INTRODUCTORY REMARKS

Some recent publications and official documents referring to the repercussions of inflation on public households create the impression of some sort of roulette gambling, rather than describing an interplay of economic actions and reactions with a more or less predictable outcome. This is a new phenomenon, since in the past the prevailing thought of economists and politicians was the conviction that, eventually, government would come out as the winner in the game. Today, one recognises that striking a balance between budgetary losses and gains from inflationary processes is a very difficult and complicated task. It is not astonishing, therefore, that the results of theoretical and empirical studies on these issues differ considerably.

Of course, one must not overlook the fact that in comparison with the good (or rather bad) old times, nearly all factors determining the influence of inflation on public revenues and expenditures have changed. Until, say, a century ago, the great majority of inflationary processes were primarily attributable to the financial behaviour of government, particularly by autocratic sovereigns pretending to represent 'the state'. Contemporary inflation, at least as far as European and northern American countries are concerned, cannot be said to be the sole or principal result of princely ostentation and/or warfare, although it is of course not independent of fiscal policy. Neither does the technique of modern inflation predominantly consist of the issue of non-convertible paper money or the clipping of coins, and similar methods. On the expenditure side, government losses from inflation were formerly rather small since civil servants, soldiers etc. were paid unchanged nominal amounts in debased money. The same was true for interest payments, provided government did not simply take recourse to repudiation, in other words, bankruptcy. Thus, in earlier times, inflation probably always brought about a net gain for government (though hardly for the economy as a whole). At present, the final result may be quite different, depending on various factors such as the strength and length of the inflationary process, the amount of outstanding debt, the structure of the tax system and the composition of public expenditures, etc. Needless to say that all these factors reflect the sociopolitical forces behind the scene which influence government's personnel and wage policy, its procurement practices, social security policy, and the struggle for balancing monetary stability against full employment.

II. EFFECTS OF INFLATION ON PUBLIC REVENUE

Beginning with the *revenue* side, possible gains for the public houshold resulting from the issue of fiduciary currency shall be left aside. In principle, the following remarks are confined to taxes in view of the fact that today, taxation yields more than 90 per cent of government revenues. However, a few words about *non-tax revenue* seem to be called for, prior to a discussion of taxes.

(1) NON-TAX REVENUE

Such revenues still play a significant role within the framework of numerous local government budgets but have, for a long time, lost their previous importance at the state and/or federal level. They consist mainly of fees, charges, and utility revenues. With respect to fees, it suffices to mention that they follow the course of inflation – if at all – with a considerable lag so that governments suffer a loss from this revenue source. In principle, the same is true of commercial revenues, with the possible exception of some utility services, particularly those found at the local government level. The most striking examples of the influence of inflationary forces on governmental commercial or semicommercial activities, however, can be found with state (federal) railways and the postal service. Whereas until the second decade of this century, state railway companies in several countries such as Prussia and Saxonia, yielded important net profits and thus formed a major revenue source in state budgets, since then they have become a heavy burden on them. This was already true in periods of reasonable monetary stability, but due to inflation and the unsatisfactory reaction to it by railway managements today, in France, Germany and elsewhere the burden has reached an almost unbearable size. In fact, in the Federal Republic of Germany, the federal government in 1975 will have to cover a railway deficit amounting to more than 10 billion deutschmarks. A similar, though by far not as important, development can be observed with regard to the postal services which almost everywhere have become a source of negative revenue. The main reason for these negative trends may be seen in the fact that in the modern welfare state, the electorate is no more willing to pay charges which, if not leaving a profit for government as until half a century ago, would at least cover the current total cost and perhaps part of outlays for investment. The same holds true of several other services at the state or local government level. Nowadays in periods of strong inflation, the reluctance to adjust charges to rising costs is much larger with public enterprises than with private firms thus causing specific, additional net losses because of time-lags. In the case of stagflation, the effects of retarded adaption are accentuated by the fact that public authorities try to avoid improvements in efficiency which would result in the dismissal of employees and workers. In any event, even aside from changes in the price and/or wage structure which, as we shall see later, may be very disadvantageous to government, the net result of the attitude of public commercial services just outlined brings about a serious worsening of a financial situation which was rather precarious even in times of a modest increase in the price level.

In conclusion, therefore, inflation has definite negative repercussions on many public enterprises and consequently on public budgets. An additional result is that the proportion of taxes on the one hand, and fees, charges and public utility revenues on the other will change in favour of taxes. Whether this is desirable or not is another question. To my mind, the general answer has to be no, although I admit that in some cases, special benefit taxes may be preferable to charges for public services and also to the common forms of taxes, in other words to those not levied on a *quid pro quo* basis. Especially with respect to local transportation enterprises, I believe that in an affluent society the great majority of people using such services are able to pay cost-covering charges and therefore should do so; as for the really poor segment, one could assist these people by individual social subsidies. For the remainder, it seems important that the adaptation of fares to cost inflation is made as fast as possible.

(2) EFFECTS OF INFLATION ON TAXES

These effects depend among other on the form of individual taxes and the structure of the overall tax system, the techniques of collecting as well as those of assessment and control, the quality of fiscal administration, and, of course, the strength and tempo of the inflationary process.

(1) Although nowadays in most Western countries, or at least the larger ones, so-called *indirect taxes* are no longer the most important tax category budgetwise, they cannot of course be neglected if one wants to obtain a correct picture of the interplay of inflation and taxation.

As far as *specific*, or unit, *taxes* are concerned, it is evident that with respect to them, government will *lose* from inflation. Other things being equal, the real burden of such taxes is doomed to decrease if one assumes that the prices of the taxed products will more or less follow the general trend of price rise. Abstracting from the not very realistic case that because of the lightening of tax burden, the relative price of the goods concerned will decline and therefore, given a rather high elasticity of substitution, the volume of their sales will go up correspondingly, one may conclude that the relative budgetary importance of unit taxes will diminish with stronger and/or more persistent inflationary pressure. In the majority of developed economies this kind of tax is in any case losing its fiscal importance. However, there still exist some countries, such as Switzerland, where, particularly at the federal level, revenue from specific taxes (custom duties included) experiences a major loss in times of inflation; this is not surprising since nearly 40 per cent of Swiss federal revenue comes from such duties.

Very much more important than specific taxes are *ad valorem taxes*, first of all in countries levying a general turnover or a net value-added tax of the consumption type. I leave aside, because of lack of space, such interesting questions as the possible effects of inflation on the distribution of disposable income among (taxable) consumption goods and savings on the one hand, and the problem of inflation-induced differentials in price movements of investment goods and consumer goods on the other hand. We may assume that *ad valorem* taxes will cause *neither gains nor losses* for the public household that can be attributed to inflation – in this regard, then, they are 'neutral'.[1] From this, we may also deduce that the yield elasticity of a net value added tax will not be affected by fluctuations of the general price level; in other words, even in periods of inflationary pressure, it remains constant namely about 1.

(2) Those taxes which are the most sensitive to changes in the purchasing power of money are *personal* (or *direct*) *taxes*, particularly *progressive* ones.

Among them, at present, the *individual income tax* is of paramount importance both from the economic and the fiscal point of view. Nevertheless, even among Western countries, there still exist great differences in this regard, as for example between France and Italy on the one hand, the United States, Great Britain, Germany, Holland, and the Scandinavian countries on the other hand. In any event, nowadays, overall tax revenue as a rule depends to a percentage varying between about 40 and 60 per cent on taxes on income in general, and those on individual income in particular. Within the latter category thanks to the more recent evolution of the level and structure of personal income but also due to the techniques of collection, it is the taxation of wages and salaries which has grown fastest in recent times. This growth has been considerably accelerated by the course of inflation.

In the field of income taxation government makes the largest gains from inflation – and inversely, taxpayers sustain the largest losses. The main reason is that on the one hand personal allowances, deductions etc., are all fixed in absolute nominal amounts, and on the other hand, open graduation of rates leads to an aggravation of absolute and relative tax burdens. If there were not this combination of indirect and direct progressivity – that is, in a case of proportional tax – one could argue that aside from time-lags, there would be no inflation-caused loss or gain, since to the extent that incomes, and consequently income taxes, increase, the purchasing power of money used for tax payments decreases. Because of progressivity the situation differs: now the real tax burden grows, and at the same time, the original distribution of the tax burdens is changed.

The following very simple numerical example may help to illustrate these

[1] The general statement above is subject to some qualifications in that government will suffer a certain loss of (real) revenue due to inflation because of lags between the accrual of tax liability and payment. This problem is of much greater importance in the field of income taxation; therefore it is treated in connection with the latter.

effects: we assume an income tax with personal allowances of 500 dollars per head; on the first 1000 dollars, the taxpayer may have to pay 5 per cent; on the following 2000 dollars 8 per cent; on the next 5000 dollars 10 per cent; on the following 10,000 dollars 15 per cent; and on the rest 20 per cent. A married individual with two children and an income of 2000 dollars would pay no tax under these rules. Six years later, the purchasing power of money is assumed to have declined by one-half. Consequently, the same individual now earning 4000 dollars is liable for a tax of 130 dollars, although his real income has not grown at all. A person whose income six years ago was 8000 dollars, and at present, after being adjusted to the inflationary rise in the cost of living index, amounts to 16,000 dollars, will have to pay a tax of 2210 dollars instead of 510 dollars, that is four times his old tax on an income the purchasing power of which has remained constant. Doubtless, our first instance represents the worst case. It shows that because of the combined effects of inflation and progressive tax rates, individuals become subject to tax who were considered by the legislator as having no ability to pay in times when the real income per head of the population was possibly, or even probably, lower. But our second example too clearly demonstrates that government thanks to inflation is profiting from increasing tax burdens in a way not intended when the original income tax act came into operation.

I do not dwell here on the much discussed problem of relations between income and corporation taxes on the one hand, changes in asset value and/or allowances for depreciation on the other hand. It is evident that in case adequate inflation adjustments are not made, the tax base is fictionally enlarged. This leads to inflation-induced budgetary gains even if proportional tax rates are applied. As to the inflation-induced changes in the distribution of the tax burden we observe that they result from the fact that in practice, there is no rate system showing a regular (symmetrical) rate graduation. Rather, the degree of progressivity decreases as income brackets increase, and finally, neglecting indirect progression resulting from allowances, we have a proportional tax (in other words: the marginal rate – almost – equals the average rate) so that repercussions of inflation will not be felt by the very richest individuals. To exemplify these distortions, I would like to point out that on the basis of the above-mentioned rate structure and allowances, we arrive at the following results: six years ago, three persons living under equal family conditions had incomes of 10,000, 50,000 and 100,000 dollars. They then paid income tax of 710, 8210 and 18,210 dollars, the proportions of their tax burdens being 100:1156:2365. Let us assume that during the last six years, these incomes were just adjusted to the rate of inflation so that they amount to double their original level. The taxes they will have to pay now are 2210, 18,210 and 38,210 dollars, the proportions accordingly 100:824:1729. Evidently, under the influence of inflation with maintenance of the old rate schedule, the distribution of tax burdens has changed considerably in that the original course of progressivity was weakened in a way very likely opposed to the ability-to-pay concept harboured by the fathers of the income tax act. To my mind, therefore, such changes in relative tax burdens represent unwanted and *unintended distortions* which, as a nasty byproduct, reduce tax transparency.

In passing I would like to mention that inflationary processes also give rise to *distortions in the field of intergovernmental fiscal relations*. As is well known, the different kinds of taxes are distributed among the two or three levels of government in a way varying in time and space. Roughly, we may distinguish two main groups of countries: those, like the United States, Great Britain, and Holland, where by far the largest part of direct (personal) taxes is levied by the national government, and those, such as Switzerland and, to a somewhat lesser degree, Sweden, where the opposite holds true. Now, according to the kind of intergovernmental distribution of taxes, inflation-induced gains from tax progressivity will mainly accrue to one or the other level of government. As a consequence, provided the original revenue distribution scheme corresponded more or less to the respective financial needs of each level of government, distortions caused by inflation will be a factor leading to ever more frequent debates on a revision of intergovernmental fiscal relations. One may well call this a misallocation of intellectual and political resources. In view of the fact that usually fiscal policy behaviour patterns of the various levels of government differ, distortions of the kind just mentioned will have negative repercussions on the efficiency of overall fiscal stabilisation efforts.

As to *taxes on net wealth and inheritance*, they too form part of direct (personal) taxes, and consequently are subject to influences of inflation. Theoretically, the problems mentioned with respect to income taxation are similar to those for these taxes. However, taxes on net wealth do not exist in the majority of Western countries and even where they exist and where their rates are rather high, the revenue they yield and thus possible budgetary gains due to inflation are relatively modest. This last remark applies also to inheritance taxes. For these reasons, I confine myself to the following very short observations.

In some countries, like the Federal Republic of Germany, the tax on net wealth is formally proportional; a certain graduation of tax burdens results only indirectly via personal allowances. In most other countries, however, such as Switzerland and the Scandinavian countries, there is also a rather steep progressivity of tax rates.

Such a combination of indirect and direct progressivity is the rule in the field of inheritance taxation where, moreover, one finds rather often a rate schedule graduated according to consanguinity. *Prima vista*, one may be inclined to think that this third element of progressivity will not give rise to inflation-induced aggravations and distortions of tax burdens and thus, to budgetary gains. In fact, however, because of the irregular structure of progressive rate schedules, not only progressivity according to the size of the bequest but also that depending on the relationship of the heir to the decedent causes initially not intended increases in tax liabilities; true, this disadvantage is mitigated more or less by the considerable lagging behind of assessment operations which are the rule also in the case of current wealth taxation.

(3) As already mentioned, *techniques of assessment and collection of taxes* are also very important for the inflation-caused 'profits' or 'losses' of revenue. Quite generally, government, in real terms, will lose more, the stronger and the longer the inflationary process is on the one hand, the greater the interval is between the accrual of tax liability and payment, on the other. During the last stage of German hyperinflation in the early 1920s, the effects of so-called 'cold (or disguised) tax progressivity' in favour of the treasury were many times overcompensated by the losses resulting from the day-to-day erosion of the purchasing power of the mark. Therefore, eventually, government was obliged to assess and collect taxes – even indirect ones – on the basis of a purely fictitious 'goldmark'.

So far, in no country rates and tempo of contemporary inflation have reached a degree comparable to that of the hyperinflation just mentioned. No doubt, however, that in several countries and with respect to certain taxes, the time-lag hinted at between assessment and collection is large enough to form a strong incentive for taxpayers to postpone their payments as long as legally possible. This possibility varies considerably from tax to tax, and within the same tax, from one group of taxpayers to another. This fact gives rise to further distortions in the personal distribution of tax burdens. Evidently, the crucial interval between accrual of liability and payment of a tax is at its minimum where, within the framework of income taxation, withholding is applied. With the exception of countries like France and Switzerland this today is the case in nearly all Western economies, at least with regard to wages and salaries. Rather often, the withholding technique is also applied to dividends and/or interest on bonds. Whereas so far, United States banks and business men have successfully opposed such a method which would oblige them to render unrequited services to the Internal Revenue, this method can be found in Great Britain, the Federal Republic of Germany, Holland etc. It is needless to emphasise that in a modern industrialised economy, taxation of wages has a much greater importance than that of income from capital. However, with respect to the latter, withholding in countries levying a net wealth tax assures at the same time a better control of taxable wealth.

Regarding income not subject to withholding, methods of collection differ very much from country to country. The United States system of declaration of estimated income, combined with instalment payments (sometimes called 'self-assessment'), guarantees to a rather high degree that the time-lag discussed is relatively short. In countries like Germany, there also exists a system of quarterly payments in advance plus a 'final payment'. However, this final payment (if any) is due only after definite assessment is made by the tax authorities, a procedure which requires at least two years and sometimes considerably more. Moreover, advance payments, though legally they may be adjusted by the fiscal administration to current inflationary and real increases in profits, are in fact changed only the other way round, leading to a reduction of instalments claimed by taxpayers in times of diminishing inflationary pressure and incomes. On balance, receivers of incomes not liable to withholding enjoy an interest-free loan from government. In contradiction to this, wage-earners and civil servants (and sometimes also individuals living on small incomes from shares and bonds), aside from being subject to a steeper rate progressivity on inflation-induced incremental income increases, do not dispose of the ability to profit from the erosion of money value as do persons whose tax is not withheld. This is another aspect of injustice brought about by inflationary processes.

Before concluding these remarks, I would like to point out that the incentive to postpone tax payments as much as possible depends to a high degree – other things being equal – on the course of inflation. In times of increasing rates of money depreciation as those observed until the end of last year, this incentive will become stronger and stronger. Inversely, when inflation rates, actual and/or expected ones, decrease, it tends to decline. However, this latter tendency may be compensated, or even overcompensated, by the reluctance to pay taxes in time when declining inflation rates are accompanied by diminishing profits and liquidity. Some recent studies relating to corporate tax payments in Germany seem to show that these payments are determined to a considerable degree by the liquidity situation of firms. The tendency to postpone tax payments thus may prove to be a one-way phenomenon. Evidently, whether and to what extent the said incentive is of actual relevance depends also on legal provisions and the efficiency of the tax administration. As to the rate graduation factor, I would like to point out that progressivity of corporate taxes does not exist everywhere – for example, not in the Federal Republic of Germany – but among other nations (because of a lower rate on a certain fraction of taxable profits) in the United States and Canada, and, albeit in a particular form, in Switzerland.

III. EFFECTS OF INFLATION ON PUBLIC EXPENDITURE

With respect to public revenues, there seems to exist the unanimous conviction that government is a net gainer from inflation, but opinions differ with regard to the net effects of inflation on *public expenditures*. This is so not only because of different approaches and/or methods used in empirical studies but also because of the fact – already mentioned in the introductory remarks – that the impact of inflationary price increases varies according to the structure of public outlays, governmental wage policy and the like.

(1) One of the most conspicuous phenomena to be emphased in this connection is the inflation-induced gain for the government from making *interest payments and debt retirement* in devalued currency. This, of course, is but a particular example of the general rule that in periods of inflationary pressure, debtors win and creditors lose. Other things being equal, such gains of government on current account depend on (a) the size of public debts, (b) the level of interest rates government has to pay, and (c) the degree and persistence of inflation.

As to the first factor, its importance varies greatly among the nations. The main reason for this is twofold: first, some countries did actively participate in the last war which compelled them to rely heavily on borrowing, whereas others remained neutral; secondly, countries such as Germany where a strong war-induced inflation was followed by a Draconian monetary reform, practically wiped out the largest part of their debt, in contrast to the majority of countries which maintained the nominal amount of their outstanding debt. No wonder that whatever standards are used to measure the relative size and budgetary importance of the public debt, statistics show that among others, Great Britain, the United States, Belgium, and Holland have to shoulder a burden several times heavier than that of countries like the Federal Republic of Germany, Austria, or France. It is exactly because of this earlier realisation of inflation-induced gains in the past that at present the second group of countries gains less from inflation than the first group as far as debt-related outlays are concerned.

Assuming the same nominal amount of outstanding debt, the second factor mentioned above, that is, the level of interest rates, evidently represents an independent source of budgetary gains from inflation only to the extent that these rates are not fully reflecting the rate of money depreciation. It is a realistic assumption that particularly in periods of high and fast-increasing inflation, the real interest rate tends to decline and even to become zero. Adding our third factor to the second one, we may conclude that the stronger and the more continuous the erosion of the value of money is, the larger are the gains for governments with regard to their debt. The budgetary importance of such a relief is indeed large in countries such as Great Britain, the United States and Canada where interest payments amount to between 7 per cent and 12 per cent of the expenditure total of all levels of government, as compared with a percentage of 3 per cent of 4 per cent in Italy, Denmark, and the Federal Republic of Germany. Therefore, provided a government is fiscal-minded, the existence of a rather large public debt may well tempt it to refrain from following a strict policy of monetary stabilisation.

However, one has to consider that governments are not only debtors but also creditors. Consequently, whether and to what extent they gain or lose by inflation depends also on their net capital position and the kind of public investment financed by borrowing. In the same measure as this investment consists of nominal monetary assets, government like any other creditor evidently will be negatively affected by inflation. However, assuming that nowadays governments (albeit internationally to a very different degree) are in a net debtor position, it is likely that from the viewpoint of capital as well as interest, there will remain on balance inflation-induced gains in favour of public households. Furthermore, since borrowing and interest obligations resulting from it play quite a different role at the various levels of government, inflation also for this reason may cause distortions of intergovernmental fiscal relations.

(2) According to many contemporary authors, the well-known rise of the public sector's share in G.N.P. is, at least partly, due to changes in the structure

of public outlays and changes in the price structure. Regarding the first phenomenon, one observes a general tendency towards a growing absolute and relative increase in public expenditures for services instead of goods on the one hand and for transfer payments on the other hand. This development is a consequence of the fact that in the modern welfare state, there is an ever-increasing demand for social assistance and labour-intensive public services such as education. Moreover, these latter services are not very susceptible to productivity gains from technical progress. As to the impact of changes in relative prices, in several countries the remuneration of civil servants and workers employed by government is nowadays growing just as fast as, or indeed even faster than, comparable salaries and wages in the private sector; this is a significant change from conditions prevailing in the past. Furthermore, social security measures such as the 'dynamisation' of old age pensions (to be found for example in the Federal Republic of Germany) tend, at least under certain conditions, to raise the transfer payments concerned by a percentage exceeding the concomitant growth rate of the G.N.P. Finally, several authors hold that also the price index of government purchases of goods rises more than that of goods demanded by private firms and/or households. Aside from the fact that this seems not to be a phenomenon which can be observed everywhere and at all times, it would be wrong to assume – as some writers do – that the lead in the prices for governmental purchases and the difference between public expenditures at current prices and those at constant prices are both due to inflation and thus bring about inflation-induced losses for the public household. As just mentioned, there are various *structural* factors which, *ceteris paribus*, give rise to a more than proportional increase in public expenditures. Therefore, in order to arrive at a correct calculation of possible budgetary losses attributable to inflation, one has to examine the question whether and to what extent inflationary processes tend to *aggravate* the structural forces which even in times of reasonable monetary stability make for a growing share of the public sector in G.N.P. by raising relative government prices.

Until now, there seems to exist no convincing evidence for such a development. Admittedly, here and there, one observes a reinforcement of the structural factors mentioned above which might be caused by inflation. But such a development is usually restricted to a short time and it is often overcompensated by opposite tendencies immediately afterwards. At any rate, it is indispensable for the calculation of government losses from inflation to attempt a neat separation between long-term, or structural, factors which cause an increase in public outlays, and the short-term, or cyclical, ones. In many cases, this proves to be a difficult task because the procedure implies a number of more or less arbitrary choices and estimates, particularly those relating to the selection of appropriate indices or deflators.

Thus, for the proper choice of deflators for governmental investment outlays, one probably has to distinguish between the price indices for outlays for equipment and highway construction on the one hand and those for the construction of buildings on the other hand. Available statistical data do not indicate that given differences in these price indices as they relate to the private and the public sector are reinforced by inflation. Such a development would, however, be a necessary precondition for being justified in speaking of inflation-induced government losses with respect to this category of expenditures.

There are several other public outlays which do not show the difficulties just alluded to. Assuming the non-existence of indexation practices, transfer payments fixed in absolute monetary terms such as premiums subsidising small savings, or subsidies to low-income recipients for house or apartment rents and the like lead to net government gains from inflation. Moreover, the simple application of a cost of living index to measure the effects of inflation seems indicated in these cases, as it can be applied also to interest payments *by* the government, though probably not to such payments *to* the government.

IV. CONCLUSIONS

Effects of inflationary processes on the public households are evident. They make themselves felt on both sides of the budget as well as on the capital account.

With respect to public revenues, inflation-induced losses are confined to categories which in general are not very important. Such losses are mostly due to the negative attitude of the modern welfare state towards a dogmatic application of the *quid pro quo* principle. In the field of taxation, government losses result only from taxes which today are of small and declining budgetary relevance. On the other hand, progressive personal taxes provide governments with considerable gains due to inflation.

On balance, then, as far as the revenue side of the budget is concerned, inflation is advantageous to the public household. But naturally, government gains have their exact counterpart in losses for the taxpayers. This is, however, a very general statement and is valid only in the sense of an average. In fact, inflation-induced taxpayer losses differ considerably from one group to another. There may even exist some individuals who emerge as net gainers.

Turning to the expenditure side, one encounters a much more complicated and less homogeneous situation. Government losses are combined with government gains, and it is very difficult to elucidate the correct balance. If understood and calculated in an appropriate way, alleged losses with respect to some categories of public expenditures seem not, or only to a modest degree, to be caused by inflation; rather they are due to structural factors which on the whole may be assumed to be inflation neutral. On the other hand, there are categories of public outlays which under the influence of inflationary developments bring about more or less significant gains for the public household. Although a general statement is impossible because of international and intertemporal divergences, it seems that the net result for public expenditures also is a budgetary gain.

If to all this one adds the effects of inflation on the position of the government as a creditor of monetary assets on the one hand and a debtor of monetary liabilities on the other hand, there is an overwhelming probability that under present conditions, the state gains much more from inflation than it possibly loses. Of course, this does not exclude the possibility that among individuals and groups 'behind the scenes' some will suffer a net loss. Furthermore, the different distortions mentioned above will lead to negative repercussions on welfare and social justice. Some of these effects might be avoided or mitigated by measures of indexation which are examined in the framework of other papers. Nevertheless, the rather discouraging conclusion which the present paper arrives at may be summed up as follows.

Contrary to the opinion of several contemporary authors, government, at present as in the past, seems to be a net winner from inflation. That is why only if and when socioeconomic forces who lose from inflationary processes – and who are aware of their losses! – come to dominate the scene of political decisions, governments will, in the interest of monetary stability, forego inflation-induced budgetary gains and thereby relieve large groups of the population from corresponding losses. Inflation is not the right way to a redistribution of income and wealth.

BIBLIOGRAPHY

It is impossible to indicate in a short note even the most important studies on the problems dealt with in the present paper. The following list is restricted to a few more recent (and perhaps not everywhere well known) articles which are of particular importance for the question whether government is a net gainer or loser from inflation.

U. A. Münzer and P. B. Spahn, Liquidität und Körperschaftsteueraufkommen, *Finanzarchiv*, N.F., Vol. 32, p. 406–424 (1974).

R. Lenk, R. Parsche and G. Spanakakis, 'Auch der Staat kein Inflationsgewinner, *Ifo-Schnelldienst*, 29/1973 (München 1973).

F. Neumark, 'Impôt et inflation', *Collection d'essais en l'honneur de Jean Marchal* (Paris, 1975).

A. Meier, 'Geldwertstabilität aus der Sicht des öffentlichen Sektors, *Stabilisierungspolitik in der Marktwirtschaft, Schriften des Vereins für Socialpolitik* (Berlin, 1975).

H. Pollak, 'Einige Bemerkungen zum Referat von A. Meier', *ibid.*

W. Ehrlicher, ed., 'Probleme der Indexbindung', Heft 2 der *Beihefte zu Kredit und Kapital* (Berlin, 1974).

J. Starbatty, 'Der Staat: Inflationsgewinner oder Inflationsgeschädigter?', *Finanzarchiv*, N.F. Vol. 33 (1975).

Inflation, Economic Growth and Taxation, Institut International Roue de Finances Publiques, Saarbrücken, XXIXe Session, Congrès de Barcelona 1973 (cf. particularly the papers by R. A. Musgrave, J. M. Buchanan, T. Stevers, H. Pollak and K. Messere. (Unfortunately this volume was published only after I had completed the present paper, but I could immediately see that Musgrave's ideas to a large extent correspond with my own.)

14 The Growth of the Public Sector and Inflation Pressure

A. Nussbaumer
INSTITUTE OF ECONOMICS, UNIVERSITY OF VIENNA

I. INTRODUCTION

It may be convenient in a theory of inflation to disregard the influence of the public sector or 'to assume it away altogether because we have no theory of government expenditure', as Domar has suggested originally in the context of the theory of economic growth [1] and because our theories of government income hardly go beyond the consequences of techniques used in taxation. But this probably is a more severe restriction for a theory of inflation than for the explanation of almost any other economic phenomenon. Regarding anti-inflation policy this would also imply disregarding some of the most important policy instruments. On the contrary, I believe therefore that Schumpeter was right when insisting that fiscal policy and practice were of supreme importance for the development not just of national economies but also of human civilisation and of human behaviour, and that there were only very few exceptions to this rule [2]. Because the public sectors of most industrial economies have grown faster than their G.N.P. during the last decades, this may be even more true today than when Schumpeter wrote his article.

On the other hand there is no simple solution for the influence of the public sector on inflation pressure even when dealing with nothing but the relative growth of public income and expenditure. Theoretical models would have to be extremely complex in order to be useful for simulation and forecasting. Simple models always will have to rest upon a large number of limiting assumptions and frequently explain nothing but a special case. This is especially true for Haavelmo's theorem about the multiplier effects of a balanced budget [3], which at first sight might make us believe that the growth of the public sector must necessarily lead to general economic expansion and hence to inflation under conditions of full employment. But even when accounting only for variations of the standard set of macroeconomic assumptions, it has been explained sufficiently in the meantime that Haavelmo's is only a special solution of a more general model [4], [5], and that his thesis rests on the assumptions that the rate of saving was equal for the private and for the public sectors of the economy, and that governments raise additional income via taxation and spend it on investment; hence the expansionist impact of the complete investment multiplier $\Delta Y = I \frac{1}{1-c}$ is only partially compensated for by the restrictive effect of the incomplete taxation or transfer multiplier $\Delta T = T\frac{1}{1-c} - T$ even if $I = 1$, assuming the budget to be balanced. But why should not governments use their additional income also for increasing wages in the public sector or for transfer payments in order to increase the welfare of the poor or to help depressed industries.

There is also no reason to assume that the propensity to save is necessarily equal for the private and for the public sectors of the economy, and still less so for various subsectors, such as workers, salaried personnel, entrepreneurs, corporations, central and local government. Then the average rate of saving will also change with the distribution of income.

For the public sector also the composition of income and expenditure matters. Income may not only be derived from taxes but also from fees, charges and revenues of the public utilities as well as from profits of government-owned corporations and from interest paid on money lent out by the government. Expenditure may be on investment, on wages and on goods consumed by the government sector, and on transfers to households, to enterprises, and to other public authorities. No generalising statement therefore is possible as to the effects of the growth of the public sector on inflation pressure. To do so, econometric models would have to be extremely complex and would have to rely upon a very great number of empirically determined parameters. Finally, a lag structure also would have to be inserted.

It is not the aim of the present paper to present such a general model; because of the limited space available only the most fundamental structure of it could be presented and hardly anything new could be said. Such a model for the public sector also would have to be developed as an integral part of already existing national simulation models, if the impact of the growth of the public sector was to be analysed in the short run. An analysis of the long run on the other hand would have to rest upon an explicit econometric model of economic growth.

Considering all of these limitations it seems therefore to be more rewarding to trace down the various influences which may determine the relationship between the growth of the public sector and inflation pressure. First we have to discuss the institutional structure of the public sector, which purposes it serves, and how it is financed. Then we have to analyse the growth of the public sector, its reasons, structural changes, and the limits to its growth. Finally this should enable us to understand the various reasons why inflation may be spurred by the growth of the public sector and what might be done if inflation was to be kept down.

A last introductory remark still may be important. Since the paper deals with the growth of the public sector only, no attention is being paid to all those influences of budgetary and fiscal policies on inflation and on monetary stabilisation which have nothing to do with the growth of the public sector.

The author believes however that budgetary and especially debt management policies might be some of the most effective instruments of monetary stabilisation.[1]

II. SCOPE AND ACTIVITIES OF THE PUBLIC SECTOR

When speaking about the state we usually have in mind the central government and its agencies. Yet there is also local government, and in federal states federal government, state governments, and communes may be distinguished. Local authorities also may enjoy lawmaking and administrative powers in their own right; in many countries such as Austria, the Federal Republic of Germany and Sweden communes are fairly independent of central government decisions. Their influence is not reduced to that of administrative agencies of the central government like in the French department system. There exists therefore more than one territorial authority for the same area, conflicts being avoided by constitutional regulation of jurisdiction. Local authorities may even have had historical priority in exercising governmental powers, because it was on their level that the need for common action and for the common interest to enjoy priority above the satisfaction of individual goals came to be experienced earliest [6]. In many countries still today local communities are charged with performing functions of supreme importance for the welfare of their citizens in education, health and old age insurance, and in safeguarding the public order.

But government need not even be organised on a territorial basis. Governmental funds, having independent legal status and being kept separate from the treasury may be established for performing special tasks, such as regulating supply and demand of basic agricultural commodities, or providing for irrigation and flood control. Authorities and boards providing for close co-operation between government and private interests may have to satisfy special needs of the community such as the administration of ports or of public utilities. Finally, the working population might be organised by law in groups representing economic interests and these groups may perform important functions and rights of self-government; in Austria, for example, all wage earners in the private sector, all self-employed people with only minor exceptions, and all farmers have to be members of the chambers of labour, the chambers of commerce, and the chambers of agriculture respectively. These public bodies and authorities have legal influence on federal and state legislation and administration and they also perform public functions in their own right, thus allowing for a more direct participation of the people and of groups concerned in the political process. While being independent of central and local governments they too belong to the public sector.

[1] Some sociologists and political scientists such as J. Schumpeter even believe that the phenomenon 'state' in itself can only develop in individualistic society as a corrective for individual action and as an instrument of public utility (*Die Krise des Steuerstaates* [2], p. 19).

The same is true for social security agencies. In most countries these do not form an integral part of central government but are legally independent. They draw their income from contributions of the insured as well as from their employers, and they also receive transfer payments from governmental budgets.

Besides this part of the public sector which may be referred to as government, there is still a second one consisting of public enterprises. It is not homogeneous as to purpose of operation, the degree of authority exercised, and the influence of market forces. There are state enterprises organised as part of the public administration and integrated financially into governmental budgets, such as postal services, telephone, the railroads and even state forests in some countries. Public utilities, gas, water, electricity, sewage systems generally owned and operated by communes are also frequently integrated into community budgets, but they may also be legally independent and even be organised in joint stock corporations, the stocks largely being owned by the government. Public enterprises mentioned so far usually also exercise authority, collect fees and compulsory contributions and frequently rely upon government transfers in order to cover planned deficits. The operation of such public enterprises and services therefore also changes the personal distribution of income.

Finally governments may own companies which continue to operate as independent corporate business and often compete with private firms. Basic industries frequently belong to this category, but also large banks and insurance companies. Purposes of operation may be to influence competition on important markets, to assure that the nation is supplied with basic commodities, to control credits and investment, but sometimes simply to earn profits for the government.

Regarding all of these different aspects under which the public sector may appear we should not be surprised about its great importance in modern industrial states.

But let us still regard the various functions performed by the public sector. These are not necessarily tied to different methods of organisation. But they may tell us something about the consequences of public action.

There are five different functions of government, the first of them being the exercise of public authority. This is concerned with the traditional duties of government, such as the administration of justice or defence. But authority also is involved if social security agencies collect contributions or if public electricity companies impose their rules on private citizens or introduce limitations on privately owned property.

A second function of government has to do with institutional welfare. Here too the individual is not free to decide whether he wants to participate in such schemes or not. This may be of great economic importance since more and more funds are poured into this sector. Deficits of operation may be substantial, since authorities may be reluctant to impose high contributions on the insured. Also as everyone is supplied equally, there will be losses because automatic supply will not always match with individual demand; duplication may occur because people continue to prepare for their own requirements individually even though public services are being made available. Thus function not only covers social insurance but increasingly also education and public transportation, and it may still spread to other sectors of economic activity previously privately operated. The growth of these public activities may well increase inflationary pressure due to less efficient use of resources, stimulation of additional demand, and an insufficient reduction of private purchasing power to pay for new services supplied.

The third function of the public sector concerns financial redistribution. This is what Musgrave has called the distribution branch [6]. Redistribution does not necessarily increase inflationary pressure, especially if it only concerns increments of real income. But if real income of some groups of the population is scheduled to decline while these groups are able to resist this policy by increasing their own claims on G.N.P., inflation will be the inevitable consequence.

All of the functions of the public sector mentioned so far have to rely on public authority for their financial requirements, that is, mainly on taxes, sometimes on charges levied similar to taxes, and only to a small extent on fees. The two other functions which still have to be mentioned, non-commercial banking and public enterprise, may meet their financial requirements largely by selling their products or services to individuals; thus they absorb private purchasing power directly. But to the extent that they do not make full use of their money-earning capacity because of giving priority to other policy aims, they too may have to rely upon funds raised by governments using their authority. This will also imply redistribution of incomes.

The reader may have noticed that our classification of the functions performed by the public sector, while being compatible with Musgrave's distinction between the allocation branch, the distribution branch, and the stabilisation branch, is overlapping with his classification. We have adopted our own criteria because we believe that it is especially in the fields of institutional welfare, of public enterprise, and of non-commercial banking that the public sector is growing to-day. While all functions imply a certain amount of redistribution and hence of monetary adjustments which may be inflationary, allocation effects are of traditional importance for the functions called authority and institutional welfare; but direct government intervention in hitherto private sectors increasing publicly directed allocation also gains in importance for non-commercial banking and public enterprise. Should this lead to a less efficient use being made of resources, this will also increase inflationary pressure.

Traditionally the burden of stabilisation is put upon government activity in the field of non-commercial banking, including funds being made available to private enterprises and on the management of the public debt. Also, allocation in the public sector may have stabilising effects. But inflationary pressure will result if public expenditure on stabilisation cannot be reduced again, once goals of stabilisation have been met and the public sector will therefore continue to grow. Finally it should be mentioned that redistribution of activities within the public sector may also have inflationary consequences, if concentration of the power to spend with central authorities is not accepted by local authorities hitherto in charge, and this finally results in duplication of public activities.

III. THE GROWTH OF THE PUBLIC SECTOR

There is ample historical evidence not just for the absolute growth of the public sector but also for its relative growth in percentages of gross national product. L. Johansen reports that public revenue before transfers in percentages of G.N.P. in Norway has increased steadily from 9·1 per cent in 1900 to 15·6 per cent in 1930 and to 30·7 per cent in 1962 [7]. While the percentage of total public revenue more than tripled during this period, the percentage of disposable public revenue in Norwegian G.N.P. only increased by two-and-a-half times from 7·4 per cent in 1900 to 9·7 per cent in 1930 to 18·7 per cent in 1962. The difference is due to the increase of financial transfers (subsidies, social insurance payments, interest payments) from the public sector to private households and enterprises from 1·7 per cent in 1900 to 12·0 per cent in 1962. This shows the rapid increase of institutional welfare and of financial aid given to the private production sector.

Peacock and Wiseman have presented time series for British government expenditure from 1792 to 1900 and from 1890 to 1955; while these do not show any constant or systematic increase of the public sector if compared to British G.N.P. for the first period, the relative share of the public sector increased progressively during the second period, when it has roughly tripled [8]. There was however no strict regularity in the relative growth of the public sector; different reasons were responsible for it at different times, such as wars, heavy unemployment, or a sudden increase of social benefits as it occurred when the National Health Service was set up.[1]

The tendency for the public sector to increase its relative share in G.N.P. also is especially clear for many countries during the last two decades. In the Netherlands total government expenditure inclusive of social security as a percentage of G.N.P. increased from 37·0 per cent in 1957 to 47·0 per cent in 1969; nearly all of this however is due to the increase of expenditure on social security from 7·9 per cent on G.N.P. in 1957 to 16·2 per cent in 1969 [9].

Statistics also show that an increasing part of the expenditure on social security had to be financed by tax revenue. In a cross-section study covering 52 countries for the period 1950 to 1959 R. S. Thorn has shown [10] that government revenues and expenditures as a percentage of G.N.P. were substantially higher for countries with a high per capita product than for countries with a low one, being only 15·9 per cent for countries with a per capita income of less than 200 United States dollars but 27·3 per cent for countries with a

[1] See also [8], pages 50 and 62.

per capita product of more than 1200 United States dollars. Most of the difference was found to be due to an increase of government transfers to households, which in turn was largely the result of differences in the level of social expenditures. Also urbanisation and losses suffered by public utilities and other government-owned corporations due to setting the price of output below cost and to the employment of excess workers (see [10] page 192) seem to have been responsible. On the whole the income elasticity of public revenue and expenditure was found to be considerably higher than unity, being 1·35 for government revenue, 1·22 for total government expenditure, and 1·65 for government expenditure on social services. The increase of government revenue was found to be largely due to the high income elasticity of personal income taxes, making tax cuts inevitable in times of inflation. Yields of taxes on corporate incomes and on capital increased at a much slower pace (see [10], page 194). Similar results can also be obtained for Austria, the income elasticity of taxes on non-wage incomes presently being 1·7 and declining at a rate of 0·1 per cent per annum. The income elasticity of the income tax on wage incomes, calculated as a trend including tax cuts adjusting for the consequences of inflation has proved [11] to be 1·3.

The evidence submitted so far is also supported by data for leading Western industrial countries during the period 1960–72 (see Appendix). In all the countries studied the share of general government in G.N.P. has increased from 1960 to 1972. This increase has been smallest for the United States, from 28·2 per cent to 31·4 per cent. The Federal Republic of Germany, Austria, and the United Kingdom show not only a higher level of public expenditure but also a faster increase of its share in total G.N.P., from 35·4 per cent to 39·0 per cent for the Federal Republic of Germany, 30·4 per cent to 37·2 per cent for Austria, and 30·1 per cent to 37·9 per cent for the United Kingdom. In France the public sector has grown from 33·1 per cent in 1960 to 37·8 per cent in 1972, and now has reached a share equivalent to that in the other countries. The fastest growth and the largest percentage of government expenditure in G.N.P. are both to be found in the public sector of the Swedish economy; its share in G.N.P. has increased from 32·4 per cent to 50·2 per cent between 1960 and 1972. In all countries the budgets of social security agencies have increased at a considerably faster rate than the disposable income of central government.

What are the reasons for this growth of the public sector? Already towards the end of the last century Adams in the United States suggested that government expenditure must grow in proportion to the community's output per head [12], while Wagner in Germany established the well known thesis that as a secular trend the public sector must grow even at a faster rate than the economy as a whole [13]. While in Wagner's time historical proof was not quite as evident as it is on the basis of statistical information for the last 70 years, he himself tried to explain the phenomenon by means of an organic theory of the state. Even when sceptical about the philosophical core of his argument, we have to admit that modern man evidently addresses himself increasingly to the state when looking for remedies for his problems or when being anxious to increase his welfare. The growth of public expenditure in recent times has probably been faster than Wagner himself would have expected [13].

In the long run it is above all else the increase of expenditure on general welfare, as shown by social insurance statistics, which is responsible. But government expenditure designed to meet the specific needs of particular population groups and sectors of the economy has also increased considerably (see [8], page 23). As government activities become more complex and as intervention by government increases, a growing part of national income is being spent directly or redistributed by governments. Even so, a recent inquiry has indicated in Sweden that people continue to desire still more public goods and services, even though the level of taxation and the level of services offered by the government are already high. Should productivity in the public sector be lower than in the rest of the economy, and should goods and services be offered below cost by the government, while it finds it difficult to cover the difference by raising taxes, this together with the exigencies of increased bureaucratic operation will contribute to inflationary pressures.

But there are also consequences of short-run developments which make for a permanent growth of the public sector. Public expenditure frequently is highly rigid and once it has been increased in order to fight against unemployment it may be continued even if the crisis has been overcome. The same holds true for taxation: while the people will not object to new taxes in times of emergency, governments are generally very reluctant to abolish them again once the situation has returned to normal. Furthermore a rising G.N.P. per head leads to an increase in the tax base and a progressive tax system will increase government income even further. Finally social disturbances may provoke government intervention and expenditure, while these in turn change the general view about desirable levels of public spending in the long run.

At the same time inflation contributes to the growth of the public sector. If a country's tax system is progressive, then even if tax rates remain unchanged during inflation, the real burden of direct taxes on individuals must increase. If there is any money illusion in the tax attitudes, which is likely to exist as long as inflation rates are low, inflation will enable the rate of increase of the share of government in total output to be faster than it could be otherwise (see [8], page 32) and the level of government expenditure can go up too. But government expenditure too will increase because of inflation; a study of the development of total expenditure of New York City during the period 1965 to 1972 has revealed for example that 43 per cent of the total increase of City expenditures could be attributed to inflation alone, 42 per cent to the employment of increased quantities of inputs and 15 per cent only to real cost growth. Growth of expenditure due to inflation was greater for labour costs (43·5 per cent for payrolls and 79·7 per cent for retirement costs) than for material inputs (22·3 per cent and for transfer payments (8·3 per cent) [14]. Should this pattern be true universally, it might suggest that inflationary wage-push may be a serious reason for the growth of public expenditure, and that inflation does make it very difficult to balance the budgets of public pensions funds and of social security agencies responsible for old age pensions, especially if wages in the public sector and old age pensions are being adjusted automatically to increases of average labour productivity and to inflated consumer prices.[1]

The question whether government is a net gainer or loser by inflation remains a subject of serious controversy. While it is generally believed that government income on the whole will increase more than proportionally, a detailed analysis of the expenditure side is much more complicated. The growth of public expenditure during periods of inflation also may be due as much to inflation as to more rapid structural change. Much will depend also on transfer payments within the public sector as well as in favour of private households, on the importance of indexation, and on the distribution of taxes and of financial liabilities between central and local government. There are also some who believe that at least the public utilities will get into financial difficulty due to inflation, because upward revision of rates frequently demands political action and is likely to be postponed because of its effects on the general costs of production and on the price index of consumer expenditure [15]. But should the balance be negative for government, that is to say should the growth of expenditure due to inflation exceed that of revenues, one may feel quite safe in assuming that governments will raise additional revenue rather than let the real volume of activities of the public sector shrink. Thus inflation is very likely to contribute to the growth of the public sector in any case.

But the public sector may still grow relative to national income for other reasons. If the number of public goods and services supplied by the public sector grows thus replacing activities of the private sector – sometimes this is called 'displacement effect' – this will have immediate consequences for the level of current government expenditure. But eventually such new current expenditures will force the government to engage in new capital projects too (see [8], page 80) because the new activities also call for real investment. This may help to explain why public investment in Austria has increased considerably faster than national income during the period from 1965 to 1974.[2] Whenever government increases efforts to guide individual economic decisions in the private sector, or whenever it feels that the economy should grow at a faster pace, investment aid to private enterprises will also grow. Sometimes annual increments of government transfers to the private sector for investment

[1] In Austria such dynamic adjustments exist both for wages in the public sector and for old age pensions. As to the problems involved in stabilising real income by indexing wages and pensions see D. Bös, 'Indexbindung von Einkommen und progressive Besteuerung'. *Zeitschrift für Nationalökonomie*, Vol. 23, p. 145 (1974).

[2] From 1965 to 1974 G.N.P. in Austria has increased from 247·4 billion Austrian shillings to 619 billion Austrian shillings, but federal investment expenditure has increased from 5·7 billion to 17·5 billion Austrian shillings. See A. Nussbaumer, 'Staatsschuld und Geldpolitik', *Wirtschaftspolitische Blätter* 3, Vol. 22, p. 62 (1975).

purposes may even exceed the annual net increase of the national debt,[1] the difference having to be financed by raising taxes.

As the national debt grows, so will government expenditure on interest payments; also the ratio between gross borrowing on the part of the government and the net increase of borrowed finance available will deteriorate if the maturity of government loans and bonds has to be reduced. This will persuade government to increase gross borrowing, but once it has secured a larger share in national capital markets it may not be willing to see it reduced again once adjustment to shorter maturities has succeeded.

Public corporations too may need additional finance, be it that new corporations are created in order to replace services previously operated privately, be it that public corporations and services already existing grow at a faster rate than the national economy as a whole. Since government mostly operates in the tertiary sector of the economy, should the tertiary sector grow above average, so will the activity of the government. Once again Parkinson's law may prove to operate.

Whenever functions of government are shared between central and local authorities, changes in responsibilities will also call for changes in expenditure. Substantial intergovernmental transfer payments may result [16]. Similarly the relative shares of central and local authorities in total public finance will change under conditions of inflation in favour of the authority receiving its revenue primarily from progressive taxes; should responsibilities remain unchanged this too will call for intergovernmental transfer payments. The displacement effect ensuing may provoke a relative growth of the total public sector, especially if authorities fight for retaining their relative shares in total finance and increasing total government revenue appears to be the only political solution possible. This will also be the case if the function of the stabilisation branch must be performed largely at the central level (see [6], page 181), while most sources yielding stable revenues are at the disposal of local governments only.[2]

When referring to the growth of the public sector, especially in connection with inflation, one should be careful however not to rely exclusively on the volume of gross public expenditure. Valuable as modern techniques may be such as full-employment budget surplus analysis, for estimating the influence of the public sector on the general economy, one may feel that they reduce fiscal policy to simple arithmetic [17]. Certainly all government expenditure has to be financed and some techniques used have inflationary effects. But on

[1] In Austria this has been so in the years 1965, 1966 and 1972. A. Nussbaumer, (*op. cit.*), table 1, p. 61.

[2] Some authors believe that at the local level many governments have their revenue and expenditure patterns more or less set, adjustments to changing preferences of the population or changes in economic activity therefore having to be made at the central level. See C. M. Tiebout, *A Pure Theory of Local Expenditures. Public Expenditure Analysis*, B. S. Sahni (ed.) (Rotterdam, 1972), p. 151; for empirical evidence concerning the United States see also A. M. Soloway, '*Growth of Government over the Past 50 Years*' (see [16]).

the expenditure side one should distinguish between government expenditure leading to the creation of income and property, and thus expansionist in nature and on the other hand purely financial transactions of the government only affecting the distribution of liquidity. The latter expenditures may be broken down again into sales and purchases of loans, bonds, and company shares, extension and collection of loans and debts, changes of other monetary liabilities and claims, and changes in the cash balances held by the government [18]. These transactions, most of which fall into the field of debt management, have no influence on real macroeconomic magnitudes in the Keynesian sense, but should be regarded as part of the monetary policy operated by the government. We do not have to include them, therefore, in our calculations concerning the growth of the public sector.[1] But it should be mentioned that such purely financial transactions, while adding to the growth of the public sector may also be used to fight inflation; for example if governments raise debts in order to retire the money collected with the national bank.

One question still remains to be answered: both statistical evidence and theoretical considerations indicate a tendency for the public sector to grow not only in absolute figures but also relatively to national income. Must this tendency come to an end at any particular share of the government in G.N.P.? While this question cannot be answered numerically, at least not for every national economy irrespective of the economic system practised, one may agree with Schumpeter who has argued that there are limits to taxation in any economy and society built upon the principles of individual free enterprise and competition. The state, he says, must not tax its subjects to the extent that they lose financial interest in production and no longer deploy the best of their energy. Should it be believed, nevertheless, that the public sector should be expanded indefinitely and that redistribution of private incomes to an ever-increasing extent is inevitable, then a state founded upon individual enterprise and upon taxation will necessarily have to break down and give way to a planned socialist economy (see [2], pages 24 and 31). When approaching

[1] The balance of the government budget may differ considerably when calculated so as to include or not to include these transactions of exclusively financial importance as figures for the Austrian federal budget show, in billions of Austrian shillings

	total balances	*balances net of exclusive financial transactions*
1967	−7·8	−4·2
1968	−8·4	−4·2
1969	−7·2	−0·7
1970	−7·2	−0·1
1971	−7·7	+1·9
1972	−7·7	+1·9
1973	−12·8	−3·0
1974	−18·5	−2·1

Federal Budgets and *Beirat für Wirtschafts- und Sozialfragen, Budgetvorschau 1974–1978,* op. cit. ([11]) p. 51 (balances net of exclusive financial transactions are also net of government purchases of military goods from other countries).

these limits individual resistance to taxation grows. To redistribute income via inflation may then be the only alternative left. While we have not seen evidence so far of a possible maximum share of government in the G.N.P. of market economies it seems to be clear however that there are severe limitations to the speed at which this share may be increased without giving rise to inflation and to severe social resistance.

IV. THE IMPACT UPON INFLATION

Short of a generally accepted theory of inflation it is extremely difficult to make any general statements as to the influence of the growth of the public sector on inflation pressure. Since the Second World War it has become customary to distinguish between cost-push and demand-pull inflations. Cost-push may be the consequence of autonomous wage increases, rising costs of capital or of imported inputs, of increasing marginal costs when getting close to the limits of industrial capacity, of structural changes during periods of rapid economic growth, of mark-up pricing under conditions of monopolistic competition, and of the extensive use made of depreciation benefits by leading companies. Demand-pull is frequently being attributed to an increase in general incomes, to a decline in the macroeconomic rate of savings due to a more equal distribution of incomes, to the extension of consumer credit, to accelerated demand for investment goods, to increasing exports, and to a rising demand of the public sector.

Admittedly various of these reasons for inflation frequently coincide, and today even the former exclusivity and sharp distinction between cost-push and demand-pull as theories of inflation are not being upheld any longer. Also Keynesian and monetarist theories of inflation cannot be distinguished very clearly any longer, but they give way to more flexible interpretations ([19], [20] and [21]). Even the Phillips-curve meets scepticism today, and increasing attention is being paid to exogenous influences such as rising export prices and productivity increases in the exporting sector [22], [23] and to institutional factors such as the downward stickiness of prices and wages. The growth and the size of the public sector of the economy, however, are only rarely being included explicitly into these theories, irrespective of the fact that the public sector in many developed industrial market economies accounts for not much less than 50 per cent of national income and sometimes even for more, especially if governmental transfer payments to the private sector are being included.

More attention therefore should be paid to the influence of the public sector on inflation both in theoretical and in empirical studies. In the present paper we only want to point out the most important reasons why the growth of the public sector might increase inflation pressure, reasons which therefore should be analysed in every detailed study of an inflationary process.

Much attention has been paid to the fact that, even assuming that public budgets are balanced, every growth of the public sector will be followed by an equivalent growth of national income. In Haavelmo's own words: 'If the consumption function is linear, and total private investment is a constant, a tax, *T*, that is fully spent will raise total gross national income by an amount *T* and leave total private net income and consumption unchanged. And this holds regardless of the numerical value of the marginal propensity to consume (see [3], page 339). The theorem does not regard a change in the rate of savings nor does it allow for a change in the relative distribution of incomes (see [3], page 342). Should the economy already have been fully employed initially, no real growth will be possible and inflation will result'.

It has to be pointed out, however, that the result obtained also depends on the assumption that government income is raised by taxes, that is by transfers from the private to the public sector of the economy; that it is spent on goods and services, that is on 'investment', the increase in total income being due to the difference between the investment and the transfer multipliers. In practice this may be so most frequently, but if government incomes should be raised and spent differently, for instance on transfers for welfare purposes, the results will be different, as can be judged on the basis of a more general model (see [4], pages 18–24). Haavelmo's theorem also disregards possible inflationary effects connected with increasing taxes. There will be an increase of the price level if government revenue is increased by a general sales tax rather than by taxation of income. In Austria it has been observed however that an increase in the level of indirect taxation leads to an increase of prices only after a time-lag of one year. This asks for an answer as to whether the price rise was due to the tax having been shifted on to consumers only after one year while primarily the burden of the tax had been absorbed by profits, or whether the general increase of prices was due to the increase of public demand on the basis of higher taxes collected in the meantime [24].

Inflation will also result if the propensity to consume for the government and for people receiving income from transfer payments is higher than that of those being taxed, because then total consumption will increase. These conditions generally will be met, since it is not very likely in the long run that government will increase taxation in order to keep idle balances; on the contrary it will rather keep smaller liquid reserves than is customary in the private sector. Pensioners and people receiving family benefits also may be expected to have a propensity to consume above the national average, since it is their special deprivation which justifies transfer payments. Should the money be raised however from taxes on wages and be spent on old age pensions not much lower than the salaries of those actively employed, the expansionist effect referred to need not exist.[1]

Should individual propensities to consume not be linear but fall with increasing income, cutting the relatively small number of high incomes severely in favour of a small increase of average incomes also will increase macroeconomic consumption and hence inflation under conditions of full employment.

[1] There seems to be statistical evidence for some advanced welfare states that the rate of savings by people depending upon old age pensions does not fall short of that of the actively employed.

Even a growth of the public sector for the mere purpose of making distribution within the private sector more equal therefore will increase inflation if the economy has already been running at full capacity before. This will also be so if corporate and enterpreneurial incomes are being reduced [25], and a consequent decline of investment and growth of industrial capacity will make matters worse.

As to the redistribution of income from private to public consumption, including investment in the public sector, the dangers of inflation still seem to be greater. Whenever public goods are to replace private goods, it follows from the very nature of public goods, that their production will involve a positive allocation effect and a redistribution effect both of which make for expansion of money incomes. Yet there is no, or at least no sufficient, income absorption effect since public goods are given away free or at considerably reduced prices. Since the exclusion principle is not or even cannot be applied, free rider problems arise – production costs are not being recovered, and resources may be lost because additional cost involved in further expansion of the production of public goods and services may no longer be covered by marginal utility [26]. Besides finance by taxation may have to face resistance of taxes and attempts to shift the burden of the additional taxes finally may lead to an increase of prices.

But certainly we are here in the midst of a controversy about political aims and economic institutions. Let me quote two prominent economists, Duesenberry and Domar: 'I wish to emphasise that the non-material benefits of a large class of government expenditures should be regarded as contributions to economic growth even when they do not add to gross national product in constant prices. . . . Many government expenditures will appear poor on the basis of their effect on physical productivity, we have to throw their non-material benefits into the scale. And the weight given to those benefits is, in the last analysis, a matter of taste, about which we cannot dispute' [27]. This attitude taken by Duesenberry, disregarding capacity effects of public expenditure while income-creating effects are inevitable, might easily lead to inflation. On the other side stands Domar stressing economic stability and the growth of productive capacity. He too believes 'that we could invest a higher fraction of our income, provided anti-inflationary measures were undertaken at the same time. (But) the bulk of our capital formation can be left in private hands, stimulated, if necessary, by tax, credit, and other policies [28].

An expansion of transfer payments to the private sector also will increase inflation if full employment prevails. As Musgrave points out, the stabilisation branch will provide for the required level of transfer payments, if expansion is needed, and it will impose the required level of taxation, if contraction is necessary (see [6], page 497). But as empirical evidence shows, the most important kind of transfer payments, those on social security, obviously show no signs of following an anticyclical trend but tend to grow faster than other budgetary expenditures at a fairly constant rate (see Appendix). This does not only increase general demand for goods and services at times when this is not needed. As expenditures have to be financed by increased taxes and contributions to social security, there is a good chance that at least a part of these extra costs will be shifted so as to increase prices eventually (see [25], page 223). But also public expenditure on investment will have inflationary consequences under conditions of full employment, since it will be responsible both for a cost-push due to additional demand for investment goods and for demand-pull resulting from the operation of the investment multiplier. Even under conditions of unemployment however public expenditure to improve the situation will not be very effective in increasing employment but rather speed up inflation, if trade unions continue a policy of asking for a fast increase in nominal wages. This brings us to another long-lasting controversy about the proper instruments to fight unemployment. Professor Hayek, once again refuting the Keynesian position that additional demand should be created by fiscal authorities, insisted that employment created artificially by public spending would only reduce labour productivity and generate inflation, should wages be constant or even rising.[1] This view also has been supported by Musgrave (see [6], page 497) and by Fellner [30] for economies suffering from a shortage of capital and wages being rigid in the downward direction. Then, in order to remove unemployment it would be necessary to reduce consumption, increase saving, and thus permit increased investment without inflation. Certainly the capital-shortage model does not fit best for highly industrialised economies, but present stagflation coincides with a continuing wage-push at least in a great number of countries. It may be argued therefore that Keynesian remedies may only be successful if accompanied by attempts to reduce production costs and by a restrictive wages policy, and that otherwise-increased public expenditure in order to fight unemployment will always have to cope with the danger of inflation. This danger will be still more serious, if it should be difficult to interrupt or reduce public works and welfare programmes once full employment has been reached, and since continuous full-employment without recession tends to eliminate completely the downward mobility of individual prices, reduces the need for adjustment and the mobility of factors, it will thus help to increase inflation pressure.

Structural change imposed by the growth of the public sector too might result in inflation because of consumers not adjusting their budgets, workers not being prepared to move to new occupations, and business firms being slow in changing their policies. This is what has sometimes been called 'demand-shift inflation'. It gains momentum if government programmes are over-ambitious and do not account for scarcity of factors or high input prices for what is frequently called 'political reasons'.

Also absorption of resources through public purchases of factors or products must reduce resources available for private use. This constitutes the opportunity costs of satisfying public wants, and should these be higher than

[1] F. A. Hayek, 'World Inflationary Recession'. First National Bank of Chicago, First Chicago Report. Chicago 1975. See also the interview 'The Critical Point Has Come' with Professor Hayek in Chicago, published in *Newsweek* (June 9, 1975).

the additional satisfaction reached by means of public expenditure, welfare will decrease, with costs remaining constant, and thus inflation follows. Moreover if public investment does not even aim at economic growth, consequences will still be more serious and countermeasures will have to be taken (for proposed remedies see [3]). But already the facts that most of the public sector belongs to the tertiary sector of the economy where labour productivity is lower than in industry, that the government is not exposed to competitive pressures forcing it to increase productivity of operation, and that public authorities have financially a much freer scope than private firms and households may be sufficient reasons why the relative growth of the public sector might add to inflation pressure.

Finally governments need not give absolute priority to the stability of the currency. They may follow a policy of assuring a rate of growth warranted in order to maintain stable employment rather than stable prices. Should inflation occur, the balance on government income and expenditure may either be positive due to an increase in the tax base and to progressive taxation. Should it be negative, however, due to indexation of taxes, of wages in the public sector, and of social security benefits, or because of input prices increasing faster than government revenues, or due to the time-lag involved in collecting taxes, taxation always can be increased, or the government can resort to borrowing. So we might look in vain for automatic economic checks forcing the government to stop inflation; yet there may be political ones.

Finally we have to discuss debt management. As national incomes and the public sector grow, so will the national debt. This is not just a consequence of wars; but as a result of population growth, inflation, and higher standards of public demand, the burden of civil functions resting on governments frequently grows faster than total government revenue. The management of this accumulated government debt as well as government policies of granting capital loans and credits to the private sector of the economy may have a strong influence on private savings, total liquidity and its distribution, interest rates, and even the volume of private credit agreements. The growth of government finance, both active and passive also makes for a growing influence of the public sector and of fiscal policy on the supply of money, and on money market, credit, and capital market operations. This calls for restricting government borrowing with central banks, restrictions which have existed for a long time in many countries, and for adjusting international borrowing to the requirements of monetary stability.[1]

V. CONCLUSIONS

We have learnt that there are many types of governments and of governmental institutions and that we have to pay proper attention to all of them, if the

[1] Austria: §41 Nationalbankgesetz, Federal Republic of Germany: §20 Bundesbankgesetz. For other countries see H. Aufricht, *Comparative Survey of Central Bank Law* (London, 1965), p. 110.

scope and the size of the public sector are to be estimated correctly. Budgets of social security agencies, frequently legally independent authorities, often grow faster than those of central governments. Intergovernmental transfer payments may not only create problems of accounting but sometimes also for monetary stability.

Economic theory as well as statistical evidence show a clear tendency of public sectors to grow relative to national income. Explanations for this tendency need not be the same for all countries and for all periods. But there are good reasons for the relatively rapid growth of the public sectors of many national economies in this century. While there are no definite and predetermined limits for the relative size of public sectors, the speed at which the public sector can grow is limited and inflationary pressure due to public expansion may indicate entering marginal zones.

There are many explanations why the growth of the public sector may affect monetary stability. Yet since there is no universally accepted theory of inflation, there exists no single theoretical model explaining the impact of the growth of the public sector on inflation pressure. Therefore it has been the aim of this article to investigate into the various possibilities why a growth of the public sector might increase inflation pressure, in order to show more clearly which assumptions have to be tested. We shall then know more about the most appropriate methods for fighting inflation in every individual case, even if the public sector should continue to grow.

REFERENCES

[1] E. Domar, *Essays in the Theory of Economic Growth* (New York, 1957) p. 20.
[2] J. A. Schumpeter, 'Die Krise des Steuerstaates'. *Zeitfrage aus dem Gebiet der Soziologie*, 4. Heft, 1918, quoted from: *Aufsätze zur Soziologie* (Tübingen, 1953) p. 4.
[3] T. Haavelmo, 'Multiplier Effects of a Balanced Budget', *Econometrica*. Oct. 1945, quoted from: *Readings in Fiscal Policy* (London, 1955) pp. 335.
[4] J. Hanschel, *Kreislauftheorie und Staatschaushalt*, Zürich, St. Gallen, 1967, p. 18.
[5] W. A. Salant, 'Taxes, Income Determination and the Balanced Budget Theorem'. *Review of Economics and Statistics*, Vol. 39, p. 152 (1957).
[6] R. A. Musgrave, *The Theory of Public Finance* (New York, 1959), p. 17.
[7] L. Johansen, *Public Economics* (Amsterdam, London, 1971), p. 3.
[8] A. T. Peacock and J. Wiseman, *The Growth of Public Expenditure in the United Kingdom* (London, 1967), pp. 37 and 42.
[9] E. Kertzman, 'The Development of Dutch Public Finance during the Period 1957–1969'. *Finanzarchiv*, N.F., Vol. 31, p. 127 (1972).
[10] R. S. Thorn, 'The Evolution of Public Finances during Economic Development', *Public Expenditure Analysis*, B. S. Sahni (ed.), (Rotterdam, 1972), p. 187.
[11] *Beirat für Wirtschafts- und Sozialfragen, Budgetvorschau für das Bundesbudget der Republik Österreich 1974–1978* (Wien, 1974), p. 39.
[12] H. C. Adams, *The Science of Finance* (New York, 1898), chapter 2.
[13] A. Wagner, *Finanzwissenschaft* (Leipzig, 1890), 3rd ed., part I, p. 16.
[14] D. Greytak, R. Gustely and R. J. Dinkelmeyer, 'The Effects of Inflation on Local Government Expenditures'. *National Tax Journal*, Vol. 27, p. 592 (1974).
[15] J. E. Haring and J. F. Humphrey (eds), *Utility Regulation during Inflation* (Los Angeles, 1971), p. 13.

[16] F. L. Fernbach, *The Increasing Role of Intergovernmental Transfer Payments in the Performance of State and Local Functions.* Federal Expenditure Policy for Economic Growth and Stability, Joint Economic Committee, US Government Printing Office (Washington, 1957), pp. 180.

[17] W. L. Smith, *Fiscal Policy Issues of the Coming Decade.* Materials Submitted to the Subcommittee on Fiscal Policy of the Joint Economic Committee, US Government Printing Office (Washington, 1965), p. 134.

[18] *Beirat für Wirtschafts- und Sozialfragen, Empfehlungen zur Budgetpolitik. Vorschläge zur Neuklassifizierung der Transaktionen der öffentlichen Hand* (Wien, 1965).

[19] E. S. Phelps (ed), *Microeconomic Foundations of Employment and Inflation Theory* (New York, 1969).

[20] D. Laidler, 'Information, Money and the Macroeconomics of Inflation', *Swedish Journal of Economics*, Vol. 76 (1974).

[21] P. Davidson and S. Weintraub, 'Money as Cause and Effect', *Economic Journal*, Vol. 83 (1973).

[22] G. Edgren, K. O. Faxen and C. E. Odhner, 'Wages, Growth and the Distribution of Income'. *Swedish Journal of Economics*, Vol. 71 (1969).

[23] O. Aukrust and I. Prim, *A Model of the Price and Income Distribution Mechanism of an Open Economy* (Oslo, 1970).

[24] F. Schebeck and H. Suppanz, 'Ökonometrische Inflationsanalyse für Österreich 1060/1975. *Empirica*, Vol. 2, p. 180, p. 197 (1974).

[25] J. Werner, 'Verteilungspolitik – wachstumspolitische und stabilitätspolitische Aspekte', *Beiträge zur Wirtschafts- und Gesellschaftspolitik.* Festschrift für Theodor Pütz (Berlin, 1975), pp. 221.

[26] H. Schleicher, *Staatshaushalt und Strategie* (Berlin, 1971), pp. 22 and 238.

[27] J. S. Duesenberry, *Government Expenditures and Growth.* Federal Expenditure Policy for Economic Growth and Stability. Joint Economic Committee (Washington, 1957), pp. 289 and 291.

[28] E. D. Domar, *Contribution of Federal Expenditures to Economic Growth and Stability.* Federal Expenditure Policy. Joint Economic Committee (Washington, 1957), p. 269.

[29] G. Bombach, 'Möglichkeiten und Grenzen einer Verteilungspolitik. Lohnpolitik und Einkommensverteilung'. *Schriften des Vereins für Socialpolitik*, N.F., Vol. 51, p. 834 (1969).

[30] W. Fellner, *Trends and Cycles in Economic Activity* (New York, 1956), pp. 212–215 and 357–367.

[31] E. Matzner, *Consequences and Preconditions of Retarded Economic Growth.* Institut für Finanzwissenschaft und Infrastrukturpolitik der Technischen Hochschule in Wien, No. 7, pp. 8–12 (1975).

APPENDIX

Statistical information on the growth and composition of the public sectors of various countries has been collected from the *Yearbook of National Accounts Statistics 1973*, United Nations, New York, 1975 and from national sources.

Figures on G.N.P. taken from the national accounts, data on the public sector were collected from the same sources, that is, data on general government and on current income and expenditure of public authorities. Taking budget data would have made necessary a large number of statistical corrections.

Data printed in lines 2, 3a, 4a refer to public revenue. By definition this is public revenue = public expenditure + public saving. If there are no other subsectors of the public sector the sum total from lines 3b + 4b + 5 equals the value indicated in line 2.

The *Yearbook* contains two accounts for some countries. Differences between them, however, are very small. Data on Austria only contain federal income and expenditure; additional information has been collected therefore from national sources.

(thousand million United States dollars)

(1) G.N.P. *former* S.N.A.	509·0	596·3	874·8	942·6	999·5	1078·1	1178·1
present S.N.A.			862·7	927·9	983·2	1060·3	1159·3
(2) General government *former* S.N.A.	143·7	173·0	264·9	298·0	304·2	323·5	370·0
present S.N.A.			254·2	285·5	289·7	306·2	349·8
(3) Central government (a) Total *former* S.N.A.	80·4	93·3	134·0	149·9	142·1	142·6	164·2
present S.N.A.			134·0	149·8	142·0	142·5	164·1
(b) Total (= a) minus transfers to other subsectors of general government *former* S.N.A.	73·9	84·2	115·3	126·2	112·9	108·7	121·5
present S.N.A.			115·3	126·1	112·8	108·6	121·4
(4) State and local government (a) Total *former* S.N.A.	41·4	51·3	83·6	93·8	128·5	145·0	168·8
present S.N.A.			72·9	81·5	114·0	127·8	148·8
(b) Total (= a) minus transfers to other subsectors of general government *former* S.N.A.	47·9	60·4	102·3	114·1	128·5	145·0	168·8
present S.N.A.			91·6	101·8	114·0	127·8	148·8
(5) Social security agency (total) *former* S.N.A.	22·0	28·4	50·3	57·6	65·1	72·5	82·7
present S.N.A.			50·3	57·6	65·1	72·5	82·7
(6) Ratio general government (2)/G.N.P. (1) *former* S.N.A.	28·2%	29·0%	30·3%	31·6%	30·4%	30·0%	31·4%
present S.N.A.			29·5%	30·8%	29·5%	28·9%	30·2%
(7) Ratio Δ general government/Δ G.N.P. *former* S.N.A.				48·8%	10·9%	24·6%	46·5%
present S.N.A.				48·0%	7·6%	21·4%	44·0%
(8) Ratio (4b)/(3b) *former* S.N.A.	64·8%	71·7%	88·7%	90·4%	113·8%	133·4%	138·9%
present S.N.A.			79·4%	80·7%	101·1%	117·7%	122·6%

Source: *Yearbook of National Accounts Statistics 1973.* Hrsg.v.United Nations, Department of Economic and Social Affairs, Statistical Office (New York, 1975), Vol. II.

FRANCE	*1960*	*1963*	*1968*	*1969*	*1970*	*1971*	*1972*
		(thousand million francs)					
(1) G.N.P. *former* S.N.A.	301·4	411·4	629·3	733·3	819·2	903·7	
present S.N.A.					803·8	894·0	997·1
(2) General government							
former S.N.A.	102·7	149·7	237·3	279·0	308·3	340·2	
present S.N.A.					304·7	336·5	377·1
(3) Central government							
(a) Total *former* S.N.A.	63·2	87·3	131·3	155·2	168·9	182·5	
present S.N.A.					173·9	189·0	212·6
(b) Total (= a) minus transfers to other subsectors of general government							
former S.N.A.	59·4	81·8	121·1	142·6	154·5	166·8	
present S.N.A.					155·5	168·4	187·0
(4) State and local government							
(a) Total *former* S.N.A.	11·2	16·4	27·6	32·2	35·8	40·3	
present S.N.A.					35·0	38·9	45·7
(b) Total (= a) minus transfers to other subsectors of general government							
former S.N.A.	11·1	16·1	27·0	31·6	35·0	39·5	
present S.N.A.					34·2	38·3	44·8
(5) Social security agency							
(total) *former* S.N.A.	33·8	53·8	92·2	10·58	119·3	136·2	
present S.N.A.					103·6	116·9	133·1
(6) Ratio general government							
(2)/G.N.P.(1) *former* S.N.A.	33·1%	36·4%	34·7%	38·0%	37·6%	37·7% (= 37·65)	
present S.N.A.					37·9%	37·6% (= 37·64)	37·8%
(7) Ratio Δ general government/							
Δ G.N.P. *former* S.N.A.				40·1%	34·1%	37·8%	
present S.N.A.						35·3%	39·4%
(8) Ratio (4b)/(3b)							
former S.N.A.	18·7%	19·7%	222·3%	22·2%	22·7%	23·7%	
					22·0%	22·7%	24·0%

Source: *Yearbook of National Accounts Statistics 1973* United Nations, Department of E…

SWEDEN	*1960*	*1963*	*1968*	*1969*	*1970*	*1971*	*1972*
		(thousand million kronen)					
(1) G.N.P.	72·0	91·6	140·1	152·4	170·3	182·9	199·2
(2) General government	23·3	33·3	62·8	69·8	78·3	89·4	99·9
(3) Central government							
(a) Total	14·2	19·4	31·2	34·8	39·5	44·8	47·1
(b) Total (= a) minus transfers to other subsectors of general government	10·6	14·2	20·5	23·1	26·0	29·5	29·9
(4) State and local government							
(a) Total	8·6	11·9	25·8	28·4	31·5	35·6	42·4
(b) Total (= a) minus transfers to other subsectors of general government	8·1	11·2	24·9	27·5	30·5	34·5	41·1
(5) Social security agency (total)	3·9	5·6	11·1	12·2	14·0	16·4	18·4
(6) Ratio general government (2)/G.N.P.(1)	32·4%	36·4%	44·8%	45·8%	46·0%	48·9%	50·2%
(7) Ratio Δ general government/ Δ G.N.P.				56·9%	47·5%	96·3%	64·4%
(8) Ratio (4b)/(3b)	76·4%	78·9%	121·5%	119·1%	117·3%	120·7%	137·5%

Source: *Yearbook of National Accounts Statistics 1973.* Hrsg. v. United Nations, Department of Economic and Social Affairs, Statistical Office (New York, 1975), Vol. II.

AUSTRIA	*1960*	*1963*	*1968*	*1969*	*1970*	*1971*	*1972*
			(thousand million schillings)				
(1) G.N.P.	163·2	207·3	302·8	331·7	371·2	413·1	474·7
(2) General government	50·5	69·7	108·4	120·3	136·2	154·0	176·8
(3) Central government							
(a) Total	27·7	37·7	55·0	60·6	68·1	76·1	87·8
(b) Total (= a) minus transfers to other subsectors of general government	27·7	37·7	55·0	60·6	68·1	76·1	87·8
(4) State and local government							
(a) Total	–	–	–	–	–	–	–
(b) Total (= a) minus transfers to other subsectors of general government	10·8	14·8	24·5	27·8	32·8	37·5	43·4
(5) Social security agency (total)	10·7	15·5	26·4	29·2	32·4	37·2	42·1
(6) Ratio general government (2)/G.N.P.(1)	30·4%	33·6%	35·8%	36·3%	36·7%	37·3%	37·2%
(7) Ratio Δ general government/ Δ G.N.P.	–	–	–	41·2%	40·3%	42·5%	37·0%
(8) Ratio (4b)/(3b)	39·0%	39·3%	44·6%	45·9%	48·2%	49·3%	49·4%

Source: *Yearbook of National Accounts Statistics 1973*, Hrsg. v. United Nations, Department of Economics and Social Affairs, Statistical Office. New York 1975, Vol. I.
Österreichisches Statistisches Zentralamt und Österreichisches Institut für Wirtschaftsforschung, Österreichs Volkseinkommen 1972 und 1973 (Wien, 1974), Ubersicht A4–A21.

FEDERAL REPUBLIC OF GERMANY	*1960*	*1963*	*1968*	*1969*	*1970*	*1971*	*1972*
		(thousand million deutsche mark)					
(1) G.N.P.	302·5	384·8	540·5	605·7	687·0	759·4	829·4
(2) General government	107·2	141·5	196·7	231·3	256·7	292·1	323·2
(3) Central government							
(a) Total	41·0	54·0	73·0	86·2	93·9	105·8	107·2
(b) Total (= a) minus transfers to other subsectors of general government	29·5	38·9	51·3	64·5	71·0	80·1	75·9
(4) State and local government							
(a) Total	37·9	49·8	67·8	78·8	83·8	95·8	113·7
(b) Total (= a) minus transfers to other subsectors of general government	35·8	47·3	64·7	75·7	80·8	92·6	110·6
(5) Social security agency (total)	41·9	55·3	80·8	91·1	105·0	119·6	136·6
(6) Ratio general government (2)/G.N.P.(1)	35·4%	36·8%	36·4%	38·2%	37·4%	38·5%	39·0%
(7) Ratio Δ general government/ Δ G.N.P.	–	–	–	53·1%	31·2%	48·9%	44·4%
(8) Ratio (4b)/(3b)	121·4%	121·6%	126·1%	117·4%	113·8%	115·6%	145·7%

Source: *Yearbook of National Accounts Statistics 1973*. United Nations, Department of Economic and Social Affairs, Statistical Office (New York, 1975), Vol. I.

UNITED KINGDOM	*1960*	*1963*	*1968*	*1969*	*1970*	*1971*	*1972*
			(thousand million pounds)				
(1) G.N.P.	25·434	30·189	42·855	45·736	49·961	55·648	61·185
(2) General government	7·652	9·530	16·131	18·183	20·611	21·908	23·193
(3) Central government							
(a) Total	6·006	7·247	12·406	14·247	16·129	17·054	17·590
(b) Total (= a) minus transfers to other sub-sectors of general government	5·036	5·980	10·142	11·780	13·253	13·702	13·713
(4) State and local government							
(a) Total	1·733	2·284	3·902	4·301	4·870	5·557	6·305
(b) Total (= a) minus transfers to other sub-sectors of general government	1·733	2·284	3·902	4·301	4·870	5·557	6·305
(5) Social security agency (total)	996	1·418	2·376	2·446	2·732	2·945	3·505
(6) Ratio general government (2)/G.N.P.(1)	30·1%	31·6%	37·6%	39·8%	41·3%	39·4%	37·9%
(7) Ratio Δ general government/Δ G.N.P.	–	–	–	71·2%	57·5%	22·8%	23·2%
(8) Ratio (4b)/(3b)	34·4%	38·2%	38·5%	36·5%	36·8%	40·6%	46·0%

Source: *Yearbook of National Accounts Statistics 1973.* Hsg. v. United Nations, Department of Economics and Social Affairs, Statistical Office (New York, 1975), Vol. I.

Discussion of the Papers by F. Neumark and A. Nussbaumer

Professor Neumark explained that the conference would discuss the two papers together. As Professor Robinson had said as chairman of the session, this gave Professor Neumark the double role of both rapier and shield. He was to introduce the paper by Professor Nussbaumer and take part in the discussion of his own.

Professor Neumark went on to say that it seemed to him that the often-quoted 'money-printing' by Government was an inflation technique belonging to the past. For our own inflationary process, a thorough examination of the relations between government and central banks was much more important. However, most discussants seemed to have forgotten that earlier, war-related inflations were the most frequent and most dangerous ones. Perhaps the way the United States Government financed the Vietnam war should not be ignored when studying the (doubtless manifold) causes of inflationary pressures since the late 1960s.

As a fiscal policy man, Professor Neumark was very glad that Professor Nussbaumer had examined the possible relationships between public sector growth and inflation. Most of his paper was devoted to a description of the scope, activities and growth of the public sector. Less than a third dealt with the influence of the growth of public households on inflation, but Professor Neumark wanted to concentrate on this latter point.

Quite rightly, Professor Nussbaumer refuted the opinion that the influence of inflation on the public sector could, or should, be 'assumed away altogether'. He rather shared Schumpeter's view that fiscal policy was supremely important for national economic development, human civilisation and human behaviour. After briefly examining the Haavelmo theorem, Professor Nussbaumer stated that he did not aim to present a general model, but believed it would be more rewarding to trace the different influences which might determine the relationship between public sector growth and inflation. He therefore began by discussing the institutional structure of public households, including the social security administration, and analysing the various functions of today's public sector.

The author went on to depict the more recent growth of the public sector and possible reasons for this. While inflation was thought to play an important role, other facts mentioned were the Peacock–Wiseman 'displacement effect'. It seemed remarkable to Professor Neumark that the author should also distinguish between government expenditures influencing the creating of income and property and therefore expansionist; and purely financial transactions of government, influencing the distribution of liquidity.

Finally, Professor Nussbaumer dealt with problems of the impact of the growth of public households on inflation. Here, the structure of public expenditure and of the tax system were mentioned as reinforcing inflation, but the increase in the level of public activities was another factor.

In the hundred years since Adolph Wagner stated his famous 'law', the absolute and relative size of public sector had grown considerably. What was debatable was the why, the how and the consequences.

On the first point, Professor Nussbaumer gave an able survey of both and contemporary theories, though he somewhat neglected the methodological subtleties in arriving at an economic meaningful assessment of the size, and the changes in size, of the public sector. More important, the analysis understated the fundamental differences in the repercussions of increased public expenditures according to the method of finance. Indeed, readers might arrive at the conclusion that Professor Nussbaumer believed that every kind of public activity would increase inflationary pressure and that growth-stimulating public expenditures and/or tax measures did not exist.

While Professor Nussbaumer would clearly not go so far, he did not always seem sufficiently aware that between, say, 1864 and 1914 a considerable expansion of the public sector had not been accompanied by greater inflationary pressure. Even in our time we observed – at least until 1970 – neither a steady relative growth of public expenditure nor a long-term correlation between this and inflation. There were certainly large differences between countries, as the author acknowledged in his statement: 'Since there is no universally accepted theory of inflation, there can be no single theoretical model explaining the impact of the growth of the public sector on inflation pressure'.

Professor Neumark did not believe that the growth of public households was as important a fact in current inflation as some peculiarities of growing public revenue and expenditure. While inevitably overlapping with his own paper, Professor Nussbaumer approached the core of the matter on the other side of the question – namely, the impact of inflation on public sector growth. Thus: 'Inflation itself contributes to the growth of the public sector'. If the tax system was progressive, and there was money illusion among tax payers, 'the real burden of direct taxes on individuals must increase'. This must be the crucial factor, if the *overall* tax system were progressive. Even non-inflationary economic growth would cause a more-than-proportional increase in tax revenue. This, in turn, permitted government and parliament to propose and vote supplementary expenditure without the unpopular need to raise tax rates. Thus the belief spread that the proceeds of built-in flexibility in the tax system would always be available, so that neither executive or legislator shrank from introducing large programmes, whose costs were doomed to rise considerably in future.

Naturally, Professor Nussbaumer was right to stress that there were limits to taxation. But these varied in time and space. Further, at least in many developed countries, they were much wider and more flexible than around 1900. The famous French economist Paul Leroy–Beaulieu had tried to show the inapplicability of the 'single tax' theory by pointing out that income tax, as a single tax, would have to reach an unbearable rate of 7 to 8 per cent. Some decades later, Colin Clark pretended that taxation beyond 25 per cent of G.N.P. must lead to inflation.

Professor Nussbaumer pointed out that 'when approaching these limits, individual resistance to taxation grows'. While accurate, Professor Neumark wondered whether the conclusion was correct, namely 'to redistribute income via inflation may be the only alternative left'. His doubts were mainly because the distributive effects of inflation were largely the exact opposite of what redistribution policies intended. There was little doubt that, under inflation, the personal distribution of income, and still more of wealth, would become increasingly unequal.

However, he agreed that 'the growth of public expenditure during periods of inflation . . . may be due as much to inflation as to more rapid structural change'. One could not exclude the possibility that inflation might accentuate tendencies towards structural change. Suppose, for example, that the share of expenditure on construction, as a proportion of total public expenditure, increased and that individuals and businesses saw real estate as having a stable value during inflation. So, the price index, both of real property and of construction, rose faster than for other goods. Then, evidently, one could speak of a process of reciprocal money depreciation.

Professor Neumark's final comment was on an issue which had been a sort of hobby for about fifty years. His first book had been on *The Notion and Nature of Inflation* (1922). The question was whether it was more sensible to use the word inflation to mean a general increase in the price level or the creation of supplementary money which might lead to such money depreciation. Definitions, of course, were matters of convenience or expediency. To him, the second version had the advantage of permitting a clear distinction between an increase in the price level mainly due to monetary operations and one caused by other factors. He raised this because of something Professor Nussbaumer had said about the Haavelmo theorem. According to Nussbaumer, this 'disregards possible inflationary effects connected with increasing taxes'. Later, he said: 'There will be an increase of the price level if government revenue is increased by a general sales tax rather than by taxation of income'. He agreed with the fact, but he refused to designate such a price increase as 'inflationary'. Otherwise, one arrived at the nonsensical conclusion that even an increase in net value added tax, whose proceeds were deactivated by the central bank, would have to be called inflationary. This would be so, even if it were designed as an anti-inflation measure, and worked by reducing private demand for consumer goods wherever tax shifting were possible. Even if the government spent the whole additional tax yield on consumer goods, the likely rise in the price level would be once-for-all, and not the continuous upward pressure characteristic of inflation proper.

Professor Levhari noted that the legislative and executive branches of government had both expenditure and revenue plans, and that Professor Neumark had asked how far these were distorted, or not realised, because of inflationary pressure.

On the revenue side, the real value of revenue from sales of services could fall sharply with inflation. A major question here, was the structure of lags. On the tax side, specific taxes might well fall too during inflation, but *ad valorem* taxes would keep roughly in line. Lags were therefore crucial in determining the real value of revenue. The effect of inflation on revenue from deductable income taxes depended on the progressivity of the system. Delays in payment could lead a progressive system to become effectively a proportional one.

If local government got the revenue from specific taxes, and central government the revenue from general income tax, the final relationship between the two branches of government could be significantly altered by inflation.

The situation was similar with inheritance and profits taxes. Again, long delays in collection would reduce their real value significantly, but one could attempt to increase the payment period as well as shifting from, for example, F.I.F.O. to L.I.F.O. in tax calculations.

On the expenditure side, if the government did not, for example, adjust interest payments, this would lead to a fall in the real value of debt. Indeed, with a very high inflation rate, the real value of debt could fall dramatically. Expenditure on health, etc. would increase quickly because there was no technological progress there, and with high inflation, this element in the economy could actually lead it.

Most of the paper assumed that there was a price inflation resulting from an independent monetary expansion. There was random transfer of money – as from the famous helicopter. With this kind of inflation, the tax system could provide an ideal remedy if one could index the tax schedule, the rate of interest, and social security payments.

But the source of the problem was often not a purely monetary one. Transfer payments were often more important. So perhaps one should put the problem in the framework of a discussion of optimal taxation. If, for example, the oil price increased, the government would pay more for the use of oil and the real income of the economy would fall – along with real government receipts – unless the progressiveness of tax rates offset it.

One had to remember that, under a profit or capital gains tax, without adjustment, income was distorted because tax was levied on imaginary profits. For example, the tax on bond interest was a tax on the returns from capital eroded by inflation. It would depend on the type of system whether this offset the lower real value of tax receipts in other parts of the system. Tax collection methods might well be more important than tax rates. For example, delays in collection could reduce the tax burden significantly.

As for what the government should do to stay in power, this was an important question, but was it beyond the scope of this discussion.

Professor Robinson thought one should distinguish the relatively direct effects of inflation on the tax system from lags between the initial earning of income, its assessment for tax, and the payment of the tax. In the United Kingdom, and in some Asian countries, these lags were important. In the United Kingdom, the lag could be as much as two years. Over such a period, the difference in the price level in some countries was so considerable that government underestimation of the rate of inflation of its expenditures led to real difficulties, for instance, in financing a budget deficit of a size which had never been foreseen or intended.

Professor Tsuru explained that the situation in Japan was the reverse of this. Japan had a good pay-as-you-go income tax system, which raised a major part of revenue. The problems arose on the expenditure side. The Japanese government had always had a surplus in recent years, despite attempts to adjust the system to adapt to inflation, and the government was compelled to use half any budget surplus to reduce debt, as had happened in each year since 1960. Inflation therefore had a deflationary effect on budgetary policies.

Mr Plessz pointed to the important problem of tax shifting. Before the oil crisis, an OECD consultant had been looking at tax-push inflation. His results suggested not only that, in general, increased direct taxes were shifted into prices through wage claims, but that the same happened with indirect taxes. This indicated that anti-inflationary policies based on increases in indirect taxation tended to be self-defeating. The study showed 'tax-push' coefficients varying typically from 0·5 to 0·8.

This was a central policy issue because it seemed to mean that it was unimportant whether one tried to tax the population through inflation or more normal forms of taxation. If one used taxation, one merely led to inflation later on. Where, as now, there was not full employment, but still inflation, perhaps the worst thing was to use an increase in indirect taxes as an anti-inflationary measure. Certainly, at some moments, one merely added to cost-push.

Professor Robinson said that there had been considerable discussion in the United Kingdom of whether one should put taxes into the cost of living index. This led to difficulties if the cost of living index included commodities whose taxation one would want to increase when one sought to deflate.

If government expenditure on a welfare state represented a rising proportion of the total economy, and the lags in assessment and collection of direct taxation were considerable one would like to be able to use indirect taxation to finance that expenditure. But it was difficult to do this if the cost of living index included tax and was then used in wage bargaining.

Professor Hague said it was obviously impossible in this type of conference to write a completely up-to-date paper which looked comparatively at a number of countries. He would therefore like to tell Professor Nussbaumer that, if one looked at more recent figures for the United Kingdom, instead of the 40 per cent of G.N.P. represented by government expenditure shown in the paper, one would have a figure of over 50 per cent. This related to what Mr Plessz had said. It was not only that transfer payments in the United Kingdom were indexed. Many of them were indexed not so much to the cost of living as to average wages. This could represent a big burden if average wages were rising rapidly and the number of, for example, pensioners was large.

As the authors had pointed out, productivity did not go up rapidly in sectors like health and education. Worse still, these sectors were also highly labour-intensive. This led to an interesting phenomenon, which must also be having an impact on the British government deficit. In recent months, there had been considerable increases in wages throughout the British economy. A point that was perhaps too often overlooked was that this led to differential rates of inflation in different parts of the economy. In particular, it had led in the United Kingdom to a tremendous increase in expenditure by central and local government because they were so highly labour-intensive.

At the same time, there was a good deal of negative fiscal drag in the United Kingdom, because specific tax rates could not be altered quickly enough. As Professor Robinson had said, if one did alter them, there was then the danger of a feedthrough effect. These were examples of serious fiscal problems arising from inflation in the United Kingdom which had not been taken seriously enough until a few months previously.

Professor Malinvaud wanted to point to a relevant case in recent French history. Tax rates in France had been reduced in 1973. He had thought at the time that this was inflationary. Admittedly, reducing the tax reduced the rate of increase in the cost of living. However, since there was a high pressure of demand, it increased demand and, in the end, probably increased the level of prices beyond what it would otherwise have been.

One ought therefore to distinguish between differences of circumstance when the government reduced indirect taxes. If they were reduced at a time when there was slack in the economy, any resultant change in demand pressure was not important for inflation. But the reduction of tax in France had been made at an inappropriate time.

Professor Hague said the situation in the United Kingdom was worse even than that. In the summer of 1974, taxes had been reduced in a pre-election period and this had probably added to inflationary pressure. More recently, they had been increased and this had led to attempts to recoup them in wage increases.

Professor Duesenberry suggested that when the economy was slack there was another distributional issue. Part of the mechanism was the attitude of the labour force and its willingness to strike unless wage increases were awarded. Perhaps the real rate of wage increase that was sought reflected real take home pay. If so, this had implications for reactions to tax changes, import price increases, etc.

The reaction to tax changes depended in part on how far they were accepted by the population. The legislature could increase payroll taxes to finance transfer payments. There was always a strong lobby in favour of such a move, but taxpayers might not be prepared to finance it. If society accepted the decision to do so, this kind of reaction, leading to wage increases, would not occur. It was not just a question of authority, but of attitudes. Did those on the shop floor want the change? That was the important issue.

Professor Bronfenbrenner argued that much depended on how the cost of living figures were calculated. A great deal of 'diddling' with the figures was possible. In the United States many cost of living figures included sales taxes. Cost of living indices would behave very differently if prices were reported net of tax.

Professor Duesenberry thought that this issue was very much like that of the money illusion. A great deal depended on what people were told had happened to the cost of living index. Nevertheless, whatever the figures said, the family still knew how far its pay cheque went. He would give Professor Bronfenbrenner part of the argument, but not the whole of it.

Professor Robinson insisted that if the percentage of income payable in tax was assessed in 1972 but not payable until 1974, this was a very different matter.

Professor Bronfenbrenner noted one thing that had happened in Japan during the American occupation. Each tax office in Japan had been assessed. If it raised less than that assessment, more was insisted on. While this was good for the Communist party, it was bad for inflation.

Professor Swoboda suggested that the study Mr Plessz had mentioned might suffer from the defect of not asking clearly the question: When could one shift an increase in tax? This shifting was only possible if the state of aggregate demand allowed. One also had to distinguish specific from *ad valorem* taxes; it was harder to shift the second. Furthermore, it was extremely important to distinguish the effect of taxes on the price level and on the rate of inflation. An increase in indirect taxation could affect the price level but not necessarily the inflation rate.

In the short run, of course, an increase in the price level would appear as an increase in the inflation rate. Policy and other reactions could perhaps accentuate this reaction of the rate of inflation to a rise in the price level. Although

Professor Neumark had already made this point, it was one that needed emphasising.

To Professor Bronfenbrenner, Professor Swoboda said that colleagues at the London School of Economics (B. Aghevli and M. Khan, on leave from the IMF) had studied the case of Indonesia. Once the rate of inflation increased, the government indeed thought of tax increases, but actually used increases in the money supply to finance real government expenditures in the short run. Furthermore, taxes had been increased by doing roughly what Professor Bronfenbrenner said the Americans had done during the occupation of Japan, namely, by accelerating and reinforcing collections rather than by increasing tax rates.

Professor Kleiman pointed out that if we all shifted our taxes forward in price increases, this would raise the price level, but everything else would remain unchanged. However, this would not be so if the subject of the shift were the government, which had real expenditure to finance. If the price level of this expenditure increased, and if the government took a big enough share of the G.N.P., the private sector might succeed in shifting the burden to it. But then the government would not get enough real resources. It would again increase taxes (and print money). This would again be shifted, through increased prices, against the government. One would then have a system where the government had to increase taxation steadily in order to get the same real resources. But one would never quite succeed.

Participants had mentioned the real value of government services. Inflation was often the result of an attempt to increase the supply of government services. This was part of Professor Duesenberry's take-home pay issue. The distinction between public and private goods was important. People resented tax the less the more closely they saw public and private goods as substitutes.

Professor Robinson noted that the interwar discussion on reparations had reached the conclusion that the tax burden would stick where one found a group which could not shift it.

Professor Duesenberry said one had to assume some lags. One group shifted tax and, because of lags, succeeded for a time. At any one moment, someone always bore the impact of the tax, but that burden changed hands. Then inflationary expectations would increase and the inflation rate would speed up. If no group could be made to bear the burden of the tax for a substantial period it was passed round. So the burden remained on each group for a limited period. Even pensioners were escalated!

A paper by Koopmans on the speed of inflation had shown the need to have sufficiently rapid inflation to enable the government to get the real resources it needed. These were not completely realistic models but they pointed to important practical truths.

Professor Aukrust thought it clear that what one could or could not do with taxation varied between countries. How far did unions understand economics, and how far did they co-operate or compete with government? He would like to quote a case where the cost of living had been considered.

Norway had gone over to V.A.T. in 1970 and, at the same time, had shifted a considerable amount of the burden of raising revenue from direct to indirect taxation. The government had made an agreement with the trade unions that they would not ask for increases in wages to match that part of the cost of living increase ascribable to this shift. The amount in question had been calculated by a reliable body – the Statistical Office – which had come to the conclusion that the increase in question was 5·8 per cent. This had not been fed through into wage increases.

Here was an example of an economic policy situation where there had been real understanding, and where the trade unions had acted with great responsibility. However, he would emphasise that what happened in Norway was not always so creditable.

Professor Mussa recalled that there was an interesting discussion of the speed of the process of inflation in Keynes's tract on *How to Pay for the War*. One reason for looking at the government deficit in analysing the process of inflation was that this deficit was frequently financed by printing money. By this route, an increase in expenditure led to monetary expansion, which fuelled inflation. Often, attempts to reduce inflation by subsidising certain commodities actually made inflation worse by creating larger deficits. In Taiwan, inflation had been halted by increasing the price of basic commodities sold through the government so that the budget deficit was reduced.

The role of money in the inflationary process could be seen by the contrast between the United Kingdom and New York City. In both, governments had run large deficits but inflation was much worse in the United Kingdom. This was because the United Kingdom had its own money and its own central bank and hence could finance its deficits by printing money. New York could not.

Professor Parkin returned to the question of reverse fiscal drag. If one took the total public sector, it was important to note that the critical thing affecting the borrowing requirement was not the rate of inflation but the rate of change in the rate of inflation. Using a simple algebraic model, one could show that if the rate of inflation was increasing more quickly than the rate at which the tax schedule was adjusted, this led to negative fiscal drag. The unstable borrowing requirement which resulted was perhaps more important than the effect of wage inflation on relative prices, mentioned by Professor Hague.

Professor Neumark told Professor Levhari that the main problem not examined had been whether structural change within the public sector had been strengthened by inflation or not. This point had been stressed by Professor Nussbaumer. It was argued that in many countries, especially Germany, inflation meant that the prices government paid for the things it bought went up more rapidly than the general price index or the G.D.P. deflator. However, it had not yet been proved that this was the case.

He was glad that speakers had emphasised the importance of lags in the assessment and collection of taxation. The judgement on the advantages and disadvantages of built-in tax flexibility had changed. We had previously seen this as a good anti-inflationary device. An important requirement was that additional proceeds due to built-in flexibility should be used either to reduce the tax rate or to sterilise funds by lodging them with the central bank.

Professor Bronfenbrenner had talked about 'diddling' calculations of the cost of living index. One needed to look at the causes of price inflation. It was not sensible to use indirect taxes as an anti-inflationary device and then include taxation in cost of living indices.

Anti-inflationary tax policy could be self-defeating. It only worked if the increase in indirect tax was not reflected in the cost of living index, and if the proceeds of such tax increases were not used to increase public expenditure. Only if this could be done, and if lags in the assessment and collection of tax were not too big, would one get a rational fiscal policy.

Professor Nussbaumer explained that he became interested in these issues because he had written a monetarist paper on fiscal policies. Money was the instrument of inflation in the private or public sectors, and monetary policy influenced the volume and distribution of liquidity. This was handled by the central bank or ministry of finance.

These ideas underlay his paper but were not wholly explicit. One needed to distinguish measures that led to an increase in money or incomes from those which merely transferred liquidity. One could construct a similar argument about debt management. He had referred to this but, in a criticism of Haavelmo, would emphasise the retirement of debt – both private (for liquidity effect) and government debt with the central bank. This kind of system was operated, in Austria, to increase potential liquidity if needed.

The issue was not merely a question of the public sector. One found similar developments in other economic systems, whatever the size of the public sector. Should we assume that structural change was often followed by credit creation? There was frequently resistance to taxation and this did lead to structural change. What difference did it make to inflation if one borrowed abroad rather than at home? There might be different effects if total credit at home was not increased. But, with tight liquidity, the central bank borrowed from the other banks and eased the system.

He thought there were three important issues on inflation in the public sector. First, allocation became less perfect because of inflation. Second, stabilisation was not necessarily the main concern of public policy. Third, income redistribution might lead to resistance. Public authority was exercised by government but there was also institutional welfare. The supply of a 'free' public good was not always seen as a substitute for private goods. There were also financial changes. In some Western European countries, the big banks were government owned, raised funds and provided credit too. There were also major nationalised industries, and one had to be clear whether one was discussing them. The public sector took many different forms and a lack of co-ordination within it could cause inflation. His conclusion was that Haavelmo's was a good theory but that its main value was in leading one to think of other alternatives.

Professor Nussbaumer agreed that inflation was linked to the creation of supplementary money. In measuring the size of the public sector, we needed first to define it. He had ignored other kinds of financing because it would have lengthened the paper but, of course, the amount of tax shifting determined the increase in credit required.

On whether inflation contributed to the growth of the public sector, he did not want to reach a specific conclusion. He also wanted to avoid the question whether the public sector price index went up faster. His own view was that there was a push where wages were important, where there was a good deal of indexing of pensions and other expenditure, and, especially, where there was a good deal of construction whose prices were going up quickly. But he did not want to get into detail on this.

As for the limits to taxation, he would not agree that there was any absolute limit, but he did think there was a limit to the speed at which one could increase the share of government in the G.N.P. A second limit was that in some European countries bigger share of government expenditure in G.N.P. made it less easy to fund a further increase.

Part 4

Policies for Inflation

15 Indexation in Israel

Reuven Brenner and Don Patinkin

THE HEBREW UNIVERSITY OF JERUSALEM

I. INTRODUCTION

The spread of 'two-digit inflation' to many parts of the Western world has led in recent years to greatly increased interest in the possible use of indexation to deal with some of the problems which arise in connection with inflation that proceeds relatively at such a rapid rate. It is accordingly the purpose of this paper to indicate in broad lines what lessons we can learn about indexation from Israel's thirty-five years of experience with it.[1]

II. ON THE NATURE OF INDEXATION

Before turning to these lessons, it is important that we clarify to ourselves the distinctive nature of indexation about which we would like to learn.[2] For it is a commonplace of both theory and practice that even in the absence of indexation, any prolonged inflationary process in a relatively free market economy generates continuously rising prices and wages in all sectors of the economy, ever-rising exchange rates (if the inflation is faster than in other countries), and a nominal rate of interest that rises the higher the expected rate of inflation.

In this commonplace observation there are two key terms: 'free market economy' and 'expected rate'. And the distinctive nature of indexation is related to these terms.

In particular, the nominal rate of interest as determined in a free market economy will correctly reflect future rates of inflation only to the extent that these rates are correctly anticipated. That this frequently does not occur in practice is evidenced by the fact that the *ex post* real rate of interest in

[1] This paper has been developed within the framework of a workshop on indexation which has been carried out at the Hebrew University during the academic year 1974–75. The authors are indebted to the participants in this seminar, and especially to Ephraim Kleiman and Reuben Gronau, for many helpful comments and discussions. They also have a particular debt to Yosef Findling for permission to make use of the paper on 'The History of the Cost-of-Living Allowance' which he presented to the workshop. Finally, they wish to express their appreciation to Nissan Liviatan and to Zvi Zussman for their valuable comments and suggestions. Needless to say, responsibility for the opinions expressed remains that of the authors alone.

[2] This section has in part made use of the discussion in Patinkin [29].

inflationary economies is frequently negative. Hence one of the primary purposes of indexation is to eliminate the necessity for correctly anticipating the rate of inflation by making contractual arrangements which, by means of the indexing clause, stipulate real rates of interest instead of nominal ones. This aspect of indexation has attracted much attention among monetary theorists in recent years, who have accordingly developed microeconomic models of portfolio choice in which one of the assets has a rate of return whose real rate of return is certain, while the nominal rate of return is not.[1]

Needless to say, the need for such indexation is greater for long-term loans than for short-term ones. Indeed, even in those countries where there are index clauses, such clauses have not been applied in the case of short-term bank loans. For it is in the nature of things that the discrepancy between what we anticipate and what actually happens is greater the longer the period for which we try to anticipate. Furthermore, the (say) loss generated by unanticipated inflation is, *ceteris paribus*, greater the longer the period in question. Thus an individual who gives a loan for three months at an annual rate of 10 per cent on the assumption that inflation will proceed at a rate of 4 per cent, and is instead unexpectedly confronted by an inflation that proceeds at an annual rate of 12 per cent will lose 0·5 per cent of the real value of his initial principle; in contrast, if he gives a loan to be repaid with accumulated interest at the end of five years he will, under the same circumstances, suffer a corresponding loss of almost 10 per cent. All this is simply a reflection of the fact that even though in both cases the lender is receiving a negative interest rate of roughly 2 per cent *per annum*, instead of the positive real rate of roughly 6 per cent that he had expected, the short-term lender will suffer this loss only for three months, after which he will be able to make a new loan that will reflect the changed inflationary conditions; whereas the long-term lender is forced to continue to suffer the consequences of these unexpected developments for five years. In brief, the shorter the term of the loan, the more quickly the lender will effectively be able to recontract it, and hence the smaller the possible loss from the unexpected.

Besides the role that indexation can play in solving this problem of unanticipated inflation, it can also play a role that derives from the fact that there is no economy in which *all* prices are determined by a freely functioning market. The absence of such a market can take the form, at one extreme, of an economy operating under an extensive system of price, wage, and foreign-exchange controls. But even in an economy in which such controls do not formally exist, there are always some administered prices, particularly of goods and services sold by or under the supervision of government (for example, exchange rates – until they recently became flexible – public-utility rates, and the like). There are also other nominal money quantities determined by governments, such as income tax brackets.

[1] See Fischer [12], as well as the paper by Liviatan and Levhari also presented in this Conference. Such a model is also the subject of an unpublished paper by Brenner.

In all these cases, a prolonged inflationary process will in practice ultimately bring about an increase in the nominal quantities in question. Thus in the face of a continued inflation, even controlled prices and exchange rates will ultimately be raised. And the same will be true of such nominal quantities as income tax brackets and the like. Such upward adjustments, however, will usually be made only with a lag – either because of the cumbersomeness of the bureaucratic procedure, or possibly the need to take even more cumbersome legislative action. And the lagging of such controlled prices behind the general inflationary process will then lead to serious distortions of the price structure and all that follows from that.

The purpose of indexation in such cases is then to lessen or even eliminate the lag in adjusting official prices. As such, its role is that of preventing the distortions – and changes in distribution of real income – that are generated by the lags that would otherwise exist. But it is not indexation in the strict sense of removing uncertainty about future real quantities.

We have so far not discussed the role of indexation in the determination of wages. In this context, however, what is called indexation is frequently actually a form of wage or income policy which does not necessarily even assure the maintenance of a constant wage rate. The outstanding example of this is Brazil, where in the three years immediately following the introduction of wage indexation (or, to use the Brazilian term, 'monetary correction'), the real minimum wage rate (and possibly also the actual one) declined – and this despite the rapid increase in per capita G.N.P. at that time; [14], page 273, and [1], page 45.

Again, the references to changes in the cost of living in the annual collective bargaining which determines money wages in large sectors of the United States and British economy do not really involve indexation. For what is involved here is not an automatic adjustment of money wages to changes in the price index so as to keep their real value constant, but one bargaining point among others in the negotiating process that determines wages. That is, the reference to cost of living allowances in these cases is only one of the headings under which workers, free of money illusion, bargain for a money wage rate that will *inter alia* also take account of the change in the value of money generated by inflation. We shall return to both of these points below.

It is clear from what has just been said that the use of indexation to decrease lags in adjusting official prices or in wage negotiations does not (in distinction to its use in loan contracts) introduce any basically new element into microeconomic theory. But it does raise a question with respect to the macroeconomic theory of inflation. For the use of indexation in these contexts may speed up the inflationary process, particularly in the case where it is one in which demand and cost inflation are interacting. In this context there are two points that should be emphasised. First, the crucial question is the difference (if any) between the rate at which inflation will proceed with (say) automatically indexed wages, and the rate at which it would proceed in a situation in which wage contracts are renegotiated (say) every year. For it is naive to assume that, in the absence of indexation, money wages would not rise in an inflationary process. Second, the fact that indexation may speed up the inflationary process does not imply that the process thereby becomes more injurious to the economy. For the welfare loss generated by inflation is a function not only of the rate of inflation (and it is not a monotonic function of that either), but also of the distortion in relative prices caused by the lagged adjustment of administered prices. Hence even if the wider application of indexation might increase the loss from the first factor, it will definitely diminish the loss from the second one.

In theory, it is of course possible that indexation may so increase the rate of inflation so as to destabilise the process. But Cagan's study of hyperinflation [8] shows how rarely divergent inflationary processes have occurred even in the most extreme cases. In any event, it has not occurred in those countries like Israel and Brazil which have had the most experience with indexation.

III. THE INFLATIONARY PROCESS IN ISRAEL

As background for the discussion which follows, let us now provide a brief description of the inflation in Israel. That such inflation is endemic to the country can be seen from figure 15.1, which shows that the cost of living index has increased 45 times in the 36 years from 1939 to 1975. This represents an average annual rate of inflation of a little more than 11 per cent. But the use of an overall average in this case is misleading; for figure 15.1 also

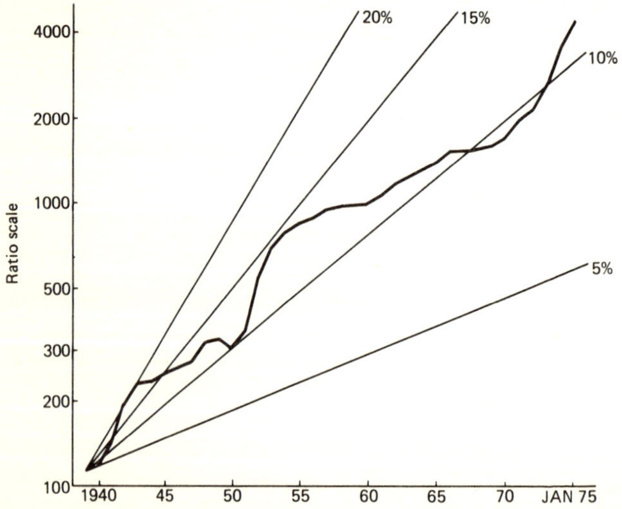

Fig. 15.1 Consumers' Price Index: 1939–1975
Sources: 1939–47: *Statistical Handbook for Jewish Palestine* (1947)
1948–75: *Statistical Abstract of Israel* (various years)

shows us that most of the inflation was concentrated in three periods which constitute only about one-third of those 36 years. Those periods were (1) the one connected with the Second World War, January 1940–December 1943; (2) the one connected with the Israeli War of Independence of 1948 and the mass immigration which almost doubled Israel's population in the three years that followed, January 1950–October 1953; and finally (3) the one connected with the boom of the early 1970s and then with the economic consequences of the Yom Kippur War, which has continued until the present date (though there are indications of a levelling off in recent months). During each of these periods, the price level increased by roughly 2·5 times, so that in all three together it increased by a multiple of roughly 15 (which represents an annual rate of inflation of 23 per cent). This is to be contrasted with the developments of the remaining 23 years of the period 1939–75, during which the price level increased by a multiple of 3 (which represents an annual rate of inflation of 5 per cent) [16], [26], [27].

In particular, the 16-year period from the end of 1954 to the beginning of 1970 was one of relative stability, during which the price index rose at an average annual rate of 4·6 per cent, representing an average quarterly rate of 1 per cent. Furthermore, as we can see from figure 15.2, in 18 of the 64 quarters in this 16-year period there was no change in prices, and in almost two-thirds of the quarters, the quarterly rate of inflation was less than or equal to 1·5 per cent. It was this relative stability which has been so radically

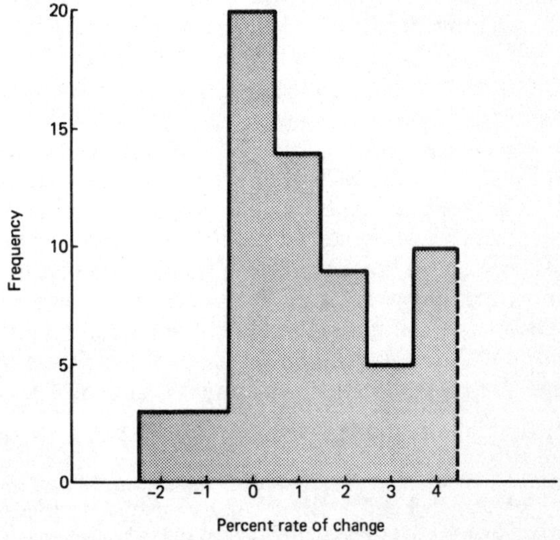

Fig. 15.2 Quarterly Rates of Change of Consumers' Price Index (January 1954–January 1970)
Source: *Statistical Abstract of Israel.*

upset by the very rapid inflation which has characterised the Israel economy during the past five years.

Insofar as the use of indexation is concerned, in one way or another, money wages have been tied to a cost of living allowance since the onset of the inflationary process in 1939. On the other hand, the indexing of long-term loans did not really begin until the mid-1950s, though (as we shall see) there were isolated instances of it already in 1948 and 1951. Similarly, pension payments have been indexed since 1950; furthermore, in many cases pensions are indexed not to the cost of living allowance, but to the nominal basic salary paid to the rank which the pensioner held upon retirement. In this way pensioners have also been able to benefit from the increases in the productivity of the economy which take place after the retirement.[1]

These have been the only applications of indexation in the Israel economy. In particular, despite the fact that there have been foreign exchange controls throughout the period, the exchange-rate itself has not been indexed. Instead, from the establishment of the state and until the end of 1974, there has been a series of official devaluations which has increased the price of a dollar (in terms of Israel pounds) almost 25 times: from IL 0·248 in 1948 to IL 6·00 in November 1974. In this way, the official exchange rate has over the period as a whole, been more than adjusted to the inflationary changes in the price index (which increased by roughly 13 times during the same period).[2] By definition, however, during the respective subperiods between these discrete changes, the official exchange rate has lagged behind the inflationary process. It is therefore important to emphasise that besides these discrete official devaluations of the exchange rate (for which formal approval of the government as a whole was necessary), there has existed in Israel a system by which more continuous administrative changes in the effective exchange rates on imports and exports, respectively, have been carried out, by means of a variety of special import duties and export subsidies. All this is shown by figure 15.3.

Thus the exchange rate effectively accorded to most transactions on current account has been fairly rapidly adjusted by administrative action to the inflationary developments; correspondingly, the major impact of the official devaluations has been on the rate accorded to transactions on capital account. We might also note that just recently (in June 1975) a cabinet subcommittee (consisting of the ministers of finance, trade and industry, and justice, and enjoined to consult with the governor of the Bank of Israel) was granted authority to make formal devaluations up to a maximum of 2 per cent during

[1] See Sarnat [32], chapter 2; [33], pages 38–39. In practice, however, the system failed to achieve this purpose fully because of the fact that, in order to avoid income tax, an increasing proportion of salaries in Israel were effectively paid in the form of 'expense allowances', which were not included in the basic salary to which the pension payment was tied. Hopefully, however, this situation will be radically changed now as a result of the reform in the income tax which has abolished such 'expense allowances'.

[2] Which is a reflection of the government's deliberate policy to increase the ratio of prices of internationally-traded goods to those of domestic goods, in order to improve Israel's chronic deficit on current account in its balance of payments.

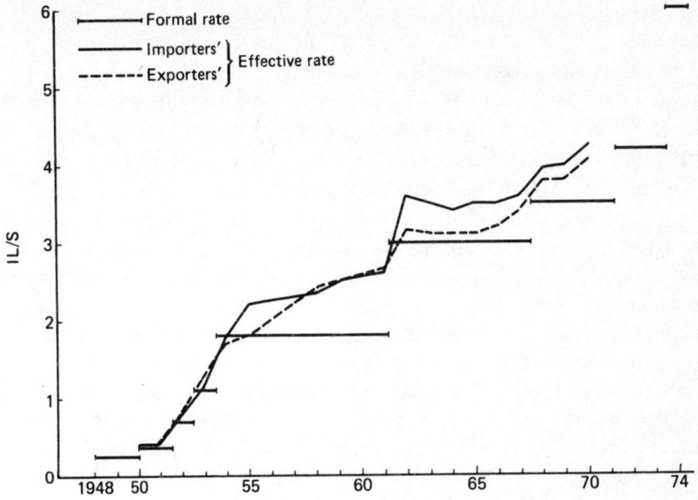

Fig. 15.3 Official and Effective Exchange Rates
Sources: 1949–61: Michaely (1968) Tables D-1 and D-3. (During 1952–54 there were several formal rates. The figures are averages weighted by value of transactions.)
1962–67: Halevy [15], p. 47.
1967–70: Valery [34].

any 30-day period, and as of this date (August 1975) has already twice exercised this power. But even now the exchange rate has not been automatically tied to the price index.

Similarly, the income-tax brackets have been changed over time more or less in accordance with the inflationary process, though without tying them automatically to the price index. Thus, for example, in 1954 a family with two children whose annual income did not exceed IL 1800 was exempt from income tax; whereas the maximum exempt income for 1966 (by which time the price index had almost doubled) was IL 4000.[1] We should however note that in the major reform of the income tax which has just taken place, the income tax brackets have been defined in a way that for the first time takes formal account of the price index.

IV. THE INDEXATION OF MONEY WAGES

Israel labour is highly organised in the Workers' Organisation of Israel (Histadrut Ovdei Eretz Yisroel), which is commonly known as the Histadrut. Similarly, Israel's manufacturing firms are organised in the Manufacturers' Association

[1] Economic Planning Authority, *Israel Economic Development* (1968), pp. 196–97.

(Hitachdut Baaley Taaseeya). The wage agreements reached by these two bodies usually set the pattern for the economy as a whole. On the nature and operation of the Histadrut, see [16], chapter 11.

Wage agreements are usually made on an annual basis. The wages themselves have three components: basic salary, fringe benefits, and a cost of living allowance. During most of the period under discussion, the exact nature of this allowance was determined by an agreement reached by the Histadrut and Manufacturers' Association; since 1970, however, the Government has also been a party to this agreement, and has indeed played an increasingly important role in determining its details. Insofar as the basic salary and fringe benefits are concerned, these are determined for each sector of the economy (or each profession) by negotiations between the specific employers' association and Histadrut trade union that are respectively involved, though here too the Government has in recent years played an important role. It should be noted that the agreed-upon increase in basic salary has generally been specified as a percentage increase of the salary as adjusted by the cost of living allowance – so that to a certain extent (see below) the specification has been in real terms.

The first cost of living agreement between the Histadrut and Manufacturers' Association was signed in December 1940. At that time Palestine (as it then was) was under a British Mandate, and as such its economy was harnessed to the British war effort. In particular, relatively large pressures of demand were exerted on its infant manufacturing sector by orders for war material from the Middle East Supply Centre [25], chapter 25. It was this excess demand that created the inflationary pressures that have been described in figure 15.1.

This inflation led to the first cost of living agreement between the Histadrut and the Manufacturers' Association in December 1940, providing a one-time cost of living allowance of 20 per cent on the basic wage, roughly corresponding to the percentage price increase since the preceding year. As the inflationary increase continued, the Mandatory Government became concerned that it should not create labour unrest, and so appointed a special 'Joint Committee on Problems of Wage Adjustment' consisting of G. E. F. Wood (then chief statistician of the mandatory government) and David Horowitz (then economist for the Jewish Agency, and later to become first governor of the Bank of Israel).[1] This committee described the policy of wage indexation that had been adopted since the onset of the war by many other countries of the British Commonwealth, and recommended that there also be an automatic cost of living adjustment for the Palestinian economy. This recommendation was immediately adopted in the cost of living agreement that was then signed between the Histadrut and Manufacturers' Association in 1942, and has been a permanent feature of Israel labour contracts ever since.

It would, however, be a serious mistake to think that the existence of a cost of living allowance has caused money wages in Israel ever since to increase

[1] In a recent newspaper article [17], Horowitz has provided some interesting recollections of the origins and operation of this Committee.

automatically in the same proportion as the official consumer's price index. The major reason for this lack of proportionality has been the fact that the 1942 agreement and all subsequent ones have specified a ceiling up to which the cost of living allowance was to be paid: that is, incomes less than or equal to this ceiling are compensated proportionately to the price increase,[1] whereas incomes above the ceiling are compensated with a fixed nominal sum equal to the compensation on the ceiling income. The use of this ceiling reflects the fact that the agreement on the cost of living allowance was intended primarily to protect the weaker, low-income groups from the effect of inflation. In fact, this differential protection for the lower-income groups may also have been a reflection of the egalitarian philosophy of the government.[2]

In any event, it is ironic to note that the ceiling-income itself was not automatically tied to the price index. Thus, for example, the nominal ceiling remained constant in the decade following 1964, even though prices more than doubled. And even when this ceiling was adjusted in 1974, it was increased by less than 50 per cent. A further adjustment of the ceiling has, however, now been carried out.

There is, however, an even more direct manifestation of the fact that indexation in Israel has not led to increases in money wages in the same proportion as the price index – and that is the simple fact shown by figure 15.4 that *real* wages in Israel have steadily increased. In practice, the cost of living allowance has frequently served as the point of departure of the collective bargaining whose purpose it essentially was to allocate the increased productivity of the economy between workers and employers. From this viewpoint, the cost of living clause in Israel labour negotiations has not played a more distinctive role than, say, in labour negotiations in certain industries in the United States. This point is particularly highlighted by the fact that in the short (though sharp) recession and unemployment of 1966 the Histadrut did not insist on the payment of the cost of living allowance.[3]

There have, however, been many periods during which the cost of living clause has fulfilled a distinctive function: that is, it has operated as a device of indexation in the proper sense of the term – by which we mean an automatic mechanism to modify the terms of an existing contract in accordance with unexpected inflationary developments. In particular, it has been an explicit or implicit provision of the cost of living agreements in Israel that if the rate of inflation should exceed a certain figure, then the cost of living allowance would be increased accordingly even during the course of the existing labour

[1] Actually, the 1942 agreement stipulated a compensation that was not in the same proportion as the price increase, but only 80 per cent of it; this was replaced by an agreement on equal proportionality in 1943. Nevertheless, because of certain technical points, the principle of equal proportionality has not always been carried out in practice.

[2] On the other hand, a provision which operated in the opposite direction was the exemption (from 1953–75) of the cost of living allowance from income tax, whose rates are very progressive. This exemption, however, has now been abolished.

[3] See *Report of the Committee of Experts' Inquiry into the Cost of Living Allowance* (1966), Part II, p. 23.

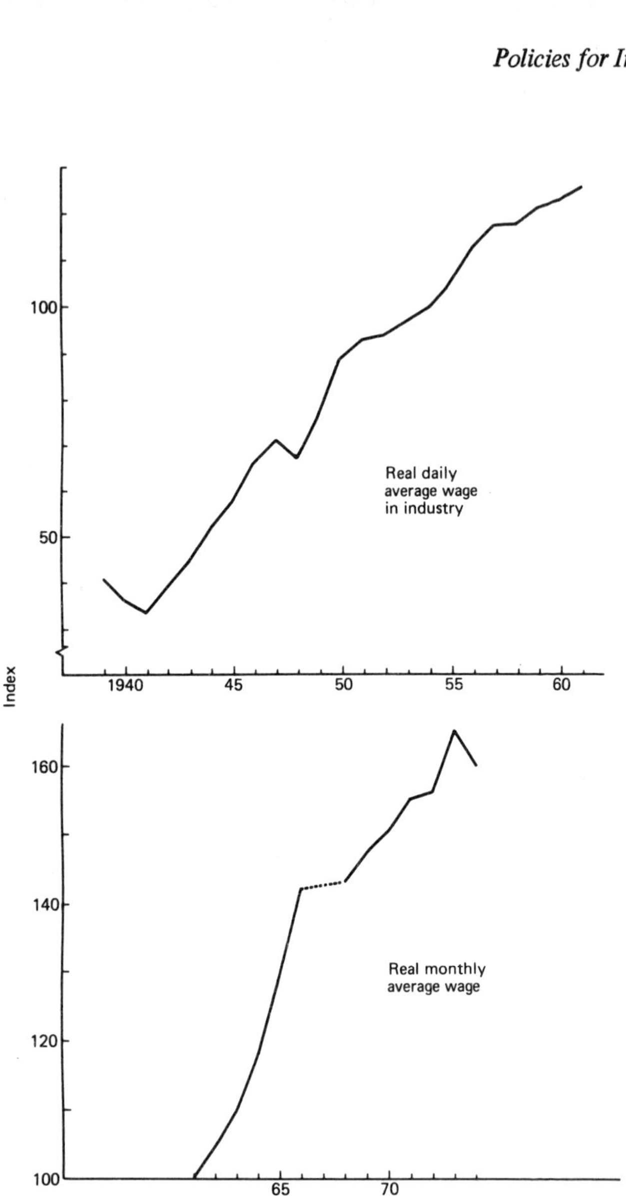

Fig. 15.4 Average Real Wage
Sources: 1939–58: Bahral (1965), Table C-3
1958–61: Bank of Israel *Annual Reports*
1962–74: Report of the 'Committee to Examine the Cost of Living Allowance Agreement'.

contract. For example, the agreement in 1957 stipulated that if price index should rise by more than 3 per cent above the index used to determine the existing cost of living allowance, then the allowance would be immediately increased accordingly. By application of such clauses, the cost of living allowances was, for example, increased in seven of the twelve months of 1952 (during which the official price index increased by roughly 60 per cent) and in four of the months of 1953 (annual price increase of 18 per cent). Indeed, in almost half of the 27 years since the existence of Israel, an additional cost of living allowance has been paid in the course of the contractual year. We should, however, note that in recent years this payment has not been automatic, but both its scope and timing have been the subject of intensive negotiations carried out with the direct participation of the government.

In any event, the fact that workers in Israel were thus 'insured' against unexpected rates of inflation should – on the assumption of risk-aversion – have caused the contractual level of nominal wages to have been somewhat less than otherwise. Unfortunately, however, the available data do not permit an empirical test of this hypothesis.

Another context in which the cost of living allowance has functioned like indexation has been in those periods in which the Histadrut has agreed to a 'wage freeze', subject only to adjustments in lieu of price increases (for instance, in 1953–55, 1959–60, 1968–69, and 1975). It should, however, be noted that such 'freezes' have generally not been successful, and that a 'wage drift' has led to increases in real wages even in these periods [16], page 74.

In the course of the many years that the cost of living allowance has been applied in Israel, questions have frequently been raised – and increasingly so in recent years – about the consistency between this allowance and other policy objectives of the government. Such questions arose in the wake of the 67 per cent devaluation of the Israel pound in 1962, when the rapid rise in money wages quickly offset the intended effect of devaluation.[1] And they have arisen once again during the past year in the wake of the 43 per cent devaluation of November 1974, and the two successive 2 per cent devaluation of recent months. Similarly, the attempts of the government to increase its tax revenues by levying additional indirect taxes has raised in its full severity the question of the effect of such taxes on the price index and hence on the cost of living allowance. In brief, in both cases the question has been raised as to whether the system of the cost of living allowance does not promote a cost inflation that negates the respective objectives of the aforementioned policies.

These problems received detailed attention from a Committee of Experts appointed jointly in 1964 by the Histadrut and the Manufacturers' Association.[2] In many ways, this was the first time since the inception of the cost of

[1] Actually, the major reason for the failure of the 1962 devaluation was the rapid monetary expansion (roughly, one-third) generated by the inflow of capital; see Beham [3], chapter 3.

[2] The members of this Committee were Baruch Ber, David Golomb, Ephraim Kleiman, and David Levhari. Its report was published in 1966. Some aspects of its approach had been adumbrated by Kleiman [18].

living allowance system over twenty years before that its rationale was subject to a systematic analysis. As a result of this analysis, the Committee distinguished between a price rise caused by demand inflation and one caused by cost inflation, and showed that the cost of living allowance could appropriately deal with the first of these rises, but not the second. Correspondingly, it recommended that changes in prices caused by variations in the effective exchange rate, changes in international prices, or changes in government taxation be removed from the price index used to compute the cost of living allowance.

As a simple way of explaining the economic logic of this distinction, let us pose the following question: under what conditions will the indexing of money wages to the cost of living index suffice to define a consistent wage policy? The conditions implicit in the discussions of many advocates of wage indexation are ones which are highly reminiscent of those that ensure the neutrality of money: namely, the condition that tastes and conditions of production are constant, and only the quantity of money in the economy changes. More specifically, the case which is implicit in many discussions of wage indexation is one in which the real output available to the private sector remains constant, while the government levies an inflation tax – either instead of another existing tax, or (in the case of a growing economy) as an additional tax which enables it to acquire for its own needs the increase in real output. It is also implicitly assumed that it is the purpose of wage-earners and profit-recipients to maintain an unchanged level of real income. In such a case, wage indexation carried out uniformly over the economy as a whole is a consistent policy: that is, it allocates the total available output between workers and employers in a way in which both groups achieve their respective goals. As a corollary, the resulting increase in money wages caused by the demand-inflation will not generate a further process of cost-inflation, for (prices having increased) the wage increase will not cause a reduction in profits.

In the real world, however, this is not generally the kind of problem with which an economy is faced. Thus most economies are characterised by a growth in per capita output over time, so that even though the application of wage indexation would keep the real income of workers constant, it would lead to a constant decrease in their relative share in the real national income. And this is hardly consistent with the observed objectives of labour. In other words, the policy of wage-indexation in such a case does not, by definition, offer any guidance on the essential question of how to divide the increased output between labour and other groups in the economy.

Our primary concern at the present moment, however, is with the opposite kind of case in which, for example, the government (because, say, of the necessity of obtaining additional resources for its defence budget) may have to *reduce* the real volume of goods and services available to the private sector. Alternatively, such a real reduction may be the consequence of a devaluation whose objective is to reduce the import surplus and thus improve the balance of payments. Assume that in the first case the government attempts to finance its additional expenditures by levying indirect taxes; similarly, in the case of devaluation, the internal prices of internationally traded goods necessarily rise. Assume further that in both cases there is an accommodating monetary policy which permits these taxes and price increases to generate corresponding increases in the general price level. Under these circumstances the attempt of labour to raise money wages in accordance with a general price index (and this could take place even in the absence of an automatic indexation clause) can succeed in its objective of maintaining labour's absolute real income constant only at the expense of the other sectors of the economy, and of profit-recipients in particular. Correspondingly, if these profit-recipients are not willing to accept a reduction in their real income, they will raise the prices of their output (again, on the assumption of a permissive monetary policy). In this way the tying of money wages to a general price index will generate a further cost inflation which in turn will generate further wage demands – and the spiral will have begun. Note, however, that under the same assumption of a permissive monetary policy, such an inflationary spiral would be generated even in the absence of indexation.

It was because the government on such occasions viewed the cost of living allowance from this cost inflation viewpoint, that it waged a vigorous struggle with the Histadrut to decrease the frequency of the payment of the allowance during the term of the labour contract.[1] The implicit and sometimes explicit rationale for this view was twofold: first, the government hoped that the postponement of the payment would provide a period during which other factors (for example, increased productivity, possible decrease in prices of domestic goods, and the like) might reduce the costs of production and thus decrease the overall pressures toward cost inflation; second, it also hoped to avoid the generation of extreme expectations which might further strengthen the inflationary process before it would be partially offset by the aforementioned factors. From both of these viewpoints, wage indexation – under certain assumptions – may increase the rate of inflation.

In any event, it was concern with the danger of generating a wage-price inflationary spiral that led the 1966 Committee of Experts to make its already described recommendation that the price index to which money wages should be tied should exclude taxes (both direct and indirect) as well as prices of imported goods. And it also emphasised that the use of such a modified index would under the foregoing circumstances assure the constancy of labour's relative share in the disposable income of the economy.

Unfortunately, this recommendation was not carried out at the time.[2] At

[1] Another – and more direct – motivation for the government's struggle against rapid wage increases was the fact that it was and is the largest employer in the economy!

[2] However, another recommendation of the Committee – based on a nice theoretical point – was carried out: namely, its recommendation that in view of the fact that about two-thirds of Israel's families lived in apartments which they owned, that component of the consumers' price index which represented the cost of dwelling services should be omitted in the computation of the cost of living allowance: for an increase in this component was offset by the corresponding increase in the imputed rental income of the average family.

the end of 1974, however, the Histadrut did agree that that part of the price increase which had been directly caused by the 43 per cent devaluation of November 1974 (estimated at about 16 per cent of the total price increase in question) would be 'sterilised' and not taken account of in computing the cost of living allowance that was due at that time. And more recently the Histadrut has accepted the recommendation of the 'Committee to Examine the Cost of Living Allowance Arrangement[1] (appointed jointly by it, the Manufacturers' Association, and the Finance Ministry) that the cost of living allowances henceforth reflect only 70 per cent of the increase in the consumers' price index, on the assumption that on the average the remaining 30 per cent represents increases due to increased nominal taxes and import prices.

Though this recommendation has the advantage of simplicity, in principle it does not really deal with the basic problem that has frequently arisen in the past – and may well arise again[2] – from the occurrence of discontinuous and significant changes in the internal prices of internationally traded goods and in the nominal level of taxes. Furthermore, since the application of this recommendation *per se* implies a continuous decrease in real wages, it also makes it clearer than ever before that the cost of living allowance is only one component in the collective bargaining process which actually determines real wages.

V. THE INDEXATION OF LONG-TERM DEBT

As a necessary background for our discussion of the role of indexed long-term debt in Israel, we should emphasise three basic facts (see on this and the following paragraphs Sarnat [33], chapters 2 to 3 and Rubner). First, that throughout the Second World War and the early years of the State, the capital market in Israel was very limited. Second, when in the mid-1950s the market began to develop, it was rapidly dominated by the government, and this situation has continued to the present. Third, and in part related to the preceding point, the government has from the very beginning served as the major financial intermediary of the economy: on the one hand, it has received funds from the sale of Independence Bonds, from the United States government (in the very early years, in the form of loans from the United States Export–Import Bank), from German reparations, and from other sources abroad, and it has supplemented these with borrowings from the domestic market; on the other hand, the government has lent these funds through the development budget, which has been the primary instrument for the financing of domestic capital formation. Thus the government has been both the major borrower and major lender in the economy.

[1] The members of this Committee were Zvi Zussman (chairman), Yosef Alschech, Amir Barnea, David Golomb, and Ben-Ami Zuckerman. Its report was published in July 1975.

[2] Though in view of the recent adoption of a 'crawling peg', probably not as a result of further discrete, large devaluations.

During the Second World War and the armed conflict that began in Palestine almost immediately afterwards, there was practically no private long-term borrowing. Only in the beginning of 1950 – a little more than a year after the complete cessation of hostilities – did this situation change. This was the period of 'austerity' (1949–51) which was accompanied by an extensive system of rationing and price controls. As a result of these controls, the official price index remained constant, and even declined during 1949–50. But both as a result of the memories of recent wartime inflation, as well as the justified feeling that the constancy of the price index was an artificial phenomenon that did not reflect the true inflationary pressures, individuals were not willing to make loans in nominal terms. Correspondingly, the attempt of the government to obtain funds from the sale of such bonds did not succeed.

Interestingly enough, the first ones to issue indexed bonds in these circumstances were private firms, and not the government.[1] And what is of further interest is the fact that the linkage in these cases was not to a general price index, but to the prices of the specific commodities respectively produced by the firms in question. Thus the first issue of linked bonds by a corporation in Israel was the Israel Land Development Company's flotation in 1951 of bonds convertible into common stock or land. This was followed in 1952 by a series of bond issues by Nesher Cement Company linked to the official price of cement. At the beginning of 1955 two more companies issued bonds linked to the prices of their respective products: Mehadrin Orange Groves Ltd. (to the price of citrus orchards) and Isras Construction Co. (to the price of apartments) [33], pages 37–38. The preference of these firms for linking their borrowings to the specific prices of their own products has an immediate economic explanation: for it is reasonable to assume that the correlation between the price of the specific product a firm sells and its profits (and it is from these profits that the firm must repay its loan) is much greater than the corresponding correlation with a general price index.

The inflationary developments which more than doubled the price level during the early 1950s led to the government's adoption in 1955–56 of a policy of linking both its borrowing and its lending. On the borrowing side, this was made necessary by its already noted inability to sell nominal bonds in this period. This was reinforced by the necessity of supplying the pension funds with a linked asset that would enable them to undertake the obligation to pay linked pensions (see section II above). On the lending side, the experience of being repaid by borrowers from the development budget with pounds which had lost half their value made it clear to the government that it must

[1] There are, however, two unconventional issues that should be mentioned here: First, in May 1948, just before the establishment of the State, the Jewish Agency floated a National Loan of £P 5 millions linked to the dollar; but this linkage at least in part reflected the fact that the monetary unit of the future State had not yet been defined. Second, when in accordance with the exchange controls that it enacted, the Government required all residents to sell all their foreign-exchange assets, it made the compensation in the form of bonds linked to the dollar (see Sarnat [33], chapter 3).

henceforth link its loans. The necessity for doing so was made most concrete by the simple fact that with the Israel pounds which it received in repayment from borrowers from the development budget, the government could not, for example, repay the dollars it had originally borrowed from the Export–Import Bank as a means of financing its development budget.

Though recognising the necessity of linkage in principle, the government did not in practice carry it out in a comprehensive and uniform manner. Instead, in accordance with the recommendation of 'The Public Committee on Indexing Government Loans',[1] the government decided: (1) to link all loans from the development budget, with certain exceptions in the case of agriculture; (2) to let the borrower choose (at the time of undertaking the loan) between linkage to the rate of exchange on the dollar and the consumers' price index; and (3) to apply linkage only to loans for periods exceeding two years, and to raise the percentage of linkage from 50 per cent to a maximum of 70 per cent as the term of the loan increased from two years to eight or more.

Clearly, there is no economic justification for determining the extent of linkage in accordance with the destination or term of a loan – and this point was forcefully made in the minority opinion submitted by Abba Lerner, who was a member of the Committee and who advocated linking all loans for all purposes in their entirety. For to subsidise any development project with a loan which is not entirely linked is in effect to provide a subsidy whose exact magnitude will ultimately be arbitrarily determined by the rate of inflation that will actually occur during the term of the loan. To a certain extent this situation was improved in 1959 when the government tied to the exchange rate on the dollar the full principal of any loan from the development budget given for the purpose of importing equipment; and tied to the cost of living index, 80 per cent of the principal of any loan made for other purposes.

Thus beginning with 1955 – and ending (for reasons to be explained) in 1962 – the government applied the principle of indexation to both its borrowing and lending. Correspondingly, as a result of its issuing linked bonds (some linked to dollar exchange rate, some to the cost of living index, and some to both in equal proportions) the sale of new issues of bonds quintupled from 1955 to 1956 and quintupled again from 1956 to 1962. Practically all of these bonds were in effect issued by the government, and 85 per cent of them were linked in one way or another. Similarly, it can be assumed that most of the loans made from the development budget were linked, though there are unfortunately no data on the exact nature and extent of this linkage [5], page 283, [22], page 152, and [33], page 43.

All this came to an abrupt end on 9 February 1962 when, as a result of the 67 per cent devaluation which was then carried out, many debtors of the development budget had the traumatic experience of finding their nominal debt increased overnight by the same 67 per cent. The public outcry was

[1] The so-called 'Lehman Committee', after the name of its chairman, Ernst Lehman.

immediate, and the government rapidly yielded to the pressure. Correspondingly, within a week or two it retroactively abolished or modified the terms of the linkage on which it had made these loans from the development budget.

The experience with this devaluation also revealed a basic weakness of one of the ways in which the government had chosen to link the bonds it had sold. In particular, it is a commonplace that a necessary condition for a successful devaluation is that it be accompanied by restrictive monetary policy. But the existence in the portfolios of the public of a financial asset (that is to say, dollar-linked bonds) whose nominal value would automatically increase as a result of the devaluation itself works in precisely the opposite direction. Indeed, some economists at the time felt that the government would have made an even greater devaluation to have taken an even fuller account of the inflationary process that had occurred since the preceding devaluation, were it not for its fears of the counter-productive financial expansion that would thus be generated by these dollar-linked bonds [22], pages 154–55.

In order to deal with this problem, the government decided quite rationally to cease the further issue of bonds linked to the rate on the dollar. Correspondingly, from 1962 onwards the government has linked its bond issues only to the consumers' price index. In this context the government also issued an interesting (and possibly unique) type of 'option bond' which gave its purchaser the right of choosing *at the time of its redemption* (five years after issue) either the 'nominal option' (which yielded a *nominal* return of 10·76 per cent per annum) or the 'linked option' (which yielded a *real* return of 4·84 per cent).

The corresponding rational solution for the problem that arose on the lending side would have been for the government to have realised that it was not only a financial intermediary, but also a government – and that this imposed upon it the obligation of providing the public service of borrowing from abroad in dollars on behalf of the economy as a whole, and then permitting the economy to borrow from it in real IL pounds. That is, the fact that it was a government meant that it was not restricted to following the conventional financial wisdom of hedging dollar-denominated borrowings from abroad with corresponding dollar-denominated lendings at home. For while Israeli firms might be expected to undertake obligations tied to the domestic price level, most of them (those not producing export goods) could not be expected to undertake obligations tied to the dollar. Thus the government should have adopted the policy of tying all loans from the development budget to the domestic price index, and not to the dollar. Unfortunately, the government was instead so overwhelmed by the public outcry that within a few years it abandoned the principle of linkage entirely insofar as its lending activities were concerned.

In particular, ever since 1966, there has been no linkage of loans from the development budget. Instead, borrowers have been required to pay an additional annual 'premium for insurance against linkage' – which during the 1960s varied from 3 to 4 per cent. The term notwithstanding, this arrangement is clearly not one of linkage, but simply a raising of the fixed nominal rate of interest on such loans.

As already noted, the period of the 1960s was one of a relatively low (less than 5 per cent) and stable rate of inflation. Indeed, throughout this period the nominal rate on the aforementioned 'option bonds' was higher than the indexed rate, so that the latter was not relevant [7]. For the same reason, the abolition of indexing on loans from the development budget during this period did not create any anomalies, and hence did not arouse any discussion.

It is sometimes considered that the indexing of government debt reduces the 'base' of the inflation tax and thus reduces the temptation of governments to carry out inflationary policies. If such a consideration is of importance for governments, then it should have been so *a fortiori* for the government of Israel during this period: for the fact that it was borrowing indexed and lending non-index meant that within a few years the net nominal financial debt of the government became negative. That is, its nominal debt to the private sector (outside money *plus* short-term debt) became less than the nominal debt of the private sector to it (on account of loans from the development budget). This was apparently the situation by, say, 1973. Correspondingly, the inflation tax in Israel at that time was actually negative. It decreased the real value of the government's nominal assets by more than it decreased that of its nominal debt [19], page 20.

It should, however, be emphasised that the contention that the existence of indexed-debt may dissuade governments from undertaking inflationary policies – as well as the immediately preceding description of the negative inflation tax in Israel in recent years – are based on the assumption that government debt is a net asset of the private sector, and correspondingly a net obligation of the government one. As is, however, emphasised in general macroeconomic theory, this will not be the case if the private sector takes full account of the future taxes that will be levied upon it in order to service the government debt which it holds [28], pages 288 ff. Similarly, the indexing of its debt will not influence government decisions if it views its future tax receipts as also being effectively indexed to the nominal G.N.P.

In any event, one fact is clear: the existence of indexed government debt did not prevent inflation in Israel. Indeed, as already noted, a reinforced and almost unprecedented wave of inflation began in 1970.

The public was somewhat slow in revising its expectations in accordance with these new developments. But by 1972 it had already reacted with a sharp shift in the composition of its portfolio from the nominal financial assets which it had accumulated at a rapid rate during the 1960s into indexed government bonds. Indeed, the increased demand for such bonds raised their nominal market price to their maturity value exclusive of indexation, so that their real rate of return became zero. That is, people were willing to buy indexed bonds solely for the purpose of preventing a decrease in the real value of their assets. In this and other ways indexed bonds became a substitute for money in the portfolios of individuals [7].

Another reason for the great popularity of indexed bonds was an anomaly in the income tax law which treated as income the full receipts of interest on a nominal bond, while not treating as income that part of the money return on an indexed bond which represented indexation. Needless to say, there is no economic logic for this distinction.

The government was even slower in reacting. Thus instead of taking advantage of the greatly increased demand for its indexed bonds (which it offered at par) to lower the real rate of interest on them, it merely increased the supply of these bonds in order to satisfy fully the increased demand. Only in February 1974 did it finally lower this real rate.

Similarly, on the lending side, not only did the government not reinstitute linkage of development loans (despite the public criticisms of many economists on this point), but it was also very slow in even raising the nominal rate of interest on such loans – which was not done until November 1974. And recently it has – most reluctantly – agreed, in the case of certain types of loans, to index development loans by the number of percentage points by which the rate of inflation exceeds 20 per cent.

Finally, we should note that the recommendation mentioned in section IV to index wages by a price index which excludes import prices and taxes has, in some quarters, also been made with respect to the price index to be used for bonds. But no decision has yet been made on this matter.

VI. CONCLUDING REMARKS

Are there any general lessons that can be learned about indexation from the Israeli experience? One such lesson is the necessity of clarifying the purpose of indexation in order to be able to define the appropriate price index to be used for the purpose. Unfortunately, this question has received very little attention in the literature.

Insofar as wage indexation is concerned, we can only emphasise again the limited extent to which in Israel (as elsewhere) this is true indexation. Instead, what is really involved here is one component among others which determine the nominal wage rate.

In the case of the indexation of bonds, there are two general questions which usually arise: first, the willingness of firms to issue indexed bonds; second the effect of the existence of such bonds on the capital market. It must be admitted that Israeli experience sheds little light on either of these questions. Insofar as the capital market is concerned, the Israel market is so limited as to be unable to provide lessons for economies with highly developed markets of this kind. Furthermore, the anomalous preferential tax treatment of index bonds in Israel means that its experience can provide no indication of the market behaviour of such bonds when such anomalies are absent.

Insofar as the willingness of firms to borrow on indexed terms is concerned, the failure of Israeli firms to do so is – during most of the period – is simply an indication that they had the much preferable alternative of borrowing from the development budget in nominal terms. And even during the period when development loans were indexed, the willingness of firms to take them reflected at least in part their belief (which was so dramatically confirmed in 1962) that the government would not enforce the indexation clause should it prove onerous. On the other hand, we do find some significance in the already noted fact that in the early 1950s – when development loans were not available – firms were willing to issue in the market bonds that were tied to their specific product prices.

From the viewpoint of the household sector, the possibility of preserving the real value of savings by investing them in indexed financial assets has undoubtedly played an important role in the maintenance of personal savings in Israel as a significant ratio of disposable income throughout the inflationary process. Similarly, such assets have provided a convenient alternative to the usual inflationary hedge of real-estate, so that the inflationary process in Israel has been accompanied less than it would otherwise have been by waste of time and energy devoted to real-estate speculation, not to speak of actual excess investment in construction that usually characterises inflationary periods. Correspondingly, the demand for indexed financial assets has served to siphon off part of the inflationary demand on the real productive resources of the economy. This is not to say that there has not been excess investment in fixed capital in certain sectors of the Israel economy; but this has stemmed more from the subsidised, unlinked loans that the government has granted for such purposes from its development budget, than from the desire *per se* to acquire physical assets as an inflationary hedge.

Let us finally note that indexation has played an important role in Israel – and could play an equally important role in other countries – with respect to such groups as pensioners and small savers. The fact that such groups in Israel have largely been protected from the severe inequities that inflation has usually inflicted upon them is itself a sufficient justification for the use of indexation at least in such contexts.

REFERENCES AND BIBLIOGRAPHY

[1] W. Baer and P. Beckerman, 'Indexing in Brazil', *World Development*, Vol. II, No. 10–12 (October–December 1974), pp. 35–47.

[2] U. Bahral, *The Effect of Mass Immigration on Wages in Israel*. (Jerusalem: Falk Project, 1965).

[3] M. Beham, *Monetary Aspects of the 1962 Devaluation*. (Jerusalem: Falk Project, 1968).

[4] H. Ben-Shahar, *Interest Rates and the Cost of Capital in Israel, 1950–1962*. (Basel: Kyklos-Verlag, 1965).

[5] H. Ben-Shahar, S. Bronfeld and A. Cukierman, 'The Capital Market in Israel' in *Israel and the Common Market*, ed. Pierre Uri. (Jerusalem: Weidenfeld and Nicolson, 1970).

[6] M. Ben-Shahar and A. Cukierman, 'The Rate of Return on Index Bonds and the Expectations for Devaluation and Changes in Price Level until 1962', *Bank of Israel Economic Review* No. 32 (1969).

[7] R. Brenner and S. Bronfeld, 'Index Bonds – a Liquid Asset', *Bank of Israel Economic Review* (1975).

[8] P. Cagan, 'The Monetary Dynamics of Hyperinflation' in *Studies in the Quantity Theory of Money* ed. Milton Friedman. (Chicago; University of Chicago Press, 1956).

[9] A. Cukierman, 'A Study on the Formation of Inflationary Expectations in Israel'. Tel-Aviv University, The Foerder Institute for Economic Research, Working Paper No. 24 (1973).

[10] A. Cukierman, 'Index-Linked Mortgages in Israel', *Federal Reserve Bank of Boston Conference Series* (forthcoming).

[11] Y. Findling, 'The History of the Cost-of-Living Allowance' unpublished seminar paper, Department of Economics, The Hebrew University of Jerusalem,(1975). (Hebrew)

[12] S. Fischer, 'The Demand for Indexed Bonds', *Journal of Political Economy*, Vol. LXXXIII. No. 3, pp. 509–534 (1975).

[13] G. Fishelson, 'An Inquiry into some Aspects of the Labor Market in Israel' in *Israel and the Common Market*, ed. Pierre Uri. (Jerusalem: Weidenfeld and Nicolson, 1970).

[14] A. Fishlow, 'Indexing Brazilian Style: Inflation without Tears?' *Brookings Papers on Economic Activity*, No. 1; pp. 261–282 (1974).

[15] N. Halevy, 'Exchange Control in Israel' in *Israel and the Common Market* ed. Pierre Uri. (Jerusalem: Weidenfeld and Nicolson, 1970).

[16] N. Halevy and R. Klinov-Malul, *The Economic Development of Israel.* (New York: Bank of Israel and Praeger, 1968).

[17] D. Horowitz, 'Cost-of-Living Allowance', *Yediot Aharonot*, (15th August, 1975), p. 11. (Hebrew)

[18] E. Kleiman, 'The Cost-of-Living Allowance and Economic Policy', *Haaretz* (8 July 1964). (Hebrew)

[19] E. Kleiman, 'Inflation and the Distribution of Public Capital', *Quarterly Economic Review*, No. 83 (1974). (Hebrew)

[20] N. Liviatan and D. Levhari, 'Risk and the Theory of Index Bonds', Hebrew University of Jerusalem. Department of Economics, Working Paper No. 67 (1975).

[21] M. Michaely, *Israel's Foreign Exchange Rate System*. (Jerusalem: Falk Project, 1968).

[22] A. Morag, *Public Finance in Israel: Problems and Development.* (Jerusalem: The Magnes Press, 1967). (Hebrew)

[23] A. Morag, *On Taxes and Inflation.* (New York: Random House, 1965).

[24] A. Morag, 'Value Linking of Loans in Israel' in *Fiscal and Monetary Problems in Developing States. Proceedings of the Third Rehovot Conference* ed. David Krivine. (New York: Praeger, 1967).

[25] R. R. Nathan, O. Gass and D. Creamer, *Palestine: Problem and Promise.* (Washington: Public Affairs Press, 1946).

[26] D. Patinkin, 'Monetary and Price Developments in Israel: 1949–1953', *Scripta Hierosolymitana*, III, Jerusalem, 1956. As reprinted in *Studies in Monetary Economics*. (New York: Harper and Row, 1972).

[27] D. Patinkin, *The Israel Economy: The First Decade*. (Jerusalem: Falk Project, 1960).

[28] D. Patinkin, *Money, Interest and Prices*. 2nd ed. (New York: Harper and Row, 1965).

[29] D. Patinkin, 'What Advanced Countries Can Learn from the Experience with Indexation', *Proceedings of a Conference on Indexation: Sao Paulo, February 1975*, National Bureau of Economic Research (1976) forthcoming.

[30] A. Rubner, *The Economy of Israel*. (London: Frank Cass, 1961).

[31] A. Rubner, 'The Abdication of the Israeli Pound as a Standard of Measurement for Medium and Long-Term Contracts', *Review of Economic Studies*, Vol. XXVIII, pp. 69–75 (1960–61).

[32] M. Sarnat, *Saving and Investment Through Retirement Funds in Israel*. (Jerusalem: Falk Project, 1966(a)).

[33] M. Sarnat, *The Development of the Securities Market in Israel*. (Basel: Kyklos-Verlag, 1966(b)).

[34] D. A. Valery, 'Effective Rates of Exchange in Israel's Foreign Trade 1962–70, *Bank of Israel Economic Review* No. 39 (1972).

OFFICIAL PUBLICATIONS

Bank of Israel *Annual Report*, Jerusalem.

Central Bureau of Statistics *Statistical Abstract of Israel*, Jerusalem.

Economic Planning Authority. *Israel Economic Development: Past Progress and Plan for the Future* (Jerusalem: Prime Minister's Office, 1968).

The Jewish Agency for Palestine, Statistical Handbook of Jewish Palestine, Department of Statistics (1947), p. 318.

Report of the Committee to Examine the Cost of Living Allowance Arrangement (Jerusalem, 1975). (Hebrew)

Report of the Committee of Experts Inquiring into the Cost of Living Allowance (Tel-Aviv, 1966). (Hebrew)

Report of the Joint Committee on Problems of Wage Adjustment, (Tel-Aviv, 1942). (Hebrew)

Report of the Public Committee on the Indexation of Government Loans (Jerusalem, 1955). (Hebrew)

Report of the Public Committee on the Indexation of Government Loans (Jerusalem, 1959). (Hebrew)

Discussion of the Paper by Reuven Brenner and Don Patinkin

Professor Paunio said the paper began with a discussion of the nature of indexation. The authors saw the distinctive feature of indexation as its link with the functioning or non-functioning of the market mechanism and with expectations. They first pointed out that the marginal rate of interest in a free market economy correctly reflected future rates of inflation only to the extent that they were correctly anticipated. Since this rarely happened, one purpose of indexation was to eliminate the necessity to anticipate the rate of inflation correctly, by stipulating real instead of nominal rates of interest.

Second, indexation could play a role because not all prices were determined by a freely functioning economy. Prices or wages might be controlled, and there were always some prices administered by the government. In inflation, the upward adjustment of these prices would be made only after a lag, whose existence might well lead to distortions in the price structure. Indexation would then shorten the lag in price adjustment and thereby prevent distortion, though, the authors pointed out that this was not indexation in the strict sense of removing uncertainty about future real values.

Third, in wage determination, what was called indexation was often a form of wage policy. References to changes in the cost of living in wage bargaining did not represent an automatic adjustment of wages to prices, but simply one element in the negotiating process. Even if the indexation of official prices and wages did not raise new problems in microeconomic theory, it might have macroeconomic consequences in speeding up the inflationary process. The authors pointed out that as this speeding up proceeded, it necessarily became increasingly injurious to the economy, because the welfare loss due to inflation was a function not only of the rate of inflation but also of the distortions in relative prices caused by the lags in adjustment. Indexation would diminish the loss from this cause.

The paper went on to outline the inflationary process in Israel since 1939. Inflation was concentrated in three periods, during which, the annual rate of inflation rose to 23 per cent. In the remaining periods, the price level increased by an average annual rate of only 5 per cent. The official exchange rate was more than adjusted to the internal inflation. Between two devaluations, the effect of exchange rates on current account transactions was rapidly adjusted to take account of inflation by administrative action, as was clear from figure 15.3.

The authors then described the process of wage negotiation and, in particular, the determination of the cost of living allowance on wages. The system for providing cost of living allowances was created during the Second World War and had become a permanent feature of Israeli labour-contracting since then. A special feature of this system was that wage agreements specified a ceiling up to which the allowance was paid, with incomes adjusted more or less proportionately for price increases. Above the ceiling, an increase in the cost of living was compensated by a fixed nominal sum of money equal to the amount of compensation for the ceiling income. In other words, the system did not automatically increase money wages in the same proportion as prices.

In the authors' view, the cost of living allowance had often served as a point of departure for collective bargaining, aimed at allocating increased productivity between workers and employers. Real wages had increased steadily, but the cost of living clause had fulfilled the function of providing an automatic mechanism to modify the terms of an existing contract, in accordance with unexpected inflationary movements. In half of the years since Israel had come into being, an additional cost of living allowance had been paid during the contractual year.

There had been discussion in Israel about the role of the cost of living allowance in the inflationary process and, in particular, whether the system promoted cost inflation, so negating the effects of other policy measures like devaluation. The authors discussed the cost inflation viewpoint, in circumstances where the aim of the government was to reduce the real volume of goods and services available to the private sector. Instead, the cost of living clause had generated an inflationary spiral. To avoid this, the Israeli government had at times attempted to reduce the frequency of payments of the cost of living allowance during the term of the labour contract. It had also been suggested, in 1966, that the price index to which money wages were tied should exclude taxes and the prices of imported goods, a recommendation not carried out until 1974. In both 1974 and 1975 the workers' organisation had agreed to some adjustment of this kind.

Finally, the paper discussed the role of indexed long-term debt in Israel. The introduction of indexed bonds was begun by pilot firms in the early 1950s, the link being not to a general price level but to the prices of the goods produced by the firms in question. In the mid-1960s, the Israeli government began to link its borrowing and lending, though not in a comprehensive and uniform way. However, the system was somewhat improved in 1959. A very high proportion of the bonds issued by the government, and of loans made by the so-called development budget, were linked.

The 67 per cent devaluation in 1962 caused a crisis. Debtors with loans linked to the dollar exchange rate found their nominal debt increased overnight by 67 per cent. The government yielded to public pressure and abolished or modified the terms of linkage in the loans. This devaluation also revealed a weakness in the system. It automatically increased the nominal value of financial assets held by the public, and so worked against the necessarily restrictive monetary policy imposed after devaluation. The government therefore decided to stop issuing bonds linked to the dollar rate and to link them only to the consumer price index. As for lending, the Israeli government abandoned index linking a few years later. Instead, borrowers were required to pay an additional annual so-called 'premium for insurance against linkage'. The newer inflationary wave which began in 1970 caused, with a lag, a sharp shift from nominal financial assets into indexed government bonds, lowering the real rate of return on these bonds to zero. Besides inflationary expectations, the special tax treatment of interest on the indexed bonds was also a factor leading to the popularity of indexed bonds.

The paper made it clear that indexation might at times be inconsistent with the general policy objectives of the government. Choosing an appropriate price index therefore became extremely important.

As for wage indexation, even if it had existed only in a limited sense, the authors put forward the hypothesis that the fact that workers had been 'insured' against unexpected inflation rates might have caused the contractual level of nominal wages to be somewhat lower than it otherwise would have been.

Israeli firms had not been willing to borrow on indexed terms, but this might have been due simply to their ability to borrow much more favourably from the development budget. The authors saw significance in the fact that firms had been willing to buy on indexed terms before development loans were available. They also stressed that indexation had protected pensioners and small savers from unfairnesses that inflation might have imposed, which was itself sufficient justification for indexation in these cases.

As a matter of comparison, Professor Paunio wanted to say a few words about the indexation widely applied in Finland during the postwar period. Beginning in 1947, the indexation policy played a part in all wage negotiations in Finland, the technical details of the process of indexation being themselves matters for negotiation. A variety of methods of index linking applied. Under the 1947 agreement, each full 5 per cent rise in the price index led to a 5·5 per cent rise in wages. An agreement made three years later settled for a 5 per cent increase for every 5 per cent increase in the index. The actual nature of the index links was changed from time to time. In 1957, it was included in wage agreements which provided for pay adjustments through a review triggered by the cost of living, instead of automatic rises. The formula provided for compensation equal to any two-thirds of the rise in the price index. In the central agreements of 1963, a system of 'thresholds' was established, the passing of each of which brought a flat rate pay rise. These rises represented approximately full compensation at the first threshold, three-quarters at the second, and so on. There was a period in the early 1960s when there was no indexation at all in wage agreements.

An agreement in 1966 contained an indexation clause according to which there was to be full compensation for cost of living increases. In the next year, full compensation was to be given for any price increase above 3 per cent between January and December of that year. The increase in December 1967 came immediately after devaluation, when the economy was prone to inflation. There was therefore considerable unanimity between unions, employers and banks in deploring the 'index jungle' which fostered inflationary shocks. Since 1968 there had been no index clauses in Finnish agreements, but there had been pressure to reintroduce them during the recent inflation.

In the financial sector, the first issue of indexed bonds was the indemnity loan of 1945, which gave 100 per cent compensation for rises in the wholesale price index and was intended to do so during a period of ten years. The first indexed bond was issued in 1953, and government securities held by private individuals had been tax exempt with one or two exceptions. In 1967, 75 per cent of total outstanding government bonds were index linked, while mortgage banks and local authorities had also issued indexed bonds. Since 1957, national pensions had been tied to the cost of living index and since 1962, all employment pensions had been linked to the general wage level. Since 1948, there had been an indexation clause in life insurance.

The banks had introduced arrangements for indexing deposits in 1965. The systems varied. Sometimes there were two kinds of account, one with 100 per cent and another with a 50 per cent compensation clause. Sometimes banks accepted only deposits with the 50 per cent clause. In 1967–68, of all term deposits, more than 30 per cent were linked.

Index charges on lending were, in general, levied only to the extent necessary to cover the index compensation due to depositors. In government lending, a 50 per cent indexation clause was generally applied. In the stabilisation agreement in 1968, a special powers act abolished index clauses from all contracts, with a few exceptions. They were continued for government bonds issued before the act as well as for all insurance policies and pensions.

The Finnish indexation system was abolished at a moment when it was clearly inconsistent with the aims of stabilisation policy after a considerable devaluation. Similar difficulties had been experienced in Israel following devaluation. It seemed that the predominant view about the nature of the inflationary process had stressed the cost inflation element. In other words, inflationary shocks from costs were frequent enough for indexation linking to spread the inflationary process. This explained why the fairly critical attitude towards indexation had developed in Finland.

Professor Bronfenbrenner thought the conference probably needed a more explicit understanding of who paid the inflation tax and how. Or had indexation eliminated the tax?

Mr Brenner replied that the Israeli government acted as a financial intermediary. It received loans in dollars and lent these out through the development budget. It later changed its policy and received indexed loans and issued indexed bonds, seeming to realise that it had a task other than that of an intermediary. Since 1968, the government had taken on itself all the risk of future and unanticipated inflation. In this context, indexation meant that the cost of inflation would be borne by future taxpayers.

Professor Patinkin said that Professor Kleiman had shown in his own paper that in Israel the inflation tax was negative, the government having more owing to it in nominal terms than it owed the public. Loans from the government development budget were made in nominal terms. Looking for rational behaviour would not help. We should not be so sure that there was macroeconomic rationality during an inflationary process. Governments were not homogeneous, rational and maximising behaviour units and one here had a reflection of the internal heterogeneity of government.

Mr Brenner explained that the meaning of a negative inflation tax in Israel was the following: index bonds, being long-term ones, an increase in the price level, while it caused an increase in the nominal debt, did not necessarily mean a present payment, but rather a future one, or future taxation.

Professor Bronfenbrenner suggested that if one did include the future, the inflation tax would become positive.

Professor Kleiman replied that future taxes would be required to pay off extra government debt. The public did not take this into account, and why should it? No-one knew who would pay in twenty years' time. Moreover, since the burden fell on taxpayers in general, any individual who refrained from buying an indexed bond now did not, by doing so, escape his liability as a taxpayer in the future. The tax would be there tomorrow whatever he did.

Professor Lundberg said his quotation about countries which made careful studies of the possibilities of indexed bonds never issuing them, and countries which did not make studies doing so, appeared to be relevant to Finland. His impression was that there had been no serious discussion of indexation, either when it was brought in or when it was ended. But Finland must have a great deal of expertise in this field. He wondered whether much research had been done, because that would be interesting. Was the reason indexation had been abandoned, because it had inflationary results? And why were there pressures to start again? That also would be an interesting study.

Professor Paunio replied that the decision to abandon indexation came from the feeling that it would lead to a wage-push. The decision was therefore taken at the political level. Moreover, the current pressure to move back to indexation was still weak. There had been studies, and these would be published.

Professor Fischer referred to cases where French firms had issued indexed bonds linked to the prices of their own products. Those firms were allowed to issue indexed bonds linked to the performance of their own businesses, but not to the general price level. One should thus not conclude that they necessarily preferred indexing to their own output price. Why were indexed bonds issued in Israel linked to the general price level rather than their own output price? Was it a basic preference of the firms, or were there legal restrictions?

Professor Kleiman thought there was a legal reason. There had been a test case in Israel, in which the court had ruled that tying one's borrowing to one's own product or share price was usury.

Professor Patinkin hoped the courts in Israel had greater discrimination than that. He would like to check what had happened, but he did not think there was any real difference between linking the value of a bond to one's own goods or to a basket of goods so far as legality was concerned. In any event, there was certainly evidence that firms in Israel were willing to borrow money indexed to their own product prices.

Professor Malinvaud, judging by what he thought was legal in France, was surprised by what Professor Fischer had said, but would assume Professor Fischer was right. It was important to recognise that relatively few indexed bonds had been issued in the period referred to. With most of these, indexation was far from complete, only part of the loan having been indexed, often only a premium. Fully indexed loans were often made by large public corporations, where the decision to do so was one by the government rather than the capital market which, in France, was far from perfect.

Professor Kleiman was not sure he agreed with the paper on wage indexation. Though wage indexation was more prevalent, there was much less interest in it in the literature than in ordinary indexation. There were three elements: first, changes in real wages; second, wage drift within the firm; and third, monetary correction for inflation, or indexation. He did not expect indexation to have much effect on real wages, the aim being simply to prevent inflation from interfering with the mechanism of wage bargaining. On how far indexation affected real wages, this was only interesting insofar as it affected what would otherwise happen.

As for inflationary subsidies and taxes, one had the curious result that one could get an inflationary subsidy to the public as a result of *less* than full indexation. The same phenomenon had been seen in Brazil. He thought there might also have been an inflationary subsidy in Finland.

Professor Lundberg thought that one weakness of the Swedish system was the fact that there were discontinuous changes in wages and prices. Many wages were increased at the same time, after which there was erosion of real wages through inflation, during the period before the next bargaining began. By the end of the year, when prices had risen, people felt poor and angry. Indexation could perhaps reduce the inflationary dynamic by removing some of the discontinuities. Was this argument used?

Professor Patinkin suggested that, without indexation, the wage increases demanded might be even bigger, though it was hard to get empirical evidence on this. He agreed with Professor Lundberg that indexation might remove some of the pressure for higher wages.

As for why wage indexation was not much discussed in the literature, he thought the answer was that it was not really indexation. Wages were paid on short-run contract, for example, for a year. If wages had to be negotiated for ten years, there would be much more indexation and much more theoretical discussion of wage indexation was well. Wage indexation was a part of incomes policy, and represented a way in which one might raise nominal wages more frequently during the year. But what was to happen was part of incomes policy. If one wanted to know how much one could raise money wages without increasing real wages, then indexation would help.

Mr Oppenheimer suggested that, in logic, Professor Lundberg's point was not really concerned with indexation. The government might well ask the trade unions and employers to arrange that a given annual wage increment be paid not all at once, but as a series of small monthly or quarterly increases throughout the year. This, however, was not indexation.

Professor Malinvaud reported that in France a number of companies gave contracts where if the cost of living increased by x per cent during two successive months, wages would increase by the same amount immediately after those months.

Professor Patinkin said that this would be true indexation.

Professor Polaczek thought the Finnish system, as described by Professor Paunio, also sounded like true indexation.

Professor Nussbaumer explained that Austrian experience supported the view that wage indexation was not true indexation. Even the trade unions did not want it. But the civil servants had been urged to introduce it because the Minister of Finance needed to know what provision to make in his budget for civil service incomes.

Professor Fischer pointed out that some wage contracts lasted for much more than a year. Many in the United States ran for three years, and longer ones did contain elements of indexation. But there was always a slight difference between indexed bonds and indexed wages. Nominal wages for the first year would be negotiated at the beginning of a contract and not adjusted *ex post* on the basis of subsequently realised inflation. Wages for the second year would be set at the beginning of the second year, and so forth. However, there was adjustment of wages in the middle of long contracts.

The last paragraph of the Brenner/Patinkin paper referred to indexing pensions and small savings. He wondered whether there would be a benefit in issuing indexed bonds over and above the payments made through the kind of social security system that existed in the United States.

Mr Brenner wondered what was the correct frequency according to which cost of living adjustments must be paid. It must be a function of the production cycle in the economy, rigidity of prices etc. In Israel, the arbitrary frequency of its payment contributed to cost-push inflation.

Professor Stahl wanted to refer back to Professor Levhari's paper. He thought one should connect the theory of indexation with the theory of contingency contracts. If one saw indexation as a second best, one might find the optimal contract contained annual renegotiation. A useful way of testing these aspects would be to look at relationships between wage and capital markets. One might study shipyards and construction, to see whether they had indexed contracts with contingency clauses. Such empirical work would help in the study of indexation but would also throw light on government interference, perhaps leading to a more general theory of indexation.

Professor Patinkin emphasised that he and Professor Brenner insisted that the indexation of wages was not like the indexation of debt. With debt, one knew that, over the length of the contract, one would receive an amount equal to the rise in the price index during the period. But, even with a sophisticated United States wage contracts, indexation was not the whole of the matter. For example, there could be wage increases because of productivity elements. Indexation was only one component of the wage change.

In Israel, workers had foregone indexation in times of unemployment. Much more obligation was undertaken by those who indexed debt than by those who indexed wages.

Arrangements made to preserve small savings by insuring the real value of those savings were important. The real rate of interest on an indexed bond to Israeli small savers in recent years was zero. The fact that they were demanded showed how strong a demand there was just to preserve the real value of what one had.

In countries with rapid inflation there was much speculation in non-monetary assets. In a sense this did not have a cost, but there was an economic cost because people spent a good deal of time searching for assets to hold. An indexed asset gave a costless way of protecting oneself.

Mr Oppenheimer said that protecting one's real wealth by acquiring physical assets was not simply a matter of time and effort spent on transactions. Where people decided to protect their wealth by putting it into property, resources were actually diverted into the construction of buildings.

Professor Robinson pointed out that when people began to hold non-monetary assets, this made the position in the near-money markets very different from normal. For example, with housing, inflation of house prices made it difficult for the young to buy houses, and for those with houses to move. These secondary effects had to be borne in mind.

Professor Liviatan pointed out that it was not correct to see a linked bond as a costless way of ensuring one's savings. The issue of indexed bonds had implications for budgetary constraints and for the tax system. These costs might well be as big as the benefits from issuing such bonds.

Dr Corden reported that Australia had indexed wages until 1953, though this was seen as a minimum. There was a big literature about the effects of the 'cost of living adjustment'. The main effect had been a downward rigidity in real wage rates, superseding the old Keynesian phenomenon of rigid money wages. The major objection to this system had been that it made it very difficult for Australia to adjust to adverse changes in the terms of trade.

Mr Brenner pointed out that an indexed loan did become a liquid asset, but only for a limited period. Only when the rate of inflation was constant did this happen.

Professor Kleiman noted that the indexation of wages, with demand-pull inflation, would ensure a constant share of wages in G.N.P. With cost-push inflation, or with increased indirect taxation, indexation would be equivalent to an attempt to increase the share of wages. This was where the downward stickiness of wages became important.

Mr Brenner thought that Israeli experience was not a good example of indexation experience. Wage indexation had been only part of the policy and it was not, in any case, really indexation at all. It was the same system as that quoted by Professor Malinvaud when he talked about a number of adjustments per annum when the rate of inflation was above some minimum level. Indexation had come from the old British régime during the Second World War, which had attempted to keep up real wages. The system had been kept without any careful study of long-run problems. Similarly, with indexed bonds, not all problems had been anticipated. It was interesting to go back to read what Abba Lerner had said about the idea. This had not been taken into account, but on many points he had later been proved right, especially over the effects of indexation on liquidity when there was a steady inflation rate.

The problem was that the government did not analyse the problem of the existence of indexed bonds, the fact that wages were indexed too, and the constraints these facts must put on its comportment.

Professor Patinkin wanted to thank Professor Paunio. He was always interested to hear from those who had adopted or rejected indexation. What Professor Paunio had said added to earlier puzzles as to why those who previously had indexation had now abandoned it.

He did not think one could learn much about the indexation of debt from Israeli experience. If firms could borrow from the government on an unindexed basis, why should they borrow on an indexed basis? Most reasonable firms could obtain funds from the development budget.

On who paid the inflationary tax, unindexed government lending from the development budget was in part a subsidy to firms. But it had an irrational aspect: the higher the inflation turned out to be, the higher was the subsidy. Clearly, the size of a subsidy should not be an arbitrary function of the rate of inflation.

In many arrangements, even where the government lent on a linked basis, it only linked part of the loan. It would be interesting to look at the theory of partial linkage.

16 A Re-evaluation of the Theory of Repressed Inflation in the Light of the Experience of Some Socialist Countries

Béla Csikós-Nagy
HUNGARIAN ECONOMIC ASSOCIATION, BUDAPEST

I. PLANNED PRICING

The economies of socialist societies are characterised by the stability of their retail prices. This is reflected in the published retail price indices, as can be seen in the following table:

TABLE 16.1
ANNUAL AVERAGE CHANGES IN THE RETAIL PRICE LEVEL[1]
IN THE PERIOD BETWEEN 1960 AND 1973

Country	*Foodstuffs*	*Others*	*Total*
Bulgaria	+1·5	+0·1	+0·8
Czechoslovakia	+0·4	+0·8	+0·5
Poland	+1·2	+0·4	+0·7
Hungary	+1·4	+0·6	+1·0
German Democratic Republic	+0·2	–0·3	–0·1
Rumania	+0·7	–0·5	+0·1
Soviet Union	+0·5	–0·6	–

[1] Owing to differences in the methods of calculation and the coverages of the trade included, the published retail price indices of the European socialist countries cannot be compared precisely. Except for one or two countries, the price statistics published represent the retail trade price index.

The socialist countries regard retail price stability as an important element of social stability. It is merely a difference in judgement that leads some socialist countries (the Soviet Union for example) to interpret stability as a stable level of consumer prices, while others (for instance Czechoslovakia) regard a slow price increase of industrial goods embodying new technologies or new fashion trends as compatible with stability and others again (for instance Hungary), while keeping their prices relatively stable, put more stress on the function of prices in maintaining equilibrium. Stability of the consumer price level is enforced despite a rise in the production costs (producers' prices).

Over the past twenty-five years the European socialist countries have progressively raised the level of agricultural procurement prices. Apart from their wish to improve the self-financing capacity of agriculture, they have adopted this policy primarily in order to ensure income parity between industrial and agricultural workers. In Western Europe this had been achieved at an earlier date. Historically the gap between agricultural and industrial prices was created in Europe by the low world market price of agricultural goods. With such price relations it would have been impossible to ensure the continuity of agricultural production in this continent.

The industrial price level rose in most European socialist countries, as a consequence not only of rising wages but also of changes in socioeconomic conditions. The creation of facilities for research and development, while accelerating technical progress and environmental protection, have increased internal costs. In certain productive branches low-cost technologies had to be discarded; the workers were no longer willing to undertake the type of labour they embodied. This, at the first stage, led to wage rises, in the second to an inevitable change of the technology. The urgent need of the masses for commodities and services can sometimes be better met with higher-cost technologies than those previously employed.

The rise in the industrial producer price level has been greater in those countries which are dependent on imported energy and materials, since their production costs are influenced by the world market price. Although the socialist countries transact the greater part of their foreign trade on the C.M.E.A. market, the C.M.E.A. contractual prices are based on the world market price after eliminating purely cyclical elements. This principle of pricing, followed from 1958 until recently has been based on an adjustment of the C.M.E.A. contract prices every five years. Since 1975 the C.M.E.A. has switched over to a yearly correction, on the basis of average international market prices during the preceding five years.

In terms of the G.N.P. the price relations of the means of production (energy, materials, semi-manufactures and capital goods) have a more functional role than those of consumer goods. When judging general price trends the export and import rates must also be taken into account. Since countries have not been prepared to calculate the implicit deflator the overall price trend cannot be quantified. But it is beyond question that the growth of the socialist economy has been associated with a rise in the general price level. In spite of this, consumer price stability has been of absolutely fundamental importance for its social effects, since the bulk of the national income is consumed by the population of the country concerned.

The socialist countries do not regard a rise in the price level as representing inflation. The elimination or diminution of the gap between agricultural and industrial prices has relaxed an increasingly acute social tension and has contributed in no small measure to enhancing the general social stability and to equilibrium in this sense. If there is a sufficient volume of commodities to satisfy the correspondingly increasing purchasing power of the peasantry, why should that be described as an inflation? If it were, any changes which increase social stability by maintaining economic equilibrium would be regarded as upsetting economic stability. Similarly, if a rise of industrial production costs due to an acceleration of the rates of technological development, of environmental protection and of increasingly stringent social requirements and other similar factors, were to be described as inflation, it would imply an identification of economic stability with the preservation of the conditions of production that have evolved historically. In this case only such changes in conditions might be considered compatible with economic stability as would decrease input and absolutely none that would increase it.

It was Lerner who first expounded a theory which could explain the standpoint of socialist countries in regard to the inflation problem. According to Lerner we can imagine a state of affairs in which there is a continuous increase in money demand in relation to supply, and a continuous rise in prices; a process which is generally foreseen. We can then have rising prices without any of the evils that we dislike in inflation. In the case of a foreseen price rise there is no excess demand. People expect to spend more money in the future, but they are also willing to pay the higher prices. The expected demand can be equal to to the expected supply [1].

The socialist countries endeavour to follow the Lerner formula. The rise in the price level, under central control, takes place in harmony with the trend of relative incomes, in the form of planned pricing. The price and incomes policy is institutionally integrated into the central control of the economy. A restrictive foreign exchange policy makes it even possible to arrange a relationship between the world market price (the C.M.E.A. contractual price) and the domestic price in a centrally organised system. Yugoslavia is an exception from this rule partly because it is the market price which best suits the system of workers' self-management and partly because Yugoslavia has an open economy. As a consequence, the effect of inflation on the world market upon the Yugoslav economy assumes the same form as in most market economies.

II. CRITERIA FOR PLANNED PRICING

The criteria of planned pricing are different in the cases of agricultural procurement, of industrial production and of consumer goods. They vary also from country to country. In the different economic systems the role played by prices in the planned development is different. In all socialist countries, however, the criteria of price planning are the same. All socialist countries try to proceed with full regard for the principle of complexity. When agricultural procurement prices or industrial producer prices are changed, they always consider the effect such changes are likely to have on the relative incomes in the productive branches concerned. In some cases price changes must not be permitted to effect the viability of the productive branch in question; in others, price changes may be aimed at providing new conditions affecting enterprise decisions. It is always in terms of such considerations that decisions regarding prices are linked up with changes in the monetary regulators, such as taxes, subsidies, credit terms, and the like.

Because of its importance the planning of consumer prices needs further elucidation. The policy in regard to consumer prices is part and parcel of the whole living standard policy. This policy embraces (1) employment policy, (2) wages policy, (3) the policy of social benefits, and (4) the policy of consumer prices. Planned pricing is thus more than merely the control of prices. It includes also the control of wages and incomes, in harmony with the prices. In this context the consumer price plan is composed of

(1) the expected changes in relative prices, regardless of whether they are administrative price decisions or whether they are determined by market factors (the planning of price changes);

(2) the expected change in the total consumer price level (the planning of the price level) as a consequence of these changes in relative prices;

(3) the differential effects of changes in the price level upon the incomes of the different strata of society (the effect planning).

The consumer price plan, is related to the various other factors in the living standard policy through its effect on the differentiation of incomes. For purposes of the policy of wages and social allowances, it is important that the price plan shall quantify the overall effect of the expected price movements for each social stratum that is regarded as forming an independent entity from the point of view of the living standard policy. What is attempted that is to say, is not only to prevent a rising consumer price level from causing a decline in the living standard of any social stratum considered as an independent entity, but also, and more important, to ensure that the real wages or real incomes of the various separate social strata comply with the plan. So regarded, the consumer price plan is satisfactory only if it makes possible the determination of the average and the minimum levels of the rises in wages and salaries, and if it keeps pensions, family allowances, social benefits, interest on money deposits, and certain other elements, at an unchanged or higher level.

III. INFLATIONARY PRESSURE

If one does not regard price movements within the control of planned pricing and offset by measures of the income policy as inflation, then inflatory manifestations consist of

(1) any rise in the price level not planned and therefore not covered by the incomes policy;

(2) any disguised price rise;

(3) any forced purchase; and

(4) any forced saving.

The possibility of an unplanned rise in the price level is a consequence of the mixed price mechanism. Even in those socialist countries in which prices are fixed in the widest sense, this is enforced in detail only for those products and for those services which are sold in socialist retail trade. It goes without saying that there are controlled prices (for public services, for example) outside this sphere; but there is also a free market on which small producers sell their goods (for instance the Kolkhoz market in the Soviet Union). Furthermore, some socialist countries (Poland, Czechoslovakia, Hungary), permit the pricing of certain non-staple commodities and services produced manufactured by state enterprises and/or co-operatives, to be subject to determination by the enterprises concerned. If, under this system, there is a rise in the price level and the consumer price plan fails to take it into consideration, which implies that it is not offset in incomes, then the price rise must be regarded as a form of inflation.

A disguised price rise represents a rise in the price level that is not measured by the price statistics. This may happen even when the price index is most scrupulously calculated. Price statistics prepared in the traditional form are neutral or indifferent in respect of changes in quality and to changes in relative weights. The price level may rise even without the price of a single product changing, partly by putting commodities of an inferior quality on the market, partly by withdrawing certain types of goods from the market and replacing them by new types only slightly different, but sold at disproportionately higher prices. It is only detailed scrutiny and the commercial enterprises themselves that are in a position to check whether both the prices and the quality comply to official regulations. If, however, there is excess demand, this supervisory function becomes much less effective.

Forced purchase is a situation in which consumer preference is restricted. The consumer is unable to find the assortment of goods on the market which he wants. Naturally, no country can rely for her supply upon commodities she does not produce. Nor can a country resort to international division of labour to improve her supply beyond the point where she is capable of keeping her international balance of payments in equilibrium. Forced purchase is a situation which indicates a deterioration of the commodity supply, caused by an imbalance and by inflationary pressure. Furthermore, with the growth of productive forces, and with a rising living standard as its result, the pattern of consumption changes and the supply structure has to follow in its track. Demand for more expensive types of goods causes a rise in the average prices of various commodity groups affected. But such a rise in average prices must not be considered as an indicator of forced purchases. In the case of excess demand, on the other hand, as part of a general rise of average prices, the quality factor contributes to the elements of inflationary pressure.

Forced savings imply that there is a shortage within a field of non-substitutable products combined with definite demand. The consumer is reluctant to spend money reserved for certain definite goods on any commodity available on the market and prefers to save his income in the hope that the desired good will be available later.

These manifestations of an inflationary pressure, with a lesser or greater intensity, exist in the economies of all socialist societies, as a consequence of the fact that excess demand has been institutionally integrated into their economy. Economists in socialist countries refer time and again to the presence of this inflationary pressure, though they generally avoid using the term 'inflation'. We meet such descriptions as a sellers' market [2], disguised price rise [3], delayed demand [4], unsatisfied demand [5], non-voluntary savings [6] and so on. It is Atlas who has objected to the term inflation not being used [7]. Konnik puts it thus: 'partial disproportions between the money in circulation and supply lead to additional demand in the retail trade and to price rises, viz. to inflationary phenomena, on the Kolkhoz market' [8].

It is a still debated issue whether this inflationary pressure is confined to consumer goods only or whether its manifestations affect economy as a whole. According to some, the means of production are not subject to the inflationary pressure since in the socialist economy the means of production are not commodities: the money available to buy them is merely a substitute for a commodity voucher.[1]

It is argued as follows: in a socialist sector of a national economy, that is in the relations between the budget and the enterprises on the one hand and as between the various enterprises on the other, no liquidity, that is, no excess demand, can exist without corresponding commodities to cover it because money without commodity coverage does not exist at all and the budget forecast never becomes an expenditure; or if it does, it is in the form of a money surplus which, after the closing of the enterprise's annual balance, is simply removed from circulation through the withdrawal of the profit. The only thing that can create a problem is if the socialist sector can draw away commodities from the population's consumption fund, by enhancing excess demand on the consumer market.

The situation examined by those who support this argument is as follows: (1) the state controls all enterprises by central plan directives; among other things it controls the composition of production and it centrally distributes the means of production; (2) money for the capital investments determined in the plan is provided by the budget; (3) the budget removes the profits of enterprises and refunds their losses.

From the Hungarian experiences, at least, it may be concluded that the inflationary pressure is felt even under such a system of economic management. What in effect we consider, with some simplifications, as the market of consumer goods, is the complete system of the commodity relations of the non-socialist, and in some cases the non-state-owned, economic sectors. In addition to consumer goods, the means of production are also sold on this market, and it is on this market that craftsmen and farmers producing 'small'

[1] Such views have been voiced recently by V. Kulizov and N. Shehet. For examination of these problems see D. Valovoy, 'On the Planned Utilisation of Commodity and Money Relations'. *Planovoye Hozyaystvo* (1974), No. 2.

commodities buy their materials, tools, machines, and it is here that the population buys building materials and similar goods.

The economists who maintain the principle that 'the means of production are not commodities' hold that the institutional segregation of the material-technological supply of socialist production from the trade turnover solves this problem. But it is impossible centrally to distribute all the means of production. Furthermore, in a system of central quotas the specifications and technical parameters of every product cannot be described in the same detail as they appear in the form of commodities in interenterprise relations. Accordingly, control by plan directives has had to assume that the most essential criteria of the means of production, including their use value, will be enforced in the enterprises's contractual relations. This also gives opportunity for manifestations of an inflationary pressure.

In the field of the means of production the opportunities for disguised price rises, induced by excess demand, are still more favourable, because the authorities can regulate only indirectly and by normative prescriptions the prices of components, subunits, special-purpose machines, all of them produced with widely varying technical parameters. In the field of the means of production the inflationary pressure appears also in various new forms, of which the excessive stocks of unfinished products, disturbances in the organisation of production and investment, delays in the completion of new projects, are typical examples.

Excess demand causes difficulties also in the management of labour. Excess demand in the consumer market, in itself, has an adverse effect on labour discipline, preventing as it does the workers from freely using their wages. Excess demand for means of production creates bottlenecks in plants; imbalances within enterprises prevent the most rational utilisation of the available manpower; the result is underemployment within the factory, in varying degrees.

In socialist countries inflationary pressure is thus not only felt but also regularly analysed during the preparation of the yearly plans. Planning, of whatever type, begins with a critical analysis of the actual economic situation, bringing together the experience accumulated in the course of continuous observation of trade in the means of production as well as in consumer goods. The information used for operative market supervision includes the utilisation of capacities, the state of order books, reports on delays in deliveries, changes in stocks, and so on. This means that the targets for economic growth which planning attempts to fix for the medium or the long range on the basis of the system of economic balances, is preceded by an analysis of the past real operations. It is this analysis which must provide an answer to the question whether economic growth can go on under conditions of equilibrium or under conditions of disequilibrium with the abolition, mitigation, continuance, or even enhancement of the inflationary pressure.

The inflationary pressure in socialist economies is the outcome of state planning based on the principle of 'equilibrium under stress'. The view that consumption should run ahead of production had been widespread, particularly in the 1950s. The assumption had been that this would be advantageous from two points of view:

(1) If growth is characterised by disequilibrium, a larger proportion of the national income must be devoted to investment, to accelerate economic growth. From this point of view the inflationary pressure may be considered as a difficulty inherent in rapid economic growth.

(2) The difficulties of growth, in the form of 'bottlenecks', guide planners in planning new capacity, and thus in structural changes. With 'planning under stress' there is an excess demand in the initial part of the plan period; stocks are depleted and shortages emerge for certain types of goods. Later on, production catches up with the demand; the extent of 'scarce' goods is reduced and stocks are gradually replenished. Finally, a genuine equilibrium is attained and, with a higher level of growth of the productive forces, a new plan once more upsets the equilibrium.

The inflationary pressure under 'planning for stress' must be distinguished from the situation in which partial imbalances occur in a state of general equilibrium. With planned pricing, even in a state of general equilibrium there may be situations in which local or nationwide shortages or surpluses arise transitionally. But the difficulties caused by such situations are negligible in comparison with the advantages inherent in planned pricing, since in a mechanism in which decisions on production are guided exclusively by the indications of market price movements, an inflationary spiral may be released, whereas in a mechanism where the price policy aims at price stability, shortages will provide guidance for economic policy. In such cases price rises provide only one of the possible alternatives to be resorted to when all other possibilities – to increase imports to increase capacity, to change the productive structure – have failed.

IV. THE ALTERNATIVES TO REPRESSED INFLATION

Excess demand with a free market mechanism tends to raise the price level (open inflation) whilst under the conditions of administrative price control it manifests itself in indirect ways (repressed inflation). The theory of repressed inflation was formulated by Novozhilov, in the light of the situation which prevailed in the Soviet economy in the period of transition from war communism to the new economic policy. The policy applied had been one of low prices related to the level of wages paid for the production of the goods concerned. These did not provide at all or only to a slight degree for any net social income. Those responsible for price policy in that period attempted to improve the market for workers in the lower income brackets. In his analysis of the situation Novozhilov found that the policy of low prices acted similarly to inflation, replacing the price rises by an increasingly acute scarcity of goods. He termed this situation 'credit inflation' [9].

In their studies of the restrictive economy during the Second World War, the debates in the West revived the discussion which had taken place in the Soviet Union in the 1920s. The difference lay only in the terminology: 'commodity shortage' was substituted by 'inflationary gap' [10], [11] and [12] and 'credit inflation' by the term 'repressed inflation' [13]. As regards the essence of the matter, there was another common element: while the debate in the West concentrated on the conditions characteristic of a war economy, the Soviet debate took place in terms of an effort to put an end to war communism.

When discussing the inflationary pressure prevailing in a socialist economy, this historical background may lead to erroneous conclusions. The theory of a repressed inflation based on a war situation was expounded most thoroughly by Bent Hansen [13]. In such a situation the fixing of prices and wages had been associated with an extensive system of rationing and coupons. Using two basic diagrams and models for the perfect competition and for monopolies Hansen attempted to bring out the significance of the inflationary gap caused by administrative freezing of the prices and wages. This may in part explain the fact that, when analysing the inflationary pressure under socialism Western economists are prone to exaggerate its negative effect [14], [15], [16] and [17]. According to them a socialist economy should be regarded as one in a state of permanent mobilisation; that is, essentially an economy of the same type as a restrictive war economy. But a socialist economy cannot be described in this way.

Hansen's models had certain weak points. Hagger drew attention to them. Hagger considered the re-examination of the model important in case of a looser price control situation. He was going out from the point that the aim of price and incomes policy is partly to freeze prices but partly to mitigate the inflationary pressure [18]. It was, among others, Polak who outlined a price control model but not with a strict price freeze. He distinguished between autonomous price increases and price adjustments [19]. But all this will not alter the essence. These debates about price control alternatives deal with the restricted war economy of a fundamentally market system.

The socialist countries control prices and wages in a fundamentally different situation. In all the European socialist countries the consumption of the population takes place under free trade, without rationing. As a general rule the only field outside the market is the distribution of housing. Rents in socialist countries are low and enable even people in the lower income brackets to live in comfortable flats. Low rents necessarily create excess demand which makes it necessary that new and empty flats shall be centrally allocated. But this does not mean an excess demand on the macroeconomic level. What is relevant is rather that under socialist conditions, as they are interpreted in our time, housing is a transitional category between public consumption and individual consumption; it has a price but it is not the price that controls distribution.

Free trade establishes certain defined requirements for the administrative price control to meet. If the administratively guaranteed price level is divorced from the equilibrium level, it not only restricts the function of money, but it affects – it weakens – the operation of planned pricing as a whole. In this connection it is worthwhile to draw attention to what Lerner said in his paper, for he used the term 'suppressed' inflation. Machlup reminded him that Röpke preferred the term 'repressed inflation' to 'suppressed inflation' because Röpke wanted to argue that prices could not be kept down for long [1].

From the point of view of the inflationary pressure under socialism, the category of the means of production must be judged by different criteria. When, that is to say, the means of production are centrally distributed, so that the allocative function of price is replaced by a system of quotas, the assumption is that the price does not need to play a compensatory role. Thus, in the sphere of the means of production the inflationary pressure may be considerably greater than in the field of consumption. It is perhaps precisely for this reason that Kraus stated that the price paid for abandoning central plan directives must be the release of the inflationary spiral [20]. This hypothesis has not, however, been verified by the experience of the socialist countries.

Large-scale experiments are going on in some regions of the Soviet Union with the introduction of free trade in the means of production and in some other commodity groups. When choosing the regions and groups of products, the initial assumption was that demand at the given price level did not exceed the demand as limited previously by quotas. Experience has proved that with free trade demand tends to diminish. This may be attributed to the fact that with free trade enterprises are disposed to keep their inventories at exactly the approved level and to adapt their purchases to the production programme already agreed. We may in this respect refer to the example of Hungary where, although the 1968 economic reform abolished the quota system for the means of production, this did not release an inflationary spiral. An economic reform of this type, that is to say, does not only activate the price function but as an organic element in the reform modifies at the same time the criteria for state planning.

V. WASTE OF RESOURCES UNDER CAPITALISM AND UNDER SOCIALISM

More rapid inflation in the industrially advanced capitalist countries has called for a comparative study of open and repressed inflation. In this field, however, scientific research has encountered almost insuperable difficulties. Open inflation can be measured by commonly known methods with price index calculations, whereas of the extent of inflationary pressure only the planners themselves can form some idea – and that only approximate – on the basis of the overall financial balance of the national economy. With these difficulties of quantitative comparison, scientific research has to resort to qualitative criteria to be able to reach any conclusions.

Similar analyses are performed, mainly in the western countries, to 'prove' why an open inflation is preferable to a repressed one, which latter is prone to introduce irrational elements into the national economy. This hypothesis is clearly reflected in the phrase 'inflation, communist style'. According to it, irrationality is created by a budgetary policy which keeps prices stable by subsidies. 'The subsidies chew up capital that would otherwise be invested in new plant and equipment, and contribute to the persistent inability of communist economies to expand fast enough to meet the demands of consumers. Consumers pay dearly in other ways for official price stability.[1]

Let us examine the budgetary price subsidy more closely. With state ownership, the entire productive organisation of the nation may be regarded as 'one enterprise' and the product as 'one product'. The state's freedom of decision operates in two directions: (1) The selection of products so as to determine how the market and non-market mechanisms shall be interrelated in the combined system of distribution. (2) The selection of the products processed into commodities, so as to determine where, in what direction and to what extent prices shall deviate from input costs. The budget may compensate for one incremental profit accrued by another one.

What the state does is essentially the same as what an enterprise does in a market economy, distributing costs between products in accordance with their cost-carrying capacities, having regard to the criterion of equilibrium prices. If the cost level of the gross national product works out as planned, there is no difficulty. For price incentives the state will use such funds only as it obtains from disincentives. This is quite natural and according to the rules since in total the price level corresponds to the value level, and the budget merely redistributes. The same happens when, to avert inflation on the world market, the budget grants subsidies to imports. If the price level of exports and imports (the terms of trade) remains unchanged, no problems will arise; the funds used by the budget to compensate for the higher import prices are equal to the extra receipts of the state, secured through a rise in the export price level.

All this may be formulated also in another way. The budget expenditure for price subsidies cannot be separated from the price and income relations in which it performs its function. The abolition of price subsidies will not increase the social capital, but will on the other hand diminish it. The state grants budgetary price subsidies mainly to keep the cost of living at a low level. In the lower income brackets it is the staples and public services which absorb the major portion of the incomes. Under such circumstances budgetary price subsidies could be abolished only if their disappearance were more than compensated for by means of wage increases. The only convincing argument would be that, if relative prices do not adapt to relative inputs, economic rationality suffers. But it is precisely this hypothesis that requires the linking of any comparative analysis of the two basic types of inflation with a similar comparative study of the value systems of capitalism and socialism. For this is the only

[1] 'Inflation, Communist Style'. *Time* (1974), VIII. No. 5.

way to prove that economic rationality in socialist systems cannot be determined in terms of the logical system of a free market.

If we regard the optimal as rational and waste as any condition which deviates from the optimal, we shall still have to determine what the optimum is. Bergson has pointed out that the optimum state must be determined as a function of social utility [21]. The social welfare function introduced by Bergson thus relates to the ideological assumptions of the economy. The concept of social utility under socialism differs widely from the notion of social utility in capitalism. From this follows that socioeconomic systems must be judged by criteria which are valid only for them. A socialist state restricts the range of those products which become commodities (individual goods); it treats part of the available products as public goods; furthermore it differentiates between the products that become commodities, and thus fall under the sphere of action of the market, according to their social significance; it sets consumer prices free from input costs according to political preferences and desires for disincentives.

The sphere of public goods is wider than in a free-market model because the communist principle of distribution in accordance with needs, so far as concerns some of its elements, already exists under socialism. The tendency is to organise the consumption of the society in respect of basic social care. This covers child care, education and schooling, health protection, and care for the aged. At the same time many products which are closely related to basic social care, have become commodities. In this case it is the task of political preferences to minimise the exclusion function of the market. The coverage for all this is provided by the disincentives on those commodities whose consumption is not essential, and especially those whose excessive consumption is harmful to health, or even harmful to society.

Inevitably, the socialist order of values replaces consumers' sovereignty with social sovereignty in a way that restricts the supply-regulating function of consumer preferences. In the final analysis, social sovereignty finds its expression in:

(1) socially organised consumption in the sphere of basic social care, whereby the concept of public goods is distinguished from the technical criteria normally applied to products, such as divisibility; and in

(2) the adjustment of the relative prices of commodities to their relative social scarcities – more precisely to the relative scarcities on the market, after correction to reflect political preferences and discouragements.

In terms of the Pareto optimum, socialism may be held to have a lower economic efficiency than capitalism. By this criterion there exists a gap in efficiency, and it may be argued that under socialism there is a waste of economic resources. But if we set out from the socialist optimum, we shall arrive at exactly the opposite result. This, however strange it may sound, directly follows from the fact that in rationality as well as in waste, an ideology equally finds expression.

It will also be clear that the income-redistributing function of the budget, the separation of prices from value, and equally price subsidies themselves, are far from being inflation-induced manifestations of the state. This budgetary function would remain necessary for social utility even if state planning were to set the targets for economic growth in such a way as to maintain equilibrium. It is at the same time beyond doubt that in the case of excess demand, this budgetary function is associated with anti-inflationary measures. It is legitimate to ask, moreover, whether the socialist order of values unequivocally requires such criteria as will lead to collective consumption being separated from the market, and price is separated from value? And if so, whether the state organises the economy in strict compliance with these criteria?

Obviously, the optimum under either socioeconomic system, can be enforced only within certain limits. In a market economy it is imperfect competition, in a planned economy it is imperfect state control which impedes the attainment of the optimum. Furthermore, in either system external effects must be taken into account. This, however, will not alter the essential fact that the waste hypothesis implied in the term 'inflation, communist style' remains wholly devoid of meaning for any Marxist economist.

Looking at the problem from the point of view of the waste of resources, open and repressed inflation require to be compared at the same time in respect of the interrelated effects of the existence and of the mitigation of excess demand. According to some views, price rationality required by excess demand is specific to repressed inflation. Thus if one approaches the problem of open and repressed inflation from the angle of the waste of economic resources, they should be distinguished in the following way: whilst in an open inflation the price clears the market, in a repressed inflation it is the rational function of price that is repressed. But in reality it is only a fiction that in an open inflation excess demand is abolished.

Current demand – as Lerner states – is equal to current supply, prices rising as much as may be needed to clear the market. Yet this clearing of the market is not an equilibrium except in the empty sense in which the supply is always equal to the demand because it is nothing but the same transaction seen from the other side. There is no real equilibrium because the buyer's expectations are not fulfilled. There is a gap between expected prices and the higher actual prices. Both controlled prices and rising actual prices restrict an excess demand, so that in neither case is the rational classical price mechanism permitted to govern the distribution of scarce goods between potential purchases [1].[1]

The freeing of price movements would not put an end to excess demand in socialist countries. The change of a repressed into an open inflation would

[1] It is noteworthy that the economic commission of the United States Congress rejected the introduction of an efficient price and wages control with the argument that it would cause distortions in the structure of prices and wages and a disparity between the United States and world market prices. *An Action Program to Reduce Inflation and Restore Economic Growth: Interim Report* (Washington, September 21, 1974).

bring matters from bad to worse. It is not the prices that should be liberated: excess demand must be abolished. Inflationary pressure does not necessarily exist in a socialist economy. It can be abolished, or at least minimised if the state (1) determines the resources to be assigned from the national income to growth in harmony with the requirement for equilibrium (2) creates more direct relations between producer and consumer, and finally (3) ensures harmony between demand and supply with a flexible price mechanism.

The debates in the Soviet Union in the twenties were significant not only from the point of view of repressed inflation but also for the establishment of a theory for an optimally operating social economy. Scientific research has ever since played an important role in the process of improving economic control.

REFERENCES

[1] Abba P. Lerner, 'The Inflationary Process. Some Theoretical Aspects'. *Review of Economics and Statistics*, Vol. XXXI (1949).
[2] Gy. Péter, 'The Significance of Economic Efficiency and Profitability in a Planned Economy'. *Közgazdasági Szemle* (1956), No. 6–8.
[3] B. Csikós Nagy, *Policy in a Transitional Economy* (Budapest, 1958).
[4] Sz. Portigul, 'Solvent Demand and Supply in Socialist Reproduction'. *Voprosy Ekonomiki* (1969), No. 12.
[5] G. Kaganov, 'On Some Theoretical and Practical Problems of Commodity and Money Circulation in Socialism'. *Dengi i kredit* (1970), No. 1.
[6] Y. Sukhorchkina, 'Conference of Statisticians on the Income of the Families'. *Vestnik Statistiki* (1970), No. 8.
[7] Z. Atlas, 'The Problem of Inflation'. *Vestnik Moskovskogo Universiteta, Seriya VII. Ekonomika* (1969), No. 3.
[8] J. Konnik, *A Course in Political Economics*, Vol. 2, Moscow (1963).
[9] V. V. Novozhilov, 'Commodity Shortages', *Vestnik Finantsov* (1926).
[10] J. M. Keynes, *How to Pay for the War*, (London, 1940).
[11] E. Lundberg, 'I kom stutveckling och köpfraftsöverkott under Krigsären', *Meddelenden fran Konjunkturinstitut*, Ser. B:2 (Stockholm, 1943).
[12] W. Salant, 'The Inflationary Gap', *American Economic Review* (1942).
[13] B. Hansen, *A Study in the Theory of Inflation*, (London, 1951).
[14] K. Bush, 'Soviet Inflation', in Y. Laulen (ed.), *Banking, Money and Credit in the U.S.S.R.*, NATO (Brussels, 1973).
[15] R. Campbell, 'Macro-economic Models and Central Price Setting in the Soviet Economy', in F. Gehrels *et al.* (eds), *Essays in Economic Analysis and Policy* (Bloomington, Indiana, 1970).
[16] G. Garvy, 'Inflation and Price Stabilisation Policies in Some Eastern European Countries', mimeographed paper presented to the C.E.S.E.S. Conference in Venice (August, 1974).
[17] G. Grossmann, 'Gold and the Sword: Money in the Soviet Command Economy', in H. Rosovsky (ed.), *Industrialisation in Two Systems* (1966).
[18] A. J. Hagger, *The Theory of Inflation* (London and New York, 1964).
[19] J. J. Polak, 'On the Theory of Price Control', *Review of Economic Statistics* (February, 1945).
[20] K. Kraus, 'Guided Economy'. *Zycie gospodarcze*, 30/3 (1969).
[21] A. Bergson, *Essays in Normative Economics* (Cambridge, Mass., 1966).
[22] L. O. Yushkov, 'The Fundamentals of the Plan Method'. *Vestnik finansov* (Nov. 10, 1928).

Discussion of the Paper by Béla Csikós-Nagy

Professor Bajt said that Professor Csikós-Nagy's paper first dealt with inflation proper. A second part discussed the welfare efficiency of the two price systems, centrally planned and market. As inflation itself was quite a problem, his comments on the second topic would be sketchy.

Professor Csikós-Nagy rejected a common reproach which ran somewhat along the lines: 'Well, you succeed in repressing inflation but your relative price system is distorted and, through suboptimum allocation, it breeds incessant loss to your economy'. Professor Csikós-Nagy's argument was that the 'socialist value system' fundamentally differed from the capitalist one, so that the welfare efficiency of the two systems could not be evaluated by common criteria. Centrally planned allocation might appear inferior, but was not. For it helped to implement planned targets and to attain the 'socialist optimum'.

He agreed with Professor Csikós-Nagy's rejection of the reproach but did not agree with his argument. He did this, if for nothing else, because the argument encouraged anybody who enjoyed sufficient social control to promote any degree of arbitrariness in social preferences. For example, how far from genuinely socialist was the planners' optimum? Nor would he comfort capitalists with the belief that their preferences were the people's preferences. This comfortable 'peaceful-coexistence' approach did not satisfy him. A definition of 'socialist relations of production' – of a humanitarian society – was obviously needed, with optima in both market and centrally planned economies evaluated through the implied criteria. This was not to suggest that Professor Csikós-Nagy should have provided such definition. The problem was broader than the discussion in the conference.

On inflation, Professor Csikós-Nagy provided data which showed that retail price levels were extremely stable in the centrally planned economies. Regrettably, these were the only data he gave on inflation. Stability of retail prices was regarded as important to social stability in centrally planned countries, he said, and was ensured despite increasing producer and import prices. This was possible, at least for a time, because retail prices were insulated from them by a powerful buffer of taxes, profits, losses and subsidies – essentially, by the state budget.

The recently achieved price increase of less than 1 per cent yearly represented almost absolute stability. It was quite a performance and many people would be satisfied with it. Professor Csikós-Nagy, however, told us that this was not regarded as inflation in central planned economies. On quantitative grounds, Professor Bajt would be inclined to agree. Almost no inflation differed a little from no inflation at all. However, Professor Csikós-Nagy gave qualitative reasons why price increases in centrally planned economies should not be regarded as inflation. One was that price increases were planned and integrated into the planned distribution and allocation process. In particular, planned economies had raised agricultural prices, and so 'relieved an increasing acute social tension and contributed in no small measure to enhancing the general social stability'.

Professor Bajt was not convinced. If price stability were an essential element of social stability, and if Professor Csikós-Nagy did not accept even 1 per cent price rises as stability, price rises must be the last resort of the planner. What accounted for 'planned' differences in price increase between socialist countries? Had the higher Hungarian price rises nothing to do with the decentralisation of her economy? To put it differently, Yugoslav planners incorporated a 20 per cent price growth in their 1975 plans. Should this rate of inflation be considered as 20 points lower than the actual rise? Or, since integration in overall planning seemed decisive, did a 30 per cent administered rise in prices in the July 1965 economic reform not qualify as inflation, because wages were adjusted by planners to maintain living standards?

He saw modern inflation as essentially a redistribution process;[1] not that it caused redistribution, but that redistribution was its prime mover. Social groups used price increases to share in the common pie and endangered groups had to fight back. Wage-profit, wage-wage, raw material-finished product prices: these relationships appeared to be one of the main gears. Market conflicts between social groups were made practically impossible in centrally planned economies, because distribution was planned. Price pressures and price increases could be explained technically. Planners simply could not accurately foresee the course of commodity and income flows. It was much easier to fulfil income than production plans, and upward adjustments of prices were much more comfortable than downward ones. In principle, planners could decrease or increase the price level, almost at will. During the last seven years of Stalin, the cost of living had been halved in the USSR and in the 1950s consumer prices were decreased in all centrally planned economies. Import prices (terms of trade) were obviously the most painful. This was understandable, since the planners were here transformed into an object of the redistribution process.

Professor Bajt therefore argued that to the extent that price increases were not generated by conflicts between social groups they should not be regarded as modern inflation. Z. V. Atlas admitted that excess money resulted in redistribution of national income, even in socialist economies, and realised that 'contrary to capitalism this redistribution has nothing to do with any class-antagonistic relations.[2] Nonetheless, Atlas missed the essential difference between the market fights of social groups and the perfect planning of commodity income flow. It all depended on definition, but Professor Bajt made this distinction both to give insight into modern inflation and to facilitate a distinction between inflation as a social and as a technical phenomenon. He found it more useful than the distinction between cost-push and demand-pull.

Professor Csikós-Nagy's second argument against describing price rises in centrally planned economies as inflationary was this. As agricultural prices had to be increased under 'increasingly acute social tension', they obviously qualified as inflation. Planners acting under social pressures were not really planners. Professor Csikós-Nagy's conclusion that such price increases should not be regarded as inflation was not convincing. Higher oil prices increased social stability by giving some underdeveloped countries a larger share in world income. Every price increase that improved the economic position of a powerful social group increased social stability, reducing strikes, riots, revolutions and wars. Should all such increase be discounted as an inflation?

[1] Z. V. Atlas, *Problema Inflacii* (Voprosi Teorii), Vestnik Moskovskojo Universitita, Serija VII, Ekonomika 14 (1969), pages 3–13.

[2] L'esperienza Inflazistica Jugloslava', *Rivista di Politica Economica*, 64 (1974).

Professor Csikós-Nagy listed four emanations of repressed inflation. First, unplanned price increases, like those on Kolkhoz markets. Second, disguised price increases resulting from lower quality, or reduced variety. Third, forced purchases, in the sense that people could buy only what they found in stores. Fourth, forced savings – money balances that could not be spent. The first two signalled an imperfectly repressed inflation. The latter two, plus Professor Csikós-Nagy's deficient labour supply ('adverse effect on labour discipline'), were emanations of repressed inflation. If one dismissed forced purchases, this left excess demand for output and labour – the typical repressed-inflation situation of Western economic theory.

With plan-fixed prices, inflationary pressures on free-market output, and labour-demand distortions, were the foreseeable outcomes of repressed inflation. The relevant question was how strong these pressures and distortions were and Professor Csikós-Nagy was not very explicit: since he was a practical economist, the inference was that they were quite strong. However, if they had been really strong, excess demand on free markets should have been increasingly pulling prices up, with forced savings accumulating to levels unknown in market economies. He shared Wiles's point[1] that it would be unrealistic to assume that centrally planned households adjusted their money balances in line with free market prices.

New flows of excess demand, as well as stocks of excess money, must have been pulling prices up. When a free market ('plan II prices') was introduced in Yugoslavia in 1948, the fraction of consumer goods channeled to it grew rapidly. In a few years, there were no goods available at 'plan I prices' at all. Nothing like that happened in centrally planned economies. Although market prices there have been increasing, their rate of increase seemed low (bad and good harvests appeared to make prices fluctuate). A recent (not yet published) recalculation of Holzman's indicator of repressed inflation by Bronson and Severin showed that Kolkhoz market pressure had been declining.[2] As for lower quality, it was a usual, but nonetheless marginal, phenomenon accompanying a steady general improvement.

Household savings were growing indeed, but not abnormally fast, and household currency holdings relative to bank deposits in Hungary and Poland were actually decreasing.[3] The total liquid asset (currency plus bank deposits)/disposal income relationship in Yugoslavia was about the same as in Hungary and Poland. The Yugoslav currency holdings/bank deposits relationship was much higher than in both countries, although Yugoslavia had no repressed inflation. While there were demand pressures on individual markets, queues did not lengthen. Rather they shortened. With fixed prices, shortages and surpluses were almost the only signals for planned corrections.

Professor Csikós-Nagy's linking of inflationary pressures to growth cycles might prove a valuable hint. It fitted quite well into the investment-cycle

[1] 'The New Inflation Consists of too Many Bankers Chasing too Few Ideas', Anti-inflationary policies: East–West, *L'Est*, Quaderni C.E.S.E.S., p. 229.

[2] G. Garvy, 'Price Stabilization Policies in some Eastern European Countries', Paper presented to the 10th International Seminar, C.E.S.E.S., (Venice, 1974).

[3] R. Portes, *Macro Economic Equilibrium under Central Planning*, Seminar Paper No. 40, Institute for International Economic Studies (University of Stockholm, 1974).

literature.[1] One should therefore expect cyclical patterns in forced savings, queues, free-market prices and labour inputs. If investigation confirmed this, we should gain more reliable information on repressed inflation and greater insight into its mechanism than by looking at trends and cross-country differences.

Professor Duesenberry wanted to ask Professor Csikós-Nagy a question. He understood that in socialist countries retail prices increased slowly or remained constant, but that there had been some significant increases in wholesale prices. He also understood that there were some subsidies. The implication was that the percentage of subsidy, or a profit margin, must be widening. Was this true, or had he missed something?

Professor de Wolff added a question. Did this not mean that subsidies cut into the rest of the state budget? The paper said that the introduction of new technology also tended to increase prices, but what of productivity increases? He could see that if a socialist country wanted to raise the standard of living it would raise wages, but surely increasing productivity worked to reduce them?

Professor Csikós-Nagy replied that one must distinguish industry from agriculture. Most socialist countries had higher retail than wholesale prices for industrial goods. So one could increase the producer price on account of higher costs for, say, tractors, and counterbalance it, if one wanted to keep the price level stable, by reducing the turnover tax incorporated in retail prices. One had almost the opposite situation in agriculture, where there were subsidies. This was not true in all countries, for example, Bulgaria. But all other socialist countries operated in this way.

Professor Duesenberry wondered, if one took the last ten years, how much increase there had been in the ratio of agricultural subsidy to the value of turnover.

Professor Csikós-Nagy answered this question by taking the example of meat in Hungary. The subsidy represented about 60 per cent of the retail price. The government could subsidise meat only by price levelling. This was a purely income redistribution function. In other words, there were items with deficit and sufficit prices. The budget subsidised goods with deficit prices by turnover taxes incorporated in sufficit prices.

Mr Kaser pointed out that farm subsidies had been introduced in the USSR in 1962. They now totalled more than in the EEC.

Professor Modigliani wanted to recall one great law of Milton Friedman. This was that if one wanted to know whether a country was developed or undeveloped, one asked whether it subsidised industry or agriculture. If it subsidised industry it was an underdeveloped country. If it subsidised agriculture, then it was developed.

He wanted to ask Professor Csikós-Nagy what had happened to the relationship between retail and wholesale prices.

Professor Csikós-Nagy answered by looking at Hungary again. The difference between retailer and producer prices in industry was now very small, perhaps

[1] A. Bajt, 'Investment Cycles in European Socialist Economies: A Review Article', *The Review of Economic Literature*, 9, 1971, pp. 53–63 and 'Spillover mechanism in a Labour-Managed Economy', Paper presented at the 3rd Riesenburg Symposium, Riesenburg, July, 1975.

10 per cent. Direct tax in Hungary took a greater percentage of revenues than in other socialist countries. As against this, the wholesale price level stood below the retail price level in the sphere of agriculture.

Professor Frisch recalled the book by Professor Sylos-Labini on *Oligopoly and Technical Progress* in which a thorough concept of mark-up pricing was developed. This concept was combined with a two-sector model of productivity growth. The first sector was characterised by a strong increase in labour productivity and the second (including services) by a smaller productivity increase.

If an increase in real wages led to a cost-push in the labour-intensive sector, there would be a fairly substantial increase in prices there. Professor Aukrust had a similar idea, in his distinction between the open and the sheltered parts of the economy. This was a model for the structural hypothesis of inflation, which related to mark-up, income distribution and productivity differences. It was perhaps outdated as an explanation of inflation in the most recent past but might be useful for socialist countries, which must experience a rather similar phenomenon.

In capitalist countries, one could see examples of downward price stickiness, but the government in a socialist country would be able to balance price increases. Why was there not a fall in prices in sectors where there was a strong productivity increase? Why was there downward stickiness in socialist countries?

Professor Tsuru noted that, under perfect competition, one theoretically should have prices falling in the industries with the biggest productivity increase. In the economy as a whole, one would get relative degrees of price fall and of price increase. One ought to get the same thing in socialist countries.

Under capitalism, of course, things were different because one there had mark-up pricing, etc. With such a price system one could get the highest-productivity industry maintaining prices at the existing level, so that the low productivity industries must increase their prices most. This was a contrast between the United Kingdom in the nineteenth century and the United States today. In planning socialist prices, one surely had to work on the basis that productivity increases were reflected in price reductions. Did socialist price planning allow for this? The paper implied that it did not, but what were socialist countries willing to do?

Professor Csikós-Nagy replied that this was a sensitive point in socialist economies, and that there were differences between countries. He thought that in the USSR, one could have increases in the prices of primary products accompanied by price reductions, say, in the machine industry. The situation was not the same in Hungary because prime cost in Hungary was partly import cost, which did not necessarily fall when productivity in the exporting country increased.

There had been special problems in Hungary since the economic reform, which had moved Hungary from a self-accounting to a self-financing system. So, the role of profit was different, and profit margins were now bigger, which also counterbalanced the increase in productivity.

Professor Bajt noted that, on Mr Kaser's first table[1] the last two columns gave an approximate answer. Food production showed a low productivity increase, but in non-food it was bigger. The low productivity sectors found difficulty in adjusting to productivity increases. Despite the buffer of price

[1] See pp. 146–50 above.

and subsidy, prices did depend on relative productivity movements.

Mr Plessz thought there had been some misunderstanding in the discussion. The argument was about price increases, not inflation. It boiled down to saying that, to some extent, adjustments in relative prices went on in planned economics, with constraints leading to price increases. This was not a sign of inflationary pressure.

He wanted to discuss a related issue. So far, the corresponding adjustment at the retail level had been very much slower than at the producer level. By influencing retail prices, socialist countries were changing income distribution. He thought it was dangerous to identify suppressed inflation in socialist countries with the system of a war economy. If one took the four manifestations of inflation noted in the paper, at least three of these were phenomena associated with underdeveloped economies. Once a reasonably advanced stage of development was reached, increases in productivity made it possible to allow for a fall in the price level, and a reduction of forced purchases and forced saving.

However, with inflationary pressure, what one had was really elements of disguised price increase. There was a continuous trend of price increase, but a variation of intensity over time. It was not a question of reducing quality, but of selling goods of the same quality at a higher price with, for example, new brand names.

Socialist countries could therefore have strong tensions and disguised price increases. The phenomena were cyclical and analagous to those of excess demand in capitalist countries, but an important point was that they were unlikely to become cumulative in times of peace.

In all countries with price controls, there were pressures to keep down prices of items in the cost of living index. Sometimes these became overwhelming. They appeared wherever it was possible to control one segment of the price structure.

Professor Duesenberry explained that one got an example of disguised price increase if one looked at a Western candy bar where the size of the bar shrank continuously but at the same price.

Professor Bajt pointed out that one could have disguised price increases even without price controls. During the last two years steaks had shrunk in countries without planned prices and not in socialist countries.

Mr Plessz pointed out that the statistical offices of Western countries had tried to measure quality changes. However, when an index had policy significance, it was likely that governments would bring in disguised price increases.

Mr Kaser pointed out that one had to remember that the retail trade in a socialist country was a monopoly. It was therefore possible to introduce higher-priced goods and to withdraw earlier brands. Often there was a quality increase, but even then the price increase exceeded its value.

Professor Duesenberry wondered whether, in Hungary, money wages rose at the same rate as average productivity.

Professor Csikós-Nagy explained that with the increase in world prices, Hungary was now using new foreign trade prices. This meant a redistribution of income internationally, with export prices up less than import prices. The increase in real wages in Hungary would have to fall transitionally (in the period 1976–77) to not more than $1\frac{1}{2}$ per cent to $2\frac{1}{2}$ per cent per annum. One could not give the whole productivity increase to the population, but would have to give some to overseas countries. However, in the first part of the 1970s it had been possible to give back something like 80 per cent of productivity increase to the population. So a 5 per cent productivity increase had been accompanied by a $3\frac{1}{2}$ per cent to 4 per cent increase in real wages.

Professor Modigliani wanted to discuss Professor Entov's paper. It had been very difficult to see any trend in inflation rates in Western countries up to 1965. At that point, there had been a significant break. So, while Professor Entov's arguments were appealing, it was hard to see that they were relevant. The break in inflation rates in the mid-1960s had surely to be explained by events other than economic structure. On the variability of price changes between periods, what one really wanted was changes in the terms of trade. When inflation was rapid, there was more dispersion of price increases. He suggested that Professor Entov needed, as the denominator of his formula, the rate of change of prices.

To Professor Csikós-Nagy, he would express surprise that there was no reference to one point. If one looked at a system with total wage and price control, it appeared that what was important was what happened to relative prices and wages. But perhaps the really important thing was savings. Socialist countries encouraged an increase in private savings in nominal terms. Since they needed to encourage savings, there was a strong incentive to keep prices stable.

Professor Lundberg got the impression that the USSR was better at long-run planning because its price formation was integrated into the social system. In capitalist countries, price and profit changes had significant effects on over-capacity and led to short-run crises. Socialist countries had much more long-run pricing processes. This made prices more reliable indicators to use in planning because price trends were quite stable.

In a visit to Sweden, Russian officials had been very impressed by the planning system of a large Swedish corporation. However, they were worried about how it could possibly work well in such a chaotic environment. Of course, socialist countries interfered with prices through taxes and subsidies, but they still had greater price stability. They used linear programming to get shadow prices and tried to adjust price trends in line with these.

He wondered about distortions and mistakes. Were those in socialist countries more fundamental than in the west? Mistakes in capitalist countries were found fairly quickly. What happened in socialist countries? Who was punished, and how? Did a socialist price system really help here?

Sir Austin Robinson said that Professor Csikós-Nagy had said very little about wages. Socialist countries had an advantage in that wage determination was in the hands of governments. But with increasing real income, there was still a problem of estimating new norms. He wondered whether socialist governments could really ignore pressures from industrial wage groups. There seemed to be a big difference between socialist and capitalist countries here, but it might be less than appeared to an outsider.

Professor Kleiman recalled that Professor Modigliani had referred to the need for Professor Entov to look at relative rather than absolute prices. Both in Professor Entov's paper and in the Kleiman–Jaffee paper this problem was taken care of because the coefficient of variation calculated was that of the *rates* of price increases. Both papers were concerned with the dispersion of relative prices.

The question of how to interpret findings connected with the rate of price increase raised questions about untapped market power. Some firms would raise prices more than others during inflation and it was interesting to ask why? One reason might be that there was a risk of governmental or public disapproval if prices were increased. If so, then the limits on prices were determined by public attitudes. In such a system of informal price control, firms waited for an excuse to increase prices. Perhaps an inflationary period gave such an excuse, though this would be the effect of the rate of inflation rather than its cause.

Professor Duesenberry wondered whether there was evidence that more concentrated industries had greater price stability than competitive ones, and whether this was true of both upward and downward stability. He thought it important to work in terms of margins calculated on the basis of standard costs. He did not think the profit margins of concentrated industries had increased over the postwar period. If one took corporate profit after tax as a ratio of sales value, and adjusted for inventory changes and capital consumption, one found there was no inflationary pressure from increasing profit margins in concentrated industries. In the mid-1950s, some firms had increased prices, but one had to distinguish between prices and profit margins to get at the cause of this.

Professor Frisch had suggested that high profits were found in concentrated industries and that this led to high wage payments. It was also suggested that firms with high profit margins were the target for big wage demands, with a kind of joint monopoly sharing of profit. There might be some of this, but he did not see much movement of the relative wages of labour in concentrated industries.

However, during booms, as Professor Bajt said happened in Yugoslavia, unorganised labour gained, and in slumps, organised labour. For example, in 1955, there had been big wage increases in the United States in the automobile industry, steel, rubber, agricultural implements, etc. It was important to note that much of Professor Entov's data came from the 1950s which meant that it was not typical.

He thought there was some truth in Professor Aukrust's theory. High profits were certainly something for union negotiators to question, but one could not hang much of the blame for inflation on rising profit margins in concentrated industries. One could hang a little on unions wanting to get excess profit margins transferred into wages.

Professor Bronfenbrenner noted that one found it difficult to *enforce* disequilibrium systems in the west over long periods during peace time. As a visitor in the USSR, he had enquired about the contribution of the legal system in this field, since enforcement seemed more effective there than in the west. What was the legal framework of enforcing supply and demand controls in an economy that remained in a disequilibrium position for a long time? In the USSR there might well be 'overkill' (unnecessarily severe enforcements) but what happened and was it worthwhile?

(1) The penalty for economic crimes was high.

(2) There was no presumption of innocence. Because of the preliminary investigation of each case, this meant that if a case went to trial, there might be some implication of guilt.

(3) There was a 25-year statute of limitations.

(4) If the accused was acquitted or received a light sentence, the government could appeal.

(5) In the west, the jury could ignore the law. In the USSR the situation was different because the judge was a member of the jury.

(6) Refusal of the accused to testify was called failure to co-operate with the investigation. It increased the danger of conviction.

(7) The accused could not choose his own defence attorney.

(8) The right to strike for higher wages existed in the USSR, but it was attenuated by the duty to work.

(9) It was also attenuated by the fact that 'peaceful picketing' carried heavy penalties.

Perhaps such a severe set of arrangements was necessary to impose controls on a disequilibrium system. While he was not judging the USSR, these arrangements must surely be a welfare cost of the system if one was interested in civil liberties.

Professor Polaczek could understand why western economists were puzzled at first sight by a situation where the state could reduce or increase both agricultural and industrial prices simultaneously. There was this situation in Poland, too. There were two phenomena. In industry, producers' prices had risen, especially because, in the past, there had been big distortions. These had to be eliminated.

For example, in the 1960s producer prices of coal, though not retail prices, were trebled, and the producer prices of the whole range of fuel-intensive goods increased *pro rata*. The reason was that Polish planners wanted to relate raw material prices to world prices. The theoretical considerations for such a move had been explained in a paper he had written then with Professor Kalecki. So the price increases in some forms of industrial goods were managed. There had been a small price reform of producers' goods in 1971, and another could take place in 1976, to correct abnormal situations inherited from the past or caused by price changes on the world market. The case of agricultural prices was different. There was a relatively slow increase in agricultural productivity in socialist countries, and the young did not want to stay on the land. So, at intervals, one had to put agricultural products on the same basis as the rest of the economy. Prices paid to farmers were increased and, later, retail prices were eventually increased as well.

What Professor Lundberg had said suggested that planning was easier than it really was. It was true that one needed price stability for short-run planning and to bring about desired changes in income distribution. However, prices were less helpful for long-range planning, especially because prices in socialist countries did adjust to world prices in the long run. So, in the mid-1960s, some Polish planners had asked whether it was correct to go on investing in coal. After hesitation, it was decided to continue. This decision, as it appeared now, was quite justified, but it showed that one could not rely on current price relations when long-term issues were involved.

To Sir Austin Robinson, Professor Polaczek said that wage control was an important instrument in planned economies, but this did not mean that there were no drawbacks. In particular, there was a danger of weakening incentives to increase production. So, Poland had started an experiment, introducing a fixed relationship between increases in output and increases in wages in big industries. If the value added tax of an industry rose 1 per cent, wages could increase – according to a stable coefficient – by, say, 0·6 per cent. Perhaps the methods of differentiating were at present not sufficiently clarified, but it meant that there had been a significant attempt to loosen the rules.

Independently of these automatic wage fund adjustments, it was also possible to raise wages in particular industries. There were periodic 'wage regulations' to adjust the real incomes of groups of workers and what was done depended on the position taken by the respective unions and on demand for products of the particular branch. Such wage regulations could change the rates of pay in particular industries relative to those in the rest of the economy

Professor Lundberg had thought that, on the coal/oil price-ratio, socialist countries would try to smooth out fluctuations in world prices, for example, by making long-run contracts. Surely socialist countries should ignore price increases resulting from inventory changes in the west.

Professor Polaczek replied that this was done. Price changes were smoothed, and this was done with an eye to the future.

Professor Csikós-Nagy reported that Hungary also used price-levelling. The beginning of the process was an increase in import prices. Hungary operated a stabilisation fund which could keep down import prices if this was wanted. So, if the trend in prices on world markets meant that the stabilisation fund was in deficit, one could either increase prices or use the budget to increase the size of the stabilisation fund.

Professor Aukrust noted that the conference had already tried to agree on what was the necessary and sufficient reason for inflation in the west. We were now looking at a group of countries which had done much better. What could the west learn? Was monetary policy in Communist countries more sensible? Or, more likely, were there institutional differences? As far as he could see, the main reason seemed to be that socialist countries could control the price of labour, the most important of all prices, which meant that other prices would easily adapt.

This was in marked contrast to the west, where governments tried to control prices in a roundabout way by managing the demand for commodities. If necessary, they would create unemployment. He hoped that the available alternative solutions were not either extreme wage control, as in the last, or the western way of sometimes creating wasteful unemployment. One needed some kind of incomes policy whereby trade unions co-operated. This was the only acceptable way forward that he could see.

Mr Oppenheimer wondered what was the *primum mobile* of inflation in the United States. He could see that oligopolistic structures were a major element in the American economy, but this did not tell us that they started inflation. If they did not, then what did? Or was this no longer an interesting question? For example, Professor Entov referred to the behaviour of big firms *in response to* price increases in factor markets and to inflationary expectations. What caused these initial price increases? Professor Entov did not explain how the process began. The monetarists gave an answer. Other economists must either give an answer of an analogous kind, or say why this was not an interesting question.

Dr Corden noted that there was evidence that there had recently been a *fall* in after-tax profit. The reasons were not wholly clear. However, Marxist analysis would suggest that this was a structural change. Changes in the money supply could explain inflation, but why should a fall in profits start inflation? And was not the evidence that to some extent the causality was the other way round, inflation helping to cause the fall in profits?

He wanted to suggest some possible reasons for the fall in profits. First, there was increasing competition in the world, because of freer trade. Perhaps multinational corporations had actually worked to reduce profit by increasing world competition. Second, there was a long-run tendency for the capital/labour ratio to rise. Neoclassical economists would expect this to lead to a falling rate of profit. Third, though he had no evidence for this, he thought the fall in profit was partly the result of inadequate allowance for the increased money cost of capital equipment. Fourth, policy measures led to a divergence between anticipated and actual rates of inflation. This led to increased real wage rates and therefore to a squeeze on profits. So there might perhaps be a temporary increase in real wages because inflationary expectations were too high.

Professor Lundberg wondered whether one ought to take more account of collusion between corporations, trade unions and government in countries like the United States. If so, one would probably find that big firms led increases in both wages and profits. Looking at profit margins alone did not show what had happened.

Professor Duesenberry reported a spectacular example of this. The last American steel wage settlement had been moderate and this had been entirely because of Japanese and German competition.

Professor Nussbaumer asked Professor Csikós-Nagy to explain what it was that prevented prices in socialist countries from increasing more rapidly than they did. He wanted him to answer this *excluding* the effect of foreign prices. Was it the control of aggregate demand that kept inflation rates so low? Did socialists countries have methods for wage and investment flexibility which reduced the need for other stabilisation methods?

On structure, changes in incomes and relative prices were probably needed in agriculture. Structural change would therefore lead to increased producer prices. But should this be shifted to consumers? If so, there would be inflation. If not, how was the process financed? Could one really shift payment for increasing agricultural costs to consumers of other goods? How did one avoid the increase in the money supply which was the cause of excess demand?

Professor Csikós-Nagy wanted, first, to thank participants for the very fruitful discussion. He would pick out the points which seemed most important.

His approach – that a rising price level could not be identified, *a priori*, with inflation – was based on earlier theory. In older textbooks, price analysis was more comprehensive than inflation/deflation analysis. The former was based on both money and commodities, with the terms inflation and deflation reserved for a certain kind of price analysis, closely connected with the money supply. Recently, this analysis had been replaced by a comprehensive inflation allowance based on cost-push, demand-pull and structural-change effects. He believed this was a retrograde change because it meant that one lost a good deal of analysis.

While one could argue that terms were pure conventions, they were also frameworks for analysis. Good terms, good classifications helped us to see the real world better. This was important, since scientific investigation must support economic policy.

He had to say this to make it clear that Professor Bajt had misunderstood him. Professor Csikós-Nagy did not pretend that price increases were inflationary in a market economy, and not in a centrally planned economy. His approach was simply that a rising price level could not be regarded, *a priori*, as inflation. Inflation meant a watering of money, and an upsetting of equilibrium. First, it redistributed incomes arbitrarily. Second, it disrupted the economy. Such a situation could be maintained temporarily but, sooner or later, must be overcome.

Moreover, the whole price flow could be understood only if one clarified secular changes. These were deep and the process was far from being completed. Some of them were:

(1) The world economy was heterocentred and not monocentred.

(2) Societies lived in different socioeconomic systems and so developed under conditions of challenge and struggle.

(3) With accelerated technical development, challenge rendered time more of a determinant than efficiency.

(4) The increasing scarcity of economic resources caused a change in rational behaviour, putting an end to cost-minimising, which allowed waste of resources.

(5) Policy used prices to redistribute national income internationally, in favour of the developing world.

(6) There was a changed relationship between society and economy, which could be characterised as a weakening mobility of societies.

(7) Full employment and proportionate incomes had come into force.

(8) The expectations of society posed new technological requirements, with environmental protection only one element.

What was important was to distinguish between what was necessary and what was avoidable; what was progressive and what regressive. Hence, Professor Csikós-Nagy advocated a prices and incomes policy to distinguish progressive elements in the flow of prices and incomes from the antisocial features of inflation.

A second point, on which he differed profoundly from Professor Bajt, was the welfare efficiency of the price system. Professor Bajt suggested that capitalist countries had an adequate political mechanism to serve peoples' preferences, whereas, in socialist countries, 'socialist preferences' could not actually come into force. To quote: 'the argument encouraged anybody who enjoyed sufficient social control to promote any degree of arbitrariness in social preferences'.

Professor Csikós-Nagy agreed only that solutions were not always perfect. This brought him to Professor Lundberg's question. He did believe that socialist planned economies was superior to market systems, but this did not mean that they had no shortcomings. Shortcomings were connected with the fact that:

(1) forecasting techniques were not good enough;
(2) time-lags were not short enough; and
(3) responses were not always what economic policies posed.

One had only to participate a little in long- or middle-range planning to see that forecasting for sectors, and of relationships, was possible only with different degrees of uncertainty. Planners could work quite accurately when interdependency in physical terms had to be forecast. Their position was weaker when values were on the agenda. Not by chance, uncertainty was greater in socialist countries that were sensitive to foreign trade, which meant that efficiency could be determined only in relation to foreign trade prices. Through this, the prediction of relative world prices was clearly connected with planning.

As for time-lags, economic policy must accept these and take them into consideration. Minimum time-lags were given by the technologies of production and distribution, which was why lags were shorter in trade than in agriculture. But actual time-lags could be longer. His own experience was that managers needed at least a year or two to adjust to new relative prices. Nor was it absolutely certain that managers' or customers' responses would be those postulated by price policy. We knew rather a lot about price elasticity from textbooks, but too little about the actual behaviour of consumers.

This gave us reason to believe that economic policy contributed to economic fluctuations, and made the presence of instability partly understandable. However, it did not follow that economic stabilisation policy could not be successful. Rather, he would say that flexibility seemed to be one precondition of successful stabilisation.

He would not say that all subsidies could be considered as justifiable from the viewpoint of the social utility function. His recent book *Socialist Price Theory and Price Policy*[1] referred, in the chapter on retail price policy, to the terms 'direct and indirect political preferences. Direct preferences were closely connected with the social utility function; indirect preferences were the consequence of freezing retail prices when production costs were changing. Direct preferences were objectively necessary in a socialist economy. Budget subsidies derived from them did not conflict with rationality as interpreted in socialism. Against this, indirect preferences were not objectively necessary and introduced elements of irrationality.

He would not say that this was the prevailing view. There were heated discussions among economists about this – as in general about the role and function of prices in a socialist economy. It was this very fact which explained the divergence of views about the interpretation of retail price stability.

The question of import subsidies, raised by Professor Nussbaumer, introduced a specific problem for socialist economies sensitive to foreign trade. Professor Csikós-Nagy would therefore take Hungary as an example. The new economic mechanism, including the mixed-price mechanism, had been introduced in Hungary in 1968, and had worked satisfactorily until the second half

[1] Publishing House of the Hungarian Academy.

of 1973. The turning point had come from inflation in the world market. The 1968 price reform had not offered a system which could permanently link foreign trade and domestic prices, giving relative price stability at home alongside inflation in the world markets. To ensure price stability, Hungary had had to resort increasingly to budget subsidies in the 1970s. In 1973, these had to counterbalance only 30 per cent of inflation; in 1974, 70 per cent of it, and this had affected the role of price as a means of orienting rational economic decisions.

In a socialist planned economy, it was, of course, possible to formulate the requirements at the strategic points of the national economy resulting from a changed situation. One could make calculations at the macrolevel and incorporate them, without price changes, into the system of planned state control. But efficiency would decline if the social interest in the new situation were not transmitted to enterprises by price changes, because enterprises would then be overwhelmed by central instructions. This would be inevitable, because harmony between social interests and those of the enterprises would have been created by prices set under different conditions. Even central instructions would not necessarily ensure a fully optimum solution, since state planning, also, had to rely on realistic prices to reveal the extremely complicated interdependencies of social production.

It had therefore been necessary to investigate the available instruments, which could be used both to ensure relative price stability and to preserve the orientation function of price. As a result, a new concept of price policy has been elaborated in 1974 and, on that basis, a medium-term plan for the period 1976–80 drawn up. Its main elements were

(1) an active policy on conversion rates, with the periodic re-evaluation of the national currency against inflated currencies;

(2) intermittent price rearrangements, to follow world market prices and to minimise budget subsidies granted on imported products;

(3) a gradual tax reform, to counteract rises in the price level and to shift taxes from production to domestic turnover;

(4) finally, the segregation of export calculations from the calculation of domestic prices.

17 Why have General Anti-inflation Policies not Succeeded?

P. M. Oppenheimer
CHRIST CHURCH, OXFORD, ENGLAND

I. INTRODUCTION

The term 'general anti-inflation policies' I take to mean macroeconomic measures in the monetary, fiscal and exchange-rate sphere, supplemented sometimes by direct restraints on prices and incomes. The period under consideration is approximately the last twenty years (1955–75) and the countries mainly those of the OECD area.

There are two possible types of explanation for the failure of macropolicies to halt inflation. One is that they were not applied in a price-stabilising manner, either because governments and central banks did not care much about price stability or because they made forecasting errors and other technical miscalculations. The second type of explanation is the more radical and controversial one that, whatever may have been the case in earlier periods of history, price stability is now beyond the power of ordinary macroeconomic policies to deliver. The basic structure and functioning of the mixed economy prevent it. Far-reaching social and institutional changes are, on this view, a necessary condition for the achievement of price stability in the western world.

These explanations should not be interpreted as mutually exclusive. Even if inflationary pressures are endemic in the mixed economy, their severity may be much affected by government policy. The endemic factors, for their part, may make price stability not literally unattainable, but just unacceptably costly in terms of other objectives.

The following sections consider first the question of government priorities, secondly that of blunders and miscalculations and finally the intrinsic difficulty of stabilising prices in the mixed economy. This last section also involves tracing the major division of academic opinion concerning the nature of inflation and its possible cure. In more technical language, section II is about the government's utility function or revealed preference and section IV about the transformation possibilities between price stability and other goals, while section III is concerned with problems of information and policy execution.

II. GOVERNMENTS' REVEALED PREFERENCES

Western governments have paid frequent lip service to the objective of stable prices, but have not accorded it much priority *vis-à-vis* full employment and continuing economic growth. Measures of monetary and fiscal restraint have been adopted for short periods (two years at most) in the face of blatantly excessive demand, but have usually been relaxed again, regardless of the trend of money wages and prices, as soon as some margin of slack became apparent. Where countries have engaged in medium-term economic programming, the emphasis has again been on real variables and on growth. Financial aspects, when not totally neglected, have been viewed in a subordinate light, and the idea of a medium-term strategy for price stability has not (to my knowledge) been explored at a practical level.

On the international plane there have been two major OECD reports on inflation (in 1961 and 1970)[1] accompanied by wide-ranging policy recommendations, as well as continuous discussion in the Organisation's Working Party No. 4 on costs of production and prices. But all this has had little apparent impact on national policies. Proposals to step up the struggle against inflation have been greeted with much less accord and enthusiasm than, for example, the G.N.P. growth target of 50 per cent in ten years which the OECD countries adopted in 1960.

The OECD's concern with inflation in 1969–70 (centering on the above-mentioned 1970 report) appears to have originated not merely in the world-wide acceleration of price increases at the end of the 1960s – from about 3 per cent to about 5 per cent a year – but also in the fact that officials responsible for international co-operation were temporarily short of other subjects to talk about. In particular, international monetary questions had diminished in prominence for the first time for some years. Agreement had been reached in 1967–68 on the form of IMF Special Drawing Rights. In 1969 the United States credit squeeze provoked a substantial flow of private funds to New York, putting the United States balance of payments (on the official settlements basis) into short-lived surplus. An imminent shortage of international liquidity was hastily diagnosed and agreement reached on the creation of $9500 million of S.D.R.'s over the years 1970–72. At the same time the devaluation of the French franc and upvaluation of the deutschmark in the late summer of 1969 removed the immediate source of exchange-market disturbance in Europe. From the autumn of 1969 until the floating of the mark in May 1971 currency questions were out of the limelight.

To ponder the course of events since then is instructive. Inflation slackened only very slightly in 1971–72; yet it all but disappeared from the agenda, as the Bretton Woods system was finally overthrown and governments endeavoured to shore up the pegged-rate regime and cope with the 'overhang' of dollar balances (of which more in the following section). Expansionary policies in 1972–73 were partly a standard reaction to the mild recession of 1970–71 (reinforced in the United States by electioneering for Mr Nixon) and partly a deliberate effort to strengthen the impact of dollar devaluation on United States exports. In addition, some of the dollar overhang found its way into

[1] W. Fellner *et al., The Problem of Rising Prices* (OEEC, 1961); and *Inflation – the Present Problem*, Report by the Secretary General (OECD, December 1970).

stockpiles of copper, wool and other commodities, while world food prices were pushed up as a result of bad harvests, particularly in the Soviet Union.

The virulently inflationary character of the 1973 boom was due partly to the sheer vigour of demand and to its synchronisation across the industrialised world. But it also reflected the nature of the main supply bottlenecks which arose. More than at any time in the previous twenty years, these were at the primary product and basic materials end, where prices are much more flexible than in the markets for finished manufactures or for labour.[1] In these circumstances, because of price/wage and price/price interactions across the economy, all prices and not only the relatively flexible ones tend to rise more steeply. During 1973 commodity prices soared and inflation rates in the industrial countries rose well into double figures. Governments and central banks moved one after another to restrain demand, and waited for the ensuing recession to restore a more normal situation. Just as the inflationary tide was turning, how-however, the oil price explosion supervened. This had a threefold impact on the economic climate. It created payments imbalances and problems of reserve management on a huge new scale. It gave another twist to the cost/price spiral, and it deepened the world recession, partly by depressing demand for automobiles and partly by causing governments in the industrial countries to intensify demand restraint policies during 1974.[2]

Recession brought a marked deceleration of prices in most industrial countries in 1974–75. Nevertheless the rate of inflation remained very high by historical standards – considerably higher even in such 'oases of stability' as Germany than it was at the time of the OECD report in 1970. Yet, as the recession deepened and unemployment climbed, policies swung with increasing force towards expansion. Two qualifications to this statement are necessary. First, the main shift to stimulus in the United States and Germany (and to some extent in Japan) was on the fiscal side; monetary authorities remained more cautious about relaxing credit. Secondly, in the United Kingdom, and perhaps in a few other countries, a shift to expansion was prevented for the time being, despite rising unemployment, by the combination of severe inflation and an external deficit. The general observation, however, stands that, as unemployment rose to post-1950 peaks, so world inflation rates receded from their peak – but the practical determination of governments to curb inflation receded even faster.

Of course, in taking these attitudes on inflation and unemployment, governments are responding to the views of their electorates. A feature of the past decade has been the apparent willingness of public opinion to tolerate higher rates of inflation, once the shock of initiation has passed. In other words, the distinction between rapid inflation and accelerating inflation appears to be

[1] Capacity utilisation in the basic materials sector of United States industry reached an astonishing 96 per cent in 1973, while in other sectors it remained in the seventies or low eighties (see *Federal Reserve Bulletin*).

[2] For a fuller statement see Bank for International Settlements, *45th Annual Report*, Basle, 1975, pp. 3–10.

important. Adaptation to steadily rising prices is for most people a straightforward, semi-automatic matter. Wages and social security payments are indexed either formally or informally. And enough money can be borrowed to purchase a dwelling (or two dwellings!), even at high nominal interest rates which may make debt servicing difficult in the early years; or else there is public housing at subsidised rents. The welfare losses bound up with such adaptations may for years remain quite slight, and even when significant may not be clearly perceived. But accelerating inflation is different. Uncertainty and a sense of insecurity soon spread, and pressure grows on the government to take firm remedial action. Once the acceleration has been halted, alarm subsides – or at least recedes from the foreground, because of the higher unemployment which almost inevitably accompanies the slowdown in credit growth.

This summary may understate the public's dislike of merely steady inflation; simultaneous fluctuation of employment and inflation rates makes the assessment difficult. It is clear, however, that standards as to what constitutes an acceptable approximation to price stability have deteriorated in the past decade. Everyone complains about rising prices, but there is a certain hollowness in the protests.

III. BLUNDERS AND MISCALCULATIONS

It is easy enough to point out errors into which economic policymakers have fallen. The difficulty is to assess how much this has contributed, over the long haul, to price inflation. My judgement is that it has contributed quite a lot in the United Kingdom, but less in other countries.

The most important point here is a propensity to exaggerate the degree of control which governments have over the functioning of the economic system, a propensity which developed in the euphoric aftermath of the Keynesian revolution and post-Second World War reconstruction. We defer to the following section the central question of the government's ability to keep the price level stable if it so desires. In this section we note that misconceptions about government power in two other areas have contributed indirectly to a worsening of inflation.

One such area is international monetary relations. The Group of Ten, discussing monetary reform from 1963 onwards, treated it as basically a diplomatic problem. Countries tabled their individual requirements for a reformed system and horsetraded their way towards a generally acceptable compromise. Whether the compromise rested on a sound technical foundation or addressed itself correctly to the weaknesses in the system was barely considered. It was taken for granted, erroneously, that whatever governments could agree on would be viable. Thus, the Group of Ten were quick to rule out of court both floating exchange rates and an increase in the price of gold.[1] However, the dis-

[1] See *Ministerial Statement of the Group of Ten, and Annex Prepared by Deputies* (1964).

equilibrium of the dollar, which was the main problem confronting them, could not be cured without recourse to one or other of these two policies. Either the dollar's convertibility into gold was to be preserved, in which case the gold price had to be raised; or it was not, in which case floating rates could be avoided only through a totally unrealistic degree of centralised management of the system. Refusal to acknowledge this dilemma prolonged the dollar disequilibrium and led to the failure of the Group of Ten and of its successor, the Committee of Twenty.

What, however, of its effect on inflation? In the 1960s some European observers saw the United States deficit as a channel through which Europe 'imported' inflation from the United States, the suggestion being that the import was involuntary. This argument is weak. European countries were happy to run their economies at the high levels of activity permitted by a strong export performance and rising reserves. Some inflation of prices also occurred; but demand management was not geared to preventing this because (as emphasised in the previous section) employment and growth were accorded higher priority. Countries where the pressure of demand became intense with the balance of payments still in surplus always had the option of upvaluing their currencies.[1] It was a regime of pegged rates, not fixed rates. The intractability of the United States deficit arose precisely from the fact that some of it was the counterpart not of unwanted surpluses in the foregoing sense, but of moderate, equilibrium surpluses which countries were happy to incur in the context of a pegged-rate system.

In the end, however, the dollar deficit did have an inflationary impact, through the mushrooming of international credit and reserves which was a feature of the system in its dying phase. From the end of 1969 to March 1973, when the attempt to maintain pegged rates on the basis of an inconvertible dollar was finally abandoned, official currency reserves (that is, excluding gold, S.D.R.s and IMF reserve positions) rose from $32 billion to $117 billion. For the first sixteen months, up to April 1971, the main proximate cause of rising dollar balances was the disparity in monetary conditions on the two sides of the Atlantic. The Federal Reserve eased credit in the recession, while the German Bundesbank in particular was tightening up. Banks in the United States repaid earlier borrowings of eurodollars on a massive scale. Thereafter it was a flight, or series of flights, from the dollar, led by United States corporations who drew on their credit lines with United States banks for the purpose. The movement continued in some measure even after the switch to floating rates in March 1973, driving the dollar rate down to levels judged excessive on

[1] Monetarists might object to this way of putting it, inasmuch as they insist that exchange-rate changes operate primarily through the real-balance effect and have no lasting impact on real variables such as output or the pressure of demand. By the same token, however, they would agree *a fortiori* with the substantive policy recommendation, that countries in surplus and wishing to escape inflation upvalue their currencies. The present context does not therefore require any sorting out of differences between the Keynesian and monetarist models of internal and external balance.

fundamental trading grounds by most informed observers. As noted earlier, the increase in reserves contributed directly to the upsurge of commodity prices, as well as indirectly to the growth of domestic credit and general economic boom in the industrial countries. The strength of exchange-market pressures and the sharpness of exchange-rate movements in 1971–73 also added to a widespread mistrust of currencies, which further stimulated demand for basic commodities, land and other real assets.

It must be emphasised that the error which governments collectively perpetrated in all this did not consist in underestimating the importance of the quantity of money, nor even in ignoring the international transmission mechanisms for inflation – though the second factor did play some part in, for instance, Germany's refusal to impose controls on international capital flows before 1971. The basic error was to tolerate chronic disequilibrium in world payments until the situation became so extreme that adjustment could no longer be postponed. The main responsibility for developments up to August 1971 lay with the United States. Thereafter it shifted towards other major countries who tried, both in the exchange market and at the conference table, to minimise the appreciation of their own currencies. The weaknesses, real and alleged, of the Bretton Woods system had been under scrutiny for years; but nobody seems to have foreseen the inflationary explosion which was to accompany the system's final breakdown.

Another area in which misconceptions about governmental power have contributed to a worsening of inflation is economic growth. This influence occurred in a few individual countries rather than in the world economy as a whole. The United Kingdom is the prime example. Successive United Kingdom governments have been concerned about the country's slow rate of growth compared with other industrial countries. Various ill-found attempts have been made to accelerate it, including a half-baked imitation of planning *à la française* in 1965–66, entry to the EEC (first attempted in 1961–63, re-attempted after 1966, finally achieved in 1971) and two episodes of deliberate fiscal and monetary expansion. It was these two episodes, one introduced by Mr Maudling as Chancellor of the Exchequer in 1963–64 (and continued by the succeeding Labour Government for a further eighteen months) and the other by Mr Barber in 1971–73, which mainly added to inflation. In both cases the inflationary effect was at first dampened by a large deterioration in the trade balance, and subsequently exacerbated as a result of the exchange-rate and other measures found necessary to restore the trading position.

The respective philosophies behind the two growth experiments differed only marginally. In the first case the idea was that faster (and steadier) growth could be achieved by maintaining a firm pressure of demand on productive capacity even in the face of an 'initial' balance-of-payments deficit. Private industrial investment would, supposedly, accelerate, and with it the long-run growth of output per man. The trend rate of increase of money wages was assumed to remain unchanged, aided if necessary by incomes policy; so faster growth of output per man would mean slower inflation, and hence rising international competitiveness (at least relative to what would have happened otherwise). Exports and the balance of payments would benefit correspondingly.

When it came to Mr Barber's turn there was less emphasis on the need for industrial investment as the alleged originator of faster growth (though there was still a lot of talk about it in relation to Britain's forthcoming membership of the EEC), and more on the need to relieve the private sector of its allegedly crippling burden of taxation. Accordingly, the fiscal side of Mr Barber's programme involved substantial cuts in taxation as well as increases in public expenditure. In addition, important changes in the mechanism of monetary policy were introduced during the summer of 1971. Direct restraints on bank lending were abolished, and flexibility of interest rates became the principal channel of monetary regulation. At the same time, reform of the system of reserve requirements and abolition of certain restrictive practices (mainly cartel arrangements on interest rates among the clearing banks)[1] widened the scope of competition in the banking sector. It is not clear whether the United Kingdom authorities believed that their new growth experiment required unfettered expansion of bank lending; or whether they thought that the interest-rate mechanism would, in some magical way, dispense them from the need to limit the aggregate total of bank credit, as well as allocate it between alternative borrowers. Perhaps there was some of each. In any case, for two years beginning in September 1971 control over the stock of money in the United Kingdom was non-existent. Bank credit to the private sector rose by 50 per cent, most of it financing either consumer outlays or real-estate transactions. Simultaneously, on the fiscal side, total borrowing by the public sector moved from a small negative figure to an annual rate of 6 per cent of G.D.P., about half as large again proportionately as the Maudling deficit of 1964.

In both episodes the problems of inflation and balance of payments were ignored, partly through shortsightedness and partly, one assumes, as part of the self-deception that rapid expansion of credit would succeed in promoting faster growth of productive capacity. The rate of money-wage increase seems to have been viewed as wholly impervious to the pressure of demand, even in the medium term. On the balance of payments, the Maudling approach offered no serious guarantee that the deficit envisaged for the early stages of the upswing would prove temporary. How then was it to be corrected without abandoning the whole strategy? If the exchange rate was at fault, it should have been lowered in the first instance, to enable exports to play a larger role in the upswing.[2] Mr Maudling was saved from the need to resolve this dilemma

[1] One should also include here the publication of clearing-bank profits. The banks had hitherto been allowed to keep their true profits secret, on the grounds that public confidence in them might be shaken by a lean year.

[2] This, if anything, was the lesson to be drawn from the discussions of 'export-led growth' which became fashionable at the time. See, for instance, Wilfred Beckerman, 'Projecting Europe's Growth', *Economic Journal*, (1962). The Maudling policy appeared to stand the doctrine on its head, expecting strong export performance to result – eventually – from an expansion of home demand.

by the General Election of October 1964 which removed the Conservatives from office. Mr Barber, however, was obliged in June 1972 to let sterling float, just as buoyant home demand was pushing the external balance into the red from the record current-account surplus in 1971. The subsequent depreciation was kept to a minimum by inducing the United Kingdom public sector to borrow abroad on a large scale. In this way the floating rate was operated as a quasi-fixed rate with extra flexibility, and the home economy was spared the worst inflationary consequences which would otherwise have resulted from the excessive growth of domestic purchasing power.

The closing stages of Mr Barber's spree were marked by miscalculation in a different area of policy, which contributed to a further acceleration of Britain's wage/price spiral in 1974–75. This was wage indexation. Stage III of the Conservative government's income policy incorporated a one-year threshold clause guaranteeing employees a pretax real-wage increase of about 3 per cent in the twelve months from October 1973. This was rash in any event, since (a) the long-run increase in United Kingdom output per man had been less than 3 per cent, (b) the long-run average would probably not be reached in 1973–74 because of the cyclical position, and (c) the 1972–73 upswing rested almost entirely on private consumer spending, and a shift towards investment – implying a shift on the income side from wages to profits – was desirable. More serious, however, was the quadrupling of oil prices which occurred just after the policy was introduced and which lowered the United Kingdom real national income by about 3 per cent at a stroke. As a result, the threshold clause was activated from May 1974 onwards, and by November had been responsible for an increase in wage rates of about 12 per cent. The figure would almost certainly have been higher, but for temporary subsidies on food, public utilities and housing rents, as well as direct restraints on other prices (the budgetary impact of which is noted below).

Britain's experiment with indexation is of interest partly because indexation, unlike other forms of incomes policy, has the approval of Milton Friedman and his disciples as being a useful anti-inflationary device.[1] It is supposed to reduce the size of pay claims by removing the rationale of allowing for future price increases when formulating them. But such reasoning is insufficient. It overlooks the possibility that an index clause may prove inflationary, as did Britain's in 1973–74, by cementing increases in real income which exceed the rise in the economy's per capita output plus or minus changes in the terms of trade. The retort that the United Kingdom inflationary spiral might have accelerated even more in the absence of the threshold arrangement is unconvincing.[2] On the other hand, it is obviously true that the year 1973–

[1] Milton Friedman, *Monetary Correction*, Institute of Economic Affairs Occasional Paper No. 14, London, (1974).

[2] It may be noted that Michael Parkin, writing in the spring of 1974, asserted on the basis of miscellaneous monetarist evidence that Britain's inflation rate would 'abate a little towards the end of the year'. (M. Parkin, 'United Kingdom Inflation: the Policy Alternatives', *National Westminster Bank Quarterly Review*, May (1974).) In actual fact

74 was atypical, with the jump in oil prices an exogenous disturbance of exceptional size. Even so, to devise a wage escalator which avoids aggravating inflation in the short term while still obtaining trade-union support can always be difficult. Friedman appears to think of indexation essentially as a long-term weapon, in line with his whole approach to the analysis of inflation; this topic is taken up in the next section.

Meanwhile, one final matter may be raised under the heading of miscalculations. In 1974–75 a few countries found themselves facing huge errors of budgetary forecasting. This was rather a new phenomenon. Britain is again the chief example. United Kingdom public-sector borrowing in 1974 totalled 8·7 per cent of G.D.P., about half of it unforeseen. The net error arose entirely on the side of expenditure, and seems to have resulted largely from the acceleration of prices and wages. Some of it was due to bad forecasting (of the public-sector wage bill), and some of it to rash attempts to hold back inflation by subsidies and direct controls (the latter accentuating financial strains on companies, thus necessitating bigger outlays in the shape of emergency government loans). In addition, local authorities seem to have been impelled by inflationary expectations to bump up their spending in *real* terms beyond the level originally envisaged. This underlines the inadequacy of United Kingdom Treasury control over local-government spending. It is too early to say how ephemeral such budgetary problems will prove to be. But they serve as a warning against easy reliance on 'automatic stabilising' effects of the fiscal mechanism in an inflationary situation. The possibility must be considered that a kind of vicious circle may develop instead, with inflation tending to enlarge the budget deficit which further feeds inflation.

IV. INFLATION AND THE MIXED ECONOMY

Is contemporary inflation curable with ordinary macroeconomic policies or is it not? The question has been debated since the mid-1950s. No firm conclusion has been reached, but on some basic aspects there is at least a certain consensus. First, the textbook proposition that expansion of purchasing power tends sooner or later to raise money prices and contraction of purchasing power to lower them still holds good. The question is how fully and swiftly the mechanism operates, and what follows from the fact that its operation is imperfect and subject to time-lags.

Secondly, the time-lags and rigidities are more conspicuous in a downward than in an upward direction. They are more conspicuous not because they are actually greater (this, although often taken for granted, has not to my knowledge been scientifically demonstrated, even for the most plausible case of wages), but because it is mainly in a downward direction that they appear unwelcome. J. C. R. Dow suggested at the I.E.A. Conference on inflation

---

the rate, while fluctuating widely from month to month during the year, ended it on an accelerating trend to reach new peaks in the first half of 1975.

fifteen years ago that inflexibility of prices reflects 'the convenience of not making frequent price adjustments, and the real cost of adapting the institutional arrangements for price – and income – determination'.[1] In other words, price changes involve costs as well as benefits, and are therefore subject to an economic calculation; it is not simply a question of 'money illusion' or institutional rigidity being either present or absent. This approach has been widely developed in the literature in recent years and has become quite familiar.[2] Where prices do not (or not immediately) adjust in the presence of disequilibrium, quantities adjust instead. If there is excess demand, the economy may to some extent be shielded from rising prices by depletion of inventories plus rationing effects such as longer delivery dates. The costs of price flexibility and inflexibility, however, vary from sector to sector; and therefore, the overall extent of price movement in any period may depend, as noted in section II above, on the sectoral pattern of demand in relation to productive capacity. If, as in 1973, major bottlenecks occur in the flexible-price sectors, then the whole price level will rise faster than otherwise. This outcome is, of course, deplored rather than welcomed. In the contrary circumstances of slack demand, inventories can be built up and delivery dates shortened. Beyond a certain point, however, if demand weakness persists and prices remain sluggish, output and employment will also decline. Only at this point does the inflexibility of prices, or rather of wages, appear to hamper the revival of economic activity (though, as Keynes and latterly Leijonhufvud have stressed, appearances may be deceptive here).

Thirdly, wage behaviour is influenced by price expectations. This helps to lower the sensitivity of wages to short-term variations in the pressure of demand. It also enables one to apply the Hicksian concept of elasticity of expectations and to envisage a kind of expectations watershed, beyond which inflation becomes more virulent and difficult to curb. This is because expectations will be a stabilising, neutral or destabilising factor according as the rate of inflation expected in the future is below, equal to or above the rate of inflation prevailing at present. Destabilising expectations are obviously liable to develop if a prolonged spell of accelerating inflation is experienced. There are indications of it having happened in the United Kingdom during 1974, though not in the industrial world at large.

So much for what is common ground. In the 1950s and early 1960s the debate over anti-inflation policies followed Keynesian categories. Attention

[1] J. C. R. Dow, 'Internal Factors Causing and Propagating Inflation – II' in D. C. Hague ed., *Inflation* (Proceedings of the 1959 I.E.A. Conference), London, Macmillan, (1962), p. 48.

[2] The contributions of the 'new microeconomics' on transactions – search – or information costs in the labour market are reviewed in the present volume by R. J. Gordon, especially Section II of his paper, pages 43–7 above. Similar ideas are important in Clower's and Leijonhufvud's reinterpretation of the Keynesian system, and in the elaboration of the general equilibrium theory of money by Hahn, Niehans, Brunner and Meltzer and others.

was focused on the extent to which price increases could be explained by the pressure of demand for productive resources, an approach derived from Keynes' 'inflationary gap' analysis in *How to Pay for the War*. Financial variables such as the stock of money or the budget deficit were not emphasised except as factors influencing real demand. The main discussion was between those who attributed inflation essentially to excess demand ('demand-pull') and those who considered that much of it was independent of demand and reflected 'cost-push', particularly wage increases forced by trade unions. Adherents of demand-pull were sceptical about incomes policy and maintained that a small permanent reduction in demand pressure would prevent prices rising. Adherents of cost-push claimed that, on the contrary, lowering demand would have but a weak and erratic effect on inflation; price stability could be achieved by this route only at an unacceptable cost in terms of extra unemployment, if indeed it could be achieved at all. Incomes policy, or a radical change in the system of collective bargaining, were advocated as the only means of curbing wage-push. It was not thought that such policies would be anything but difficult to carry through;[1] only that, without them, inflation would be incurable.

Much, though not all, of the disagreement between demand-pull and cost-push adherents concerned facts and value judgements rather than theoretical analysis. Supporters of demand-pull believed that demand was *in fact* excessive, and elements such as trade-union monopoly power therefore beside the point. They did not necessarily believe that cost-push inflation was an impossibility. And in the late 1960s some of them, such as F. W. Paish, 'changed their minds' and affirmed that inflation was indeed now being caused by wage-push. The inverted commas are appropriate, because the change of mind was not a logical volte-face; it was a consistent reaction to new evidence. As to value judgements, people held differing views on what was an 'acceptable' loss of jobs to be traded-off against greater price stability. Anyone who worried about inflation yet felt strongly that the levels of employment achieved in the first postwar decade should be maintained would tend to side with the cost-push school, even though, if pressed, he might admit that inflation had been substantially due to pressure of demand.

The demand-pull *versus* cost-push debate eventually crystallised around the Phillips-curve (Phillips' paper appearing in 1958). The demand-pull school took their stand on the stability of the curve. The cost-push school was uncommitted on this point. It asserted variously that, if the curve were stable, the volume of unemployment apparently required for price stability was unacceptably high; and that the curve was not in fact stable, but would shift outwards if government imposed higher unemployment (because the unions would get accustomed to the new unemployment level and revert to their previous behaviour). Either way, government should endeavour to shift the curve inwards by means of

[1] See, for instance, the clear and trenchant account of 'wages policy' in the 1961 OEEC report (W. Fellner *et al.*).

incomes policy. In Tinbergen–Meade language, the cost-push school saw the control of inflation as a target separate, in part, from the regulation of aggregate demand, and to that extent requiring a separate policy instrument.

In the late 1960s and early 1970s the terms of the debate were altered by the combined impact of events and monetarist economic theory. The Phillips relation turned out to be unstable in one country after another, so the demand-pull doctrine could not survive in its primitive form. The theoretical *coup de grâce* to the Phillips-curve was actually delivered from within the demand-pull school by Milton Friedman, who pointed out in his celebrated Presidential Address to the American Economic Association that Phillips had neglected the role of expectations.[1] His curve, though purporting to be a stable relationship, was actually dependent on a given state of price expectations (presumably zero or near-zero expected inflation). If inflation were faster than expected, price expectations would eventually catch on, shifting the Phillips-curve outwards. The correct long-run relationship was a locus of points at which expected and actual rates of inflation were equal. In other words, expectations could not continue indefinitely to play the stabilising role which they fulfilled up to the late 1960s. Eventually they would become neutral. Friedman does not, incidentally, go into the possibility that, as inflation accelerates, expectations may overshoot the mark and become destabilising. The expectations mechanism as he describes it is smooth and monotonic.

Friedman's critique of the Phillips-curve led (and was designed to lead) directly to a revamped version of the demand-pull thesis. Unlike the Keynesian version, this focused on long-run rather than short-run relationships and on the role of a specifically financial variable, the quantity of money. It was, in fact, the quantity theory in sophisticated form, allowing for dynamic expectations. The longer the period of inflation that one considers, so runs the argument, the greater the influence of expectations and the smaller the impact of monetary and fiscal policy upon real demand and employment. For in order to maintain unemployment at a level below that consistent with zero inflation, expansion of monetary demand must keep the actual rate of inflation ahead of the expected rate. Once expectations start moving, this implies that the rate of inflation must continuously accelerate. Ultimately the attempt to use monetary weapons to reduce unemployment below its 'natural' level must be abandoned. Financial policy thus ends up having no impact at all on the real variables and affecting only the rate of price increase. The long-run or stable Phillips-curve is vertical. There is no trade-off between unemployment and inflation.

A milder version of the model allows price expectations to adjust less than fully to the current rate of inflation, so that they retain a certain stabilising element. Some trade-off between unemployment and inflation then survives even in long-run equilibrium, but much less than in Phillips' own short-run

[1] Milton Friedman, 'The Role of Monetary Policy', *American Economic Review (Papers and Proceedings)*, (1968). As R. J. Gordon points out in his survey, the point was also developed independently by E. S. Phelps.

version. This milder variant, however, is inconsistent with the classical dichotomy between real and financial variables, on which monetarists insist. By the same token, the non-existence of wage-push inflation is, in Friedman's hands, less a matter of fact than of definition: by definition, only those who exercise immediate control over the quantity of money can cause inflation, and that does not include trade unions.

In the short run, with expectations given, there will still be a Phillips trade-off (according to the monetarist argument). But its position depends on the state of expectations. The more inflationary this is, the higher the rate of price increase remaining at any particular level of unemployment. If, however, unemployment is allowed to rise above its 'natural' level, then inflationary expectations will begin to abate and in due course die away. Until they do, significant unemployment and significant inflation will coexist. But afterwards, maintaining stable prices will require less unemployment than short-run relationships would lead one to suppose.

Thus, instead of the old demand-pull view that curing inflation requires only a small permanent cut in employment, one has the new demand-pull view that it requires a more substantial temporary cut, with 'temporary' signifying quite a long time, several years at least, but no truly permanent cut at all. A permanent cut will, however, appear to be necessary if, in the short run, employment has been pulled above its 'natural' level.

The new demand-pull view must strengthen doubts about the feasibility of eradicating inflation in a democratic society that has become accustomed to it. As a technical matter, the existence of a particular 'natural' level of unemployment at which appropriate limits on the quantity of money are sufficient, in the long run, to ensure price stability, has been assumed rather than demonstrated. We have seen that the short-run Phillips-curve is unstable. Why should the long-run one be stable, merely because it is vertical? The arguments cited below give more positive grounds for scepticism in this regard. As a political matter, the anti-inflationary recipe of the new demand-pull school clashes with the priorities discussed in section II. Governments cannot afford, electorally speaking, to give lasting priority to disinflationary demand policies. Limited doses of this medicine, following some acute worsening of the situation, are acceptable; but other objectives soon regain the upper hand.

For the same reasons, doubts arise over Friedman's advocacy of indexation, whose intended role is to hasten the reduction of inflationary expectations. It may succeed in this; but it will not necessarily do so unless two conditions are satisfied. First, the indexation formula itself must be suitably constructed (the point raised in the previous section). Second, other forces must not be allowed to aggravate inflation. In terms of the monetarist model, governments must identify a 'natural' level of unemployment and not seek to keep joblessness below it.

Believers in cost-push have all along had doubts about the feasibility of stable prices in the mixed economy. But they too have had to revise their ideas, to take account of the failure of incomes policy, in most countries that have tried it, to make any lasting impression on the rate of price increase. It seems that pay restraint, like disinflationary demand policies, is something which most governments feel able to enforce only in crisis conditions. At other times unions do not perceive compliance with it as being in their interest, any more than the electorate is content with prolonged spells of subnormal employment in the economy. Indeed, the electorate's attitude reinforces that of the unions, since it weakens still further any remaining apprehension that inflationary pay settlements may lead to loss of jobs. Even if some people do lose their jobs, they will form only a small percentage of union membership. It would be easy to construct a model along Harris–Todaro lines to demonstrate that a low probability of becoming unemployed will do little to make the trade union rank and file vote for smaller wage claims, particularly if redundant workers receive earnings-related severence pay and other benefits.[1]

It can plausibly be argued that the power of the trade unions to force inflationary behaviour on the government is only the most prominent aspect of a whole network of inconsistencies or contradictions (to use the Marxist term) inherent in the functioning of the mixed economy, and causing it to experience continuous inflation. The contradictions involve both (a) individuals behaving inconsistently in different capacities (such as voter and employee-taxpayer) and (b) different groups in society successfully pursuing conflicting policies.[2] Many of them arise from the mixture of centralised and decentralised decision-taking on resource allocation and income distribution. In a completely free market economy, with only minimal taxation to provide for indispensable collective needs such as defence and policing, individuals would accept that they had to provide for all their requirements, including education of their children, sustenance in old age, health care etc. from their own earning capacity and material wealth. On the other hand, in a fully centralised command economy, citizens would lobby the central authorities if they felt that some resources should be differently disposed. In the mixed economy the individual has no such single rule of behaviour for optimising his economic position. People can in all honesty attempt to have their cake and eat it. They can demand smaller school classes, more generous pensions and social security and better health care, but refuse to support particular taxes to pay for these things; and when the taxes are nevertheless levied, they can urge their trade union leaders to seek bigger wage awards by way of compensation. Such collisions almost inevitably have a price-inflationary outcome, which is gladly tolerated in return for continued full employment, until it becomes severe enough to be a source of widespread tension in its own right. If the govern-

[1] J. R. Harris and M. P. Todaro, 'Migration, Unemployment and Development: a Two-sector Analysis', *American Economic Review*, (1970).

[2] Wilfred Beckerman, 'Last Straw or Turning Point', in *Crisis '75*, Institute of Economic Affairs, London, (1975). For a fuller statement of the arguments see E. Dahmèn, 'Inflation: Economics or Politics?', *National Westminster Bank Quarterly Review*, (November, 1973). Professor Csikós-Nagy (this volume, chapter 16) seems to apply an analogous argument to the socialist economies of eastern Europe, maintaining that an inflation problem occurs there only in the unplanned or residual sectors.

ment then tightens credit and unemployment rises, there may be demands for better unemployment benefit, which, if granted, will encourage more voluntary unemployment, and so make it necessary for total unemployment to be still greater to achieve a given degree of disinflation.[1] A vicious circle could develop; or, more plausibly, efforts to stop inflation will not be pursued very far.

Technically, a free-market economy with hardly any public sector may also be riddled with monopolistic groups such as trade unions, cartels, workers' co-operatives in key industries and so on, whose combined pursuit of sectional interests may have a price-inflationary outcome. But the feasibility of the inflationary 'solution' depends in the long run on the presence of a central government committed to maintaining full employment and therefore to financing given levels of economic activity at ever-rising prices. Pressure to maintain such a government is thus intensified by the proliferation of monopoly and oligopoly elements, whose viability would otherwise be far more problematic.

On this line of reasoning, inflation is a phenomenon deeply ingrained in mixed economies, and perhaps in any market economy which develops substantial monopoly elements. Excess demand and wage-push are both symptoms of it. There is no reason to believe in the existence of some constant 'natural' level of unemployment guaranteed to permit stable prices in the long run. The expectations mechanism stressed by monetarists has sharpened the problem and helped to give it greater prominence; but has not made it more deep-seated than it was already.

[1] See particularly the work of Herbert Grubel and his colleagues at Simon Frazer University. For example, H. G. Grubel, D. Maki and S. Sax, 'Real and Insurance – Induced Unemployment in Canada', *Canadian Journal of Economics*, VIII, (1975), pp. 174–191.

Discussion of the Paper by P. M. Oppenheimer

Professor Lundberg pointed out that the title of the paper was 'Why have general anti-inflationary policies not succeeded?'. He would concentrate on the parts of the paper most closely related to that title. The paper itself was wider, dealing with other issues already discussed in earlier sessions. There were a lot of interesting points in the paper, but because it was short, some were missing.

The paper asserted that macroeconomic policies had failed to halt inflation; but perhaps the paper was too sweeping and too general. It was more true of some countries than of others, and even for the United Kingdom, things could have been worse. Particularly because of stop-go, inflation in the United Kingdom had at least slowed temporarily, so the statement was too sweeping.

What did we find if we compared periods during which there had been efforts to halt inflation? Were we really less successful in the 1970s, given all our social problems, the oil crisis, and the rest? He would like to have seen a more penetrating analysis of this question. To make our pronouncements scientific, we usually referred to an econometric model which compared the differences between what had occurred under an actual policy, and a target policy. This gave meaning to the question of how far a policy had damped inflation.

Of course, there had been some failures. Mr Oppenheimer gave three reasons for these. First, governments had not cared enough about halting inflation, which was a problem of priority. Second, there had been bad forecasting and technical miscalculations and errors. Third, price stability was now probably beyond the power of macroeconomic policy to provide.

However, he wondered what Mr Oppenheimer meant when he talked about price stability. Did he mean more stable than prices would have been had they equalled the norm in the mind of the government and the people? This needed to be stated.

There was a problem of interpretation. What did one mean when one spoke about the government's tolerance of inflation? Some authors even wrote of the revealed preference of the government in accepting a given rate of inflation. Sweden after the Second World War, and especially after the Korean war, had adapted to perhaps 3 per cent or 4 per cent inflation. Now, our ambitions were smaller. So, we said 7 per cent to 10 per cent was too much – our tolerance had been adapted.

One could also look at the declared intentions of governments about inflation, reflecting the preferences of the electorate. When one spoke of the trade-off between unemployment and inflation, Mr Oppenheimer said the low probability of an individual becoming unemployed reduced the fear of unemployment. But everyone was affected by inflation, though those hit hard by it were in a minority. This made it difficult to ask the electorate about its preferences. One could now add the costs of fighting inflation, which led to unemployment and distortions. Mr Oppenheimer said little about forecasting, but he did mention it and this was important.

During the discussion, participants had talked about governments choosing the inflation rate, but there was uncertainty and considerable scope for guesses. In recent years, every acceleration in the inflation rate had surprised us. The cost of fighting inflation had thereby been increased. On political errors, one of the good things about the paper was that it stopped too soon. This meant that there were fewer technicalities and more room for discussion.

Mr Oppenheimer made three points. First, he referred to the ill-fated attempts to increase economic growth in the United Kingdom, for example, in 1963–64 and 1971–73. It was true that these efforts had failed and that the United Kingdom had had both inflation and balance of payments difficulties. However, Sweden in 1974–75 had rapid expansion, low employment, growth, and a not very different rate of inflation from other countries. So the story did differ between countries.

But Mr Oppenheimer only looked at the direct effects. For example, he ignored the results of economic growth – like efforts to improve the growth of productivity. These dampened inflation and were important for the United Kingdom, whose problem was a low rate of investment leading to low productivity. Capacity was too small, leading to bottlenecks, balance of payments problems, etc. Here there was the problem of the longrun growth in productivity and Mr Oppenheimer had not taken it up. There were big differences, by comparison with Germany and Sweden. In Sweden, capacity ceilings had always been kept high. In the United Kingdom, slow growth of productivity meant that pressure for a given real wage led to more inflation than in other countries. Mr Oppenheimer referred to the British error in introducing wage indexation. This was a longer-run problem. Indexation could be stabilising or destabilising and British indexation had actually accelerated inflation, for example, because it was introduced at a time when there were problems over the terms of trade. Nevertheless, in the right circumstances, indexation could help.

The third error was in fiscal policy. An issue not discussed here was the subsidisation, for example, of agricultural products and rents, which had led to problems over the United Kingdom budget deficit. Professor Lundberg would like to know more about this, and to see it analysed in terms of a rigorous model which showed what happened if one increased subsidies to keep down prices. What effect would this have on the budget, the money supply and other variables. Mr Oppenheimer said the results would be destabilising but did not give enough evidence for this statement.

Professor Lundberg felt that a major issue left out was the destabilising effect of a high rate of personal income tax. Clearly people looked for a real disposable income of a given size after direct taxation. If one had a high marginal tax rate, there would be a multiplier effect, an increase in nominal wages, and difficulties over keeping the tax rate constant. This destabilising factor was a strong force in the inflationary machinery.

Mr Oppenheimer also missed a whole set of problems related to more selective fiscal and labour market policies. He might have referred to experience in the United Kingdom, for example with the Selective Employment Tax and the Regional Employment Premium. Sweden had arguments over such issues too, for example, whether policy was too expansionary or too contractionary because of unevennesses in the labour market. These unevennesses meant that a general expansion policy might lead to rapid inflation. It was transmitted to other areas, by the consolidated wages policy pursued in Sweden, but attempts were being made to deal with it.

There was also the problem mentioned in another discussion by Professor

Rehn that, in times of boom, there were sensitive parts of the economy where firms had rapidly increasing marginal cost curves if they took on more labour. Dealing with this problem would help with anti-inflationary policy.

At the end of the paper, Mr Oppenheimer dealt with cost-push, etc. He emphasised the role of trade union claims in the push process. Professor Lundberg understood that the trade union organisation in the United Kingdom was especially troublesome, with leapfrogging wage claims by unions, etc. This itself was a 'motor' of inflation if unemployment was kept down.

But what of employers? A true trade union push was important in given conditions, and in Sweden measures had been taken to strengthen the resistance of employers. There had also been profit squeezes and difficulties for marginal employers, strikes, labour market friction, etc. So he felt one should look at both employers and trade unions in analysing this kind of problem.

Mr Oppenheimer saw expectations as important. At the end of his paper he spoke of inconsistencies and contradictions in a mixed economy and was pessimistic about the possibility of controlling the wage/price spiral. However, Professor Lundberg missed remarks about how one might improve the bad functioning of the mixed economy in relation to inflation. He would like a discussion on whether we should, or must, improve the performance of the mixed economy in this respect. Professor Lundberg thought it important to discuss this issue. Or should we discuss how to live with the inflation our system created by making various other alterations?

He ended with a positive view. Economists in Sweden thought that one might have a better economic policy if one had better government. When there was international inflation in 1973–74, Sweden had sought a package deal – which had been accepted – with the target of stabilising expectations. It had been seen as important not to leave those inside the firm or the household to work out their own expectations, but to give a target and then to take measures to deal with problems. The idea was that the trade unions, with the employers, would find ways of keeping wage increases within the target, while increasing exports would lead to an appreciating kroner. There would also be indexation arrangements for wages to remove uncertainty.

Sir Austin Robinson had found very much of the conference difficult because it was not always clear what the monetarists were arguing. Were they reaching familiar policy conclusions by a different route, or were they using a new thought method which led to different results?

Professor Robinson was more at home with Mr Oppenheimer's paper because his thought methods were much more his own, but he was sorry that the paper had concentrated on the United Kingdom and generalised so little. The critical problem in the United Kingdom at the moment was that inflation was running at more than 20 per cent per annum, while the rate of economic growth in the country was negative rather than positive. This brought us back to the big issues. What was the trade-off between growth and inflation on the one hand, and the costs of preventing inflation, in restrictions on growth, on the other?

Up to a point, Sir Austin agreed that it was hard to separate demand and cost inflation. Over the years, different people had used these words in different senses, but he did see some value in separating rather than combining the two. He agreed that cost-push inflation might most easily be reduced in some circumstances by reducing the level of demand, but that was not the only way. One issue which needed more thought was whether there were other ways of reducing cost-push. He did not think that wage policies were wholly effective, but to say that a policy was not 100 per cent effective did not mean it was wholly ineffective.

The real problem was the actual amount of trade-off required, in the United Kingdom as an example, between unemployment and inflation. He thought there was a high economic cost of preventing inflation, and it was not clear that the Conference had adequately taken account of its dimensions. He would like to give two examples.

First, if one looked, as Professor Duesenberry had in his paper, at the effect on the United Kingdom of the recent steep increase in primary product prices, including oil, one found that the United Kingdom had lost about 25 per cent on the terms of trade. Since British imports represented about 20 per cent of G.D.P., it had lost about 5 per cent G.D.P. One should perhaps add the resultant effects on incomes within the economy, but for the moment he ignored these as internal transfers. If one could maintain a rate of growth of 3 per cent, the balance of payments cost represented about two years growth and one could deal with the real income problems this implied by allowing them to be taken up by a two-year standstill on real incomes, accompanied by normal economic expansion. This was then a short-run problem. However, if one was also obliged simultaneously to solve the inflationary problem and this reduced growth to 1 per cent or less per annum, there would be a three-year loss in G.D.P. of about 15 per cent. The short-run problem then became a long-run one and its character changed.

Second, if, in the long run, one was operating on inflation only from the demand side, this might lead to a growth rate of only 2 per cent, rather than $3\frac{1}{2}$ per cent or 4 per cent. Over the next ten years, the loss in growth would be equal to the whole of current United Kingdom imports. These were the trade-off costs and perhaps they had been too lightly treated in the conference's discussions.

During the conference, he had often felt lost. He wondered whether the monetarists believed that they had a new policy weapon to reduce inflation, additional to those used in the past. Or did they have better insights, criteria, or information on how, when and how much one should use the familiar policy weapons against inflation?

He wanted to insist that he took inflation very seriously, and that in the United Kingdom tough and unpopular things needed saying and doing. But some politicians who were bitten with the monetary bug gave the impression that they had found new, purely monetary weapons which could deal with inflation, and enable the United Kingdom to escape the tough, difficult application of the familiar anti-inflationary policy.

One who had been brought up to think as he had would expect monetary weapons to operate through the rate of interest, capital formation and borrowing to purchase consumer durables, with effects on G.D.P., wage bargaining, and so on. It would be a real service if those not singing the monetary tune could be told whether the monetarists were saying that we should go on and do even more difficult things, or whether they believed they had some new and mystical weapon which we had not thought of in the past and which enabled one to escape the painful remedies.

This led back to the really big issues. Sir Austin did not think that the polarisation of policy measures would work in a modern, mixed economy. Very tough anti-inflationary measures had literally killed four British Chancellors of the Exchequer in recent years, and he was in some cases sorry that they had perished for their faith. However, in a democratic economy one could not be as tough as the tough monetarists thought. It was equally true that to expand the economy without an effective control over cost-push might be to cause inflation. Those of us who wanted to improve the operation of mixed economies in a social democratic country had sought compromises. But was compromise possible? How could one get as much as possible of the benefits of economic expansion and growth and avoid inflation? Could one find a working compromise?

Sir Austin wanted to go back to the end of what Professor Lundberg had said. Was free wage bargaining a fundamental right? Or must we solve the problem of how to determine the level of real incomes by government intervention? Was this the price of growth without too much inflation?

Mr Plessz looked at the problems from an international point of view. Some of what was said in Professor Oppenheimer's paper reminded him of OECD discussions on the role of the synchronised expansion in the flare-up of inflation. In recent recessions, the improvement in price performance had, on each occasion, been less than in the previous recession. Governments had, therefore, been collectively aiming at some underutilisation of resources for a protracted period. Hence, the latest recession was partly the result of the collective decision of a number of governments, though it was true that it had gone much deeper than they expected.

As for the relationship between demand-pull and cost-push in a synchronised boom, we now had, in commodity markets, a national cost-push resulting from group demand-pull. The 1972–73 up-turn had been accompanied by a huge inventory boom with a particularly sharp increase in stocks of raw materials, quite out of line with the strength in final demand.

So, the real policy issue was how to deal with cost-push, in a situation when there was no excess demand. Some elements of the Mundell 'twist' might help. That is, one should use monetary policy to control the price level and fiscal policies to support overall demand, indeed to add to it in the sectors of the economy where that was particularly necessary (building construction for example). With demand as low as at present, this would have no noticeable effect in increasing inflationary pressures. One also needed sensible price and income policies.

Professor Bronfenbrenner feared that he was a convert to 'gloom and doom'. He wanted to go back to the 'uneasy triangle' noted by the London *Economist* in 1952. This identified three goals: full employment (at union wage rates); price level stability; and strong economic pressure groups, especially trade unions. The *Economist* made the point that one could have none, one, or two of these, but not three. Perhaps economists had not stressed this choice enough. Perhaps they had not insisted sufficiently on the link between wages and prices, and had made direct controls (when they worked) a convenient excuse for monetary and fiscal 'whoopee'.

His old teacher, Frank Knight, had doubted whether economists made much difference to the world because human nature was stupid. We had relied, both economists and the general public, on agreements between pressure groups of producers. This had been especially true for the Netherlands and Scandinavia, and it had not been successful, perhaps because consumers had been underrepresented. All the talk was of *group* increases in prices and wages as a reason for many of our difficulties. Perhaps these groups had less-than-perfect control over their members and could not have acted differently. In the United Kingdom this might be true of unions which did not have adequate control over their own shop stewards and members. Socialist teachers were telling their students that the mixed economy was the mixed-up economy, and that the capitalist world would blow up over inflation rather than following the Marxian path to collapse. If so, he was afraid that with the new 'inflation twist' the Marxian doctrine would be correct, and he regretted it.

Professor de Wolff discussed the issue of wage-indexation dealt with in the last section of Mr Oppenheimer's paper, emphasising the necessity of an appropriate price index for this purpose. For example, the cost of living index used should be corrected for the effects of indirect taxes. If not, the burden of indirect tax increases would only be borne by non-wage earners. An index of this kind had recently been computed for the Netherlands. A similar argument could be made over price rises resulting from a deterioration of the terms of trade.

Apart from this, he would like to point out that indexation could work in two ways. If wage earners were overestimating coming price increases and could obtain wage increases in accordance with this, wage indexation would work in an anti-inflationary way. The opposite might be equally true. He pointed to the situation, in 1975, in the Netherlands, where wage negotiations had been concluded on the assumption of a 2 per cent increase in national productivity, and had given, on average, almost full compensation for price increases, though differing for different income levels. As it turned out, productivity increased much less than the 2 per cent, so that the bargain was clearly inflationary. He concluded that indexation could be harmful and should be replaced by less inflationary types of compensation.

Professor de Wolff also wanted to comment on the effect of taxes in general on wage negotiations. Trade unions tried to shift the effects of tax increases on their real wages, particularly if they were unexpected. This could cause difficult problems for central wage negotiations, and actually did so in the Netherlands. The negotiating parties wanted to know what the government intended to do about taxes where the government, in turn, found it difficult to frame its own policy so long as it did not have a clear picture of developments on the wages front.

Professor Hague wondered whether perhaps Mr Oppenheimer's paper had reversed the title. Its subject seemed to be: Why inflationary policies do work.

As one who had worked with the British National Economic Development Council during the first period of half-baked growth policy, and for the Price Commission in the second period of half-baked, or perhaps quarter-baked, growth policy, he would like to say something in their defence.

What had been done under the NEDC might look half-baked now but had not seemed so silly at the time. He had been one of those who had pressed the Chancellor to take the gamble of increasing demand in 1964. In the previous decade there had been a clear cycle in stock building, with the balance of payments surplus moving downwards by an absolute amount roughly the same as that by which the value of inventories moved up. In 1957, the Chancellor had slowed down the economy after the top of the boom had already been reached, adding to recession as stocks ran down. In 1964, it seemed therefore worth increasing growth, to see what happened when the stock building boom ended, perhaps in 1965.

On one aspect of what happened in 1964, the paper was misleading. Despite what it said, investment had increased very rapidly in 1964. Indeed, it had perhaps increased too rapidly and, after a change in government, there was pressure from that government to reduce investment. There were clearly problems in financing investment in the United Kingdom; he simply wanted to make the point that investment in the United Kingdom did increase rapidly once growth got going.

Obviously a number of foolish things had been done in developing United Kingdom economic policy. As Professor Patinkin had said, governments were not unitary bodies; nor were the groups of civil servants who advised them. There were differences of opinion, not merely between government departments, but within them. He thought British civil servants suffered from three failings.

First, they were largely bad at economics, and when they devised methods of control, like price control, they overcomplicated the rules. His solution would be to halve the number of senior British civil servants on the basis that, with only half the time available, the policies they developed could not be so complicated as now.

Second, it was important to remember the extent to which all governments, even Labour governments, submitted to pressure, whether from the CBI, individual business leaders or trade unions when these pressure groups suggested that unemployment or other problems would be created if proposed economic measures were not toned down, governments listened very hard.

Finally, civil servants suffered, perhaps more than anything else, from loss of nerve at crucial times, as in 1957 and 1964.

Of course, there were things to be said in defence of economic policy too. In a perfect world, no doubt it was true, as Mr Oppenheimer suggested, that the British government should have revised the Stage III wage-indexing arrangements immediately after oil prices rose towards the end of 1973. But one could not expect any government to start this kind of negotiation all over again, especially when the trade unions had already been offered too much in the way of indexation. In the United Kingdom in 1973, it would have been impossible for a Conservative government to persuade them to accept something less favourable. The least-worst solution was to do what had been done and to soldier on, leaving the arrangements unchanged.

Professor Fischer suggested that the public appetite for inflation in the United States was small. It was hard to explain why the public in general appeared to accept 9 per cent unemployment with little complaint other than to say that they wanted inflation even less.

Was Professor Robinson right in suggesting that the United Kingdom could have absorbed the shock of the oil price increase in two years with a normal growth of output? To do so would have imposed other adjustments on the economy, led to changes in relative prices and called for investment to adjust the structure of the capital stock to the new set of prices. To have tried to absorb the oil price increase in the way suggested by Professor Robinson, would surely have taken a lot out of growth.

He doubted that there was any general relationship between the long-run rate of growth and the average rate of unemployment. A fall in unemployment would increase output in the short run, but the connection between average rates of unemployment and growth in the long run was less transparent.

In response to Professor Robinson's question as to whether the monetarists had a secret cure for inflation, he did not think they had. They emphasised expectations and they could logically even see an incomes policy as being a means of reaching agreement on what rate of price increase to expect. Perhaps they would say that an incomes policy could not reduce wages directly, so that wage reduction could be achieved only through market pressures. They would certainly say that if one did not reduce the rate of growth of the money supply, one would not reduce the rate of inflation, whether or not there was an incomes policy.

Dr Corden wanted to discuss a problem which existed in the United Kingdom and perhaps elsewhere. Suppose that money wages were increased at a given rate, and that the government increased the money supply more slowly than this. The likelihood was that many small firms would, one after the other, run into difficulties, with some bankruptcies leading to unemployment. This was a signalling system at work, showing the implications of failure to limit the rise in wage rates, and so limit further bankruptcies. But if there was only one coal industry and only one major motor car firm, the situation was different, because government could not then allow a whole firm to go bankrupt. So perhaps the general tendency for more nationalisation would mean that in the future there would be twenty five very large firms in the United Kingdom and it would become impossible to operate a market-based monetary policy.

Professor Duesenberry wanted to talk about the monetarists' secret weapon. His conclusion was that the monetarists were neither as dumb as they looked nor as smart as they thought. They considered the possible impact of monetary policy on inflation, but there was a fiscal version too. They saw monetary policy as operating through two channels. First, it affected real demand. Second, it had indirect effects on prices through expectations. One contribution of the monetarists had been to put greater emphasis on expectations, but the theory of expectations ran into two problems. First, one might learn from the immediate past, so that it would then be necessary to adapt expectational models. Second, people might learn from broader past experience. For example, in a gold standard world, an increase in prices was accompanied by slow expansion of the money supply, which would lead to a recession. This was difficult for those concerned with how expectations were formed, when they wanted to try to work out what would happen next. Much of the monetarist argument emphasised this, but did not spell it out clearly.

Evidence on the role of expectations came from the fact that bringing a moving average of prices into the analysis helped explanation. But this might come either from forward-looking expectations or from wage claims reflecting, for example, past increases in the cost of living. This situation related not to expectations but to what had happened already.

Professor Duesenberry thought the monetarists underestimated the effect of factors like such past changes, in the cost of living, and attributed too much to expectations.

Incomes policy related to this. Some incomes policies aimed at solving the problems resulting from earlier changes in the income distribution. Others sought to a manipulate expectations by getting agreement on what everyone would do, and common expectations on what would happen next. So most incomes policies emphasised one aspect more than others. Those monetarists who sought to restrain incomes by saying, for example, that there should not be an annual increase of more than, say, 5 per cent in the money supply, must explain what kind of transition there would be from the present rate of increase to the planned rate. At least in the United States, a restrictive monetary policy would not lead to a smooth winding down of inflation. It was liable to end in crisis, so that the monetary authorities would then back off. Under the gold standard, the guarantee that there would be no monetary expansion was the cause of frequent financial crises. The monetarists' secret weapon had explosive characteristics.

Professor Fischer suggested that while Professor Duesenberry's comment that explaining wage changes with distributed lags on past prices did not necessarily establish the role of expected inflation in wage-setting was correct, it was harder to explain away the success of distributed lags in interest rate equations. Further, in some cases the expectation variable in wage equations was taken from an interest rate equation, thus strengthening the interpretation of the role of that variable as reflecting expectations.

Sir Austin Robinson argued that the relevant expectations were about the future rate of interest, level of activity, wage demands and balance of payments. However, the desirable expectations ran three to five years ahead, and that was more than the expected life of most governments. Without interparty agreement on, for example, monetary policy for the future, one could not work on expectations to the extent assumed.

Professor Aukrust wondered why policies failed. He wanted to return to the analogy used in the conference comparing price policy to the driving of cars. First, some cars were not alone on the road; they had to follow the general traffic flow and accept the speed of others. Second, some cars were harder to drive than others; for example, the Scandinavian mini-economies were easier to handle, partly because their trade unions were well-behaved. Third, drivers were heading for different goals, some more difficult to reach than others. Fourth, drivers needed maps, and some of the politicians had maps that were not very good. Fifth, it was necessary to handle the various controls. It was hard to drive if difficult groups handled different instruments; for example, the trade unions the accelerator, the central bank the brake, and the Minister of Finance the steering wheel. And it was worse still if more than one group tried to handle the same control. In particular, one needed the trade unions to be part of a concerted agreement on how to steer the car.

Professor Patinkin wanted to make it clear that Professor Duesenberry would agree that one could not identify the gold standard with monetarism. Then Professor Fischer had overemphasised the degree to which monetarists agreed with other economists. If they were here, the monetarists would not agree that everyone else agreed with them. The monetarists clearly spent a good deal of time working on questions connected with the money supply, but how much time did they spend on persuading trade unions not to press for wage increases?

His next point was similar to the one made by Professor Fischer. Professor Robinson had indicated something of a trade-off between growth and inflation. Why? In a given year this might be true, but at a given rate of unemployment, why did not growth then continue at the same rate, whatever the monetary expansion? He could see only a once-over trade-off, while one was moving back to a lower level of unemployment.

Professor Patinkin thought that one unusual aspect of the conference was that it had given no satisfactory explanation of why there was so much inflation in the world today. Inflation was unusual in advanced European countries except in time of war. It was true there had been war in Vietnam, but that war was relatively small.

Professor Patinkin also wondered how far, in the past, European countries had used inflation to tax the foreign exchange earnings of primary producers. Primary producing countries were not fools and were now tying the prices of their primary products to inflation. He wondered whether there was this element in earlier European policies.

Professor Csikós-Nagy explained that during Hungary's negotiations to join GATT he had been able to observe the secret foreign trade practices of market economies. He had found a series of examples of government interference with trade even within GATT. So he wondered whether any discussion of global problems, based on the assumption of a free, or nearly free, market system, was valid.

Replying to the discussion, *Mr Oppenheimer* noted that there had been two interlocking sets of exchanges. The first had been concerned with the paper, and the second with the relationship between monetarist and other policy recommendations.

Professor Lundberg had given a characteristic introduction which was clear, graceful, incisive and amusing.

On the definition of price stability, he was tempted to refer to what happened after the 1967 devaluation in the United Kingdom. There had been a long time-lag before the supporting monetary and fiscal restraints were introduced, and this had been a nervous period. There were a number of visits from officials of the IMF especially concerned with credit expansion, and much argument had apparently occurred over the correct measure: was it money, whether defined broadly or narrowly, or domestic credit expansion, or some other factor? After long discussions, the head of the IMF team was reported to have declared, 'I don't care how it's measured, there's too much of it'.

He felt that the situation under discussion was a little like that. There was a gap between target and achievement in the field of price stability which had to be measured; but one could not talk as though the target were stable and agreed.

He suspected that different people had very different views about it. Some were the views of economists, some the views of the electorate and some the revealed preferences of governments, but those were affected by recent experience. For example, even in Germany a rate of inflation that had been regarded with horror in 1970 was now viewed with relief, because things had been still worse in the interim. So the definitional problem was a big one, and perhaps gave a certain haziness to the whole discussion.

He agreed (always a safe point!) on the probable need for further analysis. He did not wish to be categoric where definite conclusions were not warranted. For example, the subsidisation of some prices in the United Kingdom had recently become an important issue. The effect on the retail price index in 1975 had been, perhaps, to cause an increase of 24 per cent rather than 26 per cent; this was scarce worth having in terms of the resulting deterioration in the fiscal position. However, the figure was only his guess, and it was no more than a guess. At the same time, he pointed out that people had sometimes taken for granted that if there were a progressive income tax, then the fiscal system as a whole would act as an automatic stabiliser in the presence of inflation. It seemed a rash assumption. Mr Oppenheimer said that Professors Lundberg and Hague had referred to the possible dampening of inflation by growth, and to the lessons of the United Kingdom experience in 1963–64. He accepted that it was harder to satisfy real wage aspirations if there were no growth. Statistical evidence showed that there was greater international uniformity in movements of money wages than of real wages during the postwar period. So a country with lower productivity gains had more inflation. The question, however, was how far governments in the industrial countries were able to influence the long-run growth of productivity in their territory. He remained sceptical.

He disagreed with Professor Hague that government and civil servants should have had the nerve to go on borrowing overseas. Domestic investment did increase rapidly in certain years but this was a cyclical phenomenon, and to go on borrowing seemed too risky. It was true that the balance of payments was much affected by inventory fluctuations. The basic problem in the United Kingdom, however, was the unsatisfactory average position of the balance of payments over the cycle as a whole.

To Professor Fischer, he suggested that the reason why incomes policies had failed was partly political and partly arose from the structure of the British labour market. This was a non-monetarist answer, so it must be said that the money supply had indeed increased rapidly in recent years. However, if politics and the labour market situation had been different, it would probably have been easier to limit monetary expansion.

The willingness of the public to put up with wage restraint varied. Politicians found it easier to have pay freezes when the next election was farther ahead. In the United Kingdom the freeze in 1966 came soon after an election, and had totally disintegrated before the 1970 election. The structure of the labour market and the attitude of trade unions was the deeper problem. Trade unions mixed unity with diversity. They united on their defence of free collective bargaining and opposition to centralised control over pay. But when it came to labour market behaviour, unity vanished. It had proved impossible to obtain a practical consensus on the treatment of 'special cases' at any particular moment. Having agreed that, say, nurses or railwaymen should receive an exceptional increase, other unions promptly turned round and demanded the same increase for their own members.

18 Incomes Policies

Pieter de Wolff
UNIVERSITY OF AMSTERDAM

I. INTRODUCTION

Incomes policy is a term coined after the Second World War which covers a wide range of notions. Here it will be used in the sense that a government has a view about the sort of economic trends which are consistent with its objectives, and in particular about price stability or a reduction of the prevailing rate of inflation, and that it derives from this view certain targets for the development of incomes and takes steps to attain these targets through adequate policy measures. Although vague exhortations about restraints are thus excluded in this way the definition still covers a large number of experiments carried out in the postwar period [1].

There are some countries (for example Austria and Norway) in which a more or less permanent machinery has been set up and which continues to operate today or in which such a system has been applied for a comparatively long period (for example, the Netherlands). There are on the other hand a few countries (for example, Germany and Sweden)[1] which on grounds of principle have refrained from any policy of this kind; and in between there is a large group of countries which have only temporarily and intermittently recourse to incomes policies in situations in which such a measure seemed to be required.

In some cases the policy measures have been restricted to the publication of certain guidelines recommended to negotiating parties, as for example, the guidelines of the Kennedy administration in the United States. In other cases tripartite bodies on a voluntary basis have been set up through which the government has tried to exercise a stronger influence on the results, (for instance in Austria and Norway). Finally, there are many cases in which certain measures have been introduced on a compulsory basis. This was often the case with temporary policies (such as freezes on wages and/or prices) but this has been also the case with the Dutch more permanent incomes policy.

There has been a difference also with respect to the types of income to which the policy has been applied. In nearly all cases both wages and some form of other income have been affected, although the temporary measures introduced in France mainly relied on price control. But the policies with

[1] As was rightly pointed out at the Conference, even these exceptions have been only partial. Recently Sweden has applied price policy measures, and in Germany, as the author is well aware, concerted action has played an important role [2], [3].

respect to other incomes were not always confined to price control; in a number of cases they have been supplemented by rules for increases of dividends, profits and rents.

II. CERTAIN CONCLUSIONS FROM THE EVIDENCE

On this extensive collection of policies a still more extensive literature has been published. It shows that even with the help of econometric methods it is difficult to arrive at definite conclusions on the results of the policies mentioned. In the following a number of points has been listed and a few conclusions have been formulated based on a study of the literature as well as on the author's own experience.

(1) THE THEORETICAL ARGUMENT FOR INCOMES POLICIES

Incomes policies have always formed and still form a rather controversial subject both from a theoretical and a practical point of view. They have been proposed and applied to supplement other types of economic (fiscal and monetary) policies. The main theoretical argument behind them is that the share of wages in the national income is comparatively stable or at least only changes slowly. Thus, the rate of inflation in a country will roughly speaking be equal to the amount by which the average rate of the increase in wages exceeds the average rise in national productivity. The postwar period has been characterised by a rapid economic growth, exerting a strong pressure on national resources which has led to an upward pressure on wages and prices. To hold this pressure in check, restrictive policies are required which dampen growth and increase unemployment. The more possible it is to keep the pressures under control through an adequate incomes policy, the less will it be necessary to have recourse to policies restricting the growth of the volume of output. Consequently, effective incomes policies may be helpful in maintaining a given rate of inflation with a higher rate of growth and a lower level of unemployment than would be possible without them [4].

(2) INCOMES POLICIES ON A PERMANENT BASIS

It is clear that the effects of an incomes policy can most easily be judged in countries in which such a policy has been applied on a more or less permanent basis. The cases of Austria, Norway and the Netherlands have already been mentioned in this respect. The first conclusion to be drawn from their experience is that the political climate and the organisation of the labour market are important factors. In all three countries the incomes policy was introduced immediately after the war when there was a strong common willingness to co-operate in order to overcome the devastating consequences of the war. Labour parties held strong positions in the governments and both sides of the labour market were (and still are) strongly centralised. In Austria and Norway the degree of organisation of labour was and is relatively high. In the Netherlands it was lower (it has increased subsequently) but there already existed legislation which made it possible to declare the results of wage negotiations between unions and employers' organisations in a given industry binding on all the workers concerned. These facts facilitated the introduction of machinery for dealing with an incomes policy under which the government was in a position to exert influence on the outcome. In Austria and Norway this has been done on a voluntary basis as far as wages are concerned, though on certain occasions the government has felt it necessary to adopt compulsory measures (such as temporary freezes on wages and prices in Norway) [4], chapter 4, pages 5 to 7, [5]. In the Netherlands the policy received a legal basis from the outset, authorising the government to take final and binding decisions. In Austria and Norway it has been possible to improve the machinery over time into a tripartite co-operation supported by institutions for fact finding and analysis of the economic situation. The case of the Netherlands will be dealt with separately in section II (3) below.

A second conclusion, which is also relevant to temporary policies, is the fact that, as was mentioned earlier in the introduction, these policies nearly always related not only to wages but also to other incomes. It can be and has been argued on theoretical grounds that a restriction of the rate of increase of wages would by itself in any case lead to a similar restriction on the course of prices [6]. However, there is always a certain amount of monopolistic and administered pricing, and thus it adds to the effectiveness of the policy if it is also extended to other incomes, either directly or through an adequate price policy. But the main argument for the combination is concerned with the political feasibility of the measures. It is understandable that trade unions are only prepared to accept some form of wage restraint if they are assured that other incomes will also be kept in check.

Rules for permanent wage policies have to be simple in order to be effective and in the past there has been a preference for uniform wage rounds. This has led to the criticism that such policies were likely to be harmful to economic development by reducing the incentive for labour to move from less to more productive industries and firms. This argument does not seem to be justified by the facts. In the first place even in the case of uniform wage rounds certain deviations from the norm have been allowed. Secondly, there has always been a certain amount of wage drift, leading to a difference between the trends of actual earnings and the wage rates negotiated. Moreover, several studies have shown that there is not a very strong correlation between the rates of growth of employment by industries and the corresponding course of the wage rates, whether earned or negotiated [7]. In any case, considerable changes in employment have taken place accompanied by relatively small shifts in the ranking of earned incomes. This same comparatively uniform course of wage rates is also at the base of the well-known Scandinavian theory about the import of inflation [9]. According to this theory, which is supported by the facts, the effect of rising export prices is reinforced by the fact that productivity increases in the exporting industries are greater than in the sheltered ones, whereas wage increases in both groups are almost equal. In Norway this latter fact might be ascribed to the prevailing incomes policy but in Sweden where wage negotiations are free, this can not be the case.

Thus, it seems reasonable to conclude that the flexibility of the wage policies resulting from deliberate differentiation together with wage drift will usually be sufficient to provide for the necessary mobility of labour.

However, wage drift cannot only be considered as a safety valve to alleviate the unfavourable effects of a too-stringent wage policy. Even in the Netherlands, where deviations from the approved wage rates in either direction have not been permitted, wage drift has in fact occurred. In the other two countries, in particular in Norway, the size of the overall drift has sometimes been quite considerable and has threatened to wreck the whole system. A solution for this problem has been sought by taking a certain amount of unavoidable wage drift into consideration in the contracts concluded. A few years ago allowance for a certain amount of wage drift has been introduced as an official element in the Norwegian wage policy.

(3) THE DUTCH CASE

Although, as has been remarked already, the wage structure in a country tends to be relatively stable there is an undeniable desire on the part of both parties in the labour market to maintain some flexibility, allowing them to take account of the special circumstances of the industry or the firm concerned. If negotiations are free this condition is automatically provided. When a wage policy operates, certain rules to provide this flexibility have to be laid down and in some cases there has been recourse to so-called productivity bargaining. This method has been applied in the United Kingdom as part of the incomes policy in force during the 1960s and also during the 1959–63 phase of the Dutch incomes policy.[1] In the latter case wages were allowed to rise in accordance with a weighted average of the trends of national productivity and of the branch of industry concerned. It is clear that this policy, if applied correctly, will lead to an average wage increase equal to the increase of the national productivity. But in spite of this algebraic result the policy lacks a sound theoretical foundation. The economic argument for wage differentiation is to promote an efficient allocation of labour and although there may be a certain relation between the demand for labour by industries and their increase in productivity, it is a rather weak one and, there are even cases where both variables tend to move in opposite directions.

Apart from this theoretical objection, the practical difficulties have been

[1] A large number of articles has been published on the Dutch case; an extensive description is to be found in [2] and [3].

enormous. Strong pressure has been put on the Central Bureau of Statistics to produce the required data. This has only been possible to a limited extent, and in several cases decisions have had to be based on data supplied by the firms themselves, sometimes of a rather dubious character. (Similar difficulties were met with in Britain.) As the government feared that this practice might lead to abuse of the rules, a series of additional instructions were issued leading to confusion and irritation rather than to actual clarification.

The Dutch incomes policy is also interesting from another point of view. During the whole postwar period it has been one of the main concerns of the government to build up and maintain a favourable competitive position for the country's exports and the incomes policy has been an important instrument for the attainment of that goal. By hindsight it may now be concluded that the policy went too far. Unemployment, which for example during the recession of 1958 reached a peak of close to 4 per cent, afterwards went rapidly down and changed in the early 1960s into a strong pressure on the labour market. Certain measures were taken to alleviate this pressure (revaluation of the guilder by 5 per cent together with the Deutschmark in 1961; shortening of the working week in the same year from 48 to 44 hours with unchanged weekly earnings, and so on). But the gap between Dutch and foreign price levels still remained comparatively large and the strain resulting from it, particularly in the framework of the Common Market was underestimated. In the middle of 1963 this strain erupted into a revolt of the employers of the ship repair yards against the wage policy. Government succeeded in keeping the situation in hand by allowing a wage increase of a size so far unprecedented (it worked out at about 15 per cent) and issuing strict rules for price increases (only part of the increased wage costs were to be passed on). A more flexible incomes policy was introduced which, however, broke down in 1968. From 1964 wages rose on average much more than before. Finally in 1974, in connection with the impact of the oil crisis, the government again imposed a binding wage increase. The lesson to be drawn from this experience is not only that a too-cautious policy, leading to disparities with the outside world, runs the risk of undermining the whole system. The shock proved also to have a very favourable effect on the economy. The rising wages made labour move from low to the fast-growing high productivity industries. In the ten years preceding 1963 the national productivity rose on the average by 3·4 per cent, during the next ten years the corresponding figure was as high as 5·5 per cent. Real wages also increased much faster, the average during the ten years being 4·6 per cent and 6·3 per cent. Since over the whole period the growth of real wages exceeded that of productivity by some 1 per cent per annum the share of wages in the national income rose considerably. This is no exceptional phenomenon. It occurred in many other countries. But it is quite clear now that also the adaption process has gone too far. As a result of greatly increasing labour costs, coupled with decreasing earning capacity of the enterprises, at present a considerable amount of structural unemployment has been developing.

III. TEMPORARY INCOMES POLICIES

Thus far attention has mainly been directed to the wages side of the policy, although it has been stressed already that prices also have been kept under control. The creation of an effective price policy is one of the most difficult problems to be tackled when a permanent incomes policy is introduced. Not only is the number of prices very large but due to continuous changes in quality and the appearance and disappearance of products it is difficult to develop a watertight system of controls. In particular it is not easy to bring prices down in cases where productivity rises faster than costs. The three countries referred to have applied somewhat different systems. Usually certain basic products (for example foodstuffs) have been made subject to direct control, whereas pricing rules have been set up for other products, stipulating those cost items which were allowed to be passed on in prices (for instance the effect of increased import prices or indirect taxes) and aiming at keeping profit margins constant. Checks on the correct application of these rules were made through inspection of the administration of firms, mostly on a sampling basis. The price control, moreover, has not always been applied with uniform severity. It has been strengthened during periods of strong upward pressure on prices and relaxed when the pressure has become less.

From a theoretical point of view the price policy is more objectionable than the wages policy as it only takes into account the changes at the supply side of the markets. If the policy is rigorously applied it does not allow shifts in demand to affect profit margins through changes in prices and, therefore, it may impede the reallocation of resources. However, it is difficult to judge to what extent this objection holds in practice. Policies have not always been applied strictly and, moreover, in the small and open countries foreign competition has probably served to mitigate harmful effects.

The number of cases in which an incomes policy has been applied on a temporary basis is too large to be dealt with in any considerable detail. Thus only some general comments can be made, based on a few actual experiments.

One of these is the introduction of guideposts in the United States. Although some official recommendations had already been made during the 1950s it was, for the first time during the Kennedy administration (in 1962) that the Council of Economic Advisers (C.E.A.) issued a definite set of rules. Wages (inclusive of fringe benefits) should be increased everywhere in accordance with the trend of overall productivity. Prices should only be raised in industries in which the rise in productivity was less than the overall rise and lowered if the productivity was higher. Deviations were only allowed for if these were necessary to encourage efficient resource allocation. In 1964 these rules were tightened by noting that the exceptions were intended to apply 'to only a relatively few cases' [9].

Several studies have been made to find out whether the policy which lasted only for some four years, had any effect on the course of wages and prices. Unfortunately, their results are somewhat contradictory. But, the conclusion seems to be justified that the policy was abandoned around 1966 when demand pressure became too strong. The fact that the policy largely based on voluntary co-operation could not stand an increasing strain probably explains why the Nixon administration in 1971 had recourse to a compulsory policy when it decided that measures in the field of wages and prices were needed in order to curb down the increasing rate of inflation [10]. After a 90 days' freeze of prices and wages during the autumn of 1971 (phase I) a more flexible phase II was started, aiming at an annual wage rise of $5\frac{1}{2}$ per cent and a price rise of $2\frac{1}{2}$ per cent.

An efficient machinery was set up, to handle the vast administrative problems of so big a country. It benefited no doubt from the experience gained elsewhere. It was based on a three-tier system by which the biggest firms (annual sales over \$100 million) had to pre-notify price increases to the Pay Board, medium-size firms (sales between \$50 and 100 million) had to report only, and smaller firms (below \$50 million) obviously had to observe the rules but were only subject to spot checks.

A similar set-up was introduced for wages. Pre-notification was required for contracts affecting more than 5000 workers, reporting for those affecting 1000 to 5000 workers, smaller ones being left out of control. The price policy, in particular was efficiently organised as the bigger firms were subjected to quarterly checks of their profit accounts. A number of products and activities were exempt from the price controls, the most important being raw agricultural and fishery products. Moreover from the outset the policy was set up on a temporary basis; phase II was to last during 1972 only.

The results of the freeze were quite satisfactory, and the rate of inflation was considerably reduced. Phase II also worked quite well but the whole system was jeopardised by the rising agricultural prices due to bad harvests all over the world. Thus the policy was not terminated at the end of 1972, but in 1973 a phase III followed under which the rules in general were loosened but food prices were brought under control; at mid-1973 a 60 days' general price freeze was announced, succeeded by phase IV which brought fuel prices under control. But an increasing rate of inflation could not be prevented, mainly due to the oil crisis and the scarcity of food which added a strong impetus to the inflationary pressure. This latter factor in particular makes it difficult to judge the effectiveness of the policy, but the facts that the policy was intended to last for one year only and that it was politically impossible to bring the agricultural prices under control have most probably strongly reduced its effectiveness. In the United Kingdom the postwar history shows quite a series of efforts to contain the rise of money incomes in line with that of output. It would take too much space to describe these events in detail. Suffice it to say that periods with guidelines only or with no clear policy at all alternated with periods with more binding regulations, but due to the strongly decentralised structure of the trade union system and also as a consequence of the fact that the central TUC often was very reluctant to agree to recommendations or regulations issued by the government, the policies in general were not very successful. In an interesting study by Lipsey and Parkin [11], covering the period 1948–68, the authors derive econometric relations for the development of prices and wages in the United Kingdom both in periods of 'policy on' and 'policy off'. From these four equations they conclude that 'a policy that combines an incomes restraint with the depression of aggregate demand sufficient to remove all inflation will require a much higher level of unemployment than will a policy that solely relies on depressing aggregate demand without wage restraint'. These findings confirm the preceding conclusion and even suggest that at times the policy may have had an adverse affect. As a last example of typically temporary policies the freezes on wages and prices may be mentioned. A few examples have already been cited but, in particular during the worldwide upsurge of inflation during the years 1971–73 this type has rather often been applied, either separately or in combination with policies already in operation (in the Scandinavian countries, the Netherlands, Canada, the United Kingdom). During the period of the freeze such a policy is usually successful, the dampening effect is mostly quite clear. However, very often prices and wages resume their upward course when the freeze is lifted and the effect is more likely to take the form of a moderate postponement than of a reduction of the rate of inflation.

IV. WAGE POLICY IN THE PUBLIC SECTOR

A special problem in any type of incomes policy is presented by the wages in the public sector. Nowadays this is a very big sector, employing from 15 to 30 per cent of the wage-earning population. Thus, governments have sometimes used their influence on this sector 'to set an example' for the private sector (for instance at times in the United Kingdom). This type of policy is not very promising. Experience shows that the chances that the example will be followed on a voluntary basis are very small. Thus, the only result is that the wages of civil servants have been lagging behind those in the private sector and have had to be readjusted at a later stage. Moreover, if the backlog becomes too large the increase needed to remove it may be so big that it has a further feedback effect on the private sector. A policy where the wages of civil servants in one way or another are geared to those in the private sector (as in the Netherlands) seems to be a more sensible solution.

V. A COMMENT ON WAGE INDEXATION

Finally, a comment may be made regarding the role of wage indexation. Obviously, this method may be and is applied irrespective of the presence of other forms of incomes policy. In some countries it has already been applied for many years (as in Belgium and Denmark) but as inflation has continued and even gained force its use has been considerably extended. This is understandable, as more and more trade unions have demanded its application in order to prevent the improvements reached in their wage contracts from being swallowed up in price rises. Moreover the unions, being conscious of inflation, will anticipate it and if compensation is not granted automatically through indexation clauses they will claim this compensation in the form of higher nominal increases in their contracts. The argument is often voiced that the rate of inflation may be overestimated and this may produce an additional inflationary force. The effect of indexation is often mitigated through the application of thresholds. Compensation will only be given if prices rise more than the threshold value. But this condition becomes ineffective if inflation is sufficiently strong. In addition to this there are various reasons which render it plausible that indexation tends to add to inflation. For instance an increase in indirect taxation leads to higher prices and will reduce purchasing power; but if full indexation is agreed wage earners will automatically be exempt from this burden. Apart from the fact that this consequence may be objected to for reasons of equity, it is also to be expected that entrepreneurs and recipients of other income will try to shift their burden partly or wholly onto prices. A similar effect may occur when the price rise is due to increasing import prices if at the same time this leads to a deterioration of the terms of trade.

Indexation becomes still more harmful if the negotiated rise in real wages is based on an expected increase of productivity which is not realised in practice as the result of a recession.

VI. SOME GENERAL CONCLUSIONS

Summarising the experience which can be drawn from the examples described in the preceding paragraphs the following tentative conclusions may be drawn. For a few small countries (Austria, Norway) applying an incomes policy on a permanent basis the result seems to be positive. The argument sometimes advanced that the rate of inflation in these countries is not less than elsewhere is not justified. Small open countries cannot protect themselves against external inflationary forces unless they are prepared to revalue their currency at frequent intervals. Moreover, the case of the Netherlands shows that it may even be harmful to do better than the average for the other countries. But if one looks at the relatively smooth trends of these countries, characterised by a low degree of unemployment, a quiet labour market with very few strikes and a rather high rate of growth, it may be concluded that it fits the description given in Section I above. Table 18.1 shows these trends.

For practically all other examples the record is negative and thus the overall conclusion must be that hitherto incomes policies have been comparatively unsuccessful. But, it is questionable whether this should lead to the conclusion that in future incomes policies could be abandoned. If one looks at the experience of the years 1971–73 (before the oil crisis) when inflation in spite of all policy measures increased very strongly almost everywhere, and during which years the basis was laid for the two-digit inflation at present prevalent in many countries, it is difficult to escape the impression that certain measures in the field of wages and prices will be indispensable to turn the tide.

TABLE 18.1
TRENDS IN A NUMBER OF OECD COUNTRIES

Period	*United States*	*France*	*Germany*	*United Kingdom*	*Norway*	*Austria*	*Netherlands*
				Unemployment (%)			
1954–58	5·1	1·2	3·6	1·4	1·5	5·6	2·0
1959–63	5·8	1·2	1·0	1·9	1·6	3·3	1·4
1964–68	4·2	1·5	0·9	1·9	1·1	2·7	1·5
1969–73	5·0	2·0	0·8	3·0	0·8	2·2	2·1
				Annual increase of labour productivity in enterprises (%)			
1954–58	2·6	5·6	5·0	2·0	2·3	4·4	3·1
1959–63	3·4	5·5	5·1	3·1	2·7	4·0	3·9
1964–68	2·6	5·2	5·5	3·6	3·6	5·0	5·6
1969–73	1·9	5·4	4·9	3·8	2·5	5·5	5·4
				Annual increase of consumer prices (%)			
1954–58	1·8	5·0	1·9	3·2	3·8	2·3	3·3
1959–63	1·2	4·4	2·2	2·2	2·6	2·9	2·5
1964–68	2·2	3·3	2·6	4·1	4·2	3·1	4·4
1969–73	4·3	6·0	4·8	7·0	6·8	4·6	7·3

If this should be true it will not only be useful to appraise the methods applied hitherto but also to devise new methods which may be more effective.

In this connection attention may be drawn to the system of profit sharing which is now being discussed in many countries and which already has found application in a few countries (for instance in Germany). If such a scheme on a large scale should be acceptable to both sides of the labour market it might perhaps be possible to find unions prepared to accept moderate nominal wage increases (without indexation). They would then know they would benefit from it not only in so far as the agreement might lead to a lower rate of inflation but also if it should lead to increased profits.

This is not the place to work out the modalities of such a system. It may look impracticable, as has been the case with many other measures in the field of incomes policy. But, if adopted in a sufficient number of countries, it might play an important role in a package of measures intending to curb the present alarmingly high rate of worldwide inflation.

REFERENCES

[1] *Policies for Price Stability*, OECD (Paris, 1962), page 23.
[2] Lloyd Ulman and Robert J. Flanagan, *Wage Restraint: A Study of Incomes Policies in Western Europe* (Berkeley, 1971).
[3] Pieter de Wolff, 'The Netherlands and Germany', in *Incomes Policy: What Can We Learn from Europe*, edited by Walter Galenson (New York: Cornell University, Ithaca, 1973).

[4] 'Income in Post-war Europe', *Economic Survey of Europe in 1965*: part 2 (Geneva, 1967), chapter 1, pages 14/15.

[5] Hannek Suppanz and Derek Robinson, *Prices and Incomes Policy, the Austrian Experience,* OECD (Paris, 1972).

[6] Richard Kahn *et al., The Problem of Rising Prices*, OEEC (Paris, 1961), page 70.

[7] *Wages and Labour Mobility*, by a group of experts under the auspices of the OECD (Paris, 1965).

[8] Odd Aukrust, *Inflation in the Open Economy*, Arbeidsnotater Statistisk Centralbyrå (Oslo, 1975).

[9] G. P. Shultz and Robert Z. Aliber, *Guide Lines, Informal Controls and the Market Place* (Chicago, 1966).

[10] *Economic Report of the President* (Washington, 1972, 1973).

[11] R. G. Lipsey and J. M. Parkin, 'Incomes Policy: A Re-appraisal', *Economica* (May, 1970).

Discussion of the Paper by Pieter de Wolff

Professor Bogomolov said Professor de Wolff gave an interesting analysis of several patterns of income regulation, showing what made them effective or ineffective. His was a very realistic assessment of the opportunities open to Western states in pursuing incomes policies. Except for some small countries, the paper showed their results were more negative than positive. Professor de Wolff had given only a few indications of how Western economies could hope to succeed in income and anti-inflation policy. The latter was not just the control of incomes, especially wages, but the need to control government expenditure, exchange rates, etc. The experience of the last few years led to a need to look more deeply into the structure and outward form of inflation in market economies. Increases in the money supply, as well as credit failures, led to a rate of growth of prices which was perhaps only the outward sign of inflation. So anti-inflationary policies confined to the monetary sphere yielded few results. The roots of inflation lay in the contradictions of monopoly capitalism.

Inflation was probably a spontaneous reaction of the monetary and commodity circulation to the contradictions and disproportions of the capitalist economy, leading inevitably to rising prices and a falling exchange rate. In the process of inflation, the balance between monetary and commodity circulation was forcibly re-established. But there was no reconciliation of the other contradictions of a capitalist economy, especially the distribution of income and of property between social groups. So an anti-inflationary policy also needed to attack these disproportions. Success in combating inflation would also solve formidable problems like chronic budget deficits resulting from expansion of the arms race and the support of dying businesses. There were also problems in energy and raw materials, as well as in the sway of monopolies and monopoly pricing. The suppression of investment booms led to an oversupply of money. There was need for a new international division of labour and for doing away with differences in the level of economic development in developed and underdeveloped countries. So one needed a balanced regulation of economic life, not the support of indolent classes, and especially an end to monopoly capitalism. Inflation was a type of indirect tax which affected those in the middle and low income brackets most severely. Those whose duty it was to combat inflation frequently had a stake in it, as a source of additional income.

Socialist countries had, as the antidote, economic development. If one compared prices in East and West Germany, one saw how much more effective a socialist country was in preventing inflation. Of course, socialist countries were not insured against disproportions like lags in increasing agricultural production, and the effects of bad weather on that production. They also faced problems like an unsatisfied demand for some goods, unjustified price levels for some goods, and the growth of deferred spending power in the form of a rapid increase in savings. These were more often the result of miscellaneous planning imperfections and of economic mismanagement or crop failure. Socialist countries did increase some prices to create price disproportions and stimulate productivity, for example, on farms. But it was doubtful whether all these phenomena could be classified under the heading of inflation.

Many western economists talked about repressed inflation in Socialist countries to create the impression that the malady of inflation was universal.

In the interests of objective comparison, Professor Bogomolov wanted to emphasise the fundamental possibility, under socialism, of eliminating inflation and preventing the spontaneous reaction of money and commodities to difficulties in the economy, with grave economic and social consequences.

Professor de Wolff noted that so far there had been little discussion of incomes policy during the conference. As he had been invited to write a paper on this subject and to discuss its possibilities for fighting inflation, he had tried to describe how such policies had functioned in the past. He was not saying that incomes policies alone could prevent inflation, but that they could help to improve the trade-off between inflation and unemployment. So he had given examples where the policy was partly successful, and discussed its pros and cons. He did not suggest that incomes policy alone could lead to stable prices.

Professor Bogomolov's idea on an anti-inflationary package would probably be generally agreed. How far incomes policy would be an element in this package depended on a wide variety of social and economic institutions which differed between countries. Incomes policies had been most successful in the postwar period in countries where the political system and the organisation of the labour market were favourable to policies of this type. He mentioned Austria and Norway in this connection. In the United Kingdom, on the other hand, incomes policies had had little success. This seemed to be due, at least partly, to the fact that the labour market had been particularly unfavourable to them.

Professor Nussbaumer said the paper had referred a great deal to Austria, and he would like to comment on what was said. First, incomes policy was not an alternative to fiscal and monetary policy, but could perhaps help as an additional instrument. Second, in some countries incomes policies had been quite successful, but what was said about Austria was not entirely correct. Inflation was 9 per cent, unemployment 1·5 per cent and the rate of growth of G.N.P. 5·5 per cent. This suggested that incomes policy had been successful in Austria.

The reason for the success of incomes policy in Austria was that it worked on three levels. First, there had been good agreement between the social partners, and this had been better in 1975 than in 1974. Second, there had been no attempt to change the relative long-run shares in G.D.P. The share of wages had increased under a Conservative government and fallen under a Socialist one. There was considerable emphasis on government policy, because the social partners discussed general economic policy as well as incomes. When they suggested certain policy measures, the government found it very hard to go against labour, management and the farmers simultaneously. So there were constraints on government policy, even monetary and financial policy. The third factor was a considerable emphasis on the behaviour of firms in the labour and product markets, which led to difficulties for some international businesses. If they tried to operate in Austria as they did at home, this angered public opinion and led either to a change in policy or to the firm leaving the country.

Professor Nussbaumer thought participants would like to know that the economic research institutes gave statistical and quantitative proof for the views taken by the social partners. Sometimes the governmental statistical office was relied on for these agreed statistics.

He wondered how strong wage drift could become before it destroyed an incomes policy. If there was very strong wage pressure, incomes policy clearly would not work. However, the trade unions opposed wage drift because, if it occurred, union officials could not impress workers with what the unions were doing for them. In general, trade unions opposed wage drift just as much as management did.

Professor Nussbaumer noted that all the countries which Professor de Wolff quoted as having successful incomes policies were small, and had been afraid that they were not competitive internationally after 1945. But they were. This fear was still there now, and labour and management agreed that it was necessary to keep down wage increases to remain competitive. For example, strong competition between Austria and Germany assisted industrial efficiency in Austria. This would not be equally true of countries like France and the United Kingdom.

Professor Nussbaumer argued that incomes policy must be long-run. One could not turn it off and on. If one did, then when the policy was turned on, people would simply wait until it was turned off again.

Professor Nussbaumer thought that in Austria profit-sharing and worker participation on the boards of companies created a favourable climate.

Professor Polaczek thought one problem had not been sufficiently mentioned in the paper. Anti-inflationary policies succeeded in the 1950s, but not in the 1960s, and the paper referred to this. But he also thought that small countries could have anti-inflationary policies only so long as they were not closely integrated into a wider market. If the flow of goods and factors were free, then in order to pursue a successful anti-inflationary policy small countries had to loosen their economic ties with the rest of the world. Essentially, in an integrated world, a country had two choices. First, to pursue an anti-inflationary policy it had to loosen existing integration ties. Second, it could try to persuade the whole integrated unit to accept the common anti-inflationary policy.

Professor Kleiman queries Professor Bogomolov's statement that those in charge of monetary policy had a stake in inflation. He wondered whether this was any longer true when heads of central banks were no longer recruited among bankers but often came from other fields, such as the civil service. Most people disliked inflation, but the working class, as much as businessmen, found that their incomes kept roughly in line with prices. It was the middle class *rentiers* who were wiped out. The whole rationale of an incomes policy was that non-one was supposed to gain from it. It was this argument that was used in introducing such a policy.

Professor Kleiman noted that wage drift had an important efficiency and allocation role. It gave workers of differing quality different wages; it allowed for the fact that the quality of the labour performed by a given individual might vary with time, on-the-job training, etc.

Perhaps there was a paradox in incomes policy. It might be that there was there an analogy to the degrees of freedom open to a government under fixed and floating exchange rates. An incomes policy needed strong trade unions but if they accepted the restrictions inherent in such a policy they lost control over their members.

The neo-classical attitude seemed to be that incomes policies worked in the short run, but that in the long run the basic economic forces worked developments out in their own way whatever incomes policy were pursued. He was worried that Professor de Wolff appeared to say that there was no evidence whether incomes policies actually worked or not.

Professor Malinvaud said that if one accepted the role of expectation formation, this was a good argument for incomes policies. Perhaps their main role was to change expectations and thereby bring about a permanent shift in the rate of inflation.

He was in agreement with the whole of Professor de Wolff's paper, but would like to add something about France. A year earlier, there had been ideas of imposing a tax on nominal price increases. The idea was that one could not expect much from agreement between the social partners, but one could perhaps affect price formation in firms. The kind of tax suggested was based on the following quantity, to be computed for each firm:

$$VA_t - k \cdot \frac{F_t}{F_{t-1}} \cdot VA_{t-1} = \left(\frac{P_t}{P_{t-1}} - \frac{k}{\pi}\right) \cdot \frac{P_{t-1} \cdot VA_t}{P_t}$$

Here VA represented nominal value added, F the quantity of factor input (here, labour), P the price of value added and π the productivity increase between periods $t-1$ and t; k was a number which was an instrument of economic policy. The whole expression was multiplied by the rate of tax. Tax returns would therefore depend on the change in value added and the change in productivity. This would enable one to tax the rate of increase in price. The idea had been dropped for administrative reasons. But it had been discussed between economists who found it difficult to draw conclusions, in particular because there was no very good theory of price formation under monopolistic competition, and one could not, of course, refer to perfect competition for this problem.

Professor Patinkin had enjoyed Professor de Wolff's paper, which drew on the wisdom of experience. However, one should not regard incomes policy as a substitute for other types of policy. Despite incomes policy, a big monetary expansion would lead to inflation. One could not use incomes policy successfully in any other context than an attempt to achieve social consensus on how to operate in a free democratic society where there was freedom to express differences of opinion with respect to the levels of wages and other incomes. In this case, one might be able to get consensus, but wherever there were conflicting demands there were pressures.

Incomes policy might be able to work by stabilising expectations, but because it had worked in small countries, one was bound to make the point that it was likely to be easier to get a consensus there.

Mr Plessz explained that the OECD had recently studied experience with incomes policies. There was evidence that small countries under floating exchange rates had often succeeded, in 1973–74, in keeping out imported cost-push inflation. But it was also necessary to reduce excess demand at home. The study had concentrated on the domestic generation of inflation, and the results had been more impressive than normal analysis.

Professor Lundberg wanted to stress the last issue in the paper. It seemed likely that one could get an atmosphere of greater understanding through profit-sharing. One needed increased profit for the growth and solvency of a given sector but not all these profits needed to go to shareholders. There was a dream, much discussed in Sweden, of a more generous society where wage-push was reduced and tolerance of high profits was increased. This was a dream – with no statistical evidence to support it – but a great deal of hope. Of course, economists who believed in the Phillips-curve were not so hopeful.

Professor de Wolff welcomed the remarks by Professor Nussbaumer. The Austrian record in the field of incomes policies had been very good indeed, and on the whole what Professor Nussbaumer said supported his own views. It emphasised the basis on which such policy could succeed, in particular the great importance of a favourable social climate. He agreed with Professor Patinkin that in small countries it was easier to pursue an incomes policy. In the United States, for example, differences in regional and social structure, as well as other factors, were perhaps too big to allow an incomes policy to succeed on a more permanent basis. Also the organisation of the labour market might cause difficulties, as centralised bargaining appeared to be one of the main conditions. This fact might also explain why it had proved to be harder to maintain an incomes policy in the United Kingdom. Even so, some authors argued that incomes policy did have a positive effect in the United States, in particular during the guide-post period. But it collapsed after some years as, due to other policy measures, the climate became too inflationary.

He did not agree that a constant share of wages in G.N.P. was an essential condition for a successful incomes policy. In the Netherlands, there had been an increase in the share of wages even during the years when the policy was still in full swing. On the whole, the share of labour had increased considerably, despite what Professor Bogomolov said. The position of the working class had improved not only due to the substantial increase of the G.N.P. per capita but also due to a rising share. Otherwise, Professor de Wolff did not think that incomes policy could contribute very much to a reduction of the rate of inflation in small countries, though it could have a favourable influence on employment.

To Professor Polaczek he would say that it had been a prime target of economic policy in the Netherlands at the end of the war to keep wage and price increases low in order to restore and maintain the country's competitive position. Probably the level of wages and prices had been kept too low for too long. In the 1950s the Netherlands was a cheap country, and with hindsight the conclusion seemed justified that it would not have been possible to maintain prices at so low a level even without the EEC. But the formation of the Common Market increased the pressure that had led to wage and price inflation after 1963. The resulting rate of inflation during that period would not now be seen as so remarkable, but, at 6 per cent, it was felt to be very high at the time. Now the Netherlands was no longer a cheap country.

To Professor Lundberg he had to admit that he had been speaking a little too loosely in saying that there had been no incomes policy in Germany and Sweden. At this point his classification was not correct. But with respect to Sweden he had been thinking of the reluctance of its Government to interfere in wage negotiations. He would like to add that it was sometimes said that Sweden had an invisible incomes policy due to its centralised bargaining system and the fact that, for many decades, it had had a socialist Government maintaining good relations with the trade unions.

On the example of the French tax system mentioned by Professor Malinvaud, he observed that similar policies had been worked out for wage increases. These had depended on a rather complex formula, in which national productivity and sectoral productivity increases played a role. It was not clear to him to what extent this system had worked.

Professor de Wolff had been impressed by the paper mentioned by Mr Plessz which he had seen during the conference. It showed that during the period of floating currencies a number of small countries with prices and incomes policies (Austria, Finland, Netherlands, Norway and Sweden) had had less strong price increases than the remaining countries of Europe, though during the 1960s they had done no better or even slightly worse. But the result had to be considered with great precaution as most of the countries mentioned had still sizeable price increases in the pipe line.

Finally, again to Professor Lundberg, he would say that profit-sharing might be a useful instrument to produce a conducive social climate. Trade unions in several countries were very keen on this issue. In particular, in the Netherlands, profit-sharing could very well be a fundamental condition for making the trade unions agree to a less inflationary incomes policy.

19 Aspects of the Theory of Indexed Bonds

David Levhari and Nissan Liviatan
DEPARTMENT OF ECONOMICS
THE HEBREW UNIVERSITY OF JERUSALEM

I. INTRODUCTION

The recent worldwide inflation precipitated an intensive discussion on ways and means that will reduce the social cost of the inflationary process. One of the main proposals put forward by many economists is the use of indexation or escalator agreements to make it easier to live with inflation.[1] In particular, economists often recommend the use of index-linked bonds by government or private institutions as an appropriate tool to mitigate the cost of inflation.[2] The idea has been expressed that linked bonds could be introduced in the private capital market to the mutual benefits of lenders and borrowers in handling more efficiently inflation risks.

The problem is, of course, whether the introduction of linked-bonds markets will generate a market equilibrium satisfactory not only to lender but also to the borrower as well. It is frequently asserted that the reluctance of borrowers to engage in linked borrowing seems to prevent the development of this market. However, it is not hard to prove formally on the basis of risk theory, that without existence of legal barriers or transaction costs, a market for indexed bonds should develop to the mutual benefit of lenders and borrowers. Yet we seldom find a development of such indexed bonds in the most advanced financial markets.

We concentrate, in the following, mainly on the risk-taking aspects of indexed bonds as compared with regular bonds and not on whether the introduction of such bonds will help (or disturb) the fight against inflation. However, one of the problems discussed in our framework is whether the effects of the introduction of linked bonds may encourage savings.

The fact that private markets for linked bonds do not seem to develop easily by themselves raises the possibility of government intermediation in indexed

[1] As one example see, M. Friedman, 'Using Escalators to Help Fight Inflation', *Fortune* (July, 1974).

[2] See, e.g., G. L. Bach and R. A. Musgrave, 'A Stable Purchasing Power Bond', *American Economic Review*, 1941, pp. 823–25; R. A. Goode, 'A Constant Purchasing Power Saving Bond', *National Tax Journal* (1951), pp. 332–340; A. Morag, 'For An Inflation Proof Economy', *American Economic Review* (1962), pp. 177–85; M. Friedman, 'Using Escalators to Help Fight Inflation', *Fortune* (July, 1974).

bonds market. We analyse some aspects of this problem and state some conditions under which government intervention in the market for linked bonds may encourage savings by individuals. However, since the government's gains or losses on the linked transaction are transmitted (in general equilibrium framework) back to the consumers it is not clear whether the overall level of risk associated with inflation is reduced by government intervention in the bond market.

The analysis is generalised to a multicommodities world in which the individual is sensitive to the association of his own source of income with the price level of his consumption basket. In particular, we show that if individuals are pessimistic in their expectations concerning the prices of endowed (or produced) commodities than the reluctance of people to borrow indexed, will increase.

Index-linked bonds is a 'second best' arrangement to that of an ideal Arrow–Debreu system of contingent claims. We discuss, finally, the nature of the restriction of indexed bonds compared with the ideal markets.

II. THE MODEL[1]

Consider an individual consumer with a two-period planning horizon. The individual consumes a single commodity and has a demand for real cash balances. In the first period he has an endowment of y_1 units and consumes c units of commodity. He also has an endowment of $\overline{M}$ nominal dollars and wishes to hold M dollars (which yields direct utility as a consumers' good). He also spends B_N dollars on non-linked bonds (B_N can be negative). Assuming for the moment no linked bonds, his budget constraint for the first period is given by

$$p_1(y_1 - c) + (\overline{M} - M) = B_N \tag{1}$$

where p_1 is the price of the commodity in dollars. Let W denote the dollar value of his wealth in the second period. Then

$$W = M + iB_N + p_2 y_2 \tag{2}$$

where i is one plus the nominal interest rate on bonds and p_2 is the price of the commodity in the second period. The real value of W is then

$$\frac{W}{p_2} = w = (m + ib_N)\,\pi + y_2 \tag{3}$$

where $m = \dfrac{M}{p_1}$, $b_N = \dfrac{B_N}{p_1}$, $\pi = \dfrac{p_1}{p_2}$. Suppose that p_2, and hence π, is the only random variable in the system. Then the expected value of w (denoted $\overline{w}$) and

[1] The description of the model is identical with that of N. Liviatan and D. Levhari, 'Risk and The Theory of Indexed Bonds', *Research Report 67*, Department of Economics, The Hebrew University, Jerusalem (March, 1975).

its variance (denoted V_w) are given by

$$\bar{w} = (m + ib_N)\bar{\pi} + y;\ V_w = (m + ib_N)^2 V_\pi \tag{4}$$

where V_π is the variance of the value of money.

Consider two individuals who engage in a transaction involving non-linked bonds, i.e., for the lender $b_N > 0$ and for the borrower $b_N < 0$ and of equal absolute amount. If both individuals have no demand for money ($m = 0$) then it can be shown that their non-linked transaction is dominated by a linked one, assuming both individuals are risk-averse and have the same $\bar{\pi}$.

The linked transaction involves lending (borrowing) an amount of B_L dollars and receiving next period $rB_L \frac{p_2}{p_1}$ where r is one plus the real interest rate and $\frac{p_2}{p_1}$ represents the linkage factor. The value of w under pure linkage is then

$$w = m\pi + rb_L + y_2 \tag{5}$$

where $b_L = \frac{B_L}{p_1}$. Analogously to (4) we now have

$$w = m\bar{\pi} + rb_L + y_2,\ V_w = m^2 V_\pi. \tag{6}$$

Consider linked and non-linked transactions as *mutually exclusive* alternatives and let $b = b_N = b_L$. Let us set r to be equal to $i\bar{\pi}$ (the price-deflated nominal interest factor). Then, given the non-linked transaction, the linked one will have the same expected value. However, if $m = 0$ we have $V_w = 0$ under the linked transaction while $V_w = (ib_N)^2 V\pi > 0$ under the non-linked one. Applying the mean-variance criterion to w we find that both the lender *and* the borrower will prefer to switch from the non-linked transaction to the linked one. The foregoing result may also be applied to the non-linked part of any *mixed* (linked and non-linked) transaction. Hence there cannot exist a market for non-linked bonds, since they are dominated by the linked ones. This may be considered as a possible rationalisation of the economists' 'bias' towards linked bonds. Thus, linked bonds eliminate unnecessary risk-bearing by both lender and borrower.

This result is no longer true when the individuals hold positive amounts of money (or for that matter other nominal assets or incomes). Denoting by D_V the difference in the variance of w under non-linked and linked transactions we find

$$D_V = ib(2m + ib)\ V_\pi. \tag{7}$$

This is always positive for the lender ($b > 0$) who will therefore still prefer the linked transaction (assuming as before $r = i\bar{\pi}$). However, if the *borrower* is still to prefer the linked transaction we need the condition $2m + ib < 0$ or

$$-b > \frac{2m}{i} \tag{8}$$

in other words, the absolute value of the loan must be sufficiently in excess of his money holdings. If however his holdings of monetary assets are in excess of his borrowing (by a proper factor) then the borrower will prefer the non-linked transaction. Thus we have no longer unambiguous dominance of linked bonds.

The economic explanation for this basic difference in the attitudes of lenders and borrowers to linkage is simple. For the lender the increase in the price level reduces both the real value of his money holdings and of non-linked bonds. However, for the *borrower*, while this will still reduce the real value of his money assets, it will at the same time reduce the real burden of his debt, and hence tend to increase his net wealth. Thus for the borrower, non-linked bonds provide a hedge against inflationary losses of real balances.[1]

It may be noted that the condition $2m + ib > 0$ rules out the possibility of dominance of linked bonds for $r = i\bar{\pi}$ but not necessarily for other $r < i\bar{\pi}$. Indeed, if we set $r < i\bar{\pi}$ then, in some cases we may find a sufficiently low value of r which will induce the borrower to borrow linked and will still leave the lender better off in the linked rather than in the non-linked alternative. There is, however, no special reason to believe that this will be the case. It is just as likely that no r can be found which will make the linked transaction acceptable to both parties involved.

The foregoing analysis may suggest that the more important is the non-linked sector in the economy, the smaller is the change of a market for linked bonds to develop to sizeable proportions. It also suggests that if during the inflationary process an increasing proportion of nominal incomes is being 'indexed' the chance of a linked bonds market to develop increases. This is based on the observation that in the extreme case where all nominal incomes and money become linked, then the linked bonds must dominate the bond market.

III. MIXED PORTFOLIO

The dominance of linked bonds when $m = 0$ can also be established directly for a market in which we have both linked and non-linked bonds. The market for non-linked bonds becomes active only when we have non-linked assets (represented by m) in the economy. In fact, the size of the non-linked assets places a constraint on the equilibrium size of non-linked borrowing.

When the consumer may hold a mixed portfolio his budget, equations

[1] A similar point has been made in C. G. Fane, 'Index Linking and Inflation', *National Institute Economic Review* (November, 1974), p. 42.

become

$$b_N = y_1 - c + \overline{m} - m - b_L \tag{9}$$

$$w = (m = ib_N)\,\pi + rb_L + y_2.$$

Let us assume the following expected utility function

$$U = u\,(c, m) + f\,(\overline{w}, V_w) \tag{10}$$

which is based on the mean ($\overline{w}$)–variance (V_w) approach.

Using the first order condition for maximisation it is not hard to see that

$$\text{sign}\,(i\overline{\pi} - r) = \text{sign}\,(m + ib_N)$$

that is, assuming $\overline{\pi}$ identical for everybody, the sign of the difference of the expected real interest on nominal bonds and that on index-linked bonds is that of $m + ib_N$. So the terms $m + ib_N$ have to be of the same sign for all consumers. Summing $(m + ib_N)$ over all consumers and using $\Sigma b_N = 0$ we obtain that the sum has to be positive, and hence $m + ib_N > 0$ for all individuals. This implies $i\overline{\pi} - r > 0$. Thus in coexistence of linked and non-linked bonds, non-indexed bonds should at equilibrium command some risk premium over indexed bonds. The size of the premium depends on the individuals' composition of incomes as well as their preferences.

IV. UNSTABLE VALUE OF MONEY AND THE INCENTIVE TO INTRODUCE LINKED BONDS

We have seen that instability in the real value of money does not imply any sort of dominance of linked over non-linked bonds. Is it, however, true that as the instability of value of money *increases* the market will exhibit an increasing tendency to shift from non-linked to linked bonds? To analyse this question, we shall consider the effect of an increase in V_π on the volume of the value of transactions on linked and non-linked bond markets. We take V_π as our independent variable because it is the unanticipated variation of π which is at the heart of the linking procedure. Surely, when the value of money has zero variance, there is no need for linked bonds even when the rate of inflation is high. Thus it seems plausible to concentrate on the *variance* of the value of money (we shall also assume that other characteristics of the distribution of π are held constant).

Let us deal with a mixed market (linked and non-linked) and consider the effect of increasing V_π on the volume of transactions in the linked and non-linked markets. We can approach this problem by working out the reactions of the individual consumer to this change. To simplify the analysis we shall assume $u_{cm} \geqslant 0$ and a quadratic f in (10):

$$f(\overline{w}, V_w) - \alpha\overline{w} - \beta(\overline{w}^2 + V_w) \tag{11}$$

with $\alpha, \beta > 0$ and $\alpha - 2\beta\overline{w} > 0$. By differentiating the individual's equilibrium conditions with respect to V_π we can obtain[1] the following changes in the optimal values of c, m, b_L and b_N

$$\frac{db_L}{dV_\pi} > 0, \frac{dm}{dV_\pi} < 0, \frac{dc}{dV_\pi} < 0 \tag{12}$$

$$\frac{db_N}{dV_\pi} < 0 \quad \text{if} \quad r > \bar{\pi}. \tag{12^1}$$

Thus an increase in the variance of the value of money increases the demand for linked bonds at the expense of all other decision variables. All this is based on the assumption that $m + ib_N > 0$ which is required for market equilibrium. We also used the condition $i\bar{\pi} > r$ which is again derived from market equilibrium. This latter condition is however not required for the result $\frac{db_L}{dV_\pi} > 0$. For $\frac{db_N}{dV_\pi}$ the condition $r \geqslant \bar{\pi}$ is sufficient but not necessary. This condition will certainly be satisfied in inflation ($\bar{\pi} = E\frac{p_1}{p_2} < 1$) if the real rate of interest $(r - 1)$ is non-negative. Although in a model without production the latter condition is not necessarily satisfied, it seems still reasonable to suppose that $\bar{\pi} < r$ holds.

The main fact which we wish to emphasise with respect to $\frac{db_L}{dV_\pi} > 0$ is that it holds for both lender and borrower of linked bonds. Thus, while for the lender ($b_L > 0$) there will be a tendency to lend more when V_π increases there will be, at the same time, a tendency for the borrower ($b_L < 0$) to borrow less. Since the supply of linked bonds shrinks at the same time as demand expands, it is not clear at all what the effect on the volume of transactions will be.

For the *non-linked regime* (when linked bonds are arbitrarily excluded) we obtain under the same assumptions.[2]

$$\frac{dc}{dV_\pi} > 0, \frac{dm}{dV_\pi} > 0, \frac{db_N}{dV_\pi} < 0. \tag{13}$$

[1] See derivation of these results in Liviatan and Levhari, *op. cit.*, Appendix A-1.

[2] It should be noted that the crucial assumption in this calculation is that $m + ib_N > 0$ for everybody. This is a more natural assumption for the mixed regime, since there it must follow from market equilibrium constraints within the framework of the present model. In particular it follows from the fact that the lender of a non-linked loan will require a risk premium. This constraint does not exist in the non-linked regime. It follows therefore that in the latter regime we shall have the results stated in equation (13) for all lenders ($b_N > 0$) and for the relatively 'small' borrowers (for whom $b_N < 0$ and $ib_N + m > 0$). Thus there seems to be some tendency for the economy as a whole to react as in equation (13), especially when non-linked assets and incomes, represented by m, are quantitatively important. In view of this remark we shall assume accordingly that equation (13) holds for the economy as whole, although this need not necessarily be true for every individual.

The most interesting aspect of the foregoing comparison of equations (12) and (13) is that under the non-linked regime an increase in V_π tends to increase the demand for current consumption, while under the linked regime V_π has the opposite effect (in other words, encouraging saving). The reason for this seems to be the fact that under the non-linked regime an increase in V_π reduces the incentive to transfer wealth to the future period since all available assets become more risky. This does not happen of course when the consumer may invest in safe linked bonds.

In the foregoing models we have either fully linked or completely non-linked financial assets. In practice we have of course many types of securities with various degrees of 'linkage' to the general price level. Our results suggest, however, that when the linkage elements in the various securities is small then an increase in V_π will lead to reduced saving. In this case the introduction of a market for linked bonds will prevent the level of saving from falling under increased instability in the value of money.[1] It also means that under a non-linked regime an increase in V_π will tend to increase the inflationary pressure. In fact one of the most common arguments of governments to introduce indexed bonds is that it encourages savings and therefore reduces the inflationary pressures.

The other difference between the two regimes is that an increase in V_π increases the demand for money under the non-linked regime and reduces it under a mixed regime. The explanation for the parallel changes in c and m seems to lie in the consumption aspect of holding real balances (these enter the utility function in the same way as c). The accumulation aspect of the change in m can always be counteracted by an appropriate change in bonds.

In the foregoing analysis we compared the reaction of the two regimes to a change in V_π. Let us now consider the effects of shifting from one regime to the other holding V_π constant. Suppose that we are originally in the non-linked regime with b_L with artificially excluded. Let us consider the preliminary problem of introducing a *compulsory* indexed loan with r not exceeding $i\bar{\pi}$ Note that, since we have a perfect market for non-linked bonds, the compulsory (positive) b_L can always be sterilised by the consumer by borrowing non-linked. The effect of the compulsory loan on net saving is therefore evident immediately.

If we start with equilibrium in the non-linked regime and then free the consumer to purchase a unit of b_L, the effects on c and m are as follows:

$$\frac{dc}{db_L} < 0, \; \frac{dm}{db_L} < 0. \tag{14}$$

[1] It should be noted that in a model without production the total demand for consumption (c) must be equal to the total amount of physical endowments y_1). Thus c cannot change for the economy as a whole in equilibrium. However when production takes place an increased demand for current consumption will tend to reduce the level of real capital formation. For this result to follow it is necessary that the securities associated with the production assets should possess a low degree of linkages to the general price level.

This shows that the introduction of compulsory linked bonds tends to discourage current consumption (this may include consumption of liquidity services of money).

The foregoing analysis has some additional implication. Suppose first that instead of imposing a compulsory loan the government issues linked bonds to the public with $r < i\bar{\pi}$. Then all the individuals which originally had $\frac{\partial U}{db_L} > 0$ (at $b_L = 0$) will be interested to acquire linked bonds, while those with $\frac{\partial U}{\partial b_L} \leqslant 0$ will remain inactive, since the government does not buy bonds. However those who willingly purchase linked bonds can be assumed to behave as if they were subjected to a compulsory loan. It then follows that the introduction of linked bonds by the government will tend to discourage current consumption.

Another implication concerns the effect of introducing a private linked bonds market after it has been arbitrarily excluded. The consumers with $\frac{\partial U}{\partial b_L} > 0$ will then be interested in buying linked bonds while those with $\frac{\partial U}{\partial b_L} < 0$ will be interested in selling (that is 'reduce' b_L). It then follows from equation (14) that the former will reduce their current consumption, while the latter will increase it. The net effect on consumption of introducing a *private* market for linked bonds is therefore unclear. This is in contrast to the earlier case where the *government* alone issues linked bonds to the public. We shall later return to methods by which the government may manage the linked bonds market.

In the foregoing discussion we considered the case of an arbitrarily excluded market for linked bonds. In practice, however, we often find that a private market for linked bonds is voluntarily excluded. This phenomenon is hard to explain. Formally, the condition for non-existence of a market for linked bonds is extremely strict and cannot be expected to be fulfilled in practice. The condition is that the marginal rate of substitution between the present and future consumption will be identical for all individuals. This is the Irving Fisher condition, in a two-period world, that there will be no lender or borrowers.

In reality on the other hand, one observes the non-existence of these markets. To explain this phenomenon one probably needs to introduce transaction costs or legal impediments (such as legal difficulties in imposing a contract contingent on a change in the price index or in the proper treatment of indexed interest for income tax purposes). Since in practice we often find that no private market for linked bonds exists at all, it is important to investigate the precise nature of the foregoing barriers for the existence of these markets even on a small scale. At the present stage we cannot provide good answers to the foregoing problem. In the following discussion we shall sometimes have to assume the existence of these barriers without specifying their exact nature.

V. ENDOGENOUS INFLATION AND THE ELIMINATION OF INFLATION RISK

All the discussion up to now has been carried under the assumption that the inflation is exogenous. In this case nominal bonds have an expected risk premium $i\overline{\pi} > r$. However if we assume a purely monetary inflation where the government prints money to make transfer payments to individuals, these transfer payments constitute the basic exogenous random variable of the system.

The transfer payments T_j in the economy as a whole will of course effect p_2 and hence also π. Let us take this relationship into account by adopting a quantity approach. In particular let us assume that the value of *real* balances in the economy in the second period λ is a constant[1] (the amount of goods in the second period being constant), or

$$\frac{\Sigma \overline{M}_j + \Sigma T_j}{p_2} = \lambda \tag{15}$$

where the summation is over all individuals $j = 1, \ldots n$. It will be assumed that all individuals calculate the value of p_2 from equation (15).

It is then possible to show[2] that if individuals' price expectations are determined according to (15) then in a market equilibrium the risk premium is zero. Furthermore, the securities markets will eliminate completely the inflation risk. This is accomplished not by just using linked bonds but by using *non-linked* bonds as well as a hedge against inflationary losses on non-linked assets and incomes. A change in V_π, in the variance of purchasing power of money does not change the optimum level of any of the decision variables c, w, b_L and b_N.

VI. GOVERNMENT INTERMEDIATION IN THE BONDS MARKET

As the development of an indexed bonds market has rarely occurred in practice it has been suggested that an establishment of a government agency that would intermediate in the bonds market could be beneficial. One may consider an agency which will act on the following principles: it borrows through indexed-linked bonds and lends non-linked to the individual agents of the economy. The agency creates a supply of linked bonds for individual savers and demands non-linked-nominal bonds from 'firms' and other individual agents.

The agency pays on each dollar it borrows $r\frac{p_2}{p_1} = \frac{r}{\pi}$ and it gets i. Thus in real, second period, magnitudes its profit is $B^*(i\pi - r)$ where B^* is the value of its borrowing (or lending). Assume that the agency's 'shareholders' (all citizens) cover the company's losses and benefit from its profits. This is accomplished

[1] λ can be made to depend on interest rates and on parameters of the distribution of π without affecting the following results.

[2] Liviatan and Levhari, *op. cit.*, pp. 25–30.

through positive or negative transfer payments. For example, if the rate of inflation is higher than anticipated, that is $i\pi - r < 0$, the population is taxed to cover the agency's losses. The taxation imposed on a particular individual is independent of his own borrowing or lending and is on the average equal to $b^* (i\pi - r)$ where $b^* > 0$ is the per capita real value of the outstanding indexed bonds issued by the government agency. In the present case the individual's second period wealth constraint is:

$$\begin{aligned} w &= y_2 + b_L r + b_N i\pi + m\pi + b^* (i\pi - r) \\ &= y_2 + b_L r + [m + i(b_N + b^*)]\, \pi - rb^*. \end{aligned} \tag{16}$$

In order to evaluate the effect of the agency's operation on the private sector it is useful to distinguish between two cases. Namely, where some market for linked bonds does exist originally and the case where no such market exists at all. Let us consider first the case where a small private market for linked bonds exists and the government plans to increase its size through the agency. Now the agency creates a supply of linked bonds and a demand of equal magnitude (in value terms) on non-linked bonds. This will ordinarily result in a reduction of the price of linked bonds (increasing r) and in an increase in price of non-linked bonds (reducing i). In the ordinary model of mixed (linked and non-linked bonds) model $i\bar{\pi} - r$ is positive. Hence the operation of the agency will tend to reduce the foregoing risk premium.

One may evaluate the consequences of the agency's operation from two points of view – namely whether it tends to reduce demand for current consumption (increase saving) and whether it increases consumers' welfare. As far as the effect on the demand for c is concerned, the answer seems ambiguous since the two rates of return ($i\bar{\pi}$ and r) move in opposite directions. As for an improvement in welfare, we have argued elsewhere[1] that one cannot say definitely that something may be gained by pooling of individual risks through the agency (applying the Arrow–Lind approach).

We can make some additional comments about the welfare implications. The agency forces the economy to change the *laissez-faire* allocation of assets. This in itself cannot improve overall welfare unless there is some 'externality' involved. Now the only 'external' element which arises through the government intermediation is the transfer payments mechanism which adds to the individuals an exogenous random income $b^* (i\pi - r)$ as in equation (16). It can be shown, however, that this additional element cannot improve the individuals' welfare in a mixed market.

The more relevant case to consider is the one where initially there is no market for linked bonds. The crucial question in assessing the role of government intermediation in this case concerns the basic reason for the non-existence of a private market for linked bonds. If the reason is related to high real transaction costs then this case seems to be similar to the foregoing one and

[1] Liviatan and Levhari, *op. cit.*, p. 32.

government intervention in the *laissez-faire* system does not seem justified as means of increasing consumers' welfare.

The more relevant case for government intervention seems to be the one where the reasons for non-existence of a private market for linked bonds are not economic transaction costs. Thus suppose that the government discriminates in various ways against privately issued linked bonds. Alternatively the government may consider, for income tax purposes, the nominal capital appreciation (due to inflation) of a linked loan as a regular taxable income of the lender but it may not allow it as a deductible expense of the borrower. This practice introduces a 'wedge' between the net interest of the lender and the borrower (the net r of the former being lower). It follows that the excess demand curve for linked bonds will have a 'jump' at zero volume, as one passes from lending to borrowing. When supply of linked bonds is small relative to demand this may eliminate the market for linked bonds completely, the demand curve being below the supply curve for any volume of transactions.

The simplest way of handling these impediments to linked transactions is of course to abolish them. Suppose however that this is not possible for various reasons. Thus in the foregoing example of differential tax treatment the government will lose tax income if it allows the borrowers to deduct their nominal capital loss, due to linkage, from taxable income. We may then enquire into the effect of issuing government linked bonds to the public through the mechanism of the agency. We shall assume that the transfer payment $b^*(i\pi - r)$ is the same for every individual independently of his transaction with the agency. Consequently b^* is smaller than the amount of b_L acquired by the average lender. Similarly b^* is smaller than the amount borrowed from the agency by the representative borrower. It can be shown that the agency will have to set r lower than $i\bar{\pi}$. This means that the system cannot operate with a fair insurance principle and without a premium of non-linked over linked.

In order to examine intuitively the welfare effects of the agency's operation consider the following experiment. The agency sells a value of linked bonds with $r < i\bar{\pi}$ to the representative lender who reduces by the same value his initial non-linked lending (b_N). The representative borrower borrows from the agency a non-linked sum and reduces by the same amount his initial borrowing from private individuals (total borrowing being equal to total lending).

Ordinarily $\overline{w}$ and V_w of private individuals change in the same direction as a result of the agency's operation and consequently the effect on welfare is ambiguous. One may argue that if both lenders and borrowers trade willingly with the agency then they cannot be made worse off by it. Note however that this argument holds only for the 'trading' aspect of the agency's activity. In addition, there is a *coercive* element associated with the fiscal aspect of the transfer payments mechanism. The latter element which introduces random variability in disposable income may in many cases offset the advantages offered by better diversification.

Let us consider now the effect of the agency's operations on the demand for current consumption. We have noted earlier that the sale of linked bonds by the government tends to reduce demand for current consumption. However, in order to see the complete picture we have also to analyse the effect of the transfer payments mechanism associated with the agency's operation. To obtain some idea about this effect we consider the model with w redefined as

$$w = (m + ib_N)\pi + y_2 + b^*(i\pi - r)$$

where $b^*(i\pi - r)$ is a transfer payment of the same nature as in the case of the agency. This definition of w is appropriate for those consumers who do not buy linked bonds from the agency.[1] For those who do invest in linked agency bonds one may expect that the uncertainty generated by the transfer payment may encourage people to reduce current consumption and invest still more in linked bonds, as the results in equation (9) tend to indicate. Thus the transfer payments system seems to have different effects on different individuals with no conclusive direction for the economy as a whole.

VII. MANY COMMODITIES

Up to now we neglected the major fact that prices do not change uniformly in the same proportions. Some of the major objections to indexation come from the agents that claim that they cannot borrow through indexed linked bonds and face the extra risk that the product they supply will rise in price less than the general price level.

The rule of division of labour is such that while most individuals obtain their incomes in terms of few commodities their consumption basket includes almost all commodities. The fact that the price of the product they produce may not rise in the same proportion as the rise in the cost of their consumption basket adds another source of riskiness which should be discussed in the framework of indexed versus nominal bonds.

We assume that prices are exogenous and that each consumer obtains his income in commodities. In period $t (t = 1, 2)$ he gets y_{t_j} of good j. We denote by p_{t_j} the price of the j commodity in period t. We assume the existence of an 'ideal price index' $p_t = \Sigma\theta_j p_{t_j}, \theta_j \geqslant 0, \Sigma\theta_j = 1$. (In reality it is probable that different consumers have different price indices so that there is added uncertainty due to the fact that the 'ideal price index' for a particular consumer does not change proportionately to the index to which indexed bonds are linked.) Also, in general the ideal index, when one exists, will not be a linear function of individual prices.

We compare the cases in which with many commodities all bonds are either nominal or indexed but there is no mixed market. It turns out that the crucial element is whether the goods endowed (or produced) by the individual are

[1] It can be seen intuitively that the additional term b^* introduces additional variability in consumers' wealth. A formal analysis of the implication of this fact shows that it tends to encourage current consumption for those who do not invest in linked bonds.

relatively sticky or leading the general price index. Thus if for a particular individual his incomes are nominal or sticky then its effect is like an increase in his m or nominal assets. Hence it would *reduce* the desire of the borrower to prefer linked over non-linked transactions. The lender, on the other hand, would increase his demand for linked investment. On the other hand, if his prices are leading, for the borrower this reduces his preference for non-linked assets and his incentive to hedge by non-linked borrowing. It will increase his wish to enter into linked transactions.

It is possible that the consumers on the average are biased in the pessimistic direction assuming that their own prices will on the average change less than the general price level. Then the effect of having many endowed commodities is like increasing the amount of non-linked assets in the economy with all its implications – that is, an additional source of demand for non-linked bonds.

It is not hard to generalise the multicommodities case, with few additional single assumptions, that nominal bonds will carry a risk premium over indexed bonds – $i\bar{\pi} - r > 0$.

VIII. CONTINGENT MARKET VERSUS INDEXATION

A full set of contingent markets with appropriate possibilities of trading between individuals, contingent among other things on the level of inflation, is Pareto optimal. The question may be asked in what sense are contingent markets superior over the possibility of linking or indexing future incomes through bonds holding.

Let there be S states of nature $s = 1, 2, \ldots S$.[1] At state s the individual obtains an endowment y_s and plans to consume c_s. With Arrow–Debreu securities the individual is able to buy a contingent bond guaranteeing a nominal dollar at state s. He acquires Q_s bonds of this type with a price of v_s per bond promising to pay a nominal dollar at state s (and nothing otherwise). The price v_s is in terms of present dollars. Let us denote p_s the price level that would prevail if state s occurs.

In the case of indexed-linked bonds the consumer transfers to the second period (through index bonds acquisition) the same real resources regardless of the state of nature. This is an additional restriction which does not exist in an ideal contingent market. The question is whether the individual in a contingent market would purchase bonds in such amounts so that the transfer to the second period would be invariant to the state of nature – that is, whether $\frac{Q_s}{p_s}$ is a constant independent of S.

It is clear that it is rather accidental for a consumer in a contingent market to have $\frac{Q_s}{p_s}$ constant in his optimal behaviour. Thus the case of indexation can be looked upon as a contingent market mechanism with the additional con-

[1] The different states of the world are characterised by different initial endowments of commodities and by different amounts of government transfer payments.

straint $\frac{Q_s}{p_s} = \frac{Q_{s'}}{p_{s'}}$ for all states s and s'. We have an additional $S - 1$ constraint in the consumer maximising behaviour. Without these additional constraints the individual having different y_s across states of nature would like to transfer different amounts. Moreover, with different p_s we will have different $\frac{M}{p_s}$ and would therefore like to transfer different real values of bonds to the different states of nature. The higher the expected inflation the more we would like to transfer in contingent bonds.

As the indexed linked bond is a rather second best arrangement, one may think of a whole array of arrangements between indexation and nominal bonds. Thus one may think of partial indexation where the lender receives the nominal interest if the price rise is below a certain level and the bond is fully indexed if the price level rises above this level. The nominal rate below the critical level might be expected to be below that on full nominal bonds while the real rate for the bond above the critical level may be expected to be above that for regular linked-indexed bonds.

In fact, one may think about all sorts of different arrangements with different critical levels, or with a function of indexation which varies with the price rise. Thus it is possible that above a certain critical level we have full indexation and below it just fractional indexation with the fraction varying with the price level. All those are obviously second best arrangements to that of the existence of the full contingent markets.

20 On the Non-existence of Privately Issued Index Bonds in the United States Capital Market

Stanley Fischer[1]

MASSACHUSETTS INSTITUTE OF TECHNOLOGY

I. INTRODUCTION

'Why, if both borrower and lender benefit from them, [does] an index loan market . . . not develop spontaneously and without any government initiative'? This question, asked by Professor Arvidsson at the I.E.A. conference on inflation in 1962,[2] provides the major theme for the present paper which pursues in some detail possible reasons for the non-existence of privately issued index bonds in the United States.

In an earlier paper, I used portfolio theory and the capital asset pricing model to study the demand for index bonds and some properties of equilibrium in a capital market with equity assets as well as indexed and nominal bonds [7], and in which individuals may also own (but not sell) human capital. The major conclusions of that paper are that the equilibrium relationship between the real yields on indexed and nominal bonds depends on the extent to which equity and human capital are hedges against inflation[3] – the real yield on index bonds tends to be below that on nominal bonds to the extent that real returns on equity and human capital are negatively correlated with inflation; that, in the absence of human capital and with no relative price uncertainty, all private lending and borrowing would take place through indexed bonds; and that, with human capital, both types of bonds would in general be

[1] I am indebted to Richard Cohn, Martin Feldstein, Benjamin Friedman, Robert Merton and Stewart Myers for helpful discussions and to Olivier Blanchard and Mary Kay Plantes for excellent research assistance. Financial support from the National Science Foundation is acknowledged with thanks.

[2] Avidsson [1], p. 113. I should note that Professor Mossé, the discussant of Arvidsson's paper, was unimpressed by the question. 'Opponents of index loans said that if borrowers and lenders both wanted them, an index loan market would spring up spontaneously. This was a false argument, and needed refuting much more strongly than Professor Arvidsson had done. One might as well say that because the government built schools for children, people did not really want their children to have schools, or they would have built schools for themselves.' (From the Summary Record of the Debate, p. 402, in Hague (1962)).

[3] In the sense that their real returns are positively correlated with inflation.

expected to exist. I noted that the analysis did not throw much light on the non-existence of indexed bonds in most major capital markets.

The non-existence of privately issued index bonds in the United States is a phenomenon requiring explanation for two main reasons. First, the tying of contracts to the price level is not unknown nor even especially unusual in the United States: labour contracts, certain aspects of insurance contracts and the prices to be paid for future delivery of manufactured products have all been tied to the price level.[1] Second, there has been no dearth of innovation in the financial area over the years, although those innovations taking the form of the issue of new types of securities by existing firms – such as the certificate of deposit and the floating rate note – have been undertaken mainly by banks.

The previous paper concentrated on the demand for index bonds and equilibrium in a market composed of lifetime–utility-maximising households. However, the most likely private issuers of index bonds are corporations. Accordingly the emphasis in this paper is on the supply of index bonds by firms, whose assumed motivation is the maximisation of their stock market value.

It is well known that in the absence of bankruptcy and the differential tax treatment of equity returns and interest and under certain other assumptions, the Modigliani–Miller theorem [16] establishes that the value of the firm is independent of its debt structure – that is, that under the postulated conditions, there is no good reason for firms to issue one sort of debt rather than another. It is accordingly necessary to develop a rationale for the type of debt issued by a firm. Section II outlines a simple theory of the supply of bonds, based on the existence of bankruptcy costs and the tax treatment of interest as a business expense,[2] which is used in parts of the remainder of the paper to evaluate some arguments typically advanced to explain the non-issuance of indexed bonds by private firms [1] and [10].

Section III examines the view that firms should be more willing to issue index bonds the greater the (positive) correlation of their profits with the price level, and also presents evidence on the correlation of the real profits of some American corporations with the price level. Because the theory makes clear the crucial role of the tax treatment of indexed payments, section IV very briefly examines the ambiguous tax status of such payments in the United States. Section V considers the argument that systematic underestimation of inflation is responsible for the non-appearance of indexed bonds. Section VI

[1] The indexation of labour contracts is well-documented (see, for example Sparrough and Bolton [18]). The existence of indexation in other types of contracts is known from anecdote and personal knowledge, but the extent of such indexation has apparently not been documented.

[2] The theory is developed in greater detail in Fischer [8]; the two elements of differential tax treatment of interest and dividends and bankruptcy costs are used by Kraus and Litzenberger [14] to develop a theory of optimal financial leverage in a model where there is a full set of contingent commodities. The theory developed in Fischer [8] uses the mean variance version of the capital asset pricing model to avoid assuming a full set of contingent commodities, in which case the consumer or a mutual fund could construct an index bond.

reviews the argument that index bonds have not been issued because such bonds would saddle firms with open-ended obligations which nominal bonds with call-clause protection do not. Two further explanations for non-issuance of index bonds are considered: section VII examines the variability of the rate of inflation over the past twenty years; section VIII discusses the costs of innovation and the possibility that a large-scale change in the form of debt issues would be easier to accomplish than piecemeal changes. Conclusions are contained in section IX. An appendix compares the variability of hypothetical profit streams for sixteen United States firms, constructed on the assumption that all their long-term debt issues over the period were indexed, with the variability of their actual profit streams.

II. THE SUPPLY OF INDEX BONDS

The theory developed in Fischer [8] uses the capital asset pricing model [12] to examine the financing decision of a firm that has made an investment decision in period one which will produce (uncertain) real profits in period two. Real profits are assumed to have a random component that is uniformly distributed and independent of the price level, and also to have a component that is corelated with the purchasing power of money (the inverse of the general price level) in period two. The purchasing power of money in turn has a simple two-point symmetric distribution and its expectation for period two is the same as its value in period one.[1]

The firm is assumed to sell claims on its second period profits in the capital market. Two possible combinations of asset supplies by the firm are examined. In the first, the firm can sell indexed bonds and equity. It promises to pay an amount W in real terms to holders of index bonds, provided its profits are at least W. Such payments are treated as business expenses. Any amount of profits not paid out to index bond holders is distributed to equity holders, after payment of taxes at rate τ. If the firm's profits are less than W, it is bankrupt. In such a case, equity holders receive no payments. Certain fixed real bankruptcy costs are assumed to be incurred and bondholders receive either zero or profits minus the bankruptcy costs, whichever is greater, in the event of bankruptcy.

The elements of the theory of the supply of index bonds are accordingly simple. The issue of bonds produces a tax advantage, but the more bonds are issued, the greater the probability of bankruptcy. Thus bonds will be issued to the point at which the tax benefit balances the expected bankruptcy costs.[2] It

[1] Since it is only uncertainty about price level that matters for the analysis, no substantive results depend on the assumption that the average purchasing power of money is not expected to change.

[2] This is the essence of the view advanced by Kraus and Litzenberger [14]. This theory fails to explain the existence of bonds before the corporate income tax. Interesting papers by Jensen and Meckling [13] and Myers [17] explore the determinants of debt capacity in a longer-run perspective.

should be noted that in the absence of differential tax treatment of interest and profit distributions, no bonds would be issued by this firm.

In the capital asset pricing model assets issued by the firm are valued by the market on the basis of their expected return and the covariance of their returns with the market return. The market rate of return is assumed to have a random component that is distributed independently of the behaviour of the firm's profits except that the market rate of return is correlated with the purchasing power of money. Empirical evidence suggests that the market rate of return in the United States is negatively correlated with unexpected changes in the price level and it is accordingly assumed that the market return is positively correlated with the purchasing power of money [3].

The result of the optimisation of stock market value by the firm is a supply function for index bonds: the supply of index bonds is positively related to the maximum profits the firm expects to earn and to the tax rate on corporate profits, and negatively related to the cost of bankruptcy. The effects of price level uncertainty on the issue of index bonds depends on the relationship between the firm's profits and the price level on the one hand, and the market rate of return and the price level on the other; if the firm's profits are related to the price level in the opposite direction to which the market's return is related to the price level, price uncertainty increases the firm's issue of index bonds; if the correlation between the firm's profits and the price level is of the same sign as the correlation of the market return with the price level, then the firm's issue of index bonds is reduced by price level uncertainty. Under the empirically justifiable assumption that the market return is inversely correlated with the price level [3], the firm's supply of index bonds is greater the greater the variance of the price level, and also, the greater the correlation of its profits with the price level.

In the second situation, the firm is assumed to issue nominal bonds and equity, again with the aim of maximising its stock market value. A supply function for nominal bonds by the firm is derived and the optimised value of the firm when it can issue nominal bonds and equity is calculated. The optimised values of the firm under the two combinations of asset issues are compared and the following results obtained:

(1) Neither type of bond – indexed or nominal – dominates the other from the viewpoint of the maximisation of the firm's stock market value. There are situations in which a firm issuing nominal bonds will command a greater stock market value than one issuing indexed bonds – such situations seem to require that both the market return and the firm's profits be inversely correlated with the price level – and there are also situations in which stock market value is higher if the firm issues indexed rather than nominal bonds.[1]

[1] It should be noted that we are not here allowing the firm to issue both types of bonds simultaneously, though it is quite likely that such an option would generate a greater stock market value for the firm than the issue of only one type of bond. Our major concern, however, is to show that neither type of bond dominates the other.

(2) Given the empirically negative relationship between the market rate of return and the price level, the greater the correlation of a firm's profits with the price level, the more likely its stock market value will be higher if it issues indexed rather than nominal bonds.

(3) Increases in the variance of the price level tend to increase the relative attractiveness of issuing index bonds, at least if the effect of the price level on the market rate of return is small.

(4) Differences in tax treatment obviously affect the type of securities issued. In particular, if indexed bond interest payments are not treated as a business expense whereas nominal bond interest payments are treated as a business expense, the latter will dominate the former which will not be issued.

III. THE CORRELATION OF PROFITS WITH THE PRICE LEVEL

The analysis outlined above established that firms are more likely to have a higher stock market value by issuing indexed rather than nominal bonds if their profits are positively correlated with the price level.

In table 20.1, we present correlation coefficients between after-tax profits with an adjustment (described below) for interest payments and the consumer price index for sixteen firms. These firms were chosen from the industrial, public utilities, transportation and merchandising categories of the *Fortune* 500 firms for 1964. The criterion of selection was originally to be the largest five firms on the basis of long-term debt outstanding in 1964 in each category, subject to the firms existing in both 1954 and 1973. There are only three transportation firms because debt issues of many of the largest transportation firms were so numerous that the analysis of section V below became too costly, and there are only three merchandising firms because these firms tended to have very little debt outstanding.

Profits for each firm were adjusted by adding back to reported net profits the computed amount of interest paid on long-term debt multiplied by one minus the corporate tax rate (state plus federal) in each year. Thus we obtained a series for each firm

$$\pi_{it} = \pi_{it}^R + (1 - \tau_t)R_{it}, \quad i = 1, \ldots, 16; \quad t = 1954, \ldots, 1973 \tag{1}$$

where π_{it} will henceforth be called after tax profits, π_{it}^R is reported net income, and R_t is reported interest payments on long-term debt. We chose to work with after-tax profits because it was simpler to make the tax adjustment to interest than to compute comparable pre-tax profits for each firm.

Nominal after-tax profits, π_{it}, were then deflated by the consumer price index for each year, a linear time trend[1] was fitted to the real profit series, and the deviations of real profits from the trend values were calculated. Similarly, an exponential time trend was fitted to the annual average of the CPI for each of the twenty years, with a dummy being included for the low

[1] An exponential could not be used because profits were negative for some firms in some years.

TABLE 20.1
CORRELATIONS OF AFTER-TAX INTEREST-ADJUSTED REAL PROFITS WITH THE PRICE LEVEL, 1954–73

Firm	*(Correlation coefficient)* Price level residuals from (3)	*Price level residuals from (4) (simple time trend)*	*Total long-term debt outstanding 1973 ($ millions)*
1. US Steel	–0·06	0·08	1464
2. Mobil Oil	0·27	0·50	1052
3. Union Carbide	–0·29	–0·49	940
4. Bethlehem Steel	–0·11	0·15	670
5. I.B.M.	0·32	0·65	652
6. A.T. & T.	–0·64	–0·83	7594
7. Consolidated Edison	0·08	–0·01	2843
8. Pacific G. & E.	–0·36	–0·30	2677
9. Public Service E. & G.	0·18	–0·04	1658
10. Tennessee Gas Transmission	–0·45	–0·12	882
11. Eastern Airlines	–0·31	–0·06	785
12. American Airlines	–0·88	–0·80	692
13. Baltimore and Ohio R.R.	–0·12	0·03	361
14. Sears	0·30	0·46	956
15. May Co.	–0·24	–0·51	317
16. Woolworth	–0·44	–0·62	295

Data Sources: 1. Profits: } *Moody's* industrial manual
2. Debt position: } *Moody's* transportation manual; *Moody's* public utility manual
3. C.P.I.: B.L.S., unpublished data series, monthly seasonally adjusted O.P.I.

inflation years, 1959–65, and the residuals from that regression were calculated. The price level regression was

$$\log (CPI_t) = \alpha_0 + \beta_1 t + \beta_2 Dt \qquad (2)$$

where

$D = 1$ for $t = 1959, \ldots, 1965$
$= 0$ otherwise.

Equation (2) represents a crude estimate of the predicted path of the price level. The regression, with standard errors in parentheses, was:

$$\log (CPI_t) = \underset{(0{\cdot}0185)}{4{\cdot}3330} + \underset{(0{\cdot}0014)}{0{\cdot}0242t} - \underset{(0{\cdot}0018)}{0{\cdot}0051Dt} \qquad (3)$$

In addition, the regression was run without the dummy variable, yielding

$$\log (CPI_t) = \underset{(0{\cdot}0197)}{4{\cdot}3116} + \underset{(0{\cdot}0016)}{0{\cdot}0247t} \qquad (4)$$

Table 20.1 presents the correlations of the deviations of real after-tax profits from their trend values with the deviations of the price level from its trend value, for equations (3) and (4) respectively. In each case most of the correlations are negative. The correlations for the largest debt-issuing category – the utilities – are all either negative or close to zero, with the correlation for A.I. & T., the largest individual borrower, being strongly negative. Table 20.1 suggests that the most likely issuers of index bonds would be Mobil Oil, I.B.M. and Sears.

While it may be surprising that the correlation of deviations of real profits with deviations of the price level from their respective trends is negative for so many firms,[1] the major lesson of table 20.1 is that there exists a wide diversity of behaviour of profits with respect to the price level and that there are indeed firms that have a positive correlation of detrended profits with the detrended price level and that, according to the theory, might have been expected to issue index bonds. We conclude that the failure of indexed bonds to appear is not due to the fact that there are no firms whose profits are positively correlated with the price level.[2]

IV. THE TAX TREATMENT OF INTEREST, AND INDEXING TO THE PRICE OF THE FIRM'S OUTPUT

The analysis outlined in section II points to the tax treatment of interest as a major determinant of the type of security issued,[3] and there is some uncertainty about the tax treatment of indexed interest payments in the United States.[4] The ambiguity stems from the fact that the courts have used fixity of the interest rate as one criterion for justifying the deductibility of interest payments [19]. There are a number of other criteria, such as fixity of the maturity date, negotiability, etc., all of which an indexed bond would satisfy. Since the only criterion which puts the deductibility of indexed interest in question is fixity of the interest rate, and since interest paid on floating rate notes is

[1] It is beyond the scope of this paper to speculate on reasons for this negative correlation. One obvious 'explanation' which may be forthcoming is that all the results tell us is that profits fell over the late 1960s and early 1970s when the rate of inflation was high. Since both regressions treat the inflation rate as essentially constant over specified periods, residuals will be positive in the late 1960s and early 1970s. This explanation is probably statistically correct for the cases it fits but leaves open the question of why profits fell as the rate of inflation rose.

[2] Of course, it is possible that the financial officers of all firms believe, despite the evidence, that their real profits are negatively correlated with the price level. Presumably, though, the evidence, if it stays firm, will eventually change such beliefs.

[3] We shall not discuss the important issue of how the tax system should be adjusted for inflation but rather remain within the confines of the present United States tax structure.

[4] In my previous paper on index bonds, I stated that indexed payments would be treated as dividends, this on the basis of verbal discussion with students of the question. On further examination, I now believe that indexed interest payments would be treated as interest (see Fischer [8]).

deductible, it would now appear that in fact a very strong case could be made that indexed interest should be treated as deductible, and that there is probably no tax obstacle to the issue of indexed interest bonds. However, it should be noted that there does not appear to be any precedent precisely covering the indexed interest case, and that the issue could only be finally resolved by rulings applied to a proposed and not a hypothetical bond issue, so that some uncertainty remains.

It is also appropriate here to consider a suggestion which has been made that firms would be more willing to issue bonds indexed to their own output price than bonds linked to the general price level. If their own output price were perfectly correlated with their profits (which is the reasoning behind the suggestion) it is easy to see that the model outlined in section II would support this argument. However, it should be noted that a firm's prices can rise because of cost increases as well as demand shifts, and thus that the correlation of a firm's prices with its profits is not likely to be perfect. Further, the greater the correlation of price with profits, the more likely would it seem to be that the indexed payment on such bonds would be treated as a profit distribution. It should also be noted that in the case of the issues of such bonds by French firms in the 1950s, indexing to the own price was a device used to circumvent a series of interpretations of a law of 1895 that was taken to forbid indexation to gold or the general price level [11], and should accordingly not be treated as evidence confirming the view that firms would prefer to issue bonds tied to their own output price.

In brief, then, it appears that the tax treatment of indexed bonds, at least in the United States, should not deter their issue. The general uncertainty concerning the tax treatment of indexed bonds suggests that there has been little effort made to clarify their tax status, which in turn suggests that it is unlikely that the tax treatment of index bonds has held back potential issues.

V. EXPECTATIONS OF INFLATION AND INDEX BONDS

The experience of the last decade has been of increasing inflation. The experience of the last two decades has also been of low real yields on bonds. It is by now well known that the average pre-tax real rate of return to the holding of United States treasury bills for the 1954–73 period was 1 per cent [6].

The average real yield on long-term corporate debt for our sample of sixteen firms for 1954–73 was less than 2 per cent. Table 20.2 presents the results of a calculation in which hypothetical indexed bonds were issued by the sixteen firms of the sample described in section III. The long-term debt outstanding at the end of each half-year for each firm was calculated, and it was then assumed that each firm paid interest on outstanding debt equal to, in one case, 1 per cent at an annual rate and in the other 2 per cent annual, plus the realised rate of inflation over the preceding six months. Profits were calculated for each firm for each year on the basis of the hypothetical interest payments, and then deflated by the CPI to yield a hypothetical real profit series. Table 20.2 shows the ratio of the mean of the calculated real profit series to the mean of actual real profits over the period 1954–73. The ratios are not identical for all firms, both because the share of interest payments in profits varies among firms and because dates of debt issues vary among firms. Table 20.2 demonstrates that every firm effectively obtained bond financing at less than a 2 per cent real rate over the period, and that some, including A.T. & T., paid less than 1 per cent real.

It is tempting to conclude that the low real rate is a result of rising and therefore unexpected inflation, and that if inflation had been accurately foreseen, the real rate of interest on bonds would have exceeded 2 per cent. Thus, it is argued, firms have had little incentive to issue index bonds because real rates on nominal bonds have been low [10]. This argument obviously requires borrowers to have had systematically higher expectations of inflation than lenders. This argument is difficult to confirm or refute. It should, however, be recognised that expectations of inflation among lenders are not homogeneous: it is possible that there are enough lenders in the American economy who are sufficiently pessimistic about inflation to make it worthwhile for some corporation to issue an indexed bond at a low real rate [1]. Thus the expectations explanation, too, should be treated with suspicion.

TABLE 20.2
RATIO OF MEAN REAL PROFITS WITH INDEXED INTEREST PAYMENTS TO ACTUAL MEAN REAL PROFITS, 1954–73

Firm	*Real rate*	
	1 per cent	*2 per cent*
1. US Steel	1·003	0·988
2. Mobil Oil	1·001	0·995
3. Union Carbide	0·997	0·980
4. Bethlehem Steel	1·000	0·991
5. I.B.M.	1·003	0·999
6. A.T. & T.	0·998	0·987
7. Consolidated Edison	0·983	0·919
8. Pacific G. & E.	0·993	0·943
9. Public Service G. & E.	1·010	0·954
10. Tennessee Gas Transmission	1·027	0·982
11. Eastern Airlines	1·392	0·717
12. American Airlines	1·047	0·951
13. Baltimore and Ohio R.R.	1·101	0·982
14. Sears	1·005	1·000
15. May Co.	1·013	0·991
16. Woolworth	1·010	0·998

Note: Actual mean real profits for Eastern Airlines is close to zero

VI. THE CALL PROVISION

Corporate bonds issued in the United States typically carry a call provision by which the corporation can repay the debt on specified terms before maturity but after five years (in general) or ten years (for utilities) of its existence. Thus corporations issuing nominal bonds appear to be covered against the possibility that the nominal interest rate will fall after their debt is issued, and they are, of course, covered against increases in the nominal rate by virtue of the fixity of the coupon rate. Accordingly, the call clause protects the corporation from the risk that the interest rate and rate of inflation will fall.

There are three points to be made in connection with the argument that the call provisions has precluded the issuance of index bonds because the corporation is covered against increases in nominal interest rates by the fact that it has a fixed nominal rate on its debt and decreases in nominal rates by the call clause. First, the call clause is not free [4]. It could be, though, that the issue of call-protected nominal bonds dominates index bonds from the viewpoint of the firm; the model of section II is not equipped to analyse that issue. Second, the call clause provides protection only after five or ten years, and interest rates can change a great deal in that period. Third, there is no reason why index bonds should not have similar clauses creating minimum and maximum nominal payments.

The last two points suggest strongly that the call provision is not the explanation for the non-existence of indexed bonds.

VII. THE VARIANCE OF THE RATE OF INFLATION

The analysis of section II suggested that indexed bonds would be more likely to be issued the greater the variance of the price level. Figure 20.1 shows the time path of the CPI in the United States 1954–74 (for quarterly observations) and also the inflation rate, defined as

$$\frac{P_t}{P_{t-1}} - 1 \quad \text{where } t = 1953 \text{ II to } 1974 \text{ IV}$$

Table 20.3 presents data for the variance of the quarterly inflation rate for the four five-year subperiods of 1954–73. Although it is difficult to establish an absolute measure of variability, the second column of table 20.3 provides some notion of absolute variation: it presents the variance of the rate of inflation calculated at an annual percentage rate, and is generally of the same order of magnitude as the mean rates of inflation for the subperiods, except for 1954–58. This variance itself falls as the time interval over which the inflation rate is calculated is increased.

Perhaps the best notion of the relative variability of the inflation rate is obtained by comparing its variance with that of the stock market rate of return: the variance of the inflation rate is lower by a factor of the order of

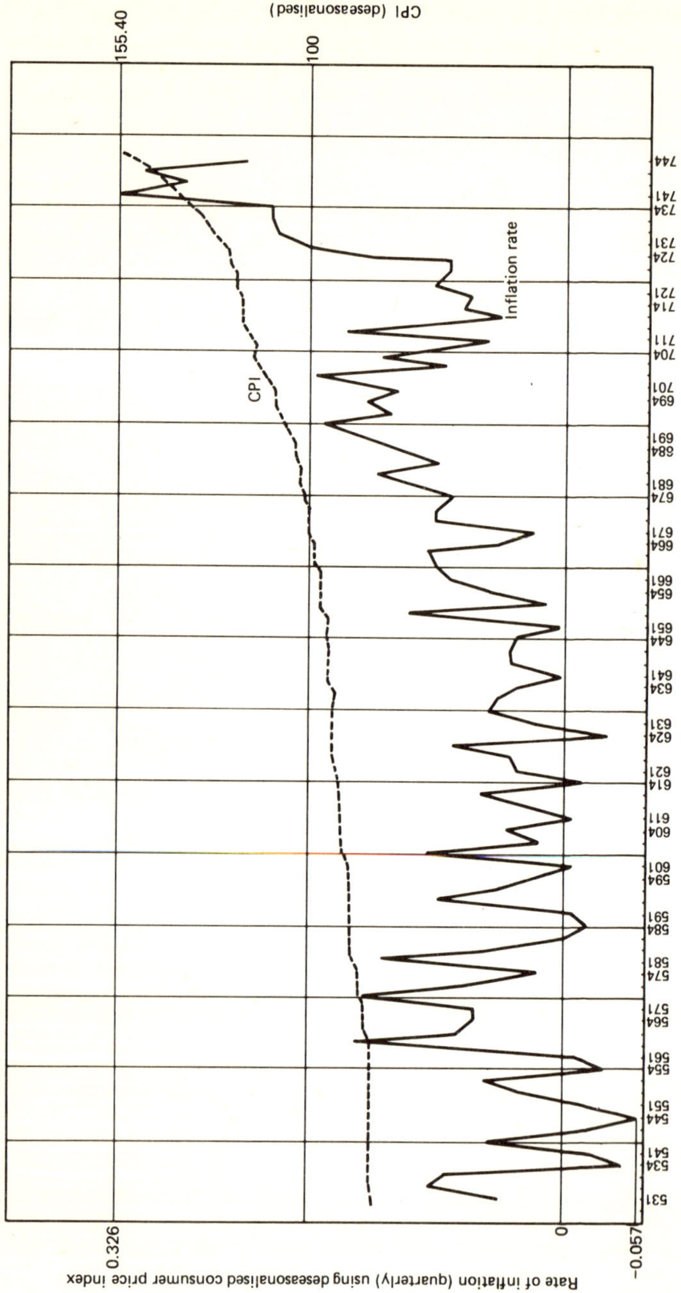

Fig. 20.1 Variations of the inflation rate

one hundred than the variance of the stock market rate of return.[1] It thus appears that in terms of the uncertainties portfolio-holders are accustomed to facing, inflation uncertainty is relatively trivial and insufficient to make the introduction of a new financial asset worthwhile. The costs of innovation are discussed in section VIII below.

TABLE 20.3
VARIANCE OF RATE OF INFLATION

Period	*Inflation rate variance*	*Variance of inflation calculated at annual % rate*
1954–73	0·3771	6·0336
1954–58	0·3346	5·3536
1959–63	0·0979	1·5664
1964–68	0·1563	2·5008
1969–73	0·2892	4·6272

Whatever the absolute magnitude of the variance of inflation, it is clear that the periods most favourable to the issue of index bonds were 1954–58 and 1969–73. These are also of course the periods in which economists were most actively discussing indexing. Further, the variance for 1970–74 (11·792) considerably exceeds that for 1969–73 (4·2672). Thus the recent instability of the inflation rate has created conditions substantially more favourable to the issue of index bonds than existed in the previous ten years.

VIII. THE COSTS OF INNOVATION

The introduction of the floating rate note[2] involved the issuer of the first such note in discussion and negotiation with the Federal Reserve System that resulted in modification of the terms of the note.[3] Such negotiation is an obvious cost of financial innovation. There are other costs of innovation such as the education of the public to the advantages and disadvantages of the new instrument. (Irving Fisher [9] attributed the failure of the Rand Kardex index bond to the unfamiliarity of the market with the instrument.) These costs are borne by the innovator and not by subsequent issuers.

The fact is, however, that the innovation was carried out in the case of the floating rate note. The note was aimed at the small borrower and thus the educational costs could be expected to be relatively high. Further, the difficulties Citicorp encountered with the Federal Reserve System stemmed largely from the fact that the issue was regarded by financial intermediaries such as

[1] This point was suggested to me by Eugene Fama. See Black, Jensen and Scholes [2] for estimates of the variance of stock market returns.

[2] See Listing Application to the New York Stock Exchange, Inc., B-4337-D, July 24, 1974, by Citicorp.

[3] *Wall Street Journal*, July 15, 1974, p. 4.

savings banks as aimed directly at their depositors,[1] and it is not certain that similar interests would be affected if an indexed bond were to be issued.

In discussing innovation, it is worthwhile distinguishing financial institutions from other corporations. Financial institutions tend to carry hedged portfolios and it is probable that they would want to innovate on both sides of their balance sheet if they innovated by issuing an indexed bond (see the model of hedging behaviour by a financial intermediary in [5]). Citicorp presumably found the floating rate note more attractive than an indexed bond because its liabilities are nominal. The desire of financial intermediaries for hedging even makes it possible that a large scale transition to indexation is as feasible as the piecemeal introduction of indexation by financial intermediaries.

Non-financial corporations have not been particularly innovative in the types of securities they issue and it may be that the costs of innovation for them are high. However, it is difficult to believe that the costs of educating a public, by now well aware of inflation, to understand the features of an indexed bond can be very high. Accordingly continuance of the current levels and variability of inflation will likely make the costs of innovation for some non-financial corporation low enough to result in the issue of an indexed bond. Similarly, if proposals for reform of the mortgage system [15] lead to the introduction of indexed mortgages, the spread of indexation could thereafter be rapid.

IX. CONCLUSIONS

Most of the explanations usually advanced for the non-issuance of private indexed bonds do not appear to explain the phenomenon. There are firms whose profits are positively correlated with the price level; the tax treatment of indexed interest would probably not be adverse; the call clause provides protection to the borrower only after a lengthy period and a similar provision could in any case be applied in the case of index bonds; the costs of innovations have not prevented sophisticated innovation aimed at small lenders. There are two arguments that may have some merit. The first is that expectations of inflation by borrowers have been systematically higher than those of lenders. However, it is difficult to believe that borrowers will always expect more inflation than lenders, or for that matter, that there are not now lenders who would accept a low real rate of interest in exchange for protection against inflation. Thus this factor would not prevent the future emergence of index bonds. The second is that the variance of inflation has been low, particularly relative to the other risks incurred in the capital markets. However, this variance is now higher than it was in the 1960s, and increased instability of the inflation rate, if maintained, may well lead to the emergence of privately issued index bonds.

[1] *New York Times*, July 6, 1974, p. 25.

APPENDIX: THE VARIABILITY OF HYPOTHETICAL PROFIT SERIES FOR SIXTEEN FIRMS ISSUING INDEXED BONDS

Closely related to the question examined in section III of the correlation of a firm's detrended profits with the detrended price level, is an issue of independent interest – the stability of after-interest profits if firms were to issue indexed rather than nominal bonds. Table 20.4 presents the results of comparisons of the variability of hypothetical real profit streams where firms issued index bonds with the variability of their actual real profit streams. The construction of the hypothetical profit series is described in section V (the real interest rate used for the construction of the appendix was 1 per cent). Each nominal profit series was deflated by the CPI to give a real profit series.

TABLE 20.4
RATIO OF VARIABILITY OF REAL PROFITS WITH INDEXED INTEREST PAYMENTS TO VARIABILITY WITH ACTUAL INTEREST PAYMENTS, 1954–73

Firm	*Rates*
1. US Steel	0·918
2. Mobil Oil	0·938
3. Union Carbide	1·033
4. Bethlehem Steel	0·969
5. I.B.M.	0·974
6. A.T. & T.	1·050
7. Consolidated Edison	2·322
8. Pacific G. & E.	2·589
9. Public Service G. & E.	2·268
10. Tennessee Gas Transmission	0·893
11. Eastern Airlines	0·567
12. American Airlines	1·011
13. Baltimore + Ohio R.R.	0·721
14. Sears	0·976
15. May Co.	1·128
16. Woolworth	1·011

Note: Eastern Airlines has mean profits close to zero and ratio is accordingly suspect as a measure of variability

A linear trend was then fitted to each hypothetical real profit series and the sum of squared residuals from that series was calculated and divided by the square of the mean of the series to give a 'coefficient of variation' of hypothetical real profits around its trend line. An identical procedure was applied to the time series for actual real profits and the corresponding 'coefficient of variation' calculated.

Table 20.2 presents the ratio of the 'coefficient of variation' for the hypothetical real profit series to that for the actual real profit series. It is seen from table 20.4 that, given the actual debt issues of firms, the profits of the industrial firms would on the whole have been more stable had they issued indexed debt rather than nominal debt, while profits for the utilities would on the whole have been less stable. The reasons the ratios in table 20.4 are not uniformly greater (less) than unity if the corresponding correlation of table 20.1 is negative (positive) is that the variability measure is affected by the dates of issue of securities. Table 20.4 shows that a number of firms, including Mobil, I.B.M. and Sears, would have had slightly more stable after-tax profit streams over the last twenty years had they issued index bonds rather than nominal bonds on every occasion on which they issued debt. Figures 20.2 and 20.3 shows hypothetical and actual real profits for Sears and Consolidated Edison for the twenty-year period.

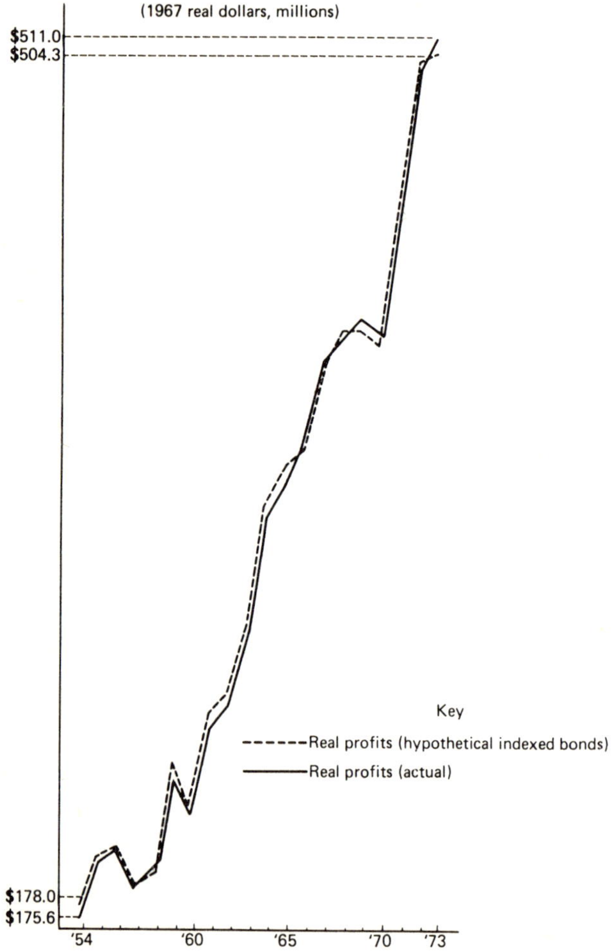

Fig. 20.2 Hypothetical and actual real profits; Sears Roebuck & Co.

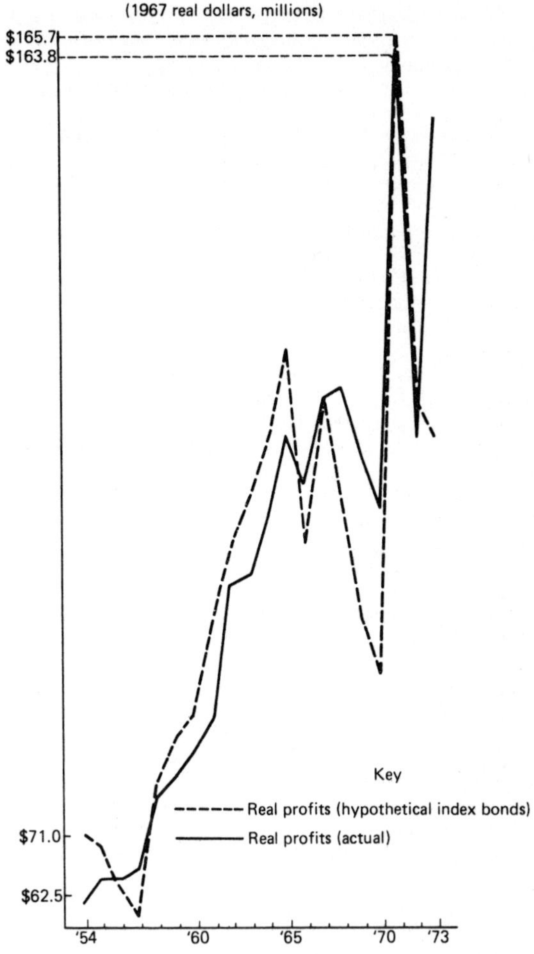

Fig. 20.3 Hypothetical and actual real profits: Consolidated Edison.

REFERENCES

[1] Guy Arvidsson, 'Should We Have Indexed Loans?', in D. C. Hague, (ed.), *Inflation*, Proceedings of a Conference Held by the International Economic Association (London: Macmillan & Co. Ltd., 1962).

[2] Fisher Black, Michael C. Jensen and Myron Scholes, 'The Capital Asset Pricing Model: Some Empirical Tests' in M. C. Jensen, (ed.), *Studies in the Theory of Capital Markets* (New York: Praeger Publishers, 1972).

[3] Zvi Body, *Hedging Against Inflation*, unpublished Ph.D. dissertation (Massachusetts Institute of Technology, 1975).

[4] Zvi Body and Benjamin M. Friedman, 'Interest Rate Expectations and the Value of Bond Call Protection', unpublished (Harvard University, 1974).

[5] Richard Cohn and Stanley Fischer, 'An Analysis of Alternative Nonstandard Mortgages', Sloan School Mortgage Study Report No. 5, (Massachusetts Institute of Technology, December 1974).

[6] Eugene F. Fama, 'Short-Term Interest Rates as Predictors of Inflation,' *American Economic Review* (June, 1975), 269–282.

[7] Stanley Fischer, 'The Demand for Index Bond', *Journal of Political Economy* (June, 1975a), 509–534.

[8] Stanley Fischer, 'Non-Indexation in the Capital Markets', unpublished manuscript (Massachusetts Institute of Technology, June, 1975b).

[9] Irving Fisher, *Stable Money* (New York: Adelphi, 1934).

[10] Milton Freidman, 'Monetary Correction', in Gierisch *et. al., Essays on Inflation and Indexation*. Washington, D.C.: American Enterprise Institute for Public Policy Research (1974).

[11] Hamel, J. 'Les Clauses D'Échelle Mobile Et La Droit Monétaire Francais', *Revue Economique* (March, 1955), 167–184.

[12] Michael C. Jensen, 'The Foundations and Current State of Capital Market Theory', in M. C. Jensen (ed.), *Studies in the Theory of Capital Markets* (New York: Praeger Publishers, 1972).

[13] Michael C. Jensen and William H. Meckling, 'Theory of the Firm: Managerial Behavior, Agency Costs and Capital Structure', unpublished (The University of Rochester Graduate School of Management, 1975).

[14] Alan Kraus and Robert H. Litzenberger, 'A State-Preference Model of Optimal Financial Leverage', *Journal of Finance* (September, 1973), 911–922.

[15] Donald Lessard and Franco Modigliani, 'Inflation and Residential Financing: Problems and Potential Solutions', forthcoming in *Innovations in Mortgage Design*, Federal Reserve Bank of Conference Series, Volume 14.

[16] Merton Miller and Franco Modigliani, 'The Cost of Capital, Corporation Finance and the Theory of Investment', *American Economic Review* (June, 1958), 261–296.

[17] Stewart C. Myers, 'A Note on the Determinants of Corporate Debt Capacity', unpublished, London Graduate School of Business Studies (1975).

[18] Michael E. Sparrough and Lena Bolton, 'Calendar of Wage Increases and Negotiations for 1972', *Monthly Labor Review* (January, 1972), 3–15.

[19] *Standard Federal Tax Reporter*, 1974: Vol. 3 and 4. (New York: Commerce Clearing House, Inc., 1973).

Discussions of the Papers by David Levhari and Nathan Liviatan and by Stanley Fischer

Professor Fischer introduced the paper by Professors Liviatan and Levhari. It had been suggested earlier that the conference was concerned with the causes, consequences and cures of inflation. Now we had to look at the consequences of the cures.

The paper presented a broader and deeper analysis than an earlier one by the same authors. He would try to compare the results contained in the present paper with those of other writers, including himself. The authors had packed a great deal into a little space. Their basic analytical tool was a model of an individual, who maximised expected utility over two time periods. The level of inflation between the two periods was uncertain, but real income in the next period was known and fixed. The individual could carry money and various bonds in his portfolio from period one to period two. The paper argued correctly that if inflation were fully expected, then even a high rate of inflation had no serious effects. The emphasis was accordingly on the uncertainty of price behaviour.

In trying to understand the authors' results, one basic point should be kept in mind. Under uncertainty, risk-averters tried to ensure the stability of future consumption flows. Most results in the paper could be traced to individuals' preferences for relative certainty of consumption flows. They would, in general, be willing to pay a premium for more stable future consumption.

The authors took up a number of issues. The first, and fundamental, question concerning index bonds was why, if indexed bonds were so desirable, there were so few private indexed bonds, and not even many governmental ones. An earlier argument by the authors had been that this reflected a congenital weakness of capital markets on the side of borrowers. It had been analysed by the authors on the basis that people had to carry money between periods. So everyone already had an asset in their portfolio that would suffer under inflation. They would thus be reluctant to issue another obligation, an indexed bond, which would also require high payments if there were unexpected inflation.

The authors, in this paper, allowed for the existence of both indexed and non-indexed bonds. Then the individual would hold some indexed bonds and some non-indexed ones, but the analysis did not explain why there were no indexed bonds. His own analysis, in the *Journal of Political Economy*, (June, 1975) was also unable to account for the non-existence of indexed bonds. Nor, for that matter, did his paper for the present conference. He would add that the present Liviatan–Levhari paper did make a small contribution to explaining why it was that indexation occurred with a high rate of inflation and not just with a more variable rate of inflation. In their paper, Professors Kleiman and Jaffee had shown that since the variability of inflation was positively correlated with the rate of inflation, one could not separate the two empirically. But now Professors Liviatan and Levhari did provide an analytical explanation for the appearance of indexing at high rates of inflation. They said that when the expected inflation was rapid, this would reduce holdings of monetary assets and lead to more willingness to issue and hold indexed ones.

He would now look at some other issues discussed in the paper. First, suppose one had two systems. In the first, one had government indexed bonds, and in the second none. There was then an interesting result. Increased variability in the rate of inflation increased savings, with indexation. Without indexation, it reduced them. But this was not necessarily true if the bonds in question were private. There was an implication that an increase in savings was therefore good. But was it? He also wondered how far the authors' result was a result of using quadratic utility functions.

Next the authors considered endogenous inflation. Earlier work, including some by himself, had taken the rate of inflation as given. The authors used a helicopter model, with money showered on the heads of the public by the government. Here, since everyone knew that the quantity theory was true, inflation was a truly nominal phenomenon. The risk premium on non-indexed bonds was therefore eliminated. The real rate of return on indexed and non-indexed bonds was the same. This was interesting, and the determination of the rate of inflation within the model was useful.

The next section was the most important. The authors took an assumption that corresponded to Israeli practice. The government set up a financial intermediary which borrowed by issuing indexed bonds and lent through non-indexed ones. There were a lot of arguments in the literature that ignored budgetary constraints on the government. The government had to pay the indexation, which imposed a constraint on it. In general, the government was in a stronger position to do this than a private business only because of its power to tax. It could back indexation by this power. However, issuing indexed bonds then implied some promise by the government that others would be taxed to pay for indexation. Unfortunately, the welfare implications of the issue of index bonds were then less clear. The Liviatan–Levhari paper showed that the use of an intermediary implied a higher real rate of return on nominal than on real bonds. The issue of such bonds would perhaps increase saving.

At the end of the paper, the authors extended their analysis to take up a situation in which there were many goods. Up to this point, the analysis had been carried out assuming there was only one good. The extension to many goods led to two difficulties. First, what was now the relevant price level? Index number problems arose both because a suitable index could not generally be defined for a given individual and because different individuals would have different price levels. Second, at this stage Liviatan and Levhari allowed second-period income to vary in real terms.

He noted that, earlier, they had treated second-period income as constant, even though there was nothing in the logic of the one-good model that required them to do so. This seemed to imply something like the assumption that one had an outside income with whatever relation to inflation one liked. Now one had to consider whether the price of the good one owned was positively or negatively correlated with those one wanted to buy. If the relationship were positive, one had an inflation hedge. So, following the general practice of diversification, one would buy nominal bonds to smooth consumption, and *vice versa*. So the issue became: what was the relationship between incomes and the price level. If the correlation between income and the rate of inflation were negative, one would tend to buy more indexed bonds.

Finally, the authors put the whole discussion into a more fundamental context. For this purpose, they used the contingent commodity model developed by Arrow, Debreu and others. There was an asset one could buy for every possible event and a corresponding insurance market. Then, indexed bonds became a second-best solution. It was possible for more sophisticated assets to be created instead. For example, one might create an asset with no indexation until the price level had increased by 3 per cent. After that, there might be indexation. This perspective was perhaps useful in giving a further way of tackling the problem.

Professor Fischer noted an interesting gap between the recent analysis of index bonds and the earlier literature, for example, that of Sweden in the late 1950s. The earlier literature had been very concerned with the assistance that the creation of indexed bonds might give to the monetary authority in controlling the rate of interest. In the Swedish case, it was argued that one could observe expectations more directly if there were both indexed and unindexed bonds. This would assist monetary policy by giving the government closer control over the real rate of interest. The literature of the 1970s had not so far addressed such questions.

As for the maturity of bonds, one found that inflation led to a shortening of the maturity structure. Indexation tended to be introduced on longer-term bonds. Why was this? Perhaps the best explanation was given by Brenner and Patinkin, in terms of the greater uncertainty of long-term bonds. However, the paper by Liviatan and Levhari, and his own papers, threw no light on the importance of indexed bonds for the debt structure.

Professor Tsuru introduced the paper by Professor Fischer. The question the paper tried to answer was: 'Why, if both borrower and lender benefit from indexed bonds, does an indexed loan market not develop spontaneously without any government initiative?'. The author analysed this problem mainly with reference to the supply side, namely private corporations which attempted to raise money by borrowing through indexed bonds.

It should be emphasised at the outset that Professor Fischer took the existing tax treatment as given. In other words, he took as given the differential tax treatment between the interest payment as a business expense and the dividend disbursement coming out of taxable income. Professor Tsuru would return to this matter at the end of his introduction. Further, Professor Fischer's argument depended partly on how the tax authorities would treat the indexed interest payment and the capital gain on the principal on the indexed bond. There was ambiguity here.

It should also, perhaps, be mentioned that Professor Fischer's analytical scheme revolved around the maximisation of the stock market value of the corporation in question. To Professor Tsuru, this issue was fairly complex and he was not certain that the formulation was sufficiently general. Incidentally, the alternatives proposed by the author were: (1) the issue of indexed bonds or equity, and (2) the issue of indexed or nominal bonds. He did not consider the case of a firm issuing both types of bond simultaneously.

It was worth remembering, if one were a non-technical reader like Professor Tsuru himself, that the choice between indexed and nominal bonds depended on the differential between the interest rates offered for each. If the rate were the same for both, there was no question that a firm would prefer to issue nominal bonds so long as there was any inflation.

Professor Fischer's conclusions were as follows. On bonds versus equity, bonds would be issued up to the point where the tax benefit balanced the expected bankruptcy costs. This was because issuing bonds produced a tax advantage, but the more bonds were issued the greater was the probability of bankruptcy. Professor Fischer then considered what the supply of indexed bonds depended on in attaining the interior maximum for the firm. First, it was positively related to the maximum profit the firm expected to earn. Second, it was positively related to the tax rate on corporate profits. Third, it was negatively related to the cost of bankruptcy. As for the effect of uncertainty about the price level on the issue of indexed bonds, the conclusions were as follows. If the firm's profits were related to the price level in the opposite direction to which the market's return was related, price uncertainty increased the amount of indexed bonds issued.

As for indexed bonds versus nominal bonds, the conclusions were as follows. First, there were situations in which the firm would have a higher value if it issued indexed bonds rather than nominal bonds. This happened, for example, when α was identical with β, which was identical with 0. The reverse was also possible. For example, when α was positive, real profits were negatively correlated with the price level. Third, an increase in the variance of the price level increased the relative profitability of issuing indexed bonds for a firm whose profits were positively correlated with the price level.

There followed another extremely interesting discussion on such issues as: a hypothetical empirical study on the correlation of profit with the price level for sixteen United States firms (a somewhat similar study could be made for other countries); the tax treatment of indexed bonds; and the relevance to the whole issue of the variance of the rate of inflation.

Professor Tsuru wanted to mention a few positive statements made in the remainder of the paper. First, it had been argued that firms had had little incentive to issue indexed bonds because the real rate of interest on nominal bonds had been too low. This argument, however, required that borrowers had a systematically higher expectation of inflation than lenders, which might have been the case. Second, it could be inferred from the earlier analysis that indexed bonds would be more likely to be issued the greater the variance of the price level. Thus, it might be that the recent instability of the inflation rate had created conditions substantially more favourable for the issue of indexed bonds than had existed in previous years.

Professor Fischer had a footnote to his paper which said that the problem 'how the tax system should be adjusted for inflation' was an important issue which should be discussed. However, Professor Tsuru wanted to raise an even more basic issue. This was the rationale of a differential tax treatment of interest payments on the one hand and dividends and investments on the other. A contractual interest payment was considered as an expense of the business whereas the dividend on equity had to come out of after-tax net income of a firm. Why was this? Once one started examining the reasons for differential tax treatment, one came to realise that the reason offered was not very convincing. A corporation had various capital needs, and they were met by resort to a varied conbination of: (1) internal saving (depreciation funds and the firm's own profit); (2) contractual borrowing; and (3) the issuing of equity shares.

The proportions of each of these had changed historically within the same country and also differed widely between countries. Japanese corporations resorted to borrowing from banks for long-term investment to a much greater degree than American ones. Sharing risk with the bank was a particular feature of the Zaibatsu system.

Theoretically, economists had often in the past spoken of interest on capital as an inclusive term. Marxists in particular would regard both interest and dividend as a part of surplus value – in other words, as a part of net income. In view of this, it appeared to him that the differential tax treatment of interest and dividend was largely a conventional matter. It should therefore be considered a subject for examination, even without any reference to an inflationary situation. This was all the more true because we now had a continuous spectrum of types of share, ranging from non-par common stocks to bond-like shares. It was extremely difficult to draw a line anywhere along this spectrum. An issue of indexed bonds provided a good opportunity for such a re-examination.

Professor Patinkin wanted to discuss the puzzle of why there were not more indexed bonds in the market. Was it related to the fact that indexed bonds were aimed to simulate a perfect market: to achieve the same nominal rate of interest as one would have if inflation were perfectly foreseen? In practice, however, the nominal rate of interest was not increased to the full extent of inflation. In Israel, bank rate had risen as far as 25 per cent, but inflation had been up to 40 per cent. So, perhaps the answer to the question of why there were in practice few indexed bonds was related to why there was no perfect capital market. There were, however, now securities in the United States which offered a variable rate of interest.

The variable rate of interest implied renegotiation at intervals, in line with the market rate. So the market was able to provide devices to overcome problems, but a perfect market was not possible.

Had the market reacted in other ways to inflation and the uncertainty of inflation? What had happened to the length of debt? Was the average term of lending now shorter than it had been when inflation rates were lower? The authors said that if one took account of tax one would get different results. This was just part of the general proposition that government debt was not a net asset if one looked at both the financing and the lending side.

Mr Oppenheimer said that nominal rates of interest were indeed slow to adjust. While he knew of no empirical studies on the matter, it was generally accepted that this was true. However, wages adjusted fairly quickly. Perhaps trade unions and the labour market adapted more readily to inflation than did the capital market. This was surprising on the face of it, but perhaps it only reflected the reluctance of the authorities to allow interest rates to go up.

Professor Stahl noted that the theory of indexed bonds had gone farther than the practice and he wondered why this was. Professor Fischer had mentioned earlier Swedish discussions and he wanted to clarify this. Those discussions were largely due to Palander, who was really interested in state intervention. If there were a market with indexed and non-indexed bonds, one would find the state forced to give its own predictions of the inflation rate, with repercussions on government policy. Professor Palander went on to note the effect of interference in the nominal market. In the short run, the nominal market, with no state interference, could be compared with an indexed market with state interference. In these circumstances, it would he hard for the state not to reveal its own expectations.

Capital markets therefore became political markets. One could ask a question like: 'Could I win a referendum by offering a variable rate of interest in inflationary times?' This was because the rate of interest was part of the political process and one could therefore impose a majority decision rule. Sweden had a good deal of experience on pseudo-indexed loans. These operated against borrowers, which was one reason why they were abandoned.

Professor Stahl thought it important to remember that institutional arrangements – including the way business accounts were set out, arrangements for mortgages among other things – were formulated in nominal terms. Very little of the civil law system had a 'real' character.

Finally, he wanted to mention that all the discussions here had considered indexed bonds in a closed economy, and capital markets were somewhat international. If Sweden were to issue indexed bonds, Swedish international firms could do well by borrowing in one market and lending in others, with differential inflation and different tax systems. The only solution would be to erect elaborate taxation sluices to prevent international capital movements aimed at exploiting differences in tax systems, and rates of interest and inflation.

Professor Robinson was glad Professor Patinkin had brought the conference back to institutions. How far had world institutions adjusted to continuing inflation? He thought that the theorists in the conference had been assuming that the adjustment was greater than it actually was.

In recent years, much of United Kingdom saving was carried out through institutions like pension funds. Here, saving was determined, not by the individual but by an institutional arrangement whereby part of his income was put into the fund. Up to now, these had worked entirely in monetary terms, but this was becoming increasingly difficult. At present, a good deal of saving was being carried out at negative real rates of interest. Individuals and institutions would therefore have to react. Pension arrangements meant that firms and universities were moving away from a pension contract stated entirely in monetary terms. It was becoming necessary, in some way, to gear the pension to the income of the same class of person at a later date rather than what the individual had earned over his whole working life.

In the past, with a negative real rate of interest over much of the economy, a considerable amount of saving had been fed back into the public sector, especially the large nationalised industries. They in turn were able to borrow at negative real rates of interest. But he wondered why, say, the electricity industry should be allowed to develop at negative rates of return. It should be able to pay a positive rate of interest. Indeed, in an ideally adjusting system it would have to. There was perhaps a long way to go before this was achieved. His own view was that indexation of borrowing was one step towards ensuring that the rate of inflation was tolerable.

Professor Kleiman wanted to try to answer the question why the theory lagged. Professor Lundberg had once said that countries which seriously studied the problem of indexation never introduced it, while countries which introduced it never stopped to consider it seriously. Perhaps this brought us back to the suggestion, made in the 1930s, that there was a great deal of unnecessary originality among non-Swedish economists because they had neither seen nor read what was being done in Sweden.

As for why private firms had not introduced indexation, he thought it was a tacit assumption of businessmen that the variability of relative prices increased with the rate of inflation. So they feared that their own revenue, and therefore profit, would not necessarily move in line with the rate of inflation. His intuitive conclusion on this seemed to be supported by the paper by Levhari and Liviatan. They showed that 'if individuals are pessimistic in their expectations concerning the prices of their endowed (or produced) commodities, then the reluctance of people to borrow linked will increased'. More research was needed on whether uncertainty increased with the rate of inflation.

There were also institutional reasons for the lack of indexed bonds. For example, there were sometimes legal ceilings on the rate of interest. In many countries, the indexed part of the payment would be considered part of the interest, which would bring the total nominal interest rate above the level permitted by usury law. There were also tax problems.

On why wages adjusted more rapidly than interest rates, Professor Kleiman thought this was due to the structure of the capital market. Banks had a monopoly position and could afford to go on lending at low real rates of interest because they were able to rob depositors. For the banks themselves to issue indexed bonds would lead to problems, because banks needed to hold their reserves in a similar kind of asset. So there would have to be a large issue of indexed government bonds to allow this.

Professor Nussbaumer also wanted to discuss the question of why there were so few indexed bonds. Keynes gave three reasons for holding liquid assets and, of these, only the speculative motive was tied to the rate of interest. The transactions motive was tied to national income, although the precise basis of precautionary holdings was more open to discussion. This meant that a large amount of savings was not related to the rate of interest. So long as one was borrowing within these 'necessary levels of saving' then there was no need to pay a rate of interest in excess of transaction costs. If one wanted to pay more, because the demand for capital exceeded 'necessary' savings, perhaps the answer was that one had been moved beyond the point where one could borrow at a given rate of interest.

Mr Brenner reminded participants that Jevons had said that one should introduce indexed bonds in deflationary times, to make the situation better for entrepreneurs.

Professor Patinkin's point about the lag which occurred before inflationary pressure appeared in an increased rate of interest might be taken as causing a tendency not to supply index bonds, though a demand was present.

Professors Levhari and Liviatan suggested that the government wanted to take real resources from the private sector. This would lead to a pessimistic attitude among private businesses and would make them less ready to issue indexed bonds because of expectations of decreased real profits.

Mr Oppenheimer argued that tax was important in practice. The arrangements currently being introduced in the United Kingdom to give pensioners the opportunity to index their savings offered a zero rate of interest in real terms, net of tax. For someone paying tax at 35 per cent on marginal income, this was equivalent to a gross yield of 40 per cent if price inflation continued at a 26 per cent annual rate. No wonder the United Kingdom authorities were reluctant to enlarge schemes of this kind!

Professor Lundberg suggested that the system participants had been discussing perhaps gave the best of all possible worlds. If it were true that the share of wages in national income was on an increasing trend, this must be related to the existence of negative rates of return on capital. This was the obverse side of the increasing share of wages. All the borrowing which seemed now to be taking place at low or negative rates of interest must help to keep up the rate of return on risk capital. This must help entrepreneurs who displayed initiative.

Professor Bronfenbrenner wondered whether there was an objection, on the collective bargaining side, to indexed bonds. If a firm had not previously issued such bonds and began to do so, perhaps there would be difficulties with the unions, who would either regard the issue as illegal or demand special compensation for permitting it. After all, one purpose of wage inflation was to squeeze the rentier!

Professor Patinkin wondered what was the link between indexation and the tax situation. In the United States, suppose a bond offered 6 per cent with indexation of principal and interest. For tax purposes, it would make a difference whether the indexed element was or was not recognised as deductible expense of the firm. If it were not, this might explain why there were so few indexed bonds.

As for the apparent difference between indexation of the rate of interest and of wages, one had to remember that one was not comparing like with like. A wage rate was a short-run phenomenon and had to be compared with a short-run rate of interest, which in general was not indexed even in countries which made use of indexation. Furthermore the wage rate altered with productivity. For example, we knew that there had been a constant rate of increase in wages over the centuries. Wages increased with economic progress. The rate of interest did not do so, and might even fall. So one would not expect wages and interest to behave in the same kind of way.

Professor Levhari wanted to compliment Professor Fischer on his good introduction to the paper. As for tax, in the long run this might be endogenous to the economic system. In the United States there were suggestions that savings and loan associations might issue bonds giving the current short-term rate of interest.

To Professor Fischer, Professor Levhari said it might be true, in general, that there was increasing variability in the purchasing power of money. However, one could not say what uncertainty did to savings. It was not true that their results were obtained from quadratic functions. Discussion was based on the new sigma approach. The criticism Professor Fischer had made applied to Professor Fischer's analysis as well. He had used an equivalent asset-pricing model which was much the same as the new sigma approach.

On the effect of indexed loans on national and multinational businesses, Professor Levhari was not sure about the tax position. To make the real rate of interest more certain would improve the position because, currently, there was a lot of uncertainty over the real rates of return. Indexation might alter nominal rates, but would at least stabilise real rates. If the argument against indexation was that it would lead to speculation, he would insist that there was speculation already.

He was not certain on the position of collective bargaining. If indexation stabilised profits, he thought it would help. In theory, in a mixed market, the expected nominal rate of interest was always greater than the indexed rate because there was always some uncertainty. In a free market, one would expect the nominal rate to be not only positive, but greater than the indexed rate. Why had this not happened?

Finally, Professor Fischer's paper had been interested in the relation between the rate of return and the rate of price increase. Professor Fischer assumed a negative relation between the market return and the rate of price increase, but a positive one between profit and the rate of price increase. Why should firms have increasing profits and falling share prices?

Professor Liviatan wanted to compare the two papers. There were some basic similarities between them. He wanted to start with a simple relationship, taking a consumer whose real wealth in the second of two periods was given by the equation

$$W_N = [m + (1 + i)b_N]\pi + y$$

W_N represented real wealth, while $(1 + i)b_N$ gave the nominal value of non-linked bonds at maturity, and m was money or nominal income. To get real value, one had to multiply by π which gave the relative value of money in the second period; Y was income in the next period. The equation therefore gave the real value of future wealth. In both the Liviatan–Levhari paper and the paper by Professor Fischer, π was assumed to be a random variable. One did not know the value of W until one knew the rate of inflation. A situation where there were index-linked bonds gave:

$$W_L = m\pi + (1 + r)b_L + y$$

These were alternatives. The first equation gave the usual arrangement in the real world. The second was the situation where the consumer had indexed bonds instead of non-indexed ones.

To see why there were few linked bonds, one should ask a consumer in the normal situation whether he would switch to linked bonds. If both borrowers and lenders wanted to switch, one would expect indexed bonds to develop. If not, there were difficulties.

Suppose one calculated the variance of wealth under each alternative and looked at the differences between the variances of W under the non-indexed (W_N) and indexed (W_L) alternatives. This difference was given by

$$D = V_N - V_L = (1 + i)b[2m + (1 + i)b]V_\pi$$

where V_N denoted the variance of W_N and so on. Now, for the lender ($b > 0$), D was always positive and he would therefore prefer the index-linked alternative (assuming the expected value of W to be the same under the two alternatives). However, for the borrower ($b < 0$), D might be negative if $2m + (1 + i)b > 0$. That was, if his non-linked assets and incomes, represented by m were sufficiently large compared to his borrowing. It should be noted that, for the borrower, his non-linked debt served as a hedge against changes in the value of money. An increase in the rate of inflation which reduced the real value of his money reduced, at the same time, the real value of his indebtedness. It was for this reason that the borrower might prefer the non-indexed alternative.

How did this relate to Professor Fischer's paper? To Professor Fischer money was not necessarily money balances but anything not linked to the price level. If firms specialised in making certain commodities that consumers consumed, then if the firm's specific product lagged in price behind the general price level, its income would be essentially part of m.

Professor Fischer considered the firm as a borrower, so that b was negative. Under what conditions would the firm prefer to issue non-indexed or indexed bonds? If the income included in m was non-indexed, then m could be bigger than b and the whole expression for D negative. So, the firm would want non-indexed bonds. But if m was zero, the firm would prefer indexed bonds.

What was the effect of increased variability in inflation? He assumed here that more inflation meant more variance. As variance ($V\pi$) increased, suppose the changes in m were small. As uncertainty over the value of money increased, lenders with positive variances would want more indexed bonds. Savers would also want more indexed bonds. But if, originally, many firms preferred non-indexed bonds, the increase in the variability of inflation would increase their aversion to the linked system. The spread would increase and this might explain the absence of an increasing tendency to index bonds with more rapid inflation.

Professor Fischer thought that Professor Liviatan had given a very useful exposition of the results of Liviatan and Levhari, but he doubted that the parallelism between the models was as strong as Professor Liviatan suggested. In Professor Liviatan's analysis, the absence of differential tax treatment made no difference to what asset was issued. In his own model, differential tax treatment of equity and bonds was crucial to the analysis. The analogy was therefore less strong than Professor Liviatan appeared to think.

On Professor Patinkin's remarks, he did discuss taxation of indexed interest in the United States in his paper. It had been thought that the tax system was unfavourable to the indexation of interest, as Professor Patinkin suggested. It had been believed that if one offered, say, 3 per cent real interest, and that a 6 per cent inflation led to a 9 per cent nominal interest payment, then only 3 per cent would be allowed as an interest deduction for the business. However, it now appeared almost certain that the tax treatment of all nominal interest payments would be the same. It was interesting that no one had bothered to do the research, pointing to the similar treatment of all nominal interest. He accordingly doubted that the tax treatment of interest was responsible for the non-issuance of indexed bonds by business in the United States.

He had been puzzled by remarks about the imperfection of the capital market in the United States. He might be using a different definition from Professor Patinkin's, but if there were a useful definition of a perfect market, he imagined the United States capital market would satisfy it.

There had been suggestions that indexing would be unnecessary if a variable nominal rate of interest were offered to lenders, equal to the short-term rate of interest at each moment of time. Such an asset, the variable rate note, had been introduced for the first time in the United States during the previous year. Its interest payment had been tied to the treasury bill rate for the previous two months. This was an important innovation, though it was not an indexed bond. He thought the reason for the form of the innovation was that the variable rate note had been introduced by a bank. Because a bank had nominal assets, it needed nominal liabilities, too. There were also many proposals for the indexation of mortgages. If savings banks introduced indexed mortgages, they would want indexed assets on both sides of their balance sheets and would issue indexed deposits.

He agreed that many institutions worked in nominal terms, including the tax system, and it would take a long time to move away from this. But he had already mentioned movements in the direction of indexation and was sure they would increase.

As for his own paper, he had examined the profit performance of sixteen United States firms, looking especially for the relationship between profits and the price level. He had found a correlation between real profits and unanticipated movements in the price level, which was, on average, negative. The fact that the movement of stock exchange prices was negatively related to unanticipated inflation was connected with this. Some firms, not unexpectedly, had profits positively correlated with the price level and this gave them an incentive to issue indexed bonds.

21 A Summing Up

D. C. Hague

MANCHESTER BUSINESS SCHOOL

Professor Hague said that the conference left him with a number of disappointments. As Professor Patinkin had pointed out, the conference had not resolved the biggest issue of all, which was why inflation was currently so severe. In the past, serious inflation had usually been linked to war. It was true that there had recently been a 'small' war in Vietnam, but Korea had only been a 'small' war too. Yet the Korean inflation had subsided quite quickly. In the inflation of 1973 and 1974 the effect on expectations, particularly in commodity markets, seemed to have been very big. And participants had expressed fears that another commodity boom might be on its way.

Some participants had suggested that one factor accounting for the current inflation was worldwide pressure from trade unions. Being as insular as most of the British, he had not realised how universal was the pressure to increase the income of the lower paid in recent years. Moreover, trade unions seemed recently to have been quite successful in ensuring that the money supply was increased to ensure that higher wages could be paid. As Professor Aukrust had said, a major problem was how to stop all pressure groups feeling they had the right to operate the economic controls.

The conference seemed to Professor Hague to have made relatively little progress in assessing the relative roles of money, trade unions, and other factors, in 'causing' inflation, though Professor Machlup had tried very hard to clarify the issue. No-one had challenged the latter's suggestion that there was no example in history of a sustained increase in the price level unaccompanied by an increase in the money stock. However, while this made the increase in the money stock a necessary and sufficient condition for inflation it did not necessarily make it the ultimate cause. Our difficulties in this field suggested that it was much harder than one might think to disentangle the chain of causality.

Professor Hague had been impressed by the suggestion that, in addition to Vietnam, a major factor leading to an increase in the world's money stock had been the move towards flexible exchange rates. These enabled a country to make do with smaller foreign exchange reserves, meeting pressure on the balance of payments by allowing the exchange rate, not the foreign currency reserves, to fall. It might well be that the move from fixed to flexible exchange rates in the early 1970s had made a substantial part of the world's foreign currency reserves unnecessary. Perhaps the recent inflation could have been reduced had there been a planned extinction of world reserves during 1972 and 1973, after the move towards more flexible exchange rates had taken place. Of course, as Professor Lindbeck had pointed out, the reverse argument held as well. A movement from flexible to fixed exchange rates, without a simultaneous increase in the money supply, would be deflationary. The conclusion seemed to be that any movement from fixed to flexible exchange rates, or back again, was to be discouraged.

Professor Hague had also been somewhat disappointed with at least one view of the role of economists. In their paper, Professors Parkin and Swoboda had argued that the line of demarcation between economics and other subjects should be drawn at the money supply. Beyond that point, they were prepared to 'give away' the subject matter to other disciplines. Professor Hague was not happy about this because of its implication for the kind of policy recommendation that economists would then feel able to give. He was also unhappy about its implication for the kind of people that economists should be. He would rather see us all try to develop a much broader social science, taking in economics as well as sociology and political science, rather than 'give away' important parts of the subject.

If we were to move in this direction it might lead, initially, to less complex models of the system economists dealt with, but he was currently more fearful of the opposite danger that the complexity and elegance of economists' models was becoming more important to them than their relevance. In the United Kingdom at least, the reputation of economists was currently very low. Perhaps part of the solution was to develop broader social scientists, on the lines he had suggested.

However, Professor Hague had a more specific unhappiness with the monetary approaches set out during the conference. On an analytical plane, he was worried that too many of them represented a 'black box' approach. There seemed to be a significant dilemma here. It might be scientifically more reputable to work in terms of black boxes, but it was certainly less satisfying. Everyone liked to have his own explanation of what was going on in his own economy or the world at large, and to be able to offer policy prescriptions to deal with current problems. That became very difficult if we were not allowed inside the black box that represented the economy. An important question not discussed by the conference was therefore how far one could legitimately get inside the black box.

The result of the Conference's approach had been that the discussion of transmission mechanisms had been very general. A good deal of it had concentrated on how likely it was that an increase in the money supply would raise output rather than prices. There had been agreement that, with 'rational expectations', an increase in the money supply would lead to an increase in prices rather than in output. With rational expectations, firms would accurately predict that further inflation was on the way and immediately adjust their prices to the predicted level. The fact that this did not often happen showed that 'rational expectations' were rarely met in practice. As Professor Gordon had argued, whether an increase in the money supply predominantly affected prices or output depended on the way in which extra money entered the economy. Hence Professor Gordon's suggestion that Anglo-Saxon economists saw the transmission process in too mechanical a way.

This led Professor Hague back to the longstanding failure of economics to link up what happened at the macroeconomic level adequately with what went on at the microeconomic level. His feeling was that we should all go away from the Conference accepting that doing something about this in a way that would make our conclusions relevant to the real world was a major obligation of economists. For example, it really was time for us to be much clearer about how pricing at the level of the individual firm or industry linked up with what happened to the general price level. One might well feel that too little work was being done to clarify what happened at the level of the firm or industry, but this was no excuse for not trying to make the linkage as quickly as we could.

Since his own interest was in pricing, Professor Hague felt that much of the discussion of the transmission problem had failed to take sufficient account of what he believed to the most important contribution to the theory of the firm in recent years. This was the work of Simon, Cyert and March of Carnegie-Mellon University, in the United States.[1] Businessmen usually ran their firms by using budgetary control systems. Because of this, while economic theory had traditionally assumed that firms were profit maximisers, Simon, Cyert and March had suggested that they were more likely to 'satisfice'. Satisficing firms pursued multiple objectives, altering course only when one or more of these objectives failed to be met. Monetary economists, working at the macroeconomic level might gain a greater understanding of inflation if they looked more carefully at the implications of satisficing behaviour for their analyses.

While Professor Hague felt that others at the conference had not taken enough account of the work of Simon, Cyert and March he had initially wondered whether he had, himself, not taken enough account of the new microeconomics. In particular, there were its hypothesis about the natural rate of unemployment and its idea of voluntary unemployment. Having listened to the discussion, he now felt that the new microeconomics did not say anything that he did not know already. Moreover, he was not sure how far people like his colleagues in the Manchester Business School, working on the dynamics of wage payment systems, would accept what the new microeconomics had to say about labour markets. He was convinced that one thing we needed to do was to bring together macroeconomists, labour-economists and those, especially in business schools who thought that they had realistic models of labour markets. This seemed to be remarkably difficult to do.

Professor Hague thought that the discussion of the international transmission of inflation had been more successful than that of domestic inflation. The conference seemed to have accepted that inflation did not enter all eco-

[1] See, especially, R. M. Cyert and J. A. March, *A Behavioural Theory of the Firm* (Prentice Hall, 1963).

nomies in the same way. With countries like Japan and the United Kingdom it came in through commodity prices. But while it travelled by many routes, and was sometimes slow in coming, there was nothing a country could do to avoid 'importing' world inflation where there were fixed exchange rates. Indeed, one of the conclusions of the conference was that, except during very short periods, a small country could never choose its 'own' rate of inflation, except in a world of completely flexible exchange rates. There seemed to have been less agreement in the conference over how much autonomy larger countries had. Most participants seemed to feel that, with fixed exchange rates, however big or small countries were, they would find it painful to deviate far from the world rate of inflation. The discussion had suggested that pursuing one's 'own' inflation rate meant very severe distortions in the economy. The case for pursuing one's 'own' inflation rate had to be very strong to make those distortions worth suffering.

The discussion of the international transmission of inflation had also suggested that, in the early 1970s, fixed exchange rates had forced more inflation on most countries than they had wished. The main deficit country, the United States, had been strong enough in the late 1960s to refuse to introduce the constraints which had been imposed on other countries by fixed exchange rates. There had been the policy of 'benign neglect'. Because the dollar was overvalued, the United States could not solve its problems by demand management: the degree of deflation would have been too severe for the rest of the world. Yet the United States had found it difficult to persuade the major European countries to allow it to devalue the dollar sufficiently. This had become possible only when the United Kingdom payments surplus had become large.

While it was not easy to sterilise funds under fixed exchange rates, there had been suggestions in the Conference that, over longish periods, Germany had been relatively successful in doing so and that perhaps other countries had 'cried wolf' too soon. Certainly one had to distinguish the short and the long term. There seemed to be a consensus in the conference that, in recent years, the rest of the world had progressively caught up with the United States on methods of production and productivity levels. Over the same period, foreign goods had become more acceptable in the United States, though it was hard to know how long this situation would persist. Professor Duesenberry had suggested that too much of the discussion had assumed a world with flows of goods, but not of capital. He had gone on to point out that the dollar was heavily influenced by capital movements and that these represented not just interest rate arbitrage, but genuine speculation.

If the move from fixed to floating exchange rates had been inflationary, Professor Giersch would insist that the only alternative was 'a Smithsonian system worked out on the backs of envelopes in Washington'. This could not survive because cost conditions in different countries were too diverse: or, at least, those countries thought they were.

Professor Hague noted that we had spent a good deal of time in the Conference discussing the welfare costs of inflation. The main welfare cost was political. Indeed, Professors Parkin and Swoboda had suggested that inflation always led to the rise of authoritarian regimes. It seemed to be agreed that this argument was too sweeping. Hitler had not come to power until well after the inflation of the early 1920s. Should Hitler be blamed on inflation or unemployment? And if on unemployment, was that unemployment the result of the preceding inflation? These subtleties would no doubt keep the economic historians busy, but there seemed to be enough truth in the suggestion of a close connection between inflation and the advent of authoritarian regimes to be worrying, especially to anyone from Britain.

Other sociopolitical costs of inflation were much more clearly the result of inflation. In 1972–73, some of the most important ones had resulted from the commodity boom, and especially the property and stock market booms. In particular, these had caused intense jealousy amongst those with few or no assets, who felt that those who did have assets were 'doing well' from inflation. It had been argued on the other hand that businessmen who wanted to avoid risks would be 'frightened' by inflation; but this factor was hard to quantify. The conference had also noted the increased search costs resulting from inflation, these being borne by those who decided that the best way to protect the real value of their wealth was to buy boats, houses or stamp collections. As Professor Modigliani had suggested, the choice seemed to be between blue chips and blue ships. A good deal of time had also been spent discussing the 'shoe leather' cost of inflation and there was general agreement that once money ceased to be a good store of value significant costs did arise. It *was* convenient to have a stable store of value which could be handled as easily as money.

Inevitably, the political problems arising from inflation had been continually stressed, not least the idea of the 'political cycle'. Some economists now argued that the reason why the current economic cycle in developed countries lasted for roughly four years was that this was the length of time between elections in some major economies. Others, and Professor Gordon in particular, did not believe in the political cycle; but Professor Hague's own view was that the idea probably represented more than half of a truth, but certainly not the whole of it. What did emerge was a belief that it would be desirable if we could lessen the synchronisation of the economic cycle in the world's major economies. This was one cost of the reduction in trade barriers resulting from various developments, including the formation of the EEC, and the work of GATT. As Professor Polaczek had pointed out, small countries found it harder to pursue their own anti-inflationary policies if they were members of integrated groups. This was an important cost of economic integration, though there was obviously very great deal to be said on the other side. For example, Mr Corden had mentioned the increase in competition which seemed to result both from moves towards freer trade and from the development of multinational corporations.

This might be linked up with the general issue of the share of profit in

G.N.P., which was an important issue in the Conference. It had been generally agreed that profits were unusually low in recent years. Mr Corden had suggested reasons. However, a major reason must have been the development of trade union pressure and, of course, the increases in the wages of the low paid.

Coming from a country like the United Kingdom, where it seemed to be difficult to maintain an adequate level of investment, Professor Hague had been worried by a suggestion from Mr Oppenheimer that there was a world rate of increase in money wages. The consequence would then be that, whatever monetary policy was pursued, inflation would be worse in countries like the United Kingdom which had a slower rate of growth of productivity. So, if capitalism were to be ended by current economic developments, the reason might not be the Marxist one that wages were squeezed down by capitalist business but that the rise in wages reduced the profitability of capitalist business so far that it could not survive.

Professor Hague had therefore been heartened by a suggestion from Professor Lundberg of the Swedish 'dream' of a society where, perhaps by profit-sharing, one was able to build a more generous society, yet one which kept the share of profit in national income high enough to sustain a genuine mixed economy. He had himself toyed with the idea, for the United Kingdom, of an investment trust in which everyone might be compelled to invest part of his income.

But perhaps falling profits would simply drive businesses out of operation and destroy the mixed economy. If so, we should all become socialist economists which perhaps made it even more important to understand the socialist countries we already had.

Professor Hague had come away from the discussion of the socialist economies as unsatisfied as he usually did. He was still not wholly clear what happened. Nevertheless, there was one interesting fact. In the west, the first term of any elementary economics course put great emphasis on the role of relative prices in the economy. Yet, once we moved on to macroeconomics, and especially to economic planning, all this was forgotten. In socialist countries, the concept of the price mechanism was somewhat disparaged. Yet Professor Csikós-Nagy had shown that relative prices were taken extremely seriously there. Thanks to effective questioning by some members of the Conference, Professor Hague thought everyone would go away rather clearer about how socialist economies used subsidies and taxes to achieve the relative prices they wanted. But he was still far from clear just how the supply of money in a socialist economy was matched up with the supply of goods. Mistakes must happen, but they did not seem to lead to inflation.

One explanation given in the Conference was that 'improved' products were brought in at higher prices, but not regarded as representing inflation. Surely this could not make much difference. Was the answer that there *was* inflation, but that the socialist systems repressed it? Professor Bronfenbrenner, for example, had pointed to the severe penalties imposed in the USSR on anyone committing economic crimes, and had wondered whether such 'overkill' made it possible to maintain a disequilibrium system for much longer than those of us who lived in the west might expect. Or was there a more fundamental solution which Professor Hague had missed?

The Conference had not found it easy to reach conclusions about economic policy. Indeed, Professor Giersch had suggested that economists would not be able to give adequate help to policymakers until they reversed their approach. They should not, as they currently tended to do, simply set out issues, but should answer questions like: What can a country do to protect itself against inflation?

Professor Hague felt that a major problem in bringing in successful anti-inflationary policies was that too many people gained, or at least did not lose, from inflation. For example, in Britain house purchasers often did extremely well. He wondered why, given that there were such benefits from owning property during inflation, a country like the United Kingdom gave tax benefits to house purchasers as well. And why did we offer house purchasers totally unindexed loans? He had already noted that the recent property boom in Britain had been even more important than the commodity boom in antagonising the British working class. It was important to try to avoid such booms in future.

As an academic, he was perhaps over-inclined to suggest that the solution to our policy failures was to use education. Perhaps, with politicians, we might be able to persuade them to work with econometric, and especially simulation, models of the economy. With the public, perhaps the main need was to convince people that complex systems often behaved counter-intuitively. For example, most people in the United Kingdom had been persuaded, by the time that the Conference began, that a major cause of inflation in recent months had been rapidly increasing wages and salaries. They had therefore drawn what appeared to be the obvious conclusion: the way to end inflation was to impose controls on wages and salaries. Any suggestion that this might be counterproductive was greeted with astonishment simply because, as he had said, this implied counter-intuitive behaviour in the economic system.

A major policy problem was that there were many groups which pushed for increases in the money supply, for reasons set out in the Parkin–Swoboda paper. He wondered whether the monetarists would accept that the most important development stemming from the renewed interest in monetarism was the realisation that we must always look at the monetary implications of policies before we introduced them. For example, he would like someone to study British, and perhaps other countries' budgets, to see whether the times when budgetary policy turned out to be less inflationary or deflationary than was expected were the occasions when monetary policy was going strongly in the opposite direction to fiscal policy.

Professor Giersch had suggested that we might pursue a Chicago-type solution, adhering strictly to an announced annual rate of increase in the money supply. Professor Giersch had also suggested variants of this: that all such announcements should relate to a period of more than one year, or that the rule might be more elaborate. For example, the government might announce that it would relate the increase in money supply to the degree of capital utilisation in the economy.

While a number of participants at the Conference had been unhappy about the failure of the 'monetarists' to make their policy recommendations clearer, their anxieties were perhaps put most clearly by Sir Austin Robinson. He wanted to know whether the monetarists believed that they had some new practical policy weapons to defeat inflation. Or did they claim to have better criteria, evidence or indicators? As a result, did they know better than the rest of us how, when and to what extent the familiar policy weapons should be used? In particular, did they believe that somehow harsh policies could be avoided? While this question was not directly answered, Professor Hague had the impression that the 'monetarists' were very anxious to avoid giving such an impression of such harshness.

As a member of the British Price Commission, Professor Hague found it interesting that nothing at all had been said in the Conference about price control. Perhaps this was right. Price control was unlikely to achieve much more than a change in expectations, especially those of consumers and trade unions. To go beyond a narrowing, or holding, of profit margins would require much more elaborate price control systems than most Western countries would be prepared to accept. Price control had only a limited role in reducing inflation, though in the right circumstances it could be an important role, particularly in the short run.

Coming from a country which had experienced great difficulty in introducing incomes policies, Professor Hague had been heartened by the optimism, especially among some of the Scandinavian economists, about the possibility of obtaining agreement on incomes policy, and all that it implied, between the various groups. Professor Giersch had suggested that the situation in Germany was currently very favourable, but that this might partly be because the German trade unions currently wanted to show that they were ready for 'participation'. It did not follow that they would always be so amenable. In the United Kingdom, the big problem was how to get the various social partners together for discussions that would actually achieve something valuable. But perhaps the situation was changing.

This left over two issues. The first was indexation. Professor Hague had found the discussions of indexation some of the most interesting and educational in the Conference. The second question was that of expectations. The Conference had been particularly concerned with whether expectations, and indeed price changes themselves, became more variable the more rapid the rate of inflation. Despite the efforts of Professor Modigliani, there was not total agreement. Perhaps further research needed to be done. On other issues, not least the well-known concepts of cost-push and demand-pull inflation, the Conference had little to say. But perhaps this was simply because we were all bored with them.

Professor Hague concluded by saying that, at the risk of being disowned by other participants, he would venture two points on which there was, if not total consensus, at least a broad measure of agreement.

First, an increase in the money supply was the *sine qua non* of all serious inflation. Second, while there might be disagreement over how such an excessive increase in the money supply might come about, a government deficit bigger than could be financed from taxation and 'genuine' savings was often the cause. Professor Mussa had put the point rather neatly. He had noted that both the United Kingdom and New York City currently had deficits which they found difficulty in financing. In New York City, the deficit did not lead to inflation. In the United Kingdom it did. The reason was that New York did not have a central bank: the United Kingdom did.

In some cases, but perhaps less often than economists sometimes implied, the cause of an increase in the money supply might be a wage push. The government could resist matching wage rises by an increase in the money supply, but only at the expense of increasing unemployment and political unpopularity.

Perhaps, as with all Conferences, all we had done during our long discussions had been to make it clearer where we disagreed. Nevertheless, he, at least, had found them valuable.

Index

Entries in **bold** type under the names of participants in the conference indicate their papers or discussions of their papers. Entries in *italic* type indicate contributions by participants to the discussions.